MAJOR GOVERNMENTS OF ASIA

MAJOR GOVERNMENTS

OF ASIA *By Harold C. Hinton,*

Nobutaka Ike, Norman D. Palmer,

Keith Callard & Richard S. Wheeler,

George McT. Kahin

EDITED BY GEORGE McTURNAN KAHIN

SECOND EDITION

✦✦✦

Cornell University Press, Ithaca, New York

© *1958 and 1963 by Cornell University*

CORNELL UNIVERSITY PRESS

First edition 1958
Second edition 1963
Second printing 1965

Library of Congress Catalog Card Number: 63-15940

PRINTED IN THE UNITED STATES OF AMERICA
BY VAIL-BALLOU PRESS, INC.

Preface

THIS second and substantially revised and expanded edition remains, I believe, the only study in comparative government devoted to the five major countries of Asia. It deals with China, India, Indonesia, Japan, and Pakistan, which in population rank respectively as first, second, fifth, sixth, and seventh among the states of the world. In Asia their size sets them clearly apart, Pakistan having a population approximately four times that of Turkey, the Asian nation next in size.

Although during the last five years there has been an impressive increase in the number of scholarly studies concerned with the governments and politics of these five states—progress which is reflected in the annotated bibliographies of our contributors—a great many important lacunae still remain, most markedly in the cases of Indonesia and Pakistan. It is possibly because of the continuing lack of such studies that there has been a continuing reluctance on the part of any one political scientist to undertake a comparative survey designed to provide a general introduction to Asian government. Presumably, such an approach, if it is to be successful, must wait a little longer. At this stage it would still appear that the best method for achieving a reasonably sound coverage is to enlist the efforts of a group of specialists, each of whom has already done extensive research and writing on one of these five countries—and that remains the basis of this book.

As in the first edition, each contributor has had to decide for himself the extent to which it was feasible to follow the plan of organization suggested by the editor. Thus, although among the contributions there remains a fair congruence of treatment, the extent of this varies. It is believed, however, that there is sufficient similarity to help the reader in understanding the material presented and in comparing some of the more important aspects of the government and politics of these five major Asian countries. Those who are interested in comparative government will encounter in this book a wide variety of political systems, with a range of differences considerably broader than is to be found among the major states of Europe, the Soviet Union included.

The authors have all, in varying degrees, continued to present considerable new and hitherto unavailable data and analyses, which it is hoped will interest specialists as well as increase the book's effectiveness as an introductory guide for students and the general reader. In addition, each contributor has prepared an extensive and in general annotated reading list, expanded and brought up to date, designed to provide guidance for readers who wish to go more deeply into various aspects of the governments and politics of these countries.

Subsequent to the publication of the first edition of this book one of our contributors, Professor Keith Callard of McGill University, has died. The circumstance of his death, sudden illness while he was engaged in field research abroad, is indicative of the kind of scholar he was—no armchair rehasher of the accounts of others, but one who insisted upon as much firsthand investigation as possible. Professor Richard S. Wheeler in his coverage of Pakistan for this second edition has retained as much as possible of the substance and spirit of Callard's contribution to the first edition. That another Pakistan specialist should wish to do so is, I think, the best testimonial possible to our late colleague's sensitive understanding of Pakistan's political development.

As with the first edition, I wish to express my appreciation to Evelyn Boyce, associate editor of the Cornell University Press, for her much-valued assistance in preparing the manuscripts for the printer and for her patience and good humor throughout this long process, despite the additional difficulties posed by the Atlantic Ocean's interposition between her and me. For her considerable help in this work I should also like to record my deep gratitude to Mrs. Susan Finch.

G. McT. KAHIN

London
February 1963

Contents

Part One: CHINA *By Harold C. Hinton*

I The Historical Background. 3

   Ancient China 4
   Imperial China 5
   The Western Impact 15
   The Revolutionary Movement 20
   The Kuomintang in Power (1928–1937) 28
   The Chinese Communist Movement (1921–1937) . . 34
   The War against Japan (1937–1945) 41
   Civil War (1945–1949) 46

II China since 1949 52

   Historical Summary 52
   The Communist Party of China 74
   Other Public Bodies 82
   Constitutional Structure and Development . . . 85
   Governmental Organization 88
   Political Realities 93
   Economic and Technological Policy and Problems . . 102
   Social and Cultural Policy and Trends 107
   Military Affairs 110
   Foreign Policy and Foreign Relations 115
   Problems and Prospects of Communist China . . . 131

The Republic of China since 1949 134

Suggested Reading 139

Part Two: JAPAN *By Nobutaka Ike*

III The Historical Background. 153

Early History 154
The Tokugawa Heritage 157
The Meiji Regime (1867–1912) 160
The Taisho Era (1912–1926) 165
The Showa Era (from 1926) 166

IV The Social and Economic Structure 173

The Individual and the Group 173
Social Stratification 176
The Social Basis of Power 179

V Governmental Organization: Past and Present . . 181

The Constitution 181
    The Prewar Constitution 181
    The Postwar Constitution 182
The Emperor 186
    The Emperor as a Symbol 186
    The Political Role of the Emperor 188
The Diet 189
    The Imperial Diet 189
    National Diet: Organization 190
The Cabinet 192
    The Prewar Cabinet 192
    The Postwar Cabinet 193
The Civil Service 195
    The Prewar Civil Service 195
    The Postwar Civil Service 197
The Judiciary 198
    The Prewar Judicial System 198
    The Postwar Judicial System 199
Local Government 201
    Prewar Local Government 201
    Postwar Local Government 202

VI Major Political Forces 204

Interest Groups 204
    Business Organizations 204
    Labor Organizations 205
    Farm Organizations 208

Contents

Women's Organizations 209
Student Organizations 209
Pressure-Group Tactics 211
Political Parties 211
Prewar Parties 211
Postwar Parties 214
Party Organization 219
The Social Basis of Parties 221

VII   The Power Structure 225

Political Power at the Local Level 225
Political Power at the National Level 228
Electoral Behavior 233
The Determinants of Voting 238
The Legislative Process 240
Bureaucratic Behavior 242

VIII   Problems of Contemporary Japan 245

Economic Problems 245
Defense Problems 250
Foreign Relations 254
Political Problems 258

Suggested Reading 259

Part Three: INDIA By Norman D. Palmer

IX   The Political Heritage of Modern India . . . 269

Patterns of Government in Hindu India 269
Mogul Government and Administration 272
British Rule to 1857 274
British Rule after 1857 277
Toward Self-Government 280
The Transfer of Power 294

X   India since Independence: The Political Record . . 301

The Cost of Partition 303
The Integration of the States 305
Constitution Making 310
The Constitutional System 312
The Constitution in Operation 321

XI   Political Parties in India 335

Attitudes toward Political Parties 335
The Indian National Congress 337
The Swatantra Party 343

Communal Parties 344
Socialist Parties 348
The Communist Party of India 353
Other Parties and Groups 359

XII   Political Dynamics 361

Elections and Electoral Procedures 361
Public Opinion 371
Pressure Groups, Conventional and Unconventional . . 375

XIII Economic Development and Foreign Relations . . 382

Economic Development 382
Foreign Relations 388
    Underlying Factors 389
    Foreign Policy of the Indian National Congress . . 390
    Nonalignment and *Panchsheel* 392
    Relations with Pakistan 394
    Other Aspects of Foreign Relations 397

Suggested Reading 403

Part Four:

PAKISTAN *By Keith Callard and Richard S. Wheeler*

XIV   Pakistan and Its Origin. 419

The Mogul Empire 420
British Rule 421
Political Awakening 423
Political Ideas 426
The Pakistan Movement 428
The New State 430
Mohammed Ali Jinnah 432
The First Year (1947–1948) 433
1948–1951 434
1951–1954 435
1954–1958 437
1958–1962 439

XV   Economic and Social Structure 442

The Economy 443
Religion 444
The Islamic State 445
The Minorities 446

XVI   The Structure of Government 449

The Central Government 450
The Central Legislature 453
Emergency Provisions 457
The Provinces and Central-Provincial Relations . . . 458
Local Government 464
The Public Service 467
The Courts 470
The Armed Forces 472

XVII   The Political Process 474

The Decline and Fall of the Muslim League 475
The Politics of East Pakistan 481
The Awami League 484
The Krishak Sramik Party 488
Non-Muslim Parties 489
The Republican Party 490
The National Awami Party 492
Religious Parties 494
Martial Law 495
Post–Martial Law Political Revival 498

XVIII   Pakistan and Its Problems 505

National Unity 506
A Free Society 507
Economic Development 510
Social Policy 514
Foreign Policy 515
Constitutional Stability 525

Suggested Reading 526

Part Five: INDONESIA *By George McT. Kahin*

XIX   The Precolonial and Colonial Background . . . 535

Precolonial History and Government 537
Netherlands Control through Indirect Rule 541
Emergence of a New Indonesian Elite and the Rise of Na-
tionalism 547

XX   The Revolution and the Revolutionary Government . 555

The Japanese Occupation 555
The Revolutionary Struggle 559
Effect of the Revolution on Indonesian Government . . 563
Government in Sumatra and in the Dutch-controlled Areas . 572

XXI   Postrevolutionary Indonesia: The Period of
       Parliamentary Democracy (1950–1957) 575

       Heightened Expectations 575
       Economic Conditions 577
       The Bureaucracy 579
       The Army 581
       The Political Elite 585
       Some Traditional Factors Affecting Decision Making . . . 587
       Formation of a Federal Government 590
       The Unitarian Movement and Creation of a Unitary Govern-
       ment 594
       Soekarno 598
       The Presidency 601
       Hatta and the Vice-Presidency 604
       Cabinet and Parliament 606
       Political Parties 609
       Political Developments (1950–1957) 618
       The Failure of Indonesia's Parliamentary Democracy . . . 626

XXII   The Introduction of Guided Democracy
       (1957–1962) 636

       Soekarno's Views 636
       The Army's Views 640
       1957–1958: A Period of Crisis 643
       Power Relationships (1958–1962) 649
       The Communist Party's Dilemma 652
       Rivalry between Partners in Power: Soekarno and the Army 655
       The Shaping of Guided Democracy (1958–1962) . . . 658

XXIII Some Major Problems 670

       The Army 670
       Regionalism and Decentralization 674
       Economic Problems 675
       Foreign Relations 680

       Suggested Reading 688

       Index 701

Maps and Charts

MAPS

1   Landforms of China and Japan   .   .   .   .   *facing*   2
2   Changing China   6
3   Communist China in 1956 .   .   .   .   .   *facing*   52
4   Japan   156
5   The Japanese empire, 1936   171
6   Present area of Japan   246
7   India and Pakistan in 1963   415
8   West Pakistan   458
9   East Pakistan   459
10   Federal Indonesia   592
11   First-level regions of Indonesia, 1963   597

CHARTS

1   The Communist Party of China   75
2   Formal governmental structure of Communist China   .   89
3   Structure of the present Japanese government   .   .   185
4   The development of self-government in British India   .   281
5   Economic differentiation in the nonagrarian sector of
     colonial Indonesian society in 1940   552

PART ONE : CHINA

By Harold C. Hinton

Map 1. Landforms of China and Japan. (Map prepared by Erwin Raisz, from *Land of the 500 Million,* by G. B. Cressey, copyright 1955, McGraw-Hill Book Co., Inc.)

· I ·

The Historical Background

"CHINA," Napoleon Bonaparte is supposed to have remarked, "there lies a sleeping giant. Let him sleep, for when he wakes he will shake the world." Napoleon's fellow Europeans proceeded to ignore his prophetic advice and to intrude themselves insistently on what he had taken for China's slumber, but what was in reality only its traditional self-containment and self-satisfaction. Within a century after Napoleon's death, China began to awaken, and its awakening, for good or ill, has indeed shaken the world.

China today demands the attention of thinking persons everywhere in the world, and of none more than of Americans. It ranks easily first among the nations of the world in population (about 700 million as of 1962). China is also among the largest political units in the world in area. It contains quantities of raw materials which may prove large enough to make it in time a major industrial and military power, provided the present Communist policy of putting the might of the state ahead of the satisfaction of consumer needs continues. Since 1949 China has been led by a strong and able leadership operating in close affiliation with the Communist bloc. This leadership wields a considerable influence throughout the underdeveloped areas af the world, and especially in Asia, by virtue of the fear and admiration that it inspires. An able and influential, but perhaps too imaginative, German writer has gone so far as to predict the emergence of China as a

3

third world power even stronger than the Soviet Union.[1] An ignorance of the nature and aims of this rising colossus, regardless of the attitude taken toward it, is a serious chink in anyone's intellectual armor.

The pages that follow will discuss the place of Communist China within the Communist bloc as well as its relationship with pre-Communist China. Necessary also, for clearer understanding, is some knowledge of how the Chinese Communists came to power and of what China was like during its long pre-Communist history.

Ancient China

The prehistory of China is something of a mystery. Archaeology shows neolithic cultures which existed in parts of North China about 2000 B.C., but it has yet to show how there happened to emerge among them, by about 1500 B.C., a very highly developed Bronze Age culture centered in the middle Yellow River Valley. This apparent sudden bound of the early Chinese into civilization is probably due in part to contacts with the Middle East, via Central Asia; the strikingly different qualities which that civilization displayed as compared with any other known early civilization is probably related to one of the basic and determining facts of China's geography and history, its relative though not complete isolation.

Bounded as it is on the west and south by deserts and mountains and on the east by an interminable expanse of water, China has been throughout its long history the most nearly isolated of all the great ancient cultural centers. Largely for the same reason, China's power to transmit its civilization to other lands has been limited to Korea, Japan, northern Indochina, and parts of Central Asia. Since the Chinese had close contact with no other civilization which was the equal of theirs, they early developed a huge cultural superiority complex which led them to think of China as the Middle Kingdom, or in other words as the only truly civilized state on earth, and as one to which all other peoples ought to pay respect and obedience.

From about 1000 B.C. until the foundation of the First Empire in 221 B.C., the Chinese people and Chinese culture were confined to an area roughly extending from the Yangtze River to the Great Wall. Over this area there reigned, with an authority that grew weaker as

[1] Wilhelm Starlinger, *Grenzen der Sowjetmacht* (Würzburg: Holzner-Verlag, 1955), pp. 115–122. A summary English translation was published in *U.S. News and World Report*, Nov. 4, 1955.

time passed, the Chou dynasty. The center of its power, as with all major Chinese dynasties until the twelfth century A.D., lay in the valley of the Yellow River, an area whose soil is easily workable with simple agricultural implements and one that has a favorable strategic location. During the last several centuries of the Chou period China, from the Great Wall to the Yangtze Valley, was organized in a way that for want of a better term can be called feudal. Both political power and social life were graded in an elaborate but decentralized fashion reminiscent of medieval Europe.

The most powerful of the various states under the increasingly nominal suzerainty of the Chou kings was that of Ch'in, located in Northwest China with its center in what is today the province of Shensi. In the fourth century B.C. the rulers of this state adopted a political philosophy of an almost totalitarian type, known as Legalism, and militarized their state in a way suggesting that of ancient Sparta. By 221 B.C. they had eliminated the Chou kings and conquered all their formal vassals. The Ch'in ruler of that period then took the title Ch'in Shih Huang Ti, meaning First Emperor of the Ch'in Dynasty. The Chinese empire, which was to endure until A.D. 1911, had begun.

Imperial China

There is need here for only the briefest summary of the history of imperial China. Its most important feature was the development of a uniquely productive system of agriculture combining the growing of rice, careful control of water, and maintenance of soil fertility through the return to the soil of all available organic wastes. This in turn made possible high levels of nutrition and rates of population growth, the result of which was first the filling up of the Yellow and Yangtze valleys and then the gradual but relentless expansion of the Chinese people into South and Southwest China. This process, which got under way on a large scale about the fourth century A.D., when North China was invaded by alien barbarians, eventually left the prolific and hardworking Chinese peasant in possession of nearly all the cultivable land in the whole of China. The aboriginal inhabitants, whose descendants still survive in South and Southwest China, were steadily pushed back into the forests and mountains to make room for the energetic Chinese rice farmer, backed by the officials and troops sent by his government.

The southward expansion of the Chinese, combined with an eastward pressure then being exerted by the Tibetans, was responsible for displacing the Thai (Siamese) and the Burmans about a thousand years ago from their original homes in Southwest China and eastern Tibet respectively into the areas they now inhabit and for pushing the Vietnamese more than a thousand years earlier still from South China

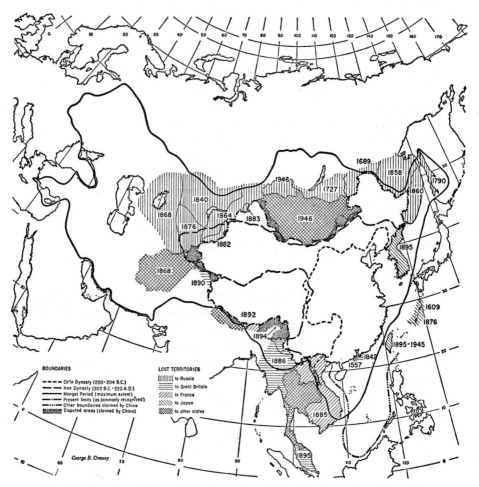

Map 2. Changing China. (By permission from *Land of the 500 Million,* by G. B. Cressey, copyright 1955, McGraw-Hill Book Co., Inc.)

into North Vietnam. Gradual penetration by Chinese merchants into Southeast Asia had begun before the beginning of the Christian era. In the late nineteenth and early twentieth centuries a large-scale migration of South Chinese to Southeast Asia took place, with the result that there are today probably 14 million Chinese in that region, where they hold a powerful economic position. A similar migration into Manchuria and Inner Mongolia has occurred during the past half century.

On this basic theme of Chinese history the rise and fall of dynasties is superimposed. During the short-lived but momentous Ch'in dynasty (221–206 B.C.) China was given a considerable degree of political unity, many of its imperial political institutions, a uniform writing system, and reasonably good communications. Under the next dynasty, the Han (202 B.C.–A.D. 220), this imperial unity was enhanced and solidified, so that the Chinese have believed ever since that all Chinese —that is, all persons of whatever race who are Chinese by culture— ought to be as united politically under a common government as they are, largely through the medium of the ideographic and comparatively unchanging written language, in the cultural realm. China in the great days of the Han (especially the second century B.C. and the first century A.D.) was a mighty empire stretching westward as far as the T'ien Shan mountains, which divide Chinese from Russian Turkestan, and was certainly the equal in power and wealth of the Roman empire, with which it had some indirect cultural and commercial contacts.

Like other Chinese dynasties after them, the Han went through a life cycle usually known as the dynastic cycle. In the first phase of this process, a given dynasty was generally governed by able and martial emperors, who in turn entrusted the tasks of administration to able ministers. These were drawn for the most part from the educated class, often known as the gentry or literati, which nearly monopolized the knowledge, enlargement, and transmission of China's rich and complex literary culture and hence was indispensable to any stable dynasty.

After a few generations, however, the character and ability of the rulers tended to decline, partly at least because of the unwholesome effects of childhood and life in the environment of an Asiatic court, with its harem and eunuchs. Nor were the Chinese emperors exempt from the operation of Lord Acton's profound observation that "power tends to corrupt, and absolute power corrupts absolutely." As emperors began to fight costlier wars and build costlier palaces for their own glorification, they necessarily had to impose increasingly heavy taxes on the peasants who made up the vast majority of their subjects. At the same time, the standards of behavior of ministers, officials, and landowners throughout the empire tended to decline correspondingly. Wealthy and powerful landowners ofter bribed or browbeat local officials into leaving their lands off the tax registers, so that a proportionately heavier part of the mounting tax burden fell on the shoulders of the peasants and small proprietors, who were least able to pay. When the peasantry had passed the limits of endurance they generally rose in revolt, and the dynasty collapsed in a welter of civil war, and sometimes also foreign invasion, to be succeeded by another dynasty.

The fall of the Han was followed by a period of about two and one-half centuries during which North China was divided among a number of kingdoms ruled by invading Turks, Mongols, and Tibetans, while South China remained under weak Chinese dynasties. In addition to accelerating the movement of Chinese southward, the turbulence of this period fostered the spread of Buddhism, which became for a time almost the national religion of China. After the restoration of imperial unity, however, Buddhism gave ground before the hostility of the Confucian literati, occasional official persecutions, and the advance of Islam in Central Asia, so that by about the year 1000 Buddhism had ceased to be an important force in Chinese life. It received its final blow from Neo-Confucianism, an eclectic philosophy formulated during the eleventh and twelfth centuries, which grafted elements of Buddhist thought onto the Confucian trunk, stole Buddhism's thunder in this way, and became the official philosophy of the Chinese empire for the rest of its days.

The reunifier of China and founder of the Second Empire was the Sui dynasty (581–617), which like the Ch'in was short-lived and violent. The counterpart of the Han was the glorious T'ang dynasty (618–907), which has a strong claim to being the greatest in the history of Asia. Once again China ruled Central Asia as far west as the T'ien Shan. So efficient and powerful was China's government and so brilliant was its culture that the Chinese were admired by all other Asian peoples who knew them, and the Japanese consciously and systematically introduced at least the externals of Chinese culture into their own country.

After a short interval of disunion following the fall of the T'ang, China came under the rule of the Northern Sung dynasty (960–1125). Being peacefully inclined and militarily weak as compared with the T'ang, this dynasty steadily lost control over its northern marches to a people of Mongolian stock, the Khitan. Turning their attention instead toward the sea, the Sung became a great naval and commercial power. The Sung period was also great in art, philosophy, and commercial prosperity.

In 1125 the Sung lost control of North China to the Juchen tribesmen of Manchuria, with whom they had foolishly allied to crush the Khitan, and they are therefore known from then on as the Southern Sung (1127–1279). Soon they were confronted with a menace far graver than the Juchen, in the shape of the Mongols. These fierce and extremely mobile nomad cavalrymen had been welded into an empire by the great conqueror Chinggis Khan (ca. 1165–1227; often misspelled Genghis or Jenghiz), who subdued most of North China and Central Asia but did not live to see his horsemen overrun Russia, Persia, and China. It is interesting that the Sung, a weak dynasty by Chinese standards, held out longer against the Mongols than any of these others, so mighty was China even in its time of relative weakness.

The conquest of the Sung was completed by Chinggis' famous grandson Khubilai, who thereupon founded the Yuan (Mongol) dynasty (1280–1368). The Mongols made few concessions to the Chinese viewpoint. Between most Central Asian peoples and the Chinese a great cultural gulf is fixed, far wider than divides the Chinese from most of the peoples of Southeast Asia. The Central Asian peoples are nomadic by necessity and warlike by preference, whereas the Chinese can fight when necessary but generally prefer not to, and they get their food from agriculture rather than from herding. The Chinese have regarded the nomads as barbarous and as a serious military problem against which precautions must be taken.

The Yuan dynasty was expelled from China by a national upsurge of Chinese patriotism and xenophobia in 1368, after a comparatively short rule. It was succeeded by a major Chinese dynasty, the Ming (1368–1644). During this period the growing wealth of South China, which had begun to outstrip that of the North during the T'ang period, found its logical reflection in the political sphere. Beginning with the Ming dynasty every major Chinese political movement, including in recent times the Communist Party, has been led mainly by South Chinese. During their early vigorous years the Ming sent out a series of seven large naval expeditions (1405–1433) which explored the shores and islands of Southeast Asia, penetrated the Indian Ocean, and even went as far west as the Red Sea, trading and enrolling local rulers in the ranks of nominal vassals of the Chinese Emperor. If these expeditions had been followed up, they might have led to the establishment of a Chinese empire in Southeast Asia and materially altered history by excluding the Europeans who came later. But they were not, mainly because of the aversion of the Confucian literati to overseas adventures and unnecessary expenditure. Instead, the Ming tended to lapse into military weakness, corruption, and conservatism, so that in the sixteenth century their northern frontiers were harassed by Mongol armies and their coasts by Japanese pirates.

It was neither of these who finally replaced the Ming, however, but the forest-dwelling Manchus to the north of the Great Wall. By the time of his death in 1626, the great Manchu leader Nurhaci had welded his people into a formidable military and political force. One of his last acts was to fix his capital at Mukden, in a fertile area farmed by Chinese colonists, where under his successors the Manchus rapidly improved their knowledge of Chinese culture and the Chinese way of governing.

Within a decade of Nurhaci's death the tribes of Inner Mongolia and the Korean kingdom had both became vassals of the Manchus, whose flanks were thereby rendered safe for a southward advance against the Ming. In 1644, when the Ming had already been overthrown by domestic rebellions, the Manchus crossed the Great Wall and began the conquest of China. They had already taken the dynastic title Ch'ing (Pure), under which they ruled until 1912.

The further conquests by which the Manchus rounded out their empire may be briefly mentioned. In 1683 Taiwan (Formosa) fell to them, and by the end of the seventeenth century most of the Outer Mongolian tribes had acknowledged themselves vassals. Tibet also became a vassal during the first half of the eighteenth century, and Sinkiang (Chinese Turkestan) was conquered in 1755–1758. The areas so far mentioned, except Korea, constituted the Manchu empire properly speaking. Around the empire lay a fringe of tributary states, of which Korea and Annam (correctly known as Vietnam after 1803) were the most faithful because the most Sinicized.

The zenith of the Ch'ing dynasty was unquestionably the reign of the wise and vigorous K'ang-hsi Emperor (1661–1722), which was the last golden age of traditional China. Under his able but warlike and arbitrary grandson, the Ch'ien-lung Emperor (1736–1795), the state and society began to groan under the burden of extravagance, growing official corruption, intolerance of unorthodox ideas, and domestic and foreign wars. The empire was still wealthy and powerful, but its foundations were being sapped. Even if its problems had not been further complicated by the intrusion of Western influences, it would have declined and perhaps fallen in the nineteenth century.

The economy of traditional China rested squarely on the production of cereal grains, especially rice, which was grown by countless peasant households using intensive methods of hand cultivation. Above the family, which was the basic economic as well as the basic social unit, the next important entity was the village, in which the peasants lived and from which they went out to tend their scattered plots of land. The village was nearly self-sufficient, except for certain commodities and implements which its residents had to buy from the nearest market town, and its near self-sufficiency imparted to traditional China something of the quality of a modern ship with its watertight compartments; a leak in one or more compartments, such as a local or regional plague or famine, did not necessarily impair the condition of neighboring compartments or the ability of the ship of state to navigate. Higher still there were cities, the imperial capital in particular, in which arts and crafts were highly developed and merchant guilds dealt in such important traditional commodities as tea, silk, porcelain, salt, and copper. These cities never developed the local self-government and political power characteristic of many medieval European cities.

Social classes in traditional China, the barriers between which were much less difficult to cross than in traditional India, were divided into two main groups, the privileged and the unprivileged, their most important representatives being the gentry and the peasantry respectively. The gentry dominated, though it never quite monopolized, the three important fields of literary activity, government service, and landownership. It was the true elite, and its support or defection was often enough to ensure the survival or fall of a dynasty. Although respected in theory as the basis of society and the producers of food, the peasants in practice enjoyed very few legal or social rights and were usually heavily taxed. They relied mainly on local custom, official inertia, and the implied or actual threat of rebellion to protect them from excessive oppression.

Two other classes, both unprivileged in theory if not always in fact, also deserve mention—the merchants and the soldiers. The Chinese are good businessmen and have always produced energetic and wealthy merchants, but the latter have generally operated under a cloud of social disapproval and have seldom exerted much political influence. Still more despised were the soldiers, who were generally conscripted peasants or semireconstructed bandits. It would be a serious mistake to conclude from this that warfare has not played an important part in Chinese history or that the Chinese are by nature more pacifistic than other peoples. They have produced many fine generals and have fought as successfully and ruthlessly as anyone else when the occasion demanded, but they have always rated the arts of peace above those of war.

For practical purposes, traditional Chinese political thought was dominated by two main philosophic schools, the Confucians and the Legalists. The Confucians succeeded in setting the tone of Chinese social and cultural life and political institutions. They preached respect for tradition (as interpreted by Confucian scholars), for conventional social relationships (including the rites in honor of deceased male ancestors that are inaccurately known as "ancestor worship"), for rule by benevolence and moral example rather than by force, for learning, and for outward proprieties. The Confucian emphasis on loyalty and conformity commended their system to the Han and later dynasties, although the Confucian injunction to rule benevolently was often violated. When a dynasty governed well, it was considered by both the Confucians and the people to hold the "mandate of heaven," which it could lose, however, through misgovernment. The people were believed under this theory to be entitled to revolt against a dynasty which had lost the mandate, but there was no idea of doing anything more revolutionary than installing a new dynasty.

The actual conduct of public affairs in imperial China was often more reminiscent of Legalism than of Confucianism. Legalism, which was espoused by the state of Ch'in in the fourth century B.C. and extended after 221 B.C. to all of what was then China, was a brutally statist philosophy. Subjects exist only for the benefit of the ruler, and those who benefit him the most are the farmers and the soldiers. All subjects must be kept in line by stringent laws and harsh punishments.

The political institutions of imperial China may be regarded as embodying a subtle and shifting blend of Confucian theory and Legalist practice. At the top of the edifice stood the Emperor, the Son of Heaven, who mediated between the people and their vaguely conceived deities. His power over his subjects was theoretically absolute and tended in practice to grow greater with the passage of time, but it was also considerably limited by precedent and by the "countervailing power" of the nobility and the gentry. Although his approval was necessary for nearly all measures and his work load was therefore great, his part in government was usually passive. Barring an exceptional Emperor or an abnormal situation, he generally waited for others to bring matters to his attention much as a modern judge does.

The Emperor was surrounded by an elaborate court, but he usually depended for the execution of his directives on a quite distinct group, the bureaucracy. This was recruited largely from the gentry class, particularly from men who had passed a series of difficult civil service examinations testing their knowledge of the classical Confucian philosophical literature. These men had a common body of knowledge, a common standard of behavior, and a common tradition. In the last analysis, the bureaucracy governed the empire, though the total number of its career members at any given time probably never exceeded 10,000. They held the professional positions in the administrative boards (Rites, Civil Office, War, Revenue, Punishments, and Works) and other agencies at the imperial capital, as well as corresponding posts at the provincial and other local levels down through the *hsien* (rural district, or county). The *hsien* magistrate was the lowest ranking official to be appointed directly from the imperial capital. Since he was by custom not appointed to his native province, he was dependent in many ways on the favor and cooperation of the local gentry and his own locally recruited staff of tax collectors, police, clerks, messengers, and the like. The people themselves were usually more affected by the actions of these subordinates than by those of the magistrate himself.

This far-flung bureaucratic system, reinforced at strategic points by garrisons of imperial troops or local levies, was held together, especially under the non-Chinese Yuan and Ch'ing dynasties, by an elaborate system of postal communications. This system permitted documents to travel in both directions between the capital and the outlying administrative centers by horse or on foot, at a speed proportional to the urgency of the document in question.

Another important bit of cement which contributed to holding the empire together was the censorate, a body of officials empowered to investigate and report abuses on the part of anyone up to and including, at least theoretically, the Emperor himself.

The revenues which nourished the system were derived from four major sources. The first and most important was the land tax, levied on all agricultural land. The second was the grain tribute, levied only in certain provinces and shipped annually up the Grand Canal to feed the bureaucracy and garrison in and near the imperial capital. The third was the salt monopoly, under which the right to deal in salt was sold to private merchants for high fees. The fourth was the "native" (or traditional) customs, imposed on foreign goods or any goods passing certain customs stations. Payment of the first two types of tax, which bore on the peasantry, was generally forgiven or postponed in times of distress. On the other hand, the actual tax burden on the people was often greatly increased by corruption and extortion in various forms.

The main traditional categories of governmental expenditure were the maintenance of the court, army, and bureaucracy, the building and repair of public works (such as the dikes along the Yellow River and the Grand Canal), and the giving of relief to the suffering in time of disaster.

The traditional structure of government in China, given the limited bureaucratic and financial resources at its disposal, rested fairly lightly on the people in ordinary times. The only governmental activities which normally and directly concerned them were the collection of taxes, the maintenance of order, and the conscription of men for the army and for labor on public works. The village, under a headman of its own choosing, was almost as autonomous in its political life as it was self-sufficient in its economic life. Where severe oppression existed, it was more likely to be the result of some local or temporary malfunctioning of the system or abuse of authority than of the nature of the system itself. The system was not perfect, its main defect being a tendency toward rigidity due to the weight of China's cultural tradition and resistance of the privileged classes to change, but it had the great virtue of stability.

Something remains to be said about traditional China's foreign relations. Not only were the Chinese convinced that all other peoples ought to admire what the Chinese regarded as their superior culture, but they tended to believe that their culture actually was so admired. In fact, the Chinese are admired and respected by their neighbors for their high culture, but they are also hated and feared for their tendency toward demographic expansion and their tremendous actual or potential military and political power. The traditional tributary relationship, already referred to, between China and many of its neighbors institutionalized these ambivalent mutual feelings. It soothed the cultural pride of the Chinese to see those they regarded as barbarians coming to the imperial capital to acknowledge a largely nominal suzerainty of the Chinese Emperor over their own rulers. For this euphoria the Chinese paid the barbarians well with rich gifts and empty titles and occasionally with more valuable protection against foreign and domestic enemies. The tributary states, for their part, derived some cultural and commercial benefit from this client relationship but (except probably in the case of Korea) felt little genuine enthusiasm for the Chinese claim to cultural superiority.

The Western Impact

The Western impact on China has been one of the most important facets of what is perhaps the salient feature of the whole of modern history, the expansion of Europe. Unlike many other areas so affected, China was not transformed into a European political dependency. It was, however, confronted with a challenge too severe for its traditional ideas and institutions to cope with.

Until the end of the nineteenth century, Western influences came to China mainly in the baggage of the Western merchant and the Western missionary. Broadly speaking, the former brought with him Western commodities and technology, and the latter Christianity and European culture.

Portuguese merchants began to come to China in limited numbers in the sixteenth century, and they were followed in the subsequent century by Dutch, French, British, and Russian rivals. China at that time was in advance of Europe in most material respects; Chinese goods, especially tea, silk, and porcelain, were in great demand in Europe, but there was no corresponding demand in China for European goods. The foreigners were therefore faced with a serious payments problem, which they solved by importing silver bullion and coins. The situation was greatly eased by the British discovery in the late eighteenth century that opium grown in the newly acquired British territories in India could be sold at handsome prices in China.

The Chinese government during this early period generally considered foreign trade a minor nuisance that should be tolerated but not encouraged. By about 1760, however, the Ch'ien-lung Emperor had banned trade with the Western nations except at the port of Canton, and even there it was subjected to very strict regulation.

By the beginning of the seventeenth century a group of Jesuit missionaries had begun to gain acceptance at the Chinese court as a first step toward Christianizing China. They hoped, very unrealistically, to convert the Emperor himself and thus create a Chinese Constantine. Unfortunately for them and their cause, the Jesuits aroused the jealousy of other Catholic missionary orders by their successes in China and by certain concessions they made to Chinese culture, such as allowing their converts to continue to perform the rites of "ancestor worship." When it became clear that the Holy See was inclining against the Jesuit position in the so-called Rites Controversy, the K'ang-hsi Emperor in 1706 decreed that only those missionaries would be allowed to preach in China who adhered to the Jesuit view on the questions in dispute. After 1742, when the Jesuit position was officially condemned at Rome, this edict had the effect of putting a virtual end to Catholic missions in China for the time being.

China's contacts with both the foreign merchant and the foreign missionary entered a new phase in the early nineteenth century. China's foreign trade was transformed during that period by two new features. The first was the growing trade in opium, which was smuggled into China and adversely affected not only the health but the finances of the coastal population of South China. The second was the industrialization of Britain, which rendered British manufacturers and exporters anxious to sell their goods, especially textiles, on the supposedly limitless Chinese market. In 1833 Parliament abolished the British East India Company's monopoly on British trade with China. The company had not taken part in the opium trade directly and had tended to act as a check valve on Sino-British trade in general. With its removal, China began to feel the full impact of British pressure for expanded trade.

The so-called Opium War (1839–1842) between Britain and China resulted from China's refusal to permit normal diplomatic relations and free trade between the European nations and itself, from the Chinese insistence on subjecting foreign nationals accused of crimes to the brutalities of Chinese criminal procedure, and from a determined Chinese effort to put an end to the opium trade. The decayed might of the Manchu empire proved no match for the small British expeditionary force sent against it. The Treaty of Nanking, imposed by the British in 1842, set the pattern for a long series of what the Chinese came to call "unequal treaties."

Under these treaties, which China was compelled to sign with all principal foreign powers including the United States and Japan, China lost much of its sovereignty. It could no longer try foreigners on its soil, but had to allow them to be tried by their own courts and under their own law. It could no longer fix its own tariffs on foreign goods entering its ports; these were set by treaty at a very low rate. It was compelled to establish conventional diplomatic relations with the treaty powers. It was forced to open numerous "treaty ports" to foreign trade and allow the establishment in them of foreign concessions, in which foreigners could lease land and carry on business and which were not subject to Chinese administration. It was made to legalize the importation of opium, to allow the establishment of foreign-owned factories in the treaty ports, and to open its inland waterways to foreign shipping.

The advantages which these treaties gave to foreign manufacturers and merchants were considerable. Foreign goods, especially opium and cotton textiles, entered in increasing quantities and tended to disrupt the Chinese economy by creating an unfavorable trade balance and wiping out local handicrafts. China's two major traditional exports, tea and silk, were almost driven off the world market about the end of the nineteenth century by British and Japanese competition respectively.

The nineteenth-century Western impact began to undermine not only China's economic self-sufficiency but also its cultural self-confidence. About the middle of the century, under the protection of the "unequal treaties," Christian missionaries both Catholic and Protestant came to China in sizable numbers and made steady but not spectacular progress in the field of conversions. They also set up schools, hospitals, and orphanages, which helped to acquaint the Chinese with Western ethics and culture. They waged war on Chinese superstitions and on cruel customs such as the binding of the feet of upper-class girls. Less tolerant than the earlier Jesuits, they denounced the Confucian basis of Chinese culture and thus sowed doubt in the minds of some and resentment in the minds of others.

In 1898 some of the powers began to establish "spheres of influence" for themselves in China: a Russian sphere in Manchuria (the southern third of which was taken over by the Japanese after the Russo-Japanese War of 1904–1905), a German sphere in Shantung, a British sphere in the Yangtze Valley, a Japanese sphere in Fukien, and a French sphere in Southwest China. Within each sphere the power in question held a near monopoly on investment and the development of communications. The fact that this trend did not lead to an outright partition of China into a number of foreign possessions was due to two main causes: the first and more important was the rivalry among the powers themselves, which culminated in the First World War and which preserved a precarious balance among their interests in China; the second was the policy of the United States.

The United States was reluctant to see China partitioned into West-ern spheres of influence or outright colonies. This reluctance found expression in Secretary of State John Hay's two famous Open Door notes, the first (1899) of which attempted to secure equality of op-portunity for American trade within the newly created foreign spheres of influence and the second (1900) of which requested the other powers to respect the "territorial and administrative entity" of China. The Open Door Policy had a slight, but only a slight, effect in check-ing foreign pressures on China; it would have had more effect if there had been any reason to think that the United States would fight to enforce it.

The Chinese response to the challenge posed by the Western im-pact in the nineteenth century was slow, uncertain, and much less effective than Japan's contemporary response to the same challenge. The Chinese were handicapped from the outset by their complacency and cultural superiority complex, as well as by their ignorance of the West and of its true strength. Few Chinese could deny after 1842, however, that Western armies and navies were stronger than those of China. During the terrible Taiping Rebellion (1850–1864), which if it had not been suppressed would have resulted in the overthrow of the Ch'ing dynasty by a pseudo-Christian successor dynasty, both sides made some use of Western weapons and military techniques. The years after the rebellion, known to the Chinese as the T'ung-chih Res-toration (1861–1874), saw the building of a limited number of mod-ern arsenals and dockyards with the help of foreign technicians, the translation of some Western technical treatises into Chinese, the train-ing of a few young Chinese in Western languages and studies, and the beginning of Chinese diplomatic representation abroad. These essentially technical innovations continued, at a moderate pace that was far from adequate to the need, during the remainder of the nine-teenth century.

The early Chinese modernizers responsible for these innovations were mainly officials committed to the traditional values of Chinese culture, though they made use of foreign advisers and Chinese com-pradors (agents for foreign firms doing business in the treaty ports). The aim of these officials was not to abandon or even modify the es-sentials of Chinese culture, but rather to preserve them by arming them with efficient modern military and economic techniques.

Toward the end of the nineteenth century it became clear to a growing number of Chinese, though not yet to the dynasty itself, that this formula was not good enough. Western technology would not flower in China unless some of the institutional soil in which it thrived at home were transplanted as well. The earliest convincing demonstration of this truth was the Sino-Japanese War (1894–1895), in which China was roundly defeated by another Asian power that had modernized far more effectively than China and had adopted not only Western techniques but also some Western institutions, such as a constitution and a parliament. The next demonstration was the "Scramble for Concessions" of 1898, which showed the Chinese how weak they still were and how close China had come to being partitioned by the powers.

The seriousness of the situation lent force to the arguments of a rising group of Chinese who favored the institutional as well as technical modernization of China under a constitutional monarchy of either the authoritarian Japanese or the liberal British type. The leaders of this group were two prominent intellectuals named K'ang Yu-wei and Liang Ch'i-ch'ao. In the spring of 1898 they gained the confidence of the young and well-meaning Kuang-hsü Emperor (1875–1908) and persuaded him to implement their program. There ensued the so-called Hundred Days Reform (June–September 1898), during which the Emperor promulgated a series of decrees aimed at modernizing the armed forces, the bureaucracy, the legal and educational system, and the economy. The people remained apathetic, however, and the bureaucracy was strongly hostile to the reforms. These reforms were nearly all canceled when the Empress Dowager Tz'u-hsi, the Emperor's aunt, who had dominated the court in her capacity of regent during most of the period from 1861 to 1889, resumed power and overthrew the reformers.

Even the Empress Dowager, however, became convinced of the urgent necessity for reform as a result of the Boxer Rebellion (1899–1900). This was an antiforeign, and especially anti-Christian, rising of lower-class Chinese in the northern provinces. The Empress Dowager lent the movement encouragement and support and even went so far as to declare war on the foreign powers (June 1900) and besiege the Legation Quarter in Peking. In mid-August, however, an international relief expedition moved up from Tientsin, took Peking, and drove the Empress Dowager and court into exile. The dynasty then had to put its seal on a humiliating peace treaty which included a large indemnity.

Convinced too late of the need for modernization, the Empress

Dowager proceeded to put into effect a reform program basically similar to the abortive one attempted by the Emperor in 1898. Usually known as the Manchu Reform Movement, this program showed some genuine if inadequate progress until the Empress Dowager's death in 1908, but thereafter tended to flounder for lack of strong leadership. The most concrete success was the almost complete eradication of opium production in China and a simultaneous agreement by the powers to eliminate gradually the importation of opium into China from abroad. Others were the creation of a modernized model army of six divisions under the able but unscrupulous official Yuan Shih-kai, a partial modernization of the bureaucracy, the promulgation of a monarchical but parliamentary constitution modeled largely on the Japanese, the construction of a sizable mileage of railways by foreign firms and groups of provincial gentry, and the drawing up of modernized legal codes.

But this official program of reform, like the private one led by K'ang Yu-wei and Liang Ch'i-ch'ao, was too little and too late. China was growing ripe for revolution.

The Revolutionary Movement

The cause of revolution in China, like that of reform, received its first major stimulus from the Japanese defeat of China in 1894–1895. The Japanese defeat of Russia in 1904–1905 gave further impetus to the revolutionary movement, especially in view of the contrast between Japan's strength and the miserable weakness that China had displayed at the time of the "Scramble for Concessions" and the Boxer Rebellion. Japan appeared to Chinese, Indians, and other Asians, suffering in varying degrees from the effects of the Western impact, as the light of Asia. Attracted also by the comparative nearness and cheapness of the Japanese schools and universities, Chinese and other Asian students flocked there in the early years of the twentieth century. Some were sent on scholarships provided by the Ch'ing dynasty, but regardless of the source of their support most of these students were extremely nationalistic, anti-Manchu, and susceptible to the propaganda of revolutionaries.

There is space here only for an account of the most important of these revolutionaries, Sun Yat-sen. Born near Canton in 1866, into a poor family, Sun received a secondary and advanced education of the Western type in Hawaii and Hong Kong. In 1895 he founded the first of a series of secret organizations dedicated to the overthrow of the

Manchus. Between then and the Revolution of 1911 he launched ten risings, some comic, some tragic, and all unsuccessful. In the intervals he spent most of his time traveling in America, Europe, and the Far East, soliciting funds and support for his movement from overseas Chinese. These he received, but the movement was doomed to frustration by its limited membership and conspiratorial methods. This political ineffectiveness acted as a check on the influence of Sun's political ideas, which had begun to take shape by about 1905.

By 1911 both the finances and the prestige of the Ch'ing dynasty had reached an extremely low point. On October 10 of that year a mutiny began in a government garrison at Wuchang, near Hankow, among troops who had been infected by revolutionary propaganda. This mutiny rapidly grew into a revolt which by the end of the year swept most of South China clear of Manchu authority. Representatives of the revolutionary groups met at Nanking in December, proclaimed the Republic of China, and elected Sun Yat-sen, then returning from the United States, its provisional President.

Meanwhile the Ch'ing government, under pressure of the crisis and at the insistence of its own National Assembly, had appointed Yuan Shih-kai Premier with dictatorial powers and the mission of suppressing the revolt. He had other ideas, however, and after inflicting some sharp defeats on the insurgents he opened secret negotiations with them in December 1911. The outcome was a celebrated agreement between Yuan and Sun Yat-sen in January 1912, under whose terms Sun resigned the provisional presidency in Yuan's favor and Yuan for his part agreed to compel the Manchu boy Emperor to abdicate and thereby to extend the authority of the revolutionary government to North China. This Yuan did in February, but he violated other commitments to the revolutionaries by removing the capital from Nanking to Peking and negotiating for a foreign loan to render himself financially independent of them. It was clear that Yuan intended to dominate, and perhaps to overthrow, the infant republic.

In preparation for the parliamentary elections scheduled for the winter of 1912–1913, a number of new political parties arose. Among these was the Kuomintang (National People's Party), which though led by Sun Yat-sen and composed of his followers was so reorganized and revitalized at that time by Sun's leading lieutenant, Sung Chiao-jen, that it may be regarded as virtually a new party. The Kuomintang won a plurality in both houses of parliament in the elections, and Sung would probably have become Premier if he had not been assassinated at Yuan Shih-kai's instigation in March 1913. Revolts, in which the Kuomintang was heavily implicated, broke out in some southern provinces during the following summer, but Yuan suppressed them without much difficulty.

He then dissolved the parliament, outlawed the Kuomintang (most of whose leaders fled to Japan), and proceeded to promulgate a constitution under which he, as President, became a virtual dictator. He ruled with an iron hand and gave China the most orderly and oppressive government it had known for more than a century. He was soon ruined, however, by Japanese enmity and his own ambition.

The Japanese government was opposed to the unification of China under a strong leader, which would render China less susceptible to Japanese influence. Yuan seemed to be such a leader, and he had earned additional hatred from the Japanese by opposing their encroachments in Korea during the decade preceding the Sino-Japanese War. In August 1914 the Japanese government entered the First World War on the Allied side, primarily in order to acquire German holdings in the Pacific. Having seized the German sphere of influence in Shantung, the Japanese presented Yuan Shih-kai in the spring of 1915 with the notorious Twenty-one Demands, which if accepted in their entirety would have transformed China into a virtual Japanese protectorate. Backed by world opinion, Yuan was able to secure a considerable modification of these demands, but he had to acquiesce in the Japanese position in Shantung.

The final Japanese blow to Yuan was delivered in connection with his plans to make himself Emperor. Late in 1915 he manipulated a show of popular support for his plans and announced that he would establish a new dynasty. This step aroused widespread opposition and even revolts in China, and the Japanese and other governments added their disapproval of the scheme. Yuan abandoned his imperial ambitions, and in June 1916 he died, while trying vainly to suppress the revolts that his announcement had touched off.

After Yuan's death the constitution and parliament of 1913 were restored. Within about a year, however, the republic was gravely weakened by the defection of the Kuomintang, which proceeded to set up a rival regime at Canton, and by widespread opposition to the government's action in taking China into the First World War on the Allied side. This it did at American insistence and mainly in order to secure a seat at the peace conference, from which it could press for abrogation of Japan's position in Shantung.

In fact, the republic soon degenerated into a dismal farce, which did much to disillusion Chinese intellectuals with Western parliamentary institutions, as embodied in the half-dozen constitutions drawn up in China between 1912 and 1928, and to pave the way for avowedly authoritarian alternatives. The recognized government at Peking became the plaything of shifting combinations of disreputable generals usually referred to as warlords. The typical warlord was a man of humble birth who had acquired at least the rudiments of a modern military education either in China or abroad and who after the Revolution of 1911 had become military governor of a province. Controlling the armed forces of the province, he also dominated its political life. He fought frequently with nearby rivals and generally treated the province as his private preserve, taxing the population almost beyond endurance. A few particularly powerful generals, who could be called superwarlords, controlled entire regions such as Manchuria (Chang Tso-lin) and Northwest China (Feng Yü-hsiang). Although often colorful and not always vicious, these warlords had a bad effect on China. Domestic militarism and Western imperialism came to rank in the eyes of Chinese revolutionaries as the two major evils which must be eliminated if China was to progress. Nevertheless, warlordism survived the fall of the republic in 1928 and continued to plague China until at least as late as 1949.

Several important trends operating during the period from 1912 to 1928 need to be mentioned before discussion of the republic and the warlords is concluded and the rise of the Kuomintang is considered. One was the tendency of the outlying parts of the former Manchu empire to separate themselves from China after 1912 and go their separate ways. The peoples of Outer Mongolia, Sinkiang, and Tibet had regarded themselves as subjects of the Manchus, not of the Chinese. Some of them, furthermore, had been antagonized by Chinese immigration into their territories, which the Manchus had encouraged after about 1900 as a precaution against absorption of the regions by Russia or Japan. After the Revolution, Outer Mongolia became independent of China in all but name and came under Soviet domination after 1921; Sinkiang fell under a succession of local Chinese warlords and was subject to powerful Soviet economic and political penetration from 1932 to 1942; and Tibet remained largely free of Chinese influence until the Chinese Communists overran it in 1950–1951.

The tendency toward gradual economic modernization, especially in the coastal regions of China, that had been in effect during the nineteenth century continued to operate during the republican period. Western commodities came increasingly into use, except in the most remote regions, and the growing of cash crops such as cotton or tobacco partially replaced subsistence farming in some coastal areas. On the whole, however, the peasant was more affected during this period by domestic political disorder than by foreign economic influences. No important change occurred in his agricultural techniques or in the trend toward more widespread tenancy. This trend was especially prevalent near the coastal cities and was the result primarily of the growth of population and the traditional preference of Chinese investors for land as the safest and most respectable outlet for their capital. Modern enterprises, both Chinese and foreign in ownership, continued to grow in the cities, but they were still far too few to make much of an impression on China's poverty and backwardness. China remained an overwhelmingly agrarian country, and the living standards of its people tended on the whole to get worse rather than better.

The most important trend of all was the growth of Chinese nationalism, in protest against both foreign imperialism and domestic militarism. One aspect of this trend was cultural and is usually known as the Chinese Renaissance. The two main leaders were Hu Shih, who had studied at Cornell and Columbia universities, and Ch'en Tu-hsiu, a professor who later became a founder of the Communist Party of China. Both men, and especially Ch'en, favored an almost complete scrapping of traditional Chinese culture and the substitution of Western culture in its materialistic and scientific aspects; Hu also led an ultimately successfully campaign for the use of *pai-hua* (the vernacular) in literature, instead of classical Chinese.

Still more important were the political manifestations of nationalism, which may be said to have begun to affect the intellectuals about 1895, the merchants a few years later, the small but growing industrial working class about 1918, and the peasants about 1925. The decision of the Versailles Conference in 1919 awarding the former German sphere in Shantung to Japan and the willingness of the pro-Japanese clique then in control of the Peking government to accept that award promptly touched off the first major manifestation of modern Chinese nationalism, the so-called May Fourth Movement. This movement, which began with student demonstrations in Peking and spread from there to other parts of the country, had the effect of preventing Chinese adherence to the Treaty of Versailles and of raising nationalist feeling to new heights. It later rose to fever pitch at the time of the May

Thirtieth Movement of 1925, which was precipitated by the shooting of Chinese demonstrators by British-officered police in the International Settlement at Shanghai. For the next two years antiforeignism in China raged unchecked, and many Christian missionaries found it wise to leave their mission stations for safer places.

This upsurge of Chinese nationalism, combined with a rising feeling in foreign countries that China had been unjustly treated and that Japan must be checked, led to some improvements in China's international position. At the Washington Conference (1921–1922), Japan agreed to evacuate Shantung, the Open Door Policy was written into treaty form for the first time (in the Nine Power Pact), and it was agreed in principle that the obnoxious features of the "unequal treaties" ought to be abrogated. Lenin's Bolshevik government made a very favorable impression on China by issuing in 1919 a ringing renunciation of former tsarist special privileges in China, though it was careful to regain in 1924 the right to operate the Chinese Eastern Railway through Manchuria to Vladivostok.

From 1913 to 1923 Sun Yat-sen's position was pathetic. His party was weak and ineffective, and he was largely dependent for what power he had on temporary alliances with unreliable warlords or other revolutionary factions. His futility was to a great extent the result of his own character, which was unselfish, patriotic, and sincere, but also impulsive, vacillating, and naïve. Even his political philosophy was not especially remarkable, but since it later became the official philosophy of China it deserves some attention.

Sun held that China could and should be transformed through the implementation of what he called the Three Principles of the People (San Min Chu I). Sun had advocated these principles as early as 1905, but they did not take final form until 1924, by which time Sun had become disillusioned with the Western democracies and favorably impressed by some aspects of Bolshevism.

The first was Nationalism, which meant the elimination of foreign imperialism and domestic militarism from China and the creation of a united but nonaggressive national state embracing not only the Chinese but also the Manchus, the Mongols, the Muslims of Northwest China and Sinkiang, and the Tibetans.

The second principle was Democracy, by which Sun meant a form of government in which the people should exercise the rights of election, recall, initiative, and referendum, but in which only educated and qualified persons should be admitted to the civil service and to political office. The government was to be divided into five branches corresponding to what Sun considered the major functions of government: executive, legislative, judicial, examination (roughly equivalent to the imperial civil service examination system), and control (roughly equivalent to the imperial censorate). Democracy as Sun defined it, however, was to be attained only in the last of three constitutional stages. During the first stage, the Kuomintang would unify China by force of arms. In the second, known as the period of Political Tutelage, the Kuomintang would exercise a monopoly of political power but use that power to train the people in the arts of self-government, so as to make possible the establishment of democracy and constitutional government.

The third principle was People's Livelihood, meaning the redistribution of land among the actual cultivators and state control of communications and heavy industry, all for the public benefit. As the comparative mildness of this program shows, Sun was far from being a Marxist.

It hardly seems necessary to comment on the vagueness and naïveté of these principles, except to emphasize Sun's unrealism in expecting a party once entrenched in dictatorial power to work for the abolition of its own dictatorship.

Sun's political ideas would not warrant even this brief summary if he had not found an ally to help him implement them. At that time Lenin and the Comintern (Third International) were casting about for Asian nationalist movements with which they might ally themselves in a joint struggle against the position of the Western powers in Asia. In 1922 they fixed on the Kuomintang as the most likely prospect in China, and a fateful alliance was accordingly concluded in 1923.

Under the terms of this alliance, the Comintern and the Soviet government provided the Kuomintang with arms, funds, and a staff of military and political advisers. The advisers reorganized the Kuomintang from top to bottom along the "democratic centralist" lines of the Soviet Communist Party and thereby transformed it for the first time into an effective political instrument. The Kuomintang also began to acquire something else it had lacked before—a reliable and effective army, which was built around an officer corps trained at the newly founded Whampoa Military Academy, near Canton.

There was another important aspect to the Kuomintang-Comintern alliance, namely, a coalition between the Kuomintang and the young and far weaker Communist Party. Sun Yat-sen insisted that Communists could enter the Kuomintang only as individuals, not as a bloc, and that they must abide by the usual conditions of membership, including party discipline. The Comintern compelled the Chinese Communists, against the better judgment of their leaders, to comply. They did so with the aim of using the Kuomintang for their own purposes, if possible.

The alliance between the Kuomintang on the one hand and the Comintern and the Chinese Communist Party on the other conferred during its brief existence considerable benefits on both parties, especially on the Kuomintang. It gave the latter not only efficient party and military machinery, but also a revolutionary zeal and a corps of agitators and propagandists, mostly Communists, who were of inestimable value in forming labor and peasant unions and in undermining the will of warlord armies to resist. The alliance, however, was an unstable one, because the parties to it had incompatible aims and distrusted each other.

The alliance began to show signs of strain not long after the death of Sun Yat-sen in March 1925. A year later General Chiang Kai-shek, the Kuomintang's leading military figure, brought off a coup which severely limited the power of the Soviet advisers and the Communists over party affairs. Stalin and the Comintern, however, decided to ignore the challenge, on the theory that everything must be subordinated to the success of the Northern Expedition, as the projected military campaign for the unification of China was called. Later, as Stalin put it, Chiang Kai-shek could be cast aside, like a squeezed lemon.

The Northern Expedition accordingly got under way in the summer of 1926 and from the beginning won brilliant successes. The rabble armies of provincial militarists melted away before the advance of the Kuomintang forces and their accompanying agitators. By the end of 1926 most of South China and the Yangtze Valley had been conquered, and the capital of the Kuomintang revolutionary regime and its party headquarters were transferred from Canton to Hankow. There they fell under the virtually complete control of the Soviet advisers, the Communists, and those elements within the Kuomintang which favored a leftist orientation for the party.

Chiang Kai-shek, whose forces were advancing farther to the east, in the lower Yangtze Valley, noted this trend with disapproval. To protect his own position and prevent the Bolshevization of the Kuomin-

tang, he prepared to strike. Against his blow his leftist opponents took
no adequate steps to protect themselves, mainly because of Stalin's
insistence that everything possible must be done to avoid giving
Chiang offense. Having entered Shanghai with the active and effective
cooperation of the Communist-led labor unions of that city, Chiang
turned on them suddenly on April 12, 1927, and crushed them. He
then set up a rival capital at Nanking in opposition to the one at
Hankow.

Stalin now had to admit that Chiang Kai-shek had betrayed the
common cause, but he still would not allow the Chinese Communists
to break off their alliance with the Kuomintang. On the contrary, he
sent them directives instructing them to seize control of the Kuomintang's party machinery and embark on a program of revolutionary
class warfare. Having learned of this policy, however, the Left Kuomintang at Hankow broke with its dangerous allies on July 15, 1927, and
expelled the Communists and the Soviet advisers. Soon afterward
most of the Left Kuomintang leaders submitted to Chiang Kai-shek.

By the spring of 1928 Chiang had consolidated his position within
the party sufficiently to resume the Northern Expedition. In spite of
a Japanese attempt to block the advance of his armies by sending
troops back to Shantung, he took Peking in June 1928. The Kuomintang
thereupon transferred the capital of China from Peking (which was
then renamed Peiping) to Nanking and officially proclaimed the military unification of China to be complete. The second of Sun Yat-sen's
three constitutional stages, that of Political Tutelage, had begun.

The Kuomintang in Power (1928–1937)

The unity achieved in 1928 was much more nominal than real. The
new government at Nanking controlled little more than the eastern
provinces; elsewhere, especially in Southwest and Northwest China,
provincial or regional militarists still exercised effective power. The
Kuomintang was never able to subdue some of these militarists; instead, it generally followed a policy of giving them high military and
political posts in their own provinces or regions, in the hope of securing their loyalty. The support purchased in this way resulted in
little of actual value, for some of these generals proved unreliable
against the Japanese and still later proved unreliable against the Communists.

After the failure of a disarmament conference in 1929 showed how
unwilling the regional militarists were to subordinate themselves in

fact to the National Government, there occurred a series of revolts against the power and policies of Chiang Kai-shek. Only the most serious of these need be mentioned. In 1929 there was a revolt by the so-called Kwangsi Clique led by Li Tsung-jen and Pai Chung-hsi; in 1930, one by a formidable combination of Feng Yü-hsiang, Yen Hsi-shan (the warlord of Shansi), and Wang Ching-wei (a prominent Left Kuomintang leader); in 1931, one by a group of Left Kuomintang politicians at Canton; in 1933, one by (non-Communist) Left Kuomin-tang generals and politicians in Fukien; and in 1936, another by the Kwangsi Clique. Chiang overcame all these revolts by force or diplo-macy. His army, trained by German advisers, was easily the strongest in China, although it could not eliminate Chiang's most dangerous and elusive enemies, the Communists.

From having been a decidedly revolutionary party under Sun Yat-sen and during the brief life of its alliance with the Communists, the Kuomintang after 1927 rapidly turned into a conservative and even reactionary party. Under Chiang Kai-shek's stultifying influence it ceased to produce able, prominent, and original political thinkers, and it therefore had no choice but to deify Sun Yat-sen and his ideas and parrot them without developing them further. Since Sun's political ideas had serious weaknesses, the uncritical propagation of them, com-bined with a rejection of the generous spirit which had been behind Sun's ideas, imparted to the Kuomintang a rigid and unattractive quality which tended to minimize popular support for it. Chiang Kai-shek and other prominent Kuomintang figures began to preach a re-turn to the ancient Confucian virtues of loyalty, propriety, and the like, ideas which no longer held compelling appeal for a people be-coming increasingly convinced of the possibility of and necessity for progress and modernization. One of the least attractive features of official Kuomintang thinking was its strong tendency toward xeno-phobia; in Chiang Kai-shek's famous tract, *China's Destiny* (published in 1943), for example, almost all China's ills and problems are at-tributed to Western influence. This strong anti-Western feeling, al-though to some extent justified, had the effect of making the Western powers less enthusiastic than they would otherwise have been about supporting the National Government against Japanese encroachments.

Another source of weakness was the fact that, although it retained the "democratic centralist" organization imparted to it during the period of the Communist alliance, the Kuomintang was never truly a "monolithic" party of the Communist type. On the contrary, it was

ridden with competing cliques whose selfish interests generally out-
weighed whatever loyalty to a common ideology, common party organization, and common cause they may have had. Basically, the
Kuomintang was an unstable coalition of military leaders, businessmen,
and rural landlords. More precisely, it was composed of the following
major cliques.

On the extreme right stood the CC (or Organization) Clique, so
called because it was controlled by the Ch'en brothers. The elder,
Ch'en Kuo-fu, was the leading specialist in party organization and
controlled most of the local party branches. He was therefore always
in a strong position at the rather infrequent party congresses (there
were six between 1924 and 1945), whose membership was elected by
the local party organs. His younger brother, Ch'en Li-fu, was a leading
party ideologist and specialist in education and public indoctrination.
He preached a strange philosophy called Vitalism, which represented
a blend of Confucianism with nineteenth-century European idealism
and enjoyed a decidedly limited popularity. The CC Clique was
strongly anti-Communist, dominant in the secret police, and very conservative in its views on social and economic questions.

Slightly less to the right stood the so-called Whampoa (or Military)
Clique. Although also conservative and anti-Communist, this group
was more concerned with problems of power than with party organization or ideology. Being specialists in force, the group generally held
the balance of power in the party, which it did not, however, entirely
dominate.

Another faction was the Political Science Clique. It was composed
largely of bureaucrats and intellectuals devoted to the goal of modern
and efficient administration, but without any clearly defined political
program.

Apart from these cliques, there were two other groups worth men-
tioning, though they were not well organized or very influential. The
first was a handful of Left Kuomintang politicians, of whom Wang
Ching-wei and Sun Yat-sen's son, Sun Fo, were the most prominent.
The other group comprised a number of wealthy businessmen, Chiang
Kai-shek's able but temperamental brother-in-law T. V. Soong being
the best known.

The keystone in the entire arch of Kuomintang power was Chiang
Kai-shek himself. He was by no means all-powerful or universally
respected within the party, yet he alone commanded both enough
power and enough loyalty to lead the party over a long period of time.

Of humble origin, having close connections with the Shanghai under-world, militaristic by training and background, conservative by inclina-tion, and intensely patriotic in a way which led him to consider the maintenance of his own power as essential to the good of the country, Chiang personified both the strengths and the weaknesses of the Kuo-mintang. A strong man himself, he could not tolerate disagreement from other strong men and preferred to surround himself with syco-phants. Personally honest, he refused to credit, or at any rate to punish, the widespread and increasing corruption among his associates and subordinates. Even more addicted than other Kuomintang leaders to multiple office holding, he held a list of posts in the party, government, and armed forces so long that it would be tedious to reproduce it. If he lacked both the dictatorial power and the charismatic appeal of a Hitler, he was nevertheless a powerful party boss with a secret police force and an army at his disposal.

During the period under consideration, China's constitutional struc-ture, like its political life, reflected the official view that the Kuomin-tang enjoyed a monopoly of legal political power. As early as 1928 the Kuomintang set up a central government containing five Yuan (branches) corresponding to the five envisioned by Sun Yat-sen: Ex-ecutive, Legislative, Judicial, Examination, and Control. This was a de-parture from Sun Yat-sen's program, for Sun had intended the fivefold governmental structure to be introduced at the end, not at the begin-ning, of the period of Political Tutelage. In most other respects the regime established in 1928 conformed to Sun's plan. The officials of the five Yuan were appointed Kuomintang members whose work was supervised by the Central Executive Committee of the Kuomintang through one of its agencies, the Political Council. Among the Yuan themselves, the executive was by far the most important, though of course it was still bound by party directives. At the top of the govern-mental structure, though also subject to control by the Kuomintang, stood the State Council, whose chairman was the nearest thing China had to a chief of state. Provincial and local offices were appointive and controlled by the central government and the Kuomintang.

In 1931 a semblance of greater constitutionality was conferred on the National Government through the adoption, by a National People's Convention whose membership had been hand-picked by the Kuomin-tang, of a provisional constitution. The main change that this con-stitution made in the preexisting situation was that it decreased the powers of the chairman of the State Council, which post Chiang Kai-shek had just given up as a sop to his opponents, who were then very vocal. He continued, however, to be very powerful in the government, in the party, and (through his chairmanship of the Military Affairs Commission) in the armed forces. The provisional constitution contained no procedure for its own amendment and vested the important power of constitutional interpretation in the Central Executive Committee of the Kuomintang. It was, in short, a legalization of Political Tutelage.

With amazing optimism the Kuomintang had promised in 1929 to complete the tasks of Political Tutelage within six years, and accordingly as early as 1933 it began work on a draft constitution for the last stage, that of constitutional government. After numerous revisions the draft was published with the party's blessing in May 1936. Unfortunately, it had several serious defects. The Executive Yuan was to be responsible, not to the Legislative Yuan in the British manner, but to a large and infrequently convened National Assembly. The powers of the President of the Republic, the chief of state, who was to be elected by the National Assembly, were so broad that it seemed likely that he would dominate the five Yuan and their respective presidents. The powers of the provincial and local governments were insufficiently protected from possible encroachments by the central government, and civil liberties were subject to restriction by legislation. It was very probable that under this constitution the Kuomintang would continue to dominate the political life of the country. It did in fact dominate elections held in 1936 for the members of a National Assembly to which the draft constitution was to be submitted for consideration; the convening of the Assembly, however, was prevented by the outbreak of war with Japan in July 1937.

The question of how the National Government of China functioned in practice during the period from 1928 to 1937 is a very important one, for it was then that the Kuomintang had its best chance to show what it could do for China. It is true that the Kuomintang was faced with enormous obstacles, such as a backward economy, domestic insurrections, and continuous Japanese pressure after 1931, but even when allowance is made for these difficulties its record remains far from impressive.

By 1937, and for that matter as late as 1949, not a single one of the 2,000-odd *hsien* in China had attained the state of local self-government that Sun Yat-sen had considered a prerequisite to the establishment of self-government on the provincial and national scales.

Nor was the mere absence of self-government the worst feature of Political Tutelage. The latter also carried with it a rigorous punitive censorship of the press, a large network of secret police and prisons, and a massive "white terror" flourishing in the cities and towns and directed not only against real or suspected Communists but also against others to whose actions or statements the Kuomintang objected. In some rural areas, especially those reconquered from the Communists, the National Government introduced after the mid-1930s the oppressive *pao-chia* system of collective responsibility for the crimes of individuals. To propagandize its official ideals of obedience and propriety, the Kuomintang inaugurated in 1934 a so-called New Life Movement, which was, however, perhaps more comic than oppressive in its actual working.

Unfortunately, the absence of freedom was not compensated by any significant increase in efficiency or mitigated by any noteworthy progress in the social and economic fields. Much praiseworthy legislation was promulgated, but it remained largely on paper. This was true, for example, of a law of 1930 fixing maximum rents on agricultural land at three-eighths of the annual crop. The unfortunate effects of the Depression, which included an outflow of silver, led to the introduction of a managed currency in 1935, under which the right of note issue was profitably confined to four central banks controlled respectively by T. V. Soong, H. H. Kung, the Ch'en brothers, and Chiang Kai-shek. The Kuomintang's approach to economic questions, at least in practice, was essentially one of dipping its hand as often as possible into a stagnant pool of wealth rather than one of trying to stir up the pool and increase its size.

In the field of foreign affairs the Kuomintang was slightly more successful. By 1931 it had successfully asserted its right to fix its own tariff rates and was on the way to abolishing the extraterritorial rights of citizens of all but the major foreign powers (the United States, Great Britain, and Japan). But these successes were dearly won, for the extreme antiforeignism of the Kuomintang tended to alienate the Western powers and render them less sympathetic to China's case against its major enemy, Japan, than they might otherwise have been.

At the hands of Japan the Kuomintang suffered a long series of injuries and humiliations: the conquest of Manchuria in 1931–1932, an attack by the Japanese navy on the "native" city of Shanghai in 1932, the occupation of Jehol province and the forced demilitarization of the Peiping-Tientsin area in 1933, an unsuccessful attempt in 1935 to make five provinces of North China and Inner Mongolia "autonomous" and thus more susceptible to Japanese penetration, and an extraordinary set of demands in 1936 which if accepted would have transformed Nationalist China into a virtual Japanese protectorate.

Until 1936 the National Government's response to these outrages was one of temporizing, for it feared the power of the Japanese and in any case was more interested in trying to suppress the Communists. This negative policy served only to whet the Japanese appetite and to arouse further the indignation of the articulate Chinese public. In 1935 the chorus of protest, to which the Communists contributed a share but only a share, reached fever heat. Thereafter the Kuomintang was under increasing pressure to stop fighting the Communists and ally with them to resist the Japanese.

The Chinese Communist Movement (1921–1937)

Until 1917 Marxism was one of the least influential intellectual currents that had entered China from the West. It would probably have remained in this state if other political movements, notably the Kuomintang, had not failed to provide any quick and spectacular answer to China's difficult and humiliating problems and if a Marxist party had not come to power in Russia in 1917. The Bolshevik Revolution was an event of incalculable importance for China. It provided China and all Asia with the spectacle of a backward nation trying energetically, if brutally, to transform itself into a modern one almost overnight through planned effort. It enabled the Soviet government to pose as a benevolent and nonimperialist friend of China in contrast to the admittedly self-interested nations of the West. It led to the formation of a Communist Party in China and provided that party with a powerful, often too powerful, leader and guide.

Shortly after the Bolshevik Revolution, Marxist study groups began to be formed among Chinese students and intellectuals in various cities of China and among groups of Chinese students abroad. By 1920 the respected intellectual Ch'en Tu-hsiu and some of his colleagues had become converts to Marxism-Leninism and had made contact with agents of the Comintern (the Third International). On July 1, 1921, the Communist Party of China (CPC) convened its First Congress and formally established itself, with Ch'en Tu-hsiu as its secretary-general. Naturally enough, the party's first major activities lay in the field of labor organization and agitation, in which it achieved considerable success. At its Second Congress, held in 1922, the party took another logical step in affiliating itself with the Comintern.

As yet the CPC was small and composed largely of intellectuals without political power or popular support. For this reason the Comintern in 1922–1923 chose the Kuomintang, rather than the CPC, as its major instrument in China and compelled the CPC to enter into its ill-fated alliance with the Kuomintang, the results of which have already been described. The CPC was nearly ruined in its infancy by Stalin's blind conviction that he could control an explosive and faraway revolutionary situation of whose power relations he actually understood very little. In spite of this disastrous error of judgment, Stalin's control over the central machinery of the CPC remained substantially unimpaired until the rise of a more independently minded CPC leadership under Mao Tse-tung about 1935.

The first reaction of Stalin and the Comintern to the disasters of 1927 was to blame Ch'en Tu-hsiu for them, to remove him from power, and to order a program of armed risings. The most important of these —the Nanchang Rising of August 1, among Communist-led units of the Kuomintang Fourth Army; the Autumn Harvest Rising, led by Mao Tse-tung in Hunan; and the bloody and short-lived Canton Commune of December 11–13—were more or less disastrous failures, but they did leave behind the nucleus of a Red Army, which in turn made possible the creation of a number of local soviets in the rural areas of Central and South China.

Rural activity of this kind offered the only prospect for the CPC, for the cities were firmly in the control of the Kuomintang or other anti-Communist factions. Furthermore, the urban labor unions, on which the CPC had placed its main reliance, were disgusted with Communist manipulation and were coming rapidly under Kuomintang control. Accordingly, the Sixth Congress of the CPC, held at Moscow in July 1928, gave permission for peasant organization and guerrilla warfare while still insisting that the main task of the CPC was to recapture leadership of the urban labor movement. The congress also confirmed the downfall of Ch'ü Ch'iu-pai, who had succeeded Ch'en Tu-hsiu as secretary-general but had been purged after the failure of the risings of 1927.

Leadership then passed into the hands of the energetic and overbearing labor organizer Li Li-san and his lieutenant Chou En-lai. Li was under almost constant pressure from the Comintern for spectacular successes in order to erase the defeats of 1927. He soon found that it was impossible to capture cities by means of proletarian risings, and his only alternative was therefore to turn to the Red Army, the most important section of which was under the control of Mao Tse-tung, and attempt to capture cities from without rather than from within. This policy, to which the Comintern gave its approval in July 1930, also failed; a Red Army force was driven out of the city of Changsha early in August after an occupation of about a week.

At first Li Li-san withstood the efforts of his opponents within the party to unseat him because of this failure, but in November 1930 he was condemned by the Comintern and thereupon resigned his posts and went into exile in Moscow. Leadership then passed into the hands of a group of young men just returned from study in Moscow and usually known as the Returned Students, or sometimes ironically as the Twenty-eight Bolsheviks. The unusually adaptable Chou En-lai managed to make himself indispensable to this new leadership, as he had to its predecessor. In their outlook and policies the Returned Students differed in no essential way from Li Li-san, except that they enjoyed greater personal favor from Stalin; they too were doctrinaire, impatient, oriented toward the cities, and subservient to the Comintern. They established the central machinery of the party briefly in Shanghai, but by the beginning of 1933 they had felt compelled to transfer it to Juichin, the capital of the central soviet government, partly as a result of Kuomintang police pressure in Shanghai and partly in order to contest with Mao Tse-tung the control of the central soviet government.

After the failure of his Autumn Harvest Rising in 1927, Mao had retreated southward with a handful of followers and set up a small soviet in the rugged terrain along the border between Hunan and Kiangsi. There he was joined by a stronger force under Chu Teh early in 1928. Together the two men began to organize a force capable of effective guerrilla warfare and to implement a program of land redistribution and peasant organization. Mao's rural orientation was not primarily attributable to his peasant origin, but rather to the impression made on him by the upsurge of antiforeignism and antilandlordism on the part of the peasants in his native province of Hunan in 1925 and to his realistic understanding of the futility of trying to base on the cities a major political movement in an agrarian country. Mao's emphasis on the revolutionary role of the peasantry earned him the disfavor of the successive leaderships of the CPC already mentioned, by whom he was deprecated as a "local Communist" who had never studied in Moscow and therefore had little understanding of Marxism-Leninism.

Nevertheless, Mao's soviet, which he transferred to Kiangsi in 1928 and thereafter steadily expanded, was the most important soviet in

China, and these soviets were virtually the only concrete success to which the CPC could point at the end of its first decade of existence. First Li Li-san, and later the Returned Students, attempted to take control of Mao's soviet away from him. Li's effort was comparatively ineffective and fairly easily resisted, but against the Returned Students Mao had less success. His principal opponents were Po Ku (secretary-general, 1932–1934) and Wang Ming (secretary-general, 1931–1932; principal CPC representative to the Comintern, 1932–1937) among the Returned Students and Chou En-lai.

Mao was elected chairman of the central soviet government (controlling in theory all soviets in China) at the First All-China Congress of Soviets held at Juichin, Kiangsi, in November 1931. Nevertheless, his actual control over the party machinery and armed forces in that area was steadily usurped by Chou En-lai and the Returned Students and their appointees. The Returned Students showed much more responsiveness to direction from the Comintern, favored a more radical and violent program of "land reform," and placed much more emphasis on regular as opposed to guerrilla warfare than did Mao.

At the end of 1930, alarmed by Li Li-san's attempt to capture Changsha, Chiang Kai-shek launched a series of so-called Annihilation Campaigns aimed at wiping out the soviets in Central China, especially the one in Kiangsi. All but the last of these campaigns were defeated by the Red Army, though with great effort and at considerable cost, by means of skillfully conducted guerrilla warfare. For the last campaign, however, which began in the summer of 1933, Chiang Kai-shek assembled an army of a million men and adopted a strategy of complete blockade and steady pressure which would probably have overwhelmed the weaker Red Army in the end regardless of the method of defense employed. It is therefore not necessary to attach complete validity to Mao Tse-tung's statement,[2] made not long afterward, in which he named the adoption of positional warfare instead of guerrilla warfare as one of the two major reasons for the destruction of the Kiangsi soviet and by implication blamed the Returned Students for this alleged error.[3]

Nor is it wise to take at face value the other reason advanced by Mao, a failure to cooperate with a Left Kuomintang revolt against

[2] Edgar Snow, *Red Star over China* (New York: Random House, 1944), p. 186.
[3] This imputation of blame has since been made explicit (e.g., Resolution on Some Questions in the History of Our Party, 1945, in *Selected Works of Mao Tse-tung* [New York: International Publishers, 1954–], IV, 196).

Chiang Kai-shek which occurred in nearby Fukien in November 1933 but was suppressed by National Government troops in January 1934.[4] There is fairly convincing evidence that the Returned Students favored active and prompt cooperation with the Fukien rebels, but that Mao advocated a more cautious policy, and that as a result of the ensuing indecision Chiang Kai-shek was enabled to move in and administer the *coup de grâce* to the rebellion.[5] According to the same source, Mao was thereupon not entirely unjustly made the scapegoat by the Comintern and the Returned Students for this disaster, which placed an implacably hostile army on the coastal flank of the Kiangsi soviet. At the Second All-China Congress of Soviets (January 1934), or shortly afterward, Mao was apparently stripped of virtually all his remaining power and sent out of Juichin. He was therefore not a party to the crucial decisions that had to be made during the ensuing months.[6]

By that time the CPC was confronted with a choice between being destroyed or attempting to break through the Kuomintang blockade and find safety elsewhere. The decision was in favor of the second course. On the night of October 15–16 the First Front Army—which had been built up by Mao Tse-tung and Chu Teh but was now largely under the control of the Returned Students and their military adviser from the Comintern, a German Communist invariably known by his Chinese name Li Teh (or Li T'e)—set out in a general westerly direction accompanied by about 30,000 civilians, mainly party functionaries.

During the first part of the Long March, as it came to be called, the Red Army followed a fairly straight and predictable course and therefore suffered heavy casualties. Indeed, there were several occasions on the Long March when the Kuomintang, with better generalship and greater energy, could have annihilated the First Front Army and thereby dealt a heavy, probably fatal, blow to the prospects of communism in China.

The military incapacity of the Returned Students, both in Kiangsi and now on the Long March, cost them the confidence of many of the

---

[4] This earlier claim is contradicted by Mao's later statement that the CPC "formed an alliance with the People's Government in Fukien" (*Selected Works*, IV, 192).

[5] Kung Ch'u (a former general in the Chinese Red Army), *Wo yü Hung Chün* [The Red Army and I] (Hong Kong: South Wind Publishing Company, 1954), pp, 362–367.

[6] *Ibid.*, pp. 395–400. See also statement by Chang Kuo-t'ao in Robert C. North, "The Rise of Mao Tse-tung," *Far Eastern Quarterly*, Feb. 1952, p. 141.

Red Army commanders. Skillfully utilizing this discontent and the support of some of his fellow Hunanese in the party hierarchy, Mao Tse-tung was able to seize control of the central party and military machinery of the CPC at a crucial conference held at Tsunyi, in Kweichow, in January 1935. His triumph received a partial endorsement from the Comintern later in 1935. Thereafter Mao's preeminent position within the CPC, which never equaled the iron dictatorship exercised by Stalin over his own party, was not seriously threatened although it was occasionally challenged.

Another important conference was held at Maoerhkai, in northwestern Szechuan, in July 1935. This time the principal antagonists were Mao and Chang Kuo-t'ao, then Mao's last remaining serious rival for power within the party. Chang considered rural soviets unsuitable for China and favored moving out of China proper, to eastern Tibet or Sinkiang; according to his own later account, he was supported in his views by the Comintern. Mao, on the other hand, upheld the suitability of soviets, refused to leave China proper, and advocated going to Shensi, where a soviet had been set up in 1930.

As a result the two men separated. Chang with his Fourth Front Army and some party functionaries who agreed with him retired to Sikang, in eastern Tibet, where they set up a central party apparatus in rivalry with that of Mao Tse-tung. Chu Teh accompanied them, for somewhat obscure reasons, and they were later joined by the Second Front Army under Ho Lung. After an unsuccessful attempt to reach Sinkiang, they finally came to Shensi to join Mao Tse-tung in October 1936.

Meanwhile, Mao and the First Front Red Army had proceeded northward through eastern Tibet into Kansu and thence into Shensi, where they arrived in October 1935 after a year on the road. The Long March had been a terrible ordeal and a feat of great military and physical endurance, which left the participants decimated and physically weakened but with greatly enhanced prestige and determination. Since that time, to have taken part in the Long March has been regarded in the CPC as a major honor.

In northern Shensi, Mao Tse-tung reestablished the central soviet government and after early 1936 proceeded to implement comparatively moderate policies, apparently under pressure from the Comintern that arose from Stalin's desire for a united front in China centering on the Kuomintang. Mao's troubles with Chang Kuo-t'ao were not over. Chang reached Shensi in October 1936, his position greatly weakened by military defeats suffered en route, and he evidently had further disputes with Mao over matters of power and policy. In 1937 the two men split openly on the question of the proper policy to be pursued toward the Kuomintang during the war against Japan. Chang favored sincere cooperation with the Kuomintang against the common enemy, Mao a policy of struggling against both simultaneously under cover of a purely nominal alliance with the Kuomintang. Mao prevailed, and in 1938 Chang was expelled from the CPC with the sanction of the Comintern.

Ever since the Japanese invasion of Manchuria in September 1931, at least some Chinese Communist leaders seem to have realized that their best and perhaps only hope of coming to power lay through a war with Japan. In April 1932 the central soviet government in Kiangsi declared war on Japan for propaganda effect. For the next three years the Comintern and the CPC repeatedly called for the overthrow of the Kuomintang and the formation of a united front, from which the Kuomintang as such would presumably be excluded, against Japan. By the time of the Seventh World Congress of the Comintern in August 1935, however, Stalin had concluded that this policy of a "united front from below" was futile. A united front against Japan must be one "from above"; in other words, it required the participation of the Kuomintang and even the leadership of Chiang Kai-shek. This view did not prevail with the CPC until reinforced by the logic of events in China.

As yet Chiang Kai-shek and the Kuomintang had given no sign of any willingness to establish a united front with the CPC. On the contrary, Chiang blockaded the soviet in Shensi as he had that in Kiangsi, though less effectively. His own blockade commanders became convinced of the futility of civil war and the desirability of united resistance to Japan. When Chiang flew to the headquarters at Sian to urge his commanders on against the Communists, they arrested him on December 12, 1936, and held him prisoner for a fortnight. They pressed him, at first without result, to form a united front with the Communists and invited a CPC delegation led by Chou En-lai to take part in the discussions. Under pressure from the Comintern and Chinese public opinion, the CPC reluctantly decided to accept Chiang Kai-shek's leadership in the war against Japan and intervened in Chiang's favor with his now-infuriated generals.

As a result, Chiang was released, apparently unconditionally, but in reality he had agreed reluctantly to a united front with the Communists. During the next several months its details were worked out, with much maneuvering and many propaganda blasts on both sides. On their part the Kuomintang and the National Government gave up their campaign against the Shensi soviet and relaxed their blockade considerably, lightened police controls and censorship of the press in the Nationalist areas, and agreed to resist the Japanese. On its side the CPC promised to abandon land redistribution and other manifestations of class warfare, cease its propaganda against the Kuomintang, and subordinate its government (renamed the Shensi-Kansu-Ningsia Border Region Government) and armed forces (renamed the Eighth Route Army) to those of the central government.

Neither side made these commitments in good faith. Nevertheless, for a short time, until nearly the end of 1938, both sides observed at least the letter of their agreement fairly faithfully, and an appreciable increase in China's unity resulted. Alarmed by this trend, the Japanese army began full-scale war against China on July 7, 1937.

The War against Japan (1937–1945)

To understand the course of the war it is necessary to recognize that the Japanese high command did not need to conquer all of China; this would probably have been impossible, and in any case not worth the effort. It would have been enough to seize and hold the major cities and lines of communication in eastern China, integrate the raw materials and manpower of that area into the economy of the Japanese empire, and if possible compel the National Government to become a Japanese puppet. Eastern China was occupied for about eight years (1937–1945). In addition, China was used as a gigantic training ground on which Japanese troops were prepared to meet more formidable enemies elsewhere. Since the Japanese did not make their main military effort in China, at least after 1941, the strength or weakness of Chinese resistance had little effect on Japan's ultimate collapse, which can be attributed almost exclusively to the efforts of the United States. Japan's adventure in China was not the drain on its strength that the campaign in Russia proved to be for Nazi Germany.

As in other Asian countries, the Japanese in China were able to find Chinese, though not very many, who were willing to collaborate with them; some did so out of sincere if misguided patriotism, some out of opportunism, and some out of a mixture of both. The leading collaborator was Wang Ching-wei, a brilliant but unstable Kuomintang politician who felt a personal jealousy toward the more powerful Chiang Kai-shek and sincerely believed that China's interests would be best served by cooperating with Japan rather than fighting it. In 1938 Wang went over to the Japanese and two years later was set up by them at the head of a puppet government in Nanking. The troops under his command became the weakest and least active of the four contestants in an extraordinarily complex military and political struggle, aptly known as a "war within a war," in which the others were the Japanese themselves, the Kuomintang, and the CPC.

Before the roles of the last two of these four opponents are considered, it would be well to summarize the major military operations of the war. The Japanese overran the North China Plain with very little difficulty, and the scene of hostilities shifted to the Yangtze Valley. After committing and losing many of his best troops in a brave but futile defense of Shanghai, Chiang Kai-shek also was forced in December 1937 to abandon his capital city of Nanking to Japanese pillaging. The Nationalist capital was then moved to Hankow, and when Hankow fell to the Japanese in October 1938 it was transferred to Chungking, in the fertile but remote province of Szechuan. At about the same time as the capture of Hankow, the Japanese also launched an amphibious assault on Canton that left them in possession of that city and a sizable beachhead around it.

By the end of 1938 the front had become nearly stable. In broad terms, it ran almost due north and south, from a point a little west of Peiping through a point a little west of Hankow to a point a little west of Canton. The Japanese were very far from controlling all the territory to the east of that line, but they controlled the cities and the principal lines of communication. To the east of the line Chinese irregular and even regular forces, mainly Communist rather than Nationalist, operated in pockets between the points held by the Japanese. In 1943, foreseeing a military crisis, the Japanese began to withdraw their troops into the cities and leave the garrisoning of outlying areas to puppet forces. In the summer of 1944 the strongest offensive since 1938 was launched by the Japanese in a successful attack on Chinese ground units and American air bases in Hunan and Kwangsi.

During the first year or two of the war, in spite of defeats suffered in the field, the position of the National Government and the Kuomintang was in some ways a strong one. The Japanese invasion and Japanese atrocities tended to rally the Chinese people behind the government. The united front with the CPC was still a reality. A consultative body known as the People's Political Council, in which all major Chinese parties and groups were represented, was appointed by the

National Government and functioned fairly effectively. Limited but
still useful military aid flowed in from the Soviet Union via Outer
Mongolia and Sinkiang and from the Soviet Union and to a lesser extent the United States and Britain over the newly constructed Burma
Road. There was a massive movement of factories, universities, and
people out of areas threatened by the Japanese and into Free China,
as it was then called.

After the removal of the capital to Chungking at the end of 1938,
however, the Nationalist position started to deteriorate alarmingly.
The terrible strain of the war began to tell, and the virtual isolation
of the government in backward Southwest China tended to promote
an increase in the influence within the Kuomintang of the reactionary
rural landlord element of the CC Clique. Relations with the CPC
showed signs of decline in 1939, the blame being attributable more to
the CPC than the Nationalists. The Kuomintang reimposed a military
blockade on the CPC-controlled areas in Northwest China, and in
1941 a semiconcealed civil war began between the two sides. Rampant
inflation set in after 1941 in the Nationalist areas, and it was aggravated
by growing corruption at all levels in the government, party, and
armed forces of Nationalist China. Despite a substantial volume of
American military aid and advice after Pearl Harbor, the Nationalist
war effort against the Japanese became, with local and temporary
exceptions, almost negligible. The effects of the war on the Nationalists
and their government were in fact disastrous, although their seriousness was not generally understood at the time, and it has been said
with much truth that the Japanese in the name of anticommunism delivered China to the Communists.

The Communists enjoyed throughout the war several unspectacular
but solid advantages over the Nationalists. They did not have to maintain a formal government or foreign relations. They stood to gain by
chaos, not lose by it. They controlled no major cities and therefore
had to feed none. They had comparatively little trouble with inflation.
Their elaborate ideology, their sense of being part of an irresistible
world movement centering in a powerful neighbor, and their disciplined party organization gave them a morale and staying power
largely absent in the case of the Kuomintang. By temperament and
training they were well suited to organizing peasant guerrilla forces
—an activity from which the Kuomintang generally preferred to ab-
stain—in order to supplement the efforts of their regular forces, which
were by no means negligible. Although they are not known to have

received any military or economic aid from the Soviet Union, they maintained communication with it throughout the war; for example, Chou En-lai, the CPC's leading expert on external relations, visited the Soviet Union in 1939 and 1940, presumably to talk with Stalin on the situation in Europe and Asia.[7]

Another important advantage of the CPC over the Kuomintang was that of superior leadership. After the expulsion of Chang Kuo-t'ao from the CPC in 1938, Mao Tse-tung remained without any serious rival for control of the party. By that time he had already elaborated a basic strategy against both the Japanese and the Kuomintang that later brought the CPC out of the war against Japan far stronger than when it had entered. His plan was to use mobile warfare conducted by regular troops and guerrilla warfare conducted by irregular forces, but seldom positional warfare. The struggle was to be masked behind a propaganda calculated to appeal to non-Communist Chinese public opinion by emphasizing resistance to Japan rather than civil war and short-term rather than long-term Communist goals.

During this period Mao was clearly moving closer to Stalin and the Soviet Communist Party, both of whom appear earlier to have regarded Mao's rise to power with some doubts and were in return regarded by Mao as largely extraneous to his own problems and those of the CPC as he saw them. By at least as early as 1939, however, Mao had become a fairly close student of Stalin's writings and had probably accepted at least the essentials of Stalin's domestic program (forced industrialization, collectivization of agriculture, and totalitarian police controls) as necessary for China once the CPC gained power. The major reasons for this *rapprochement* were probably three: Mao was beginning to formulate his program for the exercise of power, which owed almost as much to Stalin as his strategy for the seizure of power did to Lenin; Mao was being forced by the outbreak of the Second World War to pay more attention to international affairs, to which Stalin seemed a useful guide; and Mao, although in almost unchallenged control of the CPC, was preparing to apply at least some of Stalin's techniques of party control to his own party. This he did in the so-called Cheng Feng (Rectification of Working Style) Movement of 1939–1942, a purge of ideas and to some extent of individuals. To guard against a relaxation of party discipline and a dissipation of party ideology in the course of the struggle against Japan, both high-ranking and low-ranking CPC members were lectured against vari-

[7] See *New York Times*, Sept. 17, 1939, March 26, 1940.

ous failings ("subjectivism," "sectarianism," and "formalism") which seemed likely to lead to such a result. The movement appears to have had the desired effect.

Mao Tse-tung's revolutionary strategy, which he perfected during the war against Japan, resembled Stalin's formula for China somewhat, but this was mainly because the ideas of both were derived from a common Leninist base. Where Mao improved on Stalin was mainly in his keen understanding of Chinese conditions and of the consequent necessity for adaptations and flexibility. Mao himself described his strategy in 1939 as follows:

The united front and the armed struggle are the two chief weapons for defeating the enemy. The united front is a united front for carrying on the armed struggle. And the [Communist] Party organisation is the heroic fighter who wields the two weapons, the united front and the armed struggle, to storm and shatter the positions of the enemy.[8]

Mao's formula for employing these two main weapons of armed struggle and the united front was to base himself on the peasantry rather than on the proletariat (while still paying verbal tributes to the revolutionary role of the latter), in order to "encircle the cities from the countryside"; to establish local soviet governments as nuclei of further expansion; to build up a Red Army skilled at mobile and guerrilla warfare; and to isolate the Kuomintang politically and appeal to middle-of-the-road opinion by calling for a united front or "four class bloc" composed of the proletariat, the peasantry, the national (big but patriotic) bourgeoisie, and the petty bourgeoisie (including intellectuals).

By 1945 skillful application of Mao's formula and steady expansion at the expense of both the Japanese and the Kuomintang had resulted in the establishment of some twenty "liberated areas" under the control of the CPC and scattered from Manchuria to Hainan and in a rapid growth of the Red Army and of the population ruled by the CPC, to about 1 million and 85 million respectively.

In 1944, probably under Soviet pressure, the CPC began to put forward a demand for the formation of a coalition government in which the CPC, as well as the Kuomintang and certain minor middle-of-the-road parties, would participate. Although most American officials then in China, including Ambassador Hurley, inclined toward this proposal, the Kuomintang rejected it and advocated instead the conven-

[8] *Selected Works*, III, 65.

ing of the National Assembly elected in 1936, with the addition of representatives of the CPC and the minor parties. Whether the CPC seriously expected its demand for a coalition government to be accepted is impossible to say, but there is no doubt that effective propaganda was made out of it. *On Coalition Government* was the title of Mao Tse-tung's report to the Seventh Congress of the CPC, which met at Yenan (Shensi), the capital of the Shensi-Kansu-Ningsia Border Region, in April–June 1945.

The congress clearly legitimated the ascendancy of Mao Tse-tung within the CPC, which he had won since the time of the Sixth Congress in 1928. The alleged errors committed by Mao's predecessors in the party leadership were excoriated, yet three of them (Wang Ming, Po Ku, and Li Li-san) were elected to the new Central Committee in a gesture toward party harmony, and probably toward Stalin as well. A new party constitution, confirming Mao's control over the major central organs of the party and emphasizing his importance as a theorist, was adopted. The proceedings of the congress reflected an expectation of an early end to the war with Japan and of the outbreak of full-scale civil war with the Kuomintang, culminating in a Communist victory, except in the unlikely event that an acceptable coalition government could be worked out.

Civil War (1945–1949)

The Japanese government made a definitive announcement of its willingness to surrender on August 15, 1945. From their comparatively nearby bases in Southwest China and with important American help in the form of transport, Nationalist forces had little difficulty in occupying the cities in the Yangtze Valley and to the south of it which had been held by the Japanese; the CPC's New Fourth Army, which had operated in the lower Yangtze Valley since the beginning of the war, evacuated this area and moved northward, part of it going to Manchuria.

In North China it was another story. Here the Red Army had long had powerful bases, especially in Shantung. The best the Nationalists could do, again with American help, was to occupy the coastal cities without being able to maintain dependable communication between them by land.

Still more difficult was the situation in Manchuria, which both sides regarded as the major prize at stake. Soviet forces were in occupation of the entire region, and the National Government had no choice but to ratify, in a Sino-Soviet treaty signed on August 14, 1945, the right to use the principal Manchurian ports and railways which had been granted to the Soviet Union at Yalta and confirmed at Potsdam. While in occupation the Soviet forces made entry difficult for Nationalist troops, so that the latter were never able to occupy more than the major cities and rail lines from Changchun south. In violation of the Soviet government's pledge to deal only with the National Government, Soviet forces permitted CPC military units to enter Manchuria overland through Inner Mongolia and by sea from Shantung and made stocks of captured Japanese weapons available to them. A large amount of industrial equipment of Japanese origin was also shipped out of Manchuria to the Soviet Union to help restore the battered Soviet economy and to prevent Manchuria from again becoming an anti-Soviet industrial base as it had been under the Japanese, in the event that it came under Chinese Nationalist or American control. Such a possibility evidently bulked larger in Stalin's mind than the chance of Chinese Communist victory in Manchuria.

The net effect of these Soviet actions was undoubtedly to make things easier for the CPC in Manchuria. In any case the CPC was determined to control Manchuria, both because of its industrial and strategic importance and because the CPC would then have direct contact with the Soviet Union and a base with a secure rear from which it could drive southward. The Kuomintang too was determined to control Manchuria if it could, even though its control over North China was far from secure. Against American advice, but with the aid of American transport, the Kuomintang threw its best American-trained troops into the ill-fated struggle for Manchuria.

It was clear that the rapidly developing race for control of areas formerly occupied by the Japanese, and of Manchuria in particular, threatened with civil war a country which had known little peace since the collapse of the Manchus and none at all since 1937. This outlook was extremely unwelcome to Chinese public opinion and only slightly less so to the United States government, which during the Second World War had insisted on treating China as a major and essential ally. The pressure for peace from these two directions sufficed to delay, but not to prevent, the outbreak of civil war.

In December 1945 General George C. Marshall arrived in China as President Truman's special representative with instructions to urge the National Government to call "a national conference of representatives of major political elements" and to advocate a modification of the Kuomintang's dictatorship, the formation of a coalition government representing all major parties, and the establishment of a unified national army. This program resembled the one that the CPC had been advocating since 1944, but the United States government proposed it not for this reason but because it appeared to offer the only alternative to civil war.

In January–February 1946 General Marshall was able to arrange a cease-fire agreement between the two sides. Thereupon a multiparty Political Consultative Conference met and agreed on the convening of a National Assembly in May 1946, the formation of an interim coalition government, and the creation of a national army with a five-to-one ratio of divisions as between the Kuomintang and the CPC. The conference also appointed a committee to draw up a draft constitution for submission to the National Assembly; this document when completed proved to be considerably more democratic than the draft which the Kuomintang had published in 1936.

Both sides soon began to violate both the spirit and the letter of the cease-fire agreement and the resolutions voted by the Political Consultative Conference, which therefore never went into effect. General Marshall tried to enforce their observance, but in vain. He could apply sanctions only to the Kuomintang, for the CPC was beyond his reach, and he actually embargoed arms shipments to the National Government from the United States for one year (1946–1947). In the spring of 1946 fighting broke out in Manchuria, and in October the National Government further decreased the chances of peace by reinstituting conscription and announcing that it would convene the National Assembly, which the CPC and several of the minor parties had already announced they would boycott, in November. Convinced that his mission had failed, General Marshall returned to the United States in January 1947. After that the United States shifted from a policy of mediation to one of limited but still significant support for the National Government, combined with entreaties to it to reform itself.

These were to no avail; the Kuomintang continued on the same suicidal course on which it had embarked at least as early as 1941, and by 1945 it was probably past saving. The influence of the extreme right wing within the party increased, and so did oppression and corruption. High-ranking officials rushed to gain control of former Japanese assets and exploit them for private profit. The territories reoccupied from the Japanese were lamentably misgoverned, and in one such area, Taiwan, there were serious popular risings against the Kuomintang beginning on February 27, 1947. Despite the adoption of a reasonably democratic permanent constitution by the National Assembly in December 1946 and its inauguration a year later, the grip of the Kuomintang on the governmental machinery remained unbroken. Inflation continued to mount at an almost geometric rate, and the government's last effort to check it and save the national currency, by introducing in August 1948 a currency backed by gold, was a miserable failure. The intellectuals and students were increasingly alienated from the Kuomintang by its police terror and its denial of freedom of expression. Small businessmen were disgusted at speculation by high officials and ruined by inflation. The peasants were more than ever indifferent, if not actually hostile, to a regime which showed no interest in their welfare and left them to be exploited by their landlords and local officials or organized and propagandized by the Communists. Since the Kuomintang's dictatorship had always inhibited the growth of middle-of-the-road parties, those who were disillusioned with the Kuomintang had in effect nowhere else to go except to the Communists, to whom many of them turned as a probable lesser evil rather than as a positive good.

Given these conditions, there is nothing surprising in the fact that the Kuomintang suffered almost continuous defeats in the field at the hands of the Communists. That these defeats were more the result than the cause of the conditions just described can be easily shown. The National Government entered the civil war in 1946 with roughly a three-to-one advantage in population, territory, and troops under arms and an even greater superiority in industrial potential. It also enjoyed considerable, though by no means total, diplomatic, economic, and military support from the United States, whereas the CPC is not known to have received any material aid from the Soviet Union during the civil war apart from the Soviet actions in Manchuria already mentioned. Furthermore, the Japanese weapons which the CPC acquired in Manchuria were more than counterbalanced by Japanese weapons surrendered to Nationalist forces in China proper.

On paper, then, the Kuomintang was vastly superior and ought to have won, but the morale and fighting effectiveness of its troops were progressively undermined by strategic decisions taken above them by inept commanders and by the deterioration of the home front behind them. Provincial warlords serving in the governmental forces, never much more than nominally loyal to the National Government, often deserted when the military pressure from the Communists increased.

The Communists took full advantage of their enemy's weaknesses by means of skillful organization, training, propaganda, strategy, and tactics. Until 1947 they waged a largely defensive war of maneuver and under its cover began a reorganization of their forces into larger and more powerful units which became known after 1948 as field armies. In 1948 they opened an offensive in the Yellow River area from their bases in Shantung. The same year another such offensive, led by the outstanding Communist field commander Lin Piao, completed the conquest of Manchuria and thereby deprived the National Government of most of its best troops. At the beginning of 1949 the Communists took Peiping, Tientsin, and the important rail junction of Hsuchow not far north of Nanking. In April and May the Yangtze Valley cities, including Nanking and Shanghai, fell to the People's Liberation Army, as it was now officially called. The Nationalist capital was moved successively to Canton, Chungking, and Chengtu, as each city fell before the advancing Communists. By the end of 1949 the Kuomintang had transferred most of its party and governmental apparatus to Taiwan, and the CPC controlled all of China proper and the outlying regions except Taiwan itself and Tibet.

The speed with which the civil war on the Chinese mainland came to an end was probably a surprise to nearly everyone concerned. It seems likely that Stalin was one of the most surprised of all, for he had given signs that he did not take the Chinese Communists or their prospects very seriously. For good or ill, the CPC had now become of necessity a major factor in the calculations of all other powers, Communist and non-Communist alike. The most significant reasons for its triumph, in descending order of probable importance, appear to have been the Japanese invasion of China, the shortcomings of the Kuomintang, and the revolutionary strategy of Mao Tse-tung.

The CPC gave several indications during 1949 of the course it would pursue after completing the seizure of power in China. In March its Central Committee announced that the center of gravity of party work had shifted from the countryside to the cities and exhorted all party members to devote themselves to economic reconstruction. In his important work *On the People's Democratic Dictatorship*, published on July 1, Mao Tse-tung clearly stated his intention to introduce into China the essentials of Stalinism: forced heavy industrialization, socialized agriculture, and a police state equipped to suppress "counterrevolutionaries." He also announced that the "new" China would "lean to one side," toward the Soviet Union, and denied forcefully that China or any other country could remain neutral as between the Soviet and American "camps." This essentially uncompromising program Mao softened somewhat by elaborating the fiction that the new state would not be a pure Communist dictatorship or a "dictatorship of the proletariat" but would be a multiclass dictatorship "of the people," led by the CPC and exercised by the workers, the peasants, the national bourgeoisie, and the petty bourgeoisie. Minor "democratic" parties would be allowed to exist within the framework of a "united front" led by the CPC. Both the essential sternness and the superficial reasonableness of this pronouncement were to mark the history of the regime which the CPC proceeded to establish in the autumn of 1949.

· II ·

China since 1949

COMMUNIST China since the "Liberation" of 1949 is a phenomenon unique in the contemporary world. It is a Communist regime which came to power in the most populous country on earth after a generation of armed struggle against domestic and foreign enemies and with the active or passive support of a considerable section of the Chinese people. Abroad, the impact of this phenomenon on the rest of Asia has been even greater than that of the Bolshevik Revolution, because it is closer to home. Domestically, the Chinese Communists have been able to consolidate their power more rapidly and thoroughly than the Bolsheviks in Russia were able to do during the first few years after their seizure of power in 1917. The Bolsheviks had to fight a civil war after seizing power whereas in China the civil war came first.

If knowledge of China's history before 1949 is necessary to adequate understanding of Chinese government and politics since 1949, so is knowledge of the main events in China's history since the "Liberation."

Historical Summary

The Chinese People's Republic (CPR) was officially proclaimed at Peking, which became its capital, on October 1, 1949. The necessary preliminaries had been managed by the Chinese People's Political Consultative Conference, a large body nominated by the CPC to represent

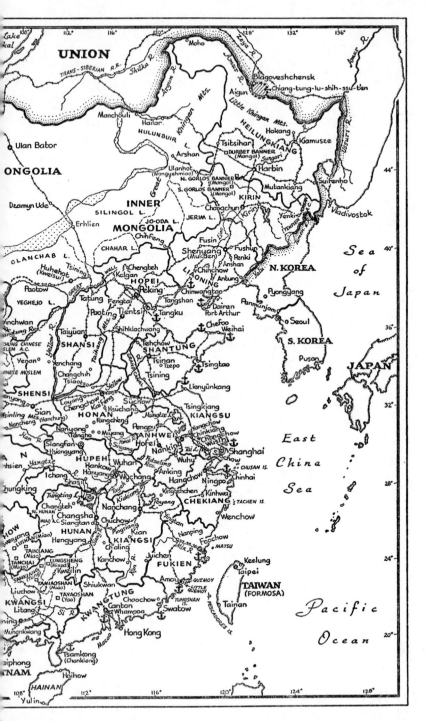

Peter S. H. Tang, copyright 1957, Frederick A. Praeger, Inc.)

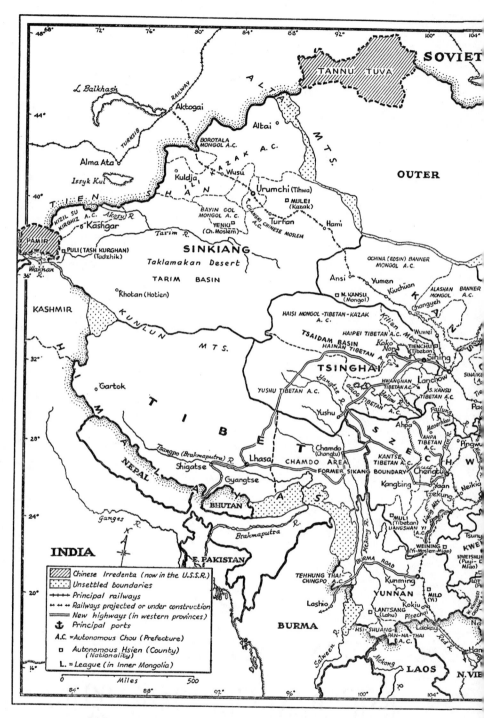

Map 3. Communist China in 1956. (From *Communist China Today*, by

various elements in the "united front" such as the CPC itself, the "democratic" political parties, various occupational groups, national minorities, and the like. The conference elected a Central People's Government Council, the highest governmental body under the new regime, designated Peking as the capital, and approved a new flag and a national anthem. It also adopted two important semiconstitutional documents: the Common Program, a statement purporting to represent the aims of the "united front" but actually elaborating some of the principles set forth by Mao Tse-tung in *On the People's Democratic Dictatorship,* and the Organic Law, which specified the organization of the Central People's Government.

By 1949 war and inflation had nearly ruined the Chinese economy and brought production almost to a standstill. The most urgent initial task of the CPC in power was to rehabilitate the economy by checking inflation and restoring production. To these tasks it devoted most of its energy during 1950, and with considerable success. It was able to check inflation after a time by bringing the whole economy under control and by the simple but effective method of computing the value of bank deposits in terms of the prices of essential commodities; thus the value of a deposit would increase in proportion to any subsequent rise in prices. The restoration of production was more difficult, and it was not until about 1952 that the output of the economy reached a level roughly equivalent to the highest achieved before 1949. In this field the major effort was made in Manchuria, which in spite of its partial sacking by the Soviet Army was still the most highly industrialized region in China.

Like the Bolsheviks in revolutionary Russia, the CPC was faced with the difficult problem of controlling the countryside so as to ensure a reasonably adequate supply of food for the cities and for export. To do this and break the power of the potentially dangerous landlord class, the CPC undertook a nation-wide program of "agrarian reform." In line with the views of Lenin, the CPC had long divided the rural population into the following major categories, on the basis of type of labor performed and relationship to the land: landlords, rich peasants, middle peasants, poor peasants, and landless peasants or "rural proletariat." Except for an interval of about a decade after the outbreak of war with Japan, the CPC had generally pursued a policy of confiscating landlords' land without compensation and redistributing it among poor and landless peasants. This was not in the main done out of benevolence, but rather to bring the rural areas under Communist control by breaking the power of anti-CPC elements in the countryside and gaining support for the CPC and recruits for the Red Army from among the poorer elements.

The same basic principles inspired the Agrarian Reform Act of June 30, 1950, which provided for the confiscation and redistribution of land belonging to landlords, but not of land belonging to rich peasants. This policy was implemented with great brutality during 1950–1952 in all major agricultural regions of China except those inhabited by national minorities. In the course of the "reform," CPC cadres (fieldworkers) put into the landlord classification and accordingly "liquidated," economically or physically, many thousands of individuals who were actually not landlords at all, or at any rate had not been exploiters.

On this bloodbath others were superimposed after China's intervention in the Korean War. The most spectacular was a campaign against "counterrevolutionaries," during which hundreds of thousands of persons accused of disloyalty to the regime and to "the people" were tried and sentenced to prison or executed in the presence of howling mobs. Two similar but distinct campaigns also conducted during 1951–1952 were the San Fan [1] campaign against corruption on the part of governmental personnel and the Wu Fan [2] campaign against alleged similar offenses on the part of private businessmen. The Wu Fan campaign, which resulted in the fining or imprisonment of many businessmen and the suicide of some, was probably prompted by the weak state of the CPR's budget and by a desire to break the power of the bourgeoisie and netted the regime perhaps as much as US$2.2 billion.

The CPC was keenly aware that two regions, Taiwan and Tibet, remained to be "liberated." At the end of 1949, accordingly, it began preparations for an amphibious assault on Taiwan. It was frustrated by its own unpreparedness for such an ambitious operation and by an epidemic of liver-fluke disease among the troops involved, most of whom were North Chinese unaccustomed to the unhealthy conditions of South China. Soon an invasion of Taiwan was rendered impossible by the outbreak of war in Korea, which led to the interposition of

---

[1] That is, "Three Anti," so called because directed against corruption, waste, and bureaucratism.

[2] "Five Anti," so called because directed against bribery, tax evasion, fraud, theft of state property, and divulgence of state economic secrets.

the United States Seventh Fleet between Taiwan and the mainland. No such obstacles prevented the conquest of Tibet, which was invaded from the east in October 1950 by troops of the Second Field Army. The completion of the campaign required about a year, during which Tibetan forces offered spirited but hopeless guerrilla resistance and the Chinese troops suffered severely from the weather and food shortages. The "liberation" of Tibet from the fiction of "Anglo-American imperialism" and its incorporation into Communist China were officially proclaimed on May 23, 1951.

The energy and ruthlessness displayed by the CPC during its first two or three years in power were of course motivated mainly by a desire to consolidate the CPC's political control as rapidly and thoroughly as possible. But there also seems to have been a sense of urgency and fear of possible satellitization by the Soviet Union and of possible "counterrevolutionary" intervention by the United States and the Kuomintang, similar to what happened in postrevolutionary Russia.

Accordingly, it was a task of the highest priority for the CPC to regulate its relations with Big Brother. This was a difficult task, for Stalin clearly would have liked to receive from the CPC the same subservience he had imposed on the Communist regimes of Eastern Europe. Mao Tse-tung, acting officially as Chairman of the Central People's Government rather than as leader of the CPC and taking his first trip outside his native country, arrived in Moscow in time to help Stalin celebrate his seventieth birthday on December 21, 1949. Later Mao and his delegation were reinforced by the arrival of Premier and Foreign Minister Chou En-lai, an able negotiator whom Stalin admired greatly.

Weeks of secret and probably hard bargaining preceded the signing of a treaty on February 14, 1950. The core of this treaty was a thirty-year defensive alliance directed against Japan or "any state allied with Japan," meaning the United States. The relationship between the Soviet Union and the CPR was proclaimed to be one of friendship based on a set of principles very similar to those which later came to be known as the Five Principles of Peaceful Coexistence. A supplementary agreement provided that the Soviet Union should continue to share in the use of the principal Manchurian railways (known collectively as the Chinese Changchun Railway) and the naval base of Port Arthur until the conclusion of a peace treaty with Japan or the end of 1952, whichever came earlier, but should immediately turn over to the CPR all its property in the nearby commercial port of Dairen. Another agreement committed the Soviet Union to lend the CPR $300 million; the loan was to be used to buy industrial equipment from the Soviet Union and was to be repaid in raw materials and currency beginning no later than the end of 1954. This scarcely constituted an act of princely generosity on Stalin's part. Such were the major published terms of the treaty, but there were numerous reports, some of them fantastic, of additional secret clauses.

Among the other subjects probably discussed were actual or proposed developments in Japan, Korea, Vietnam, and India, as well as the CPC's increasingly vocal claim to provide inspiration and perhaps leadership to Communist movements throughout Asia.

Of the large number of Sino-Soviet cultural and economic agreements signed in the wake of the treaty of February 14, 1950, the most important was a series of agreements signed on March 27 providing for the sending of Soviet military and economic advisers to China and creating four Sino-Soviet "joint-stock" companies. One was to operate a civil airline between the two countries; another was to extract nonferrous and rare minerals (including uranium) in Sinkiang; a third was to extract and refine petroleum in Sinkiang; and the fourth was to build and repair ships at Dairen. Although nominally operated on a footing of equality between the two partners, these companies were strongly reminiscent of the notorious joint companies through which the Soviet Union was draining the economies of Eastern European satellites and constituted a serious infringement of Chinese sovereignty, especially in Sinkiang.

By far the most serious crisis faced by the CPR during its early years was the Korean War. Its leaders had at least a general foreknowledge that such a war was in the offing. The Soviet Union was much more deeply involved, however, for North Korea was a Soviet rather than a Chinese satellite. The Communist side cannot have expected the United States to react as it did; otherwise the Soviet delegation would not have been boycotting the United Nations Security Council in protest against the presence of Chinese Nationalist delegates when the war began on June 25, 1950.

Already the CPC had begun to concentrate troops in Manchuria, many of them withdrawn from the Taiwan Strait. These dispositions, combined with the military aid and advice which the People's Liberation Army (PLA) had already begun to receive from the Soviet Union, placed the PLA in a position to intervene in Korea if necessary. Early in October, Chou En-lai announced that the CPC would not tolerate a northward crossing of the 38th parallel by non-Korean United Nations forces. It is possible that the cautious Stalin was reluctant to see the CPR intervene, but the CPC was determined to keep a hostile force away from its Manchurian frontier and to a lesser extent to prevent the destruction of another Communist state; in 1593 another Chinese army had intervened similarly to save a client Korean state from Japanese conquest. Not to act, furthermore, would have jeopardized the CPR's self-appointed status as the leader of Asia.

In Korea the Chinese People's Volunteers, as the PLA expeditionary force formed on October 25, 1950, was officially called in order to avoid the possible consequences of formal involvement in a war, won striking initial successes by using the methods of mobile warfare to which they were accustomed. After the disastrous failure of the two great Chinese thrusts toward Seoul in the spring of 1951 and the subsequent respite gained through the initiation of truce talks, the front became nearly stationary and all possibility of a breakthrough with conventional arms by either side disappeared.

The war imposed a serious strain on Communist China. In addition to the heavy losses of men and matériel at the front, there were heavy payments to the Soviet Union for needed military equipment. The entire country was put under a virtual state of siege and racked with the bloody campaigns already mentioned. Forced donations under the guise of voluntary "contributions" were extracted from the public. Many hundreds of thousands of people were mobilized for compulsory labor, especially in Manchuria, including service as ammunition carriers behind the front. For this strain the regime, if not the people, was compensated to some extent by more effective control over the country and a great increase in international prestige, especially elsewhere in Asia, as a result of the very respectable showing which the Chinese People's Volunteers made against a technically superior opponent in Korea.

Local defeat in Korea, in the spring of 1951, apparently taught the CPC to avoid direct collisions with American military power and contributed to a lower estimate of the utility of force as a means of advancing communism in Asia. Having preached Communist-led insurrection in Southeast Asia since early 1948, the CPC in 1951 began to soften its line, which was having little success except in Vietnam, and to search for a less military and more political approach.

The history of the tedious armistice negotiations in Korea conveys a strong impression that the CPC would have been willing to make peace in the autumn of 1952 on the basis of the compromise Indian resolution on the last major question in dispute—the disposition of prisoners of war who were unwilling to be repatriated—but that Stalin vetoed the idea. Within less than a month after the announced date of his death on March 5, 1953, the CPC proclaimed its willingness to reopen negotiations, and a truce agreement was accordingly concluded on July 27, 1953. The truce left a large Chinese force in Korea.

Meanwhile a less overt but equally important Chinese intervention had been taking place in another direction, in Vietnam. There a Communist-led guerrilla war against the French had been in progress since 1946. Unlike their North Korean colleagues, the Vietnamese Communists were never threatened with military extinction, nor was there any threat to Chinese territory; full-scale Chinese intervention was therefore both unnecessary and undesired by the Vietnamese and (after the defeat in Korea) by the Chinese. Instead, after the Korean armistice the CPC increased its flow of military aid and advice to the Vietminh forces under Ho Chi Minh. Without this aid the Vietminh would probably not have been able to defeat the French and expel them from North Vietnam, at least not for a much longer period of time.

Even before the disastrous siege of Dienbienphu in the spring of 1954 it was clear that the French had been beaten. Accordingly, a major international conference met at Geneva in the spring and early summer of 1954 to deal with both the Korean and the Indochinese questions. For the first time the CPR took part in a major international conference, the other participants being the Soviet Union, the United Kingdom, France, the (Communist) Democratic Republic of Vietnam, the three (non-Communist) Associated States of Indochina, and to a limited extent the United States. Although nothing significant was decided concerning Korea, the Soviet Union and the CPR accepted a surprisingly moderate Indochina settlement. The essence was that Vietnam was divided at the 17th parallel, instead of at about the 14th as the military situation would have indicated. This constituted a serious setback for Ho Chi Minh, but the CPC apparently wanted to prevent him from growing too strong and also to enhance its own international standing as a champion of "peaceful coexistence." [3] The CPR emerged from the Geneva Conference with its prestige considerably increased.

It won another striking triumph at the Asian-African Conference at Bandung, Java, held in April 1955. Here, as at Geneva, the CPR was represented mainly by Chou En-lai, who again performed brilliantly. He succeeded in allaying at least some of the fear and suspicion with which the CPR was regarded by its non-Communist Asian neighbors because of its domestic dictatorship, its antireligious policies, its manipulation of overseas Chinese communities, its tendency to pick boundary disputes with its neighbors, and its maintenance of a very large army. Chou appears to have returned from Bandung more than ever convinced that the policy, which the CPR had been implementing increasingly since 1954, of stressing "peaceful coexistence" in its relations with non-Communist states would be a fruitful one.

Even if such a policy had not seemed advantageous to the CPR's long-range international interests, it would still have been rendered advisable by the strain of the Korean War and the CPC's decision to devote itself to intensive internal economic development. By 1952 the CPC considered that it had sufficiently rehabilitated the economy to prepare for the launching of a Five Year Plan similar to the one inaugurated in the Soviet Union by Stalin in 1928. The Chinese plan, which was not put into final shape until about the beginning of 1955, envisaged a strenuous program of industrialization, with strong emphasis on heavy industry, and the beginning of "socialization" (collectivization, nationalization) of agriculture, handicrafts, and commerce. This Stalinist program signaled the end of the New Democracy period (1949–1952) and the beginning of the "transition to Socialism."

In November 1952 the Central People's Government announced the establishment of a State Planning Committee to draw up and super-

---

[3] As a sop to Ho, the Soviet Union and the CPR inserted in the Geneva agreements, after the signatures, a proviso that nation-wide elections be held in Vietnam within two years. These elections were never held, however, because the Diem government in South Vietnam was strongly opposed to them and because early in 1956 the Soviet government accepted the British government's contention that the holding of elections was less important than the preservation of peace in Vietnam. The indefinite postponement of the elections must have been a serious disappointment to the Vietnamese Communists.

vise the First Five Year Plan. The committee was headed by Kao Kang, a member of the CPC's Politburo and the powerful regional satrap of Manchuria.

The First Five Year Plan encountered serious difficulties from the start. It appears to have been drawn up on the assumption that a very substantial volume of aid would be forthcoming from the Soviet Union. Yet prolonged Sino-Soviet economic negotiations in Moscow (August 1952–June 1953) produced no results sufficient to justify this optimism. When the results of the negotiations were finally announced in Peking on September 15, 1953, it developed that the Soviet Union had agreed, for a consideration, to help with equipment and technicians in the building or reconstruction of 141 industrial enterprises, of which 50 had been contracted for before Stalin's death. Again the Soviet Union had demonstrated its inability or unwillingness, or both, to contribute to China's modernization on a scale commensurate with the need and with what the CPC probably wanted.

The insufficiency of Soviet aid led to some downward revisions in the Plan and may have shaken the position of Kao Kang. In addition to his misfortune in the industrial field, Kao had also made the mistake of adopting a comparatively moderate viewpoint on agriculture by advocating the mechanization of agriculture before collectivization, whereas in 1953 the CPC leadership clearly demonstrated its preference for the reverse order of priorities. Worse still, Kao and his ally Jao Shu-shih, the regional satrap of East China, attempted to gain for Kao a position in the CPC hierarchy second only to that of Mao Tse-tung. This was evidently done at the end of 1953, when Mao was seriously ill, and there was probably some connection between this affair and the fall of Beria in the Soviet Union. If Kao had succeeded, he would have moved over the heads of Liu Shao-ch'i and Chou En-lai, who probably combined against him. Kao and Jao were sternly warned in February 1954 to give up their errors and submit to party discipline. When they refused they were crushed in the ensuing spring, Kao allegedly committing suicide and Jao suffering some unannounced fate. The CPC's official statement on their case was not published until April 5, 1955, nearly a year later.

Determined to eliminate regional power from its supposedly "monolithic" regime, the CPC leadership proceeded during the summer and autumn of 1954 to abolish the regional organs in the three main systems of power: the party (the regional committees of the CPC Central Committee), the government (the regional governments or Major

Administrative Committees), and the armed forces (the field armies).[4] This program of centralization was legitimated, at least in the governmental sphere, in a formal constitution adopted in September 1954.

The major use to which the authorities at the center put their increased power over the provinces was to accelerate the socialization and development of the economy in the absence of massive Soviet aid. Among the approaches adopted was a faster collectivization of agriculture, a program intensely unpopular with many peasants and opposed by some within the CPC. Overriding all objections, Mao Tse-tung delivered a speech on July 31, 1955 (not published until October 16 in order not to disrupt the gathering of the autumn harvest, which was good that year), in which he urged an acceleration of collectivization to bring some 43 per cent of all peasant households into semisocialist "cooperatives" by 1957. At the Sixth Plenary Session of the CPC Central Committee in October 1955, this percentage was raised to 70–80.

About the same time Mao launched a program to "transform" private businesses into "joint state-private enterprises" which would be state-controlled and from which the former owners would receive a modest rate of interest on their investments in lieu of profits; this program was virtually completed during 1956. At a Supreme State Conference held in January 1956 it was decided to complete the collectivization of agriculture in 1957, thus bringing all peasants into "fully Socialist cooperatives" (i.e., collective farms). By the end of 1956, 83 per cent of all Chinese peasant families were in collective farms.

In October 1954 a Soviet delegation led by Khrushchev came to Peking in an effort to improve the state of Sino-Soviet relations. It agreed to dissolve the four joint-stock companies mentioned earlier, to evacuate Port Arthur, to cooperate in the construction of one Sino-Soviet railway through Outer Mongolia and another through Sinkiang, and to allow the CPR an additional 520 million rubles' worth of economic credits to be used, among other things, for the construction of 15 additional industrial enterprises. The two regimes publicly subscribed to the Five Principles of Peaceful Coexistence and joined in a conciliatory declaration of willingness to establish "normal" relations with Japan. There can be no doubt that this agreement, and the fact that it was signed in Peking rather than in Moscow, represented a substantial gain for the CPC leadership.

A problem much less easy of solution was posed by Khrushchev's

_____

[4] The dissolution of the field armies had probably begun in 1953.

heated secret denunciation of Stalin at the Twentieth Congress of the Soviet Communist Party in February 1956. After an ominous silence of six weeks, the CPC published on April 5, 1956, a statement agreeing that Stalin had been guilty of conceit, "subjectivism," and certain errors of policy, but defending the essentials of the system which he had imposed on the Soviet Union (and which, indeed, Khrushchev had not attacked). Peking probably feared that a denigration of one link in the chain of Marxist-Leninist ideological succession—and Mao Tse-tung was considered in China to be another such link—might lead to the depreciation of others, and it may have also foreseen the disorders which usually follow a relaxation of dictatorial controls. This statement appears to mark the CPC's first public claim to ideological leadership in the Communist world.[5]

Disorders were not long in coming. In the summer of 1956 disturbances began in Poland, and by the second half of October they had reached the proportions of a national anti-Soviet movement. The CPC appears to have given the Polish Communists prior encouragement to assert themselves against Moscow, and it may well have interceded to prevent the suppression of the movement by Soviet troops that at one time seemed imminent. From Poland the contagion soon spread to Hungary, where it assumed still more dramatic proportions. On November 1, in the initial (radio) version of its first important public statement on the crisis, the CPC indicated a considerable measure of sympathy with both the Polish and the Hungarian insurgents. Three hours later, outraged by Nagy's attempt, which had been announced in the meanwhile, to take Hungary out of the Communist bloc, it began to support, at least in public, the brutal Soviet military intervention. Its determination was perhaps strengthened by an ominous event much nearer home, a rising of peasants in North Vietnam on November 5 in protest against the enforcement of collectivization in the Chinese Communist manner.

On December 29, while Chou En-lai was touring South and South-

---

[5] This document had an interesting sequel. Within two days Mikoyan had arrived in Peking and concluded the largest Sino-Soviet economic aid agreement to be signed during 1956. This sequence of events is an example of one of the outstanding trends in Sino-Soviet relations, a tendency for limited economic aid to be exchanged for partial ideological support. In the case in question, a further part of the bargain came to light in mid-April, when the biography of Kao Kang, which inaccurately described him as mainly responsible for the "liberation" of Manchuria in 1948, was belatedly ordered deleted from the *Great Soviet Encyclopedia*.

east Asia in an effort to assess the impact of recent events on the Soviet bloc's standing in that area, the CPC published a definitive interpretation of the Stalin question that also attempted to define the essentials of Communist belief. The main points of this document were that "Stalin's mistakes take second place to his achievements," that in any case disputes over Stalin must not be allowed to impair the relations among Communist parties, and that those relations ought to be characterized by essential equality and ideological solidarity with the Soviet Union, rather than by chauvinism on either side.

In January 1957, after a brief visit to Peking, Chou En-lai spent two weeks in the Soviet Union and Eastern Europe, attempting to heal the wounds inflicted by the Polish and Hungarian crises. He seems to have had some success, for all parties concerned were apparently anxious not to let such a thing happen again.

The main lesson which the Polish and Hungarian crises would convey to a Communist mind, that "de-Stalinization" was necessary but must be carefully controlled, the CPC had already absorbed. After attributing popular dissatisfaction and unrest during 1955 to "counter-revolutionaries" and trying to suppress them by terror, the CPC in the spring of 1956 began to make some concessions. It promised to allow greater freedom of debate (the "Hundred Flowers"), to pay more attention to the production of consumer goods, to increase wages and introduce the eight-hour day, to pay higher interest rates to businessmen whose enterprises had been "transformed," and to allow some private retail trade in food and other basic commodities; and some steps were taken toward implementing these pledges. The CPC did nothing, however, to abandon or modify its control over the government and over the whole of public life; it merely relaxed that control a little. Indeed, 1956 was a year of industrial overexpansion, which, combined with poor harvests, necessitated a general retrenchment in the first half of 1957.

For this real if slight "de-Stalinization" a theoretical justification had to be found. Mao Tse-tung, citing earlier writings by Lenin and himself, told a Supreme State Conference which met on February 27, 1957, that "contradictions" can and do exist even in a "Socialist" society. They exist, he said, both within the ranks of "the people" and between "the people" and the Communist Party, and they are legitimate as long as they do not worsen into "antagonisms." In other words, it is not necessary or right automatically to label anyone who criticizes the Communist Party or its regime a "counterrevolutionary." The "contradiction" that gives rise to his criticism needs to be removed if the latter is valid. If not, the critic should be "countercriticized" and convinced of his error, but not abused. This doctrine of "contradictions" had little theoretical originality but considerable practical importance. It was well received in Eastern Europe, especially in Poland and Yugoslavia, although less so in the Soviet Union, where it was apparently regarded as an unwelcome assertion of Chinese ideological leadership.

Following Mao's speech, a "rectification" campaign was launched within the CPC, and prominent non-Communists were invited to criticize it and the government. After much encouragement some of them decided that it was safe to do so and proceeded to denounce the CPC, with considerable boldness, for the severity of its dictatorship. This plain speaking shocked the CPC, some of whose leaders seem to have been doubtful all along of the wisdom of Mao's speech of February 27. Worse still, there were widespread student demonstrations, and substantial numbers of peasants withdrew from the collective farms. Early in June 1957 the CPC struck back with an "antirightist struggle," in which manipulated public denunciations of the "rightist" critics, reinforced by thinly veiled hints that they were on the verge of aggravating "contradictions" into "antagonisms" and might therefore be treated as counterrevolutionaries, sufficed to wring public confessions and retractions from most of them. On June 18 Mao Tse-tung's speech of February 27 was published for the first time, in an edited version stating that criticism must not go so far as to challenge the "leadership" of the CPC or the validity of its version of "Socialism." If this warning had been in the original, the "rightists" would almost certainly not have spoken out as they did.

In fact, the affair destroyed what slight reality the "united front" in Communist China had, but of course the CPC did not admit this. It tried to picture itself as being in real danger from the "rightists" in order to rally public support. In the summer of 1957 it embarked on a program of intensified indoctrination of the entire population, including the peasants, many of whom were clearly discontented. The nonexistence of the "united front" was to be compensated by making everyone pretend that popular support for the CPC was greater than ever.

In the middle of 1957 the CPC found itself faced with a serious crisis, which, however, it saw hope of turning into an opportunity, in its domestic position and international relations. Its political leadership had been shown to be unsuspectedly unpopular. The newly formed collectives seemed inadequate as instruments for mobilizing labor, constructing public works, and extracting agricultural surpluses. Soviet economic credits ceased to flow in 1957.

The Soviet intercontinental ballistic missile (August 1957) and Sputnik I (October 4) and the deep impression they produced on the world, especially the United States, then shaken by recession, seemed to offer a way out. The CPC concluded that the Soviet Union must be urged and maneuvered into using the increased power and prestige conferred by its seeming technological and military breakthrough on behalf of the entire Communist bloc, in order to inflict a series of political defeats on the "imperialists," who could be deterred from launching a world war provided they were not given time to catch up in military technology. The Soviet Union must be (and was) persuaded to begin a program of limited aid to the CPR in the production of nuclear weapons. For its own part the CPR, utilizing Soviet aid (other than credits) already committed but relying mainly on China's own material and human resources, would "catch up with Britain in fifteen years," as Liu Shao-ch'i predicted in December 1957, in gross industrial output. Less publicly, the CPC decided to deviate from "peaceful coexistence," which seemed to be producing results that were too slow and uncertain, in the direction of greater toughness toward its non-Communist neighbors, without necessarily going so far as to revert to armed struggle.

During the winter of 1957–1958, while policy debates unquestionably proceeded within the CPC, millions of peasants were mobilized for reclamation, irrigation, and other such projects. The results were considered good, and in February 1958 the CPC began to speak of a "Great Leap Forward" in industry and agriculture. As elaborated in a speech by Liu Shao-ch'i to the Second Session of the Eighth CPC Congress in May (the First Session had been held in September 1956), the Great Leap was to be based on a greatly increased exploitation of rural labor power to raise agricultural output and establish local industries.

In the third quarter of 1958, when a bumper harvest was in sight and the Great Leap was in full flood, the CPC formed throughout China some 26,000 "people's communes." A commune controlled on the average about twenty collectives (renamed production brigades) and was theoretically large enough to be economically self-sufficient and to ensure maximum exploitation and optimum utilization of labor.

Normal material incentives for the peasants were almost eliminated, for instance by the abolition of the private plots of land that had been permitted in the collectives. To sweeten this pill and to make long and exhausting hours of labor possible, peasants were allowed and even encouraged to increase their consumption of food. In general, however, the emphasis was on ideological exhortations rather than on material rewards. The CPC clearly implied that China was on the verge of attaining the ultimate stage of "communism" and that communes would sooner or later be adopted in all other countries, presumably including the Soviet Union. Of little more practical significance was the widespread production, in the communes and elsewhere, of "backyard steel" in primitive hand-operated furnaces. Another prominent feature of the Great Leap was the formation of a huge "militia," for defense in case of the destruction of the urban centers by strategic attack and as an additional means of enforcing labor discipline.

The CPC seems to have expected from the beginning of the Great Leap that, after a period of energetic experimentation, the communes would have to be standardized and some of their most unpopular features, such as the insufficient rest allowed the peasants, modified. This process was begun in October 1958 and was well under way by early December, when the CPC publicized the changes (which included a de-emphasis on "backyard steel"), abandoned the extreme ideological claims for the communes, and announced Mao Tse-tung's decision not to be a "candidate" to succeed himself as Chairman of the CPR (i.e., head of state). All this did not indicate any intention to slow the economic pace of the Great Leap. At the same time, the CPC published "preliminary" production figures for 1958, including the obviously fantastic claim that the grain harvest had amounted to 375 million tons (as against 185 million tons in 1957).[6] Even more astronomical goals, including a grain harvest of 525 million tons, were set for 1959 (see Table 1). At the National People's Congress in April 1959, these claims and targets were reiterated, and Liu Shao-ch'i was "elected" to succeed Mao as Chairman of the CPR.

Parallel with the Great Leap at home, 1958 saw a toughening of

[6] The actual harvest was probably about 195 million tons. The exaggeration seems to have been due to a thorough politicization of the statistical apparatus during 1958 and inflation of figures at all levels of the official hierarchy, for propaganda effect at home and abroad.

the CPR's international behavior. The main exception, the withdrawal of what remained of the "Chinese People's Volunteers" from Korea, is probably to be accounted for by Soviet pressure. The Soviet Union disapproved of Chinese ideological claims for the Great Leap and was alarmed by Chinese pressures for more militant Soviet behavior. The

Table 1. Chinese Communist economic goals and claims
(in millions of metric tons)

	1957 claims	1962 goals (Sept. 1956)	1958 goals (Feb. 1958)	1958 goals (May 1958)
Steel *	5.35	10.5–12.0	6.248	7.1
Coal	130.0	190–210	150.7	180.0
Grain	185.0	250.0	196.0	250.0
Cotton	1.64	2.4	1.75	
	1958 goals (Aug. 1958)	1958 claims (Dec. 1958)	1958 claims (Apr. 1959)	1958 claims (Aug. 1959)
Steel	10.7	11.0	11.08	8.0
Coal	300.0	270.0	270.0	270.0
Grain	300–350	375.0	375.0	250.0
Cotton	3.5	3.35	3.5	2.1
	1959 goals (Dec. 1958)	1959 goals (Aug. 1959)	1959 claims (Jan. 1960)	1960 goals (Mar. 1960)
Steel	18.0	12.0	13.35	18.4
Coal	380.0	335.0	347.8	425.0
Grain	525.0	275.0	270.05	300.0
Cotton	5.0	2.3	2.41	2.65

* These four categories are given because the CPC regards them as the most important indicators of over-all production levels. "Grain" refers to food grain only, not industrial crops. It includes sweet potatoes (the actual tonnages being divided by four before inclusion in Chinese Communist grain statistics) and excludes soybeans. "Cotton" refers to raw cotton.

CPC disapproved of what it considered Khrushchev's reluctance to translate his alleged technological breakthroughs into politico-military victories. In May 1958 the CPC began to use the conveniently vulnerable Tito as a public whipping boy through whom to castigate Khrushchev for his "revisionism." By the time Khrushchev seemed to justify Chinese criticism by reacting to the American landing in Lebanon in mid-July with nothing more than diplomatic maneuvers, the CPC had already decided to give him and the "imperialists" an object lesson in how truly determined "socialist" states ought to behave. Khrushchev flew secretly to Peking at the end of July and explained his view of the world political and military situation to the Chinese, but he was unable to avert the object lesson.

On August 23 PLA artillery opened a bombardment of Quemoy, an offshore island heavily garrisoned by the Nationalists, in an effort to isolate it and compel its surrender. The effort, which lasted roughly through September, was a failure, because with American support (but not actual military intervention) the Nationalists were able to keep the island supplied and to prove their superiority to the Communists in aerial combat. The first turning point in the crisis came in the first week of September, when the United States made some threatening statements, the CPC responded with an offer of Sino-American ambassadorial talks, the United States accepted the offer, and the relieved Khrushchev then (and not until then) felt it safe to make an almost meaningless declaration of Soviet military support for the CPR in the event of an American attack. The second turning point came in the first week of October; when it seemed that the Nationalists might launch an air attack against Communist gun positions on the mainland, Khrushchev made it clear that such an act by the Nationalists alone would not bring Soviet intervention, and the CPC thereupon proclaimed a partial ceasefire. The outcome was a sharp local defeat for the CPC and an additional strain on Sino-Soviet relations.

The spring of 1959 brought natural disasters to China and reopened the debate within the CPC on the wisdom of the Great Leap. The doubters, although not identified publicly by name, were denounced as "right opportunists," and a number of them were purged. Among the casualties was Politburo member and Defense Minister P'eng Te-huai, who had objected to the impact of the Great Leap (especially its demands for army labor) on the armed forces, had probably sought support from the Soviet leadership—always an unforgivable act in Chinese Communist eyes—and was quietly succeeded as Defense Minister by Lin Piao in September 1959. In August, a relatively realistic mood engendered by the natural disasters mentioned, plus a realization that the objections of the "right opportunists" to the statistical and other excesses of the Great Leap were not entirely wrong, had led the CPC to cut its claims for 1958 and its goals for 1959, especially in agriculture, to levels much closer to reality (see Table 1). Against this background the tenth anniversary of the CPR was celebrated on October 1, 1959, in an atmosphere of surprising public optimism, and as 1960 opened, plans were being made for tremendous industrial expansion and an improved harvest over the actually mediocre one of 1959.

In the summer of 1959 the smoldering Sino-Indian dispute over possession of the Aksai Chin Plateau in Ladakh (the northeast corner of Kashmir), across which the Chinese had built a military highway in 1956–1957, and of the North East Frontier Agency (between Assam and eastern Tibet) erupted. After an outbreak of fighting in Lhasa in March 1959, the Dalai Lama had fled to India, where he was given a cordial welcome that infuriated Peking. India also proceeded to behave in other ways that the CPC considered inimical, if not to Chinese interests, at least to those of communism. In particular Nehru, after accepting a large new Soviet offer of economic aid, overthrew the elected but controversial Communist government in the South Indian state of Kerala (July 31). Within a week, Chinese troops began shooting incidents near the McMahon Line, which is the northern boundary of the North East Frontier Agency, and Peking revived its claims to the two disputed territories. In late October there was a serious shooting incident in Ladakh.

Meanwhile, the CPR had become involved in a controversy with Indonesia over efforts by the Indonesian government to exclude noncitizens (i.e., Chinese residents) from retail trade in the rural areas and over the failure of the Indonesian government to agree to put the Sino-Indonesian citizenship treaty of 1955 into effect through an exchange of ratifications.

Khrushchev, who had sympathized with the "right opportunists" in China, also clearly sympathized with India and Indonesia in their disputes with Peking, whose tactics he considered more likely to harm than advance the cause of communism. The announcement that he would visit India, Burma, and Indonesia early in 1960, when he might have been expected to be in Moscow to celebrate the tenth anniversary of the Sino-Soviet treaty of February 14, 1950, raised the fear in Peking that the Soviet Union might take advantage of Chinese heavyhandedness to make major political gains in South and Southeast Asia. The American announcement of November 3, 1959, that President Eisenhower would visit India, as well as ten other countries, also had an effect. Accordingly, on November 7 Chou En-lai made overtures (rejected in effect by the thoroughly irritated Nehru) for at least a temporary settlement of the border issue. In January 1960 the CPR concluded a boundary treaty with Burma (followed soon afterward by one with Nepal) and reached an agreement with Indonesia that resulted in the citizenship treaty's going into effect.

By this time Sino-Soviet differences, compounded by mutual dislike and rivalry between Khrushchev and Mao, had decided the CPC to launch a major propaganda offensive in order to discredit Khrushchev as a "revisionist" in Communist circles around the world, although still without naming him openly. The main occasions chosen were the ninetieth anniversary of Lenin's birth (April 22, 1960) and a World Federation of Trade Unions meeting in Peking in early June. Khrushchev launched his counterattack at a conference at Bucharest in late June, and the two sides agreed to submit their quarrel to a conference of all Communist parties to be held in Moscow in November.

In the meantime it became clear that the 1960 harvest in China would be a poor one, partly because of bad weather but even more because of strains and dislocations generated by the Great Leap. Timing his blow shrewdly, Khrushchev in July and August withdrew the remaining Soviet technicians (about 3,000), who together with Soviet capital equipment had been the core of the CPR's heavy industrialization program, from China. Staggered by these two disasters, the CPC called an abrupt though partly unadmitted halt to the Great Leap and launched a program of retrenchment, to supervise which it revived the regional bureaus of the Central Committee that had been abolished in 1954. In late 1960 and early 1961 the regime broke up the communes into their smallest component parts, the "production teams"; abolished the unpopular communal mess halls; granted limited peasant incentives such as small private plots; promised greater freedom to intellectuals and students; diverted some investment from industry to agriculture; closed down some industrial installations; began to shift some 20 million people from the cities to the countrysides; cut down on nonagricultural imports; began to import grain (mainly from Canada and Australia); and postponed further social revolution in Tibet.

The Eighty-one Party Conference at Moscow, which was agreed to at Bucharest in June 1960, took place while this massive (though probably insufficient) policy shift was barely getting under way, but there is no evidence that the crisis weakened the vigor with which the CPC presented its case before its brother Communist parties. Both the draft resolution, worked out in October before the conference began, and the final declaration contained some concessions to Chinese militancy toward the West and to "national bourgeois" governments in the underdeveloped countries. Although the Chinese were outvoted on most questions, they were not without some support, mainly from militant parties in Asia and Latin America, as well as Albania. The Chinese could take pride in a respectable showing against the champion and in any case were free to continue behaving as they thought best, as long as they paid lip service to the Moscow Statement. This they did, while working hard to gain support among foreign Communists, especially in the underdeveloped countries.

In 1961 agricultural conditions in China were only slightly better than in 1960 and were certainly not good enough to permit a resumption of forced industrialization at the pre-1960 pace. There was a cumulative though not dramatic growth in malnutrition and political disaffection, expressed more in disillusionment and apathy than in readiness to revolt. The Soviet Union showed no inclination to help the CPR out of its predicament by large-scale aid of any kind, and Soviet technicians were not sent back to China.

Meanwhile, the CPR had been engaged in a politically motivated program of economic aid to Albania, which was quarreling with Khrushchev a good deal more openly and vigorously than was the CPC itself. Chinese aid alone enabled the Albanians to defy the Kremlin and probably decided Khrushchev to bring the issue to a head. This he did at the Twenty-second Congress of the Communist Party of the Soviet Union, in October 1961. Khrushchev's public denunciation of the Albanian leadership at the congress and his request to the Chinese to stop supporting it drew a polite but firm rebuke from Chou En-lai, the chief CPC delegate, and the Chinese delegation returned to Peking without waiting for the end of the congress. An article by the Hungarian Janos Kadar, which appeared in *Pravda* on Mao's birthday (December 26) and certainly must have had Khrushchev's approval, denounced Mao, without naming him, as a senile "left deviationist."

The policy of industrial retrenchment continued in effect, and agricultural conditions improved slightly but perceptibly in 1962. The spring saw an upsurge of tension along the Sino-Indian frontier, as India cut off trade with Tibet and Indian troops with the aid of Soviet equipment moved into the disputed areas in some strength, as well as near the Taiwan Strait, as the PLA massed a large force opposite Taiwan to discourage the Nationalists from attempting a landing with the idea of capitalizing on the hunger and discontent on the mainland. The United States made it clear that it would neither allow the Communists to take Taiwan nor help the Nationalists to invade the mainland, and Khrushchev spoke out in the same ambiguous way as in 1958. Both sides were thus reminded that they were at a military impasse. Under the circumstances, it is not surprising that rumors circulated of a secret political agreement between the two Chinese regimes to unite after Chiang Kai-shek's death.

Relieved, at least for the time being, of the fear of an American-supported Nationalist attack across the Taiwan Strait, the CPC turned its attention to its Himalayan frontier, where a Chinese military build-up had long been in progress. Following skirmishes in Ladakh during July 1962 and a Chinese incursion into the North East Frontier Agency early in September, the Indian government on October 12 ordered its border forces to drive the Chinese out. On October 20 the PLA struck back in both disputed areas but primarily in the east, where in some places it actually penetrated into territory not claimed by the CPR. On November 20, having inflicted a stinging local defeat on the poorly equipped and inadequately prepared Indian forces, the CPC announced a unilateral cease-fire and a withdrawal to the Mc-Mahon Line and revived its somewhat ambiguous proposal of November 1959 for a compromise settlement.

Presumably this skillfully conducted operation was designed to further to some extent the CPC's long-term policy toward the Himalayan region, that is, apparently direct and complete control of the Aksai Chin area combined with a more indirect control over a "confederation" of Himalayan states extending from Nepal through the North East Frontier Agency and Nagaland in Assam, and toward the South Asian subcontinent, apparently the greatest possible influence over a fractionated and impoverished region (rather than a relatively united and developed one, as desired by the Soviet Union among others). More immediately, the CPC wanted to protect its military highway across Aksai Chin, safeguard the security of Tibet in the face of possible Indian support for the Tibetan insurgents, humiliate India and lessen its influence not only in the Himalayas but in the world at large, and demonstrate to everyone that the CPR's economic difficulties had not eliminated it as an active factor in international politics. Among the more devious motives that may not unreasonably be attributed to the CPC is a desire to ruin the career of Indian Defense Minister Krishna Menon, who was a major link in the ties between India and the Soviet Union to which the CPC objected so strongly and who was then a candidate for the succession to Nehru; to improve the prospects of Pakistan, with which the CPR had been carrying on boundary negotiations as a partial counterweight to the Soviet-Indian alignment, for a favorable settlement of the Kashmir question with India; to compel the Soviet Union to give unequivocal support either to the CPR or to India, the result in the latter case being to expose the Soviet Union in the eyes of the left-wing "national liberation movements" in the underdeveloped areas as a nonrevolutionary power; and to compromise India's nonalignment by driving it to seek military aid from the West.

By November 20, when the CPC proclaimed a cease-fire, little but an upsurge of Indian national unity marred the CPR's record of success. The probable objectives listed above had been achieved or set on the road to realization, and the actual military invasion was approaching the point of diminishing returns. To have remained south of the passes along the McMahon Line during the winter would have imposed very difficult logistical requirements and might have invited air attacks. Menon had fallen. Pakistan's leverage on all concerned had been greatly increased; on December 27, the day when Indo-Pakistani talks on Kashmir began, Pakistan and the CPR announced the conclusion of a preliminary border agreement (in the Indian view, there is no such thing as a Sino-Pakistani border). As for the Soviet Union, it clearly resented the Chinese performance at a time when Khrushchev was preoccupied with the Cuban missile crisis, which incidentally Chinese propaganda exploited in such a way as to paint the CPR as Castro's only real foreign friend. On November 5, after Khrushchev had gained greater freedom of action through the easing of the Cuban crisis, the Soviet Union articulated a position on the Sino-Indian border dispute that was at least mildly pro-Indian. Soviet military aid to India continued on a limited scale. Thus Khrushchev had largely evaded the clear-cut choice that the CPC had probably tried to impose on him, but he left little doubt of his preference for the Indian side. Two days before the Chinese announced a cease-fire, India appealed to the United States and Britain for large-scale military aid, some of which soon began to arrive.

One of the most interesting aspects of the Sino-Indian border crisis was the considerable amount of anti-Indian and pro-Chinese feeling that it revealed in the neutral Asian countries, especially Indonesia and Cambodia, both of which the CPR had been wooing for some time. At the end of 1962 a group of neutral countries, under the chairmanship of Ceylon, undertook to reconcile the Chinese and Indian positions. The immediate difficulties, if we leave apart the problem of competing Chinese and Indian long-term ambitions in the Himalayas, appeared to stem more from considerations of face and procedure than from matters of substance. India privately conceded that it could not regain Aksai Chin, and China seemed willing to keep out of the North East Frontier Agency as long as the Indian army observed a demilitarized zone along the McMahon Line. On the other hand, India wanted to submit the dispute to the World Court and to delay a settlement while rebuilding its military position in the North East Frontier Agency, whereas the Chinese wanted prompt bilateral negotiations and a quick settlement and were unwilling to tolerate an Indian military build-up along the frontier. The would-be neutral mediators clearly had a difficult task before them.

The Communist Party of China

As with other Communist parties in power, the control that the CPC exercises over China rests on four main foundations: Marxist-Leninist ideology, which links it to international communism, points out the assumed direction of the path ahead, and gives it a fortifying conviction that it represents the "wave of the future"; organization, which blankets the entire country with party, governmental, and public bodies (see Chart 1 and also Chart 2, p. 89) all responsive to the direction of the CPC leadership; propaganda, which constantly upholds the rightness of the CPC's domestic and foreign policies and insists that it is folly to oppose them; and terror, which protects the CPC from internal enemies when ideology, organization, and propaganda fail.

Again like other Communist parties, the CPC is organized on the principle of "democratic centralism." The adjective "democratic," which is much the less important of the two words, refers to the principle that at least in theory the membership of party organs is elected by the organs at the next lower level. Furthermore, local party organs elect periodically a National Party Congress which in turn elects the Central Committee and theoretically discusses and ratifies major party policies, as well as adopts a party constitution. The word "centralism" refers to the principle that a decision, once taken by an appropriate party organ, becomes absolutely binding on lower organs under its jurisdiction.

From 1945 to 1956 the party operated under the constitution adopted

Chart 1. The Communist Party of China (simplified)

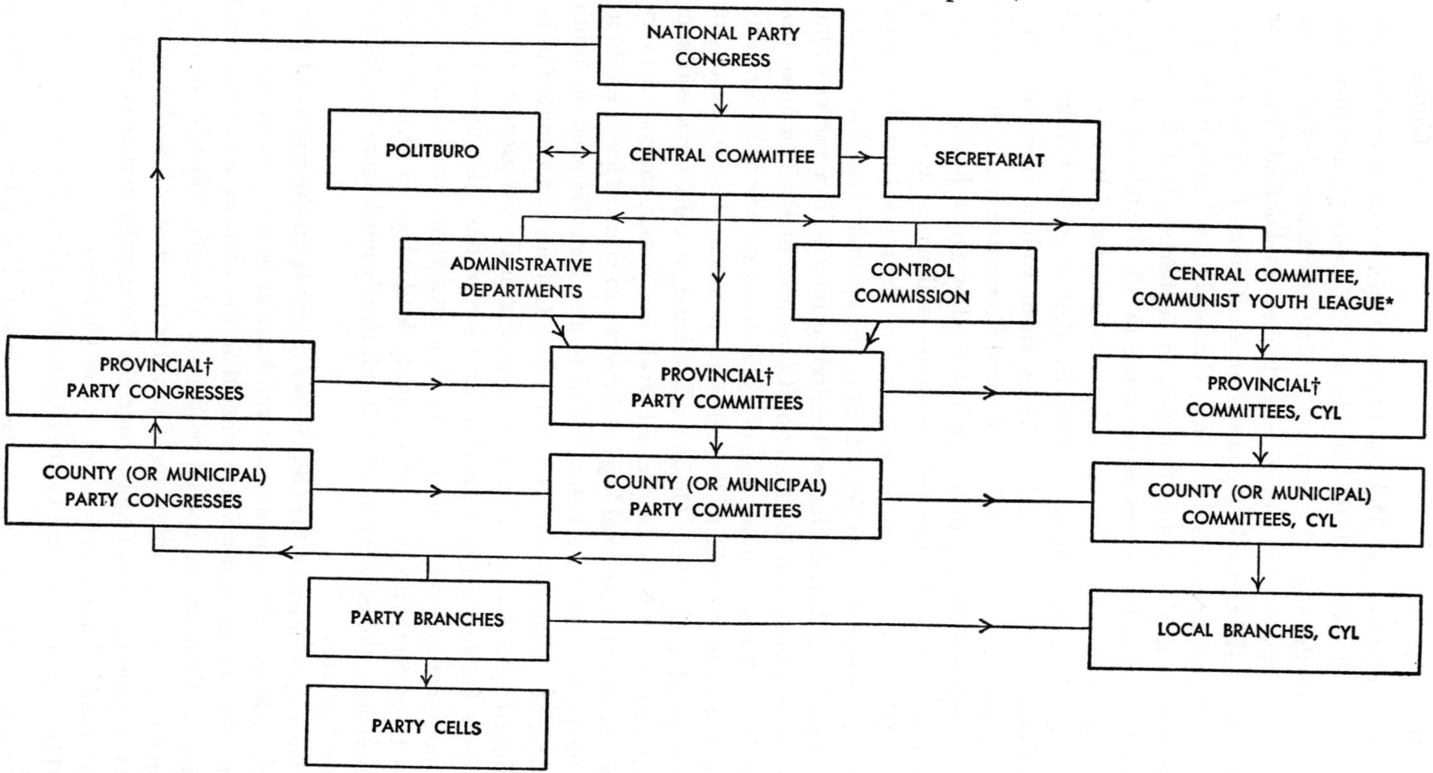

```
NATIONAL PARTY                    SECRETARIAT
CONGRESS

POLITBURO      CENTRAL COMMITTEE            CONTROL
                                           COMMISSION

               ADMINISTRATIVE
               DEPARTMENTS

PROVINCIAL†                    PROVINCIAL†           CENTRAL COMMITTEE,
PARTY CONGRESSES               PARTY COMMITTEES      COMMUNIST YOUTH LEAGUE*

COUNTY (OR MUNICIPAL)          COUNTY (OR MUNICIPAL) PROVINCIAL†
PARTY CONGRESSES               PARTY COMMITTEES      COMMITTEES, CYL

                                                    COUNTY (OR MUNICIPAL)
                                                    COMMITTEES, CYL

PARTY BRANCHES                                       LOCAL BRANCHES, CYL

PARTY CELLS
```

* The Communist Youth League has a system of congresses similar to that of the Communist Party of China.
† Or Special Municipality or Autonomous Region.

at the Seventh Congress. This constitution, which was mainly the work of Liu Shao-ch'i, stressed "the thought of Mao Tse-tung" and made the chairman of the Central Committee (Mao) ex officio also chairman of the other two most important party bodies, the Political Bureau (or Politburo) of the Central Committee and the Central Party Secretariat. The constitution presented by Teng Hsiao-p'ing and adopted by the First Session of the Eighth Congress in September 1956 introduced several changes. It contains no reference to "the thought of Mao Tse-tung" and lays great stress on "collective leadership." It does not follow the Soviet example set in 1952 by abolishing the Politburo and the Central Secretariat and replacing them with a Presidium. The post of honorary chairman of the Central Committee is created against the day when Mao may decide or be forced by age or health to retire. The chairman of the Central Committee still serves as chairman of the Politburo, but no longer necessarily as chairman (now known as general secretary) of the Secretariat of the Central Committee, which is less powerful than the former Central Secretariat. Real power within the party is vested in the Standing Committee of the Politburo. Unlike the 1945 constitution, that of 1956 makes no provision for party conferences to be held in the intervals between plenary sessions of the Central Committee. On the other hand, it calls for sessions of party congresses to be held at all levels every year, instead of every three years at the national level and every two years at lower levels, as in theory was the case before.[7] The former New Democratic Youth League is renamed the Communist Youth League and admitted to be affiliated with the party. Some provision is made for party members to get a fair hearing if accused of breaches of discipline and to hold (though not necessarily to express) their own views even if they happen to conflict with those of the party leadership. In spite of these concessions, the new constitution is still clearly much more "centralist" than "democratic."

The organization of the CPC is based largely on the territorial principle. Anyone whose permanent residence is in any part of the CPR can join no Communist Party other than the Chinese, no matter what his race; there are no special parties for Mongols, Tibetans, or other non-Chinese living within the CPR. There are also branches of the CPC among overseas Chinese, and the Communist parties of Malaya and Thailand are largely composed of Chinese.

The current or Eighth Central Committee, elected at the First Ses-

[7] No National Party Congress session was held in 1957 or has been held since 1958, however.

sion of the Eighth Congress in September 1956, consisted initially of 97 regular and 73 alternate members.[8] These are all ranked in descending order according to number of votes received at the congress, and it is probable that this order reflects a combination of relative popularity with the rank and file of the party and relative standing in the eyes of the party leadership. The elections were conducted in a carefully controlled fashion which, however, did allow for a limited freedom of nomination on the part of the delegates to the congress.

The bodies elected by the Central Committee at its first Plenary Session shortly after its own election were the Politburo (17 regular, 6 alternate members);[9] the Secretariat of the Central Committee (6 regular, 3 alternate members);[10] the Control Commission of the Central Committee, which maintains party discipline (17 regular, 4 alternate members); and the Secretariat of the Control Commission (one secretary and 5 deputies). As already mentioned, there is also a Standing Committee of the Politburo, which appears to exercise supreme power within the party and is composed of Mao Tse-tung, Liu Shao-ch'i, Chou En-lai, Chu Teh, Ch'en Yün, Lin Piao,[11] and Teng Hsiao-p'ing, in that order; they are also respectively the chairman, the five vice-chairmen, and the general secretary of the Central Committee, and before September 1956 all but Lin made up the membership of the Central Secretariat.

It seems likely that the organization of the bureaucratic apparatus under the control of the Eighth Central Committee is substantially the same as it was under the Seventh. In that case the principal departments are the Organization Department (headed by Jao Shu-shih before his fall), the Propaganda Department, the United Front Work Department (which handles relations with the non-Communist public), the Social Affairs Department (which has intelligence and espionage functions), the Rural Work Department (a fairly new body which deals with the collectivization of agriculture), the General (or Administrative) Office, the Control Commission (whose powers were increased in 1955), and the Military Committee. Each of these has supervisory power over corresponding bodies at lower levels in the party hierarchy.

Apart from the regional bureaus of the Central Committee, abol-

[8] Twenty-five additional alternates were elected at the Second Session in May 1958.

[9] Three additional regulars were elected in May 1958; one of the original regulars (Lin Po-ch'ü) died in 1960, so that the current total is 19.

[10] Two additional regulars were elected in May 1958.

[11] Lin was elected in May 1958.

ished in 1954 and revived at the end of 1960, the next lower party organ is the Communist Party organization in the province, special municipality, or autonomous region. It is organized as a smaller replica of the central party organization and has a party congress and a party committee. At the next lower level is the county or municipal party organization, which is similar in structure. Below that the most important level is that of the party branch or cell, which usually consists of about 20 party members working in the same factory, farm, and so on. It appears that every CPC member must belong to one of these branches. Although the branch is the lowest formal party organ, there also exist nuclei or fractions, small groups of party members working together within some larger nonparty body.

The CPC has expanded rapidly in recent years, until it is now the largest political party in the world. Its approximate total membership was 1.2 million in 1945, 5 million in 1949, 10.7 million at the beginning of 1956, 12 million at the end of 1956, and 17 million in 1961. The membership of the Soviet Communist Party was about 7.25 million in February 1956. Only about 10 per cent of the membership of the CPC are women, and until recently 70 per cent of the total membership were of rural origin. The rural percentage may have altered somewhat recently, for since the beginning of 1956 the CPC has been emphasizing the recruitment of "intellectuals," most of whom are actually technicians, and of workers, in order to reduce the preponderance of peasants. It should be noted that members of the small non-Communist "democratic" political parties are not encouraged, and are usually not even allowed, to join the CPC; they are more useful as window dressing.

Although the CPC constitution of September 1956 allows party members somewhat greater freedom of thought and expression than was the case before, party unity and party discipline are still the overriding goals. Erring individual members can be subjected to a variety of administrative punishments ranging from reprimand to expulsion and in extreme cases to criminal penalties at the hands of the regular courts. For dealing with undesirable tendencies within the party membership as a whole, much of which is opportunistic and insufficiently indoctrinated, the CPC evolved during its days at Yenan a purge or "rectification" technique considerably milder than Stalin's. The latest major "rectification" campaign occurred in 1957 and ran true to form. Some use is made of expulsion, but less of more drastic penalties. The emphasis is on ideological training and reassignment to other jobs, often involving manual labor and close contact with "the masses." In this way the CPC has been able to control and manipulate its rank and file with considerable success.

Attached to the CPC are two important youth organizations. The first, formerly known as the New Democratic Youth League but renamed the Communist Youth League since the First Session of the Eighth CPC Congress, contains about 25 million youths of both sexes between the ages of 15 and 25. The second, the Young Pioneers, has a membership of at least 8 million boys and girls aged from 9 to 14. The importance of these organizations as recruiting grounds for the CPC and as instruments of control and indoctrination of the rising generation is obvious and great.

The CPC like other Communist parties has also at its disposal many millions of cadres, who act as transmission belts between the party and the public. Cadres are individuals who may be CPC members, probationary members, or simply "activists" anxious to serve the party for one reason or another. They do essential work for the party, usually on a part-time basis, in military units, factories, shops, public and mass organizations, and rural villages and "people's communes" and in campaigns to suppress "counterrevolutionaries," campaigns to extract "donations" from the public, and the like. The cadres constitute an elite with considerable power and privileges.

Most cadres earn their living by serving in the governmental apparatus, in the numerous economic agencies and enterprises controlled by the government, or in the armed forces. The CPC's tight control over the government and armed forces rests, indeed, largely on the fact that virtually all important positions in both are held by CPC members. This has been true since 1949, but the percentage has become greater since 1954; for example, whereas before 1954 there were 2 non-Communist Vice-Premiers out of 5, today there are none out of 16. A corollary to the same principle is the frequency with which CPC members, and especially high-ranking ones, hold multiple offices in the party, government, and armed forces.

One of the main means of control over governmental organs and military units by the CPC is the party committees composed of CPC members working within such bodies. As in the Soviet Union, party control over the government is rendered still more obvious by a tendency for the CPC Central Committee and the State Council (cabinet) to issue joint directives on important domestic matters.

Thus the CPC has its chain of control throughout the government and armed forces, and there appears to be no way in which this control could be destroyed from the inside except in the event of a major power struggle within the top ranks of the CPC's leadership.

There appear to be differences over policy and power within the CPC, but they are between men who have long known each other and who to date have restrained their power rivalries so as not to destroy party unity. Those who have violated these rules of the game have suffered the fate of Kao Kang and Jao Shu-shih.

If the admittedly fragmentary evidence on this obscure but interesting and important subject is assembled, the existence of two major factions within the upper ranks of the CPC seems discernible. One, probably led by Liu Shao-ch'i and sometimes known as the "native radicals," is composed largely of men with comparatively little experience abroad and relatively little interest in events outside China. This faction has the upper hand within the party machinery properly speaking and dominates the CPC's pronouncements on major ideological issues. It has never viewed with favor Soviet influence on the CPC and tends to assert China's national interests and ideological views aggressively, as against the Soviet Union and the rest of the world. This faction was the driving force behind the Great Leap.

The other faction, probably led by Chou En-lai and sometimes called the "pragmatists" or "administrators," contains more men who have had extensive experience abroad. It is stronger within the government and the armed forces than within the party, but it is by no means negligible there. Although not necessarily more loyal to the Soviet Union on a strictly ideological plane than the other faction, it appears the more convinced that the CPR's own interests require a close alignment with the Soviet Union in practical matters. It has a more international and a less China-centered outlook and has been the main driving force behind the intermittent effort to base the CPR's foreign relations on at least the semblance of "peaceful coexistence." It is the more rational of the two in its domestic policies, in that it stresses technology and incentives more than ideological mobilization and indoctrination ("mass campaigns").

Apart from these differences of background and outlook, the two factions are probably involved in a limited contest for power. It is likely that neither Liu nor Chou aspires to wear Mao's mantle when he lays it down or grow to his stature, let alone to displace him in full career. It is not at all improbable, however, that each man would like to hold the first place in a "collective leadership" after the death of Mao, who is five years older than either of them. Liu's faction has two important and related advantages: it is stronger within the party, where all important decisions are made, and Mao Tse-tung clearly prefers Liu to Chou as a candidate for the succession. Liu has made his way in the party largely by devotion to Mao, whereas Chou attained a high position in the party earlier than Mao and independently of him and has had some serious disputes with him.

In order to see the question of factional differences within the CPC in true perspective, it must be realized that these differences are less important than the common outlook and background which bind CPC leaders to each other and to a common cause. This will probably remain true at least as long as Mao Tse-tung lives, for he uses his immense prestige to arbitrate between the two factions and keep them working in harness. What will happen after his death is another question.

Mao seems not to have recovered fully from his illness at the beginning of 1954, and contrary to some press reports on the state of his health he apparently has intermittent bouts of sickness—probably strokes—which temporarily immobilize him. This was certainly one reason for his decision in 1958 to retire as Chairman of the CPR. It is likely that in 1956 he had planned to turn this post over to Chou En-lai and to yield the chairmanship of the CPC Central Committee to Liu Shao-ch'i at some later date (perhaps at the time of the Ninth Congress, which should have been held in 1961 but was not, presumably because of the unfavorable state of the nation and resulting tensions within the party). Initially at least, Mao's two principal posts would in that case have been divided between two successors, not united in one. The reason why Liu, not Chou, succeeded Mao as Chairman of the CPR in April 1959, probably after an intraparty controversy, may have been a desire in upper party circles to keep Liu out of the top party post until after the end of his term as Chairman of the CPR, which expires in April 1963 or at the time of the next National People's Congress after that date. Assuming that Liu replaces Mao sooner or later at the head of the party hierarchy, as Mao intends, it will be interesting to see whether he succeeds to the fullness of Mao's statutory power by acquiring or retaining the chairmanship of the CPR as well.

No discussion of the CPC would be complete without some consideration of the theoretical framework into which it attempts to fit its own present and future position and that of the CPR. Although in a few documents, such as the Common Program of 1949 and the constitution of September 1954, the CPC used the term People's Democracy as a permissible label for the state which it controlled, it has generally evaded the efforts of Soviet writers to fasten this term officially upon it. The reason is that, as applied to the East European satellites, it connotes a dictatorship of the proletariat. The CPC insisted and still insists that the CPR is not a dictatorship of the proletariat alone but one exercised by the whole people, and in particular the "democratic" classes and groups making up the "united front," over the "reactionaries." The CPC has preferred the term People's Democratic Dictatorship to describe the state that it controls. During the Stalin controversy of 1956, however, by which time Soviet theorists had greatly broadened the meanings of the terms under discussion, the CPC began to accept the term dictatorship of the proletariat as applicable to the CPR.

Other Public Bodies

Given the importance that the CPC attaches to the maintenance of the outward appearance of a "united front," it is bound to permit the existence of other public bodies besides itself. These bodies are granted direct representation in the Chinese People's Political Consultative Conference, which is the principal institutional expression of the "united front." They are also represented indirectly (i.e., by members who are elected from geographical constituencies) in the National People's Congress, the CPR's nearest equivalent to a parliament. All these bodies are carefully supervised by the United Front Work Department of the CPC Central Committee, and none is known to have given the CPC any serious problems of control. In fact, the CPC often has more trouble in controlling its own membership and persuading it to accept some new policy than it does in controlling the non-Communist organizations, which have no access to the machinery of power. Such organizations are formally bound by the constitution of September 1954 to accept the "leadership" of the CPC.

One category of these non-Communist public bodies comprises the minor parties, or the "democratic" parties as they are officially called. They are eight in number: the Revolutionary Committee of the Kuomintang (defectors from the Kuomintang), the China Democratic League (those elements of the Democratic League, a former third-force party, which adhered to the CPC), the Democratic National Construction Association (businessmen), the Chinese Peasants and

Workers Democratic Party, the China Association for Promoting Democracy, the China Chih Kung Tang (composed largely of overseas Chinese), the Chiu San—September Third—Society (intellectuals), and the Taiwan Democratic Self-Government League. Three more parties have been dissolved by the CPC or amalgamated with other parties since 1949, for reasons that are obscure.

Although as stated earlier the number of non-Communists in high governmental posts has tended to decline since about 1954, this trend does not appear to portend an elimination of the "democratic" parties. At the time of the First Session of the Eighth CPC Congress, the *People's Daily* (the official organ of the CPC Central Committee) promised that "the Communist Party will carry out the policy of long-term coexistence and mutual supervision with other democratic parties; so long as the Communist Party exists, the other democratic parties will also exist." [12]

From shortly after the "Liberation" until about 1956, the minor parties were forbidden to build up any sort of mass support or grass-roots organization. In 1956 this ban was relaxed temporarily to the extent of allowing them to take in a sizable number of new members. Although they go through the motions of holding periodic and usually simultaneous congresses and electing central committees, the minor parties remain essentially small and powerless groups whose membership is largely middle class and therefore automatically suspect in the eyes of the CPC. Their central committees share a single newspaper, the *Kwangming Daily*. There are CPC members both overt and covert, within the minor parties; presumably they act as spies and exercise a considerable degree of control.

The so-called mass organizations have much larger memberships than do the minor parties, and they make little effort to disguise the fact that the key posts, which are not necessarily the chairmanships, are held by CPC members. The services which these organizations perform for the CPC are legion. They help to create the impression at home and abroad, which is only partially justified, that the CPC enjoys overwhelming popular support. They aid in publicizing and implementing its policies. They take part in its mass campaigns. They participate in international congresses and address communications to similar organizations in other countries.

The first major category of mass organizations consists of those that claim to represent definite and permanent interest groups. Ex-

[12] Broadcast by New China News Agency, Peking, Sept. 15, 1956.

amples are the All-China Federation of Trade Unions, which like similar organizations in all Communist countries is more concerned with
regimenting the labor force than in attempting to improve its status;
the All-China Federation of Cooperatives; the All-China Federation
of Democratic Women; the All-China Federation of Democratic
Youth; the Peasants Associations; the All-China Federation of Literary
and Art Circles; and the National Committee of the (Christian)
Churches in China for the Realization of Self-Administration, which
attempts to cut off contacts between Protestant bodies in China and
their coreligionists outside.

The other major type of mass organization exists more for a specific
purpose than as the nominal representative of some group. Examples
are the Sino-Soviet Friendship Association, which formerly carried on
an enormous volume of propaganda on behalf of the Soviet Union and
the Sino-Soviet alliance; the Chinese People's Institute of Foreign Affairs; the Red Cross Society of China; the Chinese People's Committee
for World Peace and against American Aggression; and the Asian
Solidarity Committee.

The fact that an individual is a member or officer of one of these
organizations does not necessarily indicate any real sympathy on his
part for its aims. This statement probably applies most forcefully to
the Sino-Soviet Friendship Association, which includes many non-
Communists who have no reason whatever to love the Soviet Union.
The same organization also provided a striking example of the way
in which these bodies achieve their impressive membership figures
when on November 7, 1951, it inducted all members of the People's
Liberation Army simultaneously.

Some of the theoretical implications of the CPC's policy toward
these non-Communist organizations, which is usually known as the
"mass line," seem worth exploring, and all the more so because they
show marked differences from the policy pursued in the Soviet Union.
In Bolshevik Russia, where the "dictatorship of the proletariat" was
inaugurated in 1917 and "Socialism" officially achieved in 1936, no
minor parties have been allowed to exist, and mass organizations have
flourished much less luxuriantly than they have in Communist China.
This departure from the Soviet policy toward non-Communist organizations is undoubtedly one of the major reasons why it was not until
1956 that the CPC began to accept, and even then with some reservations, the term dictatorship of the proletariat as applicable to the CPR.
The greater outward deference to non-Communist opinion in the CPR,

as compared with the Soviet Union, is partly an outgrowth of the distinctive characteristics of the "way of Mao Tse-tung," which proved so successful as a means of seizing power in China, partly an implicit encouragement to other underdeveloped countries to look with favor on the Chinese model of "socialist revolution" and "socialist construction," and partly an intimation to the Chinese Nationalists on Taiwan and to the overseas Chinese that they too may find a place in the "new" China.

Constitutional Structure and Development

As in other countries, the constitutional development of the CPR and the evolution of elected, or nominally elected, bodies have been so closely connected that they can be discussed together.

For the first five years of its existence (October 1949–September 1954) the CPR had neither a national legislature nor a formal constitution. Instead it had the Chinese People's Political Consultative Conference (CPPCC), the Common Program, and an Organic Law. The groundwork for the CPPCC had been laid during the summer of 1949, in typical CPC fashion, by the appointment of a Preparatory Committee. This committee, though of course dominated by CPC members, also included members of other parties and nonparty men, so that like the CPPCC itself it nominally represented the "united front" on which the present regime supposedly rests. Similar to other preparatory committees, this one arranged the agenda and procedure for the conference itself and gave the CPC members a chance to explain to the others what was expected of them, so that everything went smoothly.

The Common Program is essentially an elaboration of the principles set forth in Mao Tse-tung's *On the People's Democratic Dictatorship,* except that it places less emphasis on socialization of the economy and more on short-term CPC objectives such as "agrarian reform." It forecast the major domestic policies pursued by the CPC during the first few years after the "Liberation."

The Organic Law prescribes the organization of the government, which will be dealt with below, and provides that pending the convening of an All-China People's Congress elected by universal suffrage the CPPCC shall exercise its functions. Before the All-China People's Congress could be elected, People's Congresses had to be elected at the various lower levels of government. Since the election of these was not immediately feasible, the CPC in the meanwhile appointed local "representative" bodies to fulfill the same functions. Like the People's

Government Councils, which were the local executive organs, these "representative" bodies were governed by the principle of "democratic centralism."

In January 1953 preparations were begun for nation-wide elections to the People's Congresses which were scheduled to be held before the end of 1953. For reasons not quite clear but probably bearing some relation to the domestic difficulties which the CPC was facing at that time, these elections had to be postponed until 1954. In connection with the registration for these elections the authorities conducted a census, the first in the history of China, whose results as published on November 1, 1954, gave the astounding total of some 583 million people living on the Chinese mainland. The minimum voting age was 18, and about 323 million people were declared eligible to vote.

Of this number 86 per cent actually voted, usually by show of hands, for 5.5 million delegates to People's Congresses at the lowest levels, the rural district (*hsiang*) or town. Each of these then elected delegates to the People's Congresses for the *hsien* (county), and so on up through the provincial to the national level. The National People's Congress, which met in Peking in September 1954, consisted of about 1,200 delegates representing not only geographical constituencies but also the armed forces, overseas Chinese, and national minorities. One of its most important tasks was to discuss and adopt a formal constitution.

The groundwork for the constitution, like that for the National People's Congress itself, had been carefully laid. In November 1952 the Central People's Government Council, the highest government body, had appointed a 33-man committee, heavily weighted with high-ranking CPC members, to draft a constitution. Early in 1953 the CPC Central Committee helpfully submitted a draft of its own, which was never published. It is therefore impossible to say how closely this corresponded with the draft completed by the committee and approved by the Central People's Government Council in June 1954, but it can safely be assumed that the resemblance must have been very great.

After that the accepted draft was published and laid before the public for discussion. This discussion was no random affair, but was carefully organized. The draft was explained, discussed, and voted on at numerous carefully controlled gatherings of public bodies and of the general public. One case is on record in which all these things were done within the space of fifteen minutes. Numerous changes, none of them of any substance, were proposed and later transmitted to the National People's Congress for its consideration, and some were actually adopted.

The constitution, adopted by the National People's Congress on September 20, 1954, makes no very striking changes in the preexisting situation. The preamble, like that of the Common Program, stresses the concepts of the People's Democratic Dictatorship and the "united front." It describes the CPR as a unified state from which no national minority or other group has any right of secession; this view, first openly admitted by the CPC in 1949, represents a departure from the CPC's propaganda before 1949, which had sometimes promised the minorities the right of secession. The preamble and Chapter I lay much more emphasis on the socialization of the economy than had the Common Program.

Chapter II of the constitution deals with the organization of the government, to be discussed below, and Chapter III with the rights and duties of citizens. The meaning of the term citizen is not defined, but it is clear, both from the CPC's general practice and the fact that overseas Chinese are represented in the National People's Congress, that the term is intended to include all permanent residents of the CPR of whatever race (whether they belong to the ranks of "the people" or to those of the "reactionaries") and all persons of Chinese race living abroad, except as the latter's citizenship may be changed by treaty and by ensuing naturalization. Citizens of the CPR are guaranteed the usual civil liberties, including freedom of religion. They also have the right to work and to rest, as well as the obligations to pay taxes and perform military service as prescribed by law. Chapter V specifies the national flag, emblem, and capital (Peking).

It would be logical to expect that with the election of the National People's Congress and the adoption of a formal constitution the Chinese People's Political Consultative Conference would cease to exist, but something rather more complicated has happened. Shortly after the adoption of the constitution, the CPPCC was in effect superseded by its own National Committee, which has roughly twice the membership of the pre-1954 CPPCC and serves like the latter as the representative organ of the "united front." The National Committee of the CPPCC in turn has a smaller Standing Committee, which corresponds to the Standing Committee of the National People's Congress (see below), although it lacks the latter's constitutional powers, and which is under the chairmanship of Chou En-lai.

Governmental Organization

The constitution of 1954 describes the National People's Congress (see Chart 2) as the "highest organ of state power" and as the national legislature. It is elected for a term of four years and supposedly meets at least once a year.[13] It has the power to amend the constitution, elect and remove the highest officials of the government, enact legislation, and pass on important matters (such as treaties) laid before it by the government. It also elects its own Standing Committee.

The Standing Committee of the National People's Congress, whose nearest analogue before September 1954 was the Central People's Government Council, exercises at least in theory a general power of supervision over the government—and in fact exercises most of the powers of the National People's Congress when this body is not in session.

Of the officials elected by the National People's Congress, the highest ranking is the Chairman of the Chinese People's Republic (since 1959, Liu Shao-ch'i). This official exercises the ceremonial functions of a chief of state and also presides over the National Defense Council and the Supreme State Conference. The constitution does not specify whether he is eligible to succeed himself at the end of his four-year term. He is assisted, and in the event of incapacity succeeded, by a Vice-Chairman.[14]

The constitution says nothing else about the National Defense Council, except that its members are appointed by the Chairman of the CPR and confirmed by the National People's Congress. Its actual membership is much larger (13 vice-chairmen, 98 members) and has a higher proportion of non-Communists than was the case with its predecessor, the People's Revolutionary Military Council, during the 1949–1954 period. The Military Council was an extremely powerful body which actually controlled the armed forces and had military staff sections directly under it. Neither of these things appears to hold true of the National Defense Council, which meets infrequently and has much less control over the armed forces than the People's Liberation Army General Staff or the Ministry of Defense within the cabinet.

The Supreme State Conference is an *ad hoc* body composed of the Chairman and the Vice-Chairman of the CPR, the chairman of the

[13] It did not, however, meet in 1961. The 1962 session was secret.
[14] Since April 1959 there have been two Vice-Chairmen: the Communist Tung Pi-wu and the non-Communist Soong Ching-ling (Mme Sun Yat-sen).

Chart 2. Formal governmental structure of Communist China (simplified)

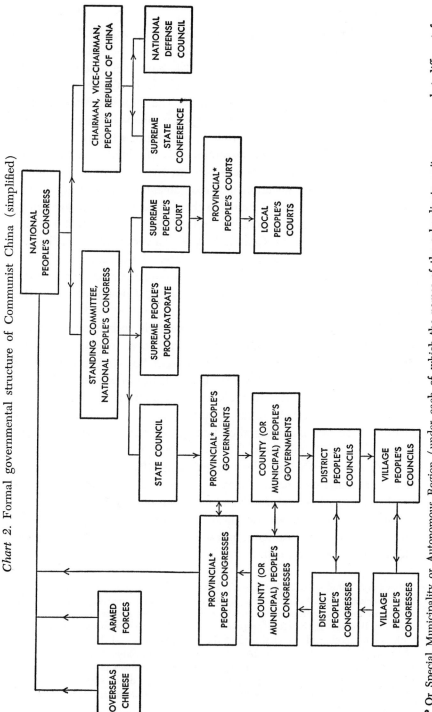

* Or Special Municipality or Autonomous Region (under each of which the names of the subordinate units are somewhat different from those shown on the chart).

Standing Committee of National People's Congress, the Premier (or chairman of the State Council), and any other persons whom the Chairman of the CPR sees fit to invite. The Supreme State Conference serves primarily as a personal forum at which the Chairman can put his own views directly before the public. The Supreme State Conference has met much less frequently since Liu Shao-ch'i became Chairman of the CPR than it did during Mao Tse-tung's tenure.

The ordinary business of government is conducted by the State Council (cabinet), known before 1954 as the Government Administration Council. The governmental reorganization of 1954 added the supervision of economic planning to the cabinet's functions by bringing the State Planning Committee under the State Council (it had formerly been under the Central People's Government Council) and at least partial control over the armed forces by creating a Ministry of Defense within the cabinet. The State Council is responsible to the National People's Congress or to its Standing Committee when the Congress is not in session.

The constitution refrains from specifying the organization of the State Council in any but the most general terms. In addition to the Premier (Chou En-lai, who was also Foreign Minister until 1958), it is headed by sixteen Vice-Premiers. Under them are six general offices and a secretary-general, which coordinate administration and are evidently bodies of considerable importance. All the cabinet officials mentioned so far, including the chairmen of the general offices, are high-ranking CPC members.

In all there are within the cabinet some fifty ministries, commissions, and affiliated agencies, most of them economic in function. The great majority of the ministers and chairmen of commissions are CPC members; those who are not have generally to do with consumer goods and technical problems, and in any event they have Communist vice-ministers under them.[15]

---

[15] Readers familiar with Parkinson's Law will realize that the cabinet's large size prevents it from functioning as a coherent unit. The same observation would also apply to the premier, vice-premiers, and chairmen of the general offices taken together. Business is therefore probably transacted by the premier in conjunction with one or another of the chairmen of the general offices and the leading officials of the appropriate ministries and/or chairmen of commissions. Each vice-premier, insofar as his other commitments permit, probably specializes in various branches of governmental work (Nieh Jung-chen, for example, deals with scientific development) and sits in when a meeting is called in which he is especially interested.

On approximately the same constitutional level with the State Council, though much less powerful in practice, and responsible like it to the National People's Congress and its Standing Committee, are two other bodies. One is the Supreme People's Court, which supervises a hierarchy of People's Courts corresponding to the various levels of the governmental structure. The other is the Supreme People's Procurator's Office, which controls a similar hierarchy of subordinate offices and acts as the public prosecutor in criminal cases.

Before 1954 the next level of government below the central government was the five Major Administrative Committees or regional governments (Northeast, Northwest, East China, Central South, and Southwest) and the North China Administrative Committee. These regional governments, whose powers were considerably curtailed at the end of 1952, were headed by very powerful and high-ranking CPC officials, who were respectively Kao Kang, P'eng Te-huai, Jao Shu-shih, Lin Piao, Liu Po-ch'eng, and Liu Lan-t'ao. These men also held high, but usually not the highest, posts in their regional party organizations. All but two of the regional government heads, Kao Kang and Jao Shu-shih, also commanded field armies, and it is probably more than a coincidence that these were the two men purged in 1954. After their elimination the regional governments, along with the regional party organizations and the field armies, were broken up.

Since the time of these changes and the adoption of the constitution of September 1954, the governmental levels directly under the central government have been of three kinds. The first is the special municipality, of which there are 2 (Peking and Shanghai); before 1954 there were 14. The second is the autonomous region, of which there are 5: the Inner Mongolia Autonomous Region, established in May 1947; the Sinkiang Uighur Autonomous Region, established in September–October 1955; Tibet, which is in the process of acquiring its "autonomy"; the Ningsia Hui Autonomous Region; and the Kwangsi Ch'uang Autonomous Region (the creation of the last two was announced in June 1957).[16] The third and most important is the province, of which there are 21.

Below this level the most important units are the rural county (*hsien*) and the municipality (*shih*), both of which come directly un-

[16] The terms Uighur, Hui (Chinese-speaking Muslim), and Ch'uang (Thai) are the names of the principal national minorities inhabiting these regions respectively.

der the government of a province or an autonomous region. At the lowest level the most important units are the rural districts (*hsiang*), the urban districts, and the towns.

The governments of all these units are remarkably uniform throughout the country and are organized as smaller replicas of the central government. That is to say, each has a People's Congress and a People's Council, the latter being elected by the former and nominally responsible to it. The chairman of a Provincial People's Council is also referred to as the chairman of the Provincial People's Government of that province or simply as the governor. The corresponding official at the municipal level is also called the mayor.

What has been said so far about governmental organization applies mainly to areas inhabited almost entirely by Han (i.e., ethnic) Chinese. In addition to the Chinese, there are within the CPR about 50 million members of minority groups, of which the most important are of Mongolian, Turkish, Tibetan, or Thai stock. These minorities live for the most part thinly scattered over the western half of the CPR. Like the minorities in the Soviet Union, many of them have kinsmen in other parts of Asia, and the CPC therefore finds it advisable to treat them with an appearance of great consideration. It has followed the general pattern worked out in the Soviet Union by Stalin, the essence of which is to give the minorities their own "autonomous" governments and allow them to enjoy the use of their indigenous language and culture at least for a time, while in reality keeping them under tight control.

In one respect the minority policy of the CPC is even less liberal than that of the Soviet Union. The Union Republics of the Soviet Union enjoy a theoretical right of secession, but even this is denied to the minorities in the CPR.

Where a sufficiently large number of people of a single minority group live together in a single area, they are organized into an "autonomous" government of one type or another. There are well over a hundred of these "autonomous" units, some of them situated in the autonomous regions and some in the provinces. In the Inner Mongolia Autonomous Region a concession is made to Mongol tradition by organizing the Mongols into units of local government known by the ancient term league (*meng*) and under them into banners (*ch'i*). "Autonomous" units lying within provinces are of course under the jurisdiction of the appropriate provincial governments. In some cases an "autonomous" government at a lower level belonging to one minority exists as an enclave within a larger "autonomous" government belonging to another. In cases where members of two or more minorities are so intermingled that it is impossible to separate them, a "democratic coalition government" is set up in which all are represented. The result is a patchwork of "autonomous" governments so complex that it would cause serious confusion if it were not for the fact that all are tightly controlled from the center by the CPC and the central government.

Political Realities

There are several ways in which the CPC ensures its control over the governmental machinery. The first and most significant is the placing of high-ranking CPC members in all really important governmental posts. Another is the maintenance of CPC party organizations within governmental agencies. A third is the custom of issuing important directives on domestic policy jointly in the name of the CPC Central Committee and the State Council, which of course guarantees the Central Committee's (or, more realistically speaking, the Politburo's) prior approval. In reality, even without this device all major administrative measures would in any case be first discussed and approved by the central CPC organs, usually the Politburo or its Standing Committee.

The governmental apparatus of the CPR completely lacks any separation of powers; in fact, that concept has been explicitly repudiated by its architects. Just as the CPC dominates the government, so within the government the executive overshadows the other branches, although their personnel seldom overlap. In actuality a legislative branch scarcely exists, for legislative functions are divided among the Politburo of the CPC, the Standing Committee of the National People's Congress, the Congress itself, and the State Council.

The concept of justice, like that of truth, has no meaning to the CPC except insofar as it serves the aims of the party. No pretense is made of administering abstract justice; the courts and laws are designed to serve "the people," whose interests are defined for them by the CPC. The result of this system of party justice is that, as in the Soviet Union, ordinary crimes are often punished no more severely than they deserve, but political offenses are sternly dealt with on the ground that they are injuries to "the people."

Like the system of justice, elections in the CPR are entirely dominated by the CPC. An election at any given level generally takes place about as follows. The voters are presented with a slate of acceptable candidates which is drawn up by the CPC organization at the next higher level, theoretically after consultation with officials of the minor parties and mass organizations. The only choice the voters have is that they may reject a few candidates as unacceptable and perhaps nominate alternates by petition; they have no way of nominating an entire alternate slate or slates. The same principle applies to the power supposedly exercised by the People's Congresses over their respective People's Councils; they may sometimes challenge the details, but never the essentials, of the policies submitted to them for discussion.

This means that the actual chain of command in the governmental apparatus does not run downward from the National People's Congress through the People's Congresses at the various lower levels and from them to the corresponding People's Councils. It runs downward from the State Council (which appears to be slightly more responsible in practice to its People's Congress than is the case at lower levels) to the People's Councils at the various lower levels.

What has been discussed so far is the main permanent, inherent, and constitutional means by which the CPC dominates the political life of the country through the machinery of the government. There are also a number of other means which are not inherent in the constitutional nature of the system but are equally important in practice.

One is the frequent redrawing of administrative boundaries by the State Council to further the aims of the CPC. In some cases this seems to be done simply to ensure more centralized control. For example, the Manchurian provinces were reduced in number from five to three (Heilungkiang, Kirin, and Liaoning) in the summer of 1954, at the same time that Kao Kang and some of his supporters were purged and many of his Manchurian appointees removed from office.

Another type of redrawing of administrative boundaries has as its aim to divide minority groups and bring them under firmer Chinese control. Here the two main examples are Tibet and the Inner Mongolia Autonomous Region. In October 1955 most of the Nationalist-created province of Sikang, which is inhabited largely by Tibetans, was absorbed into Szechuan; the remainder, the Chamdo area, has a special administrative status. When the Inner Mongolia Autonomous Region was established in May 1947, it was carved out of western Manchuria and the former province of Chahar, and it probably did contain a population of which a majority were Mongols; nevertheless, there were many Mongols living outside its boundaries, for example in Suiyuan. Since then the Inner Mongolia Autonomous Region has grown considerably by absorbing Suiyuan in 1954 and part of Jehol at the end of 1955. It is now believed to have a total population of about 8 million, of whom only about 1 million are Mongols. Another curious fact is that it was not until the absorption of Suiyuan in 1954 that the capital of the region (Huhehot, or Kweisui) lay within its borders.

Propaganda and persuasion are more prominent, and perhaps more important, features of life in Communist China than is force, although they would be much less effective if it were not for the existence of force in the background. Except in the cases of particularly dangerous times or particularly dangerous persons, the CPC seems to operate on the principle that it is better to convince an opponent or doubter of his error and get him to admit it publicly and promise to mend his ways than to liquidate him. This preference stems from the CPC's strong desire to make it appear that it is supported by the over-whelming majority of the public and from its liking for seeming to be always in the right. Since the CPC is not satisfied with mere passive support or neutrality, there is neither freedom of speech nor freedom of silence in Communist China. Everyone is expected to proclaim his loyalty to the regime and his enthusiasm for its basic policies.

The task is made much easier, though still not entirely attainable, by the CPC's monopoly of the educational system and the press. It is thus almost impossible for any idea of which the CPC does not approve, or which it is not at least prepared to tolerate, to find public expression. Other means of communication with the public which the CPC uses, and which it also controls completely, are the radio, wall posters, books and periodicals, and innumerable meetings. The meetings, which are probably the most important of these means, are of various kinds. One is the organized congress or conference held by some recognized public body. Another is the mass rally of the public in any given place to celebrate some event, listen to some message, or the like. Another is the small discussion group, at which each participant not only listens to the person in charge, who is usually a CPC cadre, but is also expected to say something. If he entertains doubts or objections to CPC policies, or has in the past, he is expected to confess this and accept gratefully the criticisms of the others present; he also criticizes them when his turn comes to do so. Sometimes individuals are required to keep diaries in which they record not only their actions but their thoughts and to produce these for inspection by CPC cadres or police officials. In their most extreme form, when applied intensively to political or military prisoners, these techniques of thought control are commonly known as "brainwashing," but it is important to realize that the entire population is exposed in varying degrees to the same techniques.

There is no doubt that "brainwashing," applied intensively to limited groups of people, can produce not only outward conformity but a great measure of inward conformity as well. Whether it can affect an entire vast population as strongly is more doubtful. The CPC is attempting to revolutionize one of the oldest, toughest, and most deeply rooted cultures in the world. The events of 1956 in Eastern Europe and the Soviet Union lead one to suspect that this culture would tend to reassert itself and that students and intellectuals would begin to demand real freedom, instead of the bogus variety which the CPC has imposed on them, under any one of three conditions: a serious and sustained failure on the part of the CPC to modernize the economy and improve living standards, a sudden relaxation of bureaucratic and police controls over the populace, or a massive exposure of the populace in some way or other to objective truth about the situation in the world at large and China's place in it. As a matter of fact, the mild "de-Stalinization" campaign of 1956 produced student disorders in China just as it did in the Soviet Union.

In the event that the method of persuasion, which seems to work fairly well under normal conditions, should fail to work for any reason, there still remains the apparatus of terror. This is presided over mainly by the Ministry of Public Security of the State Council. In June 1951 the ministry, to make things easier for itself, issued a regulation decreeing the disarming of the populace and the confining of firearms to military and governmental personnel. The ministry controls a large police force, part of which was transferred to its control from that of the armed forces in the summer of 1955 and renamed the People's Armed Police. There are also Public Security Forces within the People's Liberation Army which guard frontiers, as well as forced-labor battalions and the like.

At the end of 1954, after a period of serious floods and unrest in the countryside and a "blind influx" of peasants into the cities in search of better conditions, police controls over the populace were considerably tightened. Public Security personnel were empowered to arrest and punish persons accused of offenses against "security" without seeking a regular indictment or court trial. The urban population had already been organized into committees or teams each under the supervision of its own leaders and the police; this system was now tightened, and the regulations governing it were published.

For those who are found guilty of offenses either by the regular courts or by the police, there is a whole range of punishments from reprimand to execution. The most important, and certainly one of the most common, is forced labor or, as the CPC calls it, "reform through labor." It is also the most logical, for idleness is a vice that the CPC detests, and there are many jobs to be done for which it would be impossible or prohibitively expensive to procure machinery. The total number of forced laborers in the CPR, on which there is much less evidence than in the case of the Soviet Union, has been the subject of unrestrained speculation in some quarters. Part of the confusion arises from a failure to make a necessary distinction between true forced laborers, who are prisoners serving sentences, and what the CPC calls "unpaid labor." The latter is an ancient and probably indispensable Chinese institution under which people are conscripted in large numbers, during the agricultural slack season when possible, to perform some necessary task such as building a road or fighting a flood and are released when the job is finished. The writer would estimate—or, to put it more truthfully, guess—that the total number of true forced laborers in the CPR has never exceeded 2 million. One of the most important functions which they perform is to work under the direction of the PLA building roads, railways, and the like in distant and desolate areas such as Tibet and Sinkiang.

A logical place at which to begin a summary of the CPC's policy toward various social groups is its treatment of the intellectuals, a term under which the CPC groups technicians and advanced students as well as artists and professional people. This group has always been very active and influential in Chinese public life, and its progressive defection from the Kuomintang during the 1940s contributed greatly to the latter's downfall. There have been signs that all was not well in the CPC's relations with the intellectuals. One was a series of obviously extorted public "confessions" of alleged ideological errors issued by certain prominent intellectuals in 1952. Another was the furious denunciation in the CPC press and the disappearance, and presumably imprisonment, of a harmless fellow-traveling writer named Hu Feng in the spring of 1955. His case seems to have symbolized both growing discontent with the CPC's heavyhandedness toward intellectuals and the CPC's determination, at that time, to overwhelm this discontent with force.

In January 1956 the CPC Central Committee held a conference on the question of the intellectuals, and shortly afterward Chou En-lai told the National Committee of the CPPCC that some 40 per cent of China's intellectuals were ideologically unreliable and required further training. This seemed to foreshadow a policy of increased sternness, but such was not the outcome. In May 1956, following the first CPC pronouncement on the Stalin question and apparently taking their cue from an unpublished speech delivered by Mao Tse-tung before a Supreme State Conference earlier in the month, the CPC press and officialdom began to advocate freedom of thought and debate, as long as it was "in accordance with the consolidation of the people's regime." This policy has been described with the now-famous official slogan, "Let all flowers bloom together, let diverse schools of thought contend."

This promised increase in intellectual freedom was greeted with some skepticism on the part of adult intellectuals, who were understandably uncertain how far they dared take advantage of it, and with a certain amount of boisterous disorder on the part of students. The cause of the students' dissatisfaction, which seems to be continuing and increasing rather than diminishing, was not only the general lack of academic freedom but also the shortage of facilities for advanced and technical training and of suitable jobs after graduation. This situation has resulted in the wasting of many middle school graduates in unskilled or semiskilled jobs.

In addition to the intellectuals, the other class whose attitude contributed most to the fall of the Kuomintang and the triumph of the CPC was the peasants. The CPC's policy of "agrarian reform" or land redistribution, which was the keystone of its agrarian policy until about 1953, might seem well adapted to gain the support of at least the poorer elements among the peasantry. In actual fact, however, the CPC was more interested in mobilizing and using the peasants than it was in benefiting them, and after 1949 this became increasingly obvious.

The beginning of "cooperativization" (i.e., the herding of peasants into producer cooperatives, which were collective farms in every important respect except that machinery was generally lacking and that title to the land theoretically remained with the original owners) in earnest in 1953 was followed not long afterward by unmistakable signs of peasant unrest, aggravated by the severe floods of 1954. The CPC press admitted, sometimes directly and sometimes indirectly, that many peasants were resisting collectivization, burning crops, and destroying livestock. Peasant discontent was further increased by the inauguration in November 1953 of a system of "planned purchase and supply" of grain and other basic agricultural commodities, under which the peasant was allowed to keep only the grain considered sufficient for himself and his family and was compelled to sell the "surplus" to the state at low prices fixed by the latter. A period of debate within the CPC on agricultural policy was terminated by Mao Tsetung's decision of July 1955 in favor of accelerating "cooperativization." After the 1955 harvest "fully Socialist cooperatives," which are true collective farms except for the absence of machinery, began to be formed in large numbers, and collectivization was virtually completed in 1957, at least on paper. The peasantry seems to have received fewer benefits from the "de-Stalinization" program than any other class, the main concession granted it being the temporary opening of free markets in certain types of foodstuffs.

The process of collectivization has introduced noteworthy changes into the Chinese countryside. One of the most obvious is that land is now farmed in larger units, and many space-consuming boundaries have been eliminated. Undoubtedly large numbers of CPC cadres and much persuasion and pressure have been needed to work this change, but it seems that actual force has not been necessary in most cases. If peasant discontent should develop to the point of widespread armed resistance, it is uncertain whether the CPC could rely on its overwhelmingly peasant army to suppress it.

The industrial workers, who are theoretically the "leading" class in the CPR, have also had a difficult time, although not necessarily worse than in pre-Communist China. There can be no doubt that the workers have been driven very hard, especially since the inauguration of the First Five Year Plan in 1953. They have been subjected to various speed-up techniques and paid mainly on a piecework basis, in order to increase production. Their working hours have been long (8–10 hours, plus political classes and meetings), their wages low (about US$10–15 per month), and their housing and working conditions bad. The unions act as instruments of the state in squeezing maximum production out of the workers, rather than as their agents. Productivity is also kept up by a complex process known as "labor emulation," whose most conspicuous feature is the setting of periodically increased "norms" (production quotas) for the workers as a whole on the basis of the output of the most productive workers. Labor discipline is strict, and no worker can be hired unless he produces a "labor book" in which all his prior employment since 1949 is entered. There is an excessive differential between the wages of skilled and unskilled workers. Safety devices in the factories are scarce, and accidents are common. It is not surprising, under these conditions, that the quality of goods produced is often poor. Urban food shortages since the foundering of the Great Leap have produced widespread apathy among the workers.

Since the great "transformation" of 1956, the private businessman scarcely exists in the CPR except as a salaried employee in what was formerly his own enterprise. In the summer of 1956 he was promised that interest payments to him on his investment would be continued at least through the period of the Second Five Year Plan (1958–1962) and that the minimum rate would be 5 per cent. These promises were renewed in 1962. But there is still no provision for compensating him for the value of his capital investment in his "transformed" enterprise, which is thus in effect confiscated.

Worst of all, perhaps, is the lot of the national minorities. This is true in spite of the fact that they are outwardly treated with great consideration. The CPC has shown great skill in using this consideration to mask a reality of tight Chinese control. The key positions in the "autonomous" governments are generally held by Chinese CPC members. Even the cultural autonomy of the minorities, which is less of a fiction than their political autonomy, is manipulated for political purposes. For example, whereas the CPC has generally adopted the Latin alphabet for the minority languages in China proper, it has adopted the Cyrillic (Russian) alphabet for the Mongols of Inner Mongolia and for the Turkish peoples of Sinkiang; presumably the purpose was to give them a common writing system, and probably also a common written language, with their kinsmen in Outer Mongolia and in Soviet Central Asia and perhaps facilitate ultimate penetration of those areas by the CPR.

The nomadic minorities are especially unfortunate because the regions in which they live are very sparsely populated, undeveloped, rich in minerals, and close to strategic frontiers. Consequently these regions are receiving an influx of Chinese settlers at the rate of about 400,000 per year. If this flow continues, the minorities will eventually be drowned in a sea of Chinese. Some places in or near areas inhabited by minority groups, such as Paotow in Suiyuan, Lanchow in Kansu, and various places in Sinkiang, are becoming major centers of mining and industry. The trend toward industrialization of the minority areas will play havoc with the traditional cultures and customs of the minorities, to which most of them are passionately attached, and will force many of them into factories as unskilled laborers. For these things the increased number of schools and hospitals and the building of better communications seem questionable compensation.

Pressures by the Chinese and the CPC on the national minorities have not failed to evoke resistance. In 1951, for example, a group of Kazakh herdsmen revolted in Sinkiang, and the survivors made their way during the following winter, after suffering terrible hardships, into Kashmir. In Tibet, heavy-handed behavior by the Chinese occupation forces, an influx of Chinese settlers into the Cham region, and the beginning of preparations to grant Tibet "autonomy" were among the main causes of a revolt which broke out in the Cham region late in 1955. This revolt succeeded temporarily in interrupting land communication between Tibet and Szechuan. As a concession to the Tibetans, the CPC promised early in 1957 that "democratic reforms" (i.e., redistribution of land, including that of the monasteries) would not be introduced into Tibet during the period of the Second Five Year Plan. There was a large-scale withdrawal of Chinese cadres from Tibet, but no reduction in the PLA garrison. The probable reason for this surprisingly conciliatory policy is a fear on the part of the CPC that repression in Tibet might touch off revolts by other national minorities. By the spring of 1959, the rebellion spread westward from the Cham area to the vicinity of Lhasa, where fighting broke out in March. After a brutal though incomplete suppression of the revolt by the PLA, the CPC considered itself justified in introducing "democratic reforms" and even partial socialization into Tibet.

It is clear that by any reasonable definition the governmental system of the CPR is totalitarian. No previous government of China possessed anything like the bureaucratic apparatus, the budgetary resources, the control over local communities, or the will to transform China which the CPC has shown. It is fallacious to reason that "the totalitarian aspect of the Communist regime does not dismay the Chinese people: the Empire was also totalitarian." [17] The old empire

[17] C. P. Fitzgerald, *Revolution in China* (New York: Praeger; London: Cresset Press, 1952), p. 117.

was not totalitarian in theory and still less so in practice. Further-more, it became thoroughly discredited in the late nineteenth and early twentieth centuries, and the CPC could gain little by any re-semblance, real or imaginary, that its regime might bear to the em-pire. This generalization, it should be noted, applies only to the tra-ditional political system. It does not apply to the rest of traditional Chinese culture, most of which has shown considerable resiliency. On the whole, however, the CPC enjoys whatever popular support it has, not because it promises a return to old and tried ways, but because it promises something better.

But does the CPC enjoy popular support? It is difficult enough to gauge public opinion accurately in free countries and much more so in the case of totalitarian countries. The writer believes that until 1959 or 1960 the CPC enjoyed a very considerable measure of passive popular support because it was firmly in control, no ordinary career in Communist China was possible except for one who obeyed it, and there was no alternative in sight. The level of active support or of genuine enthusiasm was almost certainly much lower, as the case of the 14,000 Chinese prisoners in Korea who refused to be repatriated and the criticisms of the regime voiced in the spring of 1957 show. In the last few years, the failure of the Great Leap has reduced both active and passive support for the CPC greatly, although the revolts that might have been expected have been prevented by the regime's administrative and police controls.

Economic and Technological Policy and Problems

As early as 1950 the CPC formulated an economic timetable calling for three years (1950–1952) of recovery, reconstruction, and "demo-cratic reforms" (such as land reform) followed by three Five Year Plans (1953–1967), which would create a balanced and largely self-sufficient industrial system. By the end of the twentieth century, China was to be a major industrial power comparable in gross (but of course not per capita) terms with the United States and the Soviet Union. The methods to be employed were essentially Stalinist: the forced extraction of resources from the peasantry via the socialization of ag-riculture and a rapid build-up of heavy industry aided to the extent necessary by raw materials from abroad and capital equipment, tech-nology, and (if available) credits from the Soviet Union and Eastern Europe.

Through the end of the First Five Year Plan (1953–1957) progress toward the regime's economic goals appeared fairly satisfactory. The annual rate of capital formation was pushed up close to 20 per cent. In the last years of the period the gross national product grew about 7 per cent a year (the rate was much higher in industry than in agriculture) and rose to perhaps $60 billion. Neither in China nor abroad was it realized how precarious this progress actually was and how severe were the sacrifices that the peasant and the consumer were being called on to bear. Much of the growth was of the once-for-all variety resulting from such nonrepetitive factors as the cessation of civil war and the restoration of preexisting communications and industrial facilities. The heavy industrial sector, which enjoyed the highest growth rates, was heavily dependent on capital equipment and still more on technical assistance from the Soviet Union. Chinese industrial planning called for a mechanical imitation of earlier Soviet industrialization and hence was highly conventional rather than designed to take advantage of the latest developments in such fields as alloys, plastics, and electronics. Worst of all, an agricultural sector starved of investment funds could not continue for long to support both a growing population and a massive industrialization program.

The imposition on this already-overstrained economic system of the Great Leap Forward (in effect replacing the Second Five Year Plan), and in particular the denial of incentives to the peasants and the virtual wrecking of what had become during the First Five Year Plan a fairly respectable planning and statistical system, brought disaster of such dimensions that it is doubtful whether China can recover its economic momentum in less than a decade. There is a serious shortage of mechanical power in the countryside because of widespread slaughter of draft animals for food. Grain harvests since 1958 have amounted to only about 160–180 million tons per year. The average individual ration provides little more than 1,800 calories per day. Widespread malnutrition, apathy, and dejection have had the effect of pulling down production levels in all sectors of industry. A massive power shortage, due to a drop in coal production, has brought large-scale shutdowns of factories.

Obviously the key sector in which to look for an explanation of the crisis is agriculture. The short-term problem here is the weather, which since the spring of 1959 has been generally poor for agriculture. The intermediate-term, and a more fundamental, problem is Communist mismanagement—in other words, such things as excessive squeezing of the peasants and rises in weed infestation and harvesting losses because of inefficient use of labor and peasant indifference. The long-term problem is the pressure of a large and growing population on an inadequate and relatively constant amount (about 280 million acres) of cultivated land and on a depleted ecological environment ravaged by recurrent and essentially man-made "natural" disasters.

The agricultural problem has been greatly aggravated by unintelligent ecological management and water conservancy. Things have been done on a "crash," rather than a long-term, basis. Hastily planted trees have died from disease and lack of care. Overirrigation by means of large dams (built during the First Five Year Plan) and canals (built since 1958) has lowered water tables and produced salinization of agricultural land, especially in the lower Yellow River Valley.

Shortages of industrial raw materials are a much less serious limiting factor than is the agricultural crisis. Japan industrialized successfully prior to the Second World War on a far slenderer raw-material base, while importing one-fifth of its food supply, because its ecological management and agricultural technology were good. The CPR is endowed with abundant coal and iron, although much of it is of poor quality. It has uranium (in Sinkiang). It has an enormous water-power potential. Its main shortages are in the nonferrous metals (except tin and silver, of which it has plenty) and petroleum.

The CPC has accomplished something, although not enough, in the fields of power and communications. A huge nation-wide electric grid, centering on the gorges of the Yangtze River, is projected, but it has been held back by a shortage of copper (for wire) due in part to strategic trade controls that have been imposed against the CPR. The railway system, which is the most heavily overloaded in the world, is the core of the transportation network. China has added about 9,000 miles of track to the 12,000 it had before 1949 and is in fact the only major country currently building railways on an extensive scale. The railway density, however, is still totally inadequate; highways are almost nonexistent except near the major cities, and domestic air transport is more inadequate than in the last years of the Kuomintang government. There are two rail connections with the Soviet Union (via Manchuria and Outer Mongolia), and a third is under construction through Sinkiang. Railways are projected to Kashgar, Lhasa, and the Burma frontier. A strategic highway linking western Tibet with western Sinkiang was built across the Indian-claimed Aksai Chin Plateau in Kashmir in 1956–1957, another such highway has been built to the border of Sikkim, and a third is under construction to the border of Hunza in the Pakistani-held portion of Kashmir.

Shortages of skilled personnel have not necessarily been the most important factor holding back the CPR's technological progress— others have been shortages of investment funds and critical raw materials, insufficient quality controls, and the like—but they have been significant. The best scientists are mostly Western-trained, few in number, and not trusted by the regime. The younger scientists, many of whom were among the 7,000 Chinese students trained in the Soviet Union before 1957, do not appear to be of very high quality. Engineers and technicians are deficient both in quantity and quality. Nevertheless, since there is a great deal of activity in the scientific and technological fields, since much study is devoted to developments abroad in non-Communist as well as in Communist countries, and since the Chinese have ample natural aptitude, the emergence of the CPR as a major scientific and technological center, within limits imposed by its economy, is not to be ruled out.

Until the disasters of 1960, the volume of the CPR's total annual foreign trade (both ways) approximated $4 billion, three-fourths of it with the Communist bloc. Hong Kong was (and is) the biggest single non-Communist customer and hence foreign exchange earner, although it is not very important as a supplier. About three-fourths of the CPR's exports consist of processed and unprocessed agricultural products, and the balance of minerals and manufactured goods (such as cotton textiles, which have been dumped in large quantities in Southeast Asia from time to time). Imports consisted until 1960 mainly of industrial raw materials, capital equipment, and technical services. Trade with the non-Communist world has been somewhat reduced by an embargo on shipment of strategic materials to the China mainland voted by the United Nations in 1951, but less and less strictly observed except by the United States, which embargoes all trade with the CPR. In 1954 the CPR began a campaign to increase its exports to the non-Communist world, mainly no doubt in order to earn foreign exchange with which to begin repaying the credits it had received from the Soviet Union since 1950. On strictly economic grounds there would be important advantages to both parties in a greatly expanded Sino-Japanese trade, but political attitudes and obstacles on both sides have so far contributed to keeping the volume far below the prewar level.

Since 1960 the CPR's foreign trade has fallen to about half its former volume, and the composition of its imports has shifted in the direction of grain, fertilizers, and other items useful to agriculture. Imports of grain (about 9 million tons), mainly from Canada and Australia, have nearly exhausted the CPR's foreign exchange reserves (as well as world stocks of grain outside the United States and the Soviet Union) and have necessitated the sale of Chinese tin and silver on the world market and sizable credits from the suppliers. In 1961 and 1962 the Communist Chinese authorities encouraged overseas Chinese to send food parcels to friends and relatives in China. In its economic relations with the Soviet Union, the CPR has had to continue running a substantial export surplus (about $200 million a year) in order to pay off its indebtedness (which has probably never exceeded $1 billion at one time) for past aid and ordinary imports.

Total Soviet credits up to 1957—the CPR has received no Soviet credits since 1957—amounted to about $1.3 billion (5.3 billion yuan, the yuan being valued in Sino-Soviet economic relations at par with the old ruble, or at four to the dollar). Of this, $430 million is accounted for by two long-term economic credits announced in 1950 ($300 million) and 1954 ($130 million). The balance presumably consisted of military credits. It is almost meaningless to speak of other Soviet aid, whether military or economic, over and above these credits, since it would be repayable on a more or less current basis in goods or foreign exchange and would therefore constitute trade. The Soviet Union has made no grants of any significant size to the CPR. Since 1957 the United Arab Republic, India, and Indonesia have all received more economic aid and more sophisticated military equipment from the Soviet Union than has the CPR.

By a remarkable coincidence, the CPR has committed itself to date to a foreign aid program of its own almost exactly equal to the credits it has received from the Soviet Union—about $1.3 billion. Roughly three-fourths of this aid has gone to countries of the Communist bloc (mainly North Korea, North Vietnam, and Outer Mongolia, with smaller amounts to Hungary and Albania) since 1953. In 1956 the CPR began to make aid commitments, most of which have not yet been drawn on, to carefully selected non-Communist countries for mainly political purposes, beginning with Cambodia. Other recipients have been Indonesia, Burma, Ceylon, Nepal, Egypt, Yemen, Guinea, Cuba, and some revolutionary movements such as the National Liberation Front (FLN) in Algeria. The largest single commitment to a non-Communist country has been the $84 million credit to Burma, announced in January 1961. Until 1957, most of the CPR's commitments were in the form of grants; since then, they have been credits, either interest-free or bearing nominal interest.

Social and Cultural Policy and Trends

The population of the CPR, as of 1962, probably approximated 700 million. Until the disasters following the Great Leap Forward, it was growing at about 2 per cent a year and was 14 per cent urban—a low rate, but enough to give China in absolute terms the third largest urban population in the world. The end of the civil war and improvements in sanitation undoubtedly led to an increase in the growth rate after 1949.

The census of 1953–1954, which yielded a total (583 million) more than 100 million higher than the CPC had expected, gave the regime a shock and led it to reappraise the anti-Malthusian Marxist doctrine that since labor is the only source of wealth, the more people the more wealth. Slowly and cautiously, official encouragement of population control—later marriage, contraception, and in approved cases abortion and sterilization—began in 1954 and rose to a peak in the first half of 1957. The campaign apparently had little effect in the rural areas, where the vast majority of the population lives. Partly for this reason and partly because the regime believed that the economic program it was adopting would render population control both undesirable and unnecessary, the campaign almost disappeared during the Great Leap Forward. In 1960 the eminent and elderly economist Ma Yin-ch'u was dismissed as president of Peking University for advocating birth control and other heresies. The population-control campaign began to be revived early in 1962, when the bankruptcy of the thinking behind the Great Leap Forward had become obvious. Although quantitative statements are impossible, it is practically certain that the current food shortage has produced a falling off in the rate of population growth, as well as a decrease in the absolute size of the urban population.

One of the main initial social effects of Communist rule, in China as elsewhere, was to increase social mobility by eliminating preexisting elites and creating new ones, with the accent on youth. Within a short time, however, there began to emerge a "new class" of bureau-

crats and cadres with special privileges and also the heavy responsibility of mediating between an increasingly unpopular regime and
a restless though not yet rebellious people.

One of the most obvious features of the CPC's social policy is its
strenuous effort to pose as the emancipator of Chinese women, who
occupied an undeniably inferior position before the "Liberation." The
Marriage Law of 1950 granted women full equality with men in
marriage, divorce, and ownership of property. If the CPC has emancipated Chinese women from their husbands, however, this was partly
in order to subject them to the state. Very few women hold important
positions in public life. Women have been driven to work in factories and offices in large numbers, partly by the simple expedient
of keeping their husbands' wages too low to support their families
unaided. Working mothers have complained in the press that their
jobs left them little time or energy for their families. Another irritant
is the CPC's generally austere attitude toward feminine finery—lip-
stick, dresses with slit skirts, and the like being taboo except for a
time in 1956. Like men, women generally go swathed in shapeless
blue cotton jackets and trousers.

The CPC is of course fundamentally antireligious, but it realizes
that religion cannot be easily eradicated. To combat religion it employs not only outright persecution when feasible but also organizational manipulation and propaganda. Organized indigenous cults
with no foreign ties, such as Taoism, have been treated rather severely,
whereas Buddhism and Islam have been treated with outward deference. The regime has created a single controlling body dominated
by the CPC for each major religious community—the Taoists, Buddhists, Muslims, and Protestants—regardless of denominational differences. The strongest resistance has been encountered from the
Catholics, but an intensification of official pressure in 1957–1958 resulted in the formation of a "national" Catholic Church allegedly
maintaining spiritual ties (but nothing more) with the Holy See and
the consecration of some bishops in schism with Rome and yet with
valid orders. In 1958 the regime's wrath also fell, really for the first
time, on popular religion (including "ancestor worship"), in a presumably unsuccessful and apparently temporary effort to eliminate its
many wasteful rituals and to break its influence over the people's
minds.

Although the CPC officially proclaims its intention to replace both
traditional Chinese culture and the "bourgeois" partly Westernized

culture that emerged in the cities in the early twentieth century with a "socialist" culture, the CPC leadership naturally retains many traditional Chinese traits and attitudes and finds the survival of even more such traits and attitudes among the masses not only insuperable for the time being but in some respects useful.

This means that the CPC's assault on the traditional culture has been considerably less than total. It tolerates, and to some extent even encourages, much of the ancient political tradition (especially the concept of political unity on a cultural basis and an attitude of superiority toward peoples not of Chinese culture), traditional medicine, some of the traditional etiquette and customs, and much traditional art and literature.

On the other hand, the CPC has proceeded vigorously against traditional political theory, especially Confucianism; most aspects of the traditional family system, especially parental authority and "ancestor worship"; those aspects of traditional science and technology —except for medicine and some handicrafts—which can be replaced with something more modern; and the secret societies. The fact that the CPC has had some success in remolding the family, the kingpin of society and culture in traditional China, along modern lines is due to a large extent to the undermining of traditional family solidarity by the chaos of the twentieth century and in particular by the Second World War.

Although the standard of education in Chinese schools is not very high, except in certain specialized technical institutes, there have been great quantitative achievements. In 1956 there were approximately 380,000 students in colleges, universities, and higher technical schools; 5 million in regular or technical middle schools; and 62 million in primary schools—all these figures representing large increases since 1949. In addition, there are numerous courses for adults in basic literacy or more advanced subjects. In addition to regular full-time schools, the CPC has long had spare-time schools (after working hours) for adults. These were greatly expanded in 1958, as part of the Great Leap Forward, and at that time there also emerged a large number of half-time schools for children of middle school (i.e., high school) age in which study is combined with work.

In 1956 the CPC launched a reform of the writing system by simplifying several hundred of the most complicated written characters and announced a plan to introduce the Latin alphabet (with a few additional special symbols) as the standard means of writing Chinese in ten years. During 1957, however, the program was revised in the direction of using Latin letters mainly as an aid to the study of characters. To overcome the problem of mutually unintelligible dialects the CPC advocates a common speech (*p'u-t'ung-hua*) based on the Peking dialect of Mandarin. The literacy rate, which was about 30 per cent (of the entire population) in 1957, probably does not represent a great advance over the pre-1949 situation. The CPC's aim is apparently to modernize and streamline the Chinese language not only to promote literacy and education at home but to make Chinese eventually a world language.

In the fields of literature and art Soviet influence is strong, although less so than formerly. Russian people and Russian culture have never been popular in China, and many Chinese resent being pressed to learn Russian rather than English. There has been something of a revival of interest in China's traditional literature, taking the form of reprints of classical authors and new works done in the traditional manner. On the whole, however, the most common theme of contemporary art and literature is the glorification of "Socialist construction" in the "new" China.

Military Affairs

As one of the few Communist regimes that came to power through warfare, the CPC is keenly aware of the importance of armed force to its own survival and in international affairs in general. It has made the CPR the leading conventional military power in the Far East, although of course not a force comparable to the United States or the Soviet Union.

The basis of the CPC's military struggle for power, and officially at least of its military doctrine today, is the strategic thought of Mao Tse-tung. Mao distinguishes three types of warfare, all of which when properly conducted by a Communist Party such as his are highly politicized. These are positional warfare, fought by regular troops in attack on or defense of fixed positions and avoided whenever possible; mobile warfare, fought by regular troops as a war of maneuver, the preferred form; and guerrilla warfare by irregular forces, carefully organized as a supplement to mobile warfare or as a substitute for it if conditions require. Although admirably suited to the requirements of revolutionary warfare, Mao's military thought has only limited relevance to the problems of intercontinental warfare between organized states armed with modern weapons.

Although the CPC claims to rate men as more important than matériel, the growth in the power of the People's Liberation Army (PLA) has proceeded in step with its technical advances. The first of these was the acquisition of Japanese weapons from the Soviet Army in Manchuria in 1946. The second was the capture of large stocks of American equipment from the Nationalists shortly afterward. The third has been the receipt of Soviet arms, usually not the best available even in the conventional field, since 1950. On this technical basis an organizational modernization has also been possible. The politically dangerous and cumbersome field armies were abolished in 1953–1954 and replaced by a system of front armies and military districts under more effective central control. Conscription was introduced in 1954 and regular ranks, decorations, and terms of service for officers in 1955.

Since that time the total strength of the PLA has remained roughly constant at slightly over 2.5 million men, including ground forces of about 115 divisions, a small navy strongest in submarines and torpedo boats, and a large air force with about 2,500 Soviet jet aircraft but nothing heavier than light bombers These forces are heavily concentrated in the eastern part of the country. Their actual cost is probably greater than the announced military budget, which approximates $2.5 billion a year.

Important matters of military policy are of course decided by the Standing Committee of the CPC Politburo, but the highest body concerned exclusively with military affairs is the Military Committee of the CPC Central Committee, about which little is known. It is probably this body, rather than the Ministry of Defense, that controls the PLA General Staff, which has operational, logistical, and political functions. The Ministry of Defense, established in 1954, presumably exists to create a semblance of civilian (governmental) control and to give Premier Chou En-lai a greater voice in military policy than he would otherwise have. Similarly, the cumbersome National Defense Council, which rarely meets, was created in 1954 to give the Chairman of the CPR (then Mao, now Liu Shao-ch'i) a channel of personal contact with the armed forces.

Party control of the armed forces is ensured by the appointment of Communist Party members to all important posts, the maintenance of the proportion of Communist Party members in the PLA as a whole at about one-third, a network of informers, the presence of a political officer in each unit down to and including the battalion to check on the loyalty of the commander and the entire unit, the existence of party committees composed of key Communists in most units, and intensive propaganda and indoctrination. Nevertheless, the party never takes the reliability of the armed forces for granted, and with some reason; it has had trouble with some of its commanders (notably P'eng Te-huai), and the impact of the Great Leap Forward and the ensuing catastrophe on the morale of the rank and file has been considerable. According to the standards of most other Communist parties, there is a large proportion of military men in high party bodies, including the Politburo; this does not indicate a militarization of the party but rather the party's effort to satisfy the military by giving them a voice in policy making, keep an eye on them, and make the best use of their genuine abilities and specialized knowledge. In the event of a major power struggle following Mao's death, the PLA might well intervene to restore "collective leadership," or, failing that, to support Chou En-lai or some other relatively moderate and pragmatic leader, or as a last resort to seize power on behalf of one of its own commanders.

In 1954, probably as a result of the stimulus imparted to Soviet military doctrine by Stalin's death and the discussion by the United States government in April of possible retaliation against the CPR for its role in the Indochina war, the CPC began to awaken to the implications of nuclear warfare. In October the Soviet Union agreed to aid the CPR in an allegedly peaceful program of atomic research and development. At about this time two main schools of thought emerged within the PLA. One, centering in the General Staff, stressed the need for powerful, modern forces-in-being with their own nuclear capability to deter a possible enemy surprise attack and deprecated the relevance of Mao Tse-tung's military thought. The other, centering in the Ministry of Defense, advocated reliance on the Soviet nuclear deterrent, preparation to fight a prolonged broken-backed war, subordination of military modernization to the over-all economic and industrial needs of the country, and adherence to Mao's military precepts. The actual policy adopted was a compromise combining a Chinese nuclear weapons program with most elements of the other point of view.

There is a widespread belief, which the CPC has found it politically advantageous to foster, that the Communist Chinese leadership regards a Third World War as inevitable and even desirable in that it would tend to improve China's power position relative to a presumably devastated United States and Soviet Union. In reality, the CPC is almost certainly aware that it could not stand aside unharmed in such a case and that not only its population but its precious industrial system would suffer heavily, perhaps fatally, from a thermonuclear attack.

The CPC's actual view appears to be (or at least to have been) that American chickenheartedness, as evidenced for example in the talk of a "missile gap," would make it possible for the Soviet Union to exploit its technological breakthroughs such as Sputnik I and its resulting assumed strategic superiority to inflict on the United States, for the benefit of the entire Communist bloc, political defeats to which the United States would not dare to respond by precipitating world war. This strategy could work only until the United States redressed the strategic balance or, more important, thought it had done so. Even in the wake of Sputnik I and the announced testing of a Soviet ICBM, however, Khrushchev refused to pressure the United States, for whose industrial potential he has a high regard, as actively as the CPC would have liked, and in any case what he did was done in the Soviet and not the Chinese interest. He evidently wished to avoid arousing the United States to a major military preparedness program.

The CPC has maintained that the "imperialists," although unlikely to commit suicide by launching a Third World War, would start local wars against "national liberation movements" (i.e., revolutionary movements, especially Communist-led ones, in the underdeveloped areas). The Chinese view has been that the Communist bloc (meaning mainly the Soviet Union) had the duty to give all possible aid to the anti-"imperialist" side in such cases, up to and including the commitment of bloc troops if necessary. The "imperialists" could be deterred by the strategic power of the bloc from escalating such wars beyond the local level.

As its reliance on the Soviet Union to carry the brunt of the struggle against "imperialism" implies, the CPR suffers from severe limitations on its military capabilities. The PLA is adequate to cope with a Nationalist invasion unsupported by the United States and to project its power into adjacent areas up to the point where American retaliation becomes a likely possibility. The PLA, however, lacks the strategic power to "liberate" Taiwan and the offshore islands as long as the United States protects them and the strategic power to deter an American first strike or retaliatory attack against the mainland of China.

The immediate reason for this situation is that the Soviet Union has kept the Communist bloc's strategic power in the Far East almost entirely in its own hands, rather than sharing it with the CPR. Soviet military aid to the CPR to date has been carefully designed so as to stop short of giving the CPR the ability to take major military initiatives, such as an attack on Taiwan, that might involve the Soviet Union in a thoroughly unwanted Far Eastern war. Khrushchev has made it fairly clear, mainly at the time of the Quemoy crisis of 1958 and the threatened Taiwan Strait crisis of 1962, that the Soviet obligation to defend China applies only to a major and unprovoked American attack on the CPR. Anything less, such as American retaliation proportioned to the Chinese initiative that had evoked it, would be unlikely to produce more than a limited or even token Soviet response.

In November 1957 a Chinese military mission visited Moscow with the probable object of seeking nuclear weapons, or at least active aid to a Chinese nuclear weapons program, from the Soviet Union. The mission had only limited success, consisting so far as is known of one or possibly several research reactors, some technical assistance, and apparently some missiles. On this limited base the CPR embarked in 1958 on what its leaders knew would be a lengthy, essentially do-it-yourself effort to construct a nuclear weapons capability. It is generally accepted that the CPR will acquire such a capability sooner or later, probably in the mid-1960s, but it will be a long time before the CPR has the delivery systems and degree of strategic invulnerability necessary to challenge the United States, if it ever does.

The Soviet Union is clearly unenthusiastic about the CPR's nuclear ambitions. Khrushchev's statements at the time of his unilateral cessation of nuclear testing on March 31, 1958, made it appear that the move was designed partly to prevent the CPR from becoming a nuclear power. The same motive presumably underlay his espousal early in 1959 of a proposal, popular with the neutral Afro-Asian countries, for an "atom-free zone" in Asia and the Pacific. In each case the CPR's response was lukewarm, and the Soviet Union accordingly has begun to restrict the "atom-free zone" it is demanding to Southeast Asia and the Pacific.

To date the CPC has shown no serious interest in disarmament or arms control, beyond endorsing in its propaganda the virtually unrealizable Soviet demand for "general and complete disarmament." The CPR adds that it would adhere to no disarmament agreement to whose negotiation it had not been a party. It is conceivable, however, that recent developments may cause it to revise its negative attitude toward arms control, as distinct from the political advantages of merely making propaganda in favor of disarmament.

Early in 1962 the CPC began to see evidence, in the form of a series of tough statements by high American officials, that the United States was not only building up its nuclear and conventional strength but was regaining its self-confidence. The assumed opportunity was gone, or so it seemed. At the same time, the Soviet Union launched a campaign in its periodical press to educate the CPC in the realities of nuclear war and convince it that only "friendly" Communist countries would receive its protection. Coming as they did at a time of grave economic crisis, these developments evidently had a sobering effect. The CPC probably began to fear that the United States could and would use against the Communist bloc exactly the aggressive politico-military strategy it had been urging the Soviet Union to employ against the United States. It will be interesting to see what method if any the CPC can devise to advance its external objectives under these disadvantageous conditions.

Foreign Policy and Foreign Relations

The objectives of the CPR's foreign policy can be inferred more from the regime's behavior than from its pronouncements. The first is security through deterring any likely enemies (meaning the United States and Nationalist China, and conceivably the Soviet Union), by political as well as military means, from attacking the CPR. The second is territorial unification through the "liberation" of the offshore islands and Taiwan. The third is economic advantage, or in other words the promotion of China's industrialization through foreign economic relations. The fourth is leadership of as much of eastern Asia as possible, accompanied by an expulsion of American power and influence and perhaps by some Chinese territorial expansion. The fifth is the growth of communism and Chinese influence in all the underdeveloped areas, for which the CPC claims that its own experience in "socialist revolution" and "socialist construction" offers the best model. The sixth is superpower status, meaning power and influence comparable to those of the United States and the Soviet Union, or if that is impossible perhaps a position as balancing power between the two superpowers. The seventh is coleadership with the Soviet Union of the Communist bloc and the international Communist movement, and ultimately sole leadership if possible. The eighth is the eventual world-wide triumph of communism, if it is assumed that the term means anything more a generation or two from now than a technique of organizing political power.

The instrumentalities available to date to the CPC for the promotion of these objectives may be classified as nonviolent, semiviolent, and violent. The nonviolent instrumentalities include some that are applicable to almost any country (diplomacy, cultural relations, economic penetration and attraction through trade and aid, propaganda, and liaison with local Communist parties and fronts) and some applicable mainly to nearby Asian countries (harboring of political exiles, organized illegal migration to Burma, formation of "autonomous areas" near the frontiers designed to attract kindred minorities on the other side, and manipulation of overseas Chinese). The semiviolent category includes border disputes (mainly with India), subversion, threats of military action by regular forces or "volunteers," and military aid and advice to some foreign Communist states (North Korea and North Vietnam) and revolutionary movements (such as the FLN in Algeria). The CPR's use of violence since the Korean War has always been more or less ambiguous and has consisted of military actions in or near the Taiwan Strait (in 1954–1955 and 1958) and incursions into disputed border regions or demilitarized zones (along the frontiers with India, Nepal, and Burma).

In discussing the CPR's record in foreign affairs, it is important to distinguish those aspects in which Chinese security was thought to be involved from those in which it was merely a question of enhancing Chinese influence. In the former the CPR, since its defeat in Korea in the spring of 1951, has been cautious; in the latter, Chinese arrogance and Communist doctrinairism have combined to produce recurrent overestimates of the extent to which the international balance of psychological forces had shifted so as to permit bold Chinese initiatives.

The record of Chinese reactions to real or imagined threats to Chinese security begins with the Korean War, in which the CPC intervened only with reluctance and mainly in response to what it believed to be a serious threat to its Manchurian frontier. The defeat of April–May 1951, and the demands for expansion of the war then being voiced in the United States, produced a proposal by the Soviet Union in June for armistice talks. Since then the CPR has always stopped just short in its external behavior of seriously risking American retaliation or even (apart from the inconclusive fighting during the two years of the intermittent armistice talks in Korea) of engaging American forces in combat. Discussion in April 1954 of American retaliation against the CPR for its intervention in Indochina and Secretary Dulles' threats of retaliation in March 1955 and September 1958, at the time of the two Taiwan Strait crises, each had a profound and sobering effect on the CPR. Although a Nationalist invasion unsupported by the United States would probably not be a serious threat to the survival of the CPR unless the latter were already in a fairly advanced state of political disintegration, the CPC showed by its heavy troop movements in the spring of 1962 that it does not discount the Nationalist threat entirely.

At least as early as the end of 1947, after the tide of civil war had begun to turn, the CPC decided that its victory would bring a great upsurge of Chinese and Communist influence in East Asia, much like the gains that had accrued to the Soviet Union in Eastern Europe from its triumph over Germany. When a suitable opportunity offered, for example on the occasion of its message to the Calcutta Youth Conference in February 1948 or Liu Shao-ch'i's speech to a World Federation of Trade Unions meeting in Peking in November 1949, the CPC began to urge the Communist parties of South and Southeast Asia to follow "the way of Mao Tse-tung." This advice and the CPC's own example certainly had something to do with the wave of armed risings that broke out in those regions in 1948. The CPC was compelled by various limitations to restrict its own intervention largely to the relatively accessible and rewarding war in Vietnam. Elsewhere armed struggle did not work well. Furthermore, the Soviet Union objected to the implications for the Soviet position in Asia of the concept of "the way of Mao Tse-tung," and events in Korea convinced the CPC of the unwisdom of relying too heavily on force as a means of promoting communism.

Accordingly, the CPC de-emphasized armed struggle, stopped denouncing the leaders and governments of newly independent neutral countries, and began to search for a more political and less military approach. This process, which began in 1951, came to fruition in 1954 and 1955, when the post-Stalin Soviet leadership too was searching for subtler and more effective ways of influencing the neutral countries. This was the period when the CPC made the greatest use of the carrot (i.e., its nonviolent instrumentalities) as opposed to the stick. The result was a considerable improvement in the CPR's standing with governments and public opinon in non-Communist Asia, but also a decrease in direct Chinese Communist influence on the Communist movements in some Asian countries. Furthermore, the political gains made by some Asian Communist parties during this period, although impressive, did not seem likely to bring them to power in the near future.

The Soviet technological and military achievements of 1957, and still more the alarmed American reaction to them, seemed to the CPC to offer a way out of the difficulty. Assuming that the Soviet Union could be persuaded to employ its military power actively to deter American intervention in contested areas, the CPC saw hope of making significant advances for itself and communism in the underdeveloped areas, especially in Asia, by means of a reversion to militancy up to and possibly including armed struggle. That the CPR did not do more along these lines than it did is probably due to the fact that the Soviet Union refused to play its assigned role. Khrushchev equivocated in the Syrian crisis of 1957 and the Lebanese and Iraqi crises of 1958 and gave the CPC only the most lukewarm support in the Quemoy crisis of 1958, and he clearly disapproved of Chinese pressures on India and Indonesia in 1959. Both the Soviet Union and the United States, as indicated respectively by Khrushchev's trip to South and Southeast Asia in February 1960 and President Eisenhower's visit to South Asia in December 1959, seemed to be threatening to make political gains out of Chinese clumsiness. In the Middle East, Africa, and Latin America, on the other hand, where the CPC greatly expanded its political and economic activity during the period of the Great Leap Forward, Peking made considerable gains in the absence of conflicts of interest and inducements to direct pressure such as existed for it in Asia.

The CPC therefore moderated its policy toward neutral Asia and, having already indirectly criticized Khrushchev in 1958 by attacking Tito for "revisionism," shifted the brunt of its wrath to the Soviet Union. A nominal compromise truce achieved at the Moscow Conference in November–December 1960 was shattered in 1961 by Chinese economic and moral support for Albania's defiance of the Kremlin. Instead of breaking openly with Peking as he had with Tirana, Khrushchev apparently began to try to starve the CPC into submission by denying it food and credits. The Chinese responded with what they apparently regarded as the only means available, pressures of various kinds on third areas such as the Indian frontier probably designed among other things to embarrass the Soviet Union and force it to brand itself before the world as giving priority to its own national interests over those of international communism, at least as interpreted by the CPC.

The current Chinese Communist position on major issues bearing on the CPR's foreign policy, and especially on Sino-Soviet relations, may now be summarized. In the ideological field, the CPC holds that even a backward ("poor and blank") country like China can attain communism, whereas Khrushchev insists that only a prosperous and culturally advanced country, such as the Soviet Union is beginning to become, can do so. In the economic field the CPC, which does not cherish backwardness for its own sake, would like the Soviet Union to raise the economies of the Communist bloc to the Soviet level and help them toward self-sufficiency through large-scale aid, whereas the needs of the Soviet state and even those of the Soviet consumer tend to receive priority in Moscow. Sino-Soviet economic tensions have been aggravated by China's wide divergence during the Great Leap Forward from the Soviet model of economic development.

Probably the fundamental issues between the CPR and the Soviet Union are those relating to power and authority, or in other words those stemming from the CPC's determination (discernible as early as a work written by Mao Tse-tung in December 1936) to provide a model and leadership for Asia and to enjoy substantial autonomy from Moscow within its self-defined sphere and from its more recent ambitions for coleadership, and perhaps ultimate sole leadership, of the Communist bloc and the international Communist movement.[18] Even Khrushchev, who of necessity takes a more relaxed view of the Soviet Union's position in the Communist world than Stalin did, finds it impossible to tolerate the CPC's pretensions. Conversely, the CPC seems to see the easing of Soviet claims to control not as making Soviet leadership more acceptable but as providing an opportunity to press its own claims. Temporary Chinese insistence on Soviet leadership at the end of 1957, in the hope of securing Soviet acceptance of the international strategy advocated by the CPC and preventing further crises of the Hungarian variety, gave way in 1958 to renewed emphasis on the unique merits of the Chinese model of "socialist revolution" and

[18] The CPC's independent pronouncement on Stalin of April 5 (April 4 by European time), 1956, the anniversary of the (Old Style) date of Lenin's April Theses of 1917, marking the transfer of the center of world communism from Western and Central Europe to Russia, may be taken as indicating Chinese determination to begin moving the center to Peking.

"socialist construction." These claims are of course designed to appeal to the underdeveloped areas, and the main Chinese hope of attaining coleadership or perhaps hegemony in the Communist bloc is to help to power a number of militant, Peking-oriented Communist regimes in underdeveloped countries.

Almost as important to the parties involved, and of more practical consequence to the outside world, is a Sino-Soviet dispute over strategy, only the most basic of whose numerous aspects can be discussed here. To a great extent the source of this dispute lies in differences of national interest and revolutionary outlook resulting from geography. The Soviet Union has played a largely defensive role in the Far East since 1945, if regarded as a great power rather than as the principal center of world communism, and has given much higher priority to Europe—meaning at present mainly Berlin and the Common Market. The CPC is naturally preoccupied with Asia and objects to Khrushchev's use of his European concerns as a pretext for not attending to the CPC's needs.

The Soviet party interprets the present era (since the Second World War) as one whose primary characteristic is the growth of the "socialist camp" (i.e., the Communist bloc), a process reversible only through a major war, which must therefore not be risked. The enemy (i.e., the United States) must be respected strategically as well as tactically—whereas the CPC holds that the enemy is to be respected tactically but despised strategically. No decisive shift in the international balance of power has occurred yet, in the Soviet view, or will occur until about 1970, when the Soviet Union hopes to surpass the United States in total industrial production. In the meantime occasional negotiations with "imperialism" to ease specific tensions are a useful way to buy time in which the Soviet Union can build up its strategic and space capabilities, expand its foreign economic relations, and raise its living standards. Opportunities to exert political pressures on the West should be exploited up to, but not beyond, the brink of war. "General and complete disarmament," or even limited forms of disarmament, if attained under suitable political conditions, would be desirable as eliminating not only the sole force (i.e., the strategic striking power of the United States) that could stop the otherwise irresistible march of communism but also the means (overseas bases, aircraft carriers, etc.) by which the United States maintains the superior strategic mobility that enables it to intervene against Communist-led "national liberation movements" in the underdeveloped areas. For this reason the Soviet-sponsored "peace movement" (as exemplified by the World Conference on General Disarmament and Peace in Moscow in July 1962) serves the interests of the "national liberation struggle" as well as those of the Soviet Union and the Communist bloc. Communism can advance without wars of any kind, even local wars, which are dangerous because of the chance of escalation and are therefore to be avoided if possible. A peaceful, even parliamentary, alternative to armed struggle must be kept open to Communist parties seeking power. In many countries a long period of rule by the "national bourgeoisie" (as in Nehru's India) may be necessary and is acceptable provided the regime is friendly to the Soviet Union. A more advanced stage, still under the control of the "national bourgeoisie" but this time of a bourgeoisie that is friendly to communism as well as to the Soviet Union, is that of "national democracy" (Castro's Cuba, for example). The transfer of power from the "bourgeoisie" to the "proletariat" (i.e., the Communists) may occur, if the political condition of the country is sufficiently advanced, without violence and even through the ballot box, as it did on a local scale in Kerala (in India) in 1957 and may yet do in Indonesia.

To the CPC most of this smacks of the revolution betrayed, the subordination of international communism and the "national liberation struggle" to the interests and ambitions of the Soviet Union. In Chinese Communist eyes, the main characteristic of the present era is the decline of "imperialism" and a resulting opportunity for the "socialist camp" (not merely for the Soviet Union), an opportunity which, however, may be lost if "imperialism" is given time to recover and regain the initiative. A potentially decisive shift in the balance of power occurred in 1957 ("the East wind has prevailed over the West wind"), but the opportunity required energetic exploitation. "Imperialism" must be attacked with all available political means, and with military means up to and including local war, while being prevented by the strategic deterrent power of the Soviet Union from launching a world war. Negotiations with the enemy are useful and permissible only with the purpose of exposing his bad faith and making propaganda against him. The "national liberation struggle" must not be sacrificed on the altar of the "peace movement," disarmament, or collaboration with the "national bourgeoisie," which the CPC regards as unreliable and prone to compromise with "imperialism." Local Communist parties must fight for power by all available means, including armed struggle where feasible and protracted warfare, of the

kind that brought the CPC to power, where necessary. Legal parliamentary activity by local Communists is intrinsically too unrevo-
lutionary, and aid to non-Communist regimes is also intrinsically
too expensive, to appeal to the CPC. The latter's militancy is probably motivated in part by a belief that the sooner an underdeveloped
country goes Communist, and therefore the more backward it is at
the time, the more likely it will be to look to Peking rather than Moscow for guidance. Soviet willingness, sometimes amounting to eager-
ness, to wait for the allegedly inevitable to take its course probably
reflects among other things a similar estimate. The CPC has an important psychological advantage in that its more action-oriented program, based on its own example, is better calculated to appeal to
impatient, often extremist, Communists and fellow travelers in the
underdeveloped countries than is the more cautious and subtle Soviet program. It is doubtful, however, whether the CPR's psychological advantage will outweigh the Soviet Union's ability to offer more
to its chosen instruments in the way of economic and military aid.
As for the present situation within the Communist parties that are
not in power, those in Asia (other than the Ceylonese and Outer
Mongolian), plus perhaps some in Latin America, incline toward
Peking, whereas the others generally follow the Soviet lead.

Before discussing the CPR's relations with countries other than the
Soviet Union, it would be well to indicate those with which the CPR
has diplomatic relations. It has such relations with the entire Communist bloc, including the borderline cases of Yugoslavia and Albania;
with the Asian neutrals (India, Nepal, Ceylon, Burma, Cambodia,
Laos, and Indonesia) and Pakistan; with most, but by no means all,
of the Arab states, of the newly independent African states, and of
the underdeveloped members of the British Commonwealth wherever
located; with the United Kingdom but with none of the "old Dominions" (Canada, Australia, New Zealand, South Africa); with the
Scandinavian countries, the Netherlands, and Switzerland; and with
Cuba alone among the Latin American countries. Those countries
that do not recognize the CPR generally recognize the Republic of
China (Nationalist China); Malaya and a few others solve the problem by recognizing neither. Many countries would like to recognize
both of the "two Chinas," but one (Laos) that has tried to do so has
had relations broken off by the Republic of China.

Next to the Soviet Union, the CPR's most important relations with
Communist states are those with the three others in Asia: the Mon-

golian People's Republic (Outer Mongolia), the Democratic People's Republic of Korea (North Korea), and the Democratic Republic of Vietnam (North Vietnam). Soviet influence is much greater than Chinese in the first of these; Chinese influence has been greater than Soviet in the second since about 1961; the third is more nearly independent and attempts to mediate between the CPR and the Soviet Union. It should be noted that North Vietnam has a common frontier with Communist China but not with the Soviet Union, whereas the other two have common frontiers with both. In all three Chinese influence has tended to increase in recent years, especially since the death of Stalin. The North Korean and the North Vietnamese regimes, being obsessed with the desire to "liberate" the southern halves of their countries, feel a considerable affinity for the CPC's relatively militant international strategy. In all three countries there is Sino-Soviet competition to exercise influence and extend economic aid. The three lesser governments attempt to take advantage of this by playing the two giants against each other.

The CPR's standing with the Communist parties of Eastern Europe was high until 1957. It had done what all of them would like to do, namely, to implement a Stalinist domestic program and play a prominent role in the Communist world without accepting dictation from Moscow. Tito made no secret of his admiration, but it was only partially reciprocated; in December 1954 the CPC finally agreed to accept his offer of diplomatic relations, but it still regards him as a troublemaker and rebuked him in May 1958 for "revisionism" and disruption of the Communist bloc. The Chinese example, and perhaps even Chinese encouragement, played a large part in the Polish Communists' decision to assert themselves against the Kremlin in 1956. The excesses of Chinese Communist domestic and foreign policy since 1958 have chilled the CPR's relations with Eastern Europe severely, except for Albania.

The CPR's relations with Communist parties not in power, especially those in Asia, are somewhat obscure, because they lack a formal diplomatic aspect. Three bodies through which the CPC appears to maintain or to have maintained liaison with the other Communist parties of Asia, both in and out of power, are the Asia-Australasian Liaison Bureau (founded in 1949) of the World Federation of Trade Unions, the Peace Liaison Bureau (founded in 1952) of the World Peace Council, and the Asian Solidarity Committee (founded in 1956). Probably more important as channels of communication, however, are the

CPR's diplomatic and consular missions in the countries where they exist and frequent visits by other Asian Communist leaders to the CPR.

As for the nature of the relationship with the Asian parties, it seems that the CPC's influence and prestige are strong but fall short of domination, except probably in Thailand and Malaya. In effect the CPC and for that matter the Soviet party also have to choose between subordination and effectiveness in the smaller parties. The more subservient and manageable they are, the less effective they are likely to be on the local scene. On the whole, the CPC has tended to choose effectiveness over subordination. The choice has been made easier by the fact that any attempt by the CPC to reduce the other Asian parties to a position of complete subservience would almost certainly meet with serious objections not only from them but from Moscow.

It has already been shown that the CPR's relations with neutral Asia have oscillated opportunistically between the poles of pressures just short of war and elaborate gestures of good will. The weaker the country in question, the more likely it is to be the object of Chinese aid and friendly attention, because it offers no rivalry or obstacle to the CPR's ambitions for regional leadership and is susceptible of being converted into a Chinese quasi-satellite even in the absence of an indigenous Communist seizure of power. Thus Burma, Cambodia, and Nepal, and to a lesser extent Ceylon, have been allowed to nibble the Chinese carrot while scarcely feeling the Chinese stick, since 1961 at any rate. After being pressured since the early 1950s with Chinese claims to portions of its northern and eastern territories and by the intermittent presence of Communist Chinese troops allegedly there to cope with Nationalist irregular forces using Burmese soil as a base, Burma received a surprisingly favorable boundary settlement in 1960 and a large Chinese credit ($84 million) in 1961. A good deal of the fear formerly felt for the CPR in Burma has given way to admiration and gratitude. Burma seems to be drifting into a relationship with the CPR similar in some ways to that of Finland with the Soviet Union. In Nepal, the CPR extends aid and seeks influence in competition with India, the United States, and the Soviet Union, but the real contest is between the CPR and India. The CPR supports, for its own ends, the government of King Mahendra, whereas India seems to be aiding a rebellion that is in progress against his authority. In Cambodia, where the dominant political emotion is fear of the Thai and Vietnamese (whether Communist or non-Communist), the CPR has leapfrogged North Vietnam, which aspires to control of all of what was formerly French Indochina, by establishing since 1956 a powerful and superficially friendly economic and political presence. Cambodia relies on the CPR, apparently with some success, to restrain North Vietnam's urge to dominate Cambodia.

It is a different story with the larger neutrals, India and Indonesia, which are actual or potential obstacles to the attainment of the CPR's regional ambitions. Furthermore, India is an immediate neighbor with a border dispute with the CPR and in a vague sense offers for Asian consideration a politico-economic alternative to the Chinese model of development. India has received no economic aid from the CPR, and Indonesia only about as much as the far smaller state of Guinea. Both India and Indonesia were subjected to severe Chinese pressures in 1959. With at least tacit Soviet support, however, Indonesia has been able to establish a satisfactory *modus vivendi* with the CPR on the main issue between them (the citizenship of overseas Chinese resident in Indonesia), and India has declined to accept the temporary compromise settlement of the border dispute, to the effect that India control the North East Frontier Agency and the CPR control Aksai Chin, first proposed by Chou En-lai in November 1959.

The CPC's policy toward the anti-Communist Asian states (Pakistan, Thailand, the Republic of Vietnam, the Federation of Malaya, the Philippines, and the Republic of Korea) does not require detailed comment. The CPC tends to express hostility to them to the extent that they align themselves diplomatically and militarily with the United States. The CPC's aim seems to be to convince them of the disadvantages of alignment with the United States and the advantages of neutralism and friendly relations with the CPR. In this way it apparently hopes to persuade them eventually to enter the ranks of neutral nations, which in the Chinese Communist scheme of things are one step closer to "Socialism." In this effort the CPC has had some success, mainly with the educated public (to whom Chinese foreign propaganda is primarily addressed) rather than with the governments. For example, there has been some growth of feeling in Pakistan, Thailand, and the Philippines, the only Asian members of the Southeast Asia Treaty Organization, that their alignment with the West has earned them the dangerous enmity of the Communist bloc without necessarily assuring them of compensating protection by the Western powers. It would be very unwise to overlook the possibility of a drift toward neutralism on the part of the presently anti-Communist

Asian states. In fact, common hostility to India seems to be producing a Sino-Pakistani alignment to balance the Soviet-Indian combination.

The CPR is not known to have been directly involved in the recent fighting in Laos and the current fighting in South Vietnam. In both cases the North Vietnamese rather than the Chinese have the primary interest and responsibility on the Communist side, the United States is heavily involved on the non-Communist side, and in the case of Laos the Soviet Union has asserted an active interest of its own by sending overt aid to the leftist Pathet Lao. The CPR is building a road into northern Laos and certainly could intervene if it chose, but so far its aid to the Pathet Lao seems to have been limited and covert. The CPR provides North Vietnam with both economic and military aid and has also shown somewhat more enthusiasm for its effort to "liberate" South Vietnam by guerrilla warfare than has the Soviet Union, but apparently not as much as the North Vietnamese would like.

Japan occupies a special position in the CPR's calculations as a former foe and occupier, as the only industrialized non-Communist neighbor, and as a possible serious rival for leadership in Asia. Japan's significance to the CPR is likely to be enhanced by the policy recently adopted by the Soviet Union of greatly broadening its economic relations with Japan, presumably with the idea of overcoming the intense anti-Soviet feeling in Japan, increasing Soviet political influence, and adding Japan to India and Indonesia on the list of Asian countries that the Soviet Union is using as counterweights to the CPR. Until recently, the CPR has shown little serious interest in increasing its trade with Japan but a great deal in trying to work with and through Japanese leftists or even in some cases conservatives to harass the Japanese government, to prevent the rearmament and remilitarization of Japan (which in any case is not very likely in the near future), and to generate political pressures for the elimination of the extensive American base facilities. Since the economic disasters that began in 1960 and the beginning of Soviet trade offers to Japan in 1961, the CPR has seemingly become more serious about trade with Japan, although its arrogant militancy has continued increasingly to strain its relations with the Japanese Socialist Party. It remains to be seen whether Chinese political and cultural attraction for the Japanese left can outweigh the economic inducements that the Soviet Union can offer and whether either country can make significant headway against the powerful American politico-economic position in Japan.

In several countries of Southeast Asia—especially Burma, Thailand, South Vietnam, the future Federation of Malaysia (Malaya, Singapore, and the British Borneo territories), and Indonesia—Chinese make up a significant fraction of the population and one with a very powerful economic position and a slowly growing political role. Of the residents of Southeast Asia who are essentially of Chinese culture (about 14 million), only a minority are Chinese in the political sense and therefore actively exploitable by one or the other Chinese regime. The majority of these are pro-Communist, only a minority pro-Nationalist. Until 1954, the CPC's policy was one of fairly active manipulation of the overseas Chinese. After that, except in predominantly Chinese Singapore, the CPC began to show more restraint, including an admission that an overseas Chinese could renounce Chinese citizenship and take that of his country of residence if he wished. The short-term motive for this concession was undoubtedly a desire to improve relations with the governments and peoples of the Southeast Asian countries; but a possible long-term consideration was that resident Chinese might be more useful to the CPR's aims in the area if they acquired political influence, to which citizenship was a prerequisite. The CPC continues to manipulate and propagandize the overseas Chinese, but in a relatively subdued way.

Significant Chinese Communist interest and activity in the Middle East and Africa began after the Bandung Conference. In 1956 Egypt became one of the first countries in the area to recognize the CPR and, at the time of the Suez crisis, was the recipient of some token Chinese aid and a vague promise of "volunteers." The pace of Chinese activity in Africa and the Middle East quickened in 1958 and has remained fairly intense ever since. The region appeals to the CPC as an exploitable one because of its backwardness, instability, and intense anti-"imperialist" feeling, although the local Communist movements are weak and political power is generally in the hands of authoritarian "national bourgeois" or even "feudal" regimes. In the Middle East and Africa the CPR hopes to gain, and to some extent has already gained, important raw materials (possibly including oil) and political influence in left-wing circles through which it may undercut the "imperialists" and the Soviet Union, sway the immature local Communist movements, and acquire diplomatic recognition and support for the CPR's entry into the United Nations. To these ends the CPR employs a rather wide range of nonviolent and semiviolent instrumentalities, including prompt recognition of the independence of new African states and more or less covert military aid to certain "national liberation movements." One of the main themes of the extensive Chinese propanda addressed to the Middle Eastern and African countries is the allegation that they can learn from the Chinese example how to develop themselves without much foreign aid, and with little or no Western or Soviet aid.

Infuriated with Nasser for frustrating a Communist take-over of Syria by forming the United Arab Republic early in 1958, the CPR showed its displeasure by, among other things, publishing a denunciation of him by a Syrian Communist speaking in Peking in October 1959. During the Lebanon crisis in 1958 the CPR threatened to send "volunteers," and the following year it gave moral support to the unsuccessful rising of the Iraqi Communists against Kassem, who was favored by the Soviet Union. The CPR supported the non-Communist FLN's armed struggle against the French in Algeria more consistently than did the Soviet Union, granting the FLN diplomatic recognition and a credit in 1958 and apparently sending it some military aid. In the Congo, the CPR offered credits and some military aid to the short-lived Lumumba regime in 1960, although it refused his request for "volunteers," and after his fall transferred its recognition to Gizenga, not to the central government in Leopoldville. Among the African states in which the CPR has shown particular interest and has managed to acquire some influence are Somalia, Zanzibar, and (at least until its recent turn away from the Communist bloc) Guinea.

Latin America offers the CPR political and economic inducements comparable to those of Africa and the Middle East, plus a somewhat higher level of development and more mature Communist movements. Although the CPR is much admired by Latin American leftists, cultivates them industriously, and has limited economic and cultural relations with several countries of the region, the only one with which it has diplomatic relations is Cuba. The CPR regarded the establishment of the Castro regime as the first major step forward for communism in the New World. It has traded with Cuba fairly extensively and sent some aid. Especially since the missile crisis of October 1962, the CPR has given loud propaganda support to Castro, not only as against American but also as against Soviet pressures on him. The CPR's stock with Castro is therefore high and seems to be growing. In terms of influence on the local Communist Party, Chinese penetration is perhaps deepest in Chile. Like the rest of the Communist bloc, the CPR has high hopes for Brazil, where economic distress and political unrest constitute fertile soil for the growth of communism.

Although the CPR has little regard for the Charter of the United Nations, it objects to being excluded from that body in favor of the Republic of China and to being in effect represented there by the Soviet Union. The CPR certainly wants China's permanent seat on the Security Council. In the event, however, that the CPR were voted into the General Assembly but were unable to replace the Republic of China in the Security Council because of the latter's veto, the CPR might content itself for the time being with representation in the General Assembly. From 1950, when the issue of Chinese representation became acute, through 1960, the United States and its allies were able to vote through the General Assembly each year a resolution declaring a "moratorium" on the question; in other words, the substance of the issue would not be discussed and the Republic of China's position would therefore be left undisturbed. The Afro-Asian countries tended to become dissatisfied with this procedure, and in 1961 the United States therefore did not press for a vote on the moratorium but succeeded instead in getting the General Assembly to adopt a resolution declaring the question of Chinese representation to be an important one requiring a two-thirds majority for any change. A Soviet resolution calling for the replacement of the Republic of China by the CPR and an amendment proposed by Ceylon, Cambodia, and Indonesia and calling in effect for both Chinas to be represented failed of even a simple majority, much less a two-thirds majority. The outcome in 1962 was similar.

One of the very important determinants of the CPR's foreign policy is the state of near-belligerent hostility existing between it and the United States. The CPR is trying to eliminate American influence from the Far East and in fact from the entire world, and the United States has designed its Far Eastern policy since 1950 mainly to contain the CPR. Some remarks on the question of responsibility for this hostility may be in order. In late 1949 the Department of State was clearly preparing to recognize the CPR at the earliest opportunity. At that time, however, and perhaps for that reason, the CPR proceeded to maltreat American consular personnel remaining in China. The United States thereupon withdrew its officials and abandoned the idea of recognition, but it did not commit itself to the defense of Taiwan and the preservation of the Republic of China until after the outbreak of the Korean War in June 1950. The CPR is one of the states that require external enemies ("imperialists") and internal enemies ("counterrevolutionaries") to justify repression at home and assertiveness abroad. From Peking's standpoint the United States, if it did not exist, would have to be invented. There is little doubt that if it had not been for American containment and opposition, the CPR's power and influence in Asia would be vastly greater. The rest of Asia may therefore be grateful that some country has been able and willing not only to shoulder the onerous burden but to tolerate the criticisms that many Asians make of its policy, for reasons which include a desire to reinsure their relations with the CPR in case it ultimately prevails.

Beginning immediately after the outbreak of war in Korea, the Truman Administration announced that the United States Seventh Fleet would prevent offensive operations across the Taiwan Strait by either Chinese regime and inaugurated programs of economic and military aid to the Republic of China and a number of other Asian countries threatened by Communist, including Chinese, pressures. It also negotiated the ANZUS Treaty (with Australia and New Zealand) and bilateral defense agreements with the Philippines and Japan. The Eisenhower Administration added bilateral pacts with the Republic of Korea and the Republic of China (ratified early in 1955, at the time of the first Taiwan Strait crisis) and formed SEATO (the Southeast Asia Treaty Organization, composed of the United States, Britain, France, Australia, New Zealand, Pakistan, Thailand, and the Philippines) to check Communist expansion in Southeast Asia. The Eisenhower Administration also nominally "unleashed Chiang Kai-shek" by removing the public prohibition against Nationalist offensive operations against the mainland, but in practice an unpublished prohibition continued in effect. The so-called Formosa Resolution, adopted by Congress in 1955 and still in effect, provides that the President, in addition to his obligation to defend Taiwan itself, may at his discretion commit American forces to the defense of the off-shore islands (mainly Quemoy off Amoy and the Matsus opposite Foochow), provided he judges a Communist attack on them to be part of an attack on Taiwan. Going beyond this, Secretary Dulles threatened American retaliation against the mainland of China in March 1955 and September 1958, at the time of the Taiwan Strait crises, each time with a markedly calming effect on Peking's behavior. The Kennedy Administration has shown signs of wanting to adopt a "Two Chinas" policy (i.e., recognition of both Peking and Taipei), to which an evacuation of the offshore islands would probably be a necessary preliminary, but American public opinion and strong objections from Taipei have prevented any serious effort to implement these ideas.

By way of conclusion to this discussion of the CPR's foreign policy and foreign relations, a comment on its relations with the Republic of China is needed. The CPC undoubtedly wants to "liberate" Taiwan, but its preoccupation with this issue is not the overwhelming and irrational obsession that it finds useful to let others believe. The CPC realizes that a military seizure of the island would be impossible, or at least too risky, as long as the United States observes its current commitments to the Republic of China. This will continue to be true at least until the CPR acquires either a powerful nuclear arsenal of its own or more active Soviet military support and collaboration than it has received so far. Even then, an attack on the island would have so many political and economic drawbacks as to be worth while only as a last resort. The CPC would prefer a political to a military "liberation," along the lines of the arrangements whereby much territory on the mainland (including Peking) passed into its hands in 1949 with very little fighting. This would require an agreement with the Republic of China and a break between the latter and the United States. Neither of these appears a practical possibility as long as Chiang Kai-shek lives, but the chances of both would probably be increased by his death. To date, the Republic of China is not known to have done more than take note of repeated Communist offers of a political accommodation. The outcome of this tug of wills obviously depends to a great extent on the future course of events on both sides of the Taiwan Strait, as well as in the cold war in general.

Problems and Prospects of Communist China

Probably the fundamental problem faced by the CPR is this: Can it modernize not only its state sector but also the consumer sector on its overstrained and overpopulated agrarian base? The answer seems to be no, unless there is not only a change of economic policy even more drastic than the one that began late in 1960 and in the same direction, but also a substantial increase in agricultural productivity and a reduction in the absolute size of the population. Of these three assumed conditions, only the first appears possible of realization in the near future.

In the political field, it seems unlikely that either Mao or Liu Shao-ch'i—if he actually succeeds Mao—would be able or willing to institute the profound changes, in the form of a carefully controlled decompression at home and a "thaw" in the CPR's relations with the Soviet Union and the United States, that would seemingly be required to maximize the CPR's prospects for long-term growth. Such changes would be very difficult for the regime to accept, because they would rule out the CPR's ambitions for industrialization and superpower status in the reasonably near future. It is possible, however, that a shift in the political balance might bring to power, more probably after than before Mao's death, a leadership with an outlook flexible enough to make the changes in policy just indicated.

Militarily, the CPR is unable either to deter, through its own efforts, an American retaliatory attack on the China mainland or to project its power far beyond its borders. There seems to be little prospect of a significant change in this situation until the CPR acquires a sizable and reasonably invulnerable nuclear capability, complete with the most sophisticated delivery systems.

Internationally, the CPR's influence and prestige are held down, except in extreme left-wing circles, by the limitations already mentioned and have been tarnished, though less than might be imagined, by the failure of the Great Leap Forward. The CPR is also hampered by its arrogance, its reputation for bellicosity, and its limited ability and desire to engage in foreign aid.

In view of its handicaps, the CPR seems unlikely to attain anything resembling the full list of its external objectives. Even the regional ones, to say nothing of the global ones, will be very difficult to realize, in part because the CPR will have to compete increasingly in the Far East not only with the United States but with the Soviet Union.

It is possible, although not probable in the near future, that the CPR might collapse as an organized state, as the Chinese empire disintegrated from time to time. The 1962 harvest was slightly better than that of 1961, but not nearly good enough to compensate for the nutritional deficiencies accumulated since 1959 or to permit a resumption of industrial expansion. The quickest way out of the CPR's short-term economic difficulties would be a loan of Soviet gold with which to buy American wheat, but both parts of this transaction appear to be out of the question for political reasons. If a collapse came, it would probably begin with large-scale hoarding of grain by officials in the less-badly-off areas, to prevent it from being shipped out to the rest. Famine would then promptly become acute in the areas producing less than the average, and the CPR might begin to break down into regional fragments, still Communist-controlled but separate. At that point the Republic of China would probably find the temptation to launch an invasion irresistible, and the result might be a prolonged period of chaos.

A somewhat more probable outlook, however, would appear to be for the survival rather than the collapse of the CPR, a cycle of partial economic recovery followed by resumption of industrial expansion followed by crisis and a repetition of the cycle, accompanied by a gradual mellowing of the regime. The latter process, if it permitted adequate investment and incentives in the agricultural sector, might enable China to become in time, like Japan before the Second World War, a rather highly industrialized country regularly importing a large percentage of its food as well as needed industrial raw materials.

It is sometimes speculated that population pressure may produce large-scale Chinese emigration to Southeast Asia or to the Soviet Far East and Soviet Central Asia. The economic advantages of such a process would be doubtful; these regions contain a great deal of marginal land, such as the CPR is trying with only indifferent success to populate and develop in its own interior. The rice surplus of Southeast Asia, which could be considerably increased under proper management and with an assurance of a market, could probably be obtained more cheaply and advantageously under an unequal international economic relationship imposed by the CPR than through outright colonization. Perhaps more basic is the consideration that overt Chinese colonial expansion into Southeast Asia would almost certainly mean war with the United States and that such expansion into the Soviet Far East or Soviet Central Asia would almost certainly mean war with the Soviet Union. It seems probable that China's economic and demographic problems will be solved, if at all, essentially within its present frontiers.

If it is assumed that Sino-Soviet relations will not deteriorate to the point of war—this, however, is a contingency not to be entirely excluded even in the absence of Chinese demographic pressures on Soviet territory—what future course are they likely to take? An open break of party or state relations, although possible, is not very probable, because each side would stand to lose something by it and because each side seems determined that if a break comes it must be precipitated by the other. Short of an open break, relations are likely to remain roughly what they are now: semiconcealed controversy and substantial noncooperation, interspersed with interludes of temporarily improved relations and crises stopping just short of a break.

The Republic of China since 1949

The beautiful island of Taiwan, to which the Chinese Nationalists transferred their headquarters from the mainland at the end of 1949, lies on the Tropic of Cancer about 120 miles off the coast of Fukien province and has an area of approximately 14,000 square miles. It is roughly comparable in area and topography to Hainan or Ceylon. For fifty years (1895–1945) it was ruled by Japan, which valued it for its rice, sugar, and camphor and its strategic location. The Japanese gave Taiwan an orderly but oppressive government and a high literacy rate, but no preparation for self-government.

As they had been authorized to do at the Cairo Conference (November–December 1943) and by General MacArthur's General Order Number One (August 15, 1945), the Chinese Nationalists promptly occupied the island after the Japanese surrender. Carpetbagging mainlanders proceeded to misgovern it so badly that on February 27–28, 1947, many of the inhabitants rose in revolt only to be massacred. Soon afterward the National Government removed the governor, Chen Yi (not to be confused with the Chinese Communist general whose name is pronounced and spelled in English in the same way); eventually Chen was shot, but for planning to go over to the Communists rather than for what he had done on Taiwan.

In January 1949 the National Government, foreseeing the possibility that Taiwan might be needed as a refuge, appointed one of its ablest and most honorable officials, Ch'en Ch'eng, as governor of the island. He set about eliminating the worst abuses and instituting a more enlightened administration. In 1950, when Ch'en became Premier, he was succeeded as governor by K. C. Wu, another official of the highest type. Beginning in the summer of 1950, municipal and county elections were held throughout the island; these elections are especially interesting because they were the first genuine local elections ever held in Nationalist China. Since then elections have also been held for a provincial assembly, all but one of whose members are Taiwanese. Most of the members of the appointive Governor's Council are also

Taiwanese. The governor himself is appointed by the central government and is a mainlander. In the various elections at the provincial level the Kuomintang (which of course includes Taiwanese members) has won most of the seats, but some have also been won by two minor parties (the Youth Party and the Democratic Socialist Party) and by nonparty candidates.

Taiwan supports not only a provincial government but also a government claiming to be that of all China. At this higher level, because of the impossibility of holding national elections, the trend toward democratization scarcely applies. The National Assembly has great difficulty in mustering a quorum, since most of its members are either dead or live elsewhere. The five Yuan are entirely dominated by the Kuomintang and by mainland Chinese rather than by Taiwanese. Chiang Kai-shek as President exercises an arbitrary power which is nearly absolute when he chooses to make it so and which tends to increase rather than diminish with time. The Vice-President, Ch'en Ch'eng, does not have much influence with the middle ranks of the Kuomintang hierarchy, although he has some with the army high command, and his chances of inheriting the full measure of Chiang's power do not appear great. The Generalissimo's elder son, Chiang Ching-kuo, exercises much power in the secret police, the political departments of the armed forces, and the Youth Corps and is probably next to his father the most powerful man on the island. The central government still keeps on its payroll, though not in positions of real power, a number of disreputable former warlords who symbolize the albatross of the past which still tends to hang round the Kuomintang's neck.

Taiwan, in short, is essentially a police state, though not a fully totalitarian one. The tendency toward dictatorship is somewhat restrained by the need for keeping on good terms with the United States and by the presence of several thousand Americans on the island. Anyone accused of Communist sympathies is harshly dealt with, usually by execution or by imprisonment on Green Island, the Kuomintang's "counterbrainwashing center," and the regime retains its unfortunate tendency to classify any public criticism of itself as the work of Communist sympathizers. The outward conformity produced by such tactics is really hypocrisy rather than loyalty, and government and people do not trust one another. On the mainland a somewhat similar situation is eased by the regime's ability to point to "Socialization" and economic transformation as a worth-while goal and by its position as the symbol of China's growing power. The Kuomintang has no such goal to which it can point except that of reconquest of the mainland—and this makes no appeal to the Taiwanese and seems increasingly unattainable even to many mainlanders on the island.

As the dominant group within the Kuomintang has become more confident of American support, it has also tended to tighten its grip on the island. This can be seen in the cases of two able officials widely respected by Americans. In 1954 Governor K. C. Wu of Taiwan broke with the Kuomintang and came to the United States, charging that Taiwan had been made into a police state. In 1955 the regime sent into disgrace and retirement one of its ablest field commanders, Sun Li-jen, who had objected to the activities of Chiang Ching-kuo's political departments within his units, had often criticized the Generalissimo himself, and had a not very sanguine view of the prospects for a reconquest of the mainland. In 1960 a respected editor, Lei Chen, was imprisoned for criticizing the government and trying to found a new political party.

It might be thought that the crushing defeat on the mainland would have taught the Kuomintang something; it has, but not enough. The Kuomintang concluded that its defeat had been caused by bad party discipline, corruption, inefficiency, and bad strategy. This was correct, but inadequate, for the Kuomintang's basic nature and philosophy had also been to blame. Both the Central Executive Committee and the Central Supervisory Committee were abolished in 1950 and were replaced by two smaller bodies, the Central Advisory Committee and the Central Reform Committee. The last-named, which was the more important of the two smaller bodies and was headed by the Generalissimo himself, was abolished in its turn in 1952 and succeeded by a Central Committee. There was considerable transfusion of new blood into the middle and upper ranks of the party, but there has been no fundamental change in its official philosophy.

The economic situation is somewhat more encouraging. By virtue of massive American aid Taiwan enjoys close to the highest standard of living in Asia. In fact, it is higher than the island can afford. The government is afraid to risk popular displeasure and a possible growth of pro-Communist feeling by diverting resources from present consumption to investment. Long-term planning and development are also inhibited by heavy military expenditures and the Kuomintang's refusal to treat Taiwan as anything more than a temporary stopping place.

This in turn makes the Kuomintang unable to get along without continued massive American aid.

In the field of agrarian reform accomplishment has been noteworthy; the tragedy is that the Kuomintang waited so long to implement legislation much of which had been on the books since 1930 but had never been enforced on the mainland, except for a time by the Communists. Rents were first reduced to a maximum of three-eighths of the annual crop, and some public lands were sold to would-be owner-cultivators; then, beginning in 1953, most landlord-owned land was bought and resold to the tenants on reasonable terms. The former owners were paid largely in industrial securities and thus transformed willy-nilly into entrepreneurs, a sensible device. Today tenancy is almost unknown, and land is equitably distributed, but by virtue of the relationship of population to cultivated land the average size of farms is small.

With the help of ample American economic and technical assistance, Taiwanese industry has considerably expanded, especially in the fields of electricity and light industry. The island does a thriving trade with other Asian states, especially Japan.

Nevertheless, all this has been aptly called progress on a treadmill. The population (about 11 million, of whom roughly three-fourths are Taiwanese and the rest mainlanders) is growing at more than 3 per cent per year, and no amount of American aid can provide land and jobs for all the surplus. Taiwan has recently become a rice importer. This economic dilemma is worsened by the island's obscure political future.

Since Nationalist China stands or falls by American aid and protection, it is important to understand what the American policy has been. From the end of 1949 to June 1950 the United States government pursued a policy of inaction and was prepared to do nothing to save Taiwan from "liberation." The outbreak of the Korean War sharply upgraded the importance of Taiwan in the eyes of American officialdom, and the Seventh Fleet was interposed between Taiwan and the mainland by President Truman with orders to prevent any major military movement in either direction. The Chinese Nationalists then began to receive military and economic aid which has amounted by now to about $3 billion. Early in 1953 the Eisenhower Administration removed the ban on Nationalist attacks on the mainland and thus theoretically "unleashed Chiang Kai-shek." Nothing happened for two reasons. The Nationalist forces, though growing stronger with American help, were still far too weak to undertake any major operations against the mainland; and in any event Washington imposed an unpublished prohibition on any such operations without prior American consent. There was thus substantially no change in the situation. This has continued to be true in spite of the offshore-islands crises of late 1954 and early 1955 and 1958, already mentioned, and the Communist military and logistical build-up opposite Taiwan in the spring of 1962.

The Kuomintang enjoys some prestige and support among overseas Chinese, especially in the Philippines, but in general far less than do the Communists. It is the Communists, after all, who control the Chinese mainland, from which all overseas Chinese originally came. There is also a sizable number of overseas Chinese, especially among those who have had some experience of both regimes, who refuse to give support to either and long for something better. It is uncertain whether any considerable number of people on the mainland of China would welcome a substitution of the Kuomintang for the CPC.

The international status of Taiwan presents an apparently insoluble problem. The island was promised to China at the Cairo Conference in 1943, and to date no government is officially committed to anything but this solution. The question of course is, to Communist China or to Nationalist China? The Japanese peace treaty of 1951 divested Japan of any claim to Taiwan, but it did not settle the actual disposition of the island. Neither Communist China nor Nationalist China has given the slightest official sign of abandoning its claim to the other's territory. But neither side is currently in a position to make good its claim.

In theory, it would be possible for the inhabitants of Taiwan to vote freely as to which of the two regimes they prefer or whether they would like to remain independent. But the Kuomintang would not permit such an election, let alone allow itself to be deprived without a struggle of control over the island in favor of an international trusteeship or an independent government. There is a weak independence movement among the Taiwanese, which finds it wise to maintain its headquarters in Tokyo.

If the future of Taiwan is settled neither by military action nor by plebiscite, a political agreement of some sort between the two sides, presumably to take effect after Chiang Kai-shek's death, is a not unlikely outcome. On each side of the Taiwan Strait, in fact, the passing of the monolithic figure currently in command may bring some surprising changes.

SUGGESTED READING

I: The Historical Background

GENERAL WORKS

Cressey, George B. *Land of the 500 Million.* New York: McGraw-Hill, 1955. An excellent geography text.

Fairbank, John K. *The United States and China.* Rev. ed. Cambridge, Mass.: Harvard University Press, 1958. Contains an excellent treatment of traditional China.

Fitzgerald, C. P. *China: A Short Cultural History.* Rev. ed. New York: Praeger; London: Cresset, 1952. Stimulating; treatment from the eighteenth century is inadequate.

Goodrich, L. C. *A Short History of the Chinese People.* Rev. ed. New York: Harper, 1951. Especially good on the material aspects of Chinese culture.

Hinton, Harold C., and Marius B. Jansen, eds. *Major Topics on China and Japan: A Handbook for Teachers.* New York: Institute of Pacific Relations, 1957. Contains useful reading lists and discussions of important historical topics.

Latourette, Kenneth Scott. *The Chinese: Their History and Culture.* New York: Macmillan, 1934. Useful but dull; good reading lists.

——. *A History of Modern China.* London: Penguin, 1954. A useful brief survey.

Pulleyblank, E. G. *Chinese History and World History.* Cambridge, Eng.: Cambridge University Press, 1955. The section here on China and that in the Sinor book below are two stimulating, brief interpretations of Chinese history by the professor of Chinese at Cambridge.

Reischauer, Edwin O., and John K. Fairbank. *East Asia: The Great Tradition.* Boston: Houghton Mifflin, 1960. A superb history of China, Korea, and Japan down to the eighteenth century.

Sinor, Denis, ed. *Orientalism and History.* Cambridge, Eng.: Heffer, 1954. Contribution on China by E. G. Pulleyblank is on pp. 57–81. See comment under Pulleyblank above.

Winfield, Gerald F. *China: The Land and the People.* New York: Sloane, 1948. A penetrating discussion of the causes and possible cure of China's economic backwardness and poverty.

ANCIENT CHINA

Creel, H. G. *The Birth of China.* New York: John Day, 1937; Ungar, 1954. A good account based mainly on archaeological evidence.

Maspero, Henri. *La Chine antique.* Rev. ed. Paris: Boccard, 1955. An excellent survey based on literary evidence.

IMPERIAL CHINA

Carter, T. F. *The Invention of Printing in China and Its Spread Westward.* 2d ed., rev. by L. C. Goodrich. New York: Ronald Press, 1955. A standard treatment of an important and interesting aspect of cultural history.

Chi Ch'ao-ting. *Key Economic Areas in Chinese History.* London: Allen and Unwin, 1936. An interesting Marxist interpretation.

Hummel, Arthur W., ed. *Eminent Chinese of the Ch'ing Period, 1644–1912.* 2 vols. Washington, D.C.: U.S. Government Printing Office, 1943–1944. An invaluable and well-indexed biographical dictionary.

King, F. H. *Farmers of Forty Centuries; or, Permanent Agriculture in China, Korea and Japan.* London: Jonathan Cape, 1927. A classic study.

Lattimore, Owen. *Inner Asian Frontiers of China.* Rev. ed. New York: American Geographical Society, 1951. A very stimulating and sophisticated treatment of Central Asia and its relations with China.

Michael, Franz H. *The Origin of Manchu Rule in China.* Baltimore: Johns Hopkins Press, 1942. Discusses the origins of the Ch'ing dynasty.

Morse, H. B. *The Trade and Administration of China.* Shanghai: Kelly and Walsh, various editions. A useful guide to China in the late nineteenth century.

Needham, Joseph. *Science and Civilisation in China.* 2 vols. to date. Cambridge, Eng.: Cambridge University Press, 1954–. Contains much interesting and important information but is marred by inadequate Sinological knowledge and a naïve fondness for Taoism and the ideal of collectivism.

Reischauer, Edwin O. *Ennin's Travels in T'ang China.* New York: Ronald Press, 1955. A fascinating account of China in the mid-ninth century as viewed by a Japanese Buddhist monk.

Wiens, Herold J. *China's March toward the Tropics.* Hamden, Conn.: Shoe String Press, 1954. A very important though difficult treatise on the historical geography of Chinese demographic expansion to the south.

Wilbur, C. Martin. *Slavery in China during the Former Han Dynasty.* Chicago: Field Museum of Natural History, 1943. Contains some excellent historical material of a general nature.

Wright, Mary C. *The Last Stand of Chinese Conservatism: The T'ung-chih Restoration, 1862–74.* Stanford: Stanford University Press, 1956. A scholarly and important study.

THE WESTERN IMPACT

Boardman, Eugene P. *Christian Influence upon the Ideology of the Taiping Rebellion.* Madison: University of Wisconsin Press, 1952. The latest major work in a Western language on this interesting subject.

Cameron, Meribeth E. *The Reform Movement in China, 1868–1912.* Stanford: Stanford University Press, 1931. An excellent study of attempts at modernization.

Latourette, Kenneth Scott. *A History of Christian Missions in China.* New York: Macmillan, 1929. A standard account.

Teng, S. Y., and John K. Fairbank. *China's Response to the West: A Documentary Survey, 1839–1923.* Cambridge, Mass.: Harvard University Press, 1954. Translations of important Chinese documents, with valuable commentaries.

THE REVOLUTIONARY MOVEMENT

Holcombe, Arthur N. *The Chinese Revolution.* Cambridge, Mass.: Harvard University Press, 1930. Very perceptive comments on the Kuomintang at the time of its coming to power.

Houn, Franklin W. *Central Government of China, 1912–1928: An Institutional Study.* Madison: University of Wisconsin Press, 1957. A good recent treatment of a neglected subject.

Isaacs, Harold R. *The Tragedy of the Chinese Revolution.* Rev. ed. Stanford: Stanford University Press, 1951. A brilliant left-wing anti-Stalinist account of the fateful Kuomintang-Communist alliance.

Li Chien-nung. *The Political History of China, 1840–1928.* Trans. and ed. by S. Y. Teng and Jeremy Ingalls. New York: Van Nostrand, 1956. A translation of a standard Chinese text, which, however, is rather dull and detailed.

MacNair, Harley F. *China in Revolution.* Chicago: University of Chicago Press, 1931. Especially good on warlord politics.

Sharman, Lyon. *Sun Yat-sen: His Life and Its Meaning.* New York: John Day, 1934. A perceptive, critical, and standard biography.

Sun Yat-sen. *San Min Chu I.* Trans. by Frank Price. Chungking: Ministry of Information of the Republic of China, 1943. Sun's last and best-known work.

Wen-han Kiang. *The Chinese Student Movement.* New York: King's Crown Press, 1948. A good treatment of intellectual and cultural currents during the late nineteenth and early twentieth centuries.

THE KUOMINTANG IN POWER (1928–1937)

Chiang Kai-shek. *China's Destiny.* Trans. by Wang Chung-hui. New York: Macmillan, 1947. An authorized translation of this celebrated antiforeign diatribe.

Ch'ien, T. S. *The Government and Politics of China.* Cambridge, Mass.: Harvard University Press, 1950. Highly critical; standard and detailed.

China Year Book, The. Articles on the Kuomintang by George Sokolsky, especially in the 1929 volume, are perhaps the best accounts available.

Linebarger, Paul M. A. *The China of Chiang K'ai-shek: A Political Study.* Boston: World Peace Foundation, 1941. Generally favorable.

Liu, F. F. *A Military History of Modern China, 1924–1949.* Princeton: Princeton University Press, 1956. Deals mainly with the Nationalist army.

North, Robert C. *Kuomintang and Chinese Communist Elites.* Stanford: Stanford University Press, 1952. Contains valuable insights into modern Chinese political history.

THE CHINESE COMMUNIST MOVEMENT (1921–1937)

Brandt, Conrad. *Stalin's Failure in China, 1924–1927.* Cambridge, Mass.: Harvard University Press, 1958. Scholarly and perceptive.

——, Benjamin Schwartz, and John K. Fairbank, eds. *A Documentary History of Chinese Communism.* Cambridge, Mass.: Harvard University Press, 1952. A valuable collection of translated documents with commentaries whose main defect is that it does not treat Mao Tse-tung and his revolutionary strategy in enough detail.

Griffith, Brig. Gen. Samuel B., ed. and trans. *Mao Tse-tung on Guerrilla Warfare.* New York: Praeger, 1961. A useful translation, with introduction, of a work written by Mao in 1937 but not included in his *Selected Works.*

Hu, Chiao-mu. *Thirty Years of the Communist Party of China.* Peking: Foreign Languages Press, 1954. An official history, still unsuperseded.

Mao Tse-tung. *Selected Works.* 4 vols. (covering 1926–1945). London: Lawrence and Wishart; New York: International Publishers, 1954–1956. Vol. V (numbered vol. IV to correspond with the original Chinese edition and covering 1945–1949), Peking: Foreign Languages Press, 1961. An indispensable source deserving careful study, but to be treated with care. Numerous, though not fundamental, changes have been made in the original texts since 1949 and prior to publication.

North, Robert C. *Moscow and Chinese Communists.* Stanford: Stanford University Press, 1953. A rather poorly organized account of the Chinese Communist movement whose main merit is its utilization of Soviet sources.

Schwartz, Benjamin I. *Chinese Communism and the Rise of Mao.* Cambridge, Mass.: Harvard University Press, 1951. An excellent study which, however, dates the triumph of Mao within the party about three years too early; see corrections set forth in his article, "On the 'Originality' of Mao Tse-tung," *Foreign Affairs,* Oct. 1955, pp. 67–76.

Snow, Edgar. *Red Star over China.* New York: Random House, 1938, 1944. A justly famous journalistic account based on a visit to the Shensi soviet in 1936; this is a primary source which is only slightly marred by the author's enthusiasm for the Chinese Communists.

Wan, Yah-kang. *The Rise of Communism in China.* Hong Kong: Chung Shu Publishing Co., 1952. A reasonably good short history.

Whiting, Allen S. *Soviet Policies in China, 1917–1924.* New York: Columbia University Press, 1953. An excellent account based on meticulous research.

THE WAR AGAINST JAPAN (1937–1945)

Chinese Communist Movement, The. (Appendix II to part 7A, Institute of Pacific Relations.) Washington, D.C.: U.S. Government Printing Office, 1952. A valuable but badly organized military intelligence study of the Chinese Communist movement during the war.

Feis, Herbert. *The China Tangle.* Princeton: Princeton University Press, 1953. A good treatment of American policy on and in China during the war.

Rosinger, Lawrence K. *China's Wartime Politics, 1937–1944.* Princeton: Princeton University Press, 1944. Useful commentary with documents.

White, Theodore H., and Annalee Jacoby. *Thunder Out of China.* New York: Sloane, 1956. A brilliant and highly critical account of the Kuomintang during the war.

CIVIL WAR (1945–1949)

Belden, Jack. *China Shakes the World.* New York: Harper, 1949. Highly colored and too receptive to the Communist viewpoint, but informative and interesting.

Gelder, Stuart. *The Chinese Communists.* London: Gollancz, 1946. Sympathetic but valuable.

Liao Kai-lung. *From Yenan to Peking.* Peking: Foreign Languages Press, 1954. A Communist account.

McLane, Charles B. *Soviet Policy and Chinese Communists, 1931–1946.* New York: Columbia University Press, 1958. A scholarly and important study.

Military Situation in the Far East (the MacArthur hearings). 5 vols. Washington, D.C.: U.S. Government Printing Office, 1951. An important source of information which can be readily exploited by means of the index.

United States Relations with China (the White Paper). Washington, D.C.: U.S. Department of State, 1949. Contains much valuable information but must be interpreted with care.

II: China since 1949

RESEARCH AIDS

Atlas of the Northern Frontier of India. New Delhi: Ministry of External Affairs, 1960. Useful, but reproduces only maps tending to support the Indian position.

China: Provisional Atlas of Communist Administrative Units. U.S. Central Intelligence Agency, 1959. Contains by far the best available maps of Communist China; unfortunately it is out of print.

Directory of Party and Government Officials of Communist China. 2 vols. U.S. Department of State, Bureau of Intelligence and Research, 1960. Invaluable.

Journal of Asian Studies (formerly *The Far Eastern Quarterly*). Annual bibliographies. The best bibliographical aid for works in Western languages.

Sorich, Richard, ed. *Contemporary China: A Bibliography of Reports on China Published by the United States Joint Publications Research Service.* New York: Joint Committee on Contemporary China of the American Council of Learned Societies and the Social Science Research Council, 1961.

Thought of Mao Tse-tung, The: A Selected List of References to the Published Works and Statements Attributed to Mao Tse-tung and to the Literature on the Chinese Communist Leader. (External Research Division, U.S. Department of State, External Research Paper 138, April 1962.) A valuable bibliography containing works in several languages, including Chinese and Japanese.

Union Research Institute. *Index to the Material on Communist China Held by the Union Research Institute.* Hong Kong: Union Research Institute, 1957.

USEFUL GENERAL PERIODICALS

The following contain occasional important articles on Communist China: American Universities Field Staff reports (New York); *Asian Survey* (formerly *Far Eastern Survey*) (University of California, Berkeley); *Foreign Affairs* (New York); *Problems of Communism* (Washington); *World Politics* (Princeton).

Note also the following issues devoted to Communist China: *Annals of the American Academy of Political and Social Science* (Jan. 1959); *Atlantic* (Dec. 1959); *Current History* (Sept. 1962).

The *New York Times* and the *Christian Science Monitor* provide the best news coverage.

PERIODICALS DEVOTED SPECIFICALLY OR LARGELY TO COMMUNIST CHINA

China News Analysis (Hong Kong); *China Quarterly* (London); *Contemporary China* (University of Hong Kong; annual); *Current Scene* (26 Garden Road, Hong Kong; available gratis to those interested); *Far Eastern Economic Review* (Hong Kong).

CHINESE COMMUNIST MATERIALS IN ENGLISH TRANSLATION [1]

The following are official or semiofficial English-language propaganda periodicals published by the Chinese Communists: *China Today* (New York 1934–1942); *China Digest* (Hong Kong, 1946–1949); *People's China* (Peking, 1950–1957); *Peking Review* (Peking, 1958–).

The titles below are all published in Peking by the Foreign Languages Press:

China and the Asian-African Conference (Documents), 1955.

Chinese People Resolutely Support the Just Struggle of the African People, The, 1961.

Chou En-lai, *Report on the Quention of Intellectuals*, 1956.

Concerning the Situation in Laos, 1959.

Documents on the Sino-Indian Boundary Question, 1960.

Drive U.S. Imperialism Out of Asia! 1960.

In Refutation of Modern Revisionism, 1958.

Long Live Leninism, 1960. An extremely important source on the Chinese Communist world outlook, at least as presented for foreign Communist consumption in 1960.

New Developments in Friendly Relations between China and Nepal, 1960.

Ten Glorious Years, 1960. An ecstatic *festschrift* on the occasion of the CPR's tenth anniversary; contains some important articles.

Victory for the Five Principles of Peaceful Co-existence, A: Important Documents on the Settlement of the Sino-Burmese Boundary Question, 1960.

American Consulate General, Hong Kong. *Survey of the China Mainland Press; Biographic Information; Current Background* (topical); *Selections* [formerly *Extracts*] *from China Mainland Magazines; Extracts from China Mainland Publications* (topical); *Index* (bimonthly).

Union Research Institute, Hong Kong. *Union Research Service*. Series of translations of the Chinese Communist press, since 1955, with some commentaries; little duplication of the American Consulate General translations.

GENERAL WORKS

Aird, John A. *The Size, Composition, and Growth of the Population of Mainland China*. Bureau of the Census, U.S. Department of Commerce, 1961. A competent technical demographic study.

Barnett, A. Doak. *Communist China and Asia: Challenge to American Policy.*

---

[1] The official distributor in the United States for Chinese Communist literature is China Books and Periodicals, 334 W. Schiller St., Chicago 10, Ill.

New York: Harper, 1960. A competent analysis, with emphasis on foreign policy and foreign relations, and a reasoned brief for a "Two Chinas" policy.

——. *Communist Economic Strategy: The Rise of Mainland China.* Washington, D.C.: National Planning Association, 1959. An extremely well-done analysis of the Communist Chinese economy, with emphasis on foreign economic relations.

Boorman, Howard L., and others. *Moscow-Peking Axis.* New York: Harper, 1957. A useful introduction to Sino-Soviet relations.

Boyd, R. G. *Communist China's Foreign Policy.* New York: Praeger, 1962. Although with a vaguely amateurish flavor, this is a remarkably balanced treatment.

Chandra-sekhar, Sripati. *Red China: An Asian View.* New York: Praeger, 1961. Of mild interest as a description by an Indian demographer; largely unfavorable.

Chao, Kuo-chün. *Agrarian Policies of Mainland China: A Documentary Study (1949–1956).* Cambridge, Mass.: Harvard University Press, 1957. Although the commentary is marred by a naïve acceptance of official statements, the documents are useful.

Chow, Ching-wen. *Ten Years of Storm: The True Story of the Communist Regime in China.* New York: Holt, Rinehart and Winston, 1960. An interesting account by a former "democratic personage" in the CPR.

Communism in China. Hong Kong: Union Research Institute, 1959. A compendium of useful information, though dated.

Communist China, 1955–1959: Policy Documents with Analysis. With a foreword by Robert R. Bowie and John K. Fairbank. Cambridge, Mass.: Harvard University Press, 1962. A very valuable collection of documents on domestic affairs, with competent commentary by an anonymous analyst.

Elegant, Robert S. *The Dragon's Seed: Peking and the Overseas Chinese.* New York: St. Martin's Press, 1959. Interesting, but somewhat overdramatized.

Fairbank, John K. *Communist China and Taiwan in United States Foreign Policy.* (The Brien McMahon Lectures, University of Connecticut, Nov. 21, 1960.) A brilliant analysis, although not necessarily useful as a basis for policy.

Faure, Edgar. *The Serpent and the Tortoise: Problems of the New China.* New York: St. Martin's Press, 1958. An interesting, though somewhat pretentious and not always very perceptive, account of a visit in 1957 by a former French Premier.

Fitzgerald, C. P. *Revolution in China.* New York: Praeger; London: Cresset, 1952. Stimulating account of the early period, but unsound on some points; too receptive to the Communist viewpoint.

Gluckstein, Ygael. *Mao's China: Economic and Political Survey.* Boston: Beacon Press, 1957. Useful, especially on economic aspects; based on considerable research.

Gould, Sidney H., ed. *Sciences in Communist China.* Washington, D.C.: American Association for the Advancement of Science, 1961. Valuable.

Guillain, Robert. *600 Million Chinese.* New York: Criterion Books, 1957. An interesting account by a distinguished correspondent.

Houn, Franklin W. *To Change a Nation: Propaganda and Indoctrination in Communist China.* Glencoe, Ill.: Free Press, 1961. A detailed survey by a competent specialist in this field.

Hsieh, Alice Langley. *Communist China's Strategy in the Nuclear Era.* Englewood Cliffs, N.J.: Prentice-Hall, 1962. An excellent treatment of the political as well as military aspects of the subject up to about the end of 1959.

Hunter, Edward. *Brain-Washing in Red China.* New York: Vanguard Press, 1951. Journalistic and highly colored, but useful.

Kalb, Marvin. *Dragon in the Kremlin: A Report on the Russian-Chinese Alliance.* New York: Dutton, 1961. A journalistic survey consisting mainly of interviews with specialists in various parts of the world.

Krader, Lawrence. *The Economic Status of Communist China, 1965–1970.* Santa Barbara, Calif.: General Electric Co., Technical Military Planning Operation, 1958. Useful though dated.

Kuo, Ping-chia. *China: New Age and New Outlook.* London: Penguin Books, 1960. A readable and interesting survey, published just too soon to take account of the failure of the Great Leap Forward.

Li, Choh-ming. *Economic Development of Communist China: An Appraisal of the First Five Years of Industrialization.* Berkeley, Calif.: University of California Press, 1959. An ambitious and largely successful analysis of plans and performance during the First Five Year Plan period.

Lindsay, Michael. *China and the Cold War.* Melbourne: University of Melbourne Press, 1955. Very stimulating but underestimates the strength of the CPC's consistent commitment to Marxism-Leninism before 1949.

London, Kurt, ed. *Unity and Contradiction: Major Aspects of Sino-Soviet Relations.* New York: Praeger, 1962. Uneven like all symposia, but contains some excellent papers.

MacFarquhar, Roderick. *The Hundred Flowers Campaign and the Chinese Intellectuals.* New York: Praeger, 1960. Useful documents, dating from 1957, and enlightening commentary.

Mende, Tibor. *China and Her Shadow.* New York: Coward-McCann; London: Thames and Hudson, 1960. A serious and valiant, but basically unsuccessful, attempt to grasp the reality behind the Great Leap Forward.

Moraes, Frank. *The Revolt in Tibet*. New York: Macmillan, 1960. Readable, generally reliable.

Orleans, Leo A. *Professional Manpower and Education in Communist China*. Washington, D.C.: U.S. Government Printing Office, 1961. An excellent technical treatment.

Panikkar, Kavalam Madhava. *In Two Chinas: Memoirs of a Diplomat*. London: Allen and Unwin, 1955. Interesting, but not the whole story.

Quigley, Harold S. *China's Politics in Perspective*. Minneapolis: University of Minnesota Press, 1960. A useful though not very profound introduction.

Rigg, Robert B. *Red China's Fighting Hordes*. Harrisburg: Military Service Publishing Co., 1951. Poorly written, but contains much important information.

Rostow, W. W., and others. *The Prospects for Communist China*. Cambridge: Massachusetts Institute of Technology, 1954. Although dated, this book is of interest as a generally perceptive analysis and prognostication by a group of writers now in important governmental and academic positions.

Shabad, Theodore. *China's Changing Map*. New York: Praeger, 1956. A competent geography.

Sino-Soviet Dispute, The. Documented and analyzed by G. F. Hudson, Richard Lowenthal, and Roderick MacFarquhar. New York: Praeger, 1961. A competent analysis, with basic documents.

Sino-Soviet Economic Offensive in the Less Developed Countries, The. (U.S. Department of State, Publ. 6632, 1958.) An excellent factual account.

Steiner, H. Arthur. *Communist China in the World Community*. (*International Conciliation*, no. 533, May 1961.) Useful as an introduction.

Tang, Peter S. H. *Communist China Today*. 2 vols., rev. ed. Washington: Research Institute on the Sino-Soviet Bloc, 1961. Useful for reference, but weak in interpretation.

Thomas, Lowell, Jr. *The Silent War in Tibet*. Garden City, N.Y.: Doubleday, 1959. Competent and interesting.

Thomas, S. B. *Government and Administration in Communist China*. Rev. ed. New York: Institute of Pacific Relations, 1953. Detailed and objective, but dated.

Union Research Institute. *Communist China* (annual since 1955). Hong Kong. A useful summary of events and trends.

United States and the Far East, The. New York: Columbia University, American Assembly, 1956. An excellent contribution by A. Doak Barnett is on pp. 105–171.

Walker, Richard L. *The Continuing Struggle: Communist China and the Free World*. New York: Athene Press, 1958. Rather successful in capturing the spirit of Chinese Communist policy in the period of the Great Leap Forward.

Warner, Denis. *Hurricane from China.* New York: Macmillan, 1961. An interesting though somewhat overdramatized account of the threat posed by Communist China to Asia and world peace.

Whiting, Allen S. *China Crosses the Yalu: The Decision to Enter the Korean War.* New York: Macmillan, 1960. Although rather poorly organized, full of jargon, and somewhat inconclusive, this is a valuable work, if only because there is no other covering the same ground.

Wilson, Tuzo. *One Chinese Moon.* New York: Hill and Wang, 1959. An interesting travel account by a Canadian geophysicist.

Wu, Yuan-li. *An Economic Survey of Communist China.* New York: Bookman Associates, 1956. Useful, detailed.

Zagoria, Donald S. *The Sino-Soviet Conflict, 1956–1961.* Princeton: Princeton University Press, 1962. Although not covering all aspects of Sino-Soviet relations, this is a major work, the first in the field to equal the best that has been published on the Soviet Union.

THE REPUBLIC OF CHINA SINCE *1949*

Ballantine, Joseph W. *Formosa, a Problem for United States Foreign Policy.* Washington, D.C.: Brookings Institution, 1952. Somewhat dated, but still authoritative and useful.

Chiang Kai-shek. *Soviet Russia in China: A Summing Up at Seventy.* New York: Farrar, Straus, and Cudahy, 1957. Under the guise of a historical retrospect, this seems to be essentially a rejection of Communist overtures for an accommodation on the ground that the record proves that the good faith of neither the CPC nor the Soviet Union can be relied upon.

Han, Lih-wu. *Taiwan Today.* Taipei: Hwa-kuo Publishing Co., 1951. Propagandistic.

Riggs, Fred W. *Formosa under Chinese Nationalist Rule.* New York: Macmillan, 1952. Critical.

United States and the Far East, The. New York: Columbia University, American Assembly, 1956. Contribution on Taiwan by Allen S. Whiting is on pp. 173–201.

PART TWO : JAPAN

By Nobutaka Ike

· III ·

The Historical Background

JAPAN lies off the eastern coast of Asia, forming an arc extending some 1,200 miles. The northern tip of this arc has about the same latitude as Montreal, and the southern tip parallels northern Florida. The country consists of four main islands, Honshu, the largest, Kyushu and Shikoku to the south, and Hokkaido to the north, plus numerous smaller islands. In total area, Japan is just under 143,000 square miles, or slightly smaller than the state of California.

The climate in Japan is influenced by the monsoon, a seasonal wind which brings warm moisture-laden air from the southeast in the summertime and cold air from Manchuria and Mongolia in the winter months, and by the ocean currents, particularly the warm Black Current, which originates near the Philippines and flows northward. Abundant rainfall together with a warm growing season makes Japan ideal for the cultivation of rice, the principal agricultural crop.

Because of its mountainous terrain, however, less than 20 per cent of the land can be cultivated. Japan, unlike China, has no great river valleys, but since its rivers are short and swift they serve as a source of hydroelectric power. All the large cities have grown up along the coast. Tokyo, the capital and one of the largest cities in the world, is located in the Kanto plain, and the cities of Osaka, Kobe, and Kyoto are in the Kansai plain to the west.

More than 90 million people live on these islands, making Japan among the half-dozen most populous countries in the world. Although the rate of population growth has declined in recent years, the total population is still increasing and is expected to reach 100 million in the 1960s. In recent years, Japan has achieved remarkable economic growth; nevertheless, the basic problem of providing employment for an increasing population remains. Japan lacks many of the natural resources necessary for an industrial economy, and thus the nation is greatly dependent on foreign trade.

Early History

The first people to settle on the islands were the Ainu, who were probably of early Caucasic stock. The Ainu, however, were displaced and gradually driven northward by successive migrations of Mongoloid peoples who came from Mongolia and Manchuria through Korea and landed in the southern part of the country. There is evidence to suggest that additional migrations of people from the south, perhaps from the coastal areas of southern China, also occurred. In any case, the modern Japanese represent a racial mixture.

It is difficult to disengage fact from myth in the early history of the Japanese people because the earliest extant writings date to the eight century A.D., when two official histories, the *Nihon Shoki* and the *Kojiki*, were compiled. In the early period there were numerous clans, each composed of households claiming a common ancestor and led by a common chieftain. These clans, each of which controlled their own lands, were settled in the area around the Inland Sea and to the south. Eventually there emerged one dominant clan, the head of which ultimately became the Emperor. One of the purposes behind the compilation of the official histories mentioned above was to justify the authority of the imperial clan.

Starting about the fifth century, Japan began to come increasingly under the influence of Chinese civilization, which was much more complex and advanced. Among the more important elements imported from China at this time were Buddhism and a centralized bureaucratic system of government. The chieftain of a leading clan was proclaimed Emperor, and a bureaucracy, chosen in accordance with Chinese practice on the basis of competitive examinations, was created to assist the Emperor. The ownership of arable land was vested in the Emperor, and land was apportioned among cultivators in allotments varying in size with the family. It was envisioned that land would be reallotted from time to time to ensure equal distribution. Cultivators were made responsible for the payment of taxes to the central government, partly in the form of produce and partly in labor or military service.

It was one thing to borrow what must have been for its time a complex political system, but quite another thing to make it work. A centralized monarchy was simply not adapted to conditions as they existed at that time, with the result that the system never functioned effectively. The competitive examination provision was ignored in giving official posts. In time various tax-dodging devices came to be used, and in addition new land which was gradually developed to the north was kept in private hands. The flow of revenue into the imperial capital eventually became a mere trickle, whereas in the outlying areas large landholding families became richer and more powerful than the imperial family. Thus the ground was laid for the development of a feudal system.

Large sections of the country came to be ruled by feudal barons who recruited armed retainers to help protect their domains. These retainers developed into the samurai, a warrior caste, who received rice stipends from their feudal superiors in return for faithful service. Gradually the warrior caste evolved a code of behavior which emphasized unswerving loyalty to the feudal lord, contempt of death, and intense sensitivity to insult.

In the shift toward a feudal system, the imperial family was rendered politically impotent, but was never eliminated from the political scene. Indeed, the feudal lords often struggled to get control of the person of the Emperor because whoever controlled him could rule in his name and thus acquire an aura of legitimacy. The decentralization of power also led sometimes to the breakdown of law and order, and there were periods when feudal barons feuded and fought. In the course of civil wars, one or two families usually emerged with enough strength to become dominant, as in the twelfth century when the Minamoto family succeeded in establishing a military government in Kamakura, a town a few miles south of present-day Tokyo. But the Minamoto hegemony could not be perpetuated, and the country was again torn by dissension and civil war. Another cycle leading to the reestablishment of some kind of central authority came around the middle of the sixteenth century, when three military leaders, Oda Nobunaga, Toyotomi Hideyoshi, and Tokugawa Iyeyasu, appeared, each carrying on the process of military unification undertaken by his predecessor. Tokugawa Iyeyasu, the last of the triumvirate, won a de-

cisive victory in the year 1600 to become the most powerful feudal
baron in the country. In 1603 he assumed the title shogun, or "generalissimo," and he set to work to establish a social and political order

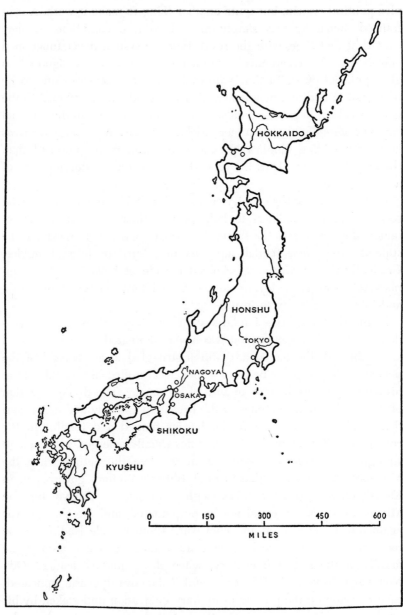

Map 4. Japan.

designed to preserve the *status quo* and prevent social change toward the end that he and his descendants would be perpetuated in power.

The Tokugawa Heritage

The British historian, Sir George Sansom, in a delightful book entitled *The Western World and Japan,* comments that in Asia before modern times one finds a "common pattern of peasant masses governed by a small class of warriors, priests or officials subsisting on revenue from land." [1] He adds that the aim of government was to maintain, by preventing change, the agrarian economy and the rigid social structure that sustained the ruling class. Moreover, the peasants, being near the margin of subsistence, were mostly concerned with matters that affected their livelihood, a condition which was "not such as to allow, still less to encourage, an interest in the problems of government." [2]

This generalized account provides a fitting introduction to the system of government which prevailed in the Tokugawa period, that is, the period between 1603 and 1867 when the Tokugawa family ruled Japan more or less as military dictators. Historians sometimes describe the political and social system which prevailed under the Tokugawa as "centralized feudalism"; and since, as can be seen, less than a century separates Japan from a feudal past, feudalism is not, as it is in the Western world, a fossilized relic described in textbooks, but in many respects a living thing which affects men's values and behavior. It is useful, therefore, to keep in mind certain salient features of the Japanese feudal system in order better to comprehend the mode of politics that characterizes the modern era.

The Tokugawa directly ruled about one-fourth of the country, and the remainder was divided among some 250 feudal nobles. The result was the division of Japan into small political units and the strengthening of local loyalties, particularly since travel between political units was discouraged. But at the same time there was present an element of centralization in that administration in the feudal domains tended to be patterned after the Tokugawa administration, and those feudal nobles who had fought against the Tokugawa in the civil wars were required to spend a part of the time in Edo (present-day Tokyo), the capital of the shogunate, and to leave their families behind as hostages when they returned to their domains.

[1] George B. Sansom, *The Western World and Japan* (New York: Knopf, 1950), p. 6.
[2] *Ibid.,* p. 5.

The shogun was the *de facto* ruler of the country. In theory he was subject to the authority of the Emperor, who, together with his court nobles, carried on ritualistic functions in Kyoto, the ancient capital. In practice, however, the Emperor was sealed off from the political life of the nation; and, indeed, it is said that the very existence of the Emperor was unknown to many of the common people.

In governing their domains, the shogun and the feudal nobles were assisted by their samurai retainers. The samurai, numbering about 5 per cent of the population, were trained as warriors and, together with the feudal nobility, formed the elite of the nation. The privileged position of the samurai vis-à-vis the common people was indicated by the fact that they were subject to their own laws and were tried in their own courts.

The remainder of the population was composed of peasants, artisans, merchants, professional people such as priests and doctors, and the eta, or outcasts. Since the economy was largely agricultural, the peasants were numerically predominant. They provided the chief source of revenue for the ruling elite in the form of a tax, usually paid in rice and amounting to as much as 40 to 50 per cent of the annual yield. In addition, the peasants were subject to numerous taxes on sundry items such as windows and female children and were compelled to provide forced labor on public works.

There were several large cities which served as focal points of commercial activity. In these cities lived artisans and merchants, some of whom succeeded in amassing large fortunes; and there developed, under merchant patronage, a sophisticated urban culture. The kabuki theater, for example, was a product of this cultural milieu.

A notable feature of life in the Tokugawa period was the extent to which the ruling authorities concerned themselves with the minute details of daily living and with the morality of the people. Everyone was admonished to be frugal, and sumptuary laws of all kinds sought to regulate the type of clothing that could be worn, the kind of dwelling that could be built, and so on; but as is so often true in matters of this kind, official prohibitions were probably not always obeyed. Nevertheless, the precedent, if not the habit, of officialdom's trying to meddle in the private lives of citizens was established.

In terms of the tasks it set for itself, the Tokugawa administrative structure was relatively simple. At the top of the structure was the shogun, but, according to the ability of the particular individual in office, actual power was sometimes in the hands of a Council of Elders or even in the hands of some palace favorite or high official. The day-to-day tasks of administration were performed by a small corps of officials who saw to it that the taxes were collected, that public morals were not allowed to deteriorate, and that order and security were maintained.

Government at the village level was more or less autonomous. In the Tokugawa period villages were relatively small in size, and they numbered some 60,000 in all the land. In every village there were several officials, generally chosen by a representative of the shogunate from among the wealthiest and long-established landowning families in the village. Their functions were to represent the villagers in any negotiations with higher authorities or other villages, to proclaim decrees and injunctions issued by the shogunate, to collect taxes, to adjudicate minor disputes, to keep records, to improve agriculture, and to keep an eye on the villagers' morals. Village leaders were assisted by a village assembly in which the landowning families had a strong voice. An important form of social and political control was the device of mutual responsibility. Groups of five families were organized into a unit; and if, for example, a family in the unit was unable to pay its taxes in full, it was the responsibility of the members of the unit to make up the difference.

The Tokugawa political system enjoyed remarkable longevity, but there was also a price to be paid. For one thing, in the 1630s those who ruled Japan decided to forbid all foreign contacts, except for carefully regulated trade with the Dutch and the Chinese at the port of Nagasaki. The adoption of this policy of national isolation appears to have rested on the fear that Christianity, considered a subversive doctrine, would spread if Europeans were allowed to enter the country and also on the fear that some of the feudal nobles might get powerful enough to challenge Tokugawa hegemony through an alliance with European nations. But by cutting itself off from neighbors in Asia and from Europe, Japan was unable to derive profit from an expanding foreign trade and to benefit from direct contact with Europe which, in the period between 1600 and 1850, underwent a technological and industrial revolution.

Moreover, the passage of time revealed serious stresses and strains within the system. Both the Tokugawa government and the smaller principalities suffered from chronic financial difficulties. Attempts were made repeatedly to overcome such difficulties by resorting to currency debasement, economy measures, higher tax levies, and forced loans, but in the long run no solution was found. Furthermore, with the passage of time, the samurai fell in debt to rice brokers and merchants so that social and political power came to be divorced from wealth. The samurai had social standing but no wealth; the merchants had wealth but no standing.

The coming of peace encouraged the growth of commerce and industry, and marked specialization in the production of goods took place. In the towns and even in the villages, merchants and landowners who had accumulated some capital began to produce goods on the basis of the "putting out" system, so that a kind of nascent capitalism began to develop within the feudal system.

In the meantime, the lot of the small agricultural producer tended to become more wretched. The amount of rice he had to turn over to the tax collector usually increased. To add to his difficulties, there were recurring natural disasters such as floods, and there were periodic famines. Peasant uprisings, varying in scale and intensity, marred the tranquillity of the countryside with increasing frequency. By the nineteenth century the "time of troubles" had come.

The travail of the ruling authorities was aggravated by attempts on the part of such countries as Great Britain, Russia, and the United States to force Japan to abandon its traditional policy of national isolation. The Tokugawa rulers were caught in a dilemma. They could not hold off indefinitely the foreign powers who possessed superior military weapons; yet they could not abandon the isolation policy without serious internal repercussions. The political history of Japan from the late 1830s to about 1870 would, if painted in detail, require a broad canvas. It would perhaps be sufficient for our purposes to note merely that the combination of internal difficulties and foreign pressure finally brought the Tokugawa shogunate to an end in 1867. In that year the last Tokugawa shogun resigned and "returned" authority to the youthful occupant of the imperial throne who came to be known as Emperor Meiji. This transfer of power is called the Meiji Restoration; and as the word Meiji, which means "enlightened government," suggests, it opened a new chapter in the political history of Japan.

The Meiji Regime (1867–1912)

There is by no means agreement among scholars as to the interpretation of the Meiji Restoration. But one thing is clear. It was not a social upheaval which brought about a transformation in the basic character of Japanese society, nor, on the other hand, was it a mere palace revolution in which one elite replaced another. Rather the Restoration may be looked upon as a kind of revolution from above in that its leadership was supplied by a small group of young samurai from several principalities in western Japan which were traditionally hostile to the Tokugawa house. In their drive to overthrow the Tokugawa, these samurai had the assistance of nobles from the imperial court, a fact which helped to give this movement an aura of legitimacy, for the ostensible objective was to "restore" the Emperor to his rightful position as the ruler of the country. Funds to finance the movement came from some of the wealthy merchant families in the big cities, and there is evidence to suggest that numerous landowner-entrepreneurs who were producing goods in the towns and villages supplied additional sums and even participated in the brief civil war which followed the resignation of the shogun. Most of the young samurai leaders who came to power were agreed on certain broad objectives. They were committed to modernizing their country. As they saw it, the Western countries were strong and powerful and rich, while their own country was backward, weak, and poor. They were convinced that survival in the modern world necessitated a well-trained army and navy equipped with new-style weapons and backed by industrial power. The national slogan of the times, "Strong army, rich country," best summarized the intellectual outlook of those in positions of leadership.

The 1870s and 1880s were a period of intense activity and considerable innovation. Numerous foreign experts and advisers were hired to teach new techniques, and Japanese students were sent abroad to study at government expense. The government took the lead in building railroads and a telegraph system. The government also set up "model" factories and subsidized the development of modern industries. New schools were built and compulsory education was decreed. A modern banking system was established.

In the social field, the legal distinction between samurai and the common people was abolished, and samurai were encouraged to take up useful occupations. Since the state could no longer afford to pay hereditary stipends, these were converted into pensions, and later these pensions were commuted into lump-sum payments. A conscript army replaced the samurai as the fighting force of the nation.

A host of political reforms were made. The feudal principalities were replaced by prefectures which were a part of a centralized administrative structure. A unified coinage system was adopted, and internal trade barriers were eliminated. Eventually a civil service based more or less on the merit system was set up. A legal code and a judicial system copied from continental European models were adopted.

The problem of the form of government proved to be a knotty one. Obviously the old feudal system was an anachronism and had to be replaced by one more appropriate to the times. It is, therefore, not surprising that considerable interest was shown in Western political thought. At first some of the intellectuals were particularly interested in the British form of parliamentary government; after all, Britain was the leading power in Europe, and therefore it appeared to provide a good model. Fundamentally, however, Meiji leaders found Western democratic ideas not to their taste. They were convinced that the task of making the country strong and rich in a short span of time called for the concentration of political power at the top. A few people who knew best, so they reasoned, should make the decisions for the majority.

The question was whether such an arrangement was acceptable to those who were excluded from power. The Meiji elite soon discovered that it was not. Opposition came from several quarters. Some samurai, refusing to accept the new order, put up sporadic armed resistance, culminating in a rebellion in southwestern Japan in 1877. The rebellion was put down by the new conscript army, and thus attempts to resist the government by the use of force were brought to an end.

Other samurai who had grievances against the government, particularly for its policy of giving a disproportionately large number of government posts to men from Choshu and Satsuma, two principalities in western Japan, organized political opposition to the government. In the beginning they formed small political clubs and societies which included in their membership peasants, especially wealthier peasants, many of whom were also engaged in small-scale rural industry. In agitating against the government, these societies drew heavily on Western political ideas, such as the social contract, natural rights, and utilitarianism. These activities led to the formation in 1881 of the first political party, the Jiyuto or Liberal Party which, according to its program, sought to broaden liberty, protect the people's rights, promote their happiness, reform society, and work for a sound constitutional system. Before long two other parties were organized, the Rikken Kaishinto or Constitutional Progressive Party, composed mostly of ex-bureaucrats, intellectuals, and urban merchants and industrialists, and the Rikken Teiseito or Constitutional Imperial Party, formed to support the government.

Although the Liberal Party originally began under the leadership of samurai, later many of its most ardent adherents were landowners who were displeased with the tax policy of the government. Japan was reluctant to borrow foreign capital for fear of compromising its political independence, and hence modernization was financed largely through taxation, internal borrowing, and currency inflation. The tax burden naturally fell most heavily on the agricultural sector of the economy, since there was no other important source of revenue. But when agriculturalists saw that taxes collected in the countryside were being used to promote industry in the cities, they became vocal in their criticism.

The opponents of the government believed that they could break the hold of the oligarchy and win for themselves a share in the government if a system of representative government could be established. Hence the great issues of the day concerned a demand for the drafting of a written constitution and the establishment of an elected parliament. The government's answer to the political movement represented by the Liberal Party and to a lesser extent by the Constitutional Progressive Party was suppression on the one hand and compromise on the other. The police frequently censored newspapers, jailed the more outspoken editors, and broke up political meetings. At the same time, in 1881, the government agreed to grant a constitution and to establish a parliament. Later the government dispatched a mission, headed by Ito Hirobumi, a former samurai from Choshu who had become an important figure, to Europe to study constitutions. Ito was much impressed by what he learned in Imperial Germany, and upon his return he and his colleagues, with the help of a Prussian adviser, set to work in strict secrecy to draft a constitution.

The government's concession to the political opposition was more in form than in substance. To be sure, those in power agreed to have a written constitution and to create a parliament, but the vital question was what kind of constitution and what kind of parliament. The political opposition could not make its influence felt in these matters, partly because the elite was able to keep the situation under control and partly because in the 1880s the popular movement in favor of parliamentary government suffered from internal dissension and hence could not continue to apply pressure on the government in an effort to carry the campaign to its logical conclusion.

In 1889 a constitution, granted, in theory, by the Emperor to his people, was promulgated; and the Imperial Diet, consisting of the House of Peers and the House of Representatives (which is composed of members chosen by a highly restricted electorate), was convened for the first time in 1890.

The constitution reserved broad powers to the Emperor, whereas the authority of the House of Representatives was greatly circumscribed. The civilian government was denied effective control of the military, for the army and navy were considered coordinate with the civilian branches, and both were responsible, in theory, to the Emperor. However, despite the dogma of imperial rule enunciated in the constitution and other documents, the Emperor practically never participated in the high-policy decisions of the government. He merely gave formal assent to decisions arrived at by others.

Who were the others? For several decades after the promulgation of the constitution, the "others" were, by and large, the small group of samurai who had participated in the Restoration movement and had worked together to build the Meiji state. These samurai formed an oligarchy, and although there was a certain amount of bickering and dissension among members of the oligarchy, they were held together by the common bond of experiences and values which they shared and by their common determination to prevent popular control of the government. At times some of the members of the oligarchy took the center of the stage and governed as Ministers of State, and at other times they lodged themselves in extralegal institutions such as the "Elder Statesmen" and the Privy Council and manipulated their protégés who occupied the formal offices of government.

The reason the oligarchy was able to maintain control was that the great mass of the population, heirs to the long tradition of Tokugawa rule, was willing to accept this state of affairs. There was, however, always a small minority which refused to accept the *status quo,* and from the beginning of the twentieth century a small band of socialists were among the dissidents. The socialist doctrine was, of course, anathema to the oligarchy, and thus the early socialists were hounded by the police and often put into jail.

The passage of time naturally decimated the ranks of the oligarchy. This was graphically symbolized by the death in 1912 of the Emperor Meiji, who had acceded the throne as a boy and had seen Japan grow into a modernized nation in his lifetime. He was succeeded by his son, Yoshihito, who came to be known as the Emperor Taisho.

The Taisho Era (1912–1926)

The Emperor Taisho, unlike his reportedly energetic and capable father, was sickly and toward the end of his reign was because of insanity forced to give way to his son, who was made a regent. Compared to the Meiji period, the tempo of change in the Taisho era appeared to be much slower; yet certain important changes took place beneath the surface, particularly in the political structure. It appears in retrospect that the years immediately following the close of the First World War marked a divide in Japanese political history. Prior to that point it had been possible to maintain oligarchic rule; but after that it became increasingly difficult to govern without some reference to the feelings and thoughts of the masses.

One can point to several factors which contributed to this lowering of the political center of gravity. First, compulsory education raised the literacy rate substantially, paving the way for the growth of mass communications and the diffusion of political ideas. Second, industrialization and urbanization contributed to increased occupational and social mobility, and as people were torn from their old social moorings, they became more receptive to new political values. Third, Japan could not remain isolated from world developments and, like others, felt the ripples of the world-wide spread of democratic ideals following the peace settlement at Versailles.

The Japanese political structure created in the Meiji period was not particularly adapted to meet the problems of the post-1919 age. As has been suggested, the institutional framework blueprinted in the Meiji constitution was not congruent with political practice, especially with regard to the fiction of the Emperor who ruled as well as reigned. The fragmentation inherent in the constitutional structure was latent so long as the Meiji oligarchy was in control, but once they disappeared from the scene, the unity and coherence they had given the government were also removed. The way was now open for one group or another to exercise power formerly wielded by the members of the oligarchy.

The 1920s were the years when party politicians were in the ascendancy. The Meiji leaders had frowned on political parties, considering them factions which tended to have a divisive effect; but, as already indicated, parties emerged even before the creation of the Imperial Diet, and after 1890 parties had in the House of Representatives a kind of forum from which to make an appeal to the people. The power of the lower house was, to be sure, greatly restricted, but still party politicians elected to that body had many an opportunity to harass the government, when they so desired, by asking embarrassing questions and delaying the passage of appropriation bills. Gradually as the members of the oligarchy became older and decreased in numbers, the sphere of action of party leaders was enlarged and they were named increasingly to cabinet posts. It was not unusual in the 1920s to name the leader of the majority party as Prime Minister, and he brought in prominent men of his party to form the cabinet. In this era, parties enjoyed the financial backing of the industrial combines known as the zaibatsu (literally, financial cliques) and the political support of small businessmen and rural landowners. Despite the parties' growing power there were certain sectors of the government which lay beyond effective control by them. The bureaucracy, recruited largely from among the graduates of the law faculty of the Tokyo Imperial University, the leading government university, was jealous of its prerogatives; and the army and navy, with their right of direct access to the throne, brooked no interference from the civilians in the government.

The fact that they lacked clear-cut authority and that certain areas of government were beyond their control was not conducive to the development of a sense of responsibility on the part of the parties. Added to this was the element of political immaturity of party leadership. The result was that corruption became rife, and as scandals were uncovered the public lost confidence in the political parties.

At the time of the death of Emperor Taisho in 1926, Japan was still in the period of party government. The reign of his son, the present Emperor, was designated Showa or "Bright Peace," but ironically forces inimicable to peace were already at work, and before long party government came to an end.

The Showa Era (from 1926)

The samurai background of Meiji leaders as well as national defense needs, particularly in the days following the end of national isolation, assured a certain bias in favor of the military within the framework of government. Under the constitution of 1889 the military achieved, as already mentioned, a position coordinate with the civilian government. Then victories in two major wars, the Sino-Japanese war, 1894–1895, and the Russo-Japanese war, 1904–1905, raised the prestige of the army and navy greatly. During the 1920s, however, military prestige suffered a setback as part of the revulsion against militarism that occurred almost everywhere throughout the world in this period. There was a reluctance in Japan, as elsewhere, to vote large appropriations for military establishments; the emphasis instead was on peace and disarmament.

The need for retrenchment was something of a blow to the Japanese army because it found itself technologically backward after the end of the First World War. Since funds needed to mechanize the army were not forthcoming, army leaders resorted to a reduction in personnel and used savings thus achieved to acquire new weapons. The reduction of personnel, by creating a feeling of insecurity among career officers and slowing down the rate of promotions, aroused resentment in army circles against the government.

Meanwhile, certain developments on the continent cast their shadow on the Japanese scene. Japan had acquired over several decades special economic and political rights in Manchuria and to a lesser extent in North China. In time many people, particularly in influential positions, came to regard these rights as something both permanent and vital to Japan's well-being. One of the goals of Chinese nationalism, on the other hand, was the elimination of special privileges and the restoration of Chinese sovereignty. It is therefore not surprising that considerable tension was generated between the two countries as the Chinese nationalist revolution went forward, leading to the establishment of the Nationalist government in Nanking in 1928.

A third complicating factor soon entered the picture. This was the world-wide economic depression. The Japanese countryside was especially hard hit by the collapse in commodity prices, especially of raw silk, which was sold in large quantities to the United States; and as a result there was widespread suffering.

Before long some of the younger army officers began to sense the gravity of the economic situation, for many of the enlisted men under them were from the poverty-stricken rural areas. These officers became very restless and thoroughly dissatisfied with the prevailing state of affairs. Much of their resentment was directed against the large industrial combines and the men who controlled them. Since these combines were a characteristic feature of Japanese capitalism, pronounced antizaibatsu sentiment amounted in effect to a crusade against capitalism. The younger officers also leveled sharp attacks against the party politicians, who, in their view, were corrupt and had sold out to the financiers. It is interesting to note that a number of these younger officers were second-generation army men, that is to say, they were sons of army officers. This meant that by and large these younger officers had grown up in a home environment which was stern, authoritarian, and highly apolitical. They were not likely to take a sophisticated view of political developments; instead they tended to view the world in a rather naïve and simple-minded fashion.

This was certainly true of the army's attitude with regard to Japan's foreign relations. There was strong criticism in army circles of the somewhat conciliatory policy pursued by the government toward the rise of Chinese nationalism. Both politicians and financiers were accused of not paying enough attention to national defense and of not using force to protect Japan's privileged position in China.

A concrete manifestation of army discontent and of the urge toward direct action in order to alter the *status quo* was the formation of secret societies within the army. One of the most important of these was the Cherry Blossom Society (Sakurakai), composed mostly of majors and lieutenant colonels. In its prospectus, the Cherry Blossom Society lamented the decline of national power and put the blame on Japan's statesmen who instead of paying attention to spiritual matters were concerned only with gaining personal power and wealth. It pointed to the decadence of political parties, the lack of sympathy for the masses on the part of the capitalistic elite, the responsibility of the mass communications media for bringing about a decline in the national spirit, the lack of patriotism among students, the economic collapse of the farming communities, unemployment, and the economic depression. "People like us," the prospectus read, "yearn for the appearance of a vigorous and clear-cut national policy which would truly rest on the masses and which would be centered on the Emperor."

Groups like the Cherry Blossom Society then began to take matters in their own hands in order to force a change in the composition of government and bring about a policy which would be more to their liking. One of their first steps was to strike in Manchuria where, they believed, the privileged position of Japan was threatened by the successes of the nationalist movement in China.

In the fall of 1931 some army units stationed in Manchuria blew up a section of the tracks of the Japanese-owned South Manchurian Railway. At the time, however, the Japanese accused the Chinese of having perpetrated the deed and, using this as a pretext, quickly took over military control of the whole of Manchuria. It appears that the affair was initiated by units in the field without authorization from the civilian government or even the supreme command in Tokyo. Once the nation was faced with a *fait accompli,* however, it supported the taking over of Manchuria. An era of militarism and intense nationalism was inaugurated.

Emboldened by their initial success, the younger officers next sought to bring about what they considered a political reformation at home. On May 15, 1932, a group of army and navy officers forced their way into the Prime Minister's residence and killed Prime Minister Inukai Tsuyoshi, a party leader, in cold blood. Other officers attacked a police station and the Bank of Japan and destroyed power stations. If the object of these attacks was to bring about political change, they were successful in a way, for with the death of Inukai, party government came to an end.

There were other acts of violence, and the most important of these was a fairly large-scale army uprising on February 26, 1936. Some 1,400 troops were involved, and in the course of the uprising the Finance Minister, the Lord Keeper of the Privy Seal, and the Inspector General of Military Education were killed. The Prime Minister, Admiral Okada Keisuke, narrowly escaped death because the officers shot his brother-in-law, who resembled him, through mistaken identity. The rebels seized some government buildings and held out for three days, after which they surrendered in obedience to an imperial order.

Some civilians were implicated in this uprising, including Kita Ikki, who was the leading theorist of the young officers' movement. Kita's ideas were given in an essay, first written around 1919, called "An Outline Plan for the Reconstruction of Japan," which became the bible of the young officers. In this essay, Kita urged that the parliament, the Privy Council, and other imperial advisers be pushed aside to permit a reform of the state by the Emperor, together with all the people, that a limitation be placed on property, including land, to be held by any one family, that large-scale enterprises be owned and operated by the state, and that workers' rights be protected, including the right to participate in management; the essay also set forth that a state had the right to start a war for self-defense and for the benefit of other states and peoples unjustly oppressed. As the theorist of the movement, Kita was executed along with other leaders of the revolt.

The February uprising turned out to be the last major effort of the young officers to bring their ideas to fruition. It should also be pointed out that the revolt represented not only a struggle between these officers and the civilians, but also the climax of a struggle between two factions in the army. The younger officers belonged mostly to the Imperial Way faction (Kodoha) which, as is evident from an analysis of Kita's views, espoused vague ideas of direct rule by the Emperor together with severe limitations on capitalistic enterprise. They were opposed by the Control faction (Toseiha) made up of officers of higher rank who were more conservative and less anti–big business. Up to 1936 the control faction had been rather tolerant of these outbreaks of violence perpetrated by the Imperial Way faction, partly, it would seem, because they were interested in utilizing the unrest to strengthen their hold on the government. But when they saw that the situation might get out of hand, as in the February incident, they took stern measures, and those responsible for the revolt were executed or severely punished.

The assassinations and revolts had the effect of intimidating sufficiently the civilians in the government so that they were more willing to accept the argument that military leaders should be put into positions of responsibility because only they could keep the unruly younger officers under control. In this way the military increased its influence in the government.

The rise of the military led to more stringent censorship and thought control. The schools were compelled to glorify militarism, and in the universities academic freedom was greatly curbed. Liberalism, to say nothing of radical ideas, was considered subversive, and individuals who subscribed to these were subjected to pressure and threats from self-appointed patriots.

In the field of foreign relations the Japanese consolidated their military seizure of Manchuria by creating a puppet state called Manchukuo. China and the Great Powers refused, of course, to recognize Manchukuo, and world opinion was brought to bear against Japan through the League of Nations, which condemned it as an aggressor. Japan then withdrew from the League.

Japanese penetration of China did not, however, end with the creation of Manchukuo. In the mid-1930s the army set up a series of so-called "autonomous" regimes in North China in order to bring the economy of this region into the Japanese economic orbit. In the summer of 1937 Japan began the military occupation of North China, and a little later fighting spread to Central China and eventually to parts of South China. Both the Chinese Nationalists and the Chinese Communists resisted Japanese encroachments by resorting to guerrilla operations as well as more conventional methods of warfare. Millions of Japanese troops were sent to China, but they could not bring about the capitulation of the Nationalist government under Chiang Kai-shek. Chinese resistance, moreover, was bolstered by moral support and material aid from the United States and other countries. The prospect of a clear-cut Japanese victory in China was slim, but Japan, on the other hand, could not withdraw without losing face.

As the war in China was prolonged, Japan's economy was put under great strain. In order to secure adequate output of arms, industrial mobilization was undertaken, and the government began to exercise more and more control over the entire economy. Mobilization also occurred on the political front. The parties, as indicated, were pushed to the background after the take-over of Manchuria, but they continued to exist and from time to time dared to make guarded criticisms of what the army was trying to do in China and at home. In 1940 the parties were put under pressure to dissolve "voluntarily" and were absorbed into a new organization known as the Imperial

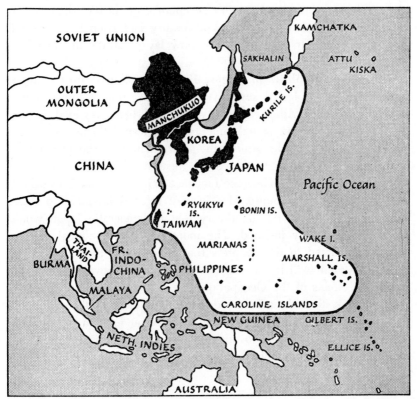

Map 5. The Japanese empire, 1936. (As redrawn from the *New York Times*.)

Rule Assistance Association (IRAA). Formally organized political parties thus disappeared from the scene.

After Japan's entry into the Second World War, the influence of the military in almost every aspect of life was increased. Japan's initial military victories following the attack on Pearl Harbor even appeared to generate considerable popular support for the military; but as Japan's fortunes took a turn for the worse, as cities were laid in ruins by bombing attacks, and as severe shortages developed, antagonism toward the military grew.

By 1945 Japan, having fought continuously since 1937, was in no condition to continue the war much longer. It was obvious that Japanese leaders, particularly military leaders, had made fatal miscalculations, but bringing the war to a close was not an easy task. There were, however, a few leaders, both civilian and military, who saw that surrender, even unconditional surrender, was preferable to national suicide; and after protracted behind-the-scenes maneuvering they were able to bring about Japan's acceptance of the Potsdam Declaration. Japan, which in less than a century had risen from a small backward nation to a great power, now lay prostrate and faced an uncertain future.

The end of hostilities in August 1945 was followed by a military occupation which lasted seven years. Legally, the Occupation was controlled by the Allied Powers which had been engaged in war against Japan, but in actual practice American influence was preponderant. Initially, the American government and the Occupation authorities took the view that steps must be taken to ensure that Japan would never again become a menace to its neighbors. Toward this end the Occupation sponsored a host of reforms intended to foster democracy in Japan, on the theory that a democratic Japan would likely be peacefully inclined. The more important political reforms will be discussed in the chapters that follow, and therefore no detailed treatment will be attempted here. As for an evaluation of the long-term effects of the Occupation, one is led to the view that it is still too early to make a final judgment. It is clear that considerable social change has taken place since 1945; yet at least in the political sphere there is evidence to suggest that basic political values and time-honored ways of behavior still persist.

· IV ·

The Social and

Economic Structure

POLITICAL Science is concerned mostly with large and complex associations, such as the state. In this respect it differs from sociology, for example, which is devoted mainly to the study of smaller social groups. It would be unwise, however, for the student of political science to ignore the behavior of man in small groups or, for that matter, the way in which man creates and distributes goods and services, because both these aspects of social life profoundly affect the character of the state and the distribution of political power within it. The purpose of this chapter is to present a sketch of the social and economic context in which Japanese politics takes place.

The Individual and the Group

A common observation in the literature on Japan is that the individual is subordinated to the group. As a general statement this observation is sound. For purposes of political analysis, however, it is useful to go a step farther and inquire into the nature of the group.

First of all, attention should be turned to the family. Everywhere the family plays a vital role in government because, as Professor MacIver says, the family is the "breeding ground of power"; [1] but in

[1] R. M. MacIver, *The Web of Government* (New York: Macmillan, 1947), ch. ii.

Japan the radiating influence of the family extends beyond anything found in the Western world. In Japan the family rather than the individual was, and is to a considerable extent today, the basic social unit. Very often the Japanese family is larger than the conjugal unit of man and wife and their offspring. It may include, and this is particularly true in the countryside, his retired father and mother and his eldest son's wife and children.

When compared to the American family, the Japanese family is as a rule much more closely knit. Emphasis is apt to be put on the welfare of the family as a whole, even if this sometimes involves individual sacrifices. Children are taught to be obedient and respectful, and it used to be said that the obligations which children owe their parents are "deeper than the ocean, higher than the mountain." In important decisions, such as the choice of a vocation or the selection of one's mate, the parents and the other members of the family have much to say. It is generally assumed that sons, particularly eldest sons, have the obligation to support their parents in their old age. Most Japanese value the idea of perpetuating the family line. When a family has no offspring, a distant relative or even someone not kin may be adopted, and this person will assume the name of the family into which he has come.

These various obligations binding members of a family are of obvious importance in regulating family life, but they also have, according to some, a wider significance. There are still many people who believe that filial piety is the basis of all morality. When the postwar constitution, which provides, among other things, for a more democratically oriented family, was being debated in the House of Representatives, one member said: "I fear that the revision of our Constitution [of 1889] will shake the foundation of the rights of the head of a house and those of parents[,] . . . that this will greatly affect the filial piety which forms the foundation of all morals." The speaker then went on to say that filial piety, which "forms the fundamentals of peace and order in the country," might be destroyed by constitutional revision and that under such revision, if it was not carefully done, a son could "marry a girl against the will of his parents, change his living place, spend money and other property ignoring the wishes of his parents, divorce a respectable wife without the consent of his parents. I fear that these undesirable matters will take place under the new Constitution." [2]

[2] Quoted in Kurt Steiner, "The Revision of the Civil Code in Japan: Provisions Affecting the Family," *Far Estern Quarterly*, IX (Feb. 1950), 173.

Underlying these fears expressed by the member of the House of Representatives was the assumption that filial piety and political loyalty are fundamentally related. According to the officially prescribed theory of state in the prewar period, the Japanese nation was a large family, headed by the Emperor, who was its patriarchal father. In theory the relationship of the Emperor to his subjects was no different from that of the father to his children. Thus to this very day Japanese of conservative persuasion insist that families must be held together by bonds of filial piety and loyalty if the social and political order is to be maintained.

Important as is the family in meeting an individual's social needs, it cannot be all-sufficing. Of necessity families must associate and work with other families. In Japan one finds several or more families coming together to create informal groupings which tend to be hierarchical in structure and relatively long enduring. These informal groupings, which may be looked upon as the "cellular units" of Japanese society, are characterized by face-to-face relationships and a strong sense of personal loyalty among its members. Needless to say, these groupings profoundly affect the values and behavior of its members, for, as George Murdock says, "it is mainly through face-to-face relations that a person's behavior is influenced by his fellows—motivated, cued, rewarded, and punished." [3]

The influence of these groupings on the individual is particularly strong in rural areas where many essential tasks are, of necessity, performed through cooperative effort. During the busy season, for instance, families exchange labor, helping each other with transplanting and harvesting. The building and maintenance of roads in the community are done cooperatively. Recreational activities, in the absence of various commercialized forms of recreation, consist of the getting together of relatives and neighbors to drink, dance, and sing. Families also obtain a kind of social security through the group, for if one's house burns down or a member of the family dies, relatives and friends come to render help. There are even forms of cooperative credit through which funds are raised to meet emergencies.

The need for cooperation is much less, of course, in urban areas, where life tends to be more impersonal. But even in the cities, there are often informal groupings of kin and nonkin which have the function of providing its members with a sense of security, both psychological and economic, attained through mutual aid.

It is not surprising, given these considerations, that in Japanese

[3] George Peter Murdock, *Social Structure* (New York: Macmillan, 1949), p. 82.

society interpersonal relationships are much more personalized than they are in contemporary America. To be sure, a complex industrialized society such as is found in Japan cannot function without formalized impersonal relationships; yet it is a fact that most Japanese still feel uncomfortable when they cannot deal with their fellow men on a highly personalized basis.

The penchant for personalized relationships has at least two social consequences. First, often the binding cement of many organizations is personal loyalty rather than common objectives, interests, or principles. Since there is a limit to the number of personal ties that individuals can have, such large organizations as political parties and labor unions are almost always torn into factions and cliques, impeding unity and concerted action.

Second, the existence of small cohesive groups has resulted in the growth of what might be called "informal government." There is a tendency to seek solutions to problems within the framework of the small group and to avoid involvement in the formal institutions of government. For example, parties involved in a dispute are likely to avoid taking the case to court and will seek instead settlement within the small group through mediation and compromise.

A particularly important role in "informal government" is played by individuals who belong to certain sections of the middle class in Japan. However, before this aspect is discussed, it is useful to take up the larger question of social stratification.

Social Stratification

Japanese society, like other complex societies, is hierarchical in structure and composed of levels or tiers of social classes. The criteria that go into determining the class to which an individual belongs are varied and, moreover, are changing with the passage of time. In general, education, occupation, income, family lineage, and style of living are important determinants.

Some significant changes have occurred at the top levels of the social hierarchy as a result of Japan's defeat and subsequent occupation. With the abolition of the peerage, aristocratic titled families, many of whom had descended from the old feudal nobility, from the samurai who held important posts in the Meiji government, and from some financial and business families which achieved prominence in the Meiji and Taisho periods, were reduced in prestige and influence. At the same time, government agencies close to the throne, such as the Privy Council, the Imperial Household Ministry, and the Elder Statesmen, and, of course, the House of Peers, through which the nobility had made their power felt, were abolished. Although some of the former peers have found positions in business and government and still enjoy a vestige of social prestige, it may be said that as a group they are no longer important politically.

Another group that has been removed from the upper levels of the social hierarchy comprises the top professional soldiers. Many of the officers in both the army and the navy were of middle-class origin, but had achieved prestige and power when the armed forces were able to push their way into the center of the political stage in the 1930s. As a result of demobilization and the revulsion against militarism, officers generally lost prestige and status, and today the political influence of professional officers is very weak indeed.

The vacuum created by the elimination of the nobility and the military from the top levels of the society has been filled by three closely related groups as they rose to power. They are the top civil servants, leaders of political parties, and executives of large financial institutions and corporations. These social groups have easy access to government bureaus and agencies and are closely allied with the conservative political parties through which they make their political influence felt.

Below the top levels of the social pyramid there is found a broad middle class. Compared to the middle class in the United States, the Japanese middle class is proportionately smaller and weaker economically, but undoubtedly it is the most important middle class in all of Asia. In this respect, Japan differs from many of the countries of present-day Asia and Africa, where one often finds under a thin layer of wealthy families the mass of the people who are forced to live on low incomes and own virtually no property.

The growth of the middle class in Japan is a product of the historical development of capitalism in Japan. For our purpose, which is to understand political phenomena, at least three features of Japanese capitalism might be mentioned. First, modern industry, as suggested in the previous chapter, was largely introduced in the Meiji period either under government auspices or with government support. Later, many of these industries were sold to private interests, thereby facilitating the growth of large industrial firms and combinations of firms, which came to be known as the zaibatsu, or industrial combine. Although the Occupation tried to dissolve these combines, it was only partially successful, and many of the prewar giants, for example the Mitsui and the Mitsubishi, remain among the leading firms in Japan today.

Among other things, the growth of modern capitalist industry has generated the need for occupational skills of all kinds. In order to function efficiently, modern industry needs skilled executives and managers, scientists to operate research laboratories, engineers to design machines, and technicians with various specialized skills, to say nothing of clerical workers, salespeople, and factory hands. Other occupations, many of which fall in the white-collar category, have also arisen in connection with modern industry. Here one thinks of professional people such as doctors and dentists, journalists, literary critics, and novelists, professors and teachers, actors, musicians, and others in the entertainment industry, civil servants, and so on. An increasing number of people residing in the big cities today are engaged in the so-called white-collar occupations.

The second characteristic of Japanese capitalism is the fact that the development of large-scale modern industry was not necessarily accompanied by the demise of the small capitalist. For example, in 1961 there were just under 31 million persons employed in nonagricultural industry, and of this total about 5.25 million persons were "self-employed" while another 3 million were "unpaid family workers." These statistics point up the fact that in Japan there are still a host of small shops and plants, owned by individuals and operated with the help of family labor and perhaps a few hired employees. The relationship between employer and employee in these instances is colored by a high degree of paternalism. The employer, like a father, is expected to provide for the welfare of his employee, and the worker is expected not only to perform his tasks but also to be loyal and devoted like a son.

As might be surmised, these small enterprises must work with a limited amount of capital, and in many instances they actually operate as subcontractors for large business firms. The economic position of small-business men is usually very precarious because of competition with the large firms as well as intense competition among themselves.

The third characteristic of Japanese capitalism is the fact that despite the growth of industry agriculture still remains a source of livelihood for a significant proportion of the population. Although the position of agriculture in the total economic picture has been declining, some 6 million families still make their living wholly or partly through farming. Thanks to the land reform program sponsored by the Occupation, the number of those who own land was increased substantially in the postwar period. It should be added, however, that the average size of the farms is still small and the majority of them are 2½ acres or less in size.

As might be expected, the amount of property, especially land, that a family owns helps determine its social position within the community, but property is not the only determinant of social prestige in the farm areas. For a family to enjoy influence, it must be able to claim in addition long residence in the community, good family lineage, education, and connections with local political figures and officials. Generally one finds in every community a few families with these attributes, and these families, even though their members may not hold formal office in local government, are usually consulted on important problems and looked to for local leadership.[4]

The Social Basis of Power

The mode of Japanese politics is affected by its social setting in several ways. As has been indicated, the choice left to the individual is generally highly circumscribed. What a man or woman thinks and, perhaps even more important, how he or she acts both socially and politically are often determined by the social groups to which the individual belongs. Of these groups the family still appears to be influential. The informal groupings of several or more families bound together by a strong sense of personal loyalty also seem to be instrumental in determining political attitudes and behavior. It is to these groups that an individual turns when he needs guidance or assistance, and this tendency to seek solutions to personal and social problems within the framework of small groups leads to what one might call "informal government."

Among those who often exercise leadership in "informal government" are individuals (and their families) who own property and have some economic reserves, such as owners of small commercial and industrial enterprises, and rural landowners. These people make their influence felt partly through economic levers, for example their position as employers or suppliers of credit, and partly through the

---

[4] For a more detailed treatment of the social and economic structure see Nobutaka Ike, *Japanese Politics: An Introductory Survey* (New York: Knopf, 1957), chs. ii, v–vii.

prestige they have in their communities. Other people also playing a part in "informal government" are schoolteachers and priests, who are respected for their specialized training, and such individuals as foremen in factories who are in a position to supervise and train those under them. In terms of political ideology, "informal government" is, of course, tradition-oriented. It rests on the continued acceptance of social hierarchy, authoritarianism, and paternalism and represents the carry-over into the twentieth century of older forms of social and political organization. "Informal government" therefore stands on the side of conservatism.

The chief challenge to conservatism comes from urban areas, which have grown manyfold in size since the Meiji Restoration. The city, the university, the office, and the factory represent sources of new ideas and new types of social organization. It is in the city and among the educated that Western influences have been most strongly felt. In the city also more impersonal and formalized social relationships occur with greater frequency.

It is incontestable that over the long run the force of tradition will be progressively weakened. What is not so clear, however, is who will be benefited, politically speaking, from social change. It might be argued that since the socialist party and the socialist movement essentially represent a break with tradition, the socialists would benefit from the weakening of tradition. The evidence to date, however, would suggest that such a conclusion would be somewhat premature. One of the important factors that is likely to determine the balance of political forces in the future is the political outlook of the white-collar class, which has steadily grown in the past and is likely to increase in the future. Whoever gets their support will enjoy a decided advantage in the future.

· V ·

Governmental Organization:

Past and Present

THE organization of government as defined in the constitution and other basic laws reveals something of the allocation of formal authority, the rules governing policy making and execution, the definition of what constitutes legitimate acts of government, and the goals implicit in the constitutional structure. Admittedly, the formal structure seldom gives a complete picture of how a political system works in practice; nevertheless, it does serve as a convenient starting point for an analysis of that system.

The Constitution

THE PREWAR CONSTITUTION

The constitution of 1889 was promulgated by the Emperor as a "gift to the people." It was issued in response to a popular movement which demanded the adoption of a written constitution and the establishment of a parliament. However, since individuals and groups outside of the government were not consulted during the drafting process, the finished document made little provision for popular control of the government.

The constitution set forth the principle of imperial rule. Thus it was proclaimed in the preamble: "The rights of sovereignty of the state, We [the Emperor] have inherited from our Ancestors, and We shall bequeath them to Our descendants. Neither We nor they shall in future fail to wield them, in accordance with the provisions of the Constitution hereby granted."

Although the constitution established executive, legislative, and judicial departments, there was a high degree of centralization since each of these departments was, in theory, responsible to the Emperor. According to the constitution, "the Emperor exercises the legislative power with the consent of the Imperial Diet"; "the respective Ministers of State shall give their advice to the Emperor, and be responsible for it," and "the Judicature shall be exercised by the Courts of Law according to law, in the name of the Emperor."

In Chapter II entitled "Rights and Duties of Subjects," a series of rights, such as the freedom of religious belief and the liberty of speech, writing, publications, and assembly, were enunciated; but in almost every instance these rights were qualified by such phrases as "within the limits of law" and "except in cases provided for in the law."

In the constitution there was provided no agency to interpret that instrument. In practice it was interpreted by the courts and in some instances by the Privy Council. Amendments to the constitution were to be made only at the initiative of the Emperor. It was necessary that at least two-thirds of the members of each house of the Imperial Diet be present to discuss the proposed amendment; and at least two-thirds of those present had to approve before it could become effective. The fact should be noted that the constitution was never amended.

The Imperial House Law, promulgated at the same time as the constitution, was second in importance only to the constitution. This law, which regulated succession and administration of the imperial family, was deemed to be superior to ordinary legislation and not subject to change by the Imperial Diet. It was to be amended only "by the Emperor, with the advice of the Imperial Family Council and with that of the Privy Council."

THE POSTWAR CONSTITUTION

The theory of imperial rule enunciated in the Meiji constitution was clearly not conducive to democratic rule; and since the prime objective of the Allied Occupation was to destroy Japanese militarism and to remake Japan into a democratic nation, it is not surprising that early attention was given to constitutional reform. During the first months of the Occupation, the Japanese government, on several occasions, was told by General MacArthur of the need for revising the constitution. As a consequence the Japanese government established a committee to study the constitutional problem, and after several months of work this committee completed a draft. This draft made clear that the committee was intent on retaining the basic philosophy of the old constitution and was not disposed to making radical changes; and as a result it was rejected. The Government Section of MacArthur's headquarters therefore set to work and quickly completed a draft in English. When this document was transmitted to the Japanese government, those in charge were taken aback; however, they realized that they had no alternative but to accede to the wishes of the Occupation authorities. Publicly both sides maintained the fiction that the proposed constitution was a Japanese document. The draft was approved by the cabinet, and after some revision it was submitted to the Diet, where it was debated, amended in certain minor respects, and approved. It became effective on May 3, 1947.

The underlying philosophy of the Meiji constitution and the postwar constitution is vastly different. In keeping with its American origin, the new constitution bears the unmistakable impress of Western liberal thought. The preamble proclaims:

We, the Japanese people, acting through our duly elected representatives in the National Diet, determined that we shall secure for ourselves and our posterity the fruits of peaceful cooperation with all nations and the blessings of liberty throughout this land, and resolved that never again shall we be visited with the horrors of war through the action of government, do proclaim that sovereign power resides with the people and do firmly establish this Constitution.

Quite clearly the theory of imperial rule has been replaced by the doctrine of popular sovereignty.

Another conspicuous feature of the new constitution is the emphasis on civil liberties. Thirty-one articles, out of a total of 103, are contained in Chapter III, which is devoted to "Rights and Duties of the People." Article 11 states, "The people shall not be prevented from enjoying any of the fundamental human rights. These fundamental human rights guaranteed to the people by this Constitution shall be conferred upon the people of this and future generations as eternal and inviolate rights." A long series of rights are enumerated:

the "right to life, liberty, and the pursuit of happiness," equality under the law, the right to choose public officials, secrecy of the ballot, the right of peaceful petition, the right to sue the state or public officials, freedom of thought and conscience, of religion, of assembly and association, of speech and press, academic freedom, equality of the sexes with reference to property rights, choice of spouse, and other matters, the right to "maintain the minimum standards of wholesome and cultural living," the right and obligation to work, the right of workers to organize and bargain collectively, and the right of access to the courts. Protection is also afforded the individual with reference to search and seizure, arrest and detention, the infliction of torture, and being compelled to testify against himself.

A unique feature of the new constitution is Article 9, which has subsequently become a matter of considerable controversy. It reads:

Aspiring sincerely to an international peace based on justice and order, the Japanese people forever renounce war as a sovereign right of the nation and the threat or use of force as a means of settling international disputes.

In order to accomplish the aim of the preceding paragraph, land, sea, and air forces, as well as other war potential, will never be maintained. The rights of belligerency of the state will not be recognized.

The power to interpret the constitution is placed in the Supreme Court, which as a court of last resort determines the "constitutionality of any law, order, regulation or official act." Amendments to the constitution are to be initiated by the Diet, and an affirmative vote of two-thirds or more of all the members of each house is required. The amendment must then be ratified by a majority of all votes cast in a special referendum. Other matters prescribed in the constitution relate to the Emperor, the Diet, the cabinet, the judiciary, finance, local self-government, and the supreme law and supplementary provisions.

Given the circumstances surrounding the drafting and adoption of the constitution, the question remains whether it is likely to become rooted in Japanese political life. Conservatives have openly expressed their desire to amend the present constitution in order to strengthen the position of the Emperor and the cabinet and generally to return, although not all the way, to the old constitution. Liberals and socialists, on the other hand, have supported the constitution and even have argued in favor of strengthening portions of it such as the section on civil liberties. In view of the lack of consensus on this problem and

Chart 3. Structure of the present Japanese government

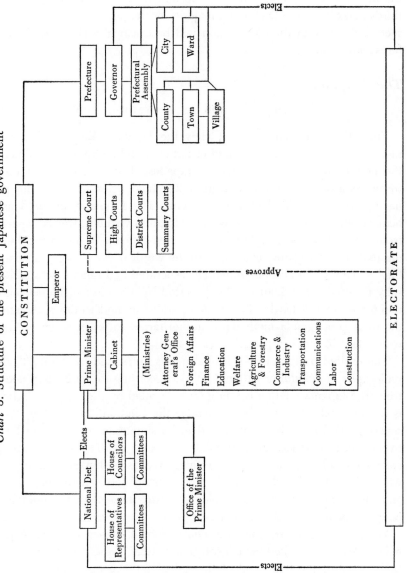

the necessity of obtaining, in order to amend the constitution, a two-thirds majority in the Diet and a majority of the popular vote, it would seem unlikely that the constitution will be drastically changed in the foreseeable future.

The Emperor

THE EMPEROR AS A SYMBOL

From the functional point of view the Japanese Emperor has, in modern times, served as a symbol of national and cultural unity. Since the end of the Tokugawa period, Japanese leaders have used the throne as a counterpoise to decentralizing tendencies and in so doing have developed a kind of Emperor cult. The Emperor, pictured as heaven-descended, divine, sacred, all-wise, and virtuous, was set apart from the nation, and people were forbidden to make of him a topic of discussion or derogatory comment. In the words of Sir George Sansom, the "concept of an absolute monarch, venerated and remote, was carefully fostered throughout the Meiji period by a process of indoctrination for which it is hard to find a close parallel in modern times, though the mass propaganda methods of authoritarian states in recent years resemble it in some respects." [1]

The exalted position of the Emperor was buttressed by the political philosophy of *kokutai* or national polity. According to the *kokutai* doctrine, the Japanese nation is a large family ruled by the Emperor, who is its patriarchal father. Consequently, the relationship between the sovereign and his subjects was said to be similar to that existing between father and son, so that filial piety and political loyalty were conceived to be one and the same thing. It was unthinkable, to those who believed in *kokutai*, that the relationship between the Emperor and his subjects could ever be changed, any more than it would be possible for father and son to switch places.

Yet according to the postwar constitutional theory this has happened. Article 1 of the new constitution states, "The Emperor shall be the symbol of the State and of the unity of the people, deriving his position from the will of the people with whom resides sovereign power." The people are now sovereign, and the Emperor derives his position from their will.

As a result of the shift in the Emperor's constitutional position, at

[1] George B. Sansom, *The Western World and Japan* (New York: Knopf, 1950), p. 356.

least two important changes have occurred. First, a considerable portion of the taboos which shrouded the imperial institution have been removed. It has become possible to discuss and write openly about the Emperor, both as a person and as an institution, even in a critical vein, without the risk of public censure or arrest. When the Emperor was prevented by his court chamberlains from attending the funeral of his brother, Prince Chichibu, in January 1953, presumably because this would have constituted a departure from tradition, the press condemned this action in no uncertain terms. Such press comments would have been inconceivable before the war.

Second, concerted attempts have been made to "humanize" the Emperor. Previously he had been so exalted that his subjects were required to bow their heads and not to look at his personage when he passed by. After the end of the war, however, the Emperor made many personal appearances, visiting farms, factories, and schools and even attending movie theaters and baseball games. Newspapers and magazines printed stories and pictures to show the daily life of the imperial household, and stories were told of how the Emperor had reduced his standard of living and simplified his daily life in order to share hardships with his subjects.

A more recent example of moves to bring the imperial family closer to the people was the marriage of the crown prince to Michiko Shoda, a daughter of a businessman, in 1959. The crown prince had met Miss Shoda on a tennis court and had fallen in love with her. The marriage was approved by the imperial family and others concerned, and Michiko Shoda, whose father was the president of Japan's largest flour-milling company, became the first "commoner" to be made a crown princess. The press and public responded with great enthusiasm to the announcement of the royal romance and marriage, and it must be said that from a public relations point of view the marriage was a master stroke. A cynic might add that historically the imperial family has allied itself with the dominant groups in society and that the crown prince's marriage illustrates the coming of age of Japanese business.

Prior to the war, many conservatives believed that any tampering with the myth of the Emperor as the exalted father of the nation would weaken the cement holding society together and would lead to social chaos. So far, at least, the conservatives have been proved wrong. Public opinion polls and other surveys, although they are not conclusive, would seem to indicate that the Emperor still enjoys con-

siderable popularity and support, especially among the rural inhabitants and the older segment of the population. The following comment by a 42-year-old lawyer may be regarded as fairly typical:

It is sheer nonsense to think that we ever believed that the Emperor was
a real god. I respect him and I support him absolutely as a human being.
This is a feeling that is strong within me and one that I am unable to
eradicate. I do not support the Emperor as a symbol of Japan, but I do
support him completely as the sovereign of our nation. Personally, I think
that the word "symbol" is too vague a term to be understood by the people.
I feel toward the Emperor much the same deep attachment that a child
feels toward its parents.[2]

THE POLITICAL ROLE OF THE EMPEROR

One reason for the remarkable capacity of the imperial house to survive the vicissitudes of history from the early period down to the
present is its noninvolvement in the give-and-take of politics. The
political role of the Emperor has been to serve as a symbol, but not to
participate in an active way in the formulation and execution of policy.
The diaries and other accounts of those individuals close to the throne
which have been recently published suggest that the Emperor on occasion asked pointed questions of his ministers and advisers, but seldom if ever took a position contrary to that suggested by them.
Clearly the Emperor's role was to give the stamp of formal approval
to decisions arrived at by others.

It goes without saying that the Emperor provided a rather convenient shield for the small group which ruled in his name. The Emperor, according to the Meiji constitution, acted on the advice of his
ministers, but since the ministers were responsible to the Emperor,
they were, in effect, responsible to no one. There were important
agencies, such as the Imperial Household Ministry, the Privy Council,
and the Supreme War Council, the legitimacy of whose actions could
not be questioned because of their intimate relation to the throne.

The constitutional position of the Emperor has changed considerably in the postwar period. He is no longer the source of all authority,
political and moral; he has been reduced to a "symbol," and sovereignty is now deemed to lie in the people. He has certain ceremonial
functions under the constitution, but he has no "powers related to
government." Because even before the war the Emperor never took

[2] Quoted in Hugh H. Smythe and Masaharu Watanabe, "Japanese Popular Attitudes toward the Emperor," *Pacific Affairs*, XXVI (Dec. 1953), 341.

part in political decisions, his present role remains substantially unchanged. The important difference, however, lies in the fact that it is no longer possible for his ministers and advisers to rule in his name. The lines of responsibility are now much more clearly drawn.

The Diet

THE IMPERIAL DIET

Japan has the longest history of parliamentary government in all of Asia. The Imperial Diet, composed of the House of Peers and the House of Representatives, was created in 1890, as a result of a popular movement extending over several decades which called for the establishment of parliamentary government.

The House of Peers was composed of princes of the blood; princes and marquises; counts, viscounts, and barons, elected from among their respective orders for seven-year terms; imperial appointees for life, selected for special service to the state or for distinguished scholarship; representatives of the Imperial Academy; and representatives elected from and by the highest taxpayers of each prefecture. The membership numbered about 400 in the 1930s, having grown by about a hundred since its establishment. It was natural, given its make-up, that the House of Peers was highly conservative; and since its powers were equal to that of the House of Representatives, it served for decades as a bulwark against popular control of the government.

In the beginning the House of Representatives was composed of 300 members, elected for a four-year term and chosen by voters who paid 15 yen or more in direct taxes. Because of the tax qualification, the landed interest was heavily represented in the lower house. With the passage of years, the membership was increased, and tax qualifications were reduced. In 1925 a universal manhood suffrage law was enacted, and under this law the size was set at 466 members. As the size of the electorate was expanded, the proportion of representatives with a background in business, industry, and law was increased substantially, whereas the number of agriculturalists declined.

The relative shortness of its sessions was indicative of the lack of power of the House of Representatives. It was generally convoked every year late in December by the Emperor, and after a recess over the New Year's holidays, it was reconvened, remaining in session until the end of March. The Emperor had the power to prorogue the Diet, but not for more than 15 days at a time, and to dissolve the Diet. In case of dissolution, a new lower house had to be convened within 5 months.

When a bill was passed by a majority of the two houses and approved by the Emperor, it became law. Bills were introduced both by the government and by members, but most legislation was government-sponsored. When a bill was passed by one house, it was sent to the other; and in case one house amended the other's bill and the amendment was not acceptable, it was referred to a committee composed of an equal number of members from each house.

Under the constitution of 1889, the government was empowered in cases of emergency to issue imperial ordinances, but Diet approval in the following session was required if such ordinances were to remain in effect. The approval of the Diet was also necessary in order to amend the constitution; but no amendments were ever made.

A serious weakness of the House of Representatives was its lack of power to exercise firm control over finances. For instance, it had no control over items in the budget for "ordinary expenditures required by the organization of the different branches of the administration and by that of the army and navy, the salaries of all civil and military officers, and expenditures that may be required in consequence of treaties concluded with foreign countries."[3] Moreover, the lower house had no control over expenditures necessitated by the legal obligations of the government or over the expenditures of the imperial household. Finally, in the event that parliament failed to pass a budget bill, the government was authorized under the constitution to "carry out the budget of the preceding year." Thus it is clear that although the prewar Diet could, if it so desired, check the actions of the executive, delay matters, and appeal to public opinion by voicing criticisms of policy, its power was greatly circumscribed.

NATIONAL DIET: ORGANIZATION

The new Diet, established under the constitution of 1947, differs substantially from its predecessor. The intent of the American framers of the constitution was to make the National Diet the core of the government. "The Diet," states the constitution, "shall be the highest organ of state power, and shall be the sole law-making organ of the State."

The present Diet consists of two houses, the House of Representatives and the House of Councilors.

---

[3] Harold S. Quigley, *Japanese Government and Politics* (New York: Century, 1932), pp. 188–189.

The House of Representatives presently consists of 467 members elected from 118 electoral districts. Each district is represented by 3 to 5 members, but each voter casts his ballot for only one candidate. Members are elected for four-year terms, but the lower house may be dissolved, in which case a new election must be held within 40 days.

The House of Councilors, which replaced the House of Peers, consists of 250 members, 150 of whom are elected from the prefectures and 100 from the nation at large. Each voter casts two votes, one for the prefectural candidate and another for the national candidate. The members of the House of Councilors, which cannot be dissolved, are chosen for six-year terms, with one-half the membership standing election every three years.

Of the two houses, the House of Representatives is more powerful. All money bills must originate in the House of Representatives. A bill passed by the lower house but voted down by the House of Councilors can become law if it is repassed by the House of Representatives by a majority of two-thirds or more of the members present.

An important innovation is the creation of a standing-committee system. The prewar Diet had 4 or 5 standing committees, but much of the work was done by each house sitting as a committee of the whole. In the National Diet there are some 15 standing committees, one for each major field of legislation, such as foreign affairs, budget, education, labor, agriculture, commerce, transportation, audit, and so on, plus a disciplinary committee and a ways and means committee. Each member of the Diet must be appointed to at least one committee, but no more than three. Committee membership and the chairmanship of committees are allocated on the basis of party strength. From time to time special committees are appointed to deal with problems that cannot be resolved effectively by the standing committees.

Much of the work of the National Diet is handled by the committees. They deliberate on legislative proposals, and the fate of these proposals is usually determined by their action. As a part of their deliberations on a measure, committees hold public hearings to which witnesses are summoned. Interested individuals and representatives of organizations affected by pending legislation can also appear to make known their views.

Unlike its predecessor, the postwar Diet is empowered to investigate the activities of the executive branch. A special committee on illegal disposal of government property, for example, undertook a lengthy probe of the disappearance of millions of dollars' worth of government property shortly after the surrender. Other committees have looked into such matters as corruption in government and the operations of government agencies.

As is true of other reforms, criticisms have been leveled at the newly created committee system. A common complaint is that committees tend to develop close ties with the ministry whose field of interest is related to it, for example the agricultural committee and the Ministry of Agriculture and Forestry, and that such ties encourage committees to become special pleaders for the ministries and their clientele.

There are several ways in which the National Diet can exercise authority over the executive branch. First of all, it is the National Diet, rather than the Emperor, who designates the Prime Minister. Moreover, the Diet can force the resignation of the cabinet, or of a cabinet member, by passing a no-confidence resolution. Unlike the prewar Diet, the present Diet enjoys the power of the purse. The budget, submitted by the cabinet, must be passed by the Diet. The Diet also has the power to tax, for no national taxes may be levied or a change made without its approval. The Diet can also exercise control over the conduct of foreign relations through its power to ratify or reject treaties concluded by the cabinet. The power to investigate the conduct of executive agencies has already been mentioned. Finally, the Diet has the authority to impeach judges, by establishing an impeachment court consisting of an equal number of members from each house. Thus it is clear that the powers of the Diet are extensive and go beyond purely legislative matters.

The Cabinet

THE PREWAR CABINET

The cabinet system was established by imperial ordinance in 1885, four years before the promulgation of the constitution. The cabinet, therefore, preceded the creation of the Diet.

The cabinet was not mentioned in the Meiji constitution and therefore was an extraconstitutional body. The constitution provided, however, that the "Ministers of State shall give their advice to the Emperor, and be responsible for it." In constitutional theory, therefore, the cabinet as a body was not responsible collectively to the Emperor. Moreover, since the responsibility of the ministers was upward to the Emperor, the cabinet ministers were very often not even members of the majority party in the Diet.

The Prime Minister was chosen by the Emperor upon the recommendation of his advisers, which included the Elder Statesmen, the Lord Keeper of the Privy Seal, the Minister of the Imperial Household, and others. In the 1920s, the heyday of party government, the leader of the majority party was often named Prime Minister; but if the history of the cabinet between 1885 and 1945 is taken as a whole, it must be said that party cabinets were the exception rather than the rule.

The person designated as Prime Minister selected his ministers, taking into account various factors such as factions within parties, the wishes of the oligarchy, and the views of the armed forces. It was required by custom and law that the Minister of War and the Minister of Navy be career officers of the rank of lieutenant general or vice-admiral or higher. Since these ministers were chosen by the Prime Minister but appointed by the Emperor on the recommendation of the leading figures in the army and navy, the armed forces were able, if they so desired, to prevent a cabinet from being formed by refusing to nominate a minister or to force the resignation of a cabinet by withdrawing a minister.

There were other ways in which cabinets could fall. Although the cabinet was not responsible to the Diet, severe attacks in the Diet forced the Prime Minister either to dissolve the lower house or to resign. Public criticism of policy, leading to riots and other disturbances, and quarrels with the Privy Council or the House of Peers usually led to resignation. Three cabinets had the support of an absolute majority in the House of Representatives; in these three instances the Prime Ministers became targets of assassins, and the cabinets fell. An important cause of resignation of cabinets was internal dissension. Although in practice the Prime Minister usually controlled his cabinet, he had no clear-cut authority over his colleagues, for in legal theory the ministers were responsible to the Emperor and not to him.

The power of the prewar cabinet, therefore, was greatly circumscribed both in theory and in practice. Nevertheless, of all the organs of government the cabinet was perhaps most consistently in the public eye; and almost all political figures came to consider appointment as Prime Minister, or even as a cabinet minister, the crowning achievement of their careers.

THE POSTWAR CABINET

The postwar cabinet is markedly different from its prewar predecessor. The new constitution states that "executive power shall be vested in the Cabinet," and it lists its functions in considerable detail. According to the provisions of the constitution the cabinet submits bills, including an annual budget, to the Diet, negotiates and concludes treaties, and in general conducts foreign relations, decides on amnesty, commutation of punishment, and so on, administers the law, directs the civil service, exercises control over the administrative branches of the government, designates the Chief Justice of the Supreme Court and appoints other judges, and issues cabinet orders to carry out the constitution and other laws.

Unlike the prewar cabinet which could function fairly independently of the Diet, the present cabinet is related closely to the legislature. First of all, the Prime Minister is designated from among its members by the National Diet. Although the Prime Minister is empowered by the constitution to appoint and dismiss his ministers, there is a provision that ministers must be civilians and that the majority of ministers must be members of the Diet.

In addition, the cabinet is required to report to the Diet on the state of national affairs and foreign relations and on the state of national finances and submit final accounts of expenditures and revenues. The cabinet has the power to dissolve the House of Representatives and to call the House of Councilors in emergency session when the House of Representatives has been dissolved.

In terms of the legal structure, the cabinet would appear to be inferior to the National Diet. In practice, however, it is the cabinet which formulates the legislative program and guides its enactment into law, particularly when the cabinet is backed by a solid majority in the lower house.

To assist the work of the cabinet, there is a Prime Minister's secretariat, headed by a director and two deputy directors. The secretariat arranges the agenda of cabinet meetings, prepares documents, and handles other business matters. Cabinet meetings, which ordinarily take place on Tuesday and Friday mornings in the Prime Minister's official residence, are presided over by the Prime Minister, but in his absence the Vice-Premier takes over the chair. There is no quorum; if decisions are made by a minority of the members, those who were absent may be later asked to sign the documents. Cabinet discussions are secret, and minutes are not published. Cabinet members are warned not to divulge what has taken place, but leaks to the press are not entirely unknown. The section of Article 66 of the constitution which states that "the Cabinet, in the exercise of executive power, shall be collectively responsible to the Diet" is interpreted to mean that cabinet decisions must be unanimous. There have been instances in which ministers have resigned because they could not agree with their colleagues.

A cabinet can stay in power so long as it has the support of the majority of members of the lower house. When it loses such support, however, and the House of Representatives passes a no-confidence resolution or rejects a confidence resolution, the cabinet must either dissolve the lower house within ten days or resign. In the latter event, the presiding officers of both houses are notified in writing by the cabinet, whereupon the Diet begins the process of choosing a new Prime Minister.

The Civil Service

The day-to-day work of the government, whose scope and functions are ever-increasing, falls largely on the thousands of civil servants who staff the ministries and agencies. The average citizen in his relationship with the government comes into contact with the civil servant, and thus for him the government is in many ways synonymous with the government official. The bureaucracy of any modern state, therefore, may be regarded as the core of government.

THE PREWAR CIVIL SERVICE

In the early years of the Meiji era, government personnel was drawn largely from the old samurai class and particularly from the geographical areas in western Japan that had provided the leadership of the Restoration movement. But with the passage of years the feeling spread that appointments went to friends of those already in the government and that able men were being kept out of public office. Accordingly, in 1885 the foundations of a modern civil service were laid with the adoption of the principle that appointments to government posts should be based on examinations. The first examinations were held in 1887 for officials of the second and third rank, the first-rank officials being exempt.

The prewar civil service was divided into the higher civil service and the ordinary civil service. Each division was subdivided. The higher civil service consisted of first-rank (*shinnin*) officials, that is, cabinet ministers, ambassadors, and highest judicial officers; second-rank (*chokunin*) officials, such as vice-ministers, bureau chiefs, and judges; and third-rank (*sonin*) officials, who held lower-level posts.

The higher civil service accounted for less than 5 per cent of the posts in the government. The ordinary civil service consisted of fourth-rank (*hanin*) officials and unclassified (*yatoi*) officials. Between three-fifths and three-fourths of the civil servants were unclassified officials.

Except for technicians, members of the higher civil service were recruited through competitive examinations given annually in Tokyo. The examinations, largely legal in character, were controlled by a committee, consisting mostly of the members of the law faculty of Tokyo Imperial University, the leading government-supported university which was originally established to train government officials. Those who passed, and they were relatively few in proportion to those who took the examinations, were put on an eligible list from which appointments were made. In making appointments, according to one account, "sons or brothers of leading officials or of those who had influence with the officials received preferential treatment. Letters of recommendation from prominent persons were presented in support of applications, and not infrequently a candidate resorted to the giving of gifts." [4] In the competition for bureaucratic posts, graduates of the Tokyo Imperial University had great advantages, and the higher civil service came to be dominated by men from this university.

The examinations for the ordinary civil service were geared for high school graduates and were given in various localities. Those in the ordinary civil service carried on much of the day-to-day work of administration, but they lacked the prestige and status accorded those in the higher civil service. Officials in the ordinary civil service were seldom promoted to the higher civil service.

In other words, a strong sense of hierarchy pervaded the Japanese civil service. It is said that those who belonged to the higher civil service ate in separate dining rooms; and status within the hierarchy was symbolized by the kind of desk one had and by the number of bookshelves and chairs for guests one had in his office.

There was also considerable jealousy among various bureaus, agencies, and ministries, and each was sensitive about its prerogatives. Proposals which required the consent and cooperation of several ministries were often held up. Another result was unnecessary duplication of work. For instance, information and documents assembled by one agency were seldom made available to another agency, so that several agencies were sometimes engaged in collecting similar data.

⁴ Maynard Shirven and Joseph L. Speicher, "Examination of Japan's Upper Bureaucracy," *Personnel Administration,* July 1951, p. 49.

In its dealings with the public the Japanese bureaucracy acquired the reputation of being arrogant and overbearing. Officials were, in theory, responsible to the Emperor, and therefore each official was vested with a segment of imperial authority. In functions at the imperial court, for example, a first-rank official was considered equal to the president of the House of Peers and the Speaker of the House of Representatives, and a second-rank official ranked with the vice-president of the House of Peers and the Vice-Speaker of the lower house. Since officials were deemed to be responsible to the Emperor and not the public, officialdom was never very much concerned with the matter of public relations.

THE POSTWAR CIVIL SERVICE

Of all the branches of the Japanese government, the civil service was probably the least affected by Occupation-sponsored reforms. This resulted partly from the fact that the Occupation avoided direct military government and instead worked through the existing Japanese government and partly from the fact that the bureaucracy was strongly entrenched and therefore reforms were difficult to make.

This is not to say that no reforms were attempted. On the contrary, a sizable number of changes were made in the institutional structure of the bureaucracy. Late in 1946, the United States Personnel Advisory Mission was sent to Japan to look into the existing system, and in line with its subsequent recommendations a National Public Service Law, providing for service-wide standards of personnel administration, was enacted by the Diet in 1947; and in 1949 a National Personnel Authority, charged with the responsibility of introducing democratic methods, providing scientific personnel management, and creating a job classification system, was established. Moreover, certain provisions affecting public officials were written into the new constitution. Thus Article 15 states in part that "all public officials are servants of the whole community and not any group thereof," and Article 17 provides that "every person may sue for redress as provided by law from the State or a public entity, in case he has suffered damage through illegal act of any public official."

It is doubtful, however, despite these institutional changes, that the Japanese bureaucracy has been altered in its basic orientation. To be sure, graduates from other universities are getting posts in the civil service in larger numbers than formerly; but graduates of the old Tokyo Imperial University are still predominant in many ministries.

Since its establishment the power of the National Personnel Authority has been whittled away, and it may eventually lose its status as an independent agency. Despite the new constitution, the Japanese bureaucracy continues to be officious and given to feelings of self-importance.

The Judiciary

THE PREWAR JUDICIAL SYSTEM

The judicial system adopted in the Meiji era was based on French and German models, with modifications to allow for Japanese conditions. The prewar legal system, therefore, was largely Continental, rather than Anglo-Saxon, in outlook.

Before the war, the judiciary was subordinated to the executive. Court administration was under the direct control of the Ministry of Justice; and certain limitations were placed on the power of the courts. The courts had no authority to rule on the constitutionality of laws, nor were they empowered to pass judgment in disputes between the government and citizens.

At the top of the court structure was the Supreme Court, which met in Tokyo. The Supreme Court, consisting of 45 justices, carried on its work in divisions composed of 5 justices each. The Supreme Court heard appeals from the courts of appeals and had exclusive jurisdiction over cases of treason and serious offenses against the imperial family.

Below the Supreme Court were high courts, one in each of the seven districts into which the country was divided. The high courts handled appeals from the lower courts. There were some 50 district courts, at least one being located in each prefecture which had jurisdiction in more serious civil and criminal cases. At the lowest level there were a little under 300 local courts in which minor cases were tried.

In addition to the ordinary courts there was the court of administrative litigation, modeled after the *cours administratives* in Germany and Austria. The administrative court was established on the theory that administrators would be inferior to the judiciary if ordinary courts were permitted to rule on the legality of administrative acts. The court of administrative litigation had authority in such matters as tax cases, disputes over the granting of licenses, cases concerning public works, disputes over boundaries between public and private lands, and cases arising out of police administration.

THE POSTWAR JUDICIAL SYSTEM

Occupation-sponsored reforms in the judicial system were extensive and ranged from changes in the structure of courts and judicial procedure to changes in the underlying philosophy of law and jurisprudence. It is perhaps not surprising, given the nature of the Occupation, that many ideas and practices of Anglo-Saxon origin were incorporated into the judicial system, thereby changing its orientation which was formerly predominantly Continental.

Under the provisions of the new constitution as well as legislation affecting the judicial branch, the courts were made independent of both the executive and the legislature. The Supreme Court, rather than the Ministry of Justice, was placed in charge of the administration of the court system. The separate administrative tribunal was abolished, and all judicial disputes were put under the jurisdiction of the ordinary courts. The courts, moreover, were given the power to pass on the constitutionality of all legislation and administrative action, provided the issue was embodied in a concrete suit of law.

The new Supreme Court consists of 15 justices, 10 of whom must have had long experience in the legal profession. The Chief Justice is appointed by the Emperor upon nomination by the cabinet, and the associate justices are appointed by the cabinet and "attested" by the Emperor. After their appointment, all justices must be approved by the electorate at the first general election of the House of Representatives following their appointment, and they must undergo similar popular review every ten years thereafter. So far no Supreme Court justice has been rejected, and it is unlikely that in the future the electorate would turn down a justice except in most unusual cases.

The work of the Supreme Court is limited to appeal cases requiring a review of the issues of law. An interesting innovation in procedure is the provision for dissenting opinions. Some important cases involving the constitutionality of law or administrative action have come before the Supreme Court. In 1959 the Supreme Court reversed the decision of a lower court which had held that the presence of American forces in Japan was contrary to the Japanese constitution.

Below the Supreme Court there are 8 high courts, which hear appeals from decisions of lower courts. Then there are 49 district courts, which have original jurisdiction over serious crimes and civil suits involving large sums and appellate jurisdiction over cases appealed from the summary courts. The summary courts, numbering 570 and located in principal cities, towns, and villages, try comparatively mild civil and criminal cases. In addition, there are 49 family courts, which handle cases involving domestic relations and juvenile delinquency.

Aside from the possible removal of Supreme Court justices through a plebiscite, judges enjoy tenure and may not be removed from office except through action taken by the impeachment court, consisting of 14 members, elected equally from the two houses of the National Diet. Reasons for impeachment include neglect of duty and conduct impairing the dignity of the court.

Court procedure in criminal cases has been modified to give more weight to the rights of the individual. Before the war, those accused of crime underwent a preliminary examination by means of questions from the bench in a closed court without the presence of a lawyer. A confession, often extorted by the use of third-degree methods, carried great weight, and in the formal trial the accused had no right to cross-examine witnesses. Moreover, the principle of habeas corpus was not recognized in Japanese law before the war.

As a result of the new constitution and the new code of criminal procedure, the preliminary examination system has been abolished, the cross-examination of witnesses is permitted, and no person may be compelled to give testimony against himself. Confession extracted by torture is not supposed to be accepted as evidence, and the court cannot convict the accused if his confession is the only evidence against him. Finally, the constitution provides that "no person shall be arrested or detained without being at once informed of the charges against him or without the immediate privilege of counsel."

Undoubtedly the intent of the Occupation reformers was to make the judiciary the guardian of the constitution and of human rights by elevating its status and by breathing into it a new philosophy. But in the last analysis, the effectiveness of the courts is dependent only partly on their ability to perform their functions. Popular attitudes toward law and legal institutions must also be taken into account. Here is encountered the unmistakable fact that traditionally people were reluctant to appeal to the courts for the adjudication of disputes and the redress of wrongs and preferred to resort to informal methods of mediation. In recent years there is a tendency for more people to take cases to the courts, and organizations such as the Japanese Civil Liberties Committee have taken the lead in getting court action against violations of civil liberties. Nevertheless, it is still true that courts play a relatively minor role. Perhaps the most eloquent testimony is the fact that there are less than 6,000 practicing lawyers out of a total population of some 90 million.

Local Government

PREWAR LOCAL GOVERNMENT

The prewar system of local government originated shortly after the Meiji Restoration when the 250-odd feudal fiefs were consolidated and replaced by prefectures. In this period, too, many new towns and villages were artificially created by government action through the amalgamation of existing towns and villages which had functioned as natural social units. In 1889 and 1890, on the eve of the convocation of the first Imperial Diet, several basic laws pertaining to local government were promulgated in order to prevent the Diet from sharing in the formation of the system of local government.

As may be inferred from this action, the basic philosophy of the Meiji oligarchs was to prevent popular control of local government and to centralize in Tokyo power over local government affairs. A stream of administrative orders flowed from Tokyo to the prefectures. The control of the police and of education was also placed in the hands of the central government. The Ministry of Home Affairs was the most important agency through which central control was exercised. The Home Minister, for example, enjoyed the power to appoint the governor of each prefecture (in 1945 there were 46 prefectures plus Hokkaido and Tokyo-to). Although there was in each prefecture a popularly elected assembly empowered to deliberate and vote on the budget, prefectural taxes, public property, and related matters, the power of the assembly was in fact advisory since the governor either dominated the assembly or could bypass it if it refused to accede to his wishes.

In the beginning, mayors of towns and cities were selected by the Ministry of Home Affairs, but with the spread of democratic ideals in the 1920s the mayor and his deputies came to be chosen by municipal assemblies. The assemblies, consisting of about 30 members or more, were elected for four-year terms and met about once a month. More frequent meetings were held by the municipal council, made up of 10 to 15 assemblymen elected by the assembly.

There seemed to be a possibility that in the 1920s more local autonomy would be granted, even leading to the popular election of governors; but with the rise of the military to power in the 1930s the trend was reversed, and during the war local government saw its most centralized form with the creation of regional administrative councils and later of regional superintendencies-general, both of which were supraprefectural organizations consisting of prefectural governors, chiefs of police, and other officials.

POSTWAR LOCAL GOVERNMENT

The Occupation authorities believed that the task of democratizing Japan would be aided by drastic changes in the system of local government. They assumed that it would be a good thing if a large measure of local autonomy were granted and that thereby "grass-roots" democracy would be fostered. Toward this end the Occupation sponsored a number of institutional changes.

The new constitution enunciates the principle of local autonomy for local public entities and stipulates that local officials shall be elected by direct popular vote, that local government bodies have the right to manage their property, affairs, and administration, and that a special law, applicable only to one local public entity, cannot be enacted by the Diet without the consent of the majority of voters of the local area concerned.

The details of local government structure were set forth in a series of laws, most important among them the lengthy Local Autonomy Law of 1947, which removed the legal power of the central government to control the prefectural government and of the latter to control the municipal governments. Other significant changes included the abolition of the Ministry of Home Affairs, provision for popular election of local officials, including governors of prefectures, creation of a system of recall and initiative, the decentralization of police and education, the creation of a local civil service, and fiscal reforms. The legal foundations of local autonomy, therefore, were laid.

But it cannot be said that as yet Japan has attained local autonomy in practice. The central government continues to exercise extensive influence over local government entities in one way or another. Although the Ministry of Home Affairs was abolished, the Local Autonomy Agency was established in 1949 to take over some of the functions formerly exercised by the Home Ministry. The Local Autonomy Agency issued directives to governors and other officials, summoned local officials to meetings in Tokyo, wrote model laws which served as a basis for legislation by prefectural and municipal assemblies, advised on local problems, and exercised indirect influence through semiofficial organizations such as the National Association of Governors. As part of the recent trend toward greater central government control over local government, in 1960 the Local Autonomy Agency was raised to the Ministry of Autonomy Affairs.

At least four reasons may be cited to explain why, despite legal and institutional changes, local government entities have not in fact achieved more independence. First, the idea of the community is relatively poorly developed, with the result that the level of civic pride is low. This is part of the general problem of political apathy, reference to which will be made later. Second, local officials by tradition and habit are not accustomed to taking the initiative in solving problems at the local level and still prefer to look to Tokyo for leadership. Third, there are many problems—social security, unemployment, economic planning, and so on—which by their nature must be dealt with at the national level. And, fourth, local government lacks the financial resources, given the present tax structure, to support numerous local undertakings and hence must rely on the central government for financial aid in the form of grants-in-aid and subsidies. As is generally true elsewhere, financial aid often leads to controls, direct or indirect.

· VI ·

Major Political Forces

ACTION—or lack of action—by the state usually has a marked impact on the economic well-being of diverse groups. Both the flow of revenue into government coffers, at the national and prefectural levels in the form of taxes, license fees, and other imposts, and the services provided by government, including subsidies it gives out, affect every citizen, whether directly or indirectly. In Japan, as in other countries, much political activity is therefore aimed at influencing government agencies in the performance of their tasks; and among those playing an important part in such activities are interest groups.

Interest Groups

BUSINESS ORGANIZATIONS

For understandable reasons, business, labor, and agriculture pay close attention to what government does (or fails to do). Individuals and groups in these sectors of the economy seek to influence government action in several ways. One way is to work through their own organizations, which by a variety of methods make their wants known to the government.

Among the principal business organizations are the Federation of Economic Organizations, the Japan Federation of Employers' Associations, the Chamber of Commerce and Industry, and the Japan

Management Association. The Federation of Economic Organizations, organized in 1946, is perhaps the most powerful and is composed of three types of members: (1) federations of business and trade associations, such as the Japan Industrial Council, the Council of Financial Organizations, and the Foreign Trade Association; (2) trade associations; and (3) business firms and businessmen. The Federation of Economic Organizations is concerned mostly with broad economic problems, such as the development of the national economy.

The Japan Federation of Employers' Associations, formed in 1948, is, as the name implies, a grouping of employers' associations which are organized on regional and prefectural levels. Its chief concern is with labor problems and Communist activities affecting labor-management relations. The Chamber of Commerce and Industry traces its history back to 1878, when the Tokyo Chamber of Commerce and Industry was established. In 1890 chambers of commerce and industry were created in various localities by law, and since then chambers of commerce and industry have had quasi-official status. The Chamber of Commerce and Industry and the local organizations promote business activities, supervise commercial organizations, engage in market research, and provide liaison between business and government. The Japan Management Association, formed in 1946, has branches in the Osaka-Kobe area, Kyushu, and Hokkaido and claims to have more than 8,000 members.

Practically all these business organizations undertake research on economic and labor problems and regularly issue journals, pamphlets, and research reports to keep their members and the business community informed and to influence public opinion indirectly. Another important function of these organizations is to attempt directly to influence public policy. From time to time these organizations issue public statements and resolutions urging the political parties or the government to follow a particular course of action. In more direct method the officials of the Federation of Economic Organizations and other groups meet both formally and informally with leading political figures and personally present their desiderata for government action.

LABOR ORGANIZATIONS

The basic objective of most labor unions is to endeavor to secure economic benefits for their members in the form of higher wages, security of employment, and improved working conditions. But, like other well-organized groups, labor unions are also endowed with the potentiality of exerting influence in the political arena. In fact, organized labor in Japan devotes considerable time and energy to political activities, but as yet its political effectiveness is not at all commensurate with the large number of workers who have become union members. An important reason for this state of affairs is to be found in the history and structure of Japanese unions.

Historically, the Japanese labor movement began at the turn of the century, but its growth was impeded by, among other things, a hostile atmosphere. Even at a 1936 high point union membership came to a little more than 400,000, and as a result of suppression unions practically ceased to exist during the war period.

Partly because of encouragement given it by the Occupation and partly in response to postwar economic and social conditions, the labor movement gained momentum after the end of the war. Today union membership totals some 7 million distributed among almost 40,000 unions.

A peculiar feature of Japanese unions is the preponderance of "enterprise" unions. The great majority of Japanese unions are organized on an enterprise basis, that is, all permanent employees, including white-collar, skilled, and unskilled workers, of a mine, shop, or factory, or of a company with several factories, are included in one union. Leadership in these unions, moreover, is often provided by white-collar employees who are better educated and more articulate and who often have ambitions of attaining management positions. Because of their structure and leadership, enterprise unions tend to be oriented inward with the result that the development of craft or industrial unions and a working-class ideology are impeded.

Enterprise unions can either remain independent or affiliate with national unions. National unions, in turn, can affiliate with large national federations. Both local and national unions sometimes shift their allegiance from one federation to another, and there are also instances of multiple affiliation.

At present there are two large national federations. The largest and most powerful is the General Council of Trade Unions of Japan, popularly known as Sohyo, and claims more than three and a half million members, which is about one-half the total membership of organized labor. The General Council has within it a great variety of unions, such as those of coal miners, metalworkers, automobile workers, and teachers. Its rival is the General Council of Japan Labor Organizations (Domei Kaigi) formed in 1962 as a result of the merger of the All-

Japan Trade Union Congress (Zenro) with several minor federations, including the National Council of Government and Public Workers' Union (Zenkanko). Historically these rival national federations go back to a common source because the All-Japan Trade Union Congress was formed in 1954 when the All-Japan Seamen's Union and the National Federation of Textile Industries Workers' Union split off from Sohyo. At present the General Council of Japan Labor Organizations claims a membership of just under one million and a half workers.

It may be said in general that the attention of the constituent enterprise unions is focused on economic problems, while the large national federations, especially the General Council of Trade Unions of Japan, concern themselves much more with political matters. Labor union leaders in Japan are ideologically oriented toward Marxism, and indeed one would be hard put to find a prominent labor leader in Japan who would publicly support the capitalist system. Hence, union leaders have maintained close ties with the Socialist Party and other left-wing organizations. But the leftist position of organized labor has not necessarily led to political unity. For one thing, national federations have shifted their political position from time to time according to the ideological point of view of those who happen to be in leadership positions. Moreover, the two rival federations often disagree on certain basic principles. The Domei Kaigi, for example, states that it supports a "free democratic labor movement," while Sohyo has sometimes joined hands with the Communists. Another area of disagreement between the two federations has been the question of the character of the Socialist Party. The General Council advocated that the Socialist Party should be a proletarian class party in contrast to the Trade Union Congress which wanted to see the Socialist Party become a national party appealing not only to workers but also to the middle class. The General Council of Japan Labor Organizations, which succeeded the Trade Union Congress in 1962, supports the Democratic-Socialist Party.

Because of differences in emphasis and interest between the local unions and the large national federations, labor is not nearly so effective politically as might be surmised. As an American observer has noted, "Enterprise unions, affiliated or not, do give a modicum of support to the national organizations simply out of recognition that political achievements favorable to labor serve to fortify their own effectiveness. This support, however, has been sporadic and largely cathartic, but seldom self-sustaining."[1] When one adds to this the fact that the national federations suffer from deep ideological differences, it is easy to understand that Japanese labor does not speak in unison.

FARM ORGANIZATIONS

Agriculture, like business and labor, has its own organizations which seek, among other things, to promote the interests of farmers. In the prewar period the most powerful farm group was the Imperial Agricultural Association (Teikoku Nokai), which evolved from several earlier farmers' associations created originally under government sponsorship. Established in 1910, the Imperial Agricultural Association was a national federation of agricultural associations organized on village, town, city, and prefectural levels.

The Imperial Agricultural Association acquired the reputation of being a landlord-dominated organization, and, according to a Japanese authority on agriculture, landlord influence was stronger at the higher levels, which were primarily concerned with political matters, and weaker at the lower levels, which were concerned mostly with technical matters involving farm production. Historically, an important function of the association was to help increase agricultural productivity, but it also became involved with rice prices and disputes between landlords and tenant farmers. Probably its most important function was to serve as a channel of communication between government bureaus interested in farm problems and the agricultural community and as an agency for distributing government subsidies to agriculture.

In the 1920s there also emerged "tenant unions" organized by socialists to defend the interests of tenant farmers against landlords. The Japan Farmers' Union (Nihon Nomin Kumiai), founded in 1922, fought for a reduction in land rents by using such methods as demonstrations, violence, and court action. The effectiveness of the Japan Farmers' Union, however, was reduced by internal dissension, caused in part by a shift in emphasis, over a period of years, from rent reduction to the socialization of land and from economic matters to political questions.

Like many other organizations, farm organizations felt an increasing amount of government control with the growth of militarism

---

[1] Solomon B. Levine, "Labor Patterns and Trends," *Annals of the American Academy of Political and Social Science*, Nov. 1956, pp. 110–111.

and the outbreak of the Second World War. In 1943 various farm organizations were combined into the Agricultural Association (Nogyo-
kai). This association, however, was abolished by law in 1947 and
was replaced by the Agricultural Cooperative Association (Nogyo
Kyodo Kumiai).

The Agricultural Cooperative Association consists of some 35,000
local cooperatives, with more than 8 million members. Although the
organization is set up primarily to act in matters related to credit, buying and selling, storage, insurance, food processing, and rural welfare, it has also become a potent political force in the rural areas. Most
of the leaders of the cooperatives are staunch supporters of the conservative Liberal Democratic Party, and hence cooperatives form
an important basis for continued conservative strength in the countryside.

WOMEN'S ORGANIZATIONS

Women were given the right to vote for the first time under the
provisions of the 1947 constitution. The granting of the franchise
to women enabled them to become active participants in the political process, and this development was reflected in the formation,
in 1948, of the Federation of Housewives (Shufu Rengo Kai), which,
as the name implies, is a national federation of women's organizations.
The federation includes several local organizations, mostly in the
Tokyo area.

The federation first attracted national attention in 1955 by its successful campaign to force dairies to reduce the price of milk. It made
arrangements with a small dairy to buy milk at wholesale prices and
then hired students and housewives to deliver the milk to consumers; in
this way it demonstrated to the public that milk could be sold somewhat cheaper. Shortly thereafter the large dairies announced a reduction in the price of milk. Today the federation is so well known
that when it sends a delegation to meet with the Prime Minister and
other important leaders to present political and economic demands
the delegation always gets a hearing.

STUDENT ORGANIZATIONS

Large-scale student participation in the demonstrations which led
to the cancellation of President Eisenhower's proposed visit to Japan
in the summer of 1960 revealed that in Japan, as in many parts of
Asia and Africa, students represent a potent political force. The or-

ganization in the main responsible for getting thousands of students out into the streets was the Zen Nihon Gakusei Jichikai Sorengo (All-Japan Federation of Student Self-Government Associations), commonly known as Zengakuren.

As its name implies, the Zengakuren is a national federation of student self-government associations which have been formed in many colleges and universities of the Tokyo and Osaka-Kyoto areas and in a few high schools. In some colleges, students automatically become members of a student association when they enroll, with the result that student organizations can acquire large memberships. At the organizing convention of the Zengakuren held in 1948, delegates from more than 250 colleges and universities claiming to represent some 200,000 students were in attendance.

Some of the activities of these student associations had to do with the welfare of college students, for example, improving student life and agitating against increases in tuition. But quite early the Japanese Communist Party decided to take an active part in student organizations, and as Communist influence increased, the Zengakuren became more and more politically oriented, and in the early 1950s the group organized strikes and mass demonstrations in support of campaigns against rearmament, the hydrogen bomb, centralization of the police, and so on.

Given the close ties between the Zengakuren and the Communist Party, it is understandable that schism within the Communist movement should be mirrored in the student organization. Following the Cominform criticism of the Japanese Communist Party in 1950, the Japanese Communists split into two factions, the so-called "main stream" and the "internationalists." The leaders of the Zengakuren followed the "internationalist" faction, that is, the minority faction, and because of this were accused by the party of being guilty of "petty bourgeois" tendencies. In retaliation, the Zengakuren refused to follow the leadership of the Japanese Communist Party.

In 1958 at the annual convention of the Zengakuren there developed a split between the group which stressed political action and the group which emphasized economic issues. The former came to be known as the "main stream" faction and the latter as the "anti–main stream" faction. Eventually the Zengakuren leaders belonging to the "main stream" were expelled from the Japanese Communist Party and accused of being "Trotskyites."

Thus the "main stream" faction in the Zengakuren regards itself as more radical than the Japanese Communists and indeed differs with them on several points of ideology. For example, the Japanese Communists speak of the possibility of peaceful coexistence between the Communist bloc and the West, whereas the Zengakuren "main stream" anticipates the outbreak of conflict between Communists and the "imperialist bourgeoisie." Another point at issue is the appraisal of imperialism. The Japanese Communist position is that Japan is under the domination of American imperialism and that the Japanese capitalists are junior partners, so to speak, of American imperialism. The Zengakuren leaders, on the other hand, argue that Japanese capitalism has reached the stage of imperialism and therefore the time is ripe for a Communist revolution in Japan.

PRESSURE-GROUP TACTICS

In order to get favorable legislative action and administrative decisions, interest groups resort to various tactics, most of which have a familiar ring to those conversant with American politics. A common maneuver is to resort to organized action. A group trying to apply pressure on the legislature to enact a particular bill might call a mass meeting of its members, pass resolutions, and send delegations with copies of such resolutions to call on the leading members of the government and the Diet. In case the organization has local regional branches, these branches are also likely to be mobilized; the local branches will also hold meetings and send letters or telegrams to Diet members and others.

A less dramatic maneuver, but one which is probably as important in the long run, is to cultivate friendly relations with key personnel in the government. Finally, many interest groups try to educate the public by printing and distributing propaganda pamphlets in order to get public opinion on their side.

Political Parties

PREWAR PARTIES

Political parties differ from pressure groups in that their objective is to get governmental positions for their leaders and in this way achieve control of the government. In Japan the idea of a political party was transplanted from the West, and the early 1870s saw the formation of political clubs and societies. These early political groupings laid the foundations for the creation of the Liberal Party (Jiyuto) in 1881, the Progressive Party (Kaishinto) in 1882, and the Imperial Party (Teiseito), a government-supported party, in 1882.

These parties were more or less voluntarily dissolved in 1885, partly as a result of continued government pressure against them and partly as a consequence of internal divisions, which were particularly acute in the case of the Liberal Party. In 1900 the Association of Political Friends (Seiyukai), which traced its lineage to the Liberal Party, was formed under the leadership of Prince Ito Hirobumi, who had played an important part in the drafting of the Meiji constitution. Like other oligarchs, Ito had been bitterly opposed to the idea of a political party, which to men of his political creed appeared to encourage disunity and weaken Japan in the community of nations. But Ito also recognized that the government needed support in the Diet once a parliament was established. Party leaders, on the other hand, had also come to understand that under the Meiji constitution the power of the Diet was to be greatly circumscribed, and hence they were more willing to compromise with the oligarchs. Those who had been affiliated with the Progressive Party did not regroup to form another party, but were content to join coalitions. Eventually between 1913 and 1915 the Constitutional Association (Kenseikai), which was the descendant of the Progressive Party, was organized.

The political parties reached the zenith of their power in the 1920s, and it appeared for a time that a full-fledged parliamentary form of government might eventually emerge. In June 1924 Kato Takaakira, who was president of the Constitutional Association and who had married into the Iwasaki family in control of the Mitsubishi industrial combine, became Prime Minister; from then until the assassination of Prime Minister Inukai Tsuyoshi in May 1932 party leaders headed cabinets, except possibly the one under General Tanaka Giichi. But even in this case, although General Tanaka was a professional soldier and not primarily a politician, he was also at the time president of the Association of Political Friends and hence enjoyed the backing of his party.

In this period the parties worked closely with the zaibatsu, who were the prime source of party funds. Large companies contributed liberally to party coffers, some supporting at the same time both the Association of Political Friends and the Constitutional Association in order to have supporters in the government no matter who won the elections. The alliance between the parties and the zaibatsu naturally caused the public to be suspicious that the government was partial to the interests of big business, and these suspicions seemed to be confirmed by the frequent charges of bribery and corruption that were aired in the Diet, principally by the party which happened to be in opposition at the moment. It was unfortunate that Japanese parties were forced to operate in an unfriendly atmosphere and with an institutional structure which impeded their attaining maturity.

The problems confronting the parties were accentuated by basic social changes which had taken place with quickened pace since the First World War. The growth of large cities, the beginnings of a labor movement, the creation of a white-collar class, and the spread of education and literacy brought increasing pressure for political participation on the part of those groups which had been denied the ballot. Most of the party leaders as well as the bureaucrats were reluctant to enlarge the electorate for fear that such a step would lead to social instability. But in the face of intense agitation on the part of the press in the large cities, urban intellectuals, and radical political groups, they were forced to enact a law in 1925 granting suffrage to all males 25 years of age and over.

It should be noted, however, that at the same time a Peace Preservation Law was also passed by the Imperial Diet to counteract the granting of suffrage. The Peace Preservation Law provided up to ten years' imprisonment for those convicted of joining societies or organizations advocating a change in the constitution, in the existing form of government, or in the system of ownership of private property. If the established parties hoped to prevent the emergence of radical parties by means of repressive legislation of this sort, they were mistaken, for the law granting universal manhood suffrage paved the way for the emergence of left-wing parties. Socialism had been imported into Japan, along with other social theories, as early as the turn of the century; and numerous socialist and anarchist-syndicalist groups had come and gone over the years. Now that the masses were put in a position of being able to participate in politics, if they so desired, the left-wing forces pushed forward with renewed vigor. However, although those on the left subscribed to Marxism, they were sharply split into several groups because of personal and doctrinal differences. In the 1928 general elections, the first held under the universal manhood suffrage act, four left-wing parties—ranging from the centrist Social Democratic Party (Shakai Minshuto) to the Communist-front organization, the Labor-Farmer Party (Rodo Nominto) —ran 88 candidates, but they succeeded in polling only about 500,000 votes, enough to elect 8 representatives to the lower house. In the years that followed, the left remained unable to achieve unity or to enlist significant popular support, and until its demise in the late 1930s, it never gained enough strength to pose a threat to the conservative parties.

The conservative parties were also afflicted by factionalism and general lack of sustained popular support. As has been noted, parties were unable to formulate constructive programs since the institutional structure prevented them from achieving significant control of the government. Moreover, their relative lack of control of the government dulled their sense of responsibility, encouraging party members in the government to engage in corrupt practices. It is therefore not altogether surprising that important sections of the public came to have little respect for political parties; and when the militarists made their bid for power after the invasion of Manchuria in 1931, parties were in a vulnerable position. The fortunes of both conservative and left-wing parties waned in the 1930s, and in 1940 they disappeared from the scene, having been amalgamated into the Imperial Rule Assistance Association (Taisei Yokusankai), a mild Japanese version of a totalitarian party. In the war period, the Imperial Rule Assistance Association was succeeded by the Political Association of Greater Japan.

POSTWAR PARTIES

With the abolition of wartime controls following Japan's surrender, old-line party politicians who had maintained informal groupings throughout the war period were now able to come together openly and reorganize parties. In the beginning literally hundreds of so-called "parties" were formed; but there eventually emerged two major conservative parties, the Liberal Party (Jiyuto) and the Progressive Party (Shimpoto), both of which were led by prewar politicians and both of which traced their lineage back to parties that existed in the 1920s and earlier.

Prewar left-wing leaders were also active in this period, and the non-Communist left succeeded in uniting sufficiently to form the Social Democratic Party (Nihon Shakaito). The Communists, who could not operate legally before 1945, now achieved legal status, and they quickly formed the Japanese Communist Party (Nihon Kyosanto), under the leadership of seasoned Communists who either had been released from jail or had returned from exile abroad. A small Cooperative Party, consisting of rural Diet members and those interested in the cooperative movement, was also formed in this period.

The first national election following the surrender took place in April 1946. The two conservative parties together secured 43 per cent of the vote and 234 seats in the lower house, and the Social Democrats managed to get 17 per cent of the vote and 93 seats. In the second election held one year later, the Social Democrats increased their strength to 143 seats, enough to become the largest single party in the House of Representatives. The two conservative parties, however, still held a combined total of 258 seats. The Social Democrats were therefore able to organize a government only by forming a co-alition with the Democratic Party (formerly Progressive Party). As this was the first time in history that they had obtained enough sup-port to install a socialist Prime Minister, the socialists were anxious to carry out their legislative program, which involved nationalization of some industries, but their efforts in this direction were thwarted mostly by the fact that they shared power with one of the conserva-tive parties. The coalition did not last long; and the cabinet was forced to resign in October 1948, giving way to the Liberals (now called Democratic Liberals) who had stayed out of the coalition. Table 2 gives the total votes obtained by the various parties in the five elec-tions that have taken place between 1952 and 1960.

The Liberal Party, under the leadership of Yoshida Shigeru, a former diplomat, went to the electorate in 1949 and won a vote of confidence by securing 264 out of a total of 466 seats. The Liberal Party victory was at the expense of the centrist groups, that is, the Democratic and the Social Democratic parties, whose number was reduced to 69 and 48 seats respectively. There was also a marked show of strength on the far left, for the Communists, who had never won more than 5 seats in any previous election, suddenly found them-selves controlling 35 seats in the lower house.

For the six years between January 1949 and February 1955 the Lib-eral Party held the reins of power, by virtue of its victories in elec-tions held in 1952 and again in 1953. In this period the opposition conservative party, the Democrats, held between 70 and 80 seats. The Social Democrats were weakened by a split into left-wing and right-wing Socialist parties. This split was caused by personal and doctrinal differences which were aggravated by the question of party attitude toward the San Francisco Peace Treaty ending the state of war between Japan and the Allied powers. The right wing favored the signing of a peace agreement even if it excluded Russia, whereas left-wing forces wanted an over-all agreement which would include the Communist countries as well as the free world.

The Liberal Party, like the Social Democratic Party, became torn by dissension as time went on. One cause was a growing feeling of antagonism to Yoshida's dictatorial methods. Perhaps an even more important reason was the difficulty that the party experienced in absorbing well-known members who were returning to political life following the rescinding of the purge. Thousands of individuals had been barred from public activities by the Occupation for having con-

Table 2. Election statistics, House of Representatives, 1952–1960

Party	1952	1953	1955	1958	1960
Democratic	6,429,450 *	9,240,920 †	13,536,044 ⎫	22,976,846 ‡	22,740,265
Liberal	16,938,221	13,476,428	9,849,457 ⎭		
Socialist					
Right-wing	4,108,274	4,677,833	5,129,594 ⎫	13,093,993 ‡	10,887,137
Left-wing	3,398,597	4,516,715	5,683,312 ⎭		
Dem-Socialist					3,464,147
Labor-Farmer	261,190	359,773	357,611	——	——
Communist	896,765	655,990	733,121	1,012,035	1,156,723
Minor parties	949,036	152,050	496,614	278,991	141,941
Independents	2,355,172	1,523,736	1,229,081	2,380,795	1,118,908

* In 1952 the Democratic Party was called the Progressive Party.

† These figures include the votes cast for the Progressive Party plus the votes cast for the Hatoyama faction of the Liberal Party.

‡ In 1956 the Democratic and Liberal parties merged to form the Liberal Democratic Party, while the right and left wings of the Socialist Party merged to form the Socialist Party.

tributed to the growth of Japanese militarism; but when Japan regained its independence the purge was rescinded, and this made it possible for purgees to return to politics. Understandably considerable tension was generated between those already in power in the Liberal Party and those who returned to the party after a period of absence. The upshot of the matter was that a dissident faction opposed to Yoshida bolted under the leadership of Hatoyama Ichiro, one of the founders of the Liberal Party who had been purged and replaced by Yoshida. This faction joined with the Progressive Party to form a new Democratic Party (Minshuto) in 1954. In the February 1955 elections, the newly formed Democratic Party gained 185 seats to become the leading party; the Liberals got 113 seats, the left-wing Socialists 89, and the right-wing Socialists 66 seats. The Communists, whose popularity had rapidly declined since the Cominform criticism of the party in 1950, secured 2 seats. Thus in 1955 the 467 seats in the House of Representatives were divided among two conservative parties, which together controlled the majority, and two socialist parties, which between them had slightly more than one-third of the seats, sufficient to block amendments to the constitution.

The logic of the situation suggested that the two conservative parties and the two socialist parties combine to form a large conservative party and an opposition socialist party. Negotiations had been going on among the socialists for some time to heal the breach between the left and right wings, but the two factions could not easily agree on a common platform. Finally, however, after lengthy conversations, a compromise was arranged and a unified socialist party was formed in the fall of 1956.

Socialist unity spurred the conservatives to settle their disagreements and create a single party that would compete with the left. Personal differences were particularly acute in the conservative camp, but after much wrangling the Democratic and the Liberal parties merged in November 1956 to form the Liberal Democratic Party, with Hatoyama Ichiro, who at the time held the post of Prime Minister, as its leader. Thus for the first time a "two-party system" emerged. This situation prevailed until 1959 when one faction left the Socialist Party to form the Democratic-Socialist Party. However, the splinter group, which took a middle-of-the-road position, did not do particularly well in the 1960 general elections, securing only 17 seats against 145 won by the regular Socialist Party.

As the foregoing historical sketch shows, parties have been formed, dissolved, and reorganized on numerous occasions in the short period after the end of the war. However, despite these changes the conservatives, except for one occasion, have remained at the helm. Why is it that in the competition for votes the conservatives have been relatively successful? There are several reasons; and one of these is that the conservative political ideology appeals to more people.

By definition conservatism is concerned with preserving what was established in the past and resisting change. In keeping with its conservative position, the Liberal Democratic Party has maintained that the Occupation-sponsored reforms broke too sharply with Japan's traditions. Accordingly, it has persistently sought to revive some of the prewar ideas and practices that were done away with under the Occupation. The conservatives, for example, have taken steps to bring about more centralization in the educational system. They have also indicated that they would like to amend the constitution, which they consider a document of alien origin, in order to strengthen the political position of the Emperor by changing his status from that of a "symbol" to the "head of the state."

In economic affairs, the Liberal Democratic Party has subscribed to a liberal philosophy which emphasizes individual initiative and free enterprise. But at the same time it has cut the ground from under its Socialist opposition by speaking in favor of a "welfare state" and the stabilization of the people's livelihood through governmental measures. Thus the party has come out publicly in favor of such social welfare measures as public health insurance, low-cost housing for workers, and expansion of care for the aged.

In foreign affairs, the Liberal Democratic Party has pledged continued cooperation with the free world. While it has favored the establishment of a small self-defense force appropriate to Japanese national strength, it has not campaigned vigorously for a full-fledged army and navy because it has realized that such a policy would run counter to public opinion. On the Communist issue, the party has declared itself to be opposed to communism and other antidemocratic activities. However, its anti-Communist stand has not deterred it from favoring increased trade with Communist nations, particularly the People's Republic of China.

The ideology of the Japanese Social Democratic Party differs substantially from that of its conservative rival. The Socialists contend that Japan is only nominally independent because foreign troops are stationed and foreign bases are maintained in Japan. They argue that monopoly capital, the capitalist class, and its instrument, the Japanese government, are under the control of the United States.

The Social Democratic Party looks upon itself as a class party led by the working class and supported by peasants, fishermen, medium and small merchants, and the intellectuals. However, it pledges to seek political power through democratic means.

The Socialists have consistently opposed agreements between Japan and the United States relating to problems of defense. They have also taken a strong stand against attempts to rearm Japan. Their argument is that Japanese security would be better assured if Japan were to negotiate security pacts with Soviet Russia and Communist China on a bilateral basis or if Japan were to conclude collective security arrangements involving Japan, Russia, and the United States.

The Socialists have affirmed that they stand for democracy, peace, and the preservation of the present constitution. It is somewhat ironical to find the Socialists, who are anti-American, defending the constitution, which was clearly American-inspired.

As for economic issues, the Socialists quite understandably have stated that their aim is to improve the people's livelihood, eliminate unemployment, and bring about other economic reforms. The difficulty with the Socialist position has been, however, that in recent years Japan has experienced remarkable economic growth and unprecedented prosperity under conservative leadership, with the result that Socialist appeals on economic ground have not elicited much response.

As is evident from the foregoing brief summary of the ideological positions of the two parties, a wide gulf separates the Liberal Democrats and the Social Democrats. The existence of this gulf has made it difficult for the two parties to work together in the Diet and has led to heated tempers and prolonged wrangling and on occasion to the outbreak of violence. When a party in power and the opposition party differ markedly on numerous basic issues, as do the two Japanese parties, the ability of the parliamentary mechanism to achieve some sort of accommodation between contending forces is usually severely tested.

PARTY ORGANIZATION

In terms of structure, Japanese parties are highly centralized. The headquarters of all parties are located in Tokyo, and although there are a number of prefectural and local party offices, the important work of the party is handled by the national headquarters organization.

The Liberal Democratic Party is led by its president, who is chosen by a party conference made up of party members elected to the two houses of the National Diet, plus delegates from the prefectural branches of the party. The election of the president is preceded by a good deal of behind-the-scenes maneuvering on the part of several party figures who lead the more powerful factions within the Liberal Democratic Party. At present there are, under the president, a number of important party officials, including the secretary-general, the chairman of the Executive Board, and the chairmen of the Political

Research Committee, the National Organization Committee, and the Party Discipline Committee.

The secretary-general's job is to keep the party machinery functioning, to help raise funds, to act as the party spokesman, to plan election strategy, to advise the president, and to negotiate with other parties. The secretary-general has a number of deputies to assist him in carrying out his duties.

The chairman of the Executive Board nominally oversees the work of the secretary-general and the Policy Research Committee and other prominent committees. The Executive Board shares with the party convention and the party caucus of Diet members the power to make high-level party decisions. In recent years, however, the Executive Board has been expanded in size to about forty members in order to enable various factions and groups within the party to be represented. It appears that as a result of the expansion in size the influence wielded by the Executive Board has declined.

The chairman of the Political Research Committee takes the lead in formulating party policy. The committee reviews and even drafts bills to be presented to the National Diet. The committee is organized into subcommittees which parallel the ministries and has a staff of research specialists.

The National Organization Committee has been elevated in importance, and its changing status represents an attempt to secure "grass-roots" strength for the party. This committee has established permanent prefectural branches in order to facilitate the recruitment of new party members, especially among the youth.

Many of the more routine tasks of the party are carried on by the headquarters staff, which works under the general supervision of the secretary-general. In terms of organization the staff is divided into a number of sections and divisions, such as youth, women, industry, labor, agriculture, publications, education, and so on.

Despite efforts in recent years to build a mass basis, the local organization of the Liberal Democratic Party is still weak. It was claimed in 1959 that the party had 2,200 chapters with more than 1.5 million registered party members. These claims, however, appear to be exaggerated, and the number of individuals who are actually enrolled as party members and pay dues regularly is probably closer to 300,000.[2]

[2] See Robert A. Scalapino and Junnosuke Masumi, *Parties and Politics in Contemporary Japan* (Berkeley and Los Angeles: University of California Press, 1962), pp. 83–85.

The Socialist Party does not have a president, and the official who is usually considered the leader of the party is the chairman of the powerful Central Executive Committee. Under the chairman is the secretary-general, who is in charge of the headquarters staff and who wields considerable power.

The Socialist Party's Policy Deliberation Committee corresponds roughly to the Political Research Committee of the Liberal Democratic Party. The committee, which is divided into a number of sub-committees, not only deliberates on pending policy questions, but also deals with the party platform and other problems such as the relation of the party to labor unions.

Like the conservative party, the Socialist Party has many local branches. Although the true situation cannot be certainly known, their local organizations appear to keep in closer touch with the Tokyo headquarters than do the branches of the Liberal Democratic Party. It is said that there are about 50,000 members formally registered on the roster of the Socialist Party and that of this group perhaps 30,000 pay their dues regularly. The party reputedly hopes to increase its dues-paying membership to about 100,000 persons.

Both parties hold conventions periodically (usually once a year) for the purpose of electing officers and passing on party policy. In general, conservative party conventions are cut-and-dried affairs, and beyond providing publicity for the party and an occasion for party members to get together, they do not seem to serve as a device for determining policy. The Socialist Party conventions, on the other hand, are often characterized by stormy sessions, with much argument and debate.

THE SOCIAL BASIS OF PARTIES

As already noted, there is at least from the ideological point of view a substantial difference between the conservative and the socialist parties. The former is committed to the perpetuation of an economic and social order based on capitalistic principles, and the latter seeks to reduce drastically the role of private capital. One would surmise, therefore, that these two parties would appeal to and obtain support from different social and economic groups. Because the element of personal loyalty often exerts a powerful influence, the picture can sometimes be distorted, but it may be said in a very general way that there exists a relationship between parties and social and economic groups.

The conservative party considers itself a national party and seeks support from all strata of the population. The conservatives are backed most heavily in rural communities, where traditional values persist and where the type of politician frequently found in the conservative camp has an appeal. Data taken from public opinion polls, from interviews, and from firsthand observation by journalists and others suggest that at least one-third to one-half of those engaged in agriculture and fishing prefer the conservatives. Since just under one-half of Japan's population still lives in rural communities, agrarian support is a important asset. It is also true, however, that in recent years the socialists have gained strength in certain rural areas. The change in sentiment may come in some instances from the movement of industry into the countryside and in other instances from the influence exerted on their kin by younger sons of farm families who have migrated to the cities.

Another important source of conservative strength is provided by the owners of commerical and industrial establishments in the towns and cities. The historical development of capitalism in Japan was such that small individually owned and operated enterprises survived in the face of industrialization and the growth of large industrial combines. Support from this segment of the population is important because in the smaller business enterprises, where a high degree of paternalism characterizes employer-employee relationships, employers are often able to influence the political attitudes of those who work for them.

Finally, conservative forces enjoy the support of high-level administrative personnel in government agencies and of corporation executives. Some corporations contribute funds to both parties, but there is no question that large corporate enterprise is on the side of conservatism and that it helps fill the coffers of the party, especially when an election is about to take place.

On the other hand, the Socialists, in keeping with their commitment to Marxist principles, explicitly seek to base their power on the working class. The Socialist Party enjoys the open support of many labor unions, including the General Council of Trade Unions of Japan (Sohyo), which boasts more than 3 million members. Labor unions, moreover, represent an important source of financial aid for the Socialist Party.

The fact that most labor union leaders identify themselves with the socialist cause, however, does not automatically determine the political attitudes of the rank and file. Available data indicate that somewhere between 40 and 45 per cent of the industrial workers favor the

Socialist Party. By and large it is those workers employed in large plants who are most class-conscious and inclined toward socialism.

Additional socialist support comes from intellectuals—professors, writers, and students. In recent decades the Japanese intellectual world has felt the strong impress of Marxist thought, with the result that it is a little unfashionable to be an intellectual and not cast one's lot with the socialists.

Finally, the Socialist Party has made inroads into the urban white-collar class. The complexity of Japanese industrial organization has fostered the need for numerous salesmen, clerks, office workers, and other specialists who are forced to live on low incomes and with relatively little job security. To many of these people the socialist program and promises have strong appeal.

In view of the foregoing relationship between political parties and social groupings, a sudden shift in the present balance between conservative and socialist forces appears unlikely, barring, of course, a cataclysmic change, such as a serious economic depression. It should be noted, moreover, that the present allocation of seats in the lower house works to the decided advantage of the conservatives. That is, the present allocation of seats between the urban and rural electoral districts is based on the distribution of population in the years immediately after the end of the war when large cities had lost much of their population owing to the air raids during the war. With the return of evacuees to the cities and continued cityward migration from the rural areas, the major Japanese cities have grown greatly in size in recent years. This urban growth, however, has not been reflected in the number of representatives sent by large city districts to the House of Representatives. The result has been gross underrepresentation of the big cities' vote, and since the urban areas represent the strongholds of the Socialists, this institutional arrangement has naturally worked to the disadvantage of the Socialist Party. Understandably there has been a good deal of agitation in favor of reapportionment, but since the present system operates to the advantage of the conservatives who control the House of Representatives, the chances that reapportionment will take place appear to be slim. Thus continued conservative strength seems assured.

It is also worth remembering that time seems to be on the side of the socialists. Further industrialization will undoubtedly enlarge the working class and gradually reduce the number of those engaged in agriculture. There is, moreover, a rough correlation between socialist support and the amount of formal education, and as the educational level of the nation rises the number of those who will turn to socialism should also rise. Historical experience also seems to show that in Japan those who have just reached voting age tend to vote for radical candidates, whereas the older age groups tend to vote for the conservatives. The present age composition of the Japanese population is such that the number of individuals who reach voting age every year far exceeds the number of individuals who die. Mathematically, therefore, the left-wing forces are acquiring new supporters while the conservatives tend to lose supporters through death. The net socialist increase is, of course, reduced by the shift of voters from the socialist to the conservatives as they grow older. A rough calculation of the relative annual change in party support has been made as follows—these are very crude calculations, but they suggest that if the present trend continues the left wing will gain about 500,000 votes per year. In 1955, conservatives obtained some 11 million more votes than the socialists and other radical parties. In 1960, however, the conservative edge over the radical parties was reduced to about 7.25 million votes. And thus, if the present trend continues, time appears to be on the side of the socialists. But it would also appear that the day when they will win a majority of seats in the House of Representatives is some years distant.

· VII ·

The Power Structure

WHENEVER a group of men seek to work together to achieve common objectives, there is a need for leadership. A few individuals must give directions for the majority to follow; otherwise various individuals are likely to work at cross-purposes to the detriment of the common ends. Social action, therefore, calls for leaders, but at the same time a man cannot be a leader without having followers. Thus power always involves human relationships. The relationship cannot be equal, however, for by definition the leader is the one who exercises a stronger voice in group decisions, partly by consent and partly by constraint.

In surveying the power structure of the Japanese state the situation at the local level will first be considered, then the national level, and finally the relationship between the local and national levels.

Political Power at the Local Level

In Chapter IV the relation of the individual to the group was considered, and it was pointed out that, as a rule, the individual is subordinated first to his family and then to informal local groups. Under these circumstances, an individualist who insists on following the dictates of his own conscience will often find himself ostracized and excluded from community affairs. Conversely, a willingness to cooperate and conform to accepted norms of behavior will lead to social approval. Thus it may be said that social behavior, particularly in rural areas, is highly circumscribed by tradition, custom, and community sentiments concerning what is proper and improper.

Among these sentiments are notions about the kind of persons who should hold leadership positions. Robert Ward notes that there "exist in almost all buraku [hamlets] one or more elders who are generally regarded as outstandingly wise and experienced in all lines and particularly in respect to matters such as village or prefectural politics which transcend the normal daily experience of most members of the community." [1]

Traditionally, in rural Japan, landed property and long residence in the community were determinants of social prestige and political influence, and important local government posts were rotated among a few families which possessed these qualifications. This is still true to some extent today. For example, a tenant farmer has been quoted as saying, "It is a commonplace that all official positions should be circulated among those who, having inherited wealth from their ancestors, are regarded as 'gentlemen' [*danna*], even though they may be stupid." [2]

The fact that members of long-established landed families generally enjoy power is in part because the people in the community expect them to take the responsibility of leadership and in part because those who belong to such families have at their disposal certain economic levers. Landed families often rent a portion of their holdings to tenant farmers, and this gives them a certain economic power, for the tenant's livelihood depends on the willingness of his landlord to continue to rent land to him. Moreover, since credit is difficult to obtain, wealthy families can use their loan-making ability in order to enhance their influence in the community. The exercise of power is seldom brutal and naked, but is tempered by a sense of paternalism, and there is always a degree of give-and-take between the influential and the influenced.

Not all local leaders come from long-established landed families. Both the postwar land reform program, which reduced large landholdings, and social changes, which have invaded the countryside as well as the cities, have contributed to modifications in leadership. In

---

[1] Robert E. Ward, "Patterns of Stability and Change in Rural Japanese Politics," in University of Michigan, Center for Japanese Studies, *Occasional Papers*, no. 1 (1951), p. 4.

[2] Masamichi Royama, *Noson Jichi no Henbo* [Changes in Local Government in Rural Areas] (Tokyo, 1948), p. 16.

some areas local shopkeepers, schoolteachers, Buddhist priests, and others not typically landowners can now be found among the local political elite. In any case, whatever their occupational background, there are everywhere in rural areas local leaders who are able, by the use of material wealth or the manipulation of political symbols, to affect the electoral behavior of the people in their area and influence decisions made by political bodies with which they are affiliated.

A somewhat similar situation with regard to the structure of power may be found in sectors of society other than rural communities. An interesting study of the Japanese labor-boss system among construction workers shows how a building contractor in paying low wages makes his workers dependent upon his "benevolence" and how the contractor acts as a kind of "father" to his workers by mediating their quarrels, finding wives for unmarried workers, personally taking care of them when ill, and in general looking after their welfare.[3] Hence in this case a highly personalized reciprocal relationship has been established between the boss and his workers, and the power relationship thus established can be utilized for political ends if and when it is to the advantage of the boss to do so. Similar social situations may be frequently found in fishing villages, in mining towns, and among gangs of hoodlums and racketeers.

The subordination of the individual to the group is buttressed by an ideology which places value on social harmony. Individuals who insist on their "rights" and bring dissension into the open are not welcome. For this reason, appeals to law and the courts to settle quarrels or to seek redress of wrongful acts are much less frequent than might be supposed. The socially approved way to seek solutions to these problems is through mediation and compromise with the help of local elders and other leaders. Thus, as was mentioned in an earlier chapter, there often exists what might be called "informal government" at the local level. Many problems, such as the bringing of sanctions against those who violate the mores, the adjudication of disputes, and to some extent the provision of social welfare measures, are handled by "informal government" without their being brought within the purview of the formal institutions of government.

Another consequence of the preference for social harmony is the avoidance of majority rule in arriving at group decisions. As one observer notes: "In Japan it is considered brash for an individual to make

[3] Iwao Ishino and John W. Bennett, *The Japanese Labor Boss System* (Columbus: Ohio State University Research Foundation, 1952).

a definite, clearcut decision regarding himself or others. He must maintain a reserve (enryo) and must restrain his own opinions." [4] Consequently, a group does not come to a decision through open debate of the issues involved, followed by voting. Rather a group decision is arrived at by consensus, with the chairman more or less "divining" the unexpressed will of the group.

In this connection, the following quotation taken from a news account of Hatoyama Ichiro's election as president of the Liberal Democratic Party is illuminating: "His election, however, did not come about as many of his supporters might have wished. Contrary to traditional unanimous installation of a new president in keeping with a prearranged understanding the choice this time took the form of balloting, which also publicly exposed intra-party strife." [5]

One result of this system of decision making is that unity is often very superficial and that not all those who participate in the decision are prepared to abide by it. Apparently many people believe that it is not inconsistent to agree to a course of action in a meeting and then ignore it as soon as the meeting is disbanded.

Political Power at the National Level

The tone and character of national politics depend to some extent on the men who are at the helm. As has been noted, in the Meiji period power came to be concentrated in the hands of an oligarchy which stemmed in the main from the younger men of the samurai class in several fiefs of western Japan. Although the establishment of a parliament in 1890 provided an institutional structure for a wider sharing of power, in practice the oligarchy managed to keep a tight hold on the government, at first by monopolizing the most important executive posts and later by manipulating their protégés from behind the scenes. For example, of those leaders who held cabinet posts between 1885 and 1918, about 55 per cent came from four geographical areas—the former feudals fiefs of Satsuma, Choshu, Tosa, and Hizen. It was not until about the end of the First World War that the influence of the oligarchy disappeared from the political area.

Among those who fell heir to the control of the government with the passing of the oligarchs were the higher bureaucrats, an overwhelming proportion of whom were graduates of Tokyo Imperial Uni-

[4] Fred Kerlinger, "Decision-Making in Japan," *Social Forces*, XXX, no. 1 (Oct. 1951), 38.

[5] *Japan News Letter*, no. 14 (April 6, 1956).

versity; senior army and navy officers; and party politicians, some of whom had previous experience in or connections with business. Very clearly, men with different backgrounds joined the ranks of the elite; yet it is doubtful that they represented an essentially new type of leadership. Robert Scalapino has succinctly characterized the political leaders of this era as follows:

Japanese leaders have never been accepted on the basis of their ability to sway the minds and hearts of the masses; rather, public speech-making and oratory have been classified as vulgar by a large proportion of the political elite. Neither has independent thought and action achieved acclaim. The leader prototype has been a man distinguished by age, culture, and character—an individual with many "connections" and a capacity for intricate behind-the-scenes negotiations.[6]

As the foregoing passage suggests, Japanese leaders did not base their power on a mass following, but rather on establishing and maintaining connections with other elite individuals and groups. It was as if there was a silent conspiracy to keep the masses out of the picture and prevent them from having a voice in important political decisions.

The Allied Occupation, on the other hand, with a different political philosophy, purposefully sought to widen the base of the power structure. Woman suffrage was granted for the first time; institutional changes described in Chapter V were undertaken in an attempt to make the government more responsive to the public will; and, finally, many prewar leaders were removed, at least temporarily, by the purge. Moreover, the hold which the military had on the government was destroyed, and this paved the way for resumption of full civilian control of the government. Thus, defeat and occupation provided an almost unprecedented opportunity for new leadership to come to the fore.

Since institutionally the National Diet occupies a strategic place in the power structure, it would be instructive to see what changes have occurred in its personnel. As a result of the purge in 1945, a little over 90 per cent of the prewar Diet members affiliated with the Progressive Party and some 44 per cent of those in the Liberal Party were denied the right to hold public office. It is not surprising, therefore, that in the first postwar election held in 1947 many "new faces" were elected. Of the 141 successful Liberal Party candidates, 102 or 72 per cent were newcomers. The percentages for the Progressive Party and the

---

[6] Robert Scalapino in *Modern Political Parties*, ed. by Sigmund Neumann (Chicago: University of Chicago Press, 1956), p. 328.

Social Democratic Party were even a little higher, running about 76 per cent in both cases.

Various types of people were represented among the newcomers, but an important group were men connected with business, either as owners of enterprises or as corporation executives. In fact, there has been a long-term trend in the direction of larger representation of businessmen in the Diet. It is difficult to get accurate statistical data on the occupational background of Diet members, for many of them are engaged in several occupations. Table 3, however, gives a rough outline of general trends. As might be expected, the conservative party roster has more businessmen and corporation executives, whereas the Socialist Party proportionately more lawyers and, recently in particular, officials of labor unions.

Table 3. Occupational background of the members of the House of Representatives, 1937–1949

Occupation	1937	1942	1946	1947	1949
Government officials	9	23	17	39	15
Members of armed forces	3	—	—	—	—
Doctors, pharmacists	10	7	14	7	4
Authors, publishers, journalists	51	61	30	35	34
Lawyers	87	70	51	46	43
Bank and corporation employees	72	87	109	116	153
Employees in commerce and industry	17	27	—	25	54
Agriculturalists	80	74	62	50	37
Mining employees	2	—	—	—	2
Educators	8	12	35	12	14
Other occupations	54	46	88	102	92
No occupation	73	59	38	34	36
Total	466	466	464	466	466

Source: *Jiji Nenkan*, 1952, p. 720. (The discrepancy in the columns for 1946 and 1949 between the figures and the total are not explained by the editors of the *Jiji Nenkan*.)

Between 1950 and 1951 the purge was rescinded for many individuals, and thus they were enabled to return to political life. In the 1952 national elections a little over 30 per cent of those elected from the two conservative parties, the Liberal Party and the Progressive Party, were so-called depurgees. In the 1955 national elections about 65 per cent of the successful candidates of the Democratic Party had prewar political experience, and a little less than 40 per cent of the Liberal

Party representatives had been active in the prewar period. That so many could make a successful comeback after some seven years of absence from public activity perhaps testifies to the essential continuity of political life in Japan.

When the uppermost levels of the elite structure are examined, evidence of continuity is even more apparent. Among prominent leaders of postwar parties have been such men as Ashida Hitoshi, Yoshida Shigeru, Shidehara Kijuro, and Shigemitsu Mamoru, all former foreign office officials; Hatoyama Ichiro, a prominent prewar politician; and Kishi Nobusuke, an ex-bureaucrat, who was purged by the Occupation authorities. Ikeda Hayato, who became Prime Minister in 1960, is also an ex-bureaucrat who had spent many years in the tax bureau. Scalapino notes that "conservative party leaders thus far have been older men whose political experience was first established in the prewar period. Age, experience (though not necessarily political party experience), and access to funds continue to be primary qualifications for conservative leadership in Japan."[7]

The situation with respect to top leadership in the Social Democratic Party is essentially no different. In his study of Japanese socialist leadership, George Totten concludes:

When one considers, for example, the dozen or so top leaders in each wing [of the Socialist Party], the proportion of prewar leaders is striking: only one of the Right Wing was not a party functionary before the war, while only one-fourth of the Left were not. The observation that even today's Japanese Socialist leadership stems largely from the prewar generation is borne out by the fact that 70 per cent of the Right and 45 per cent of the Left are over fifty years old, and of the dozen top-rank Right Wing leaders, all except Sone are close to or over sixty.[8]

With the possible exception of the left wing of the Socialist Party, the top levels of political parties in Japan have not been strengthened by the infusion of new blood. As already indicated, institutional change has occurred. Yet it is a fact that many people who hold key positions within the institutional structure are those who by prior experience and training are more likely to feel at home in the old structure. If the parties are to develop effective programs and win the confidence and support of the electorate, they will, of necessity, need to recruit new and energetic leaders. Furthermore, if and when new types

[7] *Ibid.*, p. 341.
[8] George Totten, "Problems of Japanese Socialist Leadership," *Pacific Affairs*, XXVIII (June 1955), 160–161.

of leaders are recruited, they will probably reach the top through particular channels. The conservative parties have four major sources of leadership recruitment.

(1) *The bureaucracy.* Since under the new constitution the majority of cabinet members must also be members of the National Diet, cabinet status, which carries with it high honor and great prestige, is denied to career civil servants. Hence, bureaucrats who have ambitions of becoming cabinet ministers must at some point run for a seat in the National Diet. Since about 1949 the number of ex-bureaucrats in the conservative parties has increased appreciably, until in recent years they represent about one-fourth of the members of the House of Representatives belonging to the Liberal Democratic Party. The influence wielded by ex-officials in the top levels of the party is even more noticeable. In four cabinets organized between 1957 and 1960 ex-bureaucrats have held about one-half of the cabinet posts. Thus it would appear that so long as the public continues to place higher value on those who hold or have held official positions, the bureaucracy will probably continue to be an important source of party leaders.

(2) *Business.* Over the long term, an increasing number of businessmen have been getting seats in the House of Representatives. With the high cost of election campaigns, as well as expenses such as entertainment, which burden those in office, men who have outside sources of income enjoy an advantage. In the postwar period representatives with a business background have been drawn from among owners of small- or medium-sized business establishments and from the middle ranks of big business.

(3) *The professions.* Of those with professional backgrounds, lawyers and journalists tend to predominate. Lawyers have a natural affinity for a job which primarily involves lawmaking. Lawyers are also able, as a rule, to maintain their practice even while holding a seat in the Diet, and this is helpful from the point of view of income. Journalists, on the other hand, can become well known through their writings and thus are in a position to capitalize on their fame for political purposes.

(4) *Local politics.* Local politics provides a suitable setting in which young ambitious politicians can acquire experience and prestige. In the case of Japan, changes in the institutional structure achieved under the Occupation have enlarged the arena of local politics. For example, in the postwar period many local government posts, such as governorships of prefectures, which were formerly appointive

have become elective. In addition, there has been a trend recently in which candidates for local office run under a party ticket rather than as independents. Thus a number of ex-governors, ex-prefectural assemblymen, and other locally elected officials have succeeded in obtaining posts in the National Diet. Yet in the over-all picture, the ex–locally elected official has not been as important as the ex-bureaucrat in recent years. One reason for this may be, as Scalapino and Masumi suggest, that the ex-bureaucrats are closer to the central government and to the "national interests" while the ex-prefectural and local officials are more closely related to local interests and local pressure groups.[9]

These same channels are, of course, available to socialist leaders, but as might be expected, there are fewer such leaders drawn from the bureaucracy or business. For the left wing of the Socialist Party, trade unions have been an important steppingstone. Many young socialist leaders have risen in the union hierarchy and then have run for office with the support of organized labor. In general, however, the socialist cause has been hampered by its inability to attract in large numbers men who have distinguished themselves and have won the admiration and respect of leading members of the community.

In the final analysis, it must be admitted that the choice of men who are put into positions of responsibility is partly related to popular attitudes regarding political leadership. It is therefore instructive to consider the matter of electoral behavior.

Electoral Behavior

Japanese writers often describe electoral behavior by reference to the three "ban," namely, *kamban* or signboard, *jiban* or foundation, and *kaban* or satchel.

Kamban, or signboard, poster, or billboard, signifies the candidate's reputation and his standing in the community. A man who has had a distinguished career as a government official, or is a prominent businessman, or is the head of an important local organization can get votes because of his name. For instance, a "big name" has an advantage particularly in the election to the House of Councilors from the nation at large. In this kind of election, *kamban* is often more important than party label, political ideology, or issues.

It used to be that candidates who were unsure of their standing

[9] Robert A. Scalapino and Junnosuke Masumi, *Parties and Politics in Contemporary Japan* (Berkeley and Los Angeles: University of California Press, 1962), p. 74.

could add to their drawing power by getting prominent individuals to speak on their behalf in their district. However, a legislator, who presumably knows from experience, has stated that nowadays voters are not so easily fooled.[10] One would suppose that voters are getting more sophisticated, for prior to the war a man who had been a cabinet minister was almost certain to be elected, but recently there have been instances where ex-ministers have not made the grade at election time.

The "attraction" exerted on voters by a candidate as an individual may be crudely measured in several ways. For instance, there are the results of a survey made on the eve of the 1949 national elections in an industrialized section of Tokyo. Voters were asked whether they cast their ballots for a candidate or for a party, and the answers have been tabulated in Table 4. As is shown, somewhere between one-fifth

Table 4. Basis for voting: candidate vs. party

Age of voter	For candidate		For party		For both candidate and party		Don't know		Other	
20–24	22%	(33%)*	30%	(41%)	25%	(21%)	23%	(5%)		(0%)
25–29	25	(33)	31	(47)	2	(20)	11	(0)		(0)
30–39	33	(39)	39	(40)	21	(19)	7	(1)		(1)
40–49	52	(34)	17	(42)	20	(21)	11	(3)		(0)
50–	48	(37)	15	(33)	20	(9)	17	(12)		(10)

* The figure in parentheses shows percentage of workers as distinguished from the population at large. The figures for the population at large in the 25–29 age group and for workers in the 50 and over age group do not total 100 per cent. The discrepancy is not explained by the author of the article.

Source: Ukai Nobushige, "Koba rodosha no tohyo kodo," *Sekai*, no. 84 (Dec. 1952), p. 93.

and one-half of those questioned said that they voted for the candidate himself. There seems to be a tendency—less obvious in the case of workers—for older voters to prefer to vote for candidates rather than for party affiliation.

Another way to get an idea of the personal influence which affects electoral behavior is to take the case of a candidate who has switched parties. Hirano Rikizo, a well-known socialist who had been active in the prewar period, ran for the House of Representatives in 1947 as a socialist and received 58,916 votes, to head the list. But he was purged by the Occupation for his wartime activities and therefore was

[10] Kan'ichi Tsuji, *Jingasa* [Rank and File] (Tokyo, 1953), pp. 37–42.

unable to continue political life until 1952, when he ran on the Co-operative Party ticket. Even though the Cooperative Party was a minor party, obtaining only 1.2 per cent of the national vote, Hirano was able to win his seat with 47,183 votes. In the next election in 1953 he returned to the socialist fold and campaigned under the right-wing Socialist banner, polling 40,727 votes. In 1955, however, he changed his affiliation to a minor party and failed to be reelected since he received only 20,794 votes. The case of Hirano demonstrates the ability of a candidate with a name to get votes regardless of changes in party affiliation, but it also shows that strength based on a personal following can decline suddenly.

A third example of the personal factor in voting is the strong sup-port a candidate often gets from his "friends and neighbors." Localism is still a strong factor in Japanese politics, and many people tend to vote for the candidate who lives in their immediate vicinity, pre-sumably on the theory that such a candidate is most likely to best represent local interests.

A run-down of election statistics indicates in numerous instances a close relationship between vote-getting ability and the place of resi-dence of the candidate. Table 5 showing the distribution of votes in

Table 5. Relationship between place of residence of candidates and votes cast, 1955

| City or town | Successful candidates | | | |
	J. Koizumi (Democrat)	S. Shimura (Left Socialist)	T. Noda (Democrat)	S. Yamamoto (Democrat)
Yokosuka-shi	38,234 *	17,149 *	5,245	17,370
Kawasaki-shi	8,592	27,116	31,948 *	15,192
Kamakura-shi	2,453	4,678	10,808	9,925 *
Zushi-shi	3,287	2,781	3,127	3,014
Miura-shi	3,130	2,603	793	3,314
Hayama-machi	1,863	835	869	1,222

* Total vote cast at place of residence of the candidate.

the second electoral district in Kanagawa prefecture illustrates this relationship. In this district two out of the four successful candidates polled very heavy votes in their home areas.

Thus it can be said in a very general way that personal qualifications are often important; but it is also true that the personal element is not equally important for all voters. The tendency to vote for candidates rather than for party is more pronounced among older voters and among peasants, fishermen, and owners of small business enterprises. On the other hand, government officials, urban white-collar workers, teachers, students, and industrial workers are more apt to vote along party lines.

The second "ban" is *jiban,* or foundation or footing, and it refers to the political organization that a successful politician needs if he is to be returned to office several times. In order to be sure of securing the necessary number of votes on election day, a politician must make himself popular with the electorate and especially with influential community leaders. One legislator has written that he carries a notebook containing 400 names of prominent individuals to whom he writes frequently. So that he could learn to know the people in his district, the same legislator studied photographs he had taken whenever he attended important social gatherings.[11] A frequently used tactic is to send picture postcards to voters, particularly when a potential candidate goes abroad. There are stories to the effect that conscientious politicians going on foreign trips have their aides at home cable lists of names of persons who were inadvertently overlooked when postcards were sent out.

There are other techniques of winning voter approval. A politician who wants to be successful must make it a point to attend public functions, speak to organized groups, such as women's groups, send flowers to funerals of prominent local leaders, contribute generously to worthy causes, distribute gifts, make social calls on such occasions as New Year's Day, entertain local dignitaries who come to visit the Diet when it is in session, find jobs for worthy young men, and do chores for constituents, such as interceding on their behalf with government agencies. The following account describes how a former representative from Tokyo, Takagi Masutaro, built his political organization:

This man [Takagi] was very thorough in what he did for elections. During festivals he was the first to present an offering with his name inscribed on it. At school graduations, he distributed cake, decorated with his name, among students. Naturally he went around making calls during the New Year holiday season; and he always assisted at weddings and funerals. During the Diet sessions he always mounted the rostrum several times. Whenever the interests of the townspeople were involved, he would attend the committee sessions, even if he was not a member of that particlular com-

---

[11] *Ibid.,* p. 36.

mittee; and he would have a transcript of the meetings distributed among the voters.[12]

As present electoral districts (for the House of Representatives) are fairly large, embracing in some instances a whole prefecture, a politician cannot hope to establish close personal ties with every voter. He must therefore rely on others to get out the vote for him on election day. A member of the lower house, for example, will have several followers, whom he more or less controls either through personal ties or through financial aid. Such followers may be active in prefectural politics, perhaps holding a seat in the prefectural assembly, and they in turn will have followers operating at a lower level, in city and town politics, for example, and so on down the line until there will be at the base of the pyramid informal neighborhood groups, tradesmen's organizations, women's groups, and the like.

No doubt it takes diligent effort to build a *jiban,* but once built, it often lasts. There have been instances in which a political organization has been inherited by a politician's widow or son and even by a favored disciple.

The third "ban" is *kaban,* or satchel, which symbolically holds money to use for election purposes. In Japan, as in the United States, large sums are needed to carry on a successful election campaign. Every candidate must open campaign headquarters, print and distribute thousands of posters and leaflets, entertain friends and supporters, and rent sound trucks to go up and down the streets calling out the candidate's name and urging voters to cast their ballots for him. There is also, in some instances, vote buying, either directly or through so-called "election brokers." A big item of expense is money needed to lubricate the political machine. Those at the top levels of the organization must provide funds for their immediate followers, who in turn pass on a portion of what they receive to their followers, down to the lowest levels of the organization.

Because money almost always lies at the root of political corruption, attempts have been made to regulate by law the amount candidates are permitted to spend on a campaign. To determine the total amount legally allowed, one divides the number of registered voters by the number of representatives elected from that district and multiplies by 4 yen. Everyone assumes that no candidate takes such legal limits

[12] Yoshinao Washio, ed., *Seikai Gojunen: Kojima Kazuo Kaikoroku* [Fifty Years in the Political World: The Memoirs of Kojima Kazuo] (Tokyo, 1951), p. 248.

seriously, and one legislator says that five to six times the amount permissible by law is generally enough.[13]

Attempts are also made to control election expenditure by requiring political parties and organizations to report to the government contributions received. These reports show that the conservatives collect funds from individual wealthy businessmen, from corporations, both large and small, and from trade associations. The socialists, on the other hand, are supported in the main by labor unions, which often assess each member for this purpose. Some corporations contribute to both the conservatives and the socialists. In addition, individual candidates raise money from sundry sources. Since about a thousand candidates compete for seats in the House of Representatives, a large amount of money goes into circulation every time an election is held.

The Determinants of Voting

The individual voter must now be considered, to determine if possible what makes him vote the way he does. As in the United States, tradition is one of the elements, although in Japan loyalty seems to be focused more on individuals than on party labels. For instance, some voters who have been consistently supporting a political leader will transfer their support to a son who succeeds him.

An element which is probably growing in importance is economic interest. The conservatives generally favor the interests of business and of property holders, and thus it is not surprising that businessmen, landowners, corporation executives, and higher bureaucrats tend to vote for conservative candidates. The socialists, because of their Marxian orientation, think of themselves as basically a class party built around the proletariat. Surveys show that socialists tend to be favored by organized workers in large plants, but that those employed in small establishments where a paternalistic relationship exists between owner and employee are more likely to prefer conservative candidates. As might be expected, the conservative strength is centered in the rural areas, whereas the industrialized cities form the strongholds of the Socialist Party.

A third element which may determine the way one votes is manipulation by others. There are always some individuals—found most often in small rural communities—who will vote according to instructions from other people, either out of indifference or of fear. For some

[13] Tsuji, *Jingasa,* p. 42.

voters, politics, especially at the national level, is difficult to understand and remote from problems of everyday life. Accordingly, they are easily persuaded by a local leader to vote for a particular candidate, as can be seen from the following account by Paul Dull:

As elections approached, the *senkyoya* [local political boss] made known the candidate he supported. However, the statement of advocacy was couched in the proper symbols, symbols to which his followers would respond. There was nothing so crude as the *senkyoya's* telling his followers to vote for a candidate. The *buraku senkyoya* [political boss of the hamlet] might be politically sophisticated (although not necessarily so); the *buraku* [hamlet] inhabitants were, for the most part, unaware of the dynamics of politics and merely responded to their leader's words conveyed through proper symbols such as a candidate's idealism, sincerity, past reputation, and his willingness to work for the tangible benefit of the *buraku*.[14]

In some instances actual coercion takes place. Let us assume that a local bigwig has promised to deliver a certain number of votes to a candidate. This local leader will then ask voters in his area over whom he can exercise persuasion to vote for his candidate, using as leverage such things as power to control credit. In rural communities it is not too difficult for a local political boss to find out whether or not a voter has actually followed his instructions. A local leader, for example, has been quoted to the effect that when a voter has cast his ballot as he has been told he will usually drop in on the way home from the polls to report the fact, whereas someone who has not will avoid him.[15]

Finally, the way in which institutional arrangements affect voting behavior must be examined. At present Japan is divided into 118 electoral districts which send between three and five representatives to the lower house. Each voter, however, writes in the name of only one candidate. This means that a candidate needs the support of merely a minority of voters in his district to be among the top three or five. The percentage of votes necessary to win will depend, of course, on the number of candidates running and the spread of votes among them.

Many Japanese voters do not like to "waste" votes, that is, they are reluctant to support a man who seems to have no chance of winning

[14] Paul S. Dull, "The *Senkyoya* System in Rural Japanese Communities," in University of Michigan, Center for Japanese Studies, *Occasional Papers,* no. 4 (1953), p. 30.
[15] "Aru Mura De Kiku" [We Heard in a Certain Village], *Asahi Shimbun,* Jan. 6, 1955.

or a man who is likely to win by a wide margin. There have been instances in which a candidate who secured the largest number of votes in one election dropped very low in the following election. Campaigning, therefore, becomes a tricky art, and candidates try to avoid giving the impression that they are sure to win.

The Legislative Process

One of the functions of elected officials is lawmaking, and it is pertinent to know something of the way in which these men make the laws. In present-day Japan, bills which are put into the legislative hopper may originate in several places. An individual member may present a bill if it has the approval of 20 or more members in the lower house and of 10 or more members in the upper house. Bills necessitating an appropriation of funds call for 50 and 20 signatures respectively. Proportionately the number of bills actually submitted by individual Diet members is small. Other sources of bills are the various committees of the Diet, policy research committees of the political parties, and the cabinet.

The great majority of bills are sponsored by government agencies and come to the Diet via the cabinet. In the course of their operations, bureaus and agencies may find that they must carry out some administrative action or that existing legislation is inadequate or unworkable. In such an instance, a section or a bureau in a ministry will draft a bill, very often with the assistance of the Bureau of Legislation. This bureau is under the cabinet, and its job is, among other things, to see that the proposed measure is in line with existing legislation, that it has no loopholes, and that it is technically and legally correct. After the bill has been discussed at various levels within the ministry concerned and has secured the backing of that ministry, it is sent to the cabinet.

In the case of important bills, steps are taken to get the views of outsiders through the medium of advisory committees. These committees—consisting of scholars, government officials, and representatives of various groups—can make known their views or, if they are so asked, can even draw up detailed provisions of the proposed law.

At the beginning of each Diet session, the cabinet gets a list of bills presented by the ministries and agencies. Those bills that are carefully drawn up and meet no opposition from other agencies usually stay on the list, are approved by the cabinet, and eventually are introduced in the Diet.

When a bill reaches the lower house, it is referred to an appropriate committee on the recommendation of the Ways and Means Committee. If the Ways and Means Committee believes the bill to be of such importance that it should be brought to the attention of all legislators as well as the public, it may be explained in a plenary session before it is referred to a committee.

As a part of its deliberations, the committee will often hold public hearings to give interested parties an opportunity to present their views, and it may summon cabinet members and other officials to provide information and answer questions. After the committee has approved a bill by a majority vote, it is put on the calendar and in due time comes before a plenary session of the Diet.

The chairman of the committee will report to the plenary session the decision of the committee, together with a summary of the deliberations. If there is a minority report, this will also be placed before the plenary session. A motion to amend the bill must have the support of at least 20 members in the lower house (10 in the House of Councilors); a bill calling for appropriations or an increase in appropriations must have 50 supporters in the lower house and 20 supporters in the upper house. Members who wish to speak on the bill must, as a rule, ask the secretariat of the House of Representatives to put their names on the list which the Speaker will use in recognizing members. The Speaker can limit the time allotted to those speaking, and an effort is made to give equal time to both proponents and opponents of the bill. When the debate comes to an end, members will vote on the bill; usually those in favor will be asked to stand. When the vote is close, however, or when more than one-fifth of those present take issue with the Speaker's decision, voting is by ballot. As soon as a bill is passed by one house, it is sent to the other.

Voting in the Diet is strictly controlled by political parties. Chitoshi Yanaga writes:

In the Diet the party caucus, which is the center of practical party politics, is used constantly. For the Japanese who have a strong predilection for consultation in making decisions in any sphere or any level, the party caucus is a natural procedure. Without it, it would be impossible to manage political affairs. Members of the Diet are rigidly bound by the decisions of the caucus and few dare to disregard them.[16]

[16] Chitoshi Yanaga, *Japanese People and Politics* (New York: Wiley, 1956), p. 267.

Bureaucratic Behavior

Although the Diet makes laws, often it is the bureaucracy which draws up proposed legislation; and it is certainly the bureaucracy which administers laws put on the statute books by the legislature. As Carl Friedrich says, "All realistic study of government has to start with an understanding of bureaucracy (or whatever else one prefers to call it), because no government can function without it." [17]

The Japanese bureaucracy has certain characteristics which affect its role in the political system. Before the war the bureaucracy was a closely knit organization, staffed largely by graduates of Tokyo Imperial University with training in law. As a result, civil servants took a highly legalistic approach to administrative problems, and in cases in which there was no statute or precedent to provide guidance, decisions were delayed. Although in the postwar period graduates from other universities have entered the civil service in somewhat greater numbers, many of the top posts are still held by Tokyo University graduates, and the bureaucracy remains to a large degree parochial and legalistic in its outlook.

Traditionally officials held an exalted place in society, and, accordingly, they were arrogant when dealing with the public. Under the 1947 constitution, "all public servants are servants of the whole community and not any group thereof," but in practice the notion that a bureaucrat is a "public servant" remains somewhat alien to Japanese mentality. Japanese government agencies still have much to learn about public relations and the art of becoming more responsive to public wishes and needs.

A third characteristic of the Japanese bureaucracy is its fragmentation. The various sections, bureaus, and ministries which make up the administrative structure are highly jealous of their status and prerogatives. One branch of the government will often refuse to share information and reports with other branches, so that sections within the government will be working at cross-purposes or will be duplicating work. In many instances there is little or no coordination of governmental activities.

In Japan, as elsewhere, what government does or fails to do affects the interests of many people. For example, the government regulates, directly or indirectly, all kinds of economic activities through its power

[17] Carl J. Friedrich, *Constitutional Government and Democracy* (Boston: Little, Brown, 1941), p. 57.

to grant licenses, its control of foreign exchange, its allocation of subsidies, its purchases of goods and services for defense and other needs, and so on. Given the nature of the bureaucracy, it is to the advantage of those who have frequent dealings with government agencies to establish close personal ties with important government officials.

There are several ways by which this may be achieved. In the past, companies hired bureaucrats, who by custom retired from government service in their forties and fifties, for the purpose of maintaining personal connections with agencies. One account states that "enterprising businessmen offer comfortable posts—virtual sinecures—to pensioned officials in exchange for public favors arranged through their junior colleagues who remain in service." [18] The National Public Service Law enacted in the postwar period attempts to discourage this practice by prohibiting an official for a period of two years from taking a post with a firm which had dealings with his agency.

Another method is to become well acquainted with important officials by entertaining them lavishly. Businessmen have been known to send their private cars to government offices to pick up officials and take them to golf courses and geisha parties. The newspaper *Asahi* once quoted a businessman as saying that if anyone wants to have an application acted upon "you have to become so friendly with officials that you can pick up the telephone and get section chiefs and bureau chiefs to act." [19]

Finally, a more permanent and institutionalized relationship between a government agency and interest groups is established through organizations known as *gaikaku dantai* or auxiliary organizations. The Ministry of Agriculture, which distributes large sums as subsidies, is said to have some 300 such organizations attached to it. These organizations, which get financial aid from the government agencies, help to provide liaison between a particular agency and the public concerned with its work and also furnish certain services such as publishing reports—some of them written by government officials—and specialized journals and magazines. Another link between government agencies and these auxiliary organizations is supplied by civil servants who retire from government service and take jobs as officers of such organizations. Finally, these organizations serve as convenient steppingstones

[18] Hugh H. MacDonald and Milton J. Esman, "The Japanese Civil Service," *Public Personnel Review,* Oct. 1946, p. 223.

[19] In the Dec. 31, 1954, issue.

to elective office. For example, an administrator in the Ministry of Agriculture may first become an officer of one of the auxiliary organizations connected with the ministry and then use his contacts with the farm population to get support for his candidacy.

· VIII ·

Problems of

Contemporary Japan

ANY government, if it is to survive, must be able to provide reasonably workable solutions to problems that confront the nation. In the case of Japan the tasks of statesmanship are formidable, for the problems to which solutions must be found are deep-seated and difficult. Because it is beyond the scope of the present work to treat these matters in detail, four topics—in the field of the economy, defense, foreign relations, and domestic political problems—which appear to be particularly significant will be discussed briefly in this chapter.

Economic Problems

Japan's economic goals are no different from those of many other nations, namely, to provide stable employment, economic and social security, and a rising standard of living for its population. It goes without saying that to attain these goals Japan must have a viable economy.

As is well known, Japan, especially when compared to the more fortunate nations like the United States which are well endowed by nature, is rather poor in resources. Japan is deficient in most of the raw materials required by the industrial machine and is dependent upon foreign sources for raw cotton, raw wool, rubber, bauxite, and phosphate rock. Japan must also import much of the iron ore, salt, zinc, and petroleum it needs and about one-third of the coking coal.

In order to pay for these essential imports Japan must convert raw materials into manufactured goods and sell them to foreign customers. Another way to pay for imports is to furnish services, such as

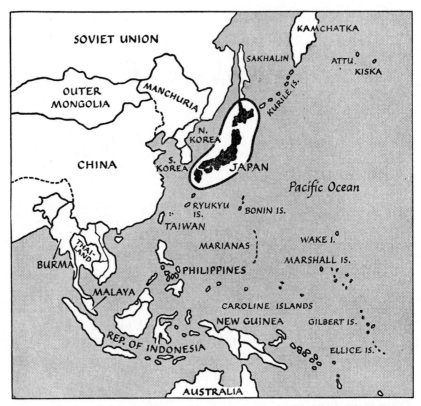

Map 6. Present area of Japan. (As redrawn from the *New York Times.*)

carrying ocean freight in Japanese-owned merchant ships, repairing jeeps and aircraft for the American forces based in Japan, and so on.

When the Japanese surrendered in 1945, the economic picture looked bleak indeed. During the war, the major cities, which were the centers of industry, had been severely damaged or even destroyed by the Allied bombing raids. Moreover, following the defeat, investments in Manchuria and China and elsewhere were confiscated, Japan's colonial empire was gone, and the traditional markets were no longer available to Japanese exporters. Despite these handicaps, Japan has achieved a remarkable recovery. In recent years Japanese economic growth has been far more impressive than that of the more advanced nations of the world, including the United States, and has reached in the best periods an amazing figure of 17 per cent annual increase in the gross national product.

How is this economic recovery to be explained? Without making any claims for comprehensiveness, one might cite the following as among the more important reasons.

First, Japanese agriculture has become increasingly productive. In the early 1950s, as much as one-fifth of Japan's food supply had to be imported, and this meant that Japan's valuable foreign exchange reserves were being used to help feed the population. But in recent years, Japanese farmers have been applying new techniques—the use of plastics to cover the ground to discourage the growth of weeds is an example—with the result that the country has experienced a series of bumper rice crops. Japan, therefore, has become more nearly self-sufficient in terms of food requirements; and, needless to say, the farmers have become more prosperous in the process.

Second, the domestic market for goods and services has been expanded appreciably. As suggested above, farmers have more money to spend for equipment, housing, and even television sets and refrigerators. The same situation applies to many workers. The growing strength of labor unions has steadily forced up wages, at least among those workers who are unionized. Rising wages, coupled with the introduction of installment-buying practices, have enabled many a wage worker to buy consumer goods such as electrical appliances which he could not previously have afforded. One also suspects that Japan's need to divert only a relatively small portion of its national income to national defense has enabled the government to spend more money for social services, and this in turn has had the effect of raising the standard of living of the Japanese people in general. In any case, it is clear that compared to the prewar situation Japan's domestic market is significantly more important.

Third, the introduction of advanced technology from abroad has greatly stimulated economic growth. Early in the 1950s Japanese industry began to modernize plant and equipment, particularly in the steel, electric power, and chemical industries. Today many of Japan's industries are up to date technologically speaking and able to compete favorably with industries in the United States and Europe.

Fourth, the role of government in encouraging business enterprises ought not to be overlooked. Traditionally government has aided industry, and this practice is still maintained. The government has helped industry largely through financial aid in the form of low-interest loans and even outright subsidies. For example, the shipping industry, which was virtually destroyed during the war, was able to make a comeback in the postwar period thanks to the generosity of the government.

Fifth, the world-wide demand for goods and services greatly enhanced opportunities to expand Japan's exports to foreign countries. The economic depression in the 1930s followed by the widespread destruction of goods and equipment during the war had created an almost unsatiable demand for goods in every part of the world. In such a situation, a country like Japan which possessed technological knowledge and an ambitious and energetic population was in a position to help meet the accumulated demand. This may be seen from statistics relating to Japan's export trade, which was at the $1.2 to $1.3 billion level in the early 1950s, but had reached the $4 billion figure in 1960.

Sixth, the contribution of the United States in the form of military spending and outright aid ought to be mentioned. American aid is a factor which Japanese writers tend to gloss over, but it would appear to be vital in helping to explain Japan's economic recovery. In the fifteen-year period between 1945 and 1960 the United States sold to Japan roughly $10 billion worth of goods and commodities. In return for this the United States obtained from Japan roughly $6 billion in goods, resulting in a deficit of about $4 billion. The Japanese were able to make up a part of this deficit by providing shipping and other services. The remainder (and larger portion of this deficit), however, was accounted for by outright U.S. aid and by the funds which the armed forces spent in Japan. In short, if Japan had not received American aid and had not allowed American forces to be stationed in the country, the Japanese would not have been able to pay for all the raw cotton, coal, iron ore, machinery, and many other items which they obtained from the United States.

The foregoing are some of the more obvious reasons which help explain Japan's recent economic success. But of course Japan has by no means solved all economic problems, and prosperity has not been without some drawbacks. For one thing Japan, which for a long time was known as a country where labor was abundant and cheap, now faces something of a labor shortage. High school graduates are partic-

ularly needed to fill semiskilled positions in electronics and other industries, and labor recruiters have been visiting high schools in search
of prospective employees. Labor shortage has tended to boost wages
paid to factory workers, and this in turn has accelerated the flow of
manpower from the farms to the factory. Over the long run Japanese
farming population has declined, as it has in the United States, but
if too many youths quit the farm to seek more lucrative employment
in the cities before farm mechanization can make up for lost manpower, Japanese agriculture, which has become so productive in recent years, could suffer a setback.

Another consequence of prosperity is that expectations of an ever-
increasing standard of living have been aroused among the population. Those who have been able to acquire refrigerators, washing machines, and television sets have now changed their goals to camping
outfits, air conditioners, and family automobiles. It is worth noting
that the conservatives, who are more sensitively attuned to popular
moods than their opposition, the socialists, have sought to capitalize
on the mass desire for a better material life. In 1960 the Economic
Deliberation Council, an advisory organ of the government, issued a
ten-year plan whose stated objective is to double the national income
between 1961 and 1970. According to this plan, the government will
set the goals and will help private business attain these goals by reducing business fluctuations through appropriate monetary measures
and by promoting social security and welfare programs.

It is recognized that certain structural changes will have to take
place in the Japanese economy if the target of a 100 per cent increase
in the national income is to be achieved by 1970. For example, there
will have to be a movement of workers into manufacturing and service industries. Above all, both imports and exports, particularly the
latter, must be greatly expanded. It is at this point that a good deal
of uncertainty enters the picture. In recent years the United States
has become Japan's best customer, but if America should suffer a
recession or if protectionist sentiment should become predominant,
the American market for Japanese goods could dwindle substantially.
As for Europe, the growth of the Common Market could result in
discouragement by European countries of the importation of goods
from Japan.

In short, the future growth of the export trade is beset with uncer-
tainties, and perhaps it is this uncertainty about the future that im-
pels many Japanese to cast glances at the Communist bloc, and

especially Communist China. Before the war, China—parts of which were under the direct or indirect control of Japan—was an excellent market for consumer goods and a source of raw materials, including coal, iron ore, and soybeans. Understandably many Japanese businessmen look back with nostalgia on the prewar China trade and argue in favor of increased trade with Communist China.

Since the end of the Second World War, Japan's trade with the Chinese mainland has remained at a low level, partly because of political reasons. For one thing, Japan does not recognize the Peking regime. The Japanese are also aware of American attitudes toward Communist China and hence are careful of American feelings in this matter. Finally, given the present state of the Chinese economy, even though Communist China could use all kinds of imports from Japan, it would have difficulty in paying for such imports. American economists tend to feel that the China market does not hold much promise for Japan.

Nevertheless, there exists a feeling among many Japanese that Japan must develop more trade with Communist China.[1] Indeed, this feeling is so strong that the conservative government has permitted private trade delegations from Japan to make barter arrangements with the Peking government and from time to time has made public statements expressing the desire to increase trade with the Communist Chinese.

In summary, it can be said that although in the recent past Japan's economic situation has brightened markedly, prosperity could turn out to be a somewhat ephemeral thing. Japan's basic problem, which is to buy raw materials from abroad and sell finished goods to foreign customers, still remains. And since the future growth of Japan's export trade will be determined in no small measure by conditions which are not subject to Japanese control, Japan's destiny to that extent rests in the hands of others.

Defense Problems

Because of its large population, its industrial capacity, and its strategic position off the continent of Asia, Japan cannot remain aloof from international developments, particularly as they relate to the Great Powers. Japan must necessarily consider the problem of national defense in a world marked by tension. Yet it must be noted

---

[1] See Douglas H. Mendel, Jr., *The Japanese People and Foreign Policy* (Berkeley and Los Angeles: University of California Press, 1961), ch. ix.

that the Japanese, despite their long record of militarism, have shown in the postwar period a preference for international cooperation and even for pacifism. They have begun to rearm only with reluctance.

The recent history of Japan's defense problems has been characterized by curious and ironical twists and turns. After the end of the war the aim of the United States and other nations was to destroy Japan's ability to wage war, and toward that end steps were taken to demobilize completely the Japanese armed forces. A provision was even written into the 1947 constitution renouncing forever "war as a sovereign right of the nation and the threat or use of force as a means of settling international disputes."

Within a few years, however, American policy was reversed because of increased tension between the United States and the Soviet Union and the Chinese Communist victory on the mainland. In June 1950, two weeks after the outbreak of war in Korea, General MacArthur authorized the creation of a National Police Reserve of 75,000 men. This marked the beginning of Japan's rearmament.

Since then there has been a gradual strengthening of Japan's armed forces. In 1952 the National Police Reserve Force was changed to a National Safety Force of 110,000 men, equipped and organized with American help. At that time seven frigates were also leased to Japan by the United States in order to provide the beginnings of a Japanese navy. Two years later, in 1954, the National Safety Force was changed into the National Defense Force, and provisions were made for an air force. In terms of size Japan's defense forces are still small, numbering a little over 200,000 men in uniform within the three branches.

To achieve even this modest build-up required extensive political maneuvering on the part of Japanese leaders. The socialists have consistently argued in favor of a policy of "neutralism," although some have advocated "armed neutralism" while others have stood for "unarmed neutralism." In any case, the socialist position has been squarely against large-scale rearmament. It is important to realize that in their stand the socialists have been supported by numerous intellectuals, women, and young men. There are probably not many Japanese who would advocate complete disarmament or go so far as to abolish the present National Defense Force; but, on the other hand, there is no popular enthusiasm for a full-fledged defense establishment.

Resistance to large-scale rearmament rests on both psychological and financial grounds. Many people share the underlying fear that rearmament will ultimately lead to the revival of militarism and that the government will again be dominated by professional soldiers. There is also the fear that rearmament will invite attack and invasion rather than prevent it. Those who think along these lines argue that it would be easier to avoid involvement in case of another war if Japan had no army, navy, or air force. Finally, some resist rearmament in the belief that Japanese forces might be used less to defend Japan's national interest than to further the policies of other nations such as the United States.

As has been mentioned, financial considerations also affect thinking on the problem of rearmament. The high cost of modern weapons of war such as radar, jet planes, guided missiles, and so on imposes a heavy burden on small nations like Japan. Because the United States has been contributing to the total cost of rearmament, Japan's outlay, although it has been increasing over the years, is still not very large. In recent years defense outlays have ranged between 10 and 15 per cent of the annual budget and between 1 and 3 per cent of the national income. However, Japan's defense costs seem certain to increase steadily in the future.

In view of the slow military build-up of Japan's armed forces, the main burden of the defense of the country has in actual practice been borne by the United States. At the time of the peace treaty with Japan in 1952 which formally ended the war, the United States signed a security treaty with Japan which provided, among other things, for the maintenance of American forces and bases in Japan, the use of American forces stationed in Japan to help maintain peace and security in the Far East (meaning Korea, Formosa, and the Ryukyus), and the use of United States forces to put down domestic revolts should Japan request such assistance. Although there was no explicit statement in the treaty which obligated the United States to defend Japan, the presence of American forces and bases most certainly served to deter an attack on Japan from without.

The Japanese reaction to these defense arrangements was not one of unqualified gratitude. The presence of foreign troops and bases offended the Japanese sense of nationalism. There was the thorny question of the jurisdiction of American personnel involved in crimes against Japanese citizens and property. There was dissatisfaction with the provisions in the treaty providing for the use of Japanese-based American troops outside of Japan and with the proviso for the use of American troops to put down domestic rebellions. There was also much controversy over the possible storing and use of nuclear weapons by American forces stationed in Japan.

These dissatisfactions eventually resulted in protracted negotiations between the two countries looking forward to a revision of the 1952 treaty. Finally, in 1960, a new security treaty was agreed upon. Unlike the first treaty, which had no terminal date, this one was to run for ten years. The United States expressly agreed to defend Japan. The treaty does not, however, commit Japan to defend the United States; Japan is to act only in territories under its control and to the extent allowed by the 1947 constitution. The United States was granted continued use of its bases and other facilities in Japan. On certain other matters, the United States agreed to "consult" Japan. Prior consultation is required, for example, in the deployment of Japan-based United States troops, in making major changes in weapons (i.e., the introduction of nuclear weapons), and in the use of bases for purposes other than the protection of Japan. The provision for prior consultation does not necessarily give the Japanese government a veto, but at the time of the signing of the treaty, a joint communiqué was issued by President Eisenhower and Prime Minister Kishi stating that the United States "has no intention of acting in a manner contrary to the wishes of the Japanese Government with respect to the matters involving prior consultation under the treaty."

The new treaty became a center of controversy in Japan. The socialists and other leftists attacked it on grounds that the United States would use Japan as a base for military operations in other parts of the Far East, that the United States would bring in nuclear weapons, and so on. Even some of the factions within the ruling Liberal Democratic Party had reservations about the treaty. The controversy, which had given rise to sporadic demonstrations led by socialists, labor unions, and the student organization, Zengakuren, reached its climax in May 1960 when Kishi Nobusuke, then Prime Minister, pushed the ratification of the treaty through the House of Representatives. President Eisenhower had announced that he would visit Japan on June 19; Prime Minister Kishi, moved by a desire to have the treaty ratified before the President's visit, called the lower house into session on May 20 (because a treaty becomes effective 30 days after passage by the House of Representatives) to act on the treaty. Since the socialists lacked the necessary votes to prevent ratification, they resorted to violence on the floor of the lower house to forestall action. At this point the Prime Minister ordered 300 policemen to clear the chamber of opposition members, and then his followers voted approval of the security treaty.

Kishi's action aroused the wrath not only of the socialists but also of the press and large sections of the public. He had also antagonized some of the powerful factions within his own party. Gigantic demonstrations aimed at both Kishi and the treaty broke out in Tokyo. When James Haggerty, the President's press secretary, arrived in Tokyo on June 10, thousands of demonstrating students surrounded his car and he had to be rescued by a U.S. Marine helicopter. After this episode, President Eisenhower's proposed visit was cancelled and Prime Minister Kishi was compelled to resign.

Although the treaty was ratified and will remain in effect until 1970, the fact that it aroused so much controversy and even led to the outbreak of violence suggests that the problem of defense is by no means settled. It seems safe to say that one of the major tasks confronting political leaders in Japan is to achieve some kind of national consensus on the vital question of Japan's defense in a world beset by tension and hostility.

Foreign Relations

Historically Japan has gone through extended periods of relative isolation from its neighbors. Even today many Japanese might find it preferable, given the world situation, to adopt an attitude of Swiss-like neutrality and avoid involvement in the power struggles among nations. However desirable such a policy might be in solving some of Japan's problems, it would be difficult to carry out. Many factors compel Japan to have continuing contacts with foreign countries— strategic position, the fact of being the most industrialized nation in Asia, dependence on foreign trade for very existence. More than many other countries, Japan is confronted with the problem of maintaining friendly relations with neighboring nations.

It is therefore unfortunate that several external and internal factors tend to impede the development of amicable relations between Japan and other countries. For instance, continued tension between the United States and its allies and the Soviet bloc has posed diplomatic problems. The policy of the conservative government in Japan is to maintain an alliance with the United States. As has been noted, Japan is heavily dependent upon the United States for national security. In addition, Japan has become closely tied to the United States in terms of economics. The United States is Japan's best customer, and Japan is America's second-best customer. Thus defense problems and economic ties pull Japan toward the United States.

At the same time Japan cannot completely ignore the Communist bloc because of geographical proximity. In these days of jet aircraft and guided missiles, Japan literally lies at the doorstep of Soviet Russia and Communist China. There are also domestic pressures from socialists and others who want a more "independent" policy. Japan therefore must arrive at some kind of working arrangement with its neighbors to the west and northwest.

Japan's relations with Russia in the past have been marked by a good deal of mutual hostility. In 1950 Russia and Communist China signed a treaty ostensibly aimed at "Japan or any nation allied with Japan." The Russians also refused to sign the peace treaty in 1952 and then persistently vetoed Japanese efforts to become a member of the United Nations, a maneuver which delayed Japan's entry into the UN until 1956. There were also several other issues between the two countries. The Russian seizure of several small islands north of Hokkaido was resented. For some years the fate of Japanese prisoners of war taken by the Soviets in the closing days of the war caused anxiety in Japan. Finally, the exclusion of Japanese fishing vessels from waters bordering on the USSR became a source of friction.

Between 1954 and 1956 talks were begun which looked forward to the settlement of some of the issues. The result was an agreement in 1956 whereby the state of war that legally existed between the two nations was terminated, diplomatic relations were resumed, and the Japanese were given rights to fish in certain Russian fishing grounds. The agreement also opened the way for the renewal of trade relations, and in recent years barter arrangements have been worked out, the Japanese getting raw materials such as coal and timber in return for machinery. But it is clear that genuinely friendly relations between the two countries cannot be achieved so long as Japan is closely tied to the United States. For instance, in 1960 the Soviets denounced the U.S.-Japanese security treaty as a military alliance against the Communist bloc.

The situation with respect to Communist China is somewhat different. Japanese feelings toward China have been affected by a number of considerations. For one thing, Japan has been under the cultural influence of China for many centuries. The Japanese also feel a racial affinity to the Chinese. Then there are some feelings of guilt with respect to Japanese behavior in China during the war. The result is that there appears to be relatively little fear of Communist China as a potentially aggressive power. The answer of the Japanese to arguments that Communist China represents a military threat is that they are not afraid because they "know" China through long association or that China is somehow "different" from Russia.

There is the added factor of potential trade with Peking, which has already been discussed. But Japan cannot promote trade on a large scale so long as the Japanese do not recognize the Peking regime. Moreover, Japan has been doing a substantial amount of business with Taiwan, to which Japan has accorded diplomatic recognition. Thus Japan's dilemma is that while on the one hand there is the desire to encourage trade with Communist China, on the other hand Japan does not want to antagonize the United States or Chiang Kaishek's regime based on Formosa. Ideally Japan would like to recognize "two Chinas," the Taiwan government and the Peking regime, but it is highly unlikely that Peking and Taiwan would agree to such an arrangement.

In the meantime, Chinese Communist policy has been to try to neutralize Japan and to remove American influence from that country. Toward this end Peking has tried a number of tactics, including working first through the Japan Communist Party and more recently through the Socialist Party which has advocated recognition of Communist China. Cultural exchange has also been used, and thousands of Japanese, including conservative businessmen, have been invited to visit China, while Chinese delegations have also come to Japan. These delegations have been welcomed by a number of Japanese organizations, such as the Japan-China Friendship Association and others, established to promote better relations between Japan and Communist China.

The future of Sino-Japanese relations will of course be determined in part by developments taking place in other parts of the world, but it is also worth noting that Yoshida Shigeru, when he was Prime Minister, stated that "Red or white, China remains our next-door neighbor. Geography and economic laws will, I believe, prevail in the long run over any ideological differences and artificial trade barriers." [2]

Japan's relations with its nearest neighbor, South Korea, have been characterized by mutual hostility. The so-called Rhee Line has proved

---

[2] Yoshida Shigeru, "Japan and the Crisis in Asia," *Foreign Affairs*, XXIX, no. 2 (Jan. 1951), 179.

to be an important point of dispute. This boundary line, established by the then President, Syngman Rhee, lies from 60 to 170 miles off the Korean coast, and Japanese fishermen are forbidden to enter the waters thus set off. Fishermen who have crossed this boundary have been seized and imprisoned. Conflicting claims over property and the treatment of Koreans residing in Japan have also engendered hostile feelings between the two countries. The United States is allied with both countries and because of the antagonism between Japan and Korea has sometimes been placed in a difficult position.

Relations with the countries of Southeast Asia will have a vital bearing on the economic future of the Japanese nation. Potentially Southeast Asia could provide some of Japan's raw materials, now procured elsewhere, and would absorb more Japanese manufactured goods as well as services. In countries such as the Philippines and Indonesia, the legacy of hatred toward Japan inherited from wartime occupation and the fear of possible revival of Japanese militarism have been greatly diminished in recent years. Agreements reached between Japan and the Southeast Asian countries for the payment of reparations by Japan have also helped to bring about more cordial relations.

Without doubt, the maintenance of friendly relations with the United States is of utmost importance from the Japanese point of view. Fortunately, when all things are considered, the two nations have succeeded to a remarkable degree in achieving harmony. This does not mean, however, that there are no areas of dispute. As has been suggested, the maintenance of military bases and the stationing of United States troops in Japan is likely to continue to be a problem.

Another issue of some duration has involved the testing of atomic weapons in the south Pacific. For understandable reasons, the people of Japan are particularly sensitive to atomic weapons, and public opinion is easily aroused on the subject. On numerous occasions Japan has protested the testing of these weapons because of the fear of fallout and the contamination of fishing grounds. Left-wing political groups have used this issue to create an image of the United States as a callous and warlike nation.

A third source of friction is the American occupation of Okinawa, which lies southwest of Japan. Okinawa was the scene of the last great battle of the war in the Pacific theater and after its seizure was converted into a mighty American military base. Under the terms of the San Francisco Treaty, "residual sovereignty" of Japan over Okinawa was recognized, with the implication that eventually the territory would be restored to Japan. But, in the meantime, the United States controls the area through the High Commissioner of the Ryukyus, who is the army commander on the island. Most Okinawans think of themselves as Japanese and would probably prefer that the island revert to some kind of Japanese administrative control. Indeed, the local legislature which was established by the United States to meet the demands of the Okinawans for local self-government has passed resolutions urging reversion to Japanese control. In Japan itself the government has taken the position that Japanese administration should be gradually exercised over the civilian population in Okinawa but that the American right to maintain bases there would be honored. It is to be hoped that American policy in the future can be so shaped that it would satisfy at least some of the desires of the Japanese and the Okinawans.

Political Problems

In a sense much of what has been said about the Japanese government and politics in the preceding chapters has explicitly or implicitly touched on a number of important political problems that confront the Japanese at the present time. But perhaps it would be appropriate in bringing the discussion of Japan to a close to take up briefly the question of the future of democracy in Japan.

Democracy as an idea is not exactly new in Japan. The writings of many of the leading Western political philosophers—Rousseau, Mill, Spencer, Bentham, Burke, and others—were translated, studied, and discussed in the latter part of the nineteenth century. There were even some, a decided minority to be sure, that urged that democratic ideas be put into practice. But for a variety of reasons, democracy as an idea was not converted into political institutions. Democracy would have greatly altered the traditional way of life, and since the development of Japan into a modern nation involved the deliberate preservation of many traditional social institutions and values, political change in the nineteenth century was not in the direction of democracy. Indeed, the constitution of 1889, although providing for a parliament, which was an imported institution, established the framework of a government controlled by an oligarchy.

It was not until after the end of the Second World War and the Allied Occupation that democracy as a set of political institutions was established in Japan. As noted previously, the postwar constitution provides a framework for a liberal democratic government.

In addition to creating new institutions, the Occupation also tried consciously to modify basic social attitudes, for example in its attempts to reform the educational system. But it is not surprising that changing political institutions proved to be an easier task than changing social attitudes. Despite all the changes that have occurred in Japan since the end of the war, Japan is still a country with a strong sense of social hierarchy, with a preference for arriving at decisions through consensus rather than through majority vote, and with an inclination to rely on highly personalized social relationships. The past still lingers in many quarters, and the result is that at the present time Japan's political institutions are "ahead," if that is the right word for it, of social attitudes. Indeed, many conservative political leaders have argued that some of the Occupation-sponsored reforms were not in keeping with Japanese traditions and have consequently urged the revival of certain of the prewar practices.

The conservatives have not had a free hand in "turning the clock back" partly because of determined resistance on the part of the socialist opposition. The socialists have been strong enough to prevent constitutional revision, but not strong enough to come to power. In view of their commitment to Marxian theory and their unwillingness to take a more pragmatic approach to politics, plus their lack of grass-roots organization, the possibility of socialist success in the near future looks most remote. Thus Japan has something approaching a permanent majority and a permanent minority, a situation which is not conducive to the smooth working of parliamentary government. The 1960 riots in connection with the revision of the security treaty pointed up weaknesses inherent in the parliamentary system as it operates in the Japanese context. What Japan needs is time—time to permit changes both in political institutions and in social attitudes toward the end that the two might come into a more harmonious balance. The question is whether democracy and parliamentary government can survive until then. On the basis of the record since 1945, there is good reason to take an optimistic view.

SUGGESTED READING

III: The Historical Background

Bellah, Robert. *Tokugawa Religion: The Values of Pre-industrial Japan.* Glencoe, Ill.: Free Press, 1957. An interesting attempt to evaluate religious factors in the development of an industrial society in Japan.

Borton, Hugh. *Japan's Modern Century*. New York: Ronald Press, 1955. A narrative account with some interpretation of major trends in recent Japanese history.

Butow, Robert J. C. *Tojo and the Coming of the War*. Princeton: Princeton University Press, 1961. A political biography of General Tojo, who was Prime Minister at the time of the outbreak of the war in the Pacific.

Kawai, Kazuo. *Japan's American Interlude*. Chicago: University of Chicago Press, 1960. The best account of the Occupation yet published.

Maxon, Yale Candee. *Control of Japanese Foreign Policy: A Study of Civil-Military Rivalry, 1930–1945*. Berkeley: University of California Press, 1957. The story of the failure to achieve coordination between the civil and military branches of the government.

Norman, E. Herbert. *Japan's Emergence as a Modern State*. New York: Institute of Pacific Relations, 1940. Somewhat outdated, but still the best introduction in English to the Meiji political and economic scene.

Reischauer, Edwin. *Japan, Past and Present*. Rev. and enl. ed. New York: Knopf, 1953. An excellent introduction to Japanese history.

Sansom, George B. *Japan: A Short Cultural History*. Rev. ed. New York: Appleton-Century, 1943. A classic work covering Japan's historical development to the early nineteenth century.

——. *The Western World and Japan*. New York: Knopf, 1950. Covers the nineteenth century with particular reference to the Western impact.

Schwantes, Robert S. *Japanese and Americans: A Century of Cultural Relations*. New York: Harper, 1955. A thoughtful study of the cultural relations between the United States and Japan.

Smith, Thomas C. *Political Change and Industrial Development in Japan: Government Enterprise, 1868–1880*. Stanford: Stanford University Press, 1955. Describes the role of government in Japanese industrialization.

Storry, Richard. *The Double Patriots: A Study of Japanese Nationalism*. Boston: Houghton Mifflin, 1957. Treats the rise of ultranationalism and militarism in the 1930's; based mostly on the Tokyo trials documents.

Yanaga, Chitoshi. *Japan since Perry*. New York: McGraw-Hill, 1950. An encyclopedic account useful mostly as a reference work.

IV: The Social and Economic Structure

Beardsley, Richard K., John W. Hall, and Robert E. Ward. *Village Japan*. Chicago: University of Chicago Press, 1959. An interdisciplinary study of a village.

Benedict, Ruth. *The Chrysanthemum and the Sword*. Boston: Houghton Mifflin, 1946. An anthropologist's interpretation of Japan; interesting and provocative, but must be used with care.

Cole, Allan B. *Japanese Society and Politics: The Impact of Social Stratification and Mobility on Politics*. Boston: Boston University, Department of Government, 1956. A brief but excellent exposition of changes in the elite structure.

Dore, R. P. *City Life in Japan: A Study of a Japanese Ward.* Berkeley: University of California Press, 1958. A perceptive study.

Haring, Douglas G. *Personal Character and Cultural Milieu.* 3d rev. ed. Syracuse: Syracuse University Press, 1956. Contains chapters on Japanese personal character.

Hollerman, Leon. "Industrial Structure and Economic Planning," *Pacific Affairs,* vol. XXXIII (Sept. 1960).

Lockwood, William L. *The Economic Development of Japan: Growth and Structural Change, 1868–1938.* Princeton: Princeton University Press, 1954. An outstanding treatment of Japanese economic development.

Maraini, Fosco. *Meeting with Japan.* New York: Viking, 1959. Poorly organized, but has many interesting personal reminiscences.

Maruyama, Masao. "The Ideology and Movement of Japanese Fascism," *Japan Annual of Law and Politics,* no. 1 (1952). An abstract of an important work by a leading Japanese political scientist.

Nagai, Michio. *Dozoku: A Preliminary Study of the Japanese "Extended Family" Group and Its Social and Economic Functions.* Columbus: Ohio State University Research Foundation, 1953. A report on the extended family system in Japan.

Norbeck, Edward. *Takashima: A Japanese Fishing Village.* Salt Lake City: University of Utah Press, 1954. An anthropological survey.

Reischauer, Edwin. *The United States and Japan.* Rev. ed. Cambridge, Mass.: Harvard University Press, 1957. An excellent general account of modern Japan.

Shiso no Kagaku Kenkyukai. *Japanese Popular Culture.* Trans. and ed. by H. Kato. Tokyo: Tuttle, 1959. Pioneering studies of changes in popular attitudes in the postwar period.

Stoetzel, Jean. *Without the Chrysanthemum and the Sword.* New York: Columbia University Press, 1955. An analysis of political and social attitudes among Japanese youth by a French sociologist.

V: Governmental Organization

Baerwald, Hans. *The Purge of Japanese Leaders under the Occupation.* Berkeley: University of California Press, 1959. Describes the way in which the purge was carried out and evaluates its effects.

Burks, Ardath W. *The Government of Japan.* New York: Crowell, 1961. Especially good on local government.

Japan, Ministry of Education. *Kokutai no Hongi.* Trans. by John Owen Gauntlett. Cambridge, Mass.: Harvard University Press, 1949. A translation of an official statement of *kokutai.*

Maki, John M. "The Prime Minister's Office and Executive Power," *Far*

Eastern Survey, vol. XXIV (May 1955). Discusses the functions of the Prime Minister's Office, to which are attached numerous specialized agencies.

Quigley, Harold S. *Japanese Government and Politics: An Introductory Study*. New York: Century, 1932. A standard work on the prewar Japanese government.

——, and John E. Turner. *The New Japan: Government and Politics*. Minneapolis: University of Minnesota Press, 1956. Particularly good on the background of the postwar constitution.

Smythe, Hugh, and Masaharu Watanabe. "Japanese Popular Attitudes toward the Emperor," *Pacific Affairs*, vol. XXVI (Dec. 1953). Quotes public opinion polls on the Emperor system.

Steiner, Kurt. "The Japanese Village and Its Government," *Far Eastern Quarterly*, vol. XV (Feb. 1956). An evaluation of reforms in local government structure.

Supreme Commander for the Allied Powers. *Political Reorientation of Japan, Sept. 1945 to Sept. 1948*. 2 vols. Washington, D.C.: U.S. Government Printing Office, 1949. An official account of the role of the Occupation in modifying Japanese political institutions.

Ward, Robert E. "The Origins of the Present Japanese Constitution," *American Political Science Review*, vol. L (Dec. 1956). Reveals the part played by the Occupation in the drafting of the new constitution.

Wildes, Harry Emerson. *Typhoon in Tokyo*. New York: Macmillan, 1954. A critique of the Occupation by a participant.

Yanaga, Chitoshi. *Japanese People and Politics*. New York: Wiley, 1956. Contains a detailed description of the organization of the postwar government.

VI: Major Political Forces

Colbert, Evelyn S. *The Left Wing in Japanese Politics*. New York: Institute of Pacific Relations, 1952. A description of the left wing with particular reference to the socialists.

Cole, Allan B. *Political Tendencies of Japanese Small Enterprises, with Special Reference to the Social Democratic Party*. New York: Institute of Pacific Relations, 1959.

Farley, Miriam S. *Aspects of Japan's Labor Problems*. New York: John Day, 1950. Discusses changes in Japanese labor under the Occupation.

Ike, Nobutaka. *The Beginnings of Political Democracy in Japan*. Baltimore: Johns Hopkins Press, 1950. Treats the origins and early growth of Japanese political parties.

Kurzman, Dan. *Kishi and Japan: The Search for the Sun*. New York: Obolensky, 1960. A semipopular biography of Kishi Nobusuke, who was forced to resign as Prime Minister after the 1960 demonstrations.

Levine, Solomon B. "Management and Industrial Relations in Postwar Japan," *Far Eastern Quarterly*, vol. XV (Nov. 1955). Discusses changes in employee-employer relationships and their implications for industrial relations.

Morris, Ivan I. *Nationalism and the Right-Wing in Japan: A Study of Postwar Trends.* London: Oxford University Press, 1960. Evaluates the strength of right-wing forces in contemporary Japan.

Saffell, John. "Japan's Post-War Socialist Party," *American Political Science Review*, vol. XLII (Oct. 1948).

Scalapino, Robert A. *Democracy and the Party Movement in Prewar Japan: The Failure of the First Attempt.* Berkeley: University of California Press, 1953. The best work in English on Japanese political parties.

——. "Japan: Between Traditionalism and Democracy," in Sigmund Neumann, ed., *Modern Political Parties.* Chicago: University of Chicago Press, 1956. A concise account of Japanese political parties.

Swearingen, Rodger, and Paul Langer. *Red Flag in Japan: International Communism in Action, 1919–1951.* Cambridge, Mass.: Harvard University Press, 1952. A detailed study of the Japanese Communist movement.

Totten, George. "Problems of Japanese Socialist Leadership," *Pacific Affairs*, vol. XXVIII (June 1955).

Uyehara, C., S. Royama, and S. Ogata. *Comparative Platforms of Japan's Major Parties.* Medford, Mass.: Tufts University, Fletcher School of Law and Diplomacy, 1955.

VII: The Power Structure

Colton, Hattie Kawahara. "The Workings of the Japanese Diet," *Pacific Affairs*, vol. XXVIII (Dec. 1955).

Colton, Kenneth. "Conservative Leadership in Japan," *Far Eastern Survey*, vol. XXIV (June 1955). An analysis of leadership recruitment among conservative groups.

Dore, R. P. *Land Reform in Japan.* London: Oxford University Press, 1959. Includes in addition to a detailed analysis of the land reform program excellent sections on Japanese politics.

Dull, Paul S. "The Senkyoya System in Rural Japanese Communities," in University of Michigan, Center for Japanese Studies, *Occasional Papers*, no. 4 (1953). Describes techniques used by a political boss.

Esman, Milton J. "Japanese Administration—A Comparative View," *Public Administration Review*, vol. VII (Spring 1947). A firsthand account of attempted reforms in the Japanese bureaucracy.

Ike, Nobutaka. *Japanese Politics: An Introductory Survey.* New York: Knopf, 1957. A study of Japanese political behavior.

Ishino, Iwao, and John W. Bennett. *The Japanese Labor Boss System.*

Columbus: Ohio University Research Foundation, 1952. A preliminary study of the behavior of labor bosses.

Langdon, Frank C. "Organized Interests in Japan and Their Influence on Political Parties," *Pacific Affairs,* vol. XXXIV (Fall 1961).

Roser, Foster. "Establishing a Modern Merit System in Japan," *Public Personnel Review,* vol. XI (Oct. 1950).

Scalapino, Robert A., and Junnosuke Masumi. *Parties and Politics in Contemporary Japan.* Berkeley: University of California Press, 1962. Very perceptive.

Ukai, Nobushige. "The Japanese House of Councillors Election of July, 1962," *Asian Survey,* vol. II (Aug. 1962).

Ward, Robert E. "The Socio-Political Role of the Buraku (Hamlet) in Japan," *American Political Science Review,* vol. XLV (Dec. 1951). Provides insight into the nature of rural politics.

——, ed. *Five Studies in Japanese Politics.* Ann Arbor: University of Michigan Press, 1957. Includes essays on the Japanese police system, political bosses, conservatism in politics, Sakhalin in Russo-Japanese relations, and law in the Tokugawa period.

Williams, Justin. "Party Politics in the New Japanese Diet," *American Political Science Review,* vol. XLII (Dec. 1948). A description of the legislature by an Occupation official who served the Japanese government in an advisory capacity.

Yoshida, Shigeru. *The Yoshida Memoirs: The Story of Japan in Crisis.* Trans. by Kenichi Yoshida. Boston: Houghton Mifflin, 1962. Yoshida was Prime Minister during the latter part of the Allied Occupation and in the years immediately after independence.

VIII: Problems of Contemporary Japan

Borton, Hugh, and others. *Japan between East and West.* New York: Harper, 1957. Contains six essays covering domestic politics, communism, economic position, diplomacy, relations with Communist China, and so on.

Cohen, Jerome B. *Japan's Postwar Economy.* Bloomington: Indiana University Press, 1958. A work by a leading authority on Japan's economy.

Hellman, Donald C. "Basic Problems of Japanese–South Korean Relations," *Asian Survey,* vol. II (May 1962).

"Japanese Intellectuals Discuss American-Japanese Relations," with introd. by Robert A. Scalapino, *Far Eastern Survey,* Oct. 1960.

Japan since Recovery of Independence. In *Annals of the American Academy of Political and Social Science,* Nov. 1956. An up-to-date appraisal of the state of affairs in Japan by 17 specialists.

Maki, John M. *Government and Politics in Japan: The Road to Democracy.*

New York: Praeger, 1962. An analysis of Japan as a constitutional democracy.

Mendel, Douglas H., Jr. *The Japanese People and Foreign Policy: A Study of Public Opinion in Post-Treaty Japan.* Berkeley: University of California Press, 1961. Based on field surveys.

Reischauer, Edwin. "The Broken Dialogue," *Foreign Affairs,* vol. XXXIX (Oct. 1960). Discusses the causes of the anti-American demonstrations in 1960.

Stockwin, J. A. A. " 'Positive Neutrality'—The Foreign Policy of the Japanese Socialist Party," *Asian Survey,* vol. II (Nov. 1962).

PERIODICALS

Contemporary Japan, a quarterly journal which carries articles on current and historical topics, particularly useful for documents and extracts of Japanese periodicals.

Japan Quarterly, published by the Asahi Newspaper Company, often contains good articles by leading Japanese writers.

Japan Times, an English-language daily published in Tokyo. Its editorial opinions are not always representative of Japanese views.

Oriental Economist, a monthly journal, is well informed on economic developments.

PART THREE : INDIA

By Norman D. Palmer

· IX ·

The Political Heritage

of Modern India

BECAUSE historical records are few and scanty, not much is known about the early inhabitants of the Indian subcontinent; but it seems likely that the pattern of conquest, infiltration, and absorption, which is so familiar in modern India, reaches far back into the darkness of prehistory. First traces of the earliest-known Indian civilization were discovered hardly more than a generation ago. Excavations at Mohenjo-Daro in Sind and at Harappa in the western Punjab unearthed the remnants of an ancient Indus Valley civilization, dating back at least to the third millennium B.C. It was an urban civilization, of considerable complexity, with highly developed arts and crafts. After a period of substantial prosperity and for reasons about which we can only speculate, this early civilization declined and died away.

Patterns of Government in Hindu India

Some centuries later, Aryan invaders entered India from the north and began to mingle with the primitive stocks, the so-called Dravidians. These Aryan peoples brought with them ideas and institutions which, under the generic name of Hinduism, have taken deep root in the Indian soil. The essence of the Hindu religious philosophy is its extraordinary fluidity, eclecticism, and adaptability. There are hundreds, even thousands, of Hindu gods and goddesses; indeed, almost

269

all ethnic strains in Indian life have contributed to the Hindu pan-
theon, and all mix together, with remarkably little jealousy or jostling.
The sacred books of Hinduism, the *Vedas* and the *Upanishads*, are
eclectic and tolerant collections, a blend of many creeds, cults, and
philosophies. From these sacred works, together with the great Sanskrit epics, the *Mahabharata* and the *Ramayana*, composed probably
between 200 B.C. and A.D. 200, and from other major writings of the
early Hindu period, many of the ideas and beliefs which have shaped
the actions and thought of Indians through the centuries have been
derived. One of the most important of the early works is the *Bhagavad
Gita,* a little gem of Hindu literature, which is buried in the vast
mass of the *Mahabharata.*

There is also a strict and rigid aspect of Hinduism. It is reflected in
the formal schools of Hindu philosophy, such as Vedanta and Yoga,
in the gradual growth of strict dietary habits, in the worship of the
cow as a sacred animal, and, above all, in the Hindu concept of caste.

Originally the Aryans were organized into tribes, with specific social functions (priests, warriors, and the like). These tribes very gradually over a period of many centuries became exclusive marriage
groups. Divided and subdivided, sometimes territorially, sometimes
according to occupation, sometimes by the sheer accidents and circumstances of history, they developed into full-fledged castes, with highly
elaborate regulations regarding not only those whom they can marry,
but also those with whom they can eat, those to whom they can talk,
and those whom they can touch.

The caste system is still one of the deepest influences in Indian social life. It is a very complicated system. Although the four main castes
are the Brahmins (the scholars), the Kshatriyas (the rulers and warriors), the Vaisyas (the merchants), and the Sudras (the workers),
there are now more than 2,000 castes and subcastes, and also a large
number of outcastes, in India today. Untouchability was officially outlawed in the Indian constitution of 1950, but it still prevails. Some
50 million Indians—over one-tenth of the total population—belong
to the so-called "scheduled castes."

In the fourth century B.C., Alexander the Great made a brief incursion into western India. Shortly after his fleeting visit the Mauryan
dynasty established a powerful empire in north India, with a capital
at Pataliputra. An important figure at the court of the first of the
Mauryan emperors was Kautilya (also known as Chanakya or Vish-
nugupta), "the greatest Indian exponent of the art of government, the

duties of kings, ministers, and officials, and the methods of diplomacy."[1] Kautilya's *Arthasastra* is one of the world's earliest classics in political science and public administration, although the text was discovered and translated only in the present century. The greatest of the Mauryan rulers was Asoka (273–232 B.C.), one of the great names in history. Asoka gave a powerful impetus to Buddhism, which is a particularly tolerant and contemplative offshoot of Hinduism. A convert to the arts of peace, he ruled benevolently over a vast empire including much of north India, the Deccan, and Afghanistan. It is wholly appropriate that the capital of one of his huge pillars, with its four lions (now in the Buddhist museum at Sarnath), is often reproduced today as a symbol of independent India and that the wheel on this capital was adopted for the national flag of India (a tricolor of orange, white, and green).

The Mauryan empire collapsed soon after the death of Asoka, and political fragmentation and disunity prevailed for six centuries, until the rise of the Gupta empire in the fourth century A.D. Under Chandragupta II (380–413), nearly all of India was united under one rule, with the center of power in north India. Indian culture reached a high point during the Gupta period. It was the golden age of Sanskrit studies, and the great university of Nalanda attracted students from all parts of Asia. The Gupta rulers also increased the prestige of India as a maritime power and sponsored the establishment of Hindu kingdoms, particularly in Southeast Asia. More than a century after the collapse of the Gupta dynasty, in the seventh century A.D., there was a momentary revival of Hindu power under Harsha, the ruler of a state north of the present site of Delhi. Harsha extended his control over most of the territory once embraced in the Gupta empire and ruled firmly and well for more than forty years; but he was the last of the great Hindu rulers of north India.

By A.D. 1000 Hindu civilization, which had reached great heights in literature and philosophy and had enjoyed occasional periods of political eminence, showed signs of fatal decay. There was, as Nehru has written, a "decline all along the line—intellectual, philosophical, political, in techniques and methods of warfare, in knowledge of and contacts with the outside world."[2]

---

[1] J. F. Fleet, Introductory Note to Kautilya's *Arthasastra*, trans. by Dr. R. Shamasastry (4th ed.; Mysore, 1951), p. v.

[2] Jawaharlal Nehru, *The Discovery of India* (New York: John Day, 1946), p. 221.

Clearly the great achievements of what might be called the Hindu period of Indian history were not in the arts of politics. The prevailing political pattern was fragmentation. The prevailing form of government, in the larger political units which rose and fell with bewildering rapidity, was absolutism. Occasionally that absolutism was benevolent, but if it was controlled at all it was limited by inefficiency or weakness in administration. There was little that could be called democratic in ancient India, any more than in other parts of the world; but some examples of representative institutions, usually local and embryonic, can be found, and these have very understandably been glorified by modern Indian nationalists.[3] If republican forms of government in fact existed, they were certainly the exception, even on local levels. The village panchayats (councils of five), in particular, merit careful study,[4] especially since the present government of India is trying to revive and extend these ancient village institutions in an organized and somewhat more democratic form.

Mogul Government and Administration

Islam was brought into India not long after it became firmly established in the Arabian peninsula in the seventh century; but the story of Islam in India really begins with Mahmud of Ghazni, who made many raids into India between 998 and 1030. In the late twelfth and early thirteenth centuries Mohammed Ghori, from what is now Afghanistan, extended his sway over a good part of northern and northwestern India. After his death in 1206, one of his generals established the Delhi Sultanate. For a century and a half the Sultans of Delhi ruled over much of north India and also conquered kingdoms in the Deccan and farther south. In the late fourteenth century the Delhi Sultanate virtually collapsed, and in 1398 Timur—or Tamerlane—swept out of Central Asia into India and sacked Delhi. By the mid-fifteenth century, the Delhi Sultanate had revived, but it never regained its former power; and in 1526 Baber, a descendant of Timur and Genghis Khan,

---

[3] For varying views and interpretations see A. S. Altekar, *State and Government in Ancient India* (Benares, 1949); U. N. Ghoshal, *A History of Hindu Political Theories* (2d ed.; London, 1927); K. P. Jayaswal, *Hindu Polity* (Calcutta, 1924); Beni Prasad, *The State in Ancient India* (Allahabad, 1928); Beni Prasad, "Political Theory and Administrative System," in R. C. Majumdar and A. D. Pusalker, eds., *The Age of Imperial Unity* (2d ed.; Bombay, 1953); Benoy Kumar Sarkar, *The Political Institutions and Theories of the Hindus* (Leipzig, 1922).

[4] See J. G. Drummond, *Panchayats in India* (Bombay, 1937); Rattan Lal Khanna, *Panchayat Raj in India* (Chandigarh, 1956).

defeated the armies of the Delhi Sultanate and established the great Mogul (or Mughal) dynasty in India.

The greatest of the Mogul rulers of India was Akbar (a grandson of Baber), who ruled from 1556 to 1605. Akbar established a control over most of India, except in the extreme south, which was firmer and more efficient than anything that India had experienced for many centuries. "The Mogul Empire at the beginning of the seventeenth century was probably the best organized and most prosperous then existing in the world." [5] The empire was organized into provinces. It was highly centralized and had an efficient civil service and tax system. Able administrators, Hindu as well as Muslim, served the Great Mogul. Akbar followed a policy of religious as well as political toleration and sought to unite Hindus and Muslims. He tried to formulate a new religion which would combine the best features of Islam, Hinduism, and other religions.

For a century following his death Akbar's successors maintained the splendor of the Mogul court and even expanded the boundaries of the empire; but they were far less able and far less tolerant than the Great Mogul. Jehangir was ineffective, and his son, Shah Jahan, builder of the Taj Mahal, not only imposed staggering burdens on the people, but reversed his grandfather's policy of religious toleration. The last of the great Mogul rulers, Aurangzeb (1659–1707), continued these oppressive policies. Obsessed with the aim of uniting India under his rule, he spent years in arduous campaigns against other Muslim kingdoms and against the Sikhs, the Rajputs, and especially the Mahrattas. For a time he ruled over more of India than any other man in the long history of the subcontinent, but he was never able to give real unity and stability to his unwieldy kingdom. Upon his death the Mogul empire fell apart. After a century and a half of dazzling magnificence and despotic power the great period of Muslim rule in India was at an end.

Obviously the Muslim contribution to Indian civilization has been a great and lasting one in many fields. Politically the Moguls determined the patterns of control on the provincial level and above, but they always had to rely upon large numbers of non-Muslim administrators, and they had to enter into agreements with many Hindu rulers. Large parts of India never experienced direct Muslim rule, and the Muslims had little effect, even during the period of imperial

[5] T. Walter Wallbank, *India in the New Era* (Chicago: Scott, Foresman, 1951), pp. 37–38.

splendor, upon the villages of India, where the great majority of the people lived. Relatively few of the many millions of Muslims in India and Pakistan today are descendants of the Moguls or other Muslim invaders of India; the great majority are descended from Hindus who (usually because of dissatisfaction with their caste position) adopted the Muslim faith and way of life. The introduction of Islam into India never produced anything like a real Hindu-Muslim synthesis. In the words of K. M. Panikkar:

The main social result of the introduction of Islam as a religion into India was the division of society on a vertical basis. Before the thirteenth century, Hindu society was divided horizontally by castes. Islam split Indian society into two sections from top to bottom. . . . It was two parallel societies vertically established on the same soil. At all stages they were different and hardly any social communication or intercourse of life existed between them.[6]

Thus the relationship between Hindus and Muslims, and the success or failure of their experiments in "peaceful coexistence," became a main theme of modern Indian history.

British Rule to 1857

The century following the death of Aurangzeb was a period of confusion in the political history of India. Mogul rule was reduced almost to impotence; Hindu power revived, especially among the Mahrattas and Sikhs; Afghan and Persian invasions were beaten back; the British and French came into conflict; and the power of the British East India Company grew steadily in importance. The political influence of this originally private corporation was extended by a curious combination of force and persuasion.

After an ineffectual revolt against Aurangzeb, the Mahratta people had slowly built up a confederation extending from the present state of Maharashtra into northern India and the frontiers of Bengal. But in 1761 their army was destroyed by invading Afghans in the Punjab, and toward the end of the century the Mahratta leader was forced to seek refuge with the British in Bombay. In 1802 he agreed, in return for a promise of protection, to receive British troops at his court and to pay an annual tribute. "The treaty," in the opinion of A. B. Keith, "unquestionably must be accepted as giving the British the Empire of India, for it reduced the head of the Mahratta confederation to a

---

[6] *A Survey of Indian History* (London, 1948), p. 162.

position of complete inferiority, and in matters external of absolute subordination, to the British." [7] Most of the lesser Mahratta chiefs refused to be bound by the treaty, and war followed in 1803–1805. As a result of the fighting, Mahratta power was checked, and it soon faded into insignificance in comparison with the growing British influence.

The French had become active in India only in the latter part of the seventeenth century, when the French East India Company was organized by Louis XIV's great finance minister, Colbert. During the confusion which followed the death of Aurangzeb, the French increased their influence and reached a peak of power during the twelve years (1742–1754) when Dupleix was Governor-General of the French East India Company's holdings, centered at Pondicherry. By force and diplomacy Dupleix more than held his own until his plans were checkmated by the activities of a young clerk of the British East India Company named Robert Clive. In 1754 Dupleix was recalled in disgrace. Shortly afterward, in 1757, Dupleix' chief ally, the Nawab of Bengal, was defeated at Plassey by forces of the British East India Company under Clive, and the main French power in India was broken. Until very recently the French maintained a foothold in Pondicherry; but after Indian independence, they yielded to strong pressure from India and ceded their holdings. Portugal, on the other hand, steadfastly refused to give up Goa and several small enclaves north of Bombay city, which it had held since the early seventeenth century. They were forced out of India only in December 1961, when Indian troops occupied Goa and the Portuguese enclaves. Since 1754, however, neither the French nor the Portuguese have had any influence in India remotely comparable to that of the British.

Robert Clive did much to lay the foundations of effective British power in India and was rewarded by appointment as Governor of Madras and later of Bengal. During succeeding decades able Governors-General, notably Warren Hastings (1774–1785), Lord Cornwallis (1786–1795), Lord Wellesley (1798–1804), Lord William Bentinck (1828–1835), and Lord Dalhousie (1848–1856), consolidated and extended the holdings of the company. By the 1840s most of the subcontinent was under British control, either directly or indirectly through treaties with princely states.

British rule in India may be divided into two main periods, with the "Sepoy Mutiny" (1857) as the watershed. The first period was one

[7] *A Constitutional History of India, 1600–1935* (2d ed.; London, 1937), p. 114.

of rule by the British East India Company, the second of rule by the British government itself, which continued to combine direct with indirect rule, as during the days of "John Company."

When it began to be a governing as well as a trading corporation, the British East India Company itself became subject to government regulations. The first bills were passed as early as 1773. Three years of investigation into Indian affairs (1781–1784) preceded the passage by Parliament of Pitt's India Act of 1784, which further limited the powers of the company. The act established a Board of Control, the President of which was virtually "a Secretary of State for India." It also provided for the appointment of the Governor-General by the British government. The parliamentary investigations of the early 1780s led to the famous trial of Warren Hastings, which started in 1788 and ended only in 1795 with Hastings' acquittal. Lord Cornwallis, the first Governor-General after the Act of 1784, laid the basis for a more honest and efficient system of administration. The governor-generalship of Lord William Bentinck (1828–1835), "the first of the modern rulers of India," was marked by significant steps in administrative and social reform. Parliament, after an intensive review, renewed the charter of the East India Company for twenty years in the Charter Act of 1833, but it closed down the company's commercial activities and gave more power to the Governor-General in Council. By this time the interests and welfare of the people of India had become matters of genuine concern to the British government, and Bentinck undertook a number of social reforms. Among these were the abolition of suttee (the suicide of widows after the death of their husbands), the suppression of lawlessness by fanatical devotees, known as Thugs, of the goddess Kali, and efforts to eliminate female infanticide.

The Charter Act of 1833 added a law member to the Governor-General's Council, who was to prove an important addition. The first law member, the famous Lord Macaulay, inaugurated a systematic codification of criminal law. In time an impressive legal structure was developed. Lord Macaulay's name is also associated with perhaps the most lasting of all Lord William Bentinck's reforms, the selection of English as the medium of education in India and the decision to follow Western methods in teaching promising young Indians. In his famous Minute on Education in 1835 Lord Macaulay recommended this step; as a result, he predicted, there would develop "a class of persons, Indian in blood and colour, but English in taste, in opinion, in morals and in intellect," and these Western-trained Indians would set the pattern for the entire country. Thus for over a century higher education in India was based on Western models, and English was the accepted medium in the schools and courts and in all government business. Even today, in independent India, this pattern still prevails, although Hindi and other Indian languages are gradually being used for purposes of instruction and although the role of English is now a hotly debated subject. Today the government of India must decide what parts of the British-imposed system of education should be preserved and what should be replaced by methods more in keeping with India's traditions and needs.

Macaulay and other English Liberals held Indian culture and customs in low esteem, and they directly challenged deep-rooted Indian practices and institutions. At the same time, unlike most of the Englishmen who helped to shape India's destiny in the half century or more following the "Mutiny," they looked forward with anticipation to the remote day when Indians would be granted self-government. "When it comes," said Macaulay, "it will be the proudest day in English history." [8]

British Rule after 1857

In 1957 both India and Pakistan commemorated the centenary of "the War of Independence," which British historians have referred to as the "Sepoy Mutiny." In *The Discovery of India* Nehru himself wrote: "It was much more than a military mutiny, and it spread rapidly and assumed the character of a popular rebellion and a war of Indian independence." [9] In a symbolic sense Nehru may be right; but the "Mutiny" was in historical fact far from "a popular rebellion and a war of Indian independence." It was confined to a limited area (starting in Meerut, spreading to Delhi, Cawnpore, Lucknow, and a few other places in north central India) and to a limited number of Indians, mostly Sepoys (Indian soldiers) of the British Indian army. The cause of the uprising was primarily a "revulsion against western influence." "The repeated annexation of territories by a foreign power, the spread of Western mode of education and new ideas of life—all

[8] Quoted in Guy Wint and Sir George Schuster, *India and Democracy* (London, 1941), p. 78.
[9] Nehru, *The Discovery of India*, p. 324.

combined revealed to the Hindu mind a consistent effort to substitute a western for a Hindu civilisation." [10] The exact occasion which set off the uprising was relatively trivial, but it "ignited the mass of combustibles which the more serious crime had collected." [11]

Although the "Mutiny" of 1857 never developed into a national resistance movement and never endangered British rule, it did have momentous consequences. It marked the end both of the East India Company as a ruling power in India and of the Mogul dynasty in even its feeblest form. It ushered in the great epoch of British rule in India, yet at the same time it unleashed forces which less than a century later were to force the British out of India entirely. After 1857 British rule was firmer and more efficient, perhaps more benevolent and farseeing as well, than it had been in the days when the British government and the East India Company were sharing the responsibilities of governing India. But the gulf between British rulers and Indian people became wider, and much of the warm intimacy of previous days gave way to aloofness and distrust. The Muslims, in particular, were at an increasing disadvantage after the "Mutiny," and they were carefully excluded from positions of trust and responsibility.[12]

In the period following the "Mutiny" the British developed an impressive structure of government and administration for India. The great parliamentary landmarks are the Indian Councils Acts of 1861 and 1892, the Morley-Minto reforms of 1909, the Government of India Act of 1919 (following the Montagu-Chelmsford report of 1918), and the Government of India Act of 1935. During these years Indians gained an increasing but never dominant voice in provincial government, in the legislative assemblies, and even in the Executive Council (after 1909). But the governors were always the key figures in the provinces, and the Governors-General (called Viceroys when acting as the representatives of the Crown) were supreme in British India as a whole, though increasingly subject to control from London. There the key figure was the Secretary of State for India, assisted by a council and by officials of the India Office. The provinces were subdivided for administrative purposes into divisions and districts. Districts were under the supervision of district officers (sometimes known as col-

---

[10] S. R., "The Sepoy Mutiny of 1857," *Radical Humanist*, XXI (May 12, 1957), 237.

[11] *Ibid.*

[12] See Chapter XIV, the "British Rule" section.

lectors), whose role in the entire system of British administration was a particularly vital one. A district officer had numerous functions and responsibilities, both official and unofficial; his chief formal duties were to administer justice, to collect revenue, and to preserve law and order. In the eyes of ordinary Indians the district officer was the British Raj.

Some efforts were made to establish advisory boards for the district officers, composed of both nominated and elected members. The results were fairly impressive in the municipalities, but disappointing in the villages and rural areas. A famous Resolution on Local Self-Government of 1882, associated with the name of the Viceroy at the time, Lord Ripon, declared: "It is not primarily with a view to improvement in administration that this measure is put forward and supported. It is chiefly designed as an instrument of political and popular education." [13] Actually, the British had little success in developing any satisfactory system of local government below the district level.

Whereas in the development of district administration there was a fusion of Indian and English traditions and usage, in the building up of local bodies almost no concession was made to native prejudices or ways of thinking. There was the great difficulty that no separate indigenous local government tradition existed (except for the village organization) distinct from the centralized administration of the state, upon which nineteenth-century officials could build.[14]

The main task of administration in British India devolved upon the members of the Indian Civil Service, who set standards of efficiency and incorruptibility which have seldom been equaled in any other civil service. Even today former ICS officers are the backbone of the administrative system in both India and Pakistan, although the withdrawal of the British members and depletions due to resignations, retirements, and deaths foreshadow the passing of this great service. One of the oldest of civil services, the ICS came into being as early as the eighteenth century. After 1853 appointments were made by the British government in place of the East India Company, on the basis of open competition. As late as 1892 the ICS numbered only 992 officers, and only 21 of these were Indians. But after 1900, increasing numbers of Indians were taken into the service, through rigid

[13] Quoted in Hugh Tinker, *The Foundations of Local Self-Government in India, Pakistan, and Burma* (London: Athlone Press, 1954), p. 44.
[14] *Ibid.*, p. 334.

examination, and on the eve of independence a major part of the service was Indian.

Just prior to the 1857 "Mutiny" the British Indian army consisted of approximately 233,000 Sepoys and 45,000 British troops, a ratio of more than five to one. After the "Mutiny" the army was completely reorganized, and the ratio of Indian to British troops was never more than two to one. Henceforth the Indian contingents were drawn more heavily than before from the "martial" races, the Sikhs, the Pathans, the Punjabi Muslims, and the Gurkas of Nepal. More than ever before the Indian army became a professional force.

After the "Mutiny," too, an earlier policy of seeking the annexation of the princely states was abandoned. Most of the Indian princes had remained loyal to the British during the "Mutiny," and as a reward the British government entered into agreements giving them assurance of British aid in retaining their holdings. Thus the princely states were brought within the British orbit. British residents were stationed in most of the more than 500 states, large and small, and often these agents had more real power than the native princes.

Toward Self-Government

Indian nationalism as an organized movement had its beginnings about 1885, the date of the founding of the Indian National Congress; but in reality its history is much longer and is associated with a wide variety of organizations and movements. There is a long background of Hindu nationalism as well as a more recent one of Muslim nationalism; and the two currents, though they often flowed alongside one another, never really mingled.

Raja Ram Mohan Roy (1770–1833) is sometimes referred to as the father of the nationalist movement among the Hindus. Although he lived several decades before the great age of Indian nationalism, his influence was manifest long after his death. In 1828 he founded the Brahmo Samaj as a Hindu reform movement. His faith was deeply rooted in the *Upanishads*, but he found in this orthodox Hindu classic a note of universal acceptance which led to a tolerant attitude toward other religions and societies. Within India, Ram Mohan Roy advocated social reform, through the adoption of Western science, religion, and educational methods. His teachings flowered in 1885 with the formation of the Indian National Congress, a party which, though it has always claimed to be nonsectarian and has always had members of

Chart 4. The development of self-government in British India *

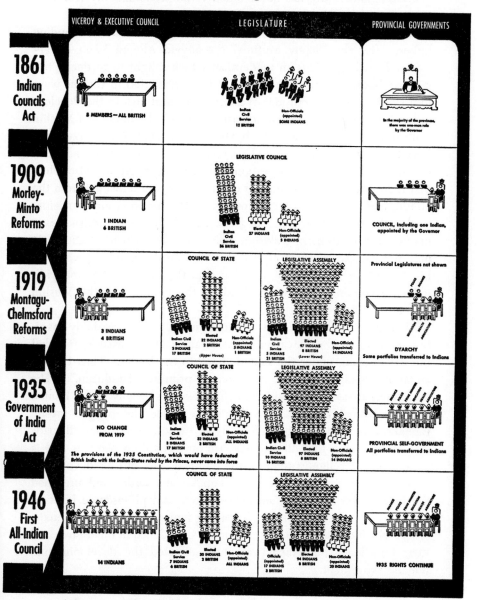

* Courtesy of British Information Services.

many religious faiths, has never failed to be predominantly Hindu in its composition and sometimes in its policies.

Muslim nationalism, though slower to develop, also had its founding father. After the "Sepoy Mutiny," Sir Sayyid Ahmad Khan (1817–1898) "launched a Muslim modernism which sought to reconcile traditional Islam with modern needs." [15] He contributed in various ways to a synthesis of Eastern and Western ideas and also to the development of a Muslim political consciousness. In 1875 he founded a Muslim College at Aligarh (now Aligarh Muslim University). Sir Sayyid believed that the Muslims should preserve their own culture and institutions, but he favored cooperation with the British. He was also "clear that there was a Muslim national consciousness quite distinct from the Hindu, and for that reason discouraged Muslims from any participation in the Indian National Congress. . . . In his whole attitude was implicit the concept of Pakistan [as a separate Muslim nation]. It only needed the prospect of British withdrawal, something which in his day still seemed remote, to bring it to the surface." [16] Sir Sayyid's influence culminated after his death in the founding of the Muslim League (1906).

After the "Mutiny," Hindu nationalism became increasingly manifest. In 1875 Swami Dayananda Saraswati, a Hindu ascetic, founded the Arya Samaj, under the slogan "Back to the Vedas." Thus Dayananda preached "a militant assertion of primitive Hinduism." [17] His movement attracted a considerable following, especially in the Punjab and the United Provinces. In this same period the Bengali mystic Ramakrishna found in the philosophy of Vedanta proof that all roads lead to truth and that all religions are one. His influence was and is greater on the religious than on the political side; but his devout follower, Vivekananda, founded the Ramakrishna Order and preached the importance of India's ancient religious and philosophic heritage for the modern world. He was a leading figure of the Indian Renaissance, which did so much to give Hindus confidence in themselves and their traditions and which profoundly affected the developing nationalist movement.

In the 1880s the nationalist movement entered a new and more concerted stage with the founding of the Indian National Congress. Among the active promoters of the Congress were Surendranath Banerjea, Dadabhai Naoroji, and an Englishman, Octavian Hume. Its

---

[15] Sir Percival Spear, *India, Pakistan, and the West* (London, 1952), p. 190.
[16] *Ibid.*, pp. 190–191.   [17] *Ibid.*, p. 184.

first meeting was held in Bombay in December 1885. Thereafter it met regularly in annual sessions. At first the British authorities looked with some favor upon the Congress. It seemed to be a moderate movement, and it proclaimed its loyalty to the British connection while it worked for a larger measure of representative government. Octavian Hume, known as the "father of the Congress," was in charge of the Congress Secretariat until 1907, and several Englishmen were elected as presidents of the Congress. As time went on, however, the Congress increased its demands and began to include in its ranks some Indians who were *persona non grata* to the British rulers of India.

Until well into the twentieth century the British authorities refused to take the Congress seriously, and they were constantly predicting its decline. "The Congress," wrote the great Viceroy, Lord Curzon, about 1900, "is tottering to its fall, and one of my great ambitions while in India is to assist it to a peaceful demise." [18] Lord Curzon not only greatly underestimated the growing strength of the nationalist movement, but he contributed unwittingly to its support by some of his own acts. Two of his "reforms," in particular, gave impetus to Indian nationalism. One was the Universities Act of 1904, which was interpreted in India as a means of making government control over education more effective and which "convulsed educated India from one end of the country to another." [19] The other was his decision to partition the province of Bengal, an act which infuriated the Hindus of Bengal.

Until the First World War the National Congress was generally controlled by moderate nationalists—men like Surendranath Banerjea and Dadabhai Naoroji and later Pherozeshah Mehta and G. K. Gokhale. Gokhale, whom Gandhi regarded as his political *guru*, "was the outstanding Indian political leader up to the First World War." [20] After 1905 the Congress adopted a stronger line and demanded a real degree of self-government (*swaraj*). For some time a struggle had been going on in the ranks of the Congress between the moderates, led by Gokhale, and the extremists, led by Tilak. Tilak was a great champion of Hindu orthodoxy. Rightly or wrongly, he became associated with a militant brand of nationalism which sometimes found expression in acts of violence. In the pages of the two newspapers which he published in Poona, one in English, the other in

[18] Lord Ronaldshay, *The Life of Lord Curzon* (London, 1928), II, 151.
[19] Surendranath Banerjea, *A Nation in the Making* (London, 1925), p. 175.
[20] Wallbank, *India in the New Era*, p. 80.

Marathi, Tilak justified the use of force in furtherance of national aims. Nationalist extremists were particularly active in Bengal during the decade following the partition of the province, as well as in Bombay and the Punjab. They received support from Congress organizations outside of India, notably in London, Paris, and San Francisco. Besides Tilak their best-known leaders were Bepin Chandra Pal in Bengal and Lala Lajpat Rai in the Punjab.

At the annual meetings of the Congress in 1906 and 1907 a showdown took place between the moderates and extremists, amid scenes of wild disorder. The moderates won the day, and in 1907 the extremists withdrew from the Congress. The triumphant moderates drew up a new constitution and remained in control of Congress machinery until the death of Gokhale in 1915. Many of the extremists, including Tilak and Lala Lajpat Rai, were either imprisoned or deported. The moderates continued to advocate peaceful and constitutional methods to achieve their goals. By the end of the First World War, however, their day was over. Most of them were essentially nineteenth-century liberals who admired British ways and institutions; and in their last years increasing dissatisfaction was felt with the slow progress of the movement.

While the Congress was torn by factional strife, various short steps in the direction of representative government were taken, in consequence of the Morley-Minto reforms of 1909. The underlying idea of these political changes was to "associate the people [of India] to a greater extent with Government in the decision on public questions"; and to this end, they granted to the Indians a few carefully hedged privileges. Through direct or indirect elections, Indians were given places in provincial councils and the central Legislative Council. For the first time, Indian members were appointed to the Viceroy's Executive Council and to the executive councils of the governors of Bombay and Madras. For the first time, also, separate electorates were provided for the Muslims. Separation of the electorates along communal lines was in one sense a forward step, as the very existence of electorates was a novelty in India. On the other hand, it implied the abrogation of all responsibility by the Hindu politician for the Muslim voter and by the Muslim politician for the Hindu voter—even though they inhabited the same village. Thus the seeds of partition were in one sense planted by the first British "liberal" reforms.

"Democratic" as they looked on the surface, the Morley-Minto reforms rested at bottom on the "fundamental principle that the executive government should retain the final decision on all questions." [21] In a famous statement in the House of Lords in December 1908, Lord Morley emphatically repudiated the idea that the proposed reforms "were in any sense a step towards parliamentary government." And he added: "If it could be said that this chapter of reforms led directly or necessarily up to the establishment of a Parliamentary system in India, I for one would have nothing at all to do with it. . . . a Parliamentary system in India is not the goal to which I for one moment would aspire." [22]

Conceived in this spirit, the Morley-Minto reforms were received with little enthusiasm in India, and they were soon overtaken by the march of events. During the First World War most Indians loyally supported the British cause, but Indian spokesmen became increasingly dissatisfied with the failure of the British to make any substantial concessions to political unrest and nationalist sentiment. The radical Tilak returned from exile in 1914, reentered the Congress, and regained a large, even a dominant, following within the organization in the remaining six years of his life.

But even at the height of the war, there were evidences that the British were aware of the need of putting their relations with India on a new footing. In 1917 the Viceroy, Lord Chelmsford, specifically recommended a greater measure of self-government. On August 20, 1917, the new Secretary of State for India, Samuel Montagu, made this historic statement in the House of Commons:

The policy of His Majesty's Government, with which the Government of India are in complete accord, is that of the increasing association of Indians in every branch of the administration and the gradual development of self-governing institutions with a view to the progressive realisation of responsible government as an integral part of the British Empire.[23]

Shortly afterward Mr. Montagu went to India where, in company with the Viceroy, he visited the major centers and heard a variety of points of view. The result of his visit was the Montagu-Chelmsford report of 1918, which led to the Government of India Act of 1919.

This famous act charted the lines of government in India until 1935. It established a kind of quasi-federal system for British India,

[21] *Report on Indian Constitutional Reforms, 1918* (London, 1918), Cd. 9109, p. 7.

[22] *Indian Speeches, 1907–1909* (London, 1909), p. 91.

[23] Quoted in *Report of the Indian Statutory Commission, 1930* (London, 1930), Cd. 3568 (Report of the Simon Commission), I, 2.

with a bicameral legislature at the Centre, consisting of the Council of State and the Assembly. In the latter body the majority of the members were elected representatives, with some official members who were nominated. In the provinces the act inaugurated the ingenious but cumbersome system of dyarchy, one of the unique features of India's constitutional system before independence.[24] In each province the government was to be of a dual nature, with the various legislative subjects classified as "reserved" or "transferred." Reserved subjects were to be handled by the governor, assisted by an executive council, but without the participation of the provincial legislature. On the other hand, transferred subjects, such as education, agriculture, and health, were entrusted to Indian ministers who were to be responsible to the provincial legislature. Generally speaking, the governor was expected to accept the advice of his ministers on these matters. The system was not as radical as it might seem, for the act included carefully worded provisions whereby the provincial governors and the Viceroy could block or override the wishes of the elected majority in the assemblies. The act also contained elaborate provisions for communal electorates. After it was passed, the franchise was given to 5,179,000 male voters (only 33,000 had been eligible to vote prior to 1919).

Liberal and forward-looking as the Act of 1919 seemed to be, it was out of date even before it was promulgated. In its very first year the central legislature, composed largely of liberals and moderates, resolved to press for further concessions. Moreover, any good effects which the act might have had were more than offset by resentment over certain unfortunate events of 1919, notably the repressive Rowlatt Acts and the Jallianwala Bagh tragedy in Amritsar, where some 400 persons were killed and 1,200 were wounded when British troops fired upon an unarmed crowd.

After the First World War the nationalist movement entered a new phase, under the leadership of Mahatma Gandhi, who had just returned to India after many years in England and South Africa. It was doubtless a fortunate thing both for India and for England that Gandhi appeared in a leading role at this time, when the stage seemed to be set for an orgy of violence and bloodshed.

It is impossible to assess the manifold contributions of Mohandas K. Gandhi to the nationalist cause. In a critical period he diverted the

[24] See A. Appadorai, *Dyarchy in Practice* (Madras, 1937), and "Kerala Putra," *The Working of Dyarchy in India* (Bombay, 1928).

movement into constructive channels—although at times it got out of control—and he identified it with the mass of the people. He related it directly to India's past and to modern needs. He preached and himself practiced the doctrines of nonviolent noncooperation (*ahimsa*) by techniques which he called *satyagraha* (soul force). He did all he could to promote good relations among all the people of India, especially between Hindus and Muslims. He gave depth and substance to India's cause, and he won for it world-wide attention and sympathy. He sought to win independence for India, not only in a political but in a spiritual sense. He gave "a moral and a spiritual standing to India's revolution." [25]

At first his efforts seemed to be unsuccessful. The Calcutta session of the Indian National Congress in 1920 accepted his policy of "progressive non-violent non-cooperation" as a weapon in support of the Khilafat movement (a Muslim protest movement in support of Turkey against threatened Allied reprisals). His methods were also viewed as a step toward greater self-government, "within the British Empire if possible, without if necessary." In December 1916 both the Congress and the Muslim League met in Lucknow, and there they agreed to cooperate in the cause of Indian unity and self-government. This "Lucknow Pact" was in effect for several years and was cemented by Gandhi's support of the Khilafat movement, in which the Muslims were intensely interested. To Gandhi this was "such an opportunity of uniting Hindus and Mohammedans as would not arise in a hundred years." But the differences between the Congress and the Muslim League were deep-seated, and the basis of their cooperation was a flimsy one. In 1922, as a result of the revolution in Turkey, the Sultan was deposed and in 1924 the caliphate was abolished. At about the same time the association between the Congress and the League came to an end. The noncooperation campaign reached a climax in 1921, but was shortly called off by Gandhi himself because of repeated acts of violence. Obviously the people of India were not yet ready to make effective use of the methods of *satyagraha*.

In 1922 Gandhi was arrested and imprisoned. In the following year, while he was still in confinement, two leaders of the Congress, C. R. Das and Pandit Motilal Nehru, were able to reverse the decision of the Congress not to cooperate in British legislative councils. The Congress thereupon contested elections; its members entered both pro-

[25] Gertrude Emerson, "Non-Violent Non-Cooperation in India," *Asia*, XXII (Aug. 1922), 674.

vincial and central legislatures and turned them into effective sounding boards for the nationalist movement.

For four years after his release from jail in 1924 Gandhi remained aloof from politics. Meanwhile the nationalist movement became increasingly radical. This trend was furthered by the rise of able, young, and militant nationalists, including Jawaharlal Nehru and Subhas Chandra Bose. Again a rift was developing between moderates and extremists, but this time there was a leader of sufficient stature and detachment to mend the rift.

In December 1928 Gandhi returned to active political work and soon was able to effect a compromise between the various groups in the Congress. At its annual meeting in 1929 in Lahore the Congress, under Gandhi's urging, adopted a pledge of complete independence and decreed that all members should take the pledge on January 26, to be observed as Independence Day. By decision of the government of a free India, January 26 twenty years later was chosen as the day on which the constitution would enter into effect and on which India would become a republic.

In March 1930 Gandhi led his famous salt march to the sea, symbolizing the national boycott of British goods, and this act was a signal for a nation-wide campaign of civil disobedience. Gandhi was arrested in May, and by mid-summer some 60,000 members and supporters of the Congress were also in prison.

Widespread disorders and moral pressures directed at England, due to the all-British composition of the Simon Commission on Indian constitutional reforms, led the Labor government in 1930 to hold a Round Table Conference in London, to discuss the whole "India problem," with the cooperation of leading Indians. Fifty-seven eminent Indians attended the first Round Table Conference, which was held in London from November 1930 to January 1931, but the Congress refused to send any representatives.

Immediately after the conference adjourned, hundreds of political prisoners, including Gandhi, were released, and in March 1931 Gandhi reached an agreement with Lord Irwin in the so-called Delhi Pact. Under this agreement the campaign of civil disobedience was to be halted and the Congress was to be represented at the second Round Table Conference. When the second conference was held, from September to December 1931, Gandhi alone spoke for the Congress. In fact, he gave the impression that he spoke for India. Unfortunately, little was accomplished either at the second Round Table Conference or at the third, where neither the Indian Congress nor the British Labor Party was represented.

Yet the pressure continued to mount for a settlement of the India problem. Finally, in the spring of 1933, Parliament appointed a Joint Committee on Indian Constitutional Reform. Its report, issued in November 1934, became the basis for the famous Government of India Act of 1935. The act was a long and complex measure, running to 451 clauses and 323 printed pages. The London *Times* of August 3, 1935, called it a "great constructive measure, the greatest indeed that a British Government has taken in hand in this century."

The Act of 1935 provided for the separation of Burma and India, and it gave a new constitution to India. Dyarchy in the provinces was abolished. The eleven provinces of British India were given a greater degree of independence from the Centre; and responsible government, limited by certain safeguards and emergency powers in the hands of the governors, was introduced in a really meaningful sense. After the act was passed, the franchise was extended to some 30,000,000 persons. A complex system of separate communal electorates was established. The Act of 1935 further provided the framework for a federal India, comprising both British India and the princely states. This significant step, however, was to be taken only when half the rulers of the princely states agreed to it. The powers of the central government and of the provincial governments were spelled out in three long lists of areas subject to federal, provincial, and concurrent jurisdiction. A kind of dyarchy appeared at the Centre through provisions giving the Governor-General full authority in defense and foreign affairs and providing for responsible government in other matters—subject, however, to the special authority of the Governor-General in finance and economics and to wide emergency powers.

The Government of India Act of 1935 was ill-fated from the beginning. As V. P. Menon remarked, "the Act had more enemies than friends." [26] One wonders whether the outcome would have been happier if the Indians had been able and willing to implement the federal provisions of the act. In spite of lengthy negotiations with the princes, the Viceroy was unable to put the federal provisions of the act into effect. Opposition to this promising experiment in central government came from many other sources. With the outbreak of the Second World War the efforts to establish a federal India along the lines

[26] *The Transfer of Power in India* (Princeton: Princeton University Press, 1957), p. 54.

charted by the Act of 1935 were shelved, never to be revived in the same form. Thus, as Menon sadly observes, "in the clash of politics, the struggle for power, the wrangle for ascendancy, and the scramble for gains on the part of the political organizations, politicians and the Princes, the scheme of federation, became a tragic casualty." [27]

After considerable delay a large measure of responsible government was actually granted to the provinces of British India for a limited period of time. The enlarged franchise was put into effect, and elections for the provincial assemblies were held early in 1937. In five of the eleven provinces the Congress obtained a clear majority. In Bombay it won nearly half the seats and soon gathered enough support to dominate the Assembly; in Assam and the North-West Frontier Province it was the largest single party. At first the Congress representatives refused to accept office because the governors would not pledge not to use their "powers of interference or set aside the advice of ministers in regard to their constitutional activities." Thus interim governments had to be organized in the five provinces where the Congress had been especially successful. Within a few months the impasse had been resolved by a statement from the Governor-General which the Congress interpreted as meeting its demands, and in July 1937 Congress ministries were formed in Bihar, Bombay, the Central Provinces, Madras, Orissa, and the United Provinces. Shortly thereafter a coalition ministry in which the Congress was the dominant group was set up in the North-West Frontier Province, and in October 1938 a similar coalition was formed in Assam. On the whole, these Congress ministries made an impressive record, and their relations with the governors were generally good; but they resigned en masse in November 1939 because of the opposition by the Congress to the circumstances under which the British brought India into the Second World War.

Various developments in 1937–1939 widened the gulf between the Congress and the Muslim League. When Congress ministries were in office in most of the provinces, no Muslims were included unless they abandoned the League and joined the Congress. It was Dr. Ambedkar, spokesman of the untouchables and not a Muslim, who said that this decision "means the political death of the Muslims as a free people." [28] Faced with the prospect that in the foreseeable future they would be a permanent minority in a Hindu-dominated state, large

---

[27] *Ibid.*, p. 57.

[28] Quoted in F. K. Khan Durrani, *The Meaning of Pakistan* (Lahore, 1944), p. 128.

numbers of Muslims began to support the League actively, and the League leaders began to think seriously in terms of a separate state. Their demands were formulated more specifically in the famous Lahore Resolution of 1940, which called for the creation of independent Muslim states in areas "in which the Muslims are numerically in the majority, as in the north-western zones of India." Thereafter the League championed partition and eventually the creation of a single Muslim state of Pakistan. These steps were naturally anathema to the Congress leaders, but by the early 1940s they were in no position to check the separatist trends.

In the spring of 1939 a crisis developed within the Congress. Subhas Chandra Bose, president in 1938 and reelected in 1939, opposed the views of Gandhi, whose retirement from politics had been no more than nominal. Gandhi won the day, and Bose was forced to resign. He immediately formed a more radical group known as the Forward Bloc. During the war he managed to escape to Germany, where he developed a great admiration for nazism, and then went to Singapore to form the Indian National Army, under the aegis of the Japanese. In October 1943 he announced the creation of the "Provisional Government of Free India," and in March 1944 he lead the INA into Indian territory, as a part of the Japanese thrust. Apparently he hoped to enter India as a conqueror, but his hopes were soon dashed, and he had to withdraw with the retreating Japanese. Thereafter his fortunes waned with those of the Japanese. Toward the end of the war he was killed in an airplane crash on Formosa. Thousands of Indians believe he is still alive, and his is still a name to conjure with in many parts of the country, especially in his native Bengal; but in 1939 his work with the Congress was over.

Meanwhile the advent of the Second World War complicated and intensified the struggle for independence. As soon as the British declared war on Germany, in September 1939, the Viceroy, Lord Linlithgow, announced that India too was at war with Germany. Promptly the Congress leaders called upon the Congress ministries in eight provinces to resign in protest. The Muslim League welcomed this move by celebrating on December 22 a Deliverance Day. Forthwith, in early 1940, the Congress accepted a recommendation of Gandhi to launch a campaign of nonviolent protest against the war. Thousands of Congressmen were arrested as they tried to launch this program. When Winston Churchill replaced Neville Chamberlain as British Prime Minister, a new round of negotiations on the subject of independence and cooperation began. But, although the Muslim League drifted ever closer to a position of all-out support for the British war effort, the Congress steadfastly refused its cooperation unless it received guarantees of immediate independence.

In 1942 Sir Stafford Cripps was sent to India on a special mission to win the cooperation of the Indians against the Japanese, who were already moving into Burma. Sir Stafford arrived in India on March 22, and a week later, at a press conference, he released the British government's draft proposals for the immediate and long-range future. Britain would not abandon its basic responsibility for the defense of India during the war, but after the fighting was over it would work with Indian representatives for "the creation of a new Indian Union." Negotiations, primarily with Congress leaders, failed to produce an agreement. On April 11 Sir Stafford admitted that "past distrust has proved too strong to allow of present agreement." The next day he left for England. As V. P. Menon observed:

The result of the Cripps negotiations, instead of bridging the gulf between the Government and the political parties in India, only served to widen it. The manner in which the negotiations had broken down tended to strengthen the doubts and suspicions in the minds of political leaders that there was no genuine desire on the part of His Majesty's Government to part with power.[29]

In August 1942 the Indian National Congress issued a sensational resolution calling on the British to "Quit India," and the party leaders set about preparing for another compaign of civil disobedience, at the very moment when the Japanese were approaching the borders of India. The British did not hesitate. They promptly arrested all the leaders of the Congress Party, and although Gandhi was released, because of ill-health, in May 1944, the majority of the Congress leadership spent the remainder of the war years in British jails.

Thus India went through the war as a divided camp, with the major nationalist movement opposed to the war effort and with the population becoming increasingly dissatisfied and disillusioned. Thousands of Indian troops who served on faraway battlefields also "recognized and felt the new trends sweeping across India."[30] Subhas Chandra Bose and his Indian National Army had many sympathizers

[29] *The Transfer of Power in India*, p. 138.
[30] Phillips Talbot, "The Independence of India," *Foreign Policy Reports*, XXIII (June 15, 1947), 77.

in India, even though they were cooperating with the Japanese; and the trial of officers of Bose's army in the Red Fort in Delhi in the latter part of 1945 aroused widespread resentment against the British and support for the accused. To the public mind of India, Bose and his followers seemed to have been trying to drive the British out of India. They were therefore national heroes, however misguided.

Relations between the Congress and the Muslim League were particularly strained by the war. Postwar elections to the central Legislative Assembly and to the provincial legislatures left no doubt that the League had won the support of the great majority of Muslims, just as the Congress had become the recognized spokesman for the great majority of non-Muslim Indians.

The growing strength of the nationalist movement in India was undoubtedly one major factor in the winning of independence; another was the impact of the war itself, for the basic discontents which brought new power to the Congress Party were precisely those which weakened the British hold on the subcontinent. But at the end of the war India was a house dangerously divided against itself. The British themselves were the first to feel that the situation was getting beyond their control. Their first action after victory in Europe was to release most political prisoners and to hold extensive conferences, in both India and England, on the subject of India's future. As a result of these conferences, Lord Wavell, who had succeeded Lord Linlithgow as Viceroy in October 1943, broadcast new proposals, designed, so he said, "to ease the present political situation and to advance India towards her goal of full self-government." He called a political conference of representative Indian leaders at Simla to form a new executive council, which was to be composed almost entirely of Indians.

The conference was held at Simla from June 25 to July 14.[31] The twenty-one Indians invited represented the major parties and groups in the country. They included Jinnah, president of the Muslim League, and Maulana Azad, then president of the Congress. Gandhi did not attend, by his own choice, but he was in Simla during the conference and available for consultation. Nehru took no part in the deliberations. It was hoped that a meeting between spokesmen of the Congress and the Muslim League, under the sponsorship of the Viceroy, would produce agreement regarding the creation of a new central government. "Very soon, however," Menon wrote many years later, "it became

[31] See Menon, *The Transfer of Power in India,* ch. viii (pp. 182–215), "The Simla Conference." Menon served as one of the secretaries of the conference.

transformed into the familiar pattern of futile discussions between the Congress and the Muslim League, and between party leaders and the Viceroy." [32] Thus the Simla Conference ended in the usual impasse. This time the failure was a particularly ominous one. As Menon regretfully noted, "The Simla Conference afforded a last opportunity for the forces of nationalism to fight a rear-guard action to preserve the integrity of the country, and when the battle was lost the waves of communalism quickly engulfed it. Only the Hobson's Choice of partition was left." [33]

The Transfer of Power

The electoral victory of the British Labor Party in July 1945 aroused great expectations in India, and the end of the war in August raised urgently the question of India's future political status. The Viceroy went to London for instructions and announced on his return in mid-September that "His Majesty's Government are determined to do their utmost to promote in conjunction with the leaders of Indian opinion the early realisation of full self-government in India." Elections for the central Legislative Assembly, held in late 1945, resulted in overwhelming victories for the Congress in non-Muslim constituencies and for the Muslim League in the Muslim constituencies, giving the Congress 57 and the League 30 of the 102 elected seats. As a result of the elections to the provincial legislatures the Congress formed ministries in six provinces, and the League in two, namely, Bengal and Sind.

In January 1946 a British parliamentary delegation of ten members toured India and talked with most of the important leaders. From March 24 to June 29 a special mission composed of three members of the cabinet—Lord Pethwick-Lawrence, Secretary of State for India; Sir Stafford Cripps, President of the Board of Trade; and A. V. Alexander, First Lord of the Admiralty—visited India to seek a reconciliation of the Congress and the Muslim League, but its efforts were in vain. In the absence of agreement among the Indians themselves the mission put forward its own proposals. Rejecting the idea of two sovereign states in the subcontinent, the mission proposed the establishment of "a Union of India, embracing both British India and the States," with residuary powers vested in the provinces or in the princely states. Special provisions were to be included for the protection of minorities, especially Muslims and Sikhs. A Constituent Assembly would be created to draw up the constitution for the new Union. In the mean-

[32] *Ibid.*, p. 214.   [33] *Ibid.*, p. 215.

time an interim government, composed of representatives of the major political parties in India, would carry on the work of administration.

Both the Congress and the Muslim League had reservations regarding the rather complicated scheme proposed by the Cabinet Mission, but both agreed to participate in elections for the 296 seats in the Constituent Assembly which were assigned to the provinces of British India (the 93 sets allotted to the Indian states were to be filled after negotiations with the rulers of the states concerned). The Congress won all of the general seats except 9, and the League won all but 5 of the seats allotted to Muslims. Now, however, the Muslim League rejected the long-term plan of the Cabinet Mission, which, it charged, had "played into the hands of the Congress." In late July the League went so far as to adopt a plan of "direct action." "This day," declared Jinnah, "we bid goodbye to constitutional methods."

With some misgivings the Viceroy decided to go ahead without the cooperation of the Muslim League. On August 6 he asked Nehru to form an interim government. With the approval of the Congress Working Committee, Nehru informed the Viceroy that the Congress would welcome the cooperation of the Muslim League but was prepared to form a government without it. The new interim government, headed by Nehru, was sworn in on September 2. In the beginning it did not include any nominees of the Muslim League, but in mid-October, after long negotiations on the part of the Viceroy with Jinnah, Gandhi, and Nehru, the League decided to participate. The five members it nominated included one member of the scheduled castes, but not Jinnah himself. As Menon notes, "The Muslim League had decided to enter the interim Government with but one purpose—and that was not to allow the Congress to consolidate its position to the detriment of the League's interest." [34] It also refused to participate in the deliberations of the Constituent Assembly until it had specific guarantees that the Muslims of India would not be dominated by the Congress and the Hindu majority. Nehru, Jinnah, Liaqat Ali Khan, and the Sikh leader Baldev Singh went to London in early December 1946 to discuss the forthcoming Constituent Assembly with leaders of the British government, but again no agreement could be reached.

In spite of the refusal of the Muslim League to participate, the Constituent Assembly met as scheduled on December 9. The highlight of the first session was the introduction by Nehru of a resolution stating that the Union of India should be "an independent Sovereign Re-

[34] *Ibid.,* p. 318.

public," with residuary powers vested in the autonomous units and with adequate safeguards for minorities and for backward communities and areas.

Early in 1947 the situation in India remained tense because of the inability of the British representatives to secure agreement on basic matters between the Congress and the Muslim League. The League continued to refuse to join the Constituent Assembly, and the Congress demanded that in the light of this refusal the representatives of the League should be dismissed from the interim government. Underlying the jockeying on immediate issues was a basic distrust which had constantly bedeviled all efforts at unified self-government. The League was insisting on a separate Pakistan, whereas the Congress wanted a single Union of India, a house of many rooms but not two separate establishments.[35]

Under these circumstances, with tension mounting in India and with increasing pressure upon it to resolve the deadlock, the British government decided to set a definite date for British withdrawal from India. On February 20 Prime Minister Attlee announced in the House of Commons that it was the "definite intention" of his government "to take the necessary steps to effect the transference of power to responsible Indian hands by a date not later than June 1948" and that if unhappily by that date a constitution for an independent India had not been worked out

by a fully representative Constituent Assembly . . . His Majesty's Government will have to consider to whom the powers of the central Government in British India should be handed over, on the due date, whether as a whole to some form of central Government for British India, or in some areas to the existing provincial Governments, or in such other way as may seem most reasonable and in the best interests of the Indian people.

On the same day the British government announced that Lord Wavell would shortly be succeeded as Viceroy by Lord Mountbatten, who would supervise the work of "transferring to Indian hands responsibility for the government of British India in a manner that will best ensure the future happiness and prosperity of India."

[35] In an interview with Eve Curie in the early 1940s Jinnah said: "How can you even dream of Hindu-Moslem unity? Everything pulls us apart: We have no intermarriages. We have not the same calendar. The Moslems believe in a single God, and the Hindus are idolatrous. Like the Christians, the Moslems believe in an equalitarian society, whereas the Hindus maintain the iniquitous system of castes and leave heartlessly fifty million Untouchables to their tragic fate, at the bottom of the social ladder." See Eve Curie, *Journey among Warriors* (Garden City, N.Y.: Doubleday, Doran, 1943), p. 463.

This announcement of the Labor government was widely hailed in both England and India. Nehru publicly described it as a "wise and courageous" declaration which "not only removes all misconception and suspicion, but also brings reality and a certain dynamic quality to the present situation in India." Jinnah refused to endorse the declaration and reiterated his demand for a separate state of Pakistan. The debates in the British Parliament revealed the grave apprehensions of many members as to the consequences of this step. Spokesmen of the Labor government admitted that the decision was fraught with grave risks, but they believed the risks were necessary.

Lord Mountbatten arrived in India on March 22, 1947. It was soon apparent to him that India was going from bad to worse, and he determined to effect the transfer of power as rapidly as possible. A new plan was drawn up after extended conferences and communications with Indian leaders and with the British cabinet in London. On June 2 and 3, after his return from London, Mountbatten met with seven Indian leaders, including Nehru and Jinnah. He also saw Gandhi, who had been preaching at his prayer meetings against partition, to explain the steps which had led to the new plan. Gandhi was observing a day of silence, but in a friendly note he indicated that he sympathized with the Viceroy's position. On June 3 Prime Minister Attlee announced the new plan in the House of Commons and in a radio broadcast. The essence of the proposal was that the British government intended to hand over its responsibilities in India before the end of the year to one or two governments, as determined by the Indians themselves. That same night, in broadcasts over All-India Radio, Lord Mountbatten explained the plan to the Indian people, and Nehru, Jinnah, and Baldev Singh followed with pleas to their people to give the plan a fair test.

By this time Lord Mountbatten and most of the Indian leaders were convinced that partition, however undesirable, was the only solution to the existing situation. Even today it is difficult to determine objectively at what point in India's history partition became "inevitable" and how the responsibility for this "solution" should be shared. Perhaps the best answer was given by Gandhi, to whom the very idea of partition was repugnant, at a prayer meeting shortly after the June 3 plan was announced: "The British Government is not responsible for partition. The Viceroy has no hand in it. In fact he is as opposed to division as Congress itself. But if both of us, Hindus and Muslims, cannot agree on anything else, then the Viceroy is left with no choice."

In June and July the decision for partition was taken by votes in the legislative assemblies of Bengal, the Punjab, and Sind, by a meeting of certain representatives of tribal groups and of the Quetta Municipality in Baluchistan, and by referenda in Sylhet and the North-West Frontier Province. Thereupon the British government began to prepare the draft of an Indian Independence Bill. Introduced in the House of Commons on July 4, it was passed by the Commons on July 15, by the Lords on the following day, and received the Royal Assent on July 18. Seldom in the history of the British Parliament had a measure of such epochal significance been put through so speedily and with so little debate. "This is a bill," declared the Secretary of State for India, "unique in the history of legislation in this country. Never before has such a large portion of the world population achieved complete independence through legislation alone." Significant though it undoubtedly was, the act simply confirmed decisions that had already been made. It provided that "as from the fifteenth day of August, nineteen hundred and forty-seven, two independent Dominions shall be set up in India, to be known respectively as India and Pakistan."

At the close of his meeting with Indian leaders on June 3 Lord Mountbatten produced a thirty-three page document entitled "The Administrative Consequences of Partition." "The effect it made on those present," reported V. P. Menon, "was indicated by the complete silence which followed. For the first time the party leaders had been made to realize the magnitude of the task that confronted them." [36] The task was indeed formidable, and the time was short. As Lord Birdwood observed (like Menon he was intimately involved in the mechanics of partition): "There was thus left just under two and a half months in which to complete the greatest political and administrative operation in history." [37] Of particular importance were the decisions regarding the division of the armed forces and the civil service and the drawing of boundaries in the two great provinces of Bengal and the Punjab, which were to be partitioned also. For each province the decisions were made by boundary commissions consisting of two High Court judges nominated by the Congress and two nominated by the Muslim League, with Sir Cyril Radcliffe as chairman of both commissions. Quite wisely, the Radcliffe awards were not announced until August 16, the day following independence for the two Dominions. They were widely criticized at the time of their announcement and at later periods, but they were nevertheless accepted as the basis

[36] *The Transfer of Power in India*, p. 397.
[37] *India and Pakistan: A Continent Decides* (New York: Praeger, 1954), p. 34.

for the redrawing of boundary lines in the Punjab and Bengal, subject to such modification as might be made by later negotiations.

Another major problem that had to be dealt with in the few weeks between early June and mid-August 1947 was that of the Indian states. There were 562 of these states in early 1947, ranging in size from Jammu and Kashmir and Hyderabad, which were larger than many independent countries in the world, to states of only a few hundred acres. Together they covered 45 per cent of the area and had 28 per cent of the population of the entire subcontinent. Some of these states, such as Mysore and Cochin, were truly progressive, and 60 of them had representative assemblies; but in general the Indian states were far behind British India in a political, economic, and social sense, and most of them were regarded as backward and autocratic, relics of the past and allies of the imperial power, Britain. Their independence guaranteed by the British, the states were a major obstacle to any federal program; they had, for example, prevented the federal provisions of the Act of 1935 from being implemented. In a declaration of May 12, 1946, the British stated clearly that although they could not and would not force the hand of the princes, they nonetheless hoped and expected that the princely states would voluntarily accede to either India or Pakistan.

In the spring of 1947 representatives of the states took their seats in the Constituent Assembly. Immediately following the historic announcement by the British government on June 3, 1947, the interim government in India created the States Ministry headed by Sardar Vallabhbhai Patel, with V. P. Menon as Secretary, to deal with the problem of the Indian states. For his success in persuading—or in some cases forcing—the princely states into the Union of India, Sardar Patel was widely hailed as the main architect of Indian unity. "The work accomplished by him at the States' Ministry amounts to a silent revolution." [38] Before August 15, 1947, the rulers of all the states contiguous to the territories of the new Union of India, with the exception of Hyderabad, Kashmir, and Junagadh, had signed an Instrument of Accession and a Standstill Agreement. Within two years after independence, the territorial unity of the Union was assured by the merger, consolidation, or integration of virtually all the states which fell within the confines of the new nation. Whether the later integra-

[38] N. Srinivasan, *Democratic Government in India* (Calcutta, 1954), p. 108. See also V. P. Menon, *The Story of the Integration of the Indian States* (New York: Macmillan, 1956).

tion was a violation of the original understandings under which the princes agreed to enter the Union of India and whether the government of India has abided by the pledges which Patel made to them in good faith are still delicate and moot questions in India today.

Thus, after long years of foreign rule and in a country divided against itself, India achieved independence in August 1947. The cost of partition, with all its attendant evils and tragic aftermath, still lay in the future. On the night of August 14 the Constituent Assembly met to usher in the nation's independence. In a moving speech Nehru declared:

Long years ago we made a tryst with destiny, and now the time comes when we shall redeem our pledge, not wholly or in full measure, but very substantially. At the stroke of the midnight hour, when the world sleeps, India will awake to life and freedom. A moment comes, which comes but rarely in history, when we step out from the old to the new, when an age ends, and when the soul of a nation, long suppressed, finds utterance. It is fitting that at this solemn moment we take the pledge of dedication to the service of India and her people and to the still larger cause of humanity.

· X ·

India since Independence:

The Political Record

IN the face of unfavorable conditions at home and abroad India's achievements since independence have been impressive indeed. The new nation has survived many crises, and Indians have a developing sense of national unity and a growing confidence that their country can face with equanimity whatever vital issues may be encountered. Step by step major obstacles have been overcome and the democratic structure has been strengthened.

At the outset two great problems involved dealing with the tragic circumstances that followed partition and ensuring the political unity of the country. The government managed very effectively the critical situation of the refugees and then turned its attention to their rehabilitation and to preparations for their entry into the normal activities of the country. Within two years after independence most of the Indian states in or contiguous to those portions of British India which were to be a part of the Union of India were integrated in various ways into the Union, thus averting what might have been a serious or even a fatal handicap to the unity of the emerging nation.

Work was begun promptly on the drafting of a constitution. After extensive discussion of the proposed draft in the Constituent Assembly and throughout the country, the constitution went into effect on

January 26, 1950, and India thereupon became a republic. As soon as preparations could be made following the adoption of the constitution, India held its first nation-wide general elections in 1951–1952, and thereafter the parliamentary institutions began to function on a more normal basis. The second general elections were held in February–March 1957, and the third in February 1962. The constitutional system that emerged was patterned heavily after Western and especially British models, but it has been adapted quite successfully to India's needs and environment, and the precedents that have been established in the first years of democratic government augur well for the future.

In 1951 India launched its First Five Year Plan (the drafting of which was finalized in late 1952), a gigantic experiment in democratic planning. At the expiration of this plan in the spring of 1956, most of the goals had been achieved, and the country immediately entered upon the even more ambitious Second Five Year Plan. Although the targets of the Second Plan were not fully realized, substantial progress was made, and in April 1961 a still more ambitious Third Plan was officially launched.

Agitation for a redrawing of the boundaries of the states of India along essentially linguistic lines was at first opposed by the government of India; but in 1953 Andhra was set up as a separate state, and on November 1, 1956, after the report of the States Reorganization Commission had been submitted and debated and after the inner circles of the Congress Party and the government had agreed upon basic matters, the map of India was redrawn internally with the creation of fourteen states and six centrally administered territories. This reorganization left the state of Bombay intact, but in 1960, as a result of continued agitation, this state was divided into the two new states of Maharashtra and Gujerat, with Bombay city as the capital of Maharashtra. In the same year the government of India agreed to the establishment of a Naga state to be known as Nagaland, and in 1961 an advisory council of representatives of the Naga tribesmen was formed, an "interim body" which was to function for three years and to assist the government in the administration of Nagaland and in the drafting of a constitution for the new state. Linguistic and regional problems are still troublesome and will doubtless stand in the way of effective national unity for many years to come. So will the divisive forces of communalism and caste, in spite of the efforts to do away with the worst features of these ancient practices.

In economic, social, and political objectives there is a remarkable degree of consensus in India. The Five Year Plans and the broad outlines of foreign policy have attracted an impressive measure of support. The tremendous popularity and prestige of Jawaharlal Nehru have won country-wide support for the dominant Congress Party and for the government which Nehru heads and have helped to consolidate the foundations of national unity and to win acceptance of the concept of the secular state. There is still, however, a vast gap between objectives and performance, between professions and deeds, between the old and the new, between social conservatism and the dynamic forces of modern life.

The Cost of Partition

India attained independence only at the cost of partition, with all its difficulties and bitterness. Rejoicing over the winning of freedom was muted by the unhappy events which marred the birth of the two nations. India awoke to independence, to use Nehru's figure of speech, to discover that a first-class crisis threatened to plunge the entire subcontinent into a bloodbath and to place an impossible burden on the already-harassed political authorities of the new states. Even before the announcement by the British government of its forthcoming abdication, communal rioting had broken out in Calcutta and other parts of the subcontinent. When it became known that two of the great provinces, the Punjab and Bengal, would likewise be cut in two, rioting and killings became more frequent. In spite of the strained relations between India and Pakistan, their leaders cooperated as best they could to avert the impending tragedy; nevertheless, during a few weeks in the fall of 1947, the subcontinent witnessed one of the greatest orgies of violence and uncontrolled fanaticism in modern times.

The worst scenes occurred in the Punjab. No one can tell how the trouble started or who should bear the major responsibility. In the western Punjab the Muslims attacked the homes and the persons of the Hindu and Sikh minority, and in the eastern Punjab the Hindus and Sikhs vented their wrath on the Muslim minority. Thousands of people were killed, often in the most brutal ways. Trains were derailed and their passengers massacred, refugee columns ambushed, homes set on fire and their inhabitants butchered in the streets. The Punjab Boundary Force had to be disbanded because its members too became infected with the communal fury.

As hundreds of Muslims began to move out of Delhi and as refugees from West Punjab streamed in, bringing harrowing tales of atrocities with them, Delhi also, in the very political center of India, witnessed terrible scenes. V. P. Menon, an eyewitness of these scenes, has given an eloquent description of the state of the refugees who came to Delhi in these trying days:

The uprooted millions were in a terrible mental state. They had been driven from their homes under conditions of indescribable horror and misery. Not many had the time to plan their evacuation; most had to move out at the shortest possible notice. They had been subjected to terrible indignities. They had witnessed their near and dear ones hacked to pieces before their eyes and their houses ransacked, looted and set on fire by their own neighbors. They had no choice but to seek safety in flight, filled with wrath at what they had seen, and full of anguish for numberless missing kinsmen who were still stranded in Pakistan and for their womenfolk who had been abducted.[1]

Fortunately, the rest of the country remained relatively unaffected by the communal frenzy, although there were threats of trouble in West Bengal. Serious rioting was averted in Calcutta only by the influence of Mahatma Gandhi, who went to India's largest city and started a fast in protest against communal disturbances. Lord Mountbatten did not exaggerate when he referred to Gandhi as "the one-man boundary force who kept the peace while a force 50,000 strong was swamped by riots."

The governments of India and Pakistan, encouraged by Lord Mountbatten, cooperated in helping to move thousands of people to and from each other's territories and in preserving some semblance of law, order, and sanity. In India an emergency committee was set up; Lord Mountbatten served as chairman, and Nehru and Patel were among its members. A special committee was created to deal with the situation in Delhi and New Delhi. In October the worst of the troubles was over, although the flow of refugees continued. By the middle of 1948 over 12 million people had crossed the Indo-Pakistan borders, creating one of the greatest refugee problems of modern times. About 5.5 million Hindus and Sikhs had moved from West Pakistan into India, about the same number of Muslims had left East Punjab and other parts of India for West Pakistan, and approximately 1.5 million non-Muslims had crossed the borders of East Pakistan into West Bengal.

[1] V. P. Menon, *The Transfer of Power in India* (Princeton: Princeton University Press, 1957), p. 418.

Nearly half a million Hindus later left Sind for India, and the influx of Hindus from East Pakistan into West Bengal still goes on.

India has made heroic efforts to cope with the tremendous refugee problem. The first task was to care for immediate needs. At one time the government of India was running some 160 camps, accommodating a million and a quarter people. There were 150,000 in two camps outside New Delhi alone. The next step was to provide centers for the rehabilitation of the refugees and to find means of integrating them into the life of the country. On the whole, the refugee problem has been largely resolved, but even today, more than a decade and a half after independence, thousands of refugees huddle in improvised shelters in Delhi, Calcutta, and other large cities of India.

Thus at the outset of independence India was faced with a human tragedy of formidable dimensions. The terrible weeks of August and September 1947 left a lasting impression on Indian minds. Trouble had been anticipated along the new frontiers of India and Pakistan, especially in divided Bengal and the Punjab, but few people foresaw mass destruction. Many Indians still find it hard to understand why such a catastrophe occurred. It was a heavy burden for the new state to bear. As V. P. Menon has observed: "The communal holocaust, the two-way exodus of refugees, their protection and the rehabilitation of those who had come to India—all these provided the Government of India, at a time when the administrative machinery was already out of joint as a result of partition, with a task as stupendous as any nation ever had to face." [2]

The Integration of the States

As soon as the communal disturbances accompanying partition had been brought under control, the government of India turned its attention to problems of consolidation and internal development. A matter of pressing importance was the necessity of integrating into the Union of India the princely states which had acceded to India prior to independence. Within two years this important task was accomplished. Again the chief credit belongs to Vallabhbhai Patel and to the States Ministry which he headed. The policy of the government of India was to subordinate the princely states to the central government by moving well beyond the Standstill Agreements that had been made prior to independence, to associate the more than 500 princely states into viable units, chiefly by consolidating them with former

[2] *Ibid.*, p. 434.

governor's provinces or chief commissioner's provinces or by forming unions of states, and to modernize and democratize the princely states to the fullest extent possible. Briefly put, the aim, as the first White Paper on Indian States declared, "was the integration of all elements in the country in a free, united and democratic India." [3] Integration meant that the princely rulers had to give up their effective power. Some continued to have appointive posts in the territories where they had once held almost absolute sway, and some took active political roles, but most were simply pensioned off.

The process of integrating the Indian states assumed three main forms. In the first place, many of the smaller states were merged and then joined to the former provinces of British India (governor's provinces). Secondly, some states were consolidated into States Unions and placed under the direct administration of the central government, and the administration of a few individual states, for special reasons, was at least temporarily of the same nature. Thirdly, many other states were joined into Unions of States. Eventually, five States Unions were thus created, and together with the only three princely states to retain their original form until the reorganization of 1956 —Mysore, Hyderabad, and Jammu and Kashmir—they became Part "B" states under the constitution of 1950. Altogether, 216 states were merged into former governor's provinces; 61 were placed under the administration of the central government, mostly merged into States Unions; and 275 were merged into five States Unions which became separate units of the Union.

A mere recital of the steps by which the more than 500 princely states were made integral parts of the Indian Union cannot even suggest the drama of the story. V. P. Menon, who was Patel's right-hand man in the States Ministry, has vividly described the negotiations which Patel and others in the States Ministry carried on with the princely rulers, trying to persuade them to relinquish their power voluntarily and thus to help in the integration of the new India. [4] Some rulers, like the fabulously wealthy Nizam of Hyderabad, were reluctant to surrender their power at all. Others took a dim view of having their territories merged with other states. Occasionally these mergers involved states whose rulers had been bitter rivals or even enemies for many

[3] See Government of India, Ministry of States, *White Paper on Indian States* (New Delhi: Government of India Press, 1st ed., 1948, rev. ed., 1950).

[4] V. P. Menon, *The Story of the Integration of the Indian States* (New York: Macmillan, 1956).

decades. To persuade the Maharajah of Gwalior and the Maharajah of Indore to join in the new state of Madhya Bharat was a feat of no small dimensions, in view of the long-standing rivalry between these two princely states. No fewer than 222 states, estates, and talukas were merged to form the United State of Kathiawar, later known as Saurashtra. Menon's lively account of the process by which Saurashtra was brought into being may be commended as a fascinating study of a most difficult operation. The accession, integration, and democratization of the princely states of India constituted a major achievement of the leaders of India and especially of Vallabhbhai Patel, who called the operation a "bloodless revolution which has affected the destinies of millions of our people."

Special problems arose with regard to Jammu and Kashmir, Hyderabad, and a small state in the Kathiawar area, Junagadh. The case of Junagadh was rather easily settled, although it caused friction between India and Pakistan and raised problems of considerable import. Located only a short distance from the southeastern borders of West Pakistan, Junagadh had a Muslim ruler and an overwhelmingly Hindu population. In September 1947 the ruler of Junagadh formally acceded to Pakistan, and Pakistan accepted the accession. When this action became known, disturbances broke out in the state. India disapproved of the arrangement and presumably encouraged the Hindus of the state to voice their protests. The ruler was forced to flee, and the Muslim Diwan, under great pressure, invited the Indian government to send in troops to restore order. On India's insistence a plebiscite was held in Junagadh in February 1948, which resulted in an almost unanimous vote for accession to India. The merger was accomplished in the following January.[5]

The case of Hyderabad posed far more serious problems for the government of India. One of the largest of the princely states and one of the most feudal, Hyderabad occupied a huge area in the center of the Deccan. From the point of view of the Indian government the integration of Hyderabad into the Union of India was a necessity. The Nizam, however, was a Muslim and had other ideas; he was strongly backed in his desire to preserve an independent existence by militant Muslim leaders and organizations inside his state and perhaps also by the government of Pakistan. He rejected the invitation to accede to India before the transfer of power. In November 1947 he did agree to sign a Standstill Agreement with India. For

[5] See *ibid.*, ch. vi.

several months Lord Mountbatten and Sir Walter Moncton, who was
the Nizam's constitutional adviser, worked with Patel and other Indian officials to persuade the Nizam to change his mind. In June 1948
the negotiations broke down, and India imposed a complete economic
blockade on the state. Within Hyderabad a campaign of violence,
spurred on by Muslim fanatics and Communists, kept the Hindu majority in a state of terror. The Nizam appealed to the Security Council
of the United Nations for aid in settling his dispute with India. While
the Security Council was considering the advisability of placing the
dispute on its agenda, in the face of India's strong insistence that
Hyderabad was not a sovereign state and therefore could not bring a
dispute before the UN, the government of India, on September 13,
1948, sent troops into Hyderabad. After no more than token resistance
the Nizam capitulated, and the state was placed under a military administration. The Indian government allowed the Nizam to continue
as head of the state. In November he acceded to India, and in January
1950 he became Rajpramukh (i.e., governor) of his state, which became a Part "B" state in the Union.[6] When all the states were reorganized along linguistic lines, in November 1956, the state of Hyderabad
passed out of existence, and the Nizam announced his retirement.
Most of what had been Hyderabad was shared by the enlarged states
of Bombay and Andhra Pradesh, and the city of Hyderabad became
the capital of the latter state.

   The government of India now regards the state of Jammu and
Kashmir as fully integrated into the Indian republic, even though the
"final" steps in this process were not completed until January 1957,
when the constitution which had been adopted by the Constituent
Assembly in Kashmir went into effect. The Pakistan government takes
an entirely different view. It maintains that the status of Kashmir is
still to be determined by a plebiscite, promised by Governor-General
Mountbatten in October 1947 and reaffirmed by Nehru and other
Indian leaders on many subsequent occasions. It holds that the principle of popular consent which motivated Indian actions in the cases
of Junagadh and Hyderabad was violated by India in the case of
Kashmir. A brochure issued by Pakistan Publications in 1957 stated:

According to its logic in the cases of Junagadh and Hyderabad, India
should have turned down the offer of a Hindu Ruler to accede to India,
in spite of the fact that 77 per cent of State's population was Muslim. . . .

   [6] *Ibid.,* chs. xvii–xix.

But in the case of Kashmir, the arguments which India had advanced in the cases of Hyderabad and Junagadh were ignored.[7]

The details of the dispute between India and Pakistan over Kashmir are discussed in the later section on foreign policy.[8] Here brief reference will be made to the evolving status of Kashmir within the Union of India.

Like the Nizam of Hyderabad, the Hindu Maharajah of Kashmir did not accept an invitation to accede to the Union of India prior to August 15, 1947. He entered into a Standstill Agreement with Pakistan, but apparently he thought in terms of preserving his independence from either of the emerging Dominions. He was subject to strong pressure from Pakistan to accede to that state. Pakistan even imposed an economic blockade on Kashmir. But tribal invasions of the Maharajah's state in October 1947 forced him to appeal to India for help. Acting on the advice of Lord Mountbatten, the government of India agreed to send military aid only if the Maharajah would accede to the Indian Union. This he did on October 26, 1947. A few hours later Indian troops landed by air in Srinagar and within a few days had pushed back the invaders. A letter from Governor-General Mountbatten to the Maharajah of Kashmir, dated October 27, 1947, made it clear that India's acceptance of the accession was provisional and that "as soon as law and order have been restored in Kashmir and her soil cleared of the invader, the question of the accession should be settled by a reference to the people." The plebiscite has never been held. In spite of the efforts of Dr. Frank Graham and other representatives of the United Nations, which has been concerned with the Kashmir dispute ever since India brought it before the Security Council on January 1, 1948, demilitarization and other essential preliminary steps could not be agreed upon by the two parties directly concerned. As time went on, new factors entered the picture, so that India's present position seems to be that the pledge of the plebiscite is no longer binding. As early as 1947 the Kashmir National Conference approved the Maharajah's decision to accede to India. Sheikh Abdullah, who was the Muslim leader of the National Conference until his dismissal and arrest in August 1953, favored close association with

[7] *Kashmir: The Powder Keg of Asia* (Karachi: Pakistan Publications, 1957), p. 5.

[8] See Lord Birdwood, *Two Nations and Kashmir* (London, 1956); Josef Korbel, *Danger in Kashmir* (Princeton: Princeton University Press, 1954); Menon, *Integration of the Indian States*, ch. xx.

India until a few weeks before his fall from power. The state of Jammu and Kashmir was listed as one of the Part "B" states of the Indian Union in the constitution of 1950, but retained a special limited relation to Union authority. The Delhi Agreement of July 1952 spelled out the details of Kashmir's special relationship with India. This agreement was ratified by both the Indian Parliament and the Constituent Assembly of Kashmir. In 1952, upon the recommendation of Sheikh Abdullah, then Prime Minister of the state, the Constituent Assembly declared that the Maharajah's rule was at an end and elected his son, Yuvraj Karen Singh, as the first Sadar-i-Riyasat or elected head of the state.

The government of Bakshi Ghulam Mohammed, which replaced Sheikh Abdullah's regime in August 1953, was strongly pro-Indian and took the position that Kashmir had irrevocably cast its lot with that of India. With the obvious approval of the Indian government, a newly elected Assembly, composed chiefly of followers of the Bakshi government, drafted and adopted a constitution for the state. Article 3, which became operative immediately on the adoption of the constitution in November 1956, stated categorically that the "State of Jammu and Kashmir is and shall be an integral part of the Union of India." When this constitution entered fully into effect on January 26, 1957, both the Bakshi regime and the government of India announced that the integration of Kashmir into the Indian republic was now complete.

Constitution Making

These three states were the last to be integrated into Indian territory; but long before this process of integration was complete, India had set about creating a constitution. Indeed, the essential character of the Indian state after the achievement of freedom was largely determined before the British government decided to withdraw from India. The new nation, it was clear, would be a democratic state, modeled mainly along British lines. The new constitution would be patterned after the Government of India Act of 1935, with such changes as seemed necessary to safeguard fundamental freedoms and to serve the needs of an independent democracy. Free India would be a federal state, and it would have a written constitution. Although the British system of cabinet responsibility would prevail, an effort would be made to adapt features of other constitutional systems as well. The new constitution would be framed by a Constituent Assembly.

Under the plan advanced by the British Cabinet Mission a Constituent Assembly was elected by the provincial assemblies in July 1946 and began to function immediately, even though its representative character was weakened when the Muslim League refused to allow its elected members to attend. The first session was held in New Delhi on December 9, 1946. Dr. Rajendra Prasad, later President of the Indian republic, was elected permanent president. An important Resolution on Aims and Objectives, moved by Nehru on December 11 and adopted on January 22, 1947, expressed the Assembly's "firm and solemn resolve to proclaim India as an Independent Sovereign Republic and to draw up for her future governance a Constitution." At its third session (April 22–May 2, 1947) the Constituent Assembly set up committees on the Union constitution and provincial constitutions, under the chairmanship of Nehru and Patel, respectively. When the fourth session met on July 14, the decision to partition the subcontinent had been announced, and only a short time remained to prepare for the assumption of full independence. The Constituent Assembly was broadened by the addition of representatives from the princely states and of members of the Muslim League from parts of the country which would be included in the Union of India. The Assembly began to discuss the principles of the new constitution, starting with the reports of the Nehru Committee. After midnight of August 14 the Assembly began to function in two capacities: as the Provisional Parliament of India, with a Speaker (G. V. Mavalankar) in the chair, and as the Constituent Assembly with sovereign powers, presided over by a president (Dr. Rajendra Prasad). The Assembly continued to function in this dual role until the work of constitution making was accomplished.

On August 29, 1947, two weeks after India became independent, the Constituent Assembly set up a drafting committee of seven distinguished members, including N. Gopalaswami Ayyangar, K. M. Munshi, Alladi Krishnaswami Iyer, and T. T. Krishnamachari, with India's most distinguished "untouchable," Dr. B. R. Ambedkar, as chairman. B. N. Rau, later a judge of the International Court of Justice, acted as constitutional adviser, and S. N. Mukerji was principal draftsman. Both because of their positions as Prime Minister and Deputy Prime Minister and because of their enormous personal influence, Nehru and Patel also played a major role in the work of constitution making. Perhaps the chief credit should go to Dr. Ambedkar, the able chairman of the drafting committee, for his vast legal knowledge, his ability as presiding officer of the committee, and his effectiveness in defending the constitutional proposals in the Constituent Assembly.

Relying heavily upon British models and upon the Government of India Act of 1935, the members of the drafting committee made a careful study of the constitutions of all the democratic countries of the world and adopted features from several. Thus the provisions regarding the Supreme Court of India owed much to the American constitution. In the framing of the vital sections dealing with fundamental rights and with the "directive principles of state policy," the committee borrowed certain provisions and ideas from the constitutions of Ireland, Australia, Canada, and the United States.

The first draft of the constitution was ready in the incredibly short time of under six months. It was the subject of extensive discussion in the country, which resulted in some changes, before it was taken up by the Constituent Assembly eight months later. The Assembly spent an entire year considering the constitutional proposals in great detail. "During this period as many as 7,635 amendments were tabled and 2,473 of these were actually discussed by the Assembly." [9] The debates in the Constituent Assembly during these months were generally on a very high level. Although they did not probe to the fundamentals of government as searchingly as did the debates in the American Constitutional Convention, they are of fundamental importance for all students of comparative government. Unfortunately India produced nothing comparable to the Federalist Papers to enlighten the people of the country on the nature and significance of the new constitution.

The third reading of the Constitutional Bill began on November 14, 1949, and was concluded on November 26 by its adoption. The final session of the Constituent Assembly was held on January 24, 1950. It elected Dr. Rajendra Prasad as President of the republic of India under the new constitution. Two days later, India was proclaimed a republic and Dr. Prasad assumed office as its President. This date is commemorated every year as Republic Day. The Constituent Assembly carried on as India's Provisional Parliament until the summer of 1952, when the first regular Parliament elected under the constitution took over.

The Constitutional System

India's constitution is the longest document of its kind in the world. It consists of 395 articles and 9 schedules. The text of the document in

[9] N. Srinivasan, *Democratic Government in India* (Calcutta, 1954), p. 138.

an official version runs to 254 pages, and the table of contents and the index to 64 pages more. For its unusual length there was both reason and precedent. "The Indian Constitution, unlike some others, is not merely a declaration of principles. It is a detailed and intricate body of organic law containing many elements that in some other countries are to be found in the statutory rather than the constitutional law." [10] Because of regional and social variations, the great variety of legal practices and customs, the relative lack of experience in self-government, and the need to provide for emergencies, the framers of the constitution took pains to be explicit. They felt that many points which might otherwise have been left to regular legislation, and even many objectives which could not be legally enforceable, should be spelled out in the basic constitutional document.

Undoubtedly the example of the Government of India Act of 1935 did not make for brevity. This act was one of the longest and most intricate ever passed by the British Parliament. As has been noted, the constitution of India borrowed heavily from it; in fact, many sections were incorporated almost without change. Professor N. Srinivasan has called the constitution "a palimpsest" of the Act of 1935. "The new Constitution may indeed be described as the working Constitution of the country under the old Act adapted to its new political status." [11]

Briefly stated, the constitution of India makes India a democratic secular state with what is essentially a parliamentary system and a federal structure. In practice, no doubt, this generalization must be qualified in many ways. Perhaps it would be more accurate to say that in India democracy is the goal rather than the reality—in other words, that India is a democracy-in-being and that the prospects for the successful evolution of democratic institutions are still unknown. The leaders of India, and most of all Nehru himself, are dedicated to the concept of the secular state, but there are strong communal forces in the country pulling in a different direction. Although India has essentially a parliamentary system, patterned, as Nehru himself stated, "largely after the British model, with necessary variations," some of the "variations," such as the emergency powers of the President and the role of the Supreme Court, suggest a strange blending of parliamentary and nonparliamentary forms.

Although India is "a Union of States," according to Article 1 of the

[10] Editorial, "A Constitution for India," *New York Times,* Nov. 28, 1949.

[11] Srinivasan, *Democratic Government in India,* p. 143.

constitution, experts in government are still arguing whether there is in fact a federal system. If so, it is a peculiar kind of federalism, with many unfederal features. Here again one notes the influence of the Government of India Act of 1935, which provided for a federation of British India and the Native States, though these provisions were never implemented. In free India the federation was peculiar in that it was created by the transfer of power from both foreign and native rulers. Thus from the outset the Indian federation had strong centralizing characteristics. These are perpetuated in the constitution, which vests residuary powers in the Centre and gives the central government an authority over the constituent units of the federation—the states— which in times of emergency may amount to a virtual suspension of the federal structure. Professor Kenneth Wheare, a distinguished British authority on constitutional systems, has expressed the view that the constitution of India "establishes, indeed, a system of government which is at most quasi-federal, almost devolutionary in character; a unitary State with subsidiary federal features rather than a federal State with subsidiary unitary features." [12] Most authorities would challenge the latter part of Professor Wheare's interpretation. They would agree that India is "at most quasi-federal," but they would in- sist that it is "a federal State with subsidiary unitary features." Most federations have felt the need to give ample authority to the central government; hence few existing federations are more than quasi-federal in character. The framers of the Indian constitution were determined to give the Centre enough power to hold the Union together against the many disruptive forces which they knew to be at work in the In- dian environment. Thus, as Professor Srinivasan has pointed out, "the new Constitution of India has effected an adjustment of federal-state relations suited to the conditions of India that is *sui generis.*" [13] It is a pattern which deserves the careful attention of students of comparative government.

A people which has known only authoritarian rule, either foreign or domestic, now has a constitution which proclaims boldly in the first words of the Preamble: "WE, THE PEOPLE OF INDIA, having solemnly resolved to constitute India into a SOVEREIGN, DEMOCRATIC REPUBLIC . . . do HEREBY ADOPT, ENACT AND GIVE TO OURSELVES THIS CONSTITU- TION." A lengthly section (Articles 12 through 35) spells out the fun-

---

[12] "India's New Constitution Analysed," *A.L.J.*, XLVIII, 21, quoted in Alan Gledhill, *The Republic of India* (London, 1951), p. 92.
[13] Srinivasan, *Democratic Government in India*, p. 147.

damental rights which are guaranteed to every person. These rights are grouped under the following subheadings: Right to Equality, Right to Freedom, Right against Exploitation, Right to Freedom of Religion, Cultural and Educational Rights, Right to Property, Right to Constitutional Remedies. Article 17 states unequivocally: " 'Untouchability' is abolished and its practice in any form is forbidden." The widespread prevalence of "untouchability" in India today does not lessen the importance of this provision in India's fundamental law; rather it points to the difficulty of trying to correct long-standing social abuses by legal means and offers a positive hope for the future.

Article 21 of the constitution reads as follows: "No person shall be deprived of his life or personal liberty except according to procedure established by law." And Article 31 (1) states: "No person shall be deprived of his property save by authority of law." These provisions call attention to the fact that there is no due process clause in the Indian constitution, such as is found in the Fifth and Fourteenth Amendments to the American constitution. American experts on constitutional law have often pointed to this omission, which was a deliberate one, as an indication that the constitution of India lacks a vital reserve power to protect the citizen against arbitrary acts of the government. In the important case of *A. K. Gopalan* v. *The State of Madras* the Supreme Court of India held that the term "procedure established by law" in Article 21 of the Indian constitution "cannot be interpreted to lay down a vague standard such as the principles of natural law" and thus was not equivalent to the American due process clause. Justice William O. Douglas of the United States Supreme Court, however, in his careful comparative study of American and Indian constitutional law, professed to "discern in Indian judicial decisions a flavor of due process when it comes to questions of *substantive* law." "Suffice it to say," he concluded, "that the concepts embodied in due process are also embodied in Indian constitutional law, where other clauses do service for a due process clause." [14]

Article 22 provides protection against arrest and detention in certain cases, but it also contains clauses which have allowed the Indian Parliament to pass the Preventive Detention Bill, one of the toughest bills on the statute books of any democratic state.

The section on fundamental rights in the constitution is followed

[14] William O. Douglas, *We the Judges: Studies in American and Indian Constitutional Law from Marshall to Mukherjea* (New York: Doubleday, 1956), pp. 28, 29.

by a brief and interesting section (Articles 36 through 50), borrowed apparently from the Irish constitution, entitled "Directive Principles of State Policy." The nature of these principles is suggested by the wording of Article 37: "The provisions contained in this Part shall not be enforceable by any court, but the principles therein laid down are nevertheless fundamental in the governance of the country and it shall be the duty of the State to apply these principles in making laws." Dr. B. R. Ambedkar stated in the Constituent Assembly that the object of the Directive Principles was "to prescribe that every government . . . shall strive to bring about economic democracy." Most of the principles are in fact concerned with economic and social policy. The broad goals are stated in Article 38: "The State shall strive to promote the welfare of the people by securing and protecting as effectively as it may a social order in which justice, social, economic and political, shall inform all the institutions of the national life."

Article 40 expreses an intention to revive an ancient institution of village democracy, the panchayat, and to make it the basis of the system of local self-government. Article 45 lays down the ambitious objective of "free and compulsory education for all children" up to the age of 14 within a period of ten years following the adoption of the constitution.

Most of the constitutional provisions, as would be expected, relate to the organization and functions of the governments in the Union and the states. India, according to Article 1, is "a Union of States." Originally the states were divided into three classes: Part "A," Part "B," and Part "C." Part "A" states were the former governor's provinces of British India, into which many princely states had been merged. Part "B" states were the five newly created Unions of Native States plus the princely states of Jammu and Kashmir, Hyderabad, and Mysore. Part "C" states were created out of the former chief commissioner's provinces, to which, after independence, some princely states had been joined. Thus in its origin the federal Union of India was composed of three main types of states, with the first two having roughly equal status, but with the Part "C" states being definitely on a lower level. Altogether there were 27 states (which became 28 in 1953 with the creation of Andhra as a Part "A" state). This division was abolished when the states reorganization went into effect in November 1956. Today there are 16 states in the republic of India, all but 2—Jammu and Kashmir and the new state of Nagaland—having equal status, plus 9 centrally administrated Union territories.

In theory all executive power of the Union of India is vested in the President. He is chosen by the elected members of both houses of the Indian Parliament and of the legislative assemblies of the states for a term of five years and is eligible for reelection. There has been much controversy and disagreement over the constitutional position and powers of the President. If the framers of the constitution had been trying to follow the British model, with such variations and adaptations as they felt to be desirable, one would assume that the President was, to use Bagehot's term, the head of the "dignified" parts of the constitution, whereas effective power would rest in the Prime Minister and the cabinet and the Parliament. That is the position which the President does in fact occupy, and it is certainly the role which the Presidents of India have thus far chosen to play. The constitution states that "the Ministers shall hold office during the pleasure of the President," but the very next article reads: "The Council of Ministers shall be collectively responsible to the House of the People." Moreover, as M. Ramaswamy has pointed out, "the President of India has no constitutional means at his disposal to implement any decision he might wish to take in the public interests when the decision depends for its execution upon legislative or fiscal action, so long as the cabinet and Parliament are hostile to the course he wishes to adopt." [15]

But the constitution of India does give the President a special position and special powers, which would seem to make him a far stronger head of state than the British sovereign. He has many powers to promulgate ordinances when Parliament is not in session and wide emergency powers, which in effect would enable him to take over the government of any state or states if he should find that the security of India is threatened "whether by war or external aggression or internal disturbances" or that "a situation has arisen in which the government" of a state "cannot be carried on in accordance with the provisions of the Constitution" or that "a situation has arisen whereby the financial stability or credit of India or any part of the territory thereof is threatened." These special powers are so sweeping that Professor B. M. Sharma has concluded:

The Constitution of India contains a vast reservoir of powers for the President, and in what manner these shall be exercised is the moot question on the answer to which shall largely depend the exact nature of the executive

[15] M. Ramaswamy, "The Constitutional Position of the President of the Indian Republic," *Canadian Bar Review*, XXVIII (June–July 1950), 651–652.

of India, whether it will be purely parliamentary, like the British king, or he will effectively exercise some of his powers independently of the Council of Ministers. For even if he adopts the latter course he will not be guilty of violating the Constitution.[16]

Article 77 of the constitution provides that "all executive action of the Government of India shall be expressed to be taken in the name of the President." He appoints the Prime Minister and other Ministers, and the Prime Minister has the duty of keeping him informed of "all decisions of the Council of Ministers relating to the administration of the affairs of the Union and proposals for legislation." The President may not be a member of either house of the Parliament, but Article 79 states that the Parliament of the Union "shall consist of the President and two houses."

The Vice-President of India is elected for a term of five years by members of both houses of Parliament in joint session. He is ex-officio chairman of the Council of States, but he may not be a member of that body or of the House of the People or of any state legislature.

Considerable speculation has been aroused by the brevity of the provisions in the constitution regarding the Council of Ministers, and particularly regarding the failure to make clear the precise relation between the President, the Prime Minister, and the Council of Ministers. The Prime Minister and the Council of Ministers are "to aid and advise the President in the exercise of his functions," but they are also "collectively responsible to the House of the People."

Parliament in India is composed of two houses, the Council of States (Rajya Sabha) and the House of the People (Lok Sabha). The Council of States has a membership of no more than 250; 12 members are nominated by the President of India, and the rest are representatives of the states, chosen for the most part by the elected members of the state assemblies. Approximately one-third of the members retire every second year, but the Council itself is not subject to dissolution. India has a weak upper chamber, without even the special dignities and privileges of, say, the House of Lords.

The House of the People has a membership of approximately 500, practically all of whom are directly elected. The maximum life of the House is five years, but it may be dissolved at any time by the President, acting upon the advice of the Prime Minister. In its organization, its procedure, the power and privileges of its members, and the rela-

---

[16] B. M. Sharma, *Federalism in Theory and Practice* (Lucknow, 1951), II, 564.

tions between the two houses, the Parliament of India is very similar to the British Parliament. In its actual operation and its place within the constitutional system the similarities are less marked.

The Supreme Court of India, consisting of a Chief Justice and ten other judges, appointed by the President and holding office until they reach the age of 65, is "placed at the apex of a single, unified judiciary which administers both federal and state laws alike throughout the country." [17] It has extensive original jurisdiction in cases which involve the government of India and any of the states, conflicts between states, or enforcement of fundamental rights. In certain cases it also has appellate jurisdiction over appeals from High Courts. The President may consult the Supreme Court on "a question of law or fact," on a matter of public importance, or on constitutional questions. To some extent the Supreme Court of India has the power of judicial review and is therefore the guardian of the constitution, but it does not have the place in the Indian system of government which the Supreme Court has in the American system. Parliament may extend the court's jurisdiction, but may also limit it. "The court's authority is intended to be more a barrier to executive arbitrariness and violations of the Constitution than to legislative acts. Any assumption of power by the court to frustrate the social policies decided upon by the Legislature can be prevented in the last resort by an amendment of the Constitution," [18] and this process is considerably easier than in the United States.

For Part "A" and Part "B" states the constitution originally provided responsible government very much along the lines of that established in the Centre, subject of course to the residuary powers of the central government. The executive power in Part "A" states was vested in a governnor and in Part "B" states in a Rajpramukh, each appointed by the President of India. The chief minister and other ministers were to be appointed by the governor or Rajpramukh, but the Council of Ministers was collectively responsible to the Legislative Assembly of the state. The state legislature was to consist either of one house, known as the Legislative Assembly, or of two houses, known as the Legislative Council and the Legislative Assembly. Each state was also to have a High Court, district courts, and such subordinate courts as might be deemed necessary. Part "C" states were to be administered by the President acting through a chief commissioner or a lieutenant gover-

---

[17] Srinivasan, *Democratic Government in India*, p. 282.
[18] *Ibid.*, p. 291.

nor. Parliament could create a legislature, either nominated or elected, for any Part "C" state and also a council of advisers or ministers. The reorganization of the Indian States in November 1956 eliminated the three classes of states and placed all fourteen new states on the same basis. Hence their government is conducted mainly along the lines charted in the constitution for Part "A" states.

In any federal union the relations between the Centre and the component units are of crucial importance. This was particularly true in India, where federalism was a novel experiment and where an effort was made to give sufficient powers to the Centre while at the same time granting as much autonomy as possible to the states. The Seventh Schedule of the constitution numerates the powers of the Centre and the states in a Union List, a State List, and a Concurrent List. Ninety-seven items are included in the Union List, 66 in the State List, and 47 in the Concurrent List. During a period of national emergency, Parliament has "power to make laws for the whole or any part of the territory of India with respect to any of the matters enumerated in the State List."

Part XIV of the Indian constitution contains provisions for recruiting and employing members of the public services, with major responsibility being vested in the Union Public Service Commission and the State Public Service Commissions. Part XV deals with elections and election procedures. An Election Commission is charged with preparation of the electoral rolls and with the conduct of all elections for the central Parliament, for legislatures of every state, and for President and Vice-President. In a country where very few people in the past had been eligible to vote, where most of the population were illiterate and backward, and where women in particular had played little part in political life, the framers of the constitution took a bold step, indeed a "calculated risk": they decreed universal adult suffrage for all the citizens of India, except those obviously disqualified, over the age of 21. Special provisions were necessary for the most backward of India's underprivileged millions, those who belonged to the so-called scheduled castes and scheduled tribes. Seats were reserved for these groups, roughly in proportion to their numbers, in the House of the People and in state legislative assemblies. The Fifth Schedule contained elaborate provisions for the administration and control of scheduled tribes, with special attention to the administration of backward tribal areas in Assam.

In a multilingual country, with strong attachments to various regional and local languages, the constitution makers took another bold step by decreeing that "the official language of the Union shall be Hindi in Devanagari script" and that "for a period of fifteen years . . . . the English language shall continue to be used for all the official purposes of the Union for which it was being used." At stated periods after the adoption of the constitution, the President was to appoint a commission to make recommendations for "the progressive use of the Hindi language" and for the use of other languages for official purposes. All proceedings in the Supreme Court and in the High Courts were to be in English, as before independence. The legislature of each state could adopt "one or more of the languages in use in the State" for official purposes. In addition to Hindi, thirteen languages of India were recognized in the constitution. These were Assamese, Bengali, Gujarati, Kannada, Kashmiri, Malayalam, Marathi, Oriya, Punjabi, Sanskrit, Tamil, Telegu, and Urdu.

A bill to amend the constitution may be introduced in either house, and in most cases the proposed amendment will become effective if it is passed in each house "by a majority of the total membership of that House and by a majority of not less than two-thirds of the members of that House present and voting" and if it receives the assent of the President. In certain cases the proposed amendment must also be ratified by the legislatures of half the states. On the whole, it is relatively easy to amend the Indian constitution.

The Constitution in Operation

The work of constitution making in India was a truly impressive performance. Few persons in the Assembly or in the country at large challenged the basic character of the document. Some wondered whether the constitution gave the government sufficient authority to deal with the many fissiparous tendencies in Indian society; others, though granting the need for authority to cope with these tendencies, expressed concern lest the extensive powers given to the Centre, especially the emergency powers, provide opportunity for a would-be dictator to overthrow the democracy. In other words, two questions basic to the success of constitutional government were raised: (1) Were the guardians of the constitution given adequate powers to discharge their responsibilities? (2) Who would guard the guardians? Neither of these potential dangers has so far developed into a direct peril to the state.

When the constitution went into effect on January 26, 1950, India became a republic and began to take steps to establish the regular institutions of democratic government. More than two years later, after the first nation-wide elections were held, the Constituent Assembly acting as the Provisional Parliament gave way to India's first regular Parliament. It had made the basic decisions and had functioned well during the first years of India's great experiment as a "sovereign, democratic republic." It had also endorsed an important extraconstitutional decision that India, though about to become a republic, wished to remain within the Commonwealth of Nations. The formula whereby a republic could remain a part of this unique association headed by a monarch was worked out in April 1949 at a conference of Commonwealth Prime Ministers convened for the express purpose of considering this problem. It was solved by a simple declaration of the governments of the Commonwealth countries. India expressed a willingness and desire "to continue her full membership in the Commonwealth of Nations and her acceptance of the King as the symbol of the free association of its independent member nations and as such the Head of the Commonwealth." The governments of the other Commonwealth countries declared that they "accept and recognize India's continuing membership in accordance with the terms of this Declaration."

However excellent the work of the draftsmen, the real test of any constitution is its actual operation. How has the constitution of India worked in the Indian environment? Obviously this question cannot be definitively answered, for less than a decade and a half has passed since the constitution went into effect. But on the whole the Indian experiment in democracy seems to be succeeding. The political leaders have been scrupulous in observing the constitution, and they have established certain conventions which augur well for the future. The successful conduct of three national elections and several elections in the states, the economic progress of the country under the Five Year Plans, tangible evidence that the government is trying to deal with ancient wrongs and to institute programs of economic and social reform—these achievements have given the people of India a growing confidence that they will be able to cope with the many grievous problems that still confront them.

The machinery of government seems to be operating well, on the formal level, although very often it is operating in ways not envisioned by those who created it. Again we are reminded that whereas the structure of the government of India is very familiar to any student of Western democratic government, in actuality the government does not operate along familiar lines. The levels of decision making differ fundamentally, and the main decisions are made to a large degree outside normal channels. This fact calls attention to the great influence of "nonpolitical" forces in India and to the role of personalities and charismatic leadership. Most of the major policies are in fact determined within the Congress Party and not by the agencies of government; and within the Congress Party they are made by Jawaharlal Nehru and a handful of associates. The Working Committee of the Party is actually the most important policy-making body in India. Thus the institutions of government are to some extent agencies to carry out decisions made elsewhere; but there is a close identification between the Congress Party and the government, and the leaders of the Congress are careful to work within the constitutional system. Nevertheless, there is a kind of unreality about the operation of the governmental agencies in India, and any examination of their functioning soon leads to other sources of influence and power.

Among the conventions that seem to be established is one that the President of the republic shall indeed be the head of the "dignified" parts of the constitution and that he shall use his extraordinary powers only upon the advice of the Prime Minister and the cabinet. In actual fact his position has been far closer to that of the English sovereign than to that of the American President or of the President of the French republic. Thus a very important precedent has been established with regard to the role and responsibilities of the head of the state.

Dr. Rajendra Prasad, India's first President, played this role in an admirable way. Dr. Prasad was a kindly gentleman, greatly beloved by the people and highly respected by all. Before his election as President of India he served with inconspicuous distinction as a president of the Indian National Congress and as president of the Constituent Assembly. He deliberately chose to remain aloof from party politics and to be a harmonizing and a unifying influence. His relations with Prime Minister Nehru were apparently close and cordial. He invariably accepted the advice of the Prime Minister on political matters, and Nehru was careful to consult him on major questions and to keep him informed at all times. At the expiration of his first term as President Dr. Prasad was unanimously reelected. He remained in office until the completion of the second term in 1962, even though he was often unable to carry out his normal duties because of illness.

Although Dr. Prasad elected to play a limited role in the Indian political system, the emergency powers bestowed upon him under the constitution were invoked several times, because of government instability and factional bickering—in the Punjab in 1951–1952, in PEPSU (Patiala and East Punjab States Union) in 1953–1954, in Andhra in 1954, in Travancore-Cochin in 1956–1957, and in Kerala in 1959–1960. In each instance the President's rule was continued for several months until, after new elections, more stable governments could be formed in the states concerned. In 1954 it seemed possible that the new state of Andhra might have a Communist government, and in 1957 India's first Communist government did in fact come to power in Kerala (formerly Travancore-Cochin). It was ousted by presidential decree in 1959, and President's rule was proclaimed. These events raised the question of using the emergency powers of the constitution in case a Communist regime in one of the states proved to be disruptive of the democratic order. Experience thus far is that the emergency provisions of the constitution are useful, indeed necessary, and have not been abused.

India has also been fortunate in its second President, Dr. Sarvepalli Radhakrishnan, a distinguished Indian educator and one of the world's great philosophers, who served as Vice-President during Dr. Prasad's two terms. He has great prestige in India and an international reputation; a former professor at Oxford, he has been President of UNESCO, and his books are read widely in many countries. He has been carefully observing the conventions followed by Dr. Prasad, he is frequently consulted by Prime Minister Nehru, and he has great personal influence in the country. If a political crisis should threaten after Nehru passes from the scene, Dr. Radhakrishnan—if he is still in office—might not hesitate to use the powers vested in the President to preserve order and stability until a successor to Nehru is firmly in power.

In India, as in other parliamentary systems, the Prime Minister is the most important official of the state; but the present Prime Minister is particularly important because he is Jawaharlal Nehru. In the last stages of the struggle for independence Nehru was overshadowed only by Gandhi in the top leadership of the Congress Party. He was Chief Minister in the interim government that was set up in India in 1946, and he has been Prime Minister of India since independence. From the time of Gandhi's assassination in January 1948 Nehru has occupied a position of unquestioned preeminence in Indian life. His great power and influence are derived less from his position as Prime

Minister than from his dominance over the Congress Party and from his unequaled personal popularity in the country. In a land where personal leadership is often more important than office or issues, Nehru is a charismatic leader par excellence; in fact, there is a real danger that as long as he lives too much reliance will be placed on his individual popularity and that when he dies or retires (and he was 73 years old in November 1962) he will leave a dangerous void. Fortunately, Nehru himself is aware of his own shortcomings and the pitfalls of great power. Fortunately, too, he is steeped in the traditions of liberal democracy and is thoroughly devoted to the democratic way. But he is also an impatient and an impulsive man, who is eager to achieve great things quickly and who sometimes rides roughshod over lesser people. On the whole, he has played his part well. That part, as he envisions it, is much greater than to be the Prime Minister of India. It is to lead the movement for the achievement of a social revolution in India.[19]

The Council of Ministers—the cabinet—in India has been very much dominated by Nehru and the Congress Party, from which its members have almost invariably been drawn, although it has contained several respected elder statesmen, such as Maulana Azad, Gopalaswami Ayyangar, Kidwai, Rajagopalachari, and Pant, and able administrators such as John Mathai, C. D. Deshmukh, and T. T. Krishnamachari. Since the death of Sardar Patel in 1950 there has been no Deputy Prime Minister, no one who could hold his own with Nehru, no one who could complement Nehru as Patel did. The collective responsibility of the Council of Ministers to the Parliament has meant very little to date, since the Congress Party has had such an overwhelming majority in the Parliament.

The Indian Parliament is playing an increasingly significant role in Indian political life, but it still does not make central decisions as one would expect in a parliamentary system. Although in its organization and procedure it closely resembles the Parliament of Britain, its actual place in Indian political life is hardly comparable to that occupied by the Mother of Parliaments. The great decisions in India are not made in or by the Parliament, or even by the dominant party in the country, but by a small group within that party.[20] Almost every lead-

[19] See Ajoy Kumar Gupta, "The Indian Parliament and States Reorganization," *Parliamentary Affairs,* X (Winter 1956–1957), 105, 107, 111.

[20] See Lanka Sunderam, "The Role of an Independent Member," in A. B. Lal, ed., *The Indian Parliament* (Allahabad, 1956), p. 68.

ing Congress M.P. holds some important post or posts in the party
hierarchy. There is close liaison between the leaders of the Congress
Party and the Congress Party in Parliament.[21] The parliamentary party
has an elected leader and a chief whip nominated by the leader. Eleven
officeholders plus twenty-one elected members form the Executive
Committee. "The constitution of the Party in Parliament lays down
that, so far as possible, all important Government motions, Bills and
resolutions should be placed before the Executive Committee in advance of their consideration by Parliament." [22] The party standing
committee provides a useful way for the Congress M.P.'s to keep informed on issues, and the state groups give them an opportunity, often
after consultation with opposition members from the same state, to
make representations on particular issues to their party leaders or to
the government.

No effective opposition to the Congress has yet developed within
the Parliament. Rarely has the vote against a measure sponsored by
the Congress ministry—that is, the government—exceeded 100, and
no one opposition party has ever had enough members in the House
of the People (50) to qualify as a recognized opposition party. "It is
. . . unfortunate that the main opposition group in the parliamentary
life of India should be the essentially non-parliamentary Communist
Party." [23]

In a sense the committees of the Parliament serve as a partial check
on the government. Standing committees were abolished in 1952. At
present the two financial committees, the Public Accounts Committee
and the Estimates Committee, are particularly influential. Regarding
the latter committee Professor Morris-Jones wrote:

The indirect influence of the Committee . . . is probably even more important than its direct influence on the Government. . . . To a very real
extent, this type of committee, inspired as it is by the idea not simply of
economy nor even of efficiency alone but also of acting as a check against
an oppressive or arbitrary executive, achieves a special political significance
as a substitute for a real Opposition.[24]

Ad hoc select committees or joint select committees are created for
every bill that is sent to committee; relatively few bills pass through

[21] See Norman D. Palmer and Irene Tinker, "Decision Making in the Indian
Parliament," in Richard L. Park and Irene Tinker, eds., *Leadership and Political
Institutions in India* (Princeton: Princeton University Press, 1959), pp. 115–136.
[22] W. H. Morris-Jones, *Parliament in India* (Philadelphia: University of Pennsylvania Press, 1957), p. 187.
[23] *Ibid.,* p. 330.   [24] *Ibid.,* pp. 307–308.

committee consideration, but these bills are usually of particular importance. In the opinion of Professor Morris-Jones:

The whole structure of Parliamentary Committees reflects and at the same time reinforces this mood of watchfulness over the Government. It provides the student of politics with an interesting if slight modification of parliamentary government of the British type. More important . . . it saves the Indian Government with its large majority from the worst temptations of autocracy.[25]

Within its limited sphere the Parliament of India is playing an increasingly useful role. The future of the Council of States seems rather uncertain; it is not yet operating well in the traditional role of an upper chamber, and its membership is not very different from that of the lower house. But the House of the People is rapidly winning for itself an established place in Indian political life. It is still a relatively new and inexperienced body, and its members are even more inexperienced. The party leaders, however, are men of long political experience, and the first Speaker of the House, G. V. Mavalankar, was a veteran parliamentarian. The language problem has been another complication and may be even more of a handicap as more members use regional languages in the debates and as the use of English diminishes.

As would be expected, the Supreme Court of India is somewhat more limited than the United States Supreme Court in its authority to act as guardian of the constitution. With respect to land reform and other social measures its jurisdiction has been further limited by the First and Fourth Amendments to the Indian constitution (in 1951 and 1955). Nevertheless it has proved to be a major bulwark of constitutional government. Although it has scrupulously refrained from passing upon political questions, it has freely exercised its extensive powers of judicial review. It has "laid down the basic principles governing the problem of delegation of legislative power,"[26] and it has done much to reconcile the fundamental rights guaranteed in the constitution with the limitations which have occasionally been placed upon these rights.

Any observer of the Indian scene is poignantly aware of the vast gap between the fundamental rights guaranteed in the Indian constitution and the limited reality of these rights in India today. Moreover, the limitations upon some of these rights are serious. For example,

---

[25] *Ibid.*, p. 315.   [26] Douglas, *We the Judges*, p. 166.

Article 22, guaranteeing protection against arbitrary arrest and detention, contains provisions which have been invoked to provide the basis
for the Preventive Detention Act, a tough measure which authorizes
the arrest and detention for many weeks without trial of persons who
are even suspected of contemplating acts which would be inimical
to public safety and order; and the amendment to Article 31, which removes from the judicial sphere the question of what is reasonable compensation for expropriated property, may seriously impair the guarantee contained in the first paragraph of Article 31 that "no person shall
be deprived of his property save by authority of law." The continued
prevalence of untouchability in many parts of the country seems incompatible with is constitutional prohibition in Article 17.

Despite all the reservations which must be entered, genuine efforts
are being made to give meaning to the constitutional provisions regarding fundamental human rights. Obviously in the area of social
reform constitutional provisions backed by court decisions cannot
immediately correct age-old injustices; but they can certainly be of
great value, and they can mark the road along which the nation desires
to move. The record of the Indian government and Parliament in the
field of social legislation is impressive; it contrasts with the British reluctance to interfere in any way, if this could possibly be avoided,
with popular customs and ways of life.[27] The Indian authorities have
not hesitated to tackle head-on some of the most deep-seated customs
which are regarded as undesirable and undemocratic, such as the
practice of untouchability, Hindu customs concerning marriage and
property matters, and other oppressive codes of behavior. A study of
the legislative history of the Hindu Code Bill and of the efforts first
to obtain consent to a comprehensive measure and then to push
through the major features in separate pieces of legislation would be
most revealing. Resistance to changes in customs was strong, but pressure for modification of certain practices was stronger. The Hindu
Marriages Act of 1955, a major piece of the Hindu Code Bill, heralded

[27] "The startling contrast between the pace of progressive legislation in India
after independence and before appears, therefore, to justify the criticism that the
policy of the British administration to interfere as little as possible with the
customs of the population in matters of personal status, family law and succession,
however well intentioned, acted as a brake on progress and retarded a possible
natural line of advancement and development of Hindu society" (K. Lipstein,
"The Reception of Western Law in India," *International Social Science Bulletin*,
IX [1957], 90). Lipstein's article is a report of the discussions on the subject indicated at the meetings of the International Association of Legal Science, held in
Barcelona in September 1956.

a revolution in the marriage law among most of the Indian population.

Among the many paradoxes of Indian political life since independence has been the simultaneous development of strong centralizing and decentralizing tendencies. These conflicting tendencies appear in the evolving relations between the Centre and the states in India. The constitution provided for a federal system having an unusual degree of central control, with residuary powers vested in the central government. The government has endorsed "the socialist pattern of society," and Indians traditionally look to the strong authority of the Centre for guidance and aid on a wide variety of matters. Hence it is hardly surprising that India presents one of the most extreme manifestations of centralization in any democratic state. In a country dedicated to democratic planning on a vast scale, the central government has given direction and leadership to this coordinated effort, and its role has been all the greater because the states have failed to make their expected contributions in finances and effort.

On the other hand, as Dr. Paul Appleby, an American specialist, has pointed out, the central government has relied on the states "for a large part of its administration." [28] In fields like development planning and education the Centre has had to rely on the states to carry out policy, and often it has encountered stubborn resistance or reluctance to act. The states have also been the strongholds of linguistic feelings. Reorganizing the political map of India along essentially linguistic lines has probably weakened a major threat to national unity. But the second general election in the bilingual state of Bombay in 1957 dramatically demonstrated that the stresses resulting from frustrated linguistic aspirations were still great. The price of nation-wide concessions to these aspirations has been high. In one of his reports on public administration in India Dr. Appleby asked: "Will India be able to maintain and develop its national unity and strength in the face of its linguistic divisions and its extraordinary dependence upon the States for a large part of its administration?" [29]

One powerful force for harmony between the Centre and the states has been the fact that the governments in New Delhi and in almost all of the states have consistently been formed by the same party. After the general elections of 1951–1952 the Congress Party formed govern-

[28] Paul H. Appleby, *Re-examination of India's Administrative System with Special Reference to Administration of Government's Industrial and Commercial Enterprises* (New Delhi: Government of India Press, 1956), p. 47.
[29] *Ibid.*

ments in all the states and maintained these governments until the second general elections in 1957, with the exception of the short-lived government formed by the minority Praja Socialist Party in Travancore-Cochin and the periods when the Punjab, PEPSU, Andhra, and Travancore-Cochin were under President's rule. Following the second general elections, the Congress maintained its control in all the reorganized states except Kerala.

After the third election in 1962, with the break-up of the shaky Congress-PSP coalition in Kerala, the Congress formed ministries in all of the states, although it had only a bare majority in Madhya Pradesh and Rajasthan. The Congress has always been careful to keep some of its leading members in the state governments. Thus some years ago five chief ministers in states—B. C. Roy in West Bengal, Pant in Uttar Pradesh, Shukla in Madhya Pradesh, Rajagopalachari in Madras, and Moraji Desai in Bombay—were sometimes referred to as Nehru's "five warlords." It is, however, perhaps a commentary on present political trends that one of these men, Desai, is now a member of the central cabinet, while Rajagopalachari is in retirement and the others are dead. Factional squabbles within the Congress Party have harried the administration in a number of the states, although in some cases strong action by the national leaders has helped to restore the party's prestige in these states and to improve the quality of the administration.

With the death of Dr. B. C. Roy on July 1, 1962, on his eightieth birthday, the last of the elder statesmen of the Congress among the chief ministers of the Indian states passed from the scene. Several of the younger chief ministers have already gained a considerable national reputation and will probably become increasingly influential in party and national affairs. One of them, Y. B. Chavan of Maharashtra, has already been brought into the central cabinet; he succeeded Krishna Menon as Minister of Defense in November 1962. Others deserving special mention are Kamaraj Naidar of Madras, Patnaik of Orissa, Sukhadia of Rajasthan, and Kairon of the Punjab. The first two seem to have a strong position in their own states; the last two have also proved to be strong and able leaders, but their position in their own states has been greatly weakened by electoral reverses and internal squabbles which they could not resolve. All of these men represent a new generation of Congress leadership, and they and others who will undoubtedly emerge in the states will unquestionably have much to say about the future course of the Congress Party and of national policy.

Although Congress ministries still control all but one of the states, in several of the state legislative assemblies there are sufficient opposition members to act as a real check upon the majority party. This gives a flavor to political life in some key states, such as Andhra Pradesh, Bihar, Madhya Pradesh, Mysore, the Punjab, Rajasthan, Uttar Pradesh, and West Bengal, which is lacking at the Centre. Possibly the composition of the state assemblies is a better barometer of trends in Indian politics than the make-up of the House of the People. Certainly there seems to be a greater popular interest in what goes on in the capitals of the states than in New Delhi, which is a long distance, psychologically as well as geographically, from most of the Indian people.

In local government and administration the district officer is still the key figure, as he was in the days of British rule. "As agents of state governments, but with national status and an all-India outlook, district officers have the job of translating the vast bulk of governmental decisions into effective action." [30] In addition to their traditional duties as chief officers for enforcing law, administering justice, and collecting taxes, they are now usually the chief development officers as well. As efforts to develop local self-government increase, agencies such as village panchayats, panchayat samitis, and zila parishads, associated with the new Panchayati Raj system, may take over many of the functions of the district officers; but "for the foreseeable future" the latter promise "to remain the key leadership figures throughout district-level India, local self-government to the contrary, notwith-standing." [31]

In the 1880s Lord Ripon made heroic efforts to reform local self-government in India. He sought "to revive and extend the indigenous system of the country" and "to make full use of what remains of the village system." [32] His primary objective was political education, not administrative efficiency; to prevent the new middle class from becoming "a source of serious political danger," he wished to give them "a training in the working of political institutions." [33] The leaders of independent India have tried to follow the same policies, though often for different reasons. One of their main objectives has been to improve the living conditions of village India, where some 80 per cent of the

---

[30] Richard L. Park, "District Administration and Local Self-Government," in Park and Tinker, eds., *Leadership and Political Institutions in India*, p. 338.

[31] *Ibid.*, p. 342.

[32] L. Wolf, *Life of Ripon* (London, 1921), II, 100.

[33] See L. S. S. O'Malley, ed., *Modern India and the West* (London, 1941), pp. 745–746.

population live. Through the Community Development Program and the National Extension Service, both integral parts of the Five Year Plans, a major effort is being made in this direction. These programs are now a part of an even more comprehensive system of local government, administration, and development known as Panchayati Raj (government by panchayats). The main agencies of Panchayati Raj are village panchayats, which the government of India is trying to revive and extend in accordance with Article 40 of the constitution, panchayat samitis (assemblies) at the development block level, and zila parishads (district committees) at the district level. The new system has been introduced, or is being introduced, in most of the states. It is one of the most exciting experiments now going on in India or in any other developing country, but it is too early to determine whether this effort at democratic decentralization will be any more successful than the many less ambitious experiments which have been tried in India and other developing countries.

Although the great majority of the Indian people live in villages, there are four cities with a population of over 2 million each (Calcutta, Bombay, Delhi–New Delhi, and Madras) and at least three others (Ahmedabad, Bangalore, and Kanpur) which are close to, or in excess of, 1 million population. There is considerable variation in the pattern of municipal government in India and in the degree of self-government which the inhabitants enjoy. In the days of the British East India Company, Bombay, Madras, and Calcutta were organized as "Presidency towns"; this implied relatively great autonomy. By 1870 there were about 200 municipalities in the subcontinent.[34] Thus Indian towns have often had a long record of experience in municipal government. Today urban areas are generally governed as townships or as corporations. Officials appointed by the state governments have the largest measure of effective authority, but there are also elected officers, and usually there is some kind of elected council. Most of the larger cities are governed as corporations, each with a commissioner appointed by the state government, an official head usually known as the mayor, and a legislative council. The municipal government is divided into departments, dealing with such matters as revenue, water, education, health and welfare, sanitation, slum clearance, and relief.

Much attention is being given in India today to problems of public

[34] See table showing "Dates of Establishment of Some Early Indian Municipalities," in Hugh Tinker, *The Foundations of Local Self-Government in India, Pakistan, and Burma* (London, 1954), pp. 30–31.

administration. There is a real danger that India may not be able to develop the necessary machinery or enough properly qualified personnel to cope with the administrative problems of running a huge underdeveloped country. Even more serious is the problem of orientation to administration. In the opinion of Dr. Paul Appleby:

Perhaps nowhere else have so many systematic barriers been erected to prevent the accomplishment of that which it has been determined shall be done. . . . Indian leadership has had the tremendous problem of shifting from the negative, antigovernmental attitude that was necessary to the drive for independence to a positive, operating, institutional responsibility appropriate and necessary to program achievements planned by independent and revolutionary India.[35]

Fortunately a good many Indians had practical experience in administration under the British, and the Indian members of the Indian Civil Service whose services were available after independence have stiffened the administrative structure of the country. Those who are still active are today in key positions in the central government or in the states. An Indian Administrative Service has been established to replace the ICS. Each year a few—far too few—young Indian college graduates are recruited by examinations for the IAS and other central services and are trained at the National Institute of Administration and in the field. Additional personnel are recruited in many other ways. The Public Service Commissions in the Centre and in the states are doing excellent work, but their efforts are limited in scope and in imagination. The Indian Institute of Public Administration provides a center for more serious study of administrative problems and for the advanced training of top administrative personnel. In general, aside from the top administrators, the work of administration in India is being carried on by relatively untrained and often unqualified persons, and no really effective measures are being taken to remedy the situation.

There is much criticism of the quality of administration in the country. According to Dr. Appleby, the four most prevalent criticisms on the popular level "are that government has too many employees, that it is permeated with dishonesty, that it is inefficient and that its work is unnecessarily hampered by 'red tape.'" He believes that many of these criticisms are overdone or miss the point. He is more concerned with administrative structures—with "personnel recruitment,

[35] Appleby, *Re-examination of India's Administrative System*, pp. 17, 46.

development and arrangement; financial provisions, fiscal policy, financial administration, and procedures, on paper and otherwise, maximizing expedition, responsibility, good judgment, effective delegation, etc." [36] Perhaps the basic question facing India's civil service is whether the people and the Parliament will pay enough to attract proper personnel and will grant those personnel scope enough to operate efficiently.

[36] Paul H. Appleby, *Public Administration in India: Report of a Survey* (New Delhi: Government of India Press, 1953), p. 9.

· XI ·

Political Parties in India

WHEN the political process in India is analyzed, not only the formal functioning of institutions should be kept in mind, but also political parties, leaders and leadership patterns, pressure groups, and public opinion. Here again much is found that is familiar and much that is unfamiliar, sometimes to a striking degree. In this chapter the Indian party system will be analyzed; in the next the focus will be upon political dynamics.

Attitudes toward Political Parties

In the newly formed democracy of India, the party system is not yet a healthy one. Some influential leaders, in fact, have advocated the development of a "new political system" in which parties in the usual meaning of the term will not exist at all. Gandhi himself often espoused this new approach, without making clear how his ideals of a *sarvodaya* society could replace the institutions of representative government. The two outstanding "nonpolitical" leaders of India today, Vinoba Bhave and Jayaprakash Narayan, whose influence in politics is perhaps greater than that of any conventional political leader except Nehru himself, would like to do away with political parties. The Radical Humanists repeatedly point to the absence of a well-developed party system and argue that parties are both unnecessary and undesirable.

335

In the political atmosphere of India, where the party system is not functioning well, where parties prior to independence had little opportunity to develop or to perform their customary roles, and where the masses of the people are illiterate, it is hardly surprising that parties are viewed with a rather jaundiced eye. Under the circumstances it could be argued that there are advantages in the absence of a balanced party structure. Richard L. Park has expressed this view in words which apply to India in particular and to other Asian countries as well:

An independence movement is not the best breeding ground for political parties in the Western sense. In the search for unity in opposition to the ruling imperial power, the Asian nationalist movements exerted every effort to bring all factions together into one independence-bound organization. . . . After independence, as was natural, these movements tended to break down, with groups of minority views leaving the parent body to form new political groupings.

. . . a well-organized political party system might have hindered the relative stability. Much of the success of the legislative and planning programs in these countries can be traced to the large, disciplined majorities held by the party in power in the respective parliaments. The hard test of parliamentary government, of course, will come when this situation no longer prevails.[1]

On the national level Indian political parties may be divided into five main groups: (1) the Congress Party; (2) the Swatantra Party, a conservative, noncommunal party; (3) the communalist parties, notably the Jan Sangh, the Hindu Mahasabha, and the Ram Rajya Parishad (the Rashtriya Swayamsevak Sangh, though ostensibly non-political, actually has considerable political influence); (4) the socialist parties, notably the Praja Socialist Party and the Socialist Party of India; and (5) the Indian Communist Party. Besides these major groupings there are numerous parties which are of some importance on the state or regional level and innumerable so-called parties which center around individual leaders. Another prominent characteristic of Indian political life is the existence of a number of groups which are both political parties and pressure groups or which are at once parties and organizations for the promotion of economic, social, or religious objectives. At the Centre, because of the dominance of the Congress, India seems to have virtually a one-party system, but in many regions

[1] "Problems of Political Development," in Philip W. Thayer, ed., *Nationalism and Progress in Free Asia* (Baltimore: Johns Hopkins Press, 1956), pp. 103–104.

and states of India opposition to the Congress is strong and is apparently growing. Moreover, there are trends within the Congress Party which may portend a lessening of its influence and power, especially after Nehru passes from the scene.

The Indian National Congress

The Indian National Congress was the directing organization of the struggle for independence in India, and since that goal was achieved it has been the dominant political party. It is the party of Gandhi and of Nehru. "It utilizes the aura of a succesful nationalist movement, to which it has added the prestige of government authority and high international importance." [2] It has both the advantages and the disadvantages of its past record and inheritance. As the spearhead of the independence movement, it attracted the support of people of very diverse viewpoints and interests who were willing to overlook their differences in the interests of the freedom struggle. When it became the ruling party of a new nation, it preserved much of the atmosphere and prestige of its past, but in the new setting it had to change many of its objectives and techniques. Under the responsibilities of authority it naturally "ceased to enjoy that overwhelming mass appeal which made it a truly national organization in the heyday of its struggle for freedom." [3] Thus the membership of the Congress has been subject to considerable variation. Indeed, almost all the political parties of modern India represent groups which split off from the main Congress Party or which have at various times been merged in the Congress.

During the Second World War the Congress took a firm stand of noncooperation and nonparticipation, as a result of which most party leaders were jailed. At this time the British naturally favored other groups, including the Muslim League and even the Communists, who supported the war effort. But the leaders of the Congress took a prominent part in the negotiations leading to independence in August 1947 and were active in the interim government and Constituent Assembly which were inaugurated in 1946. After the attainment of independence the Congress did not cease to function, as many people expected it

[2] Gene D. Overstreet and Irene Tinker, "Political Dynamics in India" (Berkeley: Modern India Project, University of California, March 1957; from material prepared for the India volume, Country Survey Series, Human Relations Area Files), p. 27.

[3] P. D. Gupta, "Political Parties and Elections in India," a lecture delivered at Subhas National College, Unnao, February 23, 1953.

would, but continued in the triple role of party, government, and social welfare organization. Gandhi, its great mentor, argued that it had outlived its usefulness "in its present shape and form, i.e., as a propaganda vehicle and parliamentary machine"; [4] he recommended that it be disbanded as a political organization and converted into a Lok Sevak Sangh, a social service organization. But, as N. V. Rajkumar explains, "Unable to contemplate the idea of dissolving an institution which was the only organizational body which could run the administration of the country and tackle the manifold problems that political freedom brought in its wake, the Working Committee with great regret dissented from Gandhiji's basic approach." [5]

Since 1947 the Congress has passed through many crises and has experienced several changes in orientation; but it has retained its unquestioned predominance at the Centre and, except for rare and not too successful experiments in a few states, has controlled the machinery of government throughout the country. It has profited greatly from its prestige as the party of national independence, although critics point out that there is a vast difference between the organization which spearheaded the independence struggle and the party which is now in power in India. It has also profited from the great popularity and prestige of Jawaharlal Nehru and from the weakness and division of the opposition. By death, retirement, or resignation it has lost some of its most important leaders. Many groups have left its ranks, including the Socialists in 1948; but it has gained new recruits, and aside from the Communist Party it is the only organized and disciplined national party of any importance in India.

Nevertheless, its organization and discipline leave much to be desired. As Nehru himself pointed out quite forcefully to his associates after the general elections of 1957, it needs to recapture some of the dynamism which it once possessed and to regain popular confidence by high standards of austerity and integrity. At the local level it seems to be losing support, and its representatives at this level are often people of inferior quality and questionable character. Its top leadership is still good, and its central organization seems to be functioning well. The major organizational problems relate to the proper relations between the agencies of the party and of the government, between the Congress Parliamentary Party and the Working Committee and other

[4] From a suggested draft for an All-India Congress Committee (AICC) resolution which Gandhi gave to the Constitution Subcommittee of the Congress on January 30, 1948, a few hours before his assassination.

[5] *Development of the Congress Constitution* (Delhi: AICC, 1948), p. 98.

top organs of the national party, and between the central agencies of the party and state and local committees. Its policy seems to involve a left-of-center orientation which, it hopes, will retain its identification with the people, enable it to resist the divisive tendencies of communalism, casteism, and linguistic differences, cut the ground from under the Socialists by embracing most of their approaches and policies, and provide a satisfactory democratic alternative to communism, whose followers now seem to be concentrating on achieving unparliamentary ends through parliamentary means.

After surviving the first crises of independence, the party found itself faced with internal conflicts in 1950. For the first three years Nehru had concentrated his personal energies on the vast tasks of national unity and survival, and he had left the internal affairs of the party largely up to others, notably to the strong hand of the Deputy Prime Minister, Vallabhbhai Patel. But Patel favored the conservative elements in the party, whereas Nehru appealed to the younger and more liberal groups. Both wanted the party to follow a moderate and middle-of-the-road policy, but Patel had little sympathy with the mounting demand for major economic and social reforms, whereas Nehru felt that the Congress must espouse a left-of-center orientation lest it cut itself off from the people and go the way of the Kuomintang in China.

Hence a crisis developed within the party in 1950 when Purshottamdas Tandon, a white-bearded orthodox Hindu "of the old school," who enjoyed the support of Patel, was elected president of the Congress over Acharya Kripalani, a candidate much more acceptable to Nehru. Nehru regarded this development as a challenge to his leadership and as a trend in the wrong direction. Above everything else he aspired to convert India into a modern secular state with a socialist orientation, and he was alarmed at the victory of the Patel-backed Hindu conservative. In the fall of 1951 the Prime Minister forced a showdown by resigning from the Congress Working Committee and other party posts. Tandon thereupon offered his resignation as president. A special meeting of the All-India Congress Committee accepted Tandon's resignation and elected Nehru as president of the Congress.[6] Although he was on record against combining the posts of Prime Minister and president of the Congress, Nehru an-

---

[6] See Susanne Hoeber Rudolph, "The Working Committee of the Indian Congress Party" (a paper prepared for the Center for International Studies, Massachusetts Institute of Technology, Jan. 14, 1955), pp. 35–37; Robert Trumbull, "Nehru Keeps His Prestige despite a Party Setback," *New York Times*, Sept. 10, 1950.

nounced that he would accept the party office because he felt that the party was moving away from the masses and because "something must be done to arrest its disintegration." He held the post as president for more than four years, until he gave way to a candidate of his choice, U. N. Dhebar, in January 1955.

During this period both the government and the party consolidated their strength and moved in a generally socialist direction. In the spring of 1953 Nehru held talks with Jayaprakash Narayan and other leaders of the Praja Socialist Party, apparently to explore the possibilities of closer cooperation, perhaps even of coalition, with his only "loyal opposition." Although these talks were suspended by mutual agreement without leading to any specific understanding, they were indicative of the direction of Nehru's thinking. His letters to Narayan revealed impatience with the pace of economic and social change and a wish to unite all like-minded persons and groups in speeding up the "social revolution." At the annual sessions of the Congress and at regular meetings of the All-India Congress Committee and of the Working Committee, resolutions were passed which culminated in the historic Avadi resolution of January 1955 laying down the objective of "a socialistic pattern of society":

In order to realize the object of the Congress as laid down in Article I of the Congress Constitution and to further the objectives stated in the Preamble and Directive Principles of State Policy of the Constitution of India, planning should take place with a view to the establishment of a socialistic pattern of society, where the principal means of production are under social ownership or control, production is progressively speeded up and there is equitable distribution of the national wealth.

This orientation greatly strengthened the position of the Congress in the country and weakened the power of the leftist parties and groups which supported similar aims.

The issue of linguistic states threatened to create serious divisions within the party and actually resulted in serious electoral setbacks for the party in Bombay state in the second general elections in 1957. On the whole, however, the Congress emerged from its many gyrations over the linguistic states issue with generally increased strength.[7] "The initial turmoil apart, States Reorganization has fulfilled the political aspirations of the people in various parts of the country and thus

[7] For a full account of the initial proposals for states reorganization see *Report of the States Reorganization Commission* (New Delhi: Government of India Press, 1955).

eliminated a factor which might have affected the party's popularity in the country." [8] The Congress has also shown a "tremendous flexibility and capacity to adapt to public opinion on specific issues." [9]

The central organs of the Congress Party are the annual Congress session, the All-India Congress Committee (AICC), and the Working Committee. On the state level the key organ is the Pradesh (State) Congress Committee, which sets up such subordinate committees, down to the level of the taluka (subdistrict), as it deems appropriate. Above the lowest levels all members of Congress committees must be "active" members. An active member must "wear khadi, be a tee-totaller, oppose untouchability, favor equality of opportunity, believe in intercommunal unity, perform 'constructive activity,' pay Rs. 1 annually and collect another Rs. 10 for Congress." There are fewer than 80,000 "active" Congress members, but some 6 million "primary" members, who accept the objectives of the party but who are not subject to the obligations and responsibilities of the "active" members.

The AICC is composed of one-eighth of the delegates of each Pradesh Congress Committee and is elected by the PCC's.[10] It meets at irregular intervals, usually on the call of the Working Committee. The Working Committee is a small and active body consisting of the president of the Congress and twenty members chosen by the president from the membership of the AICC. Two of its important subsidiary bodies are the Parliamentary Board, which exercises supervision over the Congress ministries in the states, and the Central Election Committee, which screens Congress candidates for the central Parliament and to some extent also for state assemblies. Thus "in addition to . . . power over the state parliamentary parties, the Working Committee retains a crucial hand in the all-important business of personnel selection, both for the central parliament (through the Central Election Committee) and for the state ministries (through the Parliamentary Board)." [11] It also has a "crucial hand" in the shaping of governmental policy on the national level. Of particular interest is the relationship between the Working Committee and the Congress Party in Parliament, with its separate offices and secretariat. Although

[8] S. L. Poplai, ed., *National Politics and 1957 Elections in India* (Delhi, 1957), pp. 11–12.

[9] *Ibid.*, p. 10.

[10] See Susanne Hoeber Rudolph, "The All India Congress Committee and the Annual Congress Session" (a paper prepared for the Center for International Studies, Massachusetts Institute of Technology, Jan. 14, 1955).

[11] Rudolph, "The Working Committee of the Indian Congress Party," p. 23.

at times there has been some working at cross-purposes, there can be little doubt that the Working Committee is the more important body; indeed, it is possibly the most important decision-making body in India. According to Nehru, "the basic policy of the Party is laid down by the Annual Session, and it is interpreted and implemented by the AICC. The Working Committee, as the executive of the Congress, is charged with carrying out this policy." Actually, as Susanne Rudolph has pointed out, "the real power relationship of the three national organs of the Congress Party . . . is the reverse of the stated power relationship . . . the Working Committee makes both basic and *ad hoc* policy, and submits it to the other two organs for their approval." [12]

In the more than seventy-five years of its existence the Congress has played a major role in the political life of the country. It has passed through many stages and survived many crises. Some of the greatest figures of modern India have been among its leaders. After independence it ceased to be the umbrellalike organization within which all groups took shelter and became the dominant political party in free India as well as the government of the country on both national and state levels. It is still the chief political organization in India. As long as Nehru is actively in control of the affairs of the party and of the country, the position of the Congress can hardly be effectively challenged on the national scene, and it will probably remain in power in most, if not all, of the states. Whether it can retain its influence after Nehru goes, whether it can find new momentum and dynamism under other leaders—these are great unanswered questions in India's political future.

Paradoxically, the disintegration of the Congress could be either a blessing or a tragedy. It might be a blessing if it gave way to a healthy party system, with at least two democratic parties strong enough to compete for political power; but it would be a tragedy if the removal of its strong hand impeded the progress of India's great experiment in democracy and economic development, and particularly if its passing strengthened the forces of communalism or of communism. The best-organized political opposition to the Congress today is the Communist Party; its victory would present a threat to the survival of India as a democratic state. One of the ironies of the Indian political scene is that an effective democratic opposition seems to be

[12] Rudolph, "The All India Congress Committee and the Annual Congress Session," p. 22.

out of the question as long as the Congress exists in its present form, while at the same time the disintegration of the Congress might have adverse effects on the entire prospects for democracy in India.

The Swatantra Party

In August 1959 a new conservative, noncommunal party—the Swatantra (Freedom) Party—was formally launched at a meeting at Bombay. The basic approach of the new party was suggested in a report issued after a meeting of its leaders in Madras in early June 1959:

We are of the opinion that social justice and welfare can be reached more certainly and properly in other ways than through techniques of so-called Socialism. . . . Social justice and welfare should not be brought about by violence or State compulsion . . . but must be brought into being by the spread of the doctrine of trusteeship as suggested by Gandhiji. . . . The educational activities of government, direct or indirect, should be such as to emphasize the moral obligations of those who possess wealth to hold it in trust for society, and a doctrine of life based on that moral obligation as distinguished from seeking to establish a socialistic structure based on legislative sanctions involving expropriation and loss of incentive for the individual to work and increasing dependence on the State and its officials in every walk of life.[13]

The leaders of the Swatantra Party were a heterogeneous group, almost all of whom had once been prominent in the Congress Party. They included M. R. Masani, N. G. Ranga, Homi Modi, K. M. Munshi, and, above all, C. R. Rajagopalachari. Rajiji (as Rajagopalachari is generally called) was a veteran leader of the independence struggle, the first—and last—Indian Governor-General of the Dominion of India, a former cabinet minister, and a former chief minister of the state of Madras. More than anyone else in India, except perhaps Vinoba Bhave, his name and presence evoked something of the messianic appeal that Mahatma Gandhi conveyed in large measure. Although he was in his eighties and had retired from political life, Rajiji took a leading role in the Swatantra Party from the beginning.

For a conservative, anti-Communist party, not well organized or financed, which strongly opposed the socialist orientation of the Congress and was highly critical of the foreign policy of the Congress government, the Swatantra Party, formed only a few months before the third general elections in 1962, fared rather well in these elections.

[13] Quoted in Ellen Roy, "A Closer Look at the Swatantra Party," *Radical Humanist*, XXIV (Feb. 14, 1960), 77–78.

It did not, however, have much success in Rajiji's own state of Madras and it suffered a major defeat in the overwhelming victory of V. K. Krishna Menon over Acharya Kripalani (backed by Swatantra) in North Bombay. It won eighteen seats in the Lok Sabha, which made it the second largest opposition party, and it gained significant victories in Andhra Pradesh, Bihar, Gujerat, Rajasthan, and Uttar Pradesh. In Bihar, Gujerat, and Rajasthan it became the major opposition party.

While the third general elections enhanced the prestige of the Swatantra Party, they did not indicate a major political breakthrough for the party, and they left its future in doubt. It has

already attracted more support that most political observers predicted, and it will probably be around for some time. It may well become the nucleus for a conservative opposition to existing policies of the Government. If the Congress Party itself should ever split up into conservative and socialist wings, the Swatantra Party might win the support of many conservative Congressmen, or it might merge with this group to form a really effective conservative party. It may serve as a catalytic agent, presaging a realignment of Indian political groupings. In view of the growing radicalism of Indian politics, however, it is doubtful that any political organization openly opposed to socialism in any form will gather much momentum.[14]

Communal Parties

Communalism is one of the most powerful and most divisive forces in Indian life, but thus far no communal party has had any success in national politics and very few have made much of an impact even on the state or local level, where forces of religious traditionalism and orthodoxy are stronger. Most of the communal parties represent varieties of orthodox Hinduism; among these the Jan Sangh, the Hindu Mahasabha, and the Ram Rajya Parishad are the most significant, with the Rashtriya Swayamsevak Sangh, allegedly nonpolitical, as "the Hindu communal organization of greatest potential strength." Leading non-Hindu communal parties are the Akali Dal, representing certain groups in the Sikh community, the Republican Party (formerly the Scheduled Castes Federation), devoted to the interest of the untouchables or the "scheduled castes," and the Jharkhand Party, the principal party espousing the cause of the scheduled tribes.

The most successful politically of the Hindu communal parties is

[14] Norman D. Palmer, *The Indian Political System* (Boston: Houghton Mifflin, 1961), pp. 200–201.

the Bharatiya Jan Sangh. Founded in 1951 by Dr. Shyama Prasad Mookerjee, the Jan Sangh gained the largest vote of any of the communal parties in all three general elections, returning three members to the House of the People in the first general elections, four in the second, and fifteen in the third. As long as Dr. Mookerjee was its leader, the Jan Sangh gave promise of bringing various conservative and communal groups together in a united front. Dr. Mookerjee was a former vice-chancellor of Calcutta University and the son of a distinguished Bengali jurist and educator. At one time he was president of the Hindu Mahasabha. Shortly before he formed the Jan Sangh, he was a member of the central cabinet, but he resigned over the issue of India's policy toward Pakistan. A particularly powerful speaker and an effective parliamentarian, he became a kind of unofficial leader of the opposition in the House of the People. He organized and headed a loose coalition of communal and conservative groups in the House known as the National Democratic Party. Dr. Mookerjee died in June 1953, however, while in "protective custody" in Srinagar, where he had been confined after he had made a dramatic but unauthorized entry into the state of Jammu and Kashmir in protest against the treatment of the Hindus in Jammu. After his death the communal parties had no commonly accepted spokesman, and the Jan Sangh had difficulty in holding itself together. Dr. Mookerjee's successor as president resigned to rejoin the Congress Party. In spite of its lack of leadership and internal difficulties, the Jan Sangh polled nearly twice as many votes in the second and third general elections as it did in the first. In 1962 it enjoyed a real resurgence in northern and central India, where it won some 115 seats in state assemblies, mainly in Uttar Pradesh and Madhya Pradesh, as well as 15 seats in the Lok Sabha.

The Akhil Bharat Hindu Mahasabha was formed in the early 1900s by persons who wanted to ensure the dominance of Hinduism in Indian society. It gained momentum and became active politically in opposition to the Muslim League and to the "modern" leaders of India who wanted to make independent India a secular state. In response to the Muslim League's demand for a separate Pakistan, the Mahasabha raised the slogan of "Akhand Bharat," an undivided India true to Hindu traditions. It has consistently advocated tougher policies toward Pakistan.

When Gandhi was assassinated in January 1948 by a Maharashtrian Brahmin who had been a member of the Hindu Mahasabha, the Mahasabha announced that it was retiring from the political arena;

but it rode out the storm of criticism after Gandhi's death and resumed political activity in time to contest the first general elections in 1951–1952. It fared badly in these elections, winning only four seats in the House of the People and only scattered seats in some of the state assemblies. In the second general elections in 1957 it fared even worse. Only two members of the party were returned to the House of the People, and the president, N. C. Chatterjee, the vice-president, Dr. N. B. Khare, and the general secretary, V. G. Deshpande, all lost their parliamentary seats. It was not able to increase its strength in the 1962 elections. It can no longer be regarded as important on the national level.

The Ram Rajya Parishad, the most orthodox of the leading Hindu communal parties, polled nearly 3 per cent of the votes and elected three members to the House of the People in the general elections of 1951–1952, but in 1957 it was unable to return even one member and it had little success in elections to the state legislative assemblies. It has almost disappeared as a political force.

The most important of the Hindu communal organizations, the Rashtriya Swayamsevak Sangh (RSS), is not a political party but a tightly organized, highly disciplined, paramilitary, hierarchical body of dedicated persons whose "primary aim is to establish within its own group a model of a revitalized Hindu society and eventually to secure the adoption of this cultural form in the whole country." [15] The head of the RSS is the *Sar Sanghcalak,* an office which is passed down from one incumbent to his chosen successor. Both the men who have served to date in this role, Dr. Keshav Hedgewar and Guru Madhav Rao Golwalkar, have been strong personalities. Also influential in the organization are the Organizers, an appointed executive hierarchy taking a vow to devote their lives to the work of the Sangh. Every member of the RSS is carefully screened and tested. He joins a cell of about fifty persons and participates in exercises, ceremonies, group discussions, and other forms of training.

The Rashtriya Swayamsevak Sangh, then, is today the one important Hindu communal organization in India. When communalism is at a low ebb, the devotion of its members and ancillary appeals of its organizational style

[15] Richard D. Lambert, "Hindu Communal Groups in Indian Politics," in Richard L. Park and Irene Tinker, eds., *Leadership and Political Institutions in India* (Princeton: Princeton University Press, 1959), p. 215. See also J. A. Curran, Jr., *Militant Hinduism in Indian Politics: A Study of the R.S.S.* (New York: Institute of Pacific Relations, 1951).

have kept it strong as the communal parties have faded. If communalism once again eclipses language as the primary divisive force in India, the Sangh may reemerge in a bid for general public support.[16]

For some years a militant Sikh party, the Shiromani Akali Dal, has been active in the Punjab. Its leader has been a colorful and dramatic firebrand named Master Tara Singh, an elderly and heavily bearded gentleman who looks like Michelangelo's Moses. Several of its members have held important positions in the assemblies and governments of the Punjab. It led the demand for a separate Sikh state—Sikhistan— but the majority of its members finally accepted the compromise which was proposed by the Congress Party and the central government. The agreement was so complete, in fact, that in October 1956 the majority of the ruling body of the Akali Dal voted to join the Congress Party for political activity and to continue only as a religious organization. This agreement was repudiated by Master Tara Singh himself shortly before the general elections in 1957, on grounds of bad faith on the part of the Congress, and some Akali Dal members, with their leader's blessings, ran against Congress candidates in the elections. They had very little success, however, for the majority of the members of the organization remained loyal to their new association with the Congress. Faced with this virtual repudiation by his own followers, Master Tara Singh announced that he would retire for a time to consider the proper strategy for the future.

Shortly before the third general elections the Akali leader went on a prolonged fast, which he announced would continue until death unless the demand for a Punjabi Suba was granted; but the Indian government refused to yield, and a face-saving arrangement finally persuaded Master Tara Singh to break his fast. In the 1962 elections the Akali Dal, now in opposition to the Congress, polled about 18 per cent of the votes in the Punjab and elected 19 of the 154 members of the Punjab legislative assembly.

Another type of communalism in politics is represented by the Republican Party (formerly the Scheduled Castes Federation) and the Jharkhand Party. The Federation was formed by India's most famous untouchable, Dr. B. R. Ambedkar, an English-educated lawyer, in opposition to the policies of the British government and the Indian National Congress regarding the untouchables. It is a well-known fact

[16] Lambert, "Hindu Communal Groups in Indian Politics" (a paper prepared for the conference on "Leadership and Political Institutions in India," held at the University of California, Berkeley, in August 1956), p. 19.

that Dr. Ambedkar and Gandhi did not agree on the proper treatment of the untouchables. The Federation had some influence in the negotiations in 1945–1947 leading to the transfer of power, but it faded into obscurity in 1947–1950 while its founder was Law Minister in the first cabinet of free India and chairman of the committee which drafted the Indian constitution. The constitution abolished untouchability and contained some special provisions for the scheduled castes, but Dr. Ambedkar was dissatisfied with the failure of the government and the Congress Party to institute prompt measures to implement the constitutional guarantees, and he resigned from the cabinet a few weeks before the start of the first general elections. The Scheduled Castes Federation was revived in time to contest the general elections in some areas, and it polled nearly 2.5 per cent of the votes for the House of the People. Dr. Ambedkar became increasingly embittered against the Congress Party. He publicly expressed his regrets that he had served as a member of a Congress ministry and he charged that he had been used as "a political hack" in drafting a constitution which in retrospect he repudiated. In 1956, shortly before his death, he and several thousand of his followers staged a mass public acceptance of Buddhism. After the 1957 general elections the SCF was reorganized under the name of the Republican Party, obviously having little resemblance to the American party of the same name. This party has some support among members of the scheduled castes in several Indian states, especially in Maharashtra.

Political organization among the scheduled tribes of India is still largely lacking, and the problem of the assimilation of the tribesmen into the life of the country is a vexing one. The chief tribal party, which has considerable support in Bihar, Assam, and Manipur, is the Jharkhand Party, whose leader is Jaipal Singh, an able, English-educated member of one of the tribes. The party demands a separate Jharkhand state, and it champions the interests of the tribal people generally.

Socialist Parties

In view of its present dedication to the objective of "a socialist pattern of society" the Congress itself should perhaps be discussed under this heading. Indeed, most of the prevailing trends in India seem to be socialistic. "Socialism is no longer the great divide: all are socialists now and everyone's socialism is diluted in varying degrees." [17] Nehru does not now regard himself as a Marxist, although he is frank to confess that there is much about Marxism, and also about communism, that appealed to him; but he has considered himself to be a socialist for many years, and he has been looked to as a spokesman by various leftist members and groups within the Congress.

As organized political movements socialist parties have passed through three main periods since they became a political force of some significance a quarter of a century ago. Leadership in the first period was provided by the Congress Socialist Party (CSP), which remained a party within a party until 1948. During the second period, from 1948 to 1952, the Socialist Party led a rather confused independent existence and received a rude shock in the first general elections. In 1952 the Socialist Party and the Kisan Mazdoor Praja Party merged to form the Praja Socialist Party, which has been the leading independent socialist party since that time, although it is now in another period of crisis.

In 1934 the first important socialist party in India was formed as a group within the Indian National Congress. It aspired to unite the non-Communist left wing of the nationalist movement and eventually, with the support and perhaps even under the leadership of Jawaharlal Nehru, to gain control and form the government of a free India. These hopes, of course, were never realized, although the Congress Socialist Party undoubtedly exerted some influence on Nehru and other leaders who have tried to keep the Congress Party to the left of center.

From the outset, however, the new party was characterized by internal ideological disharmonies since it embraced views ranging from the orthodox Marxist through the Fabian Socialist to a type of Gandhian socialism. This original disunity has led to a preoccupation with ideological abstractions which, along with personal disputes, have proved to be a constant source of instability and disruption.[18]

These observations hold equally true for the independent socialist parties which emerged after the Congress Socialist Party left the Congress fold. They describe difficulties and dilemmas which socialist parties in India have always faced and which are still unresolved.

In trying to unite the leftist elements in the country the CSP early admitted Communists as members. This proved to be a serious mis-

---

[17] Asoka Mehta, "The Political Mind of India," *Foreign Affairs*, XXXV (July 1957), 686.

[18] Overstreet and Tinker, "Political Dynamics in India," p. 35.

take. Communists gained positions on the CSP's National Executive and took a large section of the CSP membership with them in urging the Congress to support the war effort after 1941. During the war the CSP advocated more forceful methods of resistance to the British than the Congress leaders, under Gandhi's influence, adopted. They remained within the Congress, but they became increasingly alienated from its inner circles and from Nehru. They had little use for Patel and his staunchly conservative views. They drew closer to Gandhi, however, and he did his best to help them to improve their position within the party. They were not given any important posts in the interim government in 1946–1947 or in the Congress ministry which led India during the first years of freedom. In 1947 a new constitution for the Congress Party contained a provision which required all internal organized parties to dissolve or to leave the Congress. Reluctantly and with grave misgivings the CSP decided to leave the Congress and emerge as an independent party, appealing for support to members of the Congress and nonmembers alike.

It was . . . *not* primarily differences over ideology, program, or policies that forced the Socialists out of the Congress (although these existed) . . . but the *organizational impossibility of Socialist leadership achieving control of the Congress.* The main obstacle was Sardar Patel and the provincial leaders who worked under his control. Had this not existed, it is quite probable that the Party leadership would have been absorbed as a leading section of the Congress leadership and no opposition Socialist Party would have emerged.[19]

Thus the Socialist Party emerged from the Congress "as a *reluctant opposition,* and an *overoptimistic one.*"[20] It had a number of able leaders, but they were divided on ideological and other grounds, and in the rank and file there was little cooperation or enthusiasm. The party was badly organized and even more badly financed. Nevertheless, it entered the first general elections with high hopes. It polled over 10 per cent of the votes for the House of the People, but it won only 12 seats, whereas the Communist Party and its allies, which received only about half as many votes, elected 27 members to the House. A partial reason for this paradoxical result was the unwise So-

[19] Thomas A. Rusch, "Evolution and Devolution of Socialist Leadership: Disinheritance and Disintegration" (a paper prepared for the conference on "Leadership and Political Institutions in India," held at the University of California, Berkeley, in August 1956), p. 25. Italics in original.

[20] *Ibid.* Italics in original.

cialist policy of running candidates in many constituencies, instead of concentrating in constituencies where the chances for victory were bright, as did the Communists. All the nationally prominent members of the Socialist Party who ran for the House of the People were defeated.

In 1952 the Socialist Party joined with the Kisan Mazdoor Praja Party, which had been formed in 1951 by an orthodox Gandhian, Acharya Kripalani. The product of this fusion was the Praja Socialist Party (PSP). The new party gave a Gandhian trend to the Socialist movement. Kripalani was elected president and Asoka Mehta general secretary. For a time the merger seemed to give promise of developing into an effective opposition to both the Congress and the Communists, but soon the new party was seriously weakened by the resignation, retirement, or death of some of the key leaders and by factional disputes among those who remained.

"Six major events are responsible for bringing to fruition the basic discords inherent in the Party previously: the J. P.–Nehru talks (1952), the Bhoodan movement of Vinoba Bhave, the experience of Socialist government in the state of Travancore-Cochin (1954–55), the Avadi session of the Congress (1954), the Gaya Party Thesis adopted in 1955, and the linguistic agitations of 1956." [21] Reference has already been made to the talks between Nehru and Jayaprakash Narayan over the possibility of some kind of cooperation between the Congress and the PSP in the task of national development. The fourteen-point program which Narayan submitted to Nehru had been approved by the high command of the PSP, but some of the top leaders were not in favor of the discussions in the first place and the whole episode, which received great publicity in India and which aroused speculations that Nehru was thinking of Jayaprakash as a possible successor, provoked considerable controversy in Socialist ranks. The PSP has given its strong support to Bhave's Bhoodan Yagna movement (land gift movement), and its outstanding leader, or former leader, Jayaprakash Narayan, has presumably turned his back on politics to devote himself to Bhoodan work. When a Socialist government was formed in Travancore-Cochin in 1954, with the support of the Congress Party, which had a plurality but not a majority in the State Assembly, the national leaders of the PSP approved of the experiment; but the behavior of the Socialist-led ministry in Travancore-Cochin caused a group in the top leadership of the PSP, consisting of Ram

[21] *Ibid.*, p. 29. Jayaprakash Narayan is often referred to familiarly as "J. P."

Manohar Lohia and some of his followers, to demand the resignation of the Socialist government. Refusal of this demand led to internal friction within the central leadership of the PSP and to the election of Acharya Narendra Deva as a kind of "neutral" chairman.

The resolution adopted at the Avadi session of the Congress Party for "a socialistic pattern of society" was publicly welcomed by PSP leaders like Asoka Mehta who desired cooperation with the Congress and was publicly condemned by those, like Dr. Lohia, who wished to remain wholly aloof from the dominant party. At the PSP general conference at Gaya in 1955 a statement prepared by the national chairman of the party, Acharya Narendra Deva (who died a year later), and intended "as a compromise between various adherents of Gandhian, democratic, and Marxian socialism" [22] was adopted by the membership in the face of the opposition of such key leaders as Kripalani, Asoka Mehta, and Purshottam Tricumdas.

The socialist orientation of the Congress Party accentuated differences of viewpoint within the top leadership of the PSP over the proper policy to follow regarding the Congress. One group, of which Asoka Mehta was a leading spokesman, favored a policy of collaboration with the Congress on common objectives and warned against the dangers of playing into the hands of the Communists by ignoring "political compulsions" and realities. Another group, led by Ram Manohar Lohia, rejected the policy of collaboration with the Congress as fatal to the party and insisted that instead of being "a tail of the Congress" the PSP should become a truly revolutionary party. The divergence in viewpoint reached a climax in 1955, when the National Executive of the PSP first reprimanded and then expelled Lohia and some of his followers from the party for issuing public statements against other party leaders and party policies. Lohia promptly formed a new party, which he called the Socialist Party of India. He took with him "at least 30% of the former party's strength . . . the active leadership of six state organizations, the entire Socialist youth movement, and one-seventh of its legislative representation. His primary support lies in South and Central India and among the youthful elements in the P.S.P. who had little or no attachments to the Congress." [23]

In spite of its afflictions, however, the PSP made a good showing in the 1957 elections. By concentrating its energies (it contested only about half as many seats as had the Socialist Party and the KMPP in

[22] *Ibid.*, p. 37.   [23] *Ibid.*, p. 36.

the previous election), the party minimized its losses; and though its popular vote for the House of the People fell from over 16 per cent to about 10 per cent, its representation in the House dropped only from 20 to 18. In the State assemblies it increased its representation from 125 to 195, returning 20 or more members to the assemblies in Bihar, Bombay, Uttar Pradesh, and West Bengal. In the third general elections, after further defections, including the resignation of Acharya Kripalani, the weaknesses of the PSP were poignantly revealed. It won less than 7 per cent of the popular vote, only 12 seats in the Lok Sabha, and about 115 seats in the state assemblies.

"No party," wrote Asoka Mehta in 1957, "has gone through such hard times as the P.S.P." However, contemplating the results of the second general elections and the relatively good showing of the PSP, especially in the states, he wrote of his party: "That in spite of this it has come through unscathed suggests that it has a place among the people." [24] After the third general elections, when the party did not "come through unscathed" and when he himself lost his seat in the Lok Sabha, Mehta had to seek other evidence to support the thesis that the PSP "has a place among the people."

The Communist Party of India

In the House of the People the Communist Party of India has consistently been the largest single group in opposition to the dominant Congress Party, although Communist membership has never exceeded 30. The CPI has one or more members in most of the state legislative assemblies, and in the assemblies of three states, Kerala, West Bengal, and Andhra, it has formidable representation. In Kerala, as a result of the second general elections, it became the majority party in the Assembly (thanks to the adherence of five independent members), and it formed in this South Indian state the first Communist government in democratic India.

It is very difficult to estimate the real strength of the Communist movement in India. As in all non-Communist countries, it operates largely beneath the surface. There is much in the Indian environment which provides fertile soil for the spread of communism. Much of the appeal of communism in India is

[24] Asoka Mehta, "The Political Mind of India," *Foreign Affairs*, XXXV (July 1957), 687.

due to the extremely slow economic improvements in India, and to the inability of the masses to examine political slogans and promises critically and intelligently and to appreciate the price they would have to pay if the Communists were given a chance to fulfill their promises. . . . But the greatest asset of the Communists has always been the romantic appeal and the reflected glory of the revolutionary power of Russia and now of China. . . . If in spite of their defeat the Communists have received more votes at the polls in recent elections than is good for India, it only shows that they still benefit from their assets of poverty, popular ignorance and international tension.[25]

In spite of their efforts to exploit all kinds of popular grievances and discontent, the CPI draws its main support from the disaffected intellectuals, especially from the "educated unemployed."

Communism came to India shortly after the Bolshevik Revolution in Russia. During the 1920s Communist groups were established in a few Indian cities, and they attempted to infiltrate the trade union movement. They received guidance from M. N. Roy and other Indians who were then active in the international Communist movement, and at an early period they apparently had close contacts with the British Communist Party, which seems to have been the main channel for policy guidance and direction until at least the years after the Second World War. In the late 1940s and early 1950s it seemed that international direction was coming chiefly through the Cominform. Recently the guidance has appeared to come directly from the head centers of international communism, chiefly from Moscow.[26]

In spite of Lenin's advice to Asian Communist movements to work with the national bourgeoisie, the Indian Communists—perhaps under the influence of M. N. Roy, who publicly disagreed with Leninists regarding the proper strategy to follow in Asian countries—were extremely critical of "bourgeois nationalism" until the mid-1930s, when they conformed to the shift in the international party line and adopted

[25] Ellen Roy, "Indian Party Politics" (a lecture delivered in Chicago, June 27, 1955, under the auspices of the Chicago Council on Foreign Relations), *Radical Humanist*, XIX (July 24, 1955), 356. Mrs. Roy was the wife of M. N. Roy, who for some years was the leading Indian Communist and an agent of the Comintern and who later abjured communism and founded the Radical Humanist movement in India.

[26] For details on the relations of the Communist Party of India with the international Communist movement, see M. R. Masani, *The Communist Party of India* (New York: Macmillan, 1954); John H. Kautsky, *Moscow and the Communist Party of India: A Study in the Postwar Evolution of International Communist Strategy* (New York: Wiley, 1956); Gene D. Overstreet and Marshall Windmiller, *Communism in India* (Berkeley: University of California Press, 1959).

the strategy of the "united front." In 1934 the Communist Party of India was formed as an organized section within the Indian National Congress. Its members were able to gain representation in the higher councils of the Congress Socialist Party and of the Congress itself. But when Russia entered the Second World War the CPI, like Communist parties in all countries, called for full participation in the struggle against the Axis, whereas the policy of the Congress was one of strict noncooperation in the war effort. For this deviation from Congress policy and for its determined stand against partition, the CPI was expelled from the Congress in 1945.

Shortly after India became independent, the party, again in conformity with "the new cold war line of the international Communist movement," launched a program of direct action against the government. Although it was unable to stir up much trouble in most parts of the country, for a time in 1948 it had spectacular success in a remote Telegu-speaking section of Hyderabad state known as Telengana. There it was able to arouse the discontented peasants against the landlords and local authorities. For several months Telengana was virtually in Communist hands, in armed revolt against the government, and the Communist leaders associated with this coup gained great prestige within the inner ranks of the CPI. But the victory in Telengana was brief. Within a few months, as a result of firm and intelligent government action and Vinoba Bhave's first great crusade in his Bhoodan Yagna campaign, Communist influence in Telengana was reduced.

The Telengana affair was a warning to the rest of the country, and it did much to expose the soothing appeals of the Communists as hypocritical. The failure of the direct-action movement created confusion and division within the ranks of the Indian Communists. With some guidance from the British Communist Party, however, they veered around in time to contest the first general elections, with surprising success. The CPI received 3.3 per cent of the vote for the House of the People, and although it contested only a few constituencies, it gained 16 seats in the House and scored notable successes in West Bengal and Madras.

In 1953, reflecting the impact of the "new look" in international communism following the death of Stalin, the CPI began to take a more charitable view of the Congress Party and of Nehru. This softer line was expressed at the party's Third Congress, held at Madurai, where an effort was made to work out a compromise between various factions within the party and between the desire to oppose the Congress and yet to support the policy of "peaceful coexistence." [27] The Avadi resolution of the Congress Party and the trend of India's foreign policy raised further problems of strategy and tactics for the CPI. Although belatedly welcoming these developments, the party continued to look for opportunities to checkmate the Congress in the country. In early 1955 it undertook a major test of strength in elections in the newly created state of Andhra, where it had scored sensational victories in the general elections of 1951–1952; but its strategy backfired, and it suffered such severe losses that from being a potential threat to the Congress control of the new state it was reduced to a minority group of little influence in the State Assembly.

By the time the CPI held its Fourth Congress, at Palghat in April 1956, the effects of the Andhra debacle, the Bandung Conference, Nehru's visit to Russia, the visit of Bulganin and Khrushchev to India, and the resolutions and revelations at the Twentieth Congress of the Russian Communist Party forced the Indian Communists to reassess their position. The party declared that though it "must act as a Party of Opposition in relation to the present Government" the "democratic front" which it hoped to establish "will not be an anti-Congress front."

The CPI contested the second general elections under considerable difficulties, but the results were generally gratifying to it. It nearly doubled its vote for the House of the People and increased its representation in that body to 27. It retained its strength in West Bengal, regained some of its losses in Andhra (where elections to the State Assembly were held only in the Telengana area), won 18 seats in the Bombay State Assembly (where it had held one before), and won more seats in Kerala than the Congress. In Bombay its victories were due largely to the support of anti-Congress electoral alliances. In a constituency in Bombay city S. A. Dange, a leading Indian Communist, was elected to the House of the People by the greatest plurality accorded any candidate in India. In Kerala the Communists formed a government, with the support of five Independents they backed in the elections. The chief minister was E. M. S. Namboodiripad, later general secretary of the CPI. The unique experiment of a Communist government in an Indian state came to an abrupt end in the summer of 1959, when, amid conditions of growing disorder, the President of

---

[27] A. K. Ghosh, *On the Work of the Third Party Congress* (New Delhi: Communist Party of India, 1954), p. 5.

India dismissed the Namboodiripad regime and proclaimed President's rule, which lasted until a shaky Congress-PSP coalition government was installed following state elections in 1960.

Ruthless suppression of the uprising in Tibet by the Chinese Communists shortly before the Communist government in Kerala was ousted and the Chinese pressures along India's Himalayan frontiers shortly afterward posed further dilemmas for the CPI. Apparently the members of the Politburo were divided in their views on the proper policy to follow in the light of these new developments. One group favored support of the Chinese Communists in spite of the strong popular reactions against them in India, seemingly on the ground that Communists—especially Asian Communists—could not possibly be wrong. Another group believed that it would be wise to support Nehru's position on Tibet and on the boundary issues including the MacMahon Line. The third group advocated a middle-of-the-road position, with emphasis on the need for India and China to settle their differences by negotiations.

These events, complicated by the death of Ajoy Ghosh, the long-time general secretary of the CPI, in January 1962, seemed to put the CPI in a weak position to contest the third general election in the following month; but again, as in 1957, the results were generally gratifying to the party. It gained a larger percentage of the popular vote—10 per cent—than it had won in 1957, it returned about the same number of members to the Lok Sabha as it had had in the previous Parliament, and while it suffered some reverses in the states, it won 50 seats or more in the assemblies in Andhra and West Bengal (the comparable figures for the previous general election were 37 and 46, respectively). It continued to be a major factor in the politics of Kerala, where elections were held for the Lok Sabha but not for the State Assembly. In North Bombay it played a major part in Krishna Menon's smashing victory, but in an adjoining constituency in central Bombay, S. A. Dange, now president of the CPI and its leading vote-getter in 1956, was defeated by his Congress opponent.

Developments in the Communist world since the death of Stalin, especially Khrushchev's campaign of de-Stalinization and the growing rift between Moscow and Peking, have added to the perplexities of the CPI. In general, the top leaders of the party have supported the Moscow line, but a few have tended to be pro-Stalinist and a larger minority, with strong support in West Bengal, has been consistently pro-Chinese. The pro-China group has fallen into disfavor as a result of the Chinese attack on India in late October 1962. After this attack the National Council (as the former Politburo is now called), over the bitter protests of the pro-China members, passed a resolution condemning the Chinese actions and calling on all Indians to unite in defense of their country against Chinese aggression. At the height of the new crisis with China the government of India, acting under special emergency powers, arrested several hundred Indian Communists, especially those whose sympathies in the past had been with China.

The organization of the CPI follows the standard pattern of Communist parties generally. The basic unit on the local level is the town or local conference, in which all the cells in the area participate. Each conference, from the town or local conference through the district and provincial conferences, has an executive committee and a secretary. The party congress, at the top of the hierarchy, elects the Central Committee, which chooses the National Council and the general secretary. As in other Communist parties, the CPI has been controlled from the top, by a relatively limited number of people. There have been six general secretaries since 1934: Dr. G. Adhikari, P. C. Joshi, B. T. Randadive, Rajeshwar Rao, A. K. Ghosh, and E. M. S. Namboodiripad.[28] These men have been identified with different policies and approaches, but it is hard to decide to what extent these differences have been due to the shifts in the international party line and to what extent to differences in convictions and personalities. The parliamentary group has apparently not had a decisive influence in the inner circles of the party, although at least one of its top leaders, S. A. Dange, was a Member of Parliament from 1957 to 1962.

The Indian Communists, observed Ellen Roy, "are no different from other Communists, except that they have to their credit probably more mistakes, more turnabouts and somersaults than Communists elsewhere."[29] Indeed, "the Communist Party of India appears to be characterized by a higher degree of indiscipline . . . than any other Communist Party of which we have detailed knowledge."[30] Today the CPI "has never been so deeply divided."[31] Divisions within the party

[28] See Gene D. Overstreet, "Indian Communist Approaches to Leadership," in Park and Tinker, eds., *Leadership and Political Institutions in India,* pp. 240–241.
[29] "Indian Party Politics," p. 356.
[30] Overstreet, "Indian Communist Approaches to Leadership," in Park and Tinker, eds., *Leadership and Political Institutions in India,* p. 231.
[31] Robert A. Scalapino, "Moscow, Peking and the Communist Parties of Asia," *Foreign Affairs,* XLI (Jan. 1963), 337.

have existed ever since its founding, and at times the confusion of the Communists has been almost ludicrous. But they have survived their inner differences and the gyrations of the international party line. As the strongest opposition group in the Indian Parliament and as a major political factor in several key states, they have tangible political strength; more important, however, they are operating effectively, beneath the surface of Indian life, in trade unions, student groups, and peasant organizations, which are among the most influential and discontented segments of Indian society. They remain a disturbing element and a basic threat to democracy in India.

Other Parties and Groups

The Indian political scene is characterized by a bewildering number of political parties, most of which are hardly more than groups in local areas supporting individual personalities. Nearly 200 so-called parties announced their intention to contest the first general elections, and so many of these actually put up candidates that straight contests were the exception rather than the rule. Fourteen parties were recognized by the Election Commission as national parties in the first general elections, and 59 as state parties. Only 5 of the recognized national parties received more than 3 per cent of the vote, the minimum requirement to be recognized as a national party as stipulated by the Election Commission—the Congress, the Socialists, the Kisan Mazdoor Praja Party, the Jan Sangh, and the CPI. As a result of the showing in the first general elections, only 4 parties—the Congress, the Jan Sangh, the PSP, and the CPI—were recognized as national parties in the second election. Seven others which had been recognized as national parties were recognized only as state parties for the allotment of election symbols. For the third general elections the Election Commission recognized 16 parties, but only the Congress was allotted a symbol for all states and Union territories. The PSP was recognized for this purpose in all states and territories except the Punjab, Rajasthan, and Tripura; the Jan Sangh in five states and in Delhi; the Socialist Party in five states and Manipur; the Swatantra Party in five states and Himachal Pradesh; the Hindu Mahasabha in Madhya Pradesh, West Bengal, and Delhi; the Ram Rajya Parishad in Madhya Pradesh and Rajasthan; the Republican Party in Maharashtra and the Punjab; the Jharkhand Party in Bihar; the Muslim League in Kerala; the Dravida Munnetra Kazhagam in Madras; the Peasants and Workers Party in Maharashtra; the Ganatantra Parishad in Orissa; the Akali Dal in the Punjab; and the Forward Bloc in West Bengal.[32]

One of the most significant aspects of the second general elections was the generally good showing made by regional or state electoral coalitions. These alliances and the Independents were generally more successful than opposition parties. Indeed, Asoka Mehta is convinced that this is an important development in Indian politics:

Opposition to the Congress is emerging not in terms of rival national parties but mostly through various regional groupings: Ganatantra Parishad in Orissa, Jharkhand Party and the Janata Party in Bihar, the Dravida Munnetra Kazhagam in Madras, Samyukta Maharashtra Samiti in Maharashtra (Bombay State), Maha Gujerat Parishad in Gujarat (Bombay State), and the various tribal organizations in the tribal areas of Assam. Collectively, these parties have won more seats in the State Assemblies and the Lok Sabha than any national party in opposition to the Congress. As a matter of fact, it is not easy for a national party to satisfy and articulate the emotional discontent of a region. When a region wants to express its discontent it prefers a party whose allegiance is to the region alone and whose horizons are limited. This is perhaps the biggest danger that Indian democracy faces during the next 20 years when it will be under the severe strains of economic development.[33]

[32] S. L. Poplai, ed., *1962 General Elections in India* (Bombay: Allied Publishers, 1962), pp. 407–408.

[33] "The Political Mind of India," pp. 682–683. Material from "The Political Mind of India," by Asoka Mehta, appearing in the July 1957 issue of *Foreign Affairs*, is quoted by special permission. Copyright by Council on Foreign Relations, New York.

· XII ·

Political Dynamics

POLITICAL parties have not yet found their place in Indian political life. They have received their major tests in the three general elections which have been held since independence, and they are influenced to an indeterminate degree and in ill-defined ways by public opinion and by interest and pressure groups. In this chapter elections and electoral procedures will be discussed, and some analysis of the nebulous subjects of public opinion and pressure groups, conventional and unconventional, will be attempted.

Elections and Electoral Procedures

On every count India's three general elections were major achievements. The people of India had had little experience in voting—elections in British days were confined to a few people with special qualifications—and none at all in the complex processes of a nation-wide general election. Simply to prepare election rolls and conduct elections was a tremendous task. Over 173 million persons were eligible to vote in the first general elections, some 193 million in the second, and 210 million in the third. More than half the eligible voters actually voted in each election.

Preparations for the first general elections were started soon after India became an independent state. The constitution provided for an Election Commission and "one general electoral roll"; it also authorized the Indian Parliament to make appropriate laws regarding elections, electoral rolls, and the delimitation of constituencies. In January 1950, at about the time the constitution went into effect, the Parliament set up an Election Commission with wide powers, and in April Mr. Sukumar Sen was appointed chief election commissioner. Eventually Election Commissions were set up in all the states as well. Much of the credit for successfully preparing for the general election, conducting these elections, hearing election petitions, and carrying out basic arrangements must go to the Election Commissions and to Mr. Sen. In April 1950 Parliament passed the first electoral law dealing with the qualifications of voters and the preparation of the electoral rolls. The Representation of the People Act of 1951 dealt with procedures of elections, election expenses, election offenses, and similar matters.

The main work in preparing the electoral rolls was completed by the end of 1949, since the first general elections were originally scheduled for the spring of 1950. The rolls had to be revised almost up to the beginning of the voting in the fall of 1951. Complete accuracy in the rolls was out of the question, but the Election Commissions directed that great care should be taken to register every qualified voter. Much of the work was done by house-to-house canvass. Even then several million people were not registered; these included some 2.8 million women, who would give only the names of their husbands or fathers, and an even larger number of refugees. The delimitation of the constituencies proved to be another arduous task. Most of this work was done by Delimitation Commissions, with advisory committees consisting of members of Parliament. Eventually 3,772 constituencies were set up, 489 for the House of the People and the remainder for the state assemblies. This meant that every elected M.P. would represent approximately 720,000 persons. The decision to include in each parliamentary constituency an equal number of State Assembly constituencies helped to simplify the procedure.

Because most voters were illiterate, special arrangements had to be made to enable them to vote intelligently. Symbols were used for the parties, and the multiple-ballot-box technique allowed the voter to drop the ballot paper—a sheet bearing only a serial number stamped on it—into the ballot box bearing the symbol of the party of his choice. Special provision was also made for choosing representatives of the scheduled castes and scheduled tribes. The result was a fairly large number of double-member constituencies and even one triple-member constituency.

Because of the shortage of trained election officials and certain problems of geography and climate, the elections were held over a period of some four months in 1951–1952, with the heaviest polling in January 1952. The first elections required the preparation of 600 million ballot papers, 2.6 million ballot boxes, 132,500 polling stations, and 196,000 booths. The services of 900,000 personnel were required to supervise the voting.

Election Commissions and government agencies generally made herculean efforts to instruct the voters in their rights and duties. The work of the parties in this respect left much to be desired. Undoubtedly the elections were a great educational experience for millions of Indians, and they were conducted without major disturbances. During the campaign the candidates and party workers concentrated on local issues and interests; they also tried to make the voters identify the symbol with the party. Candidates who ran for the 489 seats to be filled in the House of the People numbered 1,874, and there were 15,361 for the seats in 22 state assemblies. Nearly 85 parties were represented, and there were also independent candidates. Over 9,000 candidates forfeited their deposits because they got less than one-sixth of the total vote in their constituencies; included in this number were nearly 5,000 Independents. Only the Congress Party put up candidates for most of the seats in the House of the People. It was therefore the only party which operated on a truly national scale.

The results of the elections were about as anticipated.[1] The Congress Party polled only about 45 per cent of the total votes cast for

[1] For details see Election Commission, *Report on the First General Elections in India, 1951–52* (2 vols.; New Delhi: Government of India Press, 1955); S. V. Kogekar and Richard L. Park, eds., *Reports on the Indian General Elections, 1951–52* (Bombay, 1956); *India Press Digests* (University of California), vol. I, no. 4, and Monograph Series no. 3 (Dec. 1956); Richard L. Park, "Indian Election Results," *Far Eastern Survey*, XXI (May 7, 1952), 61–70; Irene Tinker and Mil Walker, "The First General Elections in India and Indonesia," *Far Eastern Survey*, XXV (July 1956), 97–110; Gene D. Overstreet and Irene Tinker, "Political Dynamics in India" (Berkeley: Modern India Project, University of California, March 1957; from material prepared for the India volume, Country Survey Series, Human Relations Area Files), pp. 44–65. Many of the comments in this chapter on all three general elections are based on the observations, interviews, and investigations of the author, who was in India shortly after the conclusion of the first general elections and during the entire period of voting in the second and third general elections.

seats in the House of the People, but it elected 364 members, or 74 per cent of the total. The Communist Party returned 16 members, the Socialist Party 12, the Kisan Mazdoor Praja Party 9. No other party had any significant representation. Of the elected members 37 ran as Independents. In the state assemblies the Congress won a majority of the seats in all but 4 states. In Travancore-Cochin, Madras, Hyderabad, and West Bengal the main opposition to the Congress came from the Communists; in Orissa and Rajasthan it was from a right-wing coalition in which the princes figured prominently; in the Punjab it came from the Sikh party, the Akali Dal. Most of the nationally prominent leaders of the opposition parties were either defeated or did not run at all.

On the whole, the voters demonstrated great interest, if sometimes a bit of confusion, in the process of voting. It is of course impossible to tell what considerations influenced their decisions. Doubtless many voted for the Congress because it was the party of Gandhi and of Nehru; some may have voted for Congress candidates because their symbol was a pair of bullocks. Many villagers undoubtedly cast their ballots as directed by their headman or other leader. Women turned out in large numbers, and possibly many of them voted as their husbands had instructed. There were a number of voters who worshiped the ballot box or stuffed something besides the ballot paper into the box; there were several hundred cases of attempted impersonation and some reports of intimidation. The practice of stamping each voter's hand with a round mark in indelible ink seemed to be effective in preventing voting more than once. Since the ballot was cast in secret, it could be placed outside a box; and a voter might not deposit it at all, but retain it and perhaps sell or give it to some unscrupulous candidate who wished to rig the election. The fact that the ballot bore a serial number which was recorded opposite the name of the voter led to apprehension and to charges that the voting was not really secret at all. This practice was followed, however, only to allow an election tribunal to check the voting in case of a challenge or to check the balloting in double-member constituencies to make sure that the same voter had not cast two ballots for the same candidate.

After the general elections, the first regularly constituted Parliament of independent India met in the summer of 1952. Since its maximum life was five years, the second general elections had to be held sometime before the summer of 1957. In the interim the election lists were kept up to date by periodic revisions, the last changes being made only a few weeks before the voting began in late February 1957. For a time it seemed that the agitation and uncertainty created by reorganization of the states might force a postponement of the second general elections or even jeopardize the entire electoral process. After vigorous debate, the political map of India was redrawn, effective November 1, 1956. The changes in state boundaries and the reduction of the number of states to fourteen, each of equal status, greatly complicated the process of preparing the electoral rolls and delimiting constituencies; it also created emotional tensions where the government's decisions on state boundaries gave rise to strong feelings of frustrated regionalism. But the elections were held as scheduled, and in a much shorter period of time than the first (about three weeks, except in a few remote places). For the most part they were conducted along similar lines and, with a few exceptions, the results were not markedly different.[2] On the national level it was practically an election without issues. Naturally the opposition parties leveled a variety of charges against the Congress, but there was almost unanimous support for the broad policies of the Indian government, at home and abroad. The elections were fought largely in terms of personalities and local issues.

Peaceful as they were in most ways, in some parts of the country the second general elections gave rise to violent disagreements over the government's action in reorganizing the states just three months before the elections. Most criticisms concerned the government's failure to satisfy the demands of certain linguistic groups, particularly in Bombay and the Punjab.

Redrawing the state boundaries to conform to linguistic groupings had long been a popular issue in India. The Congress Party itself first gave strong support to linguistic demands at its Nagpur session in 1920; and in the following year regional units of the Congress were

---

[2] For background of the second general elections see S. L. Poplai, ed., *National Politics and 1957 Elections in India* (Delhi, 1957); J. R. Chandran and M. M. Thomas, eds., *Political Outlook in India Today: A Pre-election Study* (Bangalore, 1956); *Thought*, Feb. 23, 1957 (special election issue); fifteen "Election Preview" articles published in *Times of India*, Feb. 1957. For election results see Election Commission, *Report on the Second General Elections in India, 1957* (2 vols.; New Delhi: Government of India Press, 1958); Asoka Mehta, "The Political Mind of India," *Foreign Affairs*, XXXV (July 1957), 679–688; *India News*, II (April 15, 1957), 3; "India: Big Events, Few Changes," *Round Table*, no. 187 (June 1957), pp. 285–288; "India's Second General Election," *World Today*, XIII (June 1957), 232–241; James R. Roach, "India's 1957 Elections," *Far Eastern Survey*, XXVI (May 1957), 65–78.

reorganized along linguistic lines. Thus the Congress early committed itself to the linguistic principle and over the years repeatedly reaffirmed its adherence to this principle. In 1946, however, a Congress election manifesto stated that linguistic considerations would control political divisions "not in every case, but as far as it was possible in the circumstances of each case." In 1947 Nehru remarked: "First things must come first, and the first thing is the security and stability of India." The major shift in Congress policy came in 1948, with the report of the Constituent Assembly's Commission on Linguistic Provinces (the Dar Commission). This report not only stressed the financial, economic, and administrative considerations in states reorganization; it also held that formation of states exclusively or even mainly along linguistic lines would be inadvisable. Soon after this, a committee of the Congress Party headed by Nehru, Patel, and Pattabhi Sitaramayya endorsed the findings of the Dar Commission, but opened the door to widespread agitation by adding that overwhelming public opinion must be satisfied and agreeing to the possible creation of an Andhra state. The Congress as a whole held to this position in the elections of 1951. But after the elections the government found ways to delay the creation of Andhra and yielded in 1953 only after Potti Sriramulu, by fasting unto death, had roused the Telegu-speaking peoples of Madras state to violent agitation.

Finally, in December 1953, the government appointed a commission to examine "objectively and dispassionately" the question of states reorganization. The "guidance" provided by Parliament for this commission pointed clearly along the lines laid down by the Dar Commission. When its report was delivered in 1955, however, the States Reorganization Commission seemed to have followed the linguistic principle, with but two major exceptions. Of the 14 states and 3 Union territories it proposed to create, only 2 states were to remain bilingual, Bombay and the Punjab. The Marathi-speaking people of Bombay had long been demanding a unilingual state of Maharashtra with Bombay city as its capital; the Sikhs in the Punjab wanted a Punjabi-speaking state. Both demands were rejected, though all other major linguistic demands were satisfied; as a result, strong political agitation marked by occasional violence broke out in these two states, and dissatisfaction with the government's reorganization proposals was felt in virtually every state of the Union. Numerous compromises were broached by various groups and Congress policy vacillated, but the solution embodied in the States Reorganization Bill of 1956 retained a bilingual status for Bombay and the Punjab, postponing final action on the status of Bombay city for several years. Continuing agitation by the Sikhs led to a unique "regional formula" for dividing governmental functions within the Punjab along linguistic lines. The political vitality of the linguistic issue is evidenced by the resounding defeat which the Congress Party suffered in parts of Bombay state in the second general elections. Two strange electoral coalitions, the Mahagujerat Janata Parishad in Gujerat and the Samyukta Maharashtra Samiti in Maharashtra, united to bring down many Congress candidates. The parties adhering to these coalitions were united on so few other issues that the importance of the linguistic issue was strikingly demonstrated.

In the voting for state assemblies, the Congress suffered greater reverses in Bihar, Uttar Pradesh, and Bombay than were anticipated, but it still won a majority in these states and in all the other state assemblies except those of Kerala and Orissa. In all states except Kerala it was able to continue its Congress governments. Even in this problem state the gains of the Communists were not substantial, and they can be accounted for in part by the incorporation in the new Kerala state of the Malabar section of former Bombay state, where Communist strength was already great. In Orissa, where the Congress won only a few seats more than a coalition party dominated by land-lords and princes, the main opposition came not from the left but from the right. The Congress actually improved its position in a few states, including the Punjab, Rajasthan, Mysore, and Madras.

The outcome of the voting for the House of the People was remarkably similar to that in the elections of 1951–1952. The Congress won a few more seats, the Communists several and the Jan Sangh one, and the Praja Socialists lost two seats. Again, as in 1951–1952, the Congress gained approximately three-fourths of the representation in the House of the People and remained in power in all but one of the states, though polling less than half the total votes.

The techniques of campaigning and of voting were like those employed in 1951–1952. In the campaign there was more house-to-house canvassing, and fewer mass meetings were held. As in the first general elections, national leaders, including Nehru himself, campaigned vigorously. Again the All-India Radio was barred to candidates and party representatives, although the election manifestoes of the major parties were read over the air and voting instructions were broadcast frequently. On the whole, the voters cast their ballots with greater confidence and possibly with greater independence, although many voters were still unfamiliar with voting procedures, and many election irregularities were repeated. Again the campaigning and balloting passed off without serious incident.

Table 6. Lok Sabha election results * (number of seats won)

Party	1951–1952	1957	1962
Congress	364 (45.0)	371 (47.78)	361 (45.02)
Communist Party	16 (3.3)	27 (8.92)	29 (9.96)
Praja Socialist Party		19 (10.41)	12 (6.84)
Kisan Mazdoor Praja Party	9 (5.8)		
Socialist Party	12 (10.6)		
Jan Sangh	3 (3.1)	4 (5.93)	14 (6.44)
Swatantra Party			18 (6.80)
Other parties and Independents	85 (32.2)	73 (26.96)	59 † (24.94)

* Not including Jammu and Kashmir. Figures in parentheses are percentages of total vote.

† Includes 7 seats won by the DMK (Dravida Munnetra Kazhagam), 6 by the Socialists (the Lohia Socialists, a different party from the Socialist Party listed above), 4 by the Ganatantra Parishad (which merged with the Swatantra Party after the 1962 elections), 3 each by the Akali Dal, the Jharkhand Party, and the Republican Party, 2 each by the Muslim League, the Ram Rajya Parishad, the RSP (Revolutionary Socialist Party), and the Forward Bloc, and 1 by the Hindu Mahasabha.

Source: The figures for the first and second general elections are taken from the reports of the Election Commission, published in 1955 and 1958, respectively. Those for the third elections in 1962 are taken from Table I and Appendix III in the June 1962 issue of *Seminar* (no. 34, pp. 13 and 16).

Shortly after the second general elections, the government announced that it had accepted a recommendation of the Election Commission to replace the multiple-ballot-box system by a system of marked ballots, such as is used in most democratic countries. Under the new system the ballot paper contains the names of all the candidates along with party symbols. The ballot is marked in secret, but it is placed in a ballot box in the presence of polling officials, and the presiding officer checks the official mark on the back. The new method is less expensive and complicated, and it also eliminates the difficulties and abuses of the multiple-ballot-box system. On the other hand, it is more difficult and confusing for the illiterate voter.

The new ballot system was tried for the first time on a national scale in the third general elections, which were held during a period of nine days in February 1962. On the whole, it worked quite succesfully. Voters were given a small rubber stamp to mark their ballots, and they could stamp the "X" anywhere in the section of the ballot containing the name of the candidate and the symbol of the party of their choice. This process slowed the voting considerably, but it seemed to eliminate some of the abuses which had attended the use of the multiple-ballot-box technique.

As in the two previous general elections, in 1962 the campaign and the voting proceeded with little confusion or disorder.[3] Again the issues were largely local and personal in nature. There was little real discussion of national or international issues, although opponents of the Congress were critical of the foreign policies of the Congress government, especially in relation to Communist China. "The factors which affected the outcome of the election are many, and their importance varies from constituency to constituency if not from village to village."[4] The new Swatantra Party and a resurgent Jan Sangh in the north provided considerable opposition to the Congress, as did the DMK (Dravida Munnetra Kazhagam) in Madras and the Communists in Andhra, Kerala, and West Bengal; but the greatest difficulties experienced by the Congress came from within their own ranks. In many states the party was split by factional and personal rivalries, and some dissident Congressmen even supported opposition candidates or ran against the official Congress candidates themselves.

The over-all results of the 1962 elections did not change the politi-

[3] For the background of the third general elections see S. L. Poplai, ed., *1962 General Elections in India* (Bombay: Allied Publishers, 1962), especially the essay by K. P. Karunakaran on "Politics since the 1957 Elections" (pp. 1–29). This volume contains the manifestoes and important resolutions of all the major parties, articles by leading members of these parties, and valuable tables summarizing the results of the 1957 elections. The course of the campaign may be followed in the Indian newspapers and in various weekly journals, such as *Link* (New Delhi). For the results of the elections see the Indian newspapers and issues of *Link* in the period following the voting. See also Myron Weiner, "India's Third General Elections," *Asian Survey*, II (May 1962), 3–18. The *Economic Weekly* (Bombay) has published several articles on the elections, including a series of nine articles, starting with the Special Number for July 1962 (vol. XIV, nos. 28, 29, and 30), planned and organized by Myron Weiner and Rajni Kothari, under the general title: "The Third General Elections: Studies in Voting Behaviour." Statistical summaries of the results of the elections have been made available by the Election Commission.

[4] Weiner, "India's Third General Elections," p. 12.

cal picture substantially on the national scene, but they did reveal significant and sometimes unexpected changes in the balance of power in a number of states, notably Gujerat, Mysore, Madhya Pradesh, the Punjab, and Rajasthan. The Congress improved its position in a few states, notably in Maharashtra, but suffered considerable losses in several others, including Madhya Pradesh, Rajasthan, and Uttar Pradesh. The Swatantra Party scored notable success in Andhra Pradesh, Bihar, Gujerat, and Rajasthan, the Jan Sangh in Madhya Pradesh and Uttar Pradesh, the DMK in Madras, while the Communists maintained their strength in Kerala and West Bengal and increased their representation in the Andhra Assembly. The PSP lost seven seats in the Lok Sabha and maintained significant strength only in Bihar, Madhya Pradesh, Mysore, and Uttar Pradesh.

Almost all the prominent members of the opposition parties in the Lok Sabha were defeated, as were a Congress minister, three deputy ministers, the chief minister of Madhya Pradesh, and a few other leading Congressmen. The largest majorities were rolled up by two Maharanis—the Maharani of Jaipur, who stood for the Lok Sabha on the Swatantra ticket, and the Maharani of Gwalior, who was a Congress candidate for the Lok Sabha. The next largest majority was won by Krishna Menon, who defeated Acharya Kripalani, a former president of the Congress Party and a former chairman of both the Kisan Mazdoor Praja Party and the PSP, in the most highly publicized contest of the third elections. Menon was backed by the Communists and and Congress and by the personal prestige of Jawaharlal Nehru, while Kripalani stood as an Independent, with the strong support of the Swatantra, the PSP, the Jan Sangh, and almost all other parties which were active in North Bombay.

India's three general elections were great lessons in democracy which came home to almost every Indian. For the first time the humblest citizen could feel that he was participating in the processes of democracy and that his opinion counted. Even if many Indians were bewildered by the whole process, the exercise of the franchise had a continuing impact and educational value. The way the elections were conducted demonstrated that democracy, though foreign to the experience and outlook of most Indians, could be practiced in an underdeveloped Asian country among mostly illiterate people. Few of the achievements of independent India have been more impressive than this "act of faith," the adoption of universal suffrage and the successful conduct of "the world's largest democratic elections."

Public Opinion

Indian public opinion is a will-o'-the-wisp which almost defies analysis by the standard techniques of public opinion measurement that have been developed in the West. An Indian Institute of Public Opinion exists, but its observations have not yet attained anything like reliability.[5] Indians are too radically divided, on too many different levels and in too many different directions, to have distinct, formal opinions on very many topics. Such public opinions as exist concerning topics which do not touch daily life have usually been the opinions of a very small group of "intellectuals." There is hardly anything in India analogous in scope and effectiveness to the newspaper editorials, radio and television commentators, trade unions, voluntary associations, and letter-writing public in America. The vast majority of the people in India are illiterate and isolated in a more than geographical sense; they live, literally, in a world of their own. Except in a dim and negative way, they have little impact on those who make the political decisions. On the other hand, a certain tendency is evident to "Indianize" Indian politics, particularly on the regional and state levels, and here the Indian masses are slowly becoming involved and articulate. Here too, political horizons are narrower, and traditional attitudes more apparent. Here one notes the continued strength of religious orthodoxy and social conservatism, a widespread suspicion of government, a heavy burden of inertia.

Yet, over all, there can be no question that public opinion is becoming influential in India. It expresses itself in vague popular demands, unformulated, intangible, but irresistible. The issue of linguistic states was decided by a surge of public opinion that proved, ultimately, impossible to deny. Particularly in South India, resistance to the introduction of Hindi in the schools appears to be very powerful. A mass *satyagraha* movement against Portugal arose over the issue of Goa; it continued despite the appeal of the Prime Minister and the government to call it off. Even in world politics, where, at least until recently, a remarkable consensus has seemed to exist among Indians of almost all parties, the pressure of public opinion is sometimes ap-

[5] For the results of various polls conducted by the Institute see its journal, *Monthly Public Opinion Surveys.* Vol. II, nos. 16, 17, 18, and 19 (Jan., Feb., March, and April 1957), comprise a quadruple special issue containing the results of the first national public opinion poll conducted in India. It was specially designed to test public opinion research methods in India.

parent. This was illustrated by the protests within India regarding Nehru's delay in condemning the Russian brutalities in Hungary in 1956 and regarding the alleged softness and tergiversations of the government's policies toward Communist China since 1959. On the other hand, most Indians seem willing to support major decisions of foreign policy simply because Nehru makes them, even if they lead to steps whose wisdom they may question, as in the case of the dispatch of Indian troops to support the actions of the United Nations in the Congo. In a negative sense public opinion is of particular importance, and it exercises a restraining and conditioning influence on the leaders of the country, even on Prime Minister Nehru.

Thus, one senses considerable unevenness in the texture of public opinion in India. Certain issues are delicate ones, and the least tremor will touch off violent waves of protest; on others, seemingly no less important, the apathy is profound. Much of Nehru's popularity is due to his sensitivity to public moods, his efforts to keep the Congress Party in touch with the people, his innumerable public appearances. He realizes, probably far better than his idolaters, that there are definite limits to his power, that it is based on a mixture of consent and persuasion, which he must be continually on the alert to preserve.

In shaping Indian public opinion, nonpolitical organizations, individuals, and considerations are particularly important.

There is a strong tendency on the part of political forces in India to operate outside the framework of responsible political institutions, an inclination which presents a serious challenge to those institutions. Furthest removed from the framework of conventional politics are movements expressing the tradition of non-responsible leadership, exercising moral influence on formal political authority. Originating in the Brahmanic code, this tradition was strengthened by Gandhi who attempted political and social reform outside government and frequently outside party.[6]

Thus movements such as Bhoodan Yagna, extraparliamentary techniques such as fasts and *satyagraha,* and "unconventional" leaders such as Gandhi and Bhave have a tremendous influence on Indian political life. It may even be said, as Professor Morris-Jones has suggested, that these "nonpolitical" and "unconventional" aspects of Indian life are at the very heart of Indian politics.[7]

[6] Overstreet and Tinker, "Political Dynamics in India," p. 7.

[7] W. H. Morris-Jones, *Parliament in India* (Philadelphia: University of Pennsylvania Press, 1957), pp. 2, 37–40.

Because of the widespread illiteracy, geographical distances, and local patterns of Indian life, communication of all sorts is difficult, and the effective channels are often very different from those which are available in highly developed industrial states. There are no television stations, and the only radio network, All-India Radio, is controlled by the government and has only a limited impact.

Although All-India Radio broadcasts in regional languages as well as English, the audience which hears any of these broadcasts is limited both by the small number of radio sets in villages and by the variety of local dialects used throughout the nation. Motion pictures have a wider audience than does the radio, but they are widely used for escapist melodramas which tend, if anything, to reinforce traditional values of society.[8]

Foreign motion pictures, even poor ones, are popular. Indians like to boast of the fact that they have the third largest motion-picture industry in the world, surpassed only by the United States and Japan.

There are scores of newspapers, mostly weeklies and dailies, in all the regional languages and in English. Because "the press appears to be aimed primarily at national and regional elites, and its circulation is mainly urban," [9] most of the really influential newspapers are published in English. Among these are such excellent papers, with far more than a local circulation, as the *Hindu* (Madras), the *Times of India* (Bombay and Delhi), the *Statesman* (Calcutta and New Delhi), the *Amrita Bazar Patrika* (Calcutta and Allahabad), the *Hindustan Times* (New Delhi), and the *Indian Express* (published in four different cities). No Indian newspaper has a circulation of much over 100,000 copies, and most of them have far less than this. They reach a larger audience, however, than the circulation figures would suggest, for many nonpurchasers read them, and they are read to many who are illiterate. Most of the Indian newspapers are strongly political in their views, and the better ones provide, within space limitations, extensive coverage of national and international events. Lengthy and numerous editorials are common, but there are relatively few political columnists, and some of the best of these are under heavy pressure to curb their pens in writing of government policies and leaders.

Periodicals abound in India, but very few, except some film maga-

[8] Overstreet and Tinker, "Political Dynamics in India," pp. 9–10.
[9] *Ibid.,* p. 10.

zines, have a sizable circulation. Most are fly-by-night organs of opinion with a circulation of a few thousand at most. The *Eastern Economist,* published in New Delhi, is an excellent journal along the lines of the London *Economist.* The *Economic Weekly* (Bombay) is an influential journal which carries articles on political and social, as well as economic topics. Several of the scholarly or professional journals are of high quality; among these, in the field of politics and foreign affairs, are the *India Quarterly,* organ of the Indian Council of World Affairs, *International Studies,* issued by the Indian School of International Studies, and the *Indian Journal of Public Administration,* published by the Indian Institute of Public Administration.

India has one of the most effective "undergrounds" in the world. That is to say, information gets around rapidly, by word of mouth and by devious means beyond the comprehension of outsiders. Personal contacts are of the utmost importance. "In personal contact the visual impression plays a weighted role; the belief in *darshan* (the beneficial effect of being in the presence of a great man) is still strong, and to receive *darshan* one needs only to see, not listen." [10] The importance of *darshan* is generally recognized by India's leaders. Gandhi traveled ceaselessly about the countryside, often on foot, and thousands were content just to see him and to be in his presence. He used the spinning wheel and prayer meetings as effective instruments of popular education. Nehru, burdened as he is by heavy official responsibilities, devotes a considerable amount of time and energy to public appearances in all parts of India; he professes to derive strength and refreshment from his contacts with the people, and they turn out in great numbers to see and hear him. Vinoba Bhave moves about on foot from one village to another in his crusade for spiritual regeneration and sacrificial giving of land; and Jayaprakash Narayan, vowing to abjure politics, devotes most of his time to this work. These men are truly charismatic leaders. The role of charisma in Indian life cannot be overestimated, in a land where "the belief in *darshan* . . . is still strong." It is quite apparent that "the personality of leaders and their ability to have a direct impact on their audience will doubtless continue to play an outsized role in Indian politics for some time." [11]

[10] *Ibid.*

[11] *Ibid.,* p. 11. See also Myron Weiner, "Some Hypotheses on the Politics of Modernization in India," in Richard L. Parks and Irene Tinker, eds., *Leadership and Political Institutions in India* (Princeton: Princeton University Press, 1959), pp. 26–28.

Pressure Groups, Conventional and Unconventional

Like public opinion generally, the nature of pressure groups in India and their influence on Indian politics are just beginning to be topics for serious study. There are many such groups, and their influence is obviously great. One of the clearest general analyses of these groups was presented in a paper prepared for the Human Relations Area Files by Gene D. Overstreet and Irene Tinker:

Three main types of pressure groups may be distinguished in the Indian setting: 1) special-interest organizations of fairly recent origin representing modern bases of social and economic association familiar to the Western observer, such as trade unions and business groups, social welfare agencies, or youth and women's organizations; 2) organizations representing traditional social relationships, such as caste and religious groups; and 3) organizations representing the Gandhian ideological heritage.[12]

The "modern interest groups" are multiplying rapidly. They are still mostly influenced and controlled by a small group of intellectuals, and they usually have a strong political flavor. Some, in fact, are closely associated with political parties or movements. This is illustrated by trade unions, peasants' organizations, student groups, and cultural associations.

The number of industrial workers in India is still very small in comparison with the number of agricultural laborers, and they are not strongly organized; but an organized labor movement has been of some importance for a generation, and today four major unions claim a membership of approximately 3.5 million. The leadership is still concentrated markedly in the intelligentsia. "Trade Unions in India exert little influence on the policies and character of political organizations. They are rather ancillaries of the leading parties, for which they seek to extend power and further political aims."[13] The first major union was the All-India Trade Union Congress (AITUC), formed in 1920. After stormy years of intense conflict within the organization, it came strongly under Communist influence, and other political parties turned to the formation of competing unions. At present it is clearly allied with the CPI. Its general secretary, S. A. Dange, is one of India's leading Communists; he was elected to the Indian House of the People from Bombay city in the general elections of

[12] Overstreet and Tinker, "Political Dynamics in India," p. 11.
[13] Laxmi M. Singhvi and Bidyut K. Sarkar, *India: Government and Politics* (New Haven: Human Relations Area Files, 1955), p. 114.

1957, but he was defeated in 1962. To counter the AITUC the Congress Party took the initiative in forming the Indian National Trade Union Congress, which now has nearly half the members of trade unions in India. The two smaller trade unions also have political affiliations or inclinations—the Hind Mazdoor Sabha with the Socialists and the United Trade Union Congress with some of the smaller leftist parties, leaning strongly toward the Communists.

Peasant organizations (*kisan sabhas*) have existed for some time, and a number have been politically active. Among these are the All-India Kisan Sabha, which is dominated by the Communists; the Hind Kisan Panchayat, led by the Socialists; and the United Kisan Sabha, associated with smaller leftist parties. Both the Socialists and the Congress have tended in recent years to support the Bhoodan Yagna movement rather than any more politically inclined peasant associations.

Indian students are politically conscious, perhaps to an unfortunate degree, and student associations have been hotbeds of competing political activities. When the All-India Students' Federation came under Communist influence, a new association, the National Union of Students, was formed, with the blessing of the Congress Party. Many other student groups, of a national or local character, including welfare groups, philosophical societies, and debating societies, were drawn into political activity.

Cultural associations have been a fertile field for the Communists. Cultural delegations have visited Communist China and the Soviet Union, and delegations have come to India from China and Russia. The All-India Peace Council, which is associated with the Communist-dominated World Peace Movement, and the Indo-Chinese Friendship Association often parrot the international Communist line, in spite of the fact that the great majority of their members are sincere non-Communists.

Women's organizations are becoming increasingly active. At times the most important of these associations, the All-India Women's Conference, has been strongly influenced by the Communists, but it is now affiliated with the Congress Party. It is primarily concerned with welfare activities and with improving the legal and social status of women. It was particularly active as a "pressure group" while the Hindu Code Bill, in its various parts, was being considered by the Indian Parliament.

For the most part the political leaders of modern India have not been businessmen, and the policies of the Indian government since independence have placed increasing restrictions on the operations of the Indian business community. In a welfare state, dedicated to the achievement of "a socialist pattern of society," the role of "private enterprise" is limited by the over-all objectives of national planning and development. The Indian government considers that the main function of private enterprise is to help in fulfilling the goals laid down in the Five Year Plans. Indian business leaders often complain of the restrictions which are placed upon them by nationalization and social control of economic life. Partly because of the economic exploitation of the country by foreign interests, but also because of the practices of indigenous business concerns, there is widespread aversion to "predatory capitalism" in India. Thus Indian businessmen have less scope for activity and less influence on politics than the business leaders of most democratic states. On the other hand, some businessmen have had considerable influence in Indian politics, even during the days when Gandhi controlled the independence movement. It is well known that the Mahatma, who reacted against modern industrialization and was dedicated to the *sarvodaya* society, was a close friend of a great Indian industrialist, Birla, and received substantial support from the Indian business community. In India today the concentration on economic development requires the intimate association of businessmen in all phases of planning and development.[14]

Practically all the major industries in India have associations, and most of these are aligned with the most influential of the business organizations of India, the Federation of Indian Chambers of Commerce and Industry, whose headquarters are in a splendid new building in New Delhi.

The federation is an impressive organization, both in terms of the number of affiliated business firms and the efficiency of the operation. As of 1961 there were 137 member bodies (chambers of commerce and manufacturers associations) and 286 associate members (including such giant firms as Hindustan Motors, Swadeshi Mills, and Tata Iron and Steel). Many of the "member bodies" are in turn associations with a large membership. The Indian Merchants Chamber of Bombay, for example, is in the Federation and itself has a membership of almost 3000 organizations, of which over a hundred are also associations with many affiliates.[15]

[14] See Helen B. Lamb, "Business Organizations and Leadership in India Today," in Park and Tinker, eds., *Leadership and Political Institutions in India*, pp. 251–267.

[15] Bernard E. Brown, "Organized Business in Indian Politics," *Indian Journal of Political Science*, XXIII (April–June 1962), 129.

Other important national organizations of businessmen are the All-India Manufacturers Organization, which was intended to be a counterpart of the National Association of Manufacturers in the United States (though it is considerably more liberal in its policies and programs), and the Associated Chambers of Commerce of India, in which British and other foreign-owned firms are particularly active. In 1956 the Forum for Free Enterprise was founded by a number of Indian businessmen to "educate public opinion" regarding the value and accomplishments of private enterprise. The Forum has taken a decidedly conservative line and is devoting a major share of its efforts to "rousing the public to the dangers of State capitalism." Some businessmen have given open support to the new conservative Swatantra Party, but most of the business associations and the larger firms, perhaps because they wish to remain on good terms with the ruling Congress Party, have remained conspicuously aloof from the new party. "Thus, in spite of ideological antipathy to the 'socialized pattern of society' . . . there has been no massive switchover of businessmen to Swatantra." [16]

The second main type of pressure groups—caste and religious groups—includes organizations which have functioned or which still function both as political parties and as associations to promote the interests of a particular group or community. These include such important "parties" as the Republican Party, the Akali Dal, and even, to some degree, the Hindu Mahasabha. Organizations devoted to the interests of special religious groups include the All-India Conference of Indian Christians, the Parsi Central Association and Political League, and the Anglo-Indian Association. Caste groups are particularly numerous. The Marwari Association, for example, is dedicated to the interests of a community which has achieved a conspicuous place in the business life of India. The Harijan Sewak Sangh is one of the many associations which "work to ameliorate the social and economic status of the lower castes through legislation and social work . . . —a part of the complex of Gandhian constructive institutions." [17]

The third variety of pressure groups is in many respects unique to the Indian setting, performing functions and filling needs which affect all levels of Indian life. Their work appeals to the humblest villager and to the most sophisticated Westernized political leader.

These agencies formally disavow the normal pressure group function of influencing political institutions, seeking instead the fundamentally different

[16] *Ibid.*, p. 137.
[17] Overstreet and Tinker, "Political Dynamics in India," p. 18.

goal of effecting change outside the institutional framework through creating the essential moral impetus. However, they possess great prestige and exercise significant influence through the power of example and through close personal contact with government.[18]

Most of these groups have their roots in Indian tradition and attitudes. Many of them were founded by Mahatma Gandhi or came into being under the stimulus of his teachings and example. They are designed to promote the great goal of the Mahatma of a *sarvodaya* society, classless and casteless, emphasizing the regeneration of the individual and the welfare of all, a society almost without government and formal institutions, in which voluntary constructive work would provide for most needs. In this way Gandhi hoped to bring out the best in the human spirit and to avoid the abuses and complications of modern technological life. The political leaders of independent India are departing from the spirit and practice of Gandhi's teachings, but they are conscious of the profound significance of these teachings and of the great influence that they have in the country as a whole. They are encouraging the cooperation of Gandhian associations and movements in such aspects of the national effort as welfare work and the community development projects.

The all-encompassing association of the Gandhian constructive workers is called the Sarvodaya Samaj. The Samaj is a body of members only, however, and has no formal organization except an annual conference. The primary organized agency of the Sarvodaya movement is the Sarva Seva Sangh. . . . Affiliated with the Sarva Seva Sangh are a number of specialized groups, including the All-India Village Industries' Association, the Go-Seva Sangh (a society for cow protection), the All-India Spinners Association, the Hindustani Prachar Sabha (a society for the promotion of Hindustani), and the Talimi Sangh (a society for the promotion of basic education).[19]

By far the most dramatic effort to make Gandhi's ideals a living reality in Indian life is the Bhoodan Yagna movement of Acharya Vinoba Bhave. Its purpose is to achieve a nonviolent revolution of the kind that Gandhi envisioned. Acharya Kripalani has called it "the greatest revolution since Gandhiji."

Called the Bhoodan Yagna (land gift movement) because voluntary redistribution of land was its first goal, it has since added the aims of *sampattidan* (donation of wealth), *koopdan* (donation of wells), *baildan* (donation of bullocks), and *jivandan* (donation of personal service to the cause)—all

---

[18] *Ibid.*, p. 19.   [19] *Ibid.*, p. 20.

culminating in the goal of *gramdan* representing communal ownership of village land and the establishment of village democracy as envisaged by Gandhi.[20]

In the fall of 1951 Vinoba Bhave set out on foot from Sevagram on the first stage of a movement which was to attract world-wide attention and to create a tremendous stir in the Indian countryside. One of Gandhi's closest followers, he looked like a bearded Gandhi, and he wore the same scanty dress. After going to Delhi and New Delhi to explain the purpose of his movement and to dramatize it, he began a walking tour of Indian villages which won for him the sobriquet, "India's Walking Saint." [21] After his initial successes in the Telengana area of Hyderabad, where Communist propaganda had produced a state of revolt, he moved to Bihar and intensified his efforts. Within a few years he had been given several million acres of land and many other gifts, including several hundred entire villages—the *gramdan* villages. Yet the economic results of the movement have been disappointing. Very little of the land has been redistributed, and much of it is of little value anyway. Bhave was not interested in developing an organization, and he expressed a desire to eschew politics; but he has been quite willing to receive the assistance and support of government authorities in his work. Several states have enacted legislation to facilitate the redistribution of the land donated to the Bhoodan movement, and the top leaders of India, including the former President, Dr. Rajendra Prasad, himself an old Gandhian from Bihar, Prime Minister Nehru, and the present President, Dr. Radhakrishnan, have gone out of their way to visit Bhave and to express their approval of the movement. As has been noted, the Praja Socialist Party has been particularly interested in Bhoodan, and its outstanding leader, Jayaprakash Narayan, is devoting himself to this work and has presumably retired from political life. Because of its great popular appeal and potentiality, the Communists are taking a special interest in the movement, although Bhave himself is a strong critic of communism and of Communist methods.

Vinoba Bhave is generally regarded as the nearest approximation to a Gandhi in India today, and his Bhoodan movement is in the true Gandhian tradition. "Only in India, one feels, could there be such a movement. . . . It shows how powerful still is the moral force of

[20] *Ibid.*

[21] See Hallam Tennyson, *India's Walking Saint: The Story of Vinoba Bhave* (Garden City, N.Y.: Doubleday, 1955).

the Gandhian outlook." [22] Although professing to be wholly non-political, it undoubtedly has a powerful influence on Indian politics. Its main significance is perhaps more spiritual than economic or political. "But whatever may be the fate of its specific program—much of which in the long run is incompatible with the prevailing modernist goals of industrialization and secularization—the Sarvodaya movement in general," and the Bhoodan movement in particular, represent "an important predisposition to non-responsible forms of organization and action which may influence the future development of political institutions in India." [23]

[22] Lady Hartog, *India: New Pattern* (London, 1955), p. 34.
[23] Overstreet and Tinker, "Political Dynamics in India," p. 21.

· XIII ·

Economic Development

and Foreign Relations

INTERNALLY a major objective of the government of India is to increase the productive capacity and to raise the standards of living of the large and growing population. This is a task which will tax to the utmost the economic and human resources of the country. At the present time the major effort is being made through the Third Five Year Plan, which represents one of the most significant experiments in economic planning on a nation-wide scale in the world.

Externally India is interested in cultivating friendly relations with all nations, in avoiding too close commitments to any group, and in working for international peace and cooperation. In spite of the policy of "nonalignment," the leaders of India are poignantly aware of the stake which their country has in the course of world affairs and of the disastrous consequences to their country and people of another global war. The current crisis with China has forced them to reexamine the bases of their foreign policy and to take a more realistic approach to "the facts of international life."

Economic Development

"The central objective of public policy and of national endeavour in India since Independence has been promotion of rapid and balanced economic development."[1] To achieve this end, large-scale economic planning, directed and controlled by the government, has been undertaken. Even before independence the Congress Party, at Nehru's urging, established in 1938 a Planning Committee which drew upon the help not only of the Congress Party but also of numerous industrialists, labor representatives, and economists. As Frank Moraes has noted, however, "it was soon obvious to [Nehru] . . . that national planning on a comprehensive scale could only take place under a free national government prepared to introduce fundamental changes in the country's social and economic structure."[2] The resolutions passed at the annual sessions of the Congress Party, both before and after the creation of the Planning Committee in 1938, supported state intervention in the economic life of the nation. The adoption of the "socialistic pattern of society" resolution at the sixtieth annual session of the Congress Party at Avadi, Madras, in January 1955 was supported by its proponents as a logical development of Congress policy rather than as an innovation.

The constitutional basis for government action in the sphere of economic planning is found in Article 39 of Part IV, "Directive Principles of State Policy," which pledges that the state shall direct its policy toward securing:

(a) that the citizens, men and women equally, have the right to adequate means of livelihood;
(b) that the ownership and control of the material resources of the community are so distributed as best to subserve the common good; and
(c) that the operation of the economic system does not result in the concentration of wealth and means of production to the common detriment.

To translate these goals into reality, the government of India, in March 1950, established a Planning Commission, whose principal tasks were to "formulate a Plan for the most effective and balanced utilisation of the country's resources," to "appraise from time to time the progress achieved in the execution of each stage of the Plan and recommend the adjustments of policy and measures that such appraisal may show to be necessary," and to examine "the principal problems affecting the social and economic development of the country."

The Planning Commission has worked under the direct supervision

[1] Planning Commission, Government of India, *Second Five Year Plan* (New Delhi: Government of India Press, 1956), p. 1.
[2] Frank Moraes, *Jawaharlal Nehru* (New York: Macmillan, 1956), p. 421.

of the government of India and especially of the National Development Council, which was set up to provide a high-level agency to consider the place of planning in the political life of the country. The importance of this coordinated effort in national planning is suggested by the fact that Prime Minister Nehru is chairman of both the Planning Commission and the National Development Council and has been very active in these roles. Economic planning on a national scale has also involved the closest possible cooperation between the central government and the states and between the government and the "private sector" in the country, as well as the maximum public participation and support.

In July 1951 the Planning Commission prepared a draft outline of a plan of development for the period of five years from April 1951 to March 1956. After widespread review and comment by both official and private groups and individuals, the First Five Year Plan was submitted and approved by the Parliament. It called for a total outlay in the public sector of approximately $4.3 billion. A major target of the planners was to increase agricultural production, particularly food grains, and irrigation facilities. A concerted effort to expand industrial production was deliberately postponed until the Second Plan in the hope that concentration on agriculture and related areas would yield a direct rise in the living standards of the people. Fortunately the monsoons during the First Plan period were good, yielding sufficient rain to ensure abundant harvests.

The over-all results of the First Five Year Plan were encouraging. National income over the five-year period increased by some 18 per cent. Food-grain production went up by 20 per cent. Over 6 million acres of land were brought under irrigation through major works, and another 10 million through minor works. Industrial production increased steadily. The Community Development Program was launched in October 1952, and the National Extension Service in 1953. In the annual evaluation report on the progress of these programs covering the final year of the First Plan period, it was noted that distinct advances had been made "in terms of provision of basic amenities needed by the people—education, health and sanitation, water supplies, communications." [3]

Although the First Five Year Plan achieved most of its objectives, its

[3] *Evaluation Report on Working of Community Projects and N.E.S. Blocks* (New Delhi: Programme Evaluation Organisation, Planning Commission, Government of India, 1956), p. 1.

implementation revealed a number of areas where even greater effort and concentration of material resources were required. These factors came to the fore in the early stages of the drafting and implementation of the Second Five Year Plan.

The Second Plan called for an expenditure of $10.08 billion in the public sector, more than twice that of the First Plan. The principal objectives of the Second Plan were: (1) "a sizeable increase in national income"; (2) "rapid industrialization with particular emphasis on the development of basic and heavy industries"; (3) "a large expansion of employment opportunities"; and (4) "reduction of inequalities in income and wealth and a more even distribution of economic power."

Table 7. Distribution of outlay in the public sector, 1951–1966
(at 1960–1961 prices)

	First Plan		Second Plan		Third Plan	
	$ million	%	$ million	%	$ million	%
Agriculture and community development	611.1	15	1,113	11	2,242.8	14
Major and medium irrigation	651	16	882	9	1,365	9
Power	546	13	934.5	10	2,125.2	13
Village and small industries	90.3	2	367.5	4	554.4	4
Industries and minerals	155.4	4	1,890	20	3,192	20
Transport and communications	1,098.3	27	2,730	28	3,120.6	20
Social services and miscellaneous	963.9	23	1,743	18	2,730	17
Inventories					420	3
Total	4,116	100	9,660	100	15,750	100

Source: Planning Commission, Government of India, *Third Five Year Plan* (New Delhi: Government of India Press, 1961); adapted from tables on pp. 33 and 58.

As the implementation of the Second Plan proceeded, major difficulties, mostly unanticipated, developed. These included foreign exchange shortages and a serious drought in 1957,[4] a rise in prices of imported goods as a result of such factors as the closing of the Suez

[4] The drought of 1957 forced the government of India to import far more food than planned, and this factor, plus the rise in prices at home and abroad, increased the cost of the plan by about 20 per cent. See "The State of the Plan," *Eastern Economist*, XXVIII (March 22, 1957), 422.

Canal in late 1956, and inflation in many Western countries. In October 1957 the Indian government authorized the withdrawal of all $630 million of its sterling assets, held in Britain, in an attempt to solve its balance of payments problems. This, however, was at best a temporary solution since, as Finance Ministry officials noted, the sterling reserve held in Britain was the equivalent of only eight months' imports into India. India had to rely more heavily on foreign aid than had been planned, and this introduced another element of uncertainty into the planning picture.

As a consequence of these unfavorable developments, the targets of the Second Plan had to be scaled down, and the main objective came to be the preservation of the "hard core." This objective was achieved, but overall the Second Plan fell short of its original targets by some 30 per cent, and national income increased by about 20 per cent instead of the target of 25 per cent. Real progress was made in industrialization in both the public and private sectors. Three new steel plants were built, with the help of the USSR and of British and German interests, in the public sector. The expansion in employment opportunities was more than offset by additions to the labor force, so that instead of an estimated 6 million unemployed at the end of the Second Plan the actual figure was close to 9 million. If any progress at all was made in the "reduction of inequalities in income and wealth and a more even distribution of economic power," it was spotty at best and was not readily apparent.

In spite of the failure to achieve the planned targets of the Second Plan, a much more ambitious Third Plan was launched in April 1961, under what seemed to be more auspicious circumstances. This plan envisioned a total expenditure of over $15 billion in the public sector and some $9 billion in the private sector. It estimated that some $3 billion could be raised by additional taxation and that about $5 billion—one-third of the public sector expenditure and more than one-fifth of the total expenditure—would be made available by foreign aid. The announced objectives of the Third Plan were substantially the same as those of the Second, with the addition of "self-sufficiency in foodgrains" and increased agricultural production generally. The proposed increase in national income was "over 5 per cent per annum." Steel, machine building, chemicals, fuel, and power were specifically mentioned as basic industries scheduled for expansion, and the hope was expressed that the industry expansion during the Third Plan period would lay the basis for meeting the requirements of further industrialization "within a period of ten years or so mainly from the country's own resources." [5]

The success of the Third Plan has been jeopardized by serious shortfalls in steel and coal production and in transportation and power,[6] by the continuing shortage of foreign exchange, and by the new burdens placed on the economy as a result of the enlarged conflict with China. The planned increase in exports cannot be achieved unless problems of production, quality, and price can be resolved and unless international economic conditions and policies of India's major customers, notably the United Kingdom and the United States, are more favorable. The foreign exchange problem is particularly serious; indeed, "the shortage of foreign exchange may become the major obstacle to further economic progress." [7] Self-sufficiency in food grains will probably not be achieved by 1966, although some recent estimates are more hopeful than past performance. Industrial production will undoubtedly increase greatly, but India will in all probability be far from the stage of self-sustaining growth in the "ten years or so" mentioned in the Third Plan, or in any foreseeable period, unless many inhibiting factors are overcome. Unemployment, already a major problem, will almost certainly be greater at the end of the Third Plan period.

In spite of all the obstacles in the way, India has made remarkable progress during nearly a decade and a half of planned development, and it seems to be gathering momentum year by year. The Five Year Plans are regarded by most Indian and foreign experts as sound and realistic, although there have been serious lacunae and mistakes and although the gap between plans and performance has often been distressingly wide. India is, paradoxically, a static society on the move. It is in the midst of a "crisis of development," and it is experiencing many tensions and anxieties. But it is a fact of great significance, not only for India but for all of the non-Communist world,

[5] Planning Commission, Government of India, *Third Five Year Plan* (New Delhi: Government of India Press, 1961), p. 48.

[6] A study made in 220 industrial units, sponsored by the Federation of Indian Chambers of Commerce and Industry, indicated that the average loss of production due to a shortage of coal was between 20 and 25 per cent. See *Economic Weekly*, No. 4, 1961, p. 1681. "Throughout the first year of the Third Plan the Indian economy suffered from a severe shortage of electrical power, which could cause a 25 per cent shortfall in the physical program embodied in the total Plan." See Richard H. Kaufman, "India's Five Year Plans: The First of the Third," *Asian Survey*, II (Aug. 1962), 39.

[7] Kaufman, "India's Five Year Plans," p. 41.

that the largest of all the non-Communist states, embracing one-seventh of the human race, is consciously dedicated to the democratic way and has embarked on a planned course of growth as a free society, instead of succumbing to the temptations of forced development by totalitarian methods. India has embarked on a "difficult and tremendous journey" which has no ending, but which offers hope for a brighter future for its growing millions. To achieve its ambitious goals it must redouble its own efforts and receive substantial encouragement and tangible support from the other countries, particularly the developed countries, of the non-Communist world.

Foreign Relations

In spite of pressing internal problems and the policy of nonalignment India has, since 1947, played an active and generally consistent role in foreign affairs, based on a remarkable consensus at home. Whatever outside criticisms may be made of India's foreign policy, it makes sense to most Indians who have any views at all on such matters. It has given India an influence on the world which is far greater than India's actual power would seem to warrant, and it is almost the only policy which could win such widespread support within the country.[8] "The consensus still exists in large measure, but important aspects of foreign policy, and to some degree the whole basic approach to foreign affairs, are now being challenged more vigorously than ever before."[9] This new development has been occasioned in part by internal developments and divisions, but mainly by the sharp change for the worse in relations with Communist China since 1959.

In power-political terms India is a weak country, with few of the advantages which a nation must possess to be influential in world affairs. To be sure, it is the most populous of the democratic states, but in view of the extremely low standards of living, widespread illiteracy, and social fissures, the large numbers of people are perhaps more a source of weakness than of strength at the present time. India occupies a vast territory in a strategically important part of the world, but resources are limited and there are distressing problems of internal unity. Nevertheless, India is the largest non-Communist state in Asia, the largest and most important of the "underdeveloped" coun-

[8] See N. D. Palmer, "India's Outlook on Foreign Affairs," *Current History*, XXX (Feb. 1956), 69.
[9] N. D. Palmer, "India's Foreign Policy," *Political Quarterly*, XXXIII (Oct. 1962), 391.

tries, the leading nation in the "uncommitted" world, and a leading spokesman of the newly emergent nations, especially of the Afro-Asian group of states in the United Nations. India regards itself as a major bridge between East and West, whether these two terms be taken to refer to the Communist and non-Communist worlds or to Asia and the West. However irritating or shortsighted India's position of nonalignment may seem to a partisan eye, it has resulted in greater influence in the councils of the nations than association with the West would give.

UNDERLYING FACTORS

The foreign policy of India, like that of any other country, is conditioned by certain basic factors, such as geographic, strategic, and historical considerations, domestic pressures and influences, and basic characteristics of national life. It is also profoundly affected by the policies and attitudes of other states and by the general course of international developments.[10]

In geographic and strategic terms India occupies a vital part of the earth's surface.[11] Since relations with Pakistan are most unsatisfactory, there is a strategic problem within the natural frontiers of the Indian subcontinent. India is directly concerned with the security of the Indian Ocean area, but has no immediate problem in this respect, so long as the defense of the region depends essentially upon British and American sea power, with such collateral support as the Indian navy can provide. If Nepal and Bhutan are included within its strategic frontiers, India has the longest border which any non-Communist state shares with a Communist state, and the greatest of the Communist powers is not far to the northwest. India's Himalayan borders have become "live frontiers" since 1959, as a result of China's moves in Tibet and along the borders, and especially since October 20, 1962, when the Chinese launched a major attack in the North East Frontier Area and in Ladakh. India is now faced with a major security problem, with the remote and frigid Himalayan area as the immediate theater of conflict.

In countless ways India's long historical experience has shaped its policies as an independent state. Its leaders have been made particu-

[10] For summaries of basic factors in India's foreign policy see J. C. Kundra, *Indian Foreign Policy, 1947–1954: A Study of Relations with the Western Bloc* (Groningen, 1955); K. P. Karunakaran, *India in World Affairs, August 1947–January 1950* (Calcutta, 1952).

[11] See K. M. Panikkar, *Geographic Factors in Indian History* (Bombay, 1955).

larly sensitive to foreign domination in a cultural and psychological as well as a political sense, and they are especially concerned with remaining aloof from great-power politics in order to concentrate on serious internal problems. India is struggling to behave externally as well as internally in keeping with its traditions and beliefs. The present policy of nonalignment may be explained almost solely in terms of present weaknesses and opportunities as related to the existing international situation; but the careful student of Indian society and history is likely to conclude that the policy has even deeper roots in the Indian past and that somehow it is linked with the great traditions of Indian philosophy and experience, such as the Buddhist teachings of the middle way, the ancient faith in *ahimsa*—meaning nonviolence in more than a physical sense—and other Gandhian teachings based on Indian values. Many of the leaders of modern India, including Nehru himself, are inclined to shape their policies in the light of immediate considerations, such as influence the policies and actions of national leaders elsewhere, but they know that India's historical experience and traditions must affect its foreign relations, and they realize the importance of domestic considerations and pressures in shaping foreign policy.

Prior to 1947 the foreign policy of India was largely determined in Westminster, and it did not necessarily reflect the views of India's leaders or of Indians generally. During the First World War, for example, many Indians rallied around the British war effort, and thousands of them fought in Europe and elsewhere overseas. During the Second World War, Indians again fought in Europe, North Africa, and other parts of the world, and India was officially at war with the Axis powers; but the Indian National Congress was opposed to India's involvement in the struggle, so long at least as India was not free, and throughout most of the war years it advocated a policy of noncooperation. Even though India was not independent, it was a member of the League of Nations, and many Indians gained international experience in the League councils and at various international conferences. Nevertheless, India entered the family of nations in 1947 with relatively little experience and with relatively few commitments. This proved to be both an advantage and a handicap.

FOREIGN POLICY OF THE INDIAN NATIONAL CONGRESS

Well before 1947, however, a kind of Indian foreign policy did emerge in the Indian National Congress, the spearhead of the freedom movement. One of the first resolutions passed by the Congress at its first annual session in 1885 was a protest against the annexation of Upper Burma. In 1904 the Congress protested against a recent expedition to Tibet, on the ground that it was "but part of a general forward policy, which . . . threatens to involve India in foreign entanglements." [12] Until the end of the First World War, the Congress took relatively little interest in questions of foreign policy and generally supported the British position on such issues. Immediately after the war the Congress began to take a more active and independent line, in foreign as well as in domestic policies. Resolution after resolution expressed opposition to imperialism and especially to European rule, sympathy with peoples struggling to be free, hatred of war, desire for peace, and antipathy toward foreign entanglements.

In 1925 the Congress authorized the All-India Congress Committee to establish a foreign department. Jawaharlal Nehru became head of this department and the chief spokesman of the Congress in the field of foreign affairs. Thus for a generation he has been the voice of India in foreign policy; in fact, he has established a record in this field which is unequaled by any other democratic statesman. This fact should be remembered, for it helps to explain India's remarkable consistency in foreign policy and it is a reminder that, as Nehru himself stated in 1955, "our foreign policy is not a sudden growth, but a natural outcome of our thinking for many years past." [13]

Before the outbreak of the Second World War the Congress strongly dissociated itself from British policy. A resolution of the Working Committee in August 1939 declared:

The past policy of the British Government, as well as the recent developments, demonstrate abundantly that this Government does not stand for freedom and democracy and may at any time betray these ideals. India cannot associate herself with such a Government or be asked to give her resources for democratic freedom which is denied to her and which is likely to be betrayed.

This policy was carried to the point of almost complete noncooperation during the war.

After the war, Congress resolutions welcomed the emergence of

[12] N. V. Rajkumar, ed., *The Background of India's Foreign Policy* (New Delhi: All-India Congress Committee, 1952), p. 37. All subsequent quotations from Congress resolutions are taken from this very useful collection.

[13] Address at the annual session of the Congress Party in Madras in January 1955.

the United Nations, deplored the position allotted to the smaller nations, lent moral support to freedom movements everywhere, particularly in Asia, and deprecated the politics of the atom bomb which "has brought to a crisis the immoral and self-destructive elements of the present-day political, economic and spiritual structure of the world." Indian spokesmen, including Gandhi, Nehru, and Mrs. Sarojini Naidu, took a prominent part in the First Asian Relations Conference, held in New Delhi in April 1947.[14] In a sense this was a precursor to the conference on Indonesia which was held in New Delhi in January 1949, on the invitation of the government of India, and to the important Asian-African Conference at Bandung in April 1955, which was sponsored by the "Colombo Powers," including India. These meetings marked the growing role of Asian countries in world affairs. The idea is one which Nehru has often expressed. "In this crisis in world history," he declared at the Asian Relations Conference, "Asia will necessarily play a vital role. The countries of Asia can no longer be used as pawns by others; they are bound to have their own policies in world affairs."

NONALIGNMENT AND PANCHSHEEL

Thus even before they assumed the responsibilities of independence, India's spokesmen had charted the broad outlines of the foreign policies which India has followed with little deviation since 1947. "The main objectives" of India's foreign policy, stated Nehru in an address at Columbia University in October 1949, are

the pursuit of peace, not through alignment with any major power or group of powers but through an independent approach to each controversial or disputed issue, the liberation of subject peoples, the maintenance of freedom, both national and individual, the elimination of racial discrimination and elimination of want, disease, and ignorance, which afflict the greater part of the world's population.

India's foreign policy is often characterized as one of neutralism. This is a word which its spokesmen generally reject. They insist that India's policy of nonalignment is a sound policy, well suited to promote India's national interests and the cause of world peace. They indignantly deny that it is a negative or escapist policy. "I should like

[14] See *Asian Relations: A Report of the Proceedings and Documentation of the First Asian Relations Conference, New Delhi, March–April 1947* (New Delhi, 1948).

to make it clear," asserted Nehru in 1949, "that the policy India has sought to pursue is not a negative and neutral policy. It is a positive and vital policy that flows from our struggle for freedom and from the teachings of Mahatma Gandhi." [15]

The belief that nonalignment or a policy of independence in foreign affairs is the path to peace furnishes a partial explanation for India's aversion to the power politics and military pacts of the major powers. In a letter to the presidents of the Pradesh Congress Committees in July 1954 Nehru wrote: "Peace can only be preserved by the methods of peace. A warlike approach to peace is a contradiction in terms." And military pacts represent to him "a war-like approach to peace," "a wrong approach," "a dangerous approach," which "sets in motion all the wrong tendencies and prevents the right tendencies from developing." He is particularly opposed to SEATO and the Baghdad Pact, which "apart from their being, I think, basically in the wrong direction, affect us intimately and in a sense tend to encircle us from two or three directions." [16]

Instead of relying on military pacts, Nehru recommends acceptance of the *Panchsheel* (or *Panch Shila*), the five principles of peace. These principles were first spelled out in the treaty between India and Communist China regarding Tibet in the spring of 1954; they were repeated in the Nehru–Chou En-lai declaration of June 1954 and in many other pronouncements which Nehru has made. They recur in the communiqué issued at the close of the Bandung Conference in April 1955. The five principles are mutual respect for territorial integrity and sovereignty, nonaggression, noninterference in internal affairs, equality and mutual benefit, and peaceful coexistence. "These principles," said Nehru in December 1955 at the time of the visit of Bulganin and Khrushchev, "form the basis of our relations with other nations. If *Panch Shila* were fully and sincerely accepted by all countries, then peace would be assured to everyone and cooperation would follow."

A policy based upon such nebulous principles, upon "deciding each issue on its own merits," upon "independence" or nonalignment may at times be no policy at all. India's leaders have often been taxed with unwillingness or incapacity to recognize present dangers and real issues, with a tendency to take refuge in moral abstractions, and with naïveté or worse regarding the Soviet-Communist threat.

[15] Address at Columbia University on October 17, 1949.
[16] Speech in the Lok Sabha on February 17, 1953.

RELATIONS WITH PAKISTAN

India's relations with Pakistan are of central importance in the total picture of India's foreign relations. Unhappily the two nations that emerged in the Indian subcontinent began their separate existences in a state of mutual tension and recrimination, and they are still at odds on several major issues and a multitude of minor ones. Josef Korbel believes that "the real cause of all the bitterness . . . is the uncompromising and perhaps uncompromisable struggle of two ways of life, two concepts of political organization, two scales of values, two spiritual attitudes that find themselves locked in deadly conflict." [17] Other observers believe that though the Indian concept of the secular state differs widely from the Pakistan concept of an Islamic state, the two nations can settle their differences amicably and co-exist peaceably in the subcontinent.

For some years before partition, relations between Hindus and Muslims, and between the Indian National Congress and the Muslim League, steadily deteriorated. Chiefly responsible were Muslim apprehensions of their future in a predominantly Hindu state, the rather inflexible attitude of the Congress toward the League, and the League's urgent demand for a separate state of Pakistan. The tragic circumstances of partition widened the gulf between the two new nations; "they were divided by a pool of Punjabi blood." [18] Many other issues arising from partition—notably the treatment of minorities in the two countries, problems of the settlement of claims of evacuee property, and economic difficulties—have bedeviled Indo-Pakistan relations ever since 1947. Perhaps most important of all the causes of friction, aside from underlying distrust, have been the problems of the canal waters and, above all, Kashmir.

East Pakistan usually suffers from too much water; great loss of life and property is caused by the frequent floods. Most of West Pakistan, on the other hand, suffers from too little water. At least three important rivers of the Indus system, on which life depends in West Pakistan, flow in part through Indian territory. In 1948 an agreement was signed between India and Pakistan whereby over a period of years India would divert a good share of the water from the rivers running through Indian territory, and Pakistan, with considerable finan-

[17] *Danger in Kashmir* (Princeton: Princeton University Press, 1954), p. 16.
[18] Taya Zinkin, "Indian Foreign Policy: An Interpretation of Attitudes," *World Politics*, VII (Jan. 1955), 188.

cial assistance from India, would make alternate arrangements for needed water by more efficient use of the waters which run through West Pakistan and by a series of link canals. Shortly after this agreement was reached, efforts to implement it and to settle other problems arising from the canal-waters question became bogged down in endless negotiations between the two countries, in Washington and elsewhere.

After some eight years of technical discussions and diplomatic negotiations, thanks in large measure to the good offices of the International Bank for Reconstruction and Development, India and Pakistan reached an agreement regarding this most serious dispute, whereby the waters of the three eastern rivers of the Indus (the Ravi, the Beas, and the Sutlej) will be for the use of India, and those of the three western rivers (the Indus itself, the Jhelum, and the Chenab) will be for the use of Pakistan. Pakistan, with the help of India and other countries, will build a series of link canals and other works to replace the supply of water it has been receiving from the three eastern rivers. This agreement was signed in Karachi on September 19, 1960, by Mohammed Ayub Khan, Nehru, and W. A. B. Iliff, representing the World Bank. At the same time the World Bank, India, Pakistan, and six other countries signed the Indus Basin Development Fund Agreement, which pledged about $1 billion to meet the cost of the Indus Basin development program. About 70 per cent of this amount will be made available by the United States.

The signing of the Indus Water Treaty resolved one of the major issues in dispute between India and Pakistan. Unfortunately it did not lead to the expected improvement in Indo-Pakistan relations or to any progress in the settlement of the Kashmir dispute.

The Kashmir question is one of the thorniest issues in contemporary international relations, even though it is not a Communist–non-Communist dispute and even though the chief disputants are fellow members of the Commonwealth who want to find a way out of the dilemma.[19] India insists that all of the former princely state of Jammu and Kashmir is legally a part of the Republic of India and that Pakistan is illegally occupying Indian territory. Pakistan insists that the future of the disputed area should be determined by a plebiscite, in

---

[19] For fuller discussions of the Kashmir question see Michael Brecher, *The Struggle for Kashmir* (New York: Oxford University Press, 1953); Korbel, *Danger in Kashmir;* Lord Birdwood, *Two Nations and Kashmir* (London, 1956); J. B. Das Gupta, *Indo-Pakistan Relations, 1947–1955* (Amsterdam, 1958), chs. iii, iv.

accordance with India's pledge in late 1947 and repeated United Nations recommendations. India apparently has withdrawn its commitment to hold a plebiscite in Kashmir, allegedly on the grounds that Pakistan has not accepted the necessary preconditions for a plebiscite or withdrawn its troops from "Azad Kashmir" and that American arms aid to Pakistan and certain other developments have changed the whole complexion of affairs. India justifies its position in Kashmir largely on the basis of the accession of the Maharajah of Kashmir to India in late October 1947 and the alleged aggression of Pakistan in Kashmir. The Indian position on this issue is, as clearly stated by President Rajendra Prasad in his address to the Parliament on March 19, 1957, that the "Jammu and Kashmir State is and has been a constituent State of the Union of India since October 1947, like other States which acceded to the Union." To Indians the inauguration of a constitution for Kashmir on January 26, 1957, was simply a formal recognition of a status which had in fact existed for nearly a decade.

Pakistan, of course, completely rejects these claims, and the Security Council of the United Nations, which has had the Kashmir question on its agenda ever since India brought it before the Council in January 1948, seems to agree with Pakistan that the future of Kashmir is still to be determined. India has been increasingly critical of the UN's position on this question and especially of the position taken by Britain and the United States in debates and votes in the Security Council. Thus India's attitude on this issue has hardened at a time when Pakistan's spokesmen and many of its people are becoming increasingly vehement on Kashmir.

In 1962, at the request of Pakistan, the Kashmir question was again discussed in the Security Council of the United Nations. In June, after sharp exchanges between the Indian and Pakistani representatives, V. K. Krishna Menon and Zafrulla Khan, a resolution to which India strongly objected, calling upon the two countries to try to resolve the dispute by direct negotiations, was defeated by a Soviet veto. In December, however, after the Chinese attack on India, Duncan Sandys of the United Kingdom and Averell Harriman of the United States persuaded Nehru and Ayub Khan to agree to direct talks on Kashmir. These talks began later in the same month, on the ministerial level, in a generally favorable atmosphere and without mutual recrimination, but little if any progress was made in the efforts to find bases of agreement or of compromise on the major issues in dispute.

Until some agreement is reached regarding the status of Kashmir, relations between India and Pakistan will continue to be jeopardized by tension and suspicion, with even some danger of an explosion in the subcontinent. If an amicable agreement could be reached on this issue, Indo-Pakistan relations generally might be very much improved; and in a more relaxed atmosphere the two countries could reduce their defense expenditures, deal more hopefully with the other issues in dispute between them, and concentrate more effectively on basic problems of economic development, social welfare, and political survival.

OTHER ASPECTS OF FOREIGN RELATIONS

India is also greatly concerned about relations with other near neighbors, notably Nepal, Burma, Ceylon, Afghanistan, and the two great Communist powers whose vast territories extend to, or close to, the frontiers of India.

The Indian attitude toward the Soviet Union and communism has often been characterized as ambivalent, although to most Indians it seems consistent. The example of Soviet Russia had exercised an almost hypnotic fascination for many Indians, few of whom are Communists. They are particularly impressed with the success of the Soviet efforts to change Russia within a remarkably short space of time from an underdeveloped country to one of the two most powerful states of the world. They also admire Soviet policies toward nationalities within the borders of the USSR and toward Asians generally. They tend to exaggerate the successes of the Soviet experiment and to minimize or ignore the costs in human terms.

As relations between India and China have deteriorated, relations between India and the Soviet Union have become closer and more cordial. Indians appreciate the position of the USSR regarding Kashmir and Goa, Soviet economic aid, including assistance in financing and building a great steel plant at Bhilai, and above all the Soviet attitude toward the new tensions in Sino-Indian relations. The Soviet Union has been careful to avoid endorsing recent Chinese moves and has given India the impression that it might be useful in helping India to restrain Peking's ambitions.[20]

When the Soviet Union refrained from criticizing the Chinese attack on India in October–November 1962, urged India to enter into negotiations with China on China's terms, and announced that it was forced

---

[20] Palmer, "India's Foreign Policy," pp. 395–396.

to "postpone" delivery of a few MIG-21 jet fighter planes that it had promised to send to India, many Indians began to question the wisdom of relying on the Soviet Union in any controversy involving a fellow-Communist state; but Nehru continued to believe in the *bona fides* of the Russians and in their desire not to contribute to the expansion of Chinese power in Asia.

India has posed as the leading champion of Communist China's claims to membership in the United Nations and to a major role in world affairs. Indian spokesmen were assiduous in cultivating the leaders of the People's Republic of China, in playing upon the theme of the long friendship between the two great Asian countries, and in emphasizing the doctrine of peaceful coexistence as embodied in the *Panchsheel*.

The Chinese actions in Tibet and along India's northern borders in 1959 hit India like an icy blast from the Himalayas and were greeted with a mixture of incredulity, indignation, and alarm. The Dalai Lama and several thousand Tibetans escaped to India and were given asylum there. Some 12,000 square miles of Indian territory, according to Indian claims, in the North East Frontier Agency and in Ladakh were occupied by Chinese troops. Charges and countercharges were exchanged between the former friendly Asian neighbors.[21] India hastily built roads toward the frontier areas, trained and dispatched troops to these areas, and in many other ways prepared for rugged Himalayan operations. Numerous clashes between Indian and Chinese troops in these remote areas kept Sino-Indian relations in a state of growing tension.

The crisis was further aggravated in October–November 1962, when the Chinese suddenly launched a major offensive in the North East Frontier Agency and Ladakh. This attack aroused India as no other incident since its emergence as an independent nation had done. Nehru himself confessed that "we were getting out of touch with the realities of the modern world" and that "we were living in an artificial atmosphere of our own creation." He described the Chinese attack as "the greatest menace that has come to us since we became independ-

[21] The Government of India has issued eight white papers, containing "Notes, Memoranda, and Letters Exchanged between the Governments of India and China" from 1954 to January 1963. See also *Report of the Officials of the Governments of India and the Peoples' Republic of China on the Boundary Question* (New Delhi: Ministry of External Affairs, Government of India, Feb. 1961); Jawaharlal Nehru, *India's Foreign Policy* (Delhi: Publications Division, Ministry of Information and Broadcasting, Government of India, 1961), pp. 302–394.

ent" and as "a turning point not only in the history of Asia but in the history of the world." After 1959, and especially after October 1962, relations between India and China can never be the same again.

Indians are still in the dark regarding China's real motives and intentions, which seem to be linked with internal difficulties and pressures and with long-term expansionist aims. But because of China's actions a new and harsher era has set in, not only in Sino-Indian relations, but in Indian foreign policy generally.

India has sought to cultivate close relations with the Arab states of the Middle East and especially with the United Arab Republic. In part this may be due to a desire to thwart any ambitions which Pakistan might entertain of leadership in the Muslim world. As would be expected, the Indian leaders sharply denounced the British and French intervention in Egypt in the fall of 1956. They were slower and less vehement in critizing the Soviet Union for its brutal repression of the uprising in Hungary, which preceded the Suez crisis by a few days.

Many people of Indian origin live outside India, mainly in Ceylon, Burma, Malaya, and East and South Africa. Relations between India and these countries have often been colored by the treatment of these people. India has shown a special solicitude for their welfare, even though the Indian government has never claimed them as Indian citizens. This question has been a source of particular tension between India and Ceylon and South Africa. In South Africa, Gandhi first experimented with the techniques of *satyagraha* which he later applied with such effect in India. The position of persons of Indian origin in South Africa has become a matter of world concern as a result of recent policies in the Republic of South Africa, policies known as *apartheid*. Frequent discussions of the problem have occurred in the United Nations, with India in a leading role, and India has given continuous attention to the problem.[22] India has also expressed concern over the treatment of persons of Indian origin in Kenya, Uganda, and elsewhere in East Africa.

Outside of South and East Africa, Indian interest in African developments has been expressed in many ways. In the United Nations it has taken a special interest in the status of peoples of trust territories and nonself-governing areas. India has strongly supported the nationalist movements in the continent, and it has welcomed the emergence of many new African states. It seems to regard itself as a special champion and protector of the newly independent and still-dependent peo-

[22] See Karunakaran, *India in World Affairs*, ch. vii.

ples of Africa, and some African nationalist leaders look to India for guidance and support.

With independence, relations between India and Britain naturally took on an entirely different complexion, but the two countries are still bound by many ties, both tangible and intangible. Notwithstanding all the differences in culture and outlook and the bitter feeling that inevitably developed between a subject people and a paramount power, the British impact upon India was a profound one, and its influence is manifest today in countless ways. India's political, administrative, legal, and educational systems are based on British models. Even attitudes of mind and patterns of political behavior reflect the impact of the British connection. Free India chose to remain within the Commonwealth, even after becoming a republic in January 1950. It has many economic ties with Britain. It is a member of the sterling area, and its currency is tied to the British pound. After the war India had large sterling balances, steadily drawn upon in recent years, chiefly for purposes of economic development.

In recent years relations with Britain have been strained by a number of events, notably the British role in the Suez Canal crisis in 1956, the British position on the Kashmir question, British reactions to India's occupation of Goa, the Commonwealth Immigrants Act of 1962, and the steps taken by Britain to associate itself with the European Economic Community. These and other developments have provoked anti-British feeling and demands that India should withdraw from the Commonwealth; but they have not seriously weakened the innumerable ties that still bind India to the country which ruled over it for many decades.[23]

Relations with the United States have assumed a growing importance since the Second World War and particularly since India became independent. For many reasons the United States is especially interested in India, the largest of the non-Communist states of the underdeveloped world. Contacts between Americans and Indians on both official and unofficial levels have increased steadily in the post-independence era. India, too, has a special interest in the United States, the most powerful of the nations of the "free world," its second largest customer, and the main source of foreign economic assistance for its development efforts.

Indo-American relations have fluctuated markedly in the past decade and a half. They reached high points during the last months of

[23] Palmer, "India's Foreign Policy," p. 394.

the Truman Administration, when Chester Bowles was American ambassador; at the time of the visit of President Eisenhower in India in December 1959, when Indians, smarting under new strains in Sino-Indian relations, gave the American President one of the greatest receptions in their history; at the time of the Prime Minister's visit to the United States in November 1961; and especially after the Chinese attack on India on October 20, 1962, an event which led to a new attitude toward the United States, occasioned not only by the prompt American response to India's request for military assistance but also by a searching reappraisal of the bases of its foreign policy. Low points came as a result of the decision of the United States to extend military aid to Pakistan, announced in February 1954, and in the aftermath of the Goa affair in late 1961 and early 1962, when Indians reacted strongly against the American criticisms of the Indian move into Goa.

Indians have been quite outspoken in their criticisms of certain aspects of United States foreign policy. They have accused the United States of concentrating too heavily on the "so-called" Soviet-Communist threat and of giving insufficient attention to other problems. They have charged that the United States relies too heavily on "wrong approaches" to peace, such as military pacts and "collective security." They have been critical of American policy in Asia, particularly of American support of reactionary regimes and of colonial policies. They dislike American policy toward both Communist and Nationalist China. They have argued that the United States has harmed them in areas of their most immediate concern; and they point to policies such as arms aid to Pakistan, American criticism of the Indian position on the Kashmir question, and American encouragement of the formation of SEATO and the Baghdad Pact (now CENTO), which in their eyes brought the cold war to the very frontiers of India (this presumably implies that it was far away before!). In spite of all these disagreements, however, relations between India and the United States have been generally good. There is a vast reservoir of mutual good will, interest, and respect between the leading democratic states of the East and the West.[24]

[24] See Phillips Talbot and S. L. Poplai, *India and America* (New York: Harper, for the Council on Foreign Relations, 1958). This volume is based to a large extent on the data papers and discussions of two study groups, one set up by the Council on Foreign Relations in New York, the other by the Indian Council of World Affairs in New Delhi. See also N. D. Palmer, "India and the United States: Maturing Relations," *Current History*, XXXVI (March 1959), 129–134; Selig S. Harrison, ed., *India and the United States* (New York: Macmillan, 1961).

Despite India's policy of nonalignment—which has assumed a rather different complexion since the Chinese attack of October 1962—its spokesmen have not been reluctant to express their views on many international issues or to participate in a wide variety of cooperative international endeavors. Apparently they see their major role as mediatory, helping to bridge the gulf between the Communist and non-Communist worlds, between Asia and the West, between the developed and underdeveloped countries. India assumed important mediatory or supervisory roles in Korea and Indochina and at many international conferences. It has not hesitated to join international associations of a nonmilitary nature. It is a member of the Commonwealth, perhaps the most successful of all international associations, even though the central member is the former ruling power and another member is its "unfriendly" neighbor, Pakistan. It is one of the "Colombo Powers" and is a leading participant in and beneficiary of the Colombo Plan. It belongs to the sterling area, a unique international economic grouping, and is a leader of the Afro-Asian group in the United Nations. Its role in the UN has been a conspicuous and busy one. India attaches great importance to the world organization, which it regards as primarily an agency for the peaceful settlement of disputes and for international cooperation on the broadest possible front. Indian spokesmen tend to minimize the responsibilities of the UN with regard to maintaining peace and resisting aggression and to emphasize the UN's potential in the peaceful settlement of international disputes and in advancement of human rights and fundamental freedoms.[25]

Thus India is both a committed and an uncommitted nation. It believes that there is no conflict between the brand of nationalism for which it stands and the cause of international cooperation. India is allergic to military arrangements but not to international commitments of other sorts. This position was reaffirmed by Jawaharlal Nehru in July 1957. Speaking in the Lok Sabha, he said: "Broadly speaking, I am against breaking any kind of associations of nations. I want more associations and not less."

[25] See Karunakaran, *India in World Affairs*, chs. viii–xi; *India and the United Nations* (New York: Manhattan Publishing Co., 1957), a report of a study group set up by the Indian Council of World Affairs in New Delhi; Ross N. Berkes and M. S. Bedi, *The Diplomacy of India* (Stanford: Stanford University Press, 1958).

SUGGESTED READING

IX: The Political Heritage of Modern India

GENERAL WORKS

Brown, W. Norman. *The United States and India and Pakistan.* Cambridge, Mass.: Harvard University Press, 1953. An excellent introduction to Indian history, politics, and culture. A revised edition will soon be published.

Lamb, Beatrice Pitney. *India—A World in Transition.* New York: Praeger, 1963. A comprehensive introductory survey of Indian history, culture, politics, and foreign policy.

Majumdar, R. C., gen. ed. *The History and Culture of the Indian People.* Bombay, 1951–. Six of the ten volumes planned in this series, which will probably be regarded as the standard treatment of Indian history and culture, have already been published: vol. I, *The Vedic Age;* vol. II, *The Age of Imperial Unity;* vol. III, *The Classical Age;* vol. IV, *The Age of Imperial Kanauj;* vol. V, *The Struggle for Empire;* vol. VI, *The Delhi Sultanate.*

Moreland, W. H., and A. C. Chatterjee, *A Short History of India.* 3d ed. London, 1953. A standard political history.

Nehru, Jawaharlal. *The Discovery of India.* New York: John Day, 1946. A classic interpretation of Indian history and character, written in prison in 1944.

Radhakrishnan, S. *Indian Philosophy.* 2 vols. New York: Macmillan, 1922–1927. A profound and lengthy interpretation by one of India's leading modern philosophers, who is now President of India.

Riencourt, Amaury de. *The Soul of India.* New York: Harper, 1960. A provocative and stimulating interpretation of Indian history and civilization.

Sources of Indian Tradition, comp. by William Theodore de Bary, Stephen Hay, Royal Weiler, and Andrew Yarrow. New York: Columbia University Press, 1958. A valuable collection of readings, mostly from original sources.

Wallbank, T. Walter. *A Short History of India and Pakistan.* New York: New American Library of World Literature, 1958. A convenient pocketbook abridged edition of the same author's *India in the New Era* (Chicago: Scott, Foresman, 1951).

GOVERNMENT AND POLITICS IN THE PRE-BRITISH PERIOD

Altekar, A. S. *State and Government in Ancient India.* Benares, 1949. Demonstrates that monarchy was not the only form of government known to ancient India.

Basham, A. L. *The Wonder That Was India: A Survey of the Culture of the Sub-Continent before the Coming of the Muslims.* London, 1954. Especially ch. iv, "The State: Political Life and Thought." One of the best and most comprehensive one-volume treatments of Indian history, culture, and institutions during the Hindu period.

Brown, D. MacKenzie. *The White Umbrella: Indian Political Thought from Manu to Gandhi.* Berkeley: University of California Press, 1953. Part One, "Ancient Political Thought," contains a brief commentary on "The Nature of Indian Thought" and excerpts from four classics of the Hindu period: the *Manu Samhita*, the *Santiparvan* of the *Mahabharata*, Kautilya's *Arthasastra*, and the *Sukraniti*.

Ghoshal, U. N. *A History of Hindu Political Theories—From the Earliest Times to the End of the First Quarter of the Seventeenth Century A.D.* 2d ed. London, 1927. A widely known work, first published in 1923.

Jayaswal, K. P. *Hindu Policy—A Constitutional History of India in Hindu Times.* Calcutta, 1924. Jayaswal is a leading exponent of the thesis that "republican institutions" existed in ancient India.

Kautilya. *Arthasastra.* Trans. by R. Shamasastry. 4th ed. Mysore, 1951. An Indian political classic, the work of "the greatest exponent of the art of government, the duties of kings, ministers, and officials, and the methods of diplomacy."

Majumdar, R. C., and A. D. Pusalker, eds. *The Age of Imperial Unity.* (*The History and Culture of the Indian People,* vol. II.) 2d ed. Bombay, 1953. Ch. xvii, "Political Theory and Administrative System," by Beni Prasad, is particularly recommended.

Majumdar, R. C., H. C. Raychaudhuri, and Kalikinkar Datta. *An Advanced History of India.* London, 1950. A standard work.

Moreland, W. H., and A. C. Chatterjee. *A Short History of India.* 3d ed. London, 1953. A well-known brief history, chiefly political.

Prasad, Beni. *The State in Ancient India—A Study in the Structure and Practical Working of Political Institutions in North India in Ancient Times.* Allahabad, 1928.

Sarkar, Sir J. *Mughal Administration.* 3d ed. Calcutta, 1935. An excellent brief survey.

Sherwani, H. K. *Studies in Muslim Political Thought and Administration.* 2d ed. Lahore, 1945.

Srivastava, A. L. *The Mughal Empire, 1526–1803.* 2d ed. Agra, 1957. Emphasizes administrative and social aspects of Mogul rule.

GOVERNMENT AND POLITICS IN THE BRITISH PERIOD

Birdwood, Christopher Bromhead, Baron. *A Continent Experiments.* London, 1946. The last years of British rule in India, described by a man who held high rank in the British Indian army.

Campbell-Johnson, Alan. *Mission with Mountbatten.* London, 1951. A valuable account by Lord Mountbatten's private secretary.

Coupland, Sir Reginald. *India: A Re-statement.* London, 1945. A brief commentary by a recognized authority.

——. *The Indian Problem: Report on the Constitutional Problem in India.* London, 1944. 3 vols. in 1. Vol. I, "The Indian Problem, 1833–1935"; vol. II, "Indian Politics, 1936–1942"; vol. III, "The Future of India." A constitutional history of India during an eventful century.

Dodwell, H. H. F., ed. *The Indian Empire, 1858–1919, with Chapters on the Development of Administration, 1818–58.* (*The Cambridge History of India,* vol. VI.) Cambridge, Eng., 1932.

Griffiths, Sir Percival J. *The British Impact on India.* London, 1952. A remarkably objective treatment by a Britisher who had long experience in India.

——. *The British in India.* London, 1946. A brief history.

Keith, A. B. *A Constitutional History of India, 1600–1935.* 2d ed. London, 1926. A standard work.

Lumby, E. W. R. *The Transfer of Power in India, 1945–47.* London, 1954. An excellent brief survey.

Menon, V. P. *The Transfer of Power in India.* Princeton: Princeton University Press, 1957. A detailed study by a prominent Indian civil servant who participated in many of the events which he describes.

Moreland, W. H., and A. C. Chatterjee. *A Short History of India.* 3d ed. London, 1953. Especially good on constitutional questions.

O'Malley, L. S. S., ed. *Modern India and the West: A Study of the Interaction of Their Civilizations.* London, 1941. An astute interpretation.

Proceedings of the Round Table Conference. 3 sessions, 1931–1932. Cmd. 3778; Cmd. 3997; Cmd. 4238.

Report of the Indian Statutory Commission, 1930. Cmd. 3568–3569. Report of the Simon Commission.

Report on Indian Constitutional Reforms, 1918. Cmd. 9109. Montagu-Chelmsford report.

Singh, Gurmukh Nihal. *Landmarks in Indian Constitutional and National Development,* vol. I, 1600–1919. 3d ed. Delhi, 1952. By a respected Indian political scientist and government official. Widely used in India.

Tinker, Hugh R. *The Foundations of Local Self-Government in India, Pakistan, and Burma.* London, 1954. Especially good for the period 1882–1937.

Woodruff, Philip (pseud. for Philip Mason). *The Men Who Ruled India.* Vol. I, *The Founders of Modern India.* London, 1953. Vol. II, *The Guardians.* London, 1954. Delightful studies, emphasizing the role of leading personalities.

THE NATIONALIST MOVEMENT

Banerjea, Sir Surendranath. *A Nation in the Making: Being the Reminiscences of Fifty Years of Public Life*. London, 1925. The memoirs of one of the founders and early leaders of the Indian National Congress.

Bondurant, Joan. *Conquest of Violence: The Gandhian Philosophy of Conflict*. Princeton, N.J.: Princeton University Press, 1958. A sensitive interpretation of some of the guiding tenets of Gandhi's philosophy.

Brecher, Michael. *Nehru: A Political Biography*. London, 1959. The best biography of India's great leader. Contains a good summary of events in India during the past half-century.

Brown, D. Mackenzie. *The Nationalist Movement: Indian Political Thought from Ranade to Bhave*. Berkeley: University of California Press, 1961. A sequel to the same author's *The White Umbrella: Indian Political Thought from Manu to Gandhi*. Contains selections from the writings and speeches of prominent Indian leaders of the past century, with commentaries by the editor.

Buch, M. A. *Rise and Growth of Indian Militant Nationalism*. Baroda, 1940. Throws light on less-publicized aspects of the Indian nationalist movement.

Desai, A. R. *Social Background of Indian Nationalism*. Bombay, 1948. An excellent historical and sociological analysis.

Fischer, Louis. *Gandhi: His Life and Message for the World*. New York: New American Library of World Literature, 1954. A warmly human biography of the Mahatma, by a well-known American admirer.

Gandhi, Mohandas K. *Autobiography; or, The Story of My Experiments with Truth*. 2d ed. Ahmedabad, 1940. Revealing insights into Gandhi's thoughts and character. The first edition was published in 1927.

Lajpat Rai, Lala. *Young India: An Interpretation and a History of the Nationalist Movement from Within*. New York: H. B. Huebsch, 1916. By a prominent nationalist leader.

Lovett, Sir Harrington Verney. *A History of the Indian Nationalist Movement*. London, 1920. A staunch defense of the thesis that "Britain cannot abdicate her responsibilities" in India. The author spent nearly 35 years in India as an ICS officer.

Moraes, Frank. *Jawaharlal Nehru: A Biography*. New York: Macmillan, 1956. A "life and times" biography, and hence in effect a history of modern India.

Nehru, Jawaharlal. *Toward Freedom: The Autobiography of Jawaharlal Nehru*. New York: John Day, 1942. Provides revealing insights into the independence struggle as well as into the personality of the most important living Indian statesman.

Sitaramayya, P. B. *The History of the Indian National Congress (1885–1935)*. 2 vols. Allahabad, 1935. The standard official history, by a prominent member of the Congress.

——. *The Nationalist Movement in India*. Bombay, 1950. The author was a leading figure in the nationalist movement in its last phases.

Tendulkar, D. G. *Mahatma: Life of Mohandas Karamchand Gandhi*. 8 vols. Bombay, 1951–1954. A detailed record of the life and teachings of the greatest of modern Indians, the "Father of the Nation."

Varma, V. P. *Modern Indian Political Thought*. Agra, 1961. A survey of the political thinking of leading Indians of the past century and a half.

X: India since Independence

GENERAL WORKS

Birdwood, Christopher Bromhead, Baron. *India and Pakistan: A Continent Decides*. New York: Praeger, 1954. Extensive discussions of internal and external problems; eight chapters on Kashmir.

Dean, Vera M. *New Patterns of Democracy in India*. Cambridge, Mass.: Harvard University Press, 1959. An introduction to major economic, social, and political changes in the "New India."

Griffiths, Sir Percival. *Modern India*. (Nations of the World series.) New York: Praeger, 1957. One of the best volumes on India since independence.

Harrison, Selig S. *India: The Most Dangerous Decades*. Princeton: Princeton University Press, 1960. A penetrating study of the inner dynamics of Indian political and social life, with emphasis on caste, linguistic, and other divisions, especially in Andhra Pradesh.

Lyon, Jean. *Just Half a World Away: My Search for the New India*. New York: Crowell, 1954. Penetrating and well-written observations on major political and social changes now under way in India.

Menon, V. P. *The Story of the Integration of the Indian States*. New York: Macmillan, 1956. The definitive work, by Vallabhbhai Patel's right-hand man in the States Ministry.

Moraes, Frank. *India Today*. New York: Macmillan, 1960. A good general introduction to contemporary India, by a well-known Indian journalist.

Park, Richard L., and Irene Tinker, eds. *Leadership and Political Institutions in India*. Princeton: Princeton University Press, 1961. An important selected and revised group of papers by leading American, Indian, and other scholars, originally presented at a seminar at the University of California, Berkeley, in August 1956.

Parton, Margaret. *The Leaf and the Flame*. New York: Crowell, 1959. Personal reminiscences and impressions of India, by an American journalist.

Smith, Donald E. *India as a Secular State*. Princeton: Princeton University Press, 1963. A searching analysis of the bases and significance of the secular approach to politics in India.

——. *Nehru and Democracy: The Political Thought of an Asian Democrat*. New York: Longmans, Green, 1958. An interpretation of Nehru's political philosophy.

Tinker, Hugh. *India and Pakistan: A Political Analysis*. New York: Praeger, 1962. A concise and informed commentary on the politics of India and Pakistan since independence.

Trumbull, Robert. *As I See India*. New York: Sloane, 1956. The author was *New York Times* correspondent in India for seven years.

THE CONSTITUTIONAL SYSTEM

Appleby, Paul H. *Public Administration in India: Report of a Survey*. Delhi: Manager of Publications, 1953. A widely discussed report by an American expert.

Basu, D. D. *Commentary on the Constitution of India*. 3d ed. 2 vols. Calcutta, 1955. A detailed commentary.

Douglas, William O. *We the Judges: Studies in American and Indian Constitutional Law from Marshall to Mukerji*. Garden City, N.Y.: Doubleday, 1956. Stimulating comparisons between American and Indian constitutional law by a Justice of the American Supreme Court; based on lectures at the University of Calcutta.

Gledhill, Allan. *The Republic of India: The Development of Its Laws and Constitution*. London, 1951. A legal analysis by a well-known British authority on Indian jurisprudence.

Gorwala, A. D. *Report on Public Administration*. New Delhi: Planning Commission, Government of India, 1951. A famous public document.

Indian Institute of Public Administration. *The Organisation of the Government of India*. Bombay, 1958. A useful manual.

Jennings, Sir W. Ivor. *Some Characteristics of the Indian Constitution*. Madras, 1953. Lectures at the University of Madras in 1952.

Joshi, G. N. *The Constitution of India*. 3d ed. London, 1954. One of the best and most substantial commentaries.

Lal, A. B., ed. *The Indian Parliament*. Allahabad, 1956. Among the many contributors are Indian M.P.'s and others with firsthand experience in the workings of parliamentary institutions in India.

Majumdar, B., ed. *Problems of Public Administration in India*. (Indian Political Science Association, Publ. no. 1.) Patna, 1954. Contains papers by many authors.

Morris-Jones, W. H. *Parliament in India*. Philadelphia: University of Pennsylvania Press, 1957. The best treatment of the Indian Parliament.

Palmer, Norman D. *The Indian Political System*. Boston: Houghton Mifflin, paperback ed., 1961; hard-cover ed., 1962 (also London, 1962). The first comprehensive treatment of the subject by an American scholar. Contains four historical chapters, but emphasis is on the contemporary political system.

Pylee, M. V. *Constitutional Government in India.* Bombay, 1960. One of the best of the many books on the subject by Indian political scientists. The author has also written a shorter work entitled *India's Constitution* (Bombay, 1962).

Rao, K. V. *Parliamentary Democracy in India.* Calcutta, 1961. A competent survey by the head of the Department of Political Science at Utkal University in Cuttack, Orissa.

Report of the States Reorganization Commission, 1955. Detailed recommendations for the political reorganization of India, with valuable background material.

Santhanam, K. *Union-State Relations in India.* Bombay, 1960. A provocative examination of a vital aspect of the Indian federal system.

Sharma, M. P. *Local Self-Government in India.* 2d ed. Bombay, 1951. A brief text.

Srinivasan, N. *Democratic Government in India.* Calcutta, 1954. Traces the development of parliamentary government in India and presents a concise summary of the salient features of the constitution of 1950.

XI: Political Parties in India

Bhargava, G. S. *Leaders of the Left.* Bombay, 1951. Personal portraits.

Chatterjee, N. C. *Awakening of India: Problems of Today.* New Delhi, 1952. By a leader of the Hindu Mahasabha.

Curran, J. A., Jr. *Militant Hinduism in Indian Politics: A Study of the R.S.S.* New York: Institute of Pacific Relations, 1951. Mimeograph. A concise study of the Rashtriya Swayamsevak Sangh.

Kautsky, John H. *Moscow and the Communist Party of India: A Study in the Postwar Evolution of Communist Strategy.* Cambridge, Mass.: Technology Press; New York: Wiley, 1956. An analysis of the gyrations in the party line of the CPI against the background of international Communist strategy and tactics.

Lakhanpal, P. S. *History of the Congress Socialist Party,* Lahore, 1946.

Lal Bahadur. *The Muslim League: Its History, Activities, and Achievements.* Agra, 1954.

Masani, M. R. *The Communist Party of India: A Short History.* London, 1954. A brief but comprehensive study, with effective use of Communist documents.

Mehta, Asoka. *Democratic Socialism: Mid-Twentienth Century Synthesis.* 2d ed. Hyderabad, 1954. By one of the chief spokesmen and a leading theoretician of the Praja Socialist Party.

Nehru-Jayaprakash Talks. Bombay, 1953. Issued by the Praja Socialist Party. An important exchange of views in 1953, which attracted nation-wide attention and comment.

Overstreet, Gene D., and Irene Tinker. "Political Dynamics in India." Berkeley: Modern India Project, University of California, March 1957. Mimeograph based on a chapter prepared for the India volume of the Country Survey Series published by the Human Relations Area Files.

Overstreet, Gene D., and Marshall Windmiller. *Communism in India.* Berkeley: University of California Press, 1959. The most comprehensive study of the subject.

Prakash, Indra. *A Review of the History and Work of the Hindu Mahasabha and the Hindu Sanghatan Movement.* New Delhi, 1952.

Rajkumar, N. V. *Indian Political Parties.* New Delhi, 1948. Published by the All-India Congress Committee.

Rudolph, Susanne H. *The Action Arm of the Indian National Congress: The Pradesh Congress Committee. The All-India Congress Committee and the Annual Congress Session. The Working Committee of the Indian Congress Party: Its Forms, Organization, and Personnel.* Cambridge: Massachusetts Institute of Technology, Center for International Studies, 1955. Mimeograph. Three detailed studies.

Weiner, Myron. *Party Politics in India: The Development of a Multi-Party System.* Princeton: Princeton University Press, 1957. Emphasizes Socialist and communalist parties; also contains considerable material on general trends in the party system in India.

XII: Political Dynamics

ELECTIONS AND ELECTORAL PROCEDURES

All India Election Guide. Madras, 1956. A reference book published on the eve of India's second general elections.

Election Commission, India. *Report on the First General Elections, 1951–52.* 2 vols., New Delhi, 1955. *Report on the Second General Elections in India, 1957.* 2 vols., New Delhi, 1958. Detailed information regarding the first and second general elections. A similar report on the third elections in 1962 will shortly be published by the Election Commission.

"Indian Experience with Democratic Elections, The," *Indian Press Digests,* Monograph Series no. 3, Dec. 1956. Summaries of the first general elections and by-elections between 1952 and 1957.

Kogekar, S. V., and Richard L. Park, eds. *Reports on the Indian General Elections, 1951–52.* Bombay, 1956. Published under the auspices of the Indian Political Science Association. Reports on the first general elections in each of the Indian states.

Mehta, Asoka. *The Political Mind of India.* Bombay, 1952. Analysis of the first general elections by a prominent Indian Socialist.

Monthly Public Opinion Surveys. Issued by the Indian Institute of Public Opinion, New Delhi. "The Indian General Elections: An Analysis of Political Opinion Based on India's First Gallup Poll," vol. II, nos. 16, 17, 18, and 19 (Jan., Feb., March, and April 1957).

Poplai, S. L., ed. *National Politics and 1957 Elections in India.* Delhi, 1957. Published on the eve of the second general elections; contains policy statements and election manifestoes of the four major parties and an informative commentary on "Parties between the Elections" by Sisir Gupta.

——. *1962 General Elections in India.* Bombay, 1962. Published on the eve of the third general elections; contains election manifestoes, resolutions, and commentaries by leaders of the five major parties and an article by K. P. Karunakaran on "Politics since the 1957 Elections."

Rajkumar, N. V., ed. *The Pilgrimage and After: The Story of How the Congress Fought and Won the General Elections.* New Delhi, 1952. Issued by the All-India Congress Committee.

Sharma, Bodh Raj. *Report on Elections in the Punjab.* Jullundur, 1952.

Singh Sud, S. P., and Ajit Singh Sud. *Indian Elections and Legislators.* Ludhiana, 1953.

Venkatarangaiya, M. *The General Election in the City of Bombay, 1952.* Bombay, 1953.

PUBLIC OPINION AND PRESSURE GROUPS

Misra, B. R. *V for Vinoba.* Calcutta, 1956. Examines "the significance of the Bhoodan movement in the context of the agrarian problems of Indian economy." The author is a great admirer of Vinoba Bhave.

Monthly Public Opinion Surveys. Issued by the Indian Institute of Public Opinion, New Delhi. These surveys are particularly valuable and pertinent. They include frequent reports on "The Structure of Indian Public Opinion" and on Indian views on a great variety of questions of a tangible and intangible nature.

Overstreet, Gene D., and Irene Tinker. "Political Dynamics in India." Berkeley: Modern India Project, University of California, March 1957. Especially the sections on "Political Awareness and Activity in India" and "Pressure Groups."

Singvi, Laxmi M., and Bidyut K. Sarkar. *India: Government and Politics.* New Haven: Human Relations Area Files, 1955. Especially ch. iii, "Political Dynamics."

Tennyson, Hallam. *India's Walking Saint: The Story of Vinoba Bhave.* Garden City, N.Y.: Doubleday, 1955. An intimate picture of Vinoba

Bhave and his Bhoodan Yagna movement, by a sympathetic Englishman.

Weiner, Myron. *The Politics of Scarcity.* Chicago: University of Chicago Press, 1962. A study of "Public Pressure and Political Response in India." The chapters on various pressure groups in India are especially important.

XIII: *Economic Development and Foreign Relations*

ECONOMIC DEVELOPMENT

Chandra, J. G. *India's Socialistic Pattern of Society.* Delhi, 1956. With a foreword by U. N. Dhebar, former president of the Congress Party. A valuable exposition of the official viewpoint.

Dasgupta, A. A. Sen, and J. K. Sengupta. *Planning and the Plans.* Calcutta, 1961.

Dey, S. K. *Panchayati Raj.* Bombay, 1961. Essays on an important new experiment in rural India, by the Indian Minister for Community Development, Panchayati Raj, and Cooperation.

Fisher, Margaret W., and Joan V. Bondurant. "Indian Approaches to a Socialist Society," *Indian Press Digests,* Monograph Series no. 2, 1956. A useful compilation and analysis of Indian viewpoints.

Gagdil, D. R. *Planning and Economic Policy in India.* Poona, 1961. Essays by one of India's leading economists.

Krishnamachari, V. T. *Planning in India. Bombay,* 1961. The most valuable parts of this book are the chapters on the Planning Commission, of which the author was deputy chairman.

Lewis, John P. *Quiet Crisis in India.* Washington, D.C.: Brookings Institution, 1962. A readable analysis of economic development in India and its implications for American policy.

Malenbaum, Wilfred. *Prospects for Indian Development.* New York: Free Press of Glencoe, 1962 (also London, 1962). A detailed and somewhat critical study by an American economist.

Mayer, Albert, and Associates, in collaboration with McKim Marriott and Richard L. Park. *Pilot Project, India.* Berkeley: University of California Press, 1958. A case study of the Etawah Project in Uttar Pradesh, which became a kind of "model" for the Community Development Program.

Nair, Kusum. *Blossoms in the Dust.* London, 1961. A challenging and rather gloomy report on "the human element in Indian development," by an Indian woman journalist. Based on a year's first-hand observations.

Narayan, Shriman. *Trends in Indian Planning.* Bombay, 1952. Essays with a strong Gandhian flavor, by a member of India's Planning Commission.

Planning Commission, Government of India. *First Five Year Plan.* 1951. *Second Five Year Plan.* 1956. *Third Five Year Plan.* 1961. *Towards a Self-Reliant Economy.* 1961.

——. *The New India: Progress through Democracy.* New York: Macmillan,

1958. An attempt "to set out for readers abroad the underlying approach and main features of India's economic and social programs." Prepared at the request of the Planning Commission by a special study group, including two representatives of the Ford Foundation.

Reddaway, W. B. *The Development of the Indian Economy.* Homewood, Ill.: Irwin, 1962. A substantial study by an English economist. The first volume in a series of Studies in the Economic Development of India, sponsored by the Center for International Studies, Massachusetts Institute of Technology.

Sovani, N. V. *Planning of Post-War Economic Development in India.* Poona, 1951. A study of government planning of economic development during the period 1947–1950, with suggestions for future planning.

Vakil, C. N., and P. R. Brahmananda. *Planning for an Expanding Economy: Accumulation, Employment, and Technical Progress in Underdeveloped Countries.* Bombay, 1956. Contains a critical evaluation of the Second Five Year Plan.

——. *Planning for a Shortage Economy: The Indian Experiment.* Bombay, 1952. An analysis of the First Five Year Plan, by two prominent Indian economists.

Venkatasubbiah, H. *Indian Economy since Independence.* 2d rev. ed. Bombay, 1961. A useful commentary on the main aspects of the Indian economy, with particular reference to the Five Year Plans.

FOREIGN RELATIONS

Bains, J. S. *India's International Disputes—A Legal Study.* Bombay, 1962. An analysis of disputes concerning Kashmir, canal waters, the treatment of persons of Indian origin in Ceylon and South Africa, Portugal's right of passage over Indian territory, Tibet, and border problems with China.

Berkes, Ross N., and M. S. Bedi. *The Diplomacy of India.* Stanford: Stanford University Press, 1958. A study, based largely on United Nations documents, of "Indian Foreign Policy in the United Nations."

Birdwood, Christopher Bromhead, Baron, *Two Nations and Kashmir.* London, 1956. One of the best books on the controversial Kashmir question.

Chakravarti, P. C. *India's China Policy.* Bloomington: Indiana University Press, 1962. A critical examination of Sino-Indian relations, especially since the revolt in Tibet in 1959.

Das Gupta, J. B. *Indo-Pakistan Relations, 1947–1955.* Amsterdam, 1958. One of the most comprehensive and objective books by an Indian scholar on this controversial area of India's foreign policy.

Gupta, Karunakar. *India's Foreign Policy in Defence of National Interest.* Calcutta, 1956.

Harrison, Selig S., ed. *India and the United States.* New York: Macmillan, 1961. A valuable summary of discussions at two conferences on Indo-

American relations—one sponsored by the U.S. National Commission for UNESCO in 1957, the other by the Committee on International Economic Growth in 1959.

India and the United Nations. (National Studies on International Organization series, sponsored by the Carnegie Endowment for International Peace.) New York: Manhattan Publishing Co., 1957. Report of a study group set up by the Indian Council of World Affairs.

India in World Affairs. A series of volumes issued under the auspices of the Indian Council of World Affairs. The first two volumes, by K. P. Karunakaran, cover the period 1947–1953; the third, by M. S. Rajan, concentrates on the years 1954–1956.

Indian Year Book of International Affairs, The. Annual volumes beginning in 1952, published under the auspices of the Indian Study Group on International Affairs, Madras University. Contributions by Indian and foreign scholars.

Jain, Girilal. *India Meets China in Nepal.* Bombay, 1959. *Panchsheel and After.* New York: Asia Publishing House, 1960. Both of these books deal mainly with the crisis in Sino-Indian relations in 1959.

Karunakaran, K. P. *Alignment and Non-Alignment in Asia.* New Delhi, 1961. These brief essays are especially valuable for the light they throw on the bases of India's foreign policy.

Kundra, J. C. *Indian Foreign Policy, 1947–1954: A Study of Relations with the Western Bloc.* Groningen, 1955. An objective and informative study.

Levi, Werner. *Free India in Asia.* Minneapolis: University of Minnesota Press, 1952.

Nehru, Jawaharlal. *India's Foreign Policy.* Delhi, 1961. An important one-volume collection of Nehru's speeches on foreign affairs between September 1946 and April 1961. Issued by the Publications Division, Ministry of Information and Broadcasting, Government of India.

Prasad, Bimla. *The Origins of Indian Foreign Policy.* Calcutta, 1960. A study of "The Indian National Congress and World Affairs, 1885–1947."

Rajkumar, N. V., ed. *The Background of India's Foreign Policy.* New Delhi, 1952. Issued by the All-India Congress Committee. A useful compilation of the resolutions of the Indian National Congress on foreign policy and international affairs, from 1885 to 1952.

Rosinger, L. K. *India and the United States: Political and Economic Relations.* New York: Macmillan, 1950.

Talbot, Phillips, and S. L. Poplai. *India and America.* New York: Harper, for the Council on Foreign Relations, 1958. Based on discussions and conclusions of two study groups, one set up by the Indian Council of World Affairs, the other by the Council on Foreign Relations.

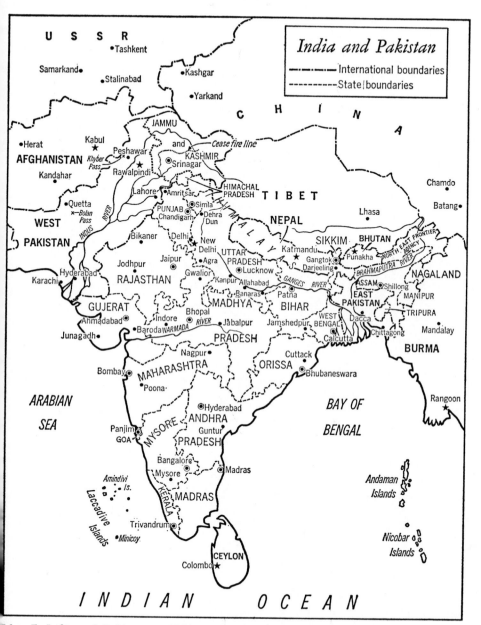

Map 7. India and Pakistan in 1963. (Adapted from *The Indian Political System,* ©
1961 by Norman D. Palmer, with the permission of Houghton Mifflin Company.)

PART FOUR : PAKISTAN

By Keith Callard

REVISED AND BROUGHT UP TO DATE

FOR THE SECOND EDITION

by Richard S. Wheeler

· XIV ·

Pakistan and Its Origin

IN AUGUST 1947 the name Pakistan appeared for the first time on the map of the world. Pakistan is not merely a new state, claiming a status of sovereign equality among nations, but a new people and a new territory. At no time in previous history had the two wings of modern Pakistan shared a common identity, whether ethnic, political, linguistic, or economic. East and West Pakistan comprise two large pieces of former Indian territory which have one feature in common —a population that is predominantly Muslim.

The process of dividing India into two new states was bitter, bloody, and costly beyond measure. The majority of India's inhabitants had no wish to see their country partitioned. They believed that, given independence and good will, a free, democratic, and progressive state could be built in which every Indian would find a place. The Muslims, one-quarter of the total, refused to cooperate. They claimed to be a separate nation, having nothing in common with the Hindu majority except the accident of living in the same country. Even though they lived together in one village and might see each other every day of their lives, Muslim and Hindu were never part of the same community. They differed in religion, in morals, in diet, in dress, in education, in family laws. They did not eat in one another's houses, and their children did not intermarry. Under such circumstances, physical nearness bred suspicion, not comradeship.

The prospect of the end of British rule brought apprehension to many Muslims. On the one hand it meant freedom and independence; but on the other it might mean the permanent status of a minority under the domination of an alien and unsympathetic majority. Mohammed Ali Jinnah, who is rightly called the founder of Pakistan, said: "We are opposed to a united India constitution with Central Government, Federal or otherwise. We are opposed to this because it will mean our transfer from the British *raj* to the Hindu *raj*. A united India means a Hindu racial and cultural majority dominating over Muslims whose civilisation, culture and social structure of life is totally different." [1]

The Mogul Empire

The earliest Muslim influence reached the shores of India in the seventh and eighth centuries, and Sindh was under the rule of an Arab commander by 712. Apart from this enclave in the extreme northwest, establishment of Muslim power in India really began with the conquests of Mahmud of Ghazni. In the early part of the eleventh century Mahmud annexed the Punjab and carried out raids to the west and south. A hundred and fifty years later the Ghaznavid power was overthrown by another Turkish dynasty—the Ghuris—who captured Delhi in 1193 and established control of most of northern India. The latter part of the fourteenth and the early fifteenth century witnessed the breakup of Turkish rule and the division of power among a series of small kingdoms. A wide area of dominion was established by the Lodi kings (1451–1526).

Substantial areas of India had been ruled by Muslims for five hundred years before the beginning of the Mogul empire. Babur, the first Emperor, captured Delhi and Agra in 1526, and his grandson Akbar (reign 1556–1605) extended the rule of the Moguls over the greater part of northern and central India. The Moguls were Central Asians who came to India by way of Afghanistan. They came as conquerors over the Khyber Pass, seeking to possess the riches of the Indian peninsula. They were sustained by a strong martial faith which made the subjugation of the infidel appear an act of piety. The India that was their prey was a land of an ancient and varied civilization, superior in material wealth and intellectual subtlety to the Central Asian homeland of the Moguls. As the invaders settled, they learned

---

[1] Jamil-ud-Din Ahmad, ed., *Some Recent Speeches and Writings of Mr. Jinnah*, II (Lahore: Shaikh Muhammad Ashraf, 1947), 380.

much from their new subjects. Akbar was a man of tolerance, which he demonstrated by attempting to found a new, composite religion.

The reign of Aurangzeb (1658–1707) was marked by a new adherence to strict Islamic orthodoxy. Under his successors, the Mogul court was remarkable for magnificence and debauchery rather than tolerance and sound administration. From this same time the power of the empire began to decay. The peacock throne remained the symbol of authority, but its effective strength was limited by over-ambitious viceroys, the increasing claims of the European foreigner, and the rebellion of Maratha and Sikh princes. The Moguls and their subordinates remained a ruling class, but they were surrounded by corruption, treason, and decay. Following the battle of Plassey (1757) the preponderance of power passed to the East India Company. In 1858, after the turmoil of the Mutiny,[2] the trappings of the Mogul court were swept away, and the ninety years of direct British rule began.[3]

British Rule

The next half century held depression and uncertainty for Muslim interests. Before 1858 the vestiges of the Mogul empire, anachronistic though it had become, had allowed Muslims to feel that they were still a ruling group. The conduct of official business in Persian (the court language) and the persistence of Islamic law in personal matters had given employment to Muslims educated in the old style and having a knowledge of Arabic, Persian, and Urdu. Direct British administration, which had been extending itself for eighty years, meant that the government carried on more of its functions in the English language and through legal and administrative devices established by Englishmen. Indians who desired a career in government service therefore had to know English and possess some of the elements of a Western-style education.

In these matters the Hindu proved himself much more adaptable than the Muslim. The Hindu had learned Persian as a language foreign to his culture and background: he was quite prepared to abandon it

[2] The uprising of 1857 has traditionally been called by British historians the Indian (or Sepoy) Mutiny. In India and Pakistan it is now fashionable to describe it as the War of Independence. In truth it was more than the first and less than the second. It is certainly a mistake to view it as the product of nationalism as that term is now understood.

[3] For a more complete discussion of the establishment of British control and for the events leading to independence see Chapter IX.

and turn to English. The Muslim, on the other hand, regarded Persian or Persianized Urdu as his own language and looked on the old form of education as an important aspect of his religion. British officials now filled the senior posts; Hindus were recruited for clerical positions, and Muslims, if employed at all, were used in inferior, manual occupations. For the Indian middle classes there were almost no careers outside the army, government service, or law. In 1871 Sir William Hunter wrote of the Muslims of Bengal:

A hundred years ago, the Musalmans monopolized all the important offices of state. The Hindu accepted with thanks such crumbs as their former conquerors dropped from their table, and the English were represented by a few factors and clerks. The proportion of the Muhammadans to Hindus . . . is now less than one-seventh . . . . in fact, there is now scarcely a Government office in Calcutta in which a Muhammadan can hope for any post above the rank of porter, messenger, filler of inkpots and mender of pens.[4]

The Muslim upper and middle classes thus found that they were badly equipped to prosper in the nineteenth century. The Indian peasant has always lived a hard life, beset by famine, disease, and oppression, and the Muslims, in some regions of India, were among the lower levels of village existence. Most of them were converts from Hinduism; many had accepted the new faith in part because of the hardship imposed on the lower castes in the Hindu social system. Islam gave them pride of spiritual equality though not of material prosperity. There was one means by which a Muslim villager, especially from the Punjab and the North-West Frontier,[5] could improve his position—that of service in the Indian army. But the vast majority of villagers depended on the soil and the weather. If crops were good, they prospered; if the crops failed, the peasants starved.

In the years after 1858 the Muslim community stood apart from other Indians. It had lost its special function as a governing elite and had found no alternative. The Muslims were distrusted by the British for having played a predominant part in the Mutiny. They were ignored or brushed aside by the Hindus, who saw them as fallen tyrants. And they lacked self-confidence, for they could perceive the

[4] W. W. Hunter, *The Indian Musalmans* (reprinted from 3d ed.; Calcutta: Comrade Publishers, 1945), pp. 161–162.

[5] The area known as the North-West Frontier is made up of the North-West Frontier Province, the princely states along the frontier, and tribal areas. This area has dominated the military scene for thousands of years as an invasion route. (The North-West Frontier Province was merged into West Pakistan in 1955.)

weaknesses of the old order and the technological superiority of the British structure, with its railways and telegraphs and its regular, disciplined armies. There was no leadership to be found in the wreckage of the old order, and there were almost no Muslims equipped to master the new sciences that the West had brought to India.

Political Awakening

Slowly and against considerable opposition there began to emerge new leaders who took much that the West had to offer without abandoning their basic faith in Islam. In the year of the Mutiny the three Presidency universities were founded at Bombay, Calcutta, and Madras. With the development of the steamship and the opening of the Suez Canal it became easier and more normal for young Indian students to go to the universities of Britain and continental Europe. In 1875 Sir Sayyid Ahmad Khan, who had been deeply impressed by his visit to England, established the nucleus of the Aligarh Muslim University.

Toward the end of the nineteenth century the British rulers of India began to take steps to associate more Indians with the upper levels of government. A few were taken into the higher civil service; municipal councils, chosen mainly by election, were given substantial powers of local administration; and the number of Indian representatives on the provincial legislative councils was substantially increased.

British policy toward India from 1830 to 1947 was always the reflection of three separate points of view. First, there was a minority who believed that Britain's finest day in India would be when power was transferred in peace to a free Indian government. Second, there was another minority who believed in a permanent Indian empire, the brightest jewel in the British crown, which must be ruled firmly, justly, and without concessions to nationalist sentiments. And third, there was the majority who at all times felt that the Indian empire was a good thing while it lasted and that, though changes would be necessary, they should be introduced with caution. This was the normal opinion of the senior administrators who spent their lives in India.

To the minds of perceptive Indians, British policy posed the issue of who was to receive the increasing share of power. If, even in the remote future, India were to become independent, there would be a struggle to determine who would rule. Half a century before the Muslim League raised its demand for Pakistan, Sir Sayyid Ahmad Khan used these words:

Now suppose that all the English . . . were to leave India . . . then who would be the rulers of India? Is it possible that under these circumstances two nations—the Mohammedan and Hindu—could sit on the same throne and remain equal in power? Most certainly not. It is necessary that one of them should conquer the other and thrust it down. To hope that both could remain equal is to desire the impossible and the inconceivable.[6]

The Muslims were a minority in India, outnumbered three to one by the Hindus. Their share of the middle class, commercial, professional, and official, was far smaller. Therefore they asked for protection against being overwhelmed by the larger community. In particular, they wanted a reserved quota in the public services and special provisions to ensure Muslim representation in the legislatures. In 1906, reform was in the air, and the Muslim community made its first organized political moves. A deputation under the Aga Khan asked the Viceroy for special safeguards in the event of an extension of representative government. Later in the same year, under equally aristocratic sponsorship, the Muslim League was formed at Dacca in East Bengal.

The Indian National Congress [7] had been in existence for more than twenty years. It had begun as a respectable, upper-middle-class organization with some British membership and guidance. It was now becoming more vigorous and more radical and falling under the influence of Hindu revivalism that was both anti-Western and uncongenial to the Muslims. Two issues at this period served to divide the interests of the two communities. The Muslim request for safeguards was conceded in the Morley-Minto reforms of 1909. The Muslim community was given reserved seats in the legislatures, to be filled by Muslims voting in separate constituencies; the number of Muslim seats was somewhat higher than their proportion of the population would have indicated. This provision led Muslim candidates to campaign along communal lines since they were appealing for Muslim votes only. Many Indians have seen in this law the true progenitor of Pakistan.

The second divisive issue arose over the partition of Bengal. This enormous province was divided in 1905, in part with the intent of allowing the mainly Muslim East Bengal to govern itself apart from the

---

[6] Quoted in Richard Symonds, *The Making of Pakistan* (3d ed.; London: Faber and Faber, 1951), p. 31.

[7] See Chapters IX and XI.

predominant influence of the Hindu middle class of Calcutta. The Hindus protested bitterly and with violence, and the partition was annulled in 1912. This was seen by the Muslims as a betrayal by the British and as an indication that they would have to fight more vigorously to preserve their status.

It would be wrong to suppose that from the establishment of the Muslim League there was nothing but antagonism between this party and the Congress. It was possible for individuals to be sincere members of both organizations. In 1916 they agreed upon the Lucknow Pact, which outlined a constitution for an autonomous India.

In the First World War the British government promised India a major advance toward full self-government. At the war's end, the leaders of Indian nationalism were determined to force the pace and were profoundly disappointed at the meagerness of the concessions offered. The Muslims also found themselves with a grievance. The Muslim world had always paid at least nominal deference to the position of the Caliph, as the successor to the Prophet Muhammad. The Caliph was then the Sultan of Turkey, which was the only surviving independent Muslim power of any magnitude. The Turks lost in the war, and as a consequence it seemed that Turkey was to be dismembered. Indian Muslims, even though they had backed the Allied war effort, protested against such harshness. They were therefore in a mood to join Gandhi's civil disobedience movement in order to further the somewhat incongruous twin objectives of self-government and the preservation of the caliphate. Ultimately the Turks preserved their territory but abandoned their Caliph, and his Indian supporters were left without a cause.

The agreement with the Indian National Congress and the caliphate agitation caused the Muslim League to recede into the background, and the reforms of 1919 enlarged the degree of representative government in the provinces and maintained the provisions for separate electorates for Muslims. The question of a final transfer of power was too remote to cause intense rivalry. The Muslim demands for continued and increased safeguards were presented to the Simon Commission and to the Round Table Conferences that followed.[8] Muslim leaders were unwilling to discuss possible powers of a future central government until they were assured of enhanced representation in the provincial legislatures.

[8] See p. 288.

Political Ideas

At this stage few Muslims had contemplated the erection of a separate state, although certain social and political ideas had begun to
produce a tendency toward Muslim separatism. Western countries
have become accustomed to the concept that loyalty is owed primarily
to the state and that the state is the nation, organized for purposes of
government. These propositions, however, were by no means obvious
to the educated Indian in the early years of the present century.

The Indian's loyalty, his sense of solidarity, began at home. First
came his family with all its ramifications. Then there were the ties
within the village, especially to those of the same caste or religious
community. Beyond this were wider religious bonds and regional
patriotism, based on language or history and connected perhaps with
loyalty to a big landowner or an Indian prince. And beyond these lay
the idea of India, remote and somewhat alien, as a British-erected and
British-controlled conglomeration. Most Indians, Muslim or Hindu,
were therefore pluralists, unable to accept one object of loyalty placed
ahead of all others. "Where God commands, I am a Muslim first, a
Muslim second and a Muslim last and nothing but a Muslim. But
where India is concerned, I am an Indian first, an Indian second and
an Indian last and nothing but an Indian." [9] These words were used
by Muḥammad Ali (1878–1930), who was to find that the two loyalties would tear him apart.

It was the idea of nationalism in any form that was new in the Indian subcontinent, not the older sectional loyalties. Muslim separatism
was one response to the new doctrine. Indian nationalism, the doctrine
that there was one nation in India, had the advantage that it promised
the quickest route to the transfer of power from British to Indian
hands. But concentration upon national unity was bound to cause
conflict with the other loyalties. The best that could be offered the
Muslims was the status of a religious minority in a secular state. And
in a cultural sense that state was likely to evolve a unified social outlook that would be predominantly Hindu in tradition and content.

Muslim social and political thought in this period was primarily
directed to insisting that the bonds of Muslim solidarity should not be
overlooked. The Muslim felt the call of Indian nationalism, but he
wished to preserve a high place also for Islam. Almost every Muslim
thinker, whichever side of the fence of nationalism he chose, tried to

[9] Quoted in Symonds, *The Making of Pakistan*, p. 43.

preserve some degree of special status for Islam and its followers. Many attempted to stay astride that fence until the events of 1940–1947 forced them to make a choice.

The first concern of Muslim middle-class thinkers was that the Muslim community should not be left hopelessly behind in the acquisition of the new ideas and techniques offered by the West. Sir Sayyid Ahmad Khan (1817–1898) was the first major writer to urge his co-religionists to learn from the European. He concerned himself with proving to the British that the Muslim community was loyal and should be trusted. He then urged Muslims to educate themselves and play a part in public life. He was not an anti-Hindu although he felt that the Muslim community would have to display much more vigor if it were to avoid submergence.[10]

Sayyid Ahmad had sought to show that Islam was no barrier to scientific inquiry and social progress. Amir Ali (1849–1928) told the Muslims that, compared with Christianity, they possessed a religion and a culture for which no apology was needed. His message was that Muslims should be proud of and true to their own heritage, which was ample enough to permit incorporation of new ideas "Sir Sayyid had maintained that Islam was not inimical to liberal progress. Amir Ali presented an Islam that is that progress." [11] The effect of this line of argument was to encourage Indian Muslims to look upon Islam as their proper object of identification rather than India. They felt themselves brothers of Muslims everywhere as well as residents of the Punjab or of the United Provinces.

This strain of pan-Islamic sentiment was in the forefront of the case presented by the exponents of the Khilafat movement (to preserve the caliphate). Muhammad Ali, the leader of the movement, was able for several years to combine his ardent desire for the end of British rule with his devotion to Islam. Even Abul Kalam Azad, who was to become president of the Congress and a minister in Nehru's cabinet, proclaimed the identity of Islamic and nationalist causes in the defense of the caliphate.[12]

The Khilafat movement was doomed to frustration, and it was barren of ideas except for the emphasis on the unity of all Muslims. The movement demonstrated, however, the readiness of large masses of

---

[10] See Wilfred Cantwell Smith, *Modern Islam in India* (London: Gollancz, 1946), pp. 24–26.

[11] *Ibid.*, p. 49.

[12] *Ibid.*, pp. 201–202.

Muslims to respond to a call based upon Islam. It was a mass movement which had many of the features of a holy war. As it declined, the line between Muslim separatism and Indian nationalism became more marked—some leaders turned primarily to the defense of Muslim communal interests and others to the cause of a united India.

Thus far the aim of Muslim thinkers had been to preserve the identity of the community. The next stage in the development of the ideas of Muslim separatism was the injection of a spirit of dynamism, and the leading figure in this regard was Sir Muhammad Iqbal (1876–1938). Iqbal was a poet, philosopher, lawyer, and politician. His primary concern was to combine the progressive driving force of the Western countries and the tradition of Islam. He condemned the tendency to accept passively the situation brought about by others. The Muslims everywhere must act, individually and collectively. He was less certain and less consistent about the nature of those actions, but he was sure that their inspiration could be found only in Islam. In 1930, when he was president of the Muslim League, he suggested the creation of a separate Muslim state in northwest India. At the time the idea seemed fantastic, but it made an impression on the minds of others, even though, for some years, it was to remain an inspiration rather than a practical objective.

The Pakistan Movement

The discussions of 1928–1932 led ultimately to the Government of India Act of 1935 which granted near autonomy in the provinces and promised a major advance toward self-government at the center. Provincial elections were held in 1937, and the result was a general victory for the Congress. The Muslim League, led by Mohammed Ali Jinnah, had contested the elections on the basis that it would cooperate fully with the Congress if its status was recognized as the true spokesman of the Muslim community. Congress ministries were formed in seven of the eleven provinces, but no gesture of cooperation as between equals was made in the direction of the League. On the contrary, in one province the Congress agreed to nominate Muslim League members to the cabinet only on the condition that they accept party discipline and cease to function as a separate entity.

For the first time Muslims found themselves in the position that they had begun to fear—that of being subject to a mainly Hindu government able to claim the sanction of an electoral victory. This fear acted as a spur to the Muslim League, which had fought the election without carrying the argument to the level of the peasants and the urban laborer.[13] In the by-elections that took place after 1937 the League showed signs of new strength and determination. Many members of minor parties (including two provincial chief ministers) also joined the League in the name of Muslim solidarity.

Soon after the outbreak of the Second World War the Congress ordered its provincial ministries to resign as a protest against the declaration of war on behalf of India without the consent of Indian leaders. This was an opportunity for the League, and Mr. Jinnah proclaimed a Day of Deliverance. The stage was then set for the League to demand an independent state. The formal adoption of this proposal came in 1940 at Lahore. The resolution demanded "that the areas in which the Muslims are numerically in a majority, as in the northwestern and eastern zones of India, should be grouped to constitute 'independent States' in which the constituent units shall be autonomous and sovereign: . . ." This was the Pakistan Resolution. It took by surprise the rest of the world, which was busy watching the battles of France and Britain. The very name Pakistan was unfamiliar. It had been coined six or seven years previously by a student at Cambridge; the idea had been advocated in general terms by the poet and philosopher Iqbal. But practical men had dismissed the scheme as unworkable, a vision incapable of fulfillment. It had scarcely been mentioned in the general elections of 1937. Now it was the official policy of a party that claimed the sole right to speak for one-fourth of India's population. There were many who called it a bluff, a propaganda device to be used in subsequent bargaining.

The later war years saw the Congress leaders in jail or in flight. The League gave conditional approval to the war effort and clung to its position of power. Moreover, it converted itself into an agency with mass influence. The campaign for Pakistan provided its spokesmen with a rallying cry that could transcend all lesser claims to loyalty and obedience. The cause could appeal to the backward-looking and the orthodox who longed to live under the rule of believers in the true faith; it could also cast its spell upon the young and the innovators who, as Muslims, would otherwise be left as a minority in a united India.

Immediately after the war the government of India took steps to hold new elections for both the central and provincial assemblies. Al-

[13] The franchise was limited by property and education qualifications, and the Muslim League had effectively represented only its more-educated portions.

though the Congress emerged clearly as the strongest party, the League carried almost all the provincial Muslim seats except in the North-West Frontier Province and took every Muslim seat in the central Assembly. Its claim to represent the large majority of Muslims could no longer be denied.

The Congress could, and did, deny the right of the League to be the sole spokesman for all the Muslims of India. The president of the Congress at this period was Abul Kalam Azad, whose presence served to vindicate the Congress's claim of being a nation-wide organization and also infuriated the League.

After the elections the British Cabinet Mission visited India [14] and produced its proposals for a loose federal system of government with the provinces ranged into "groups," two of which would have been predominantly Muslim. A Constituent Assembly was to be chosen by the elected members of the provincial assemblies, and the Viceroy's Executive Council was to be reorganized as an interim cabinet and include members drawn from both the Congress and the League.

Neither of the major parties could agree entirely to this scheme. The interim cabinet was established, however, and the Constituent Assembly constituted. After some delay League representatives entered the cabinet but stayed away from the Assembly. At this point the British government set a time limit for the transfer of power and sent Lord Mountbatten as the last Viceroy to superintend the transition to independence. It was not until June 3, 1947, that the people of India learned that the country was to be partitioned and that two new independent states—India and Pakistan—were to come into existence at midnight on August 14.

The New State

Pakistan was made up of two sizable fragments severed from the structure of the old India. The legislatures of the Punjab and Bengal met and decided upon partition, with the Muslim-majority areas— West Punjab and East Bengal—forming Pakistan. A referendum was held in the North-West Frontier Province and in the Sylhet district of Assam, and each chose Pakistan, as did Sindh and Baluchistan. The princely states were left to decide for themselves which of the new Dominions to join. Bahawalpur, Khairpur, and eight relatively minor states in Baluchistan and the Frontier acceded to Pakistan. So much for the enumeration of territories.

[14] See p. 295.

What happened in fact was that one country, even though it had been inhabited by two nations, was abruptly and brutally torn in two. Communal tension had been rising as the struggle for the succession to power intensified. Appalling riots occurred in Bombay and Calcutta, and the province of Bihar suffered widespread violence. Immediately before partition the system of law and order had effectively ceased in large sections of the Punjab. The British troops who had been available in the last resort were leaving, and so were many British civil officials.

In that summer of 1947, apart from brief rejoicings on the day of independence, fear and hatred were the principal emotions. Rumors of rape, murder, and arson augmented the horror of the immense atrocities that had in fact occurred. A Muslim surrounded by Hindus, or vice versa, never knew if he would live through the night. In some instances, especially in the princely states, the authorities participated in massacre and mass expulsion of those who belonged to the alien community. No one will ever know the full death toll. Estimates range up to 1 million, with a figure for refugees of more than 12 million.[15]

This human disruption was the harder to deal with because of the accompanying dislocation of government and commercial services. From the point of view of administration and economics, India had been a single unit before 1947. Substantial powers were centralized in New Delhi, and the main commercial centers for the whole country were Bombay, Madras, and Calcutta. The new Dominion of India inherited all these centers of government and trade. In addition, there were many large provinces which had not been divided and which had been relatively unaffected by violence or the movement of population. India suffered at partition; Pakistan was devastated. East Bengal, Pakistan's largest province, had been severed from its main urban focus in Calcutta and was separated from its new federal capital by a thousand miles of unfriendly Indian territory. The Punjab was also partitioned and had been the scene of the worst of the violence and arson. Lahore, its capital, less than twenty miles from the border, was left in flames, and its large population of Hindu and Sikh shopkeepers, clerks, and mechanics had fled. The province of Sindh had to act as host to the new central government which was established at Karachi and to refugees who poured in by the hundred thousand.

Out of this chaos the government of the new state had to bring

[15] See Symonds, *The Making of Pakistan*, pp. 83–84; E. W. R. Lumby, *The Transfer of Power in India* (London: Allen and Unwin, 1954), ch. v.

order. It had to begin by creating itself. There had been few senior Muslim civil servants, and one or two of these had elected to stay on the Indian side of the border. Hindu and some British officials had withdrawn from their posts in Pakistan to serve India or to retire. There was no organized nucleus around which a government could be built, no offices, no telephones, no typewriters, no files. Some officials and implements had arrived from Delhi, but others were delayed en route or failed to arrive. There was no reserve in provincial service to be drawn upon.

Mohammed Ali Jinnah

Above all the confusion, one figure stood forth resolute and confident. He was Mohammed Ali Jinnah (1876–1948), the first Governor-General of Pakistan and the Qaid-i-Azam (Great Leader) of the nation. No one could differ more markedly from the stereotype of the Asian nationalist politician than Mr. Jinnah. For most of his life he dressed in well-tailored European clothes, and he wore an eyeglass. Even when he adopted local costume, he chose a form of dress (*sherwani*) somewhat resembling a black frock coat with a high buttoned collar. He had an ascetic appearance, and the first impression he made was of cold but brilliant intensity. He never suffered fools gladly and disdained the tricks of the politician that win easy popularity.

In his youth Jinnah went to England for a legal education and returned to establish a highly successful practice at the Bombay bar. Politics soon claimed him, and election to the central Legislative Council followed in 1909. He was a member of both the Congress and the League and was the principal promoter of the Lucknow Pact when he first became president of the League. He was rightly regarded as a leading exponent of Hindu-Muslim unity. By temperament and reason he was unattracted by either Gandhi's civil disobedience or the movement to preserve the caliphate. He returned to active political leadership at the time of the preparation of the Muslim case for the Simon Commission and the Round Table Conferences. After the failure to reach agreement Jinnah remained in London and contemplated spending the balance of his career at the English bar. But in 1934 he was persuaded to return to his native land and to assume that command of the Muslim League which he never afterward relinquished. In no sense did he become a popular leader until after the 1937 elections and the subsequent adoption of the Pakistan Resolution.

Although he had great respect for the tradition of Islam, he was not an orthodox Muslim and could never have been described as a religious fanatic. His loyalty was primarily to the Muslim people of India and their common cultural heritage. He was far too much a master and a student of the common law to consider a return to the simplicity of the Islamic state patterned after that of the Holy Prophet and of those who immediately followed. At no stage did Jinnah want a state inhabited solely by Muslims. But he believed that a Muslim-majority state would be the best guarantee of the survival of the Muslim community throughout the subcontinent and of harmony between the two major communities. After 1937 he became convinced that no safeguards within a single state could ensure the effective preservation of the Muslim group identity.

In his capacity as president of the Muslim League, Jinnah felt himself to be almost the incarnation of the Indian Muslim nation. He towered above his subordinates and sought lieutenants who would serve him rather than colleagues who might argue with him. His will was inflexible, and his continued insistence on Pakistan was so obdurate that the Viceroy and the Congress abandoned hope of any change on his part or that of his followers.

The First Year (1947–1948)

The immediate task facing the new government was to establish its control and ensure minimum services throughout its territory. The exact boundaries were not known until immediately after partition, and it was months before the normal lines of responsibility could be established. The army had to be partitioned, and the attempt to maintain a joint command throughout the disturbed areas was never completely effective. The Hindu and Sikh civil servants, railwaymen, clerks, bankers, and shopkeepers had to be replaced with Muslims, whether qualified or not. Provision had to be made for the hundreds of thousands of refugees, to provide them with food, shelter, and some medical attention.

The government was organized according to the provisions of the 1935 Government of India Act, with some modifications introduced for Pakistan in the few weeks preceding and following the date of independence. The principal figure was the Governor-General, Mr. Jinnah. Other Dominions of the Commonwealth had reduced the office of Governor-General to that of a figurehead. In Pakistan it was the office that corresponded most closely to that of the Viceroy who had been the real head of the government of British India. The Prime

Minister, Liaqat Ali Khan, was quite content to serve as the first lieutenant of the Qaid-i-Azam, a role that he had played during the struggle to secure the new state.

The immediate task of combating the emergency fell upon the executive branch of government. The legislature, known as the Constituent Assembly, met in the week before independence, but it then adjourned for six months. It was composed, for the territories of Pakistan, on the same basis as the Constituent Assembly established in 1946 for the subcontinent as a whole. That is, its original 69 members were chosen by the provincial assemblies. Additional members were added to represent the tribal areas and the princely states, and readjustments were made to reflect the movements of population that had taken place. Its job was twofold: to write a constitution and to act as an interim parliament. Each of the four provinces (East Bengal, Punjab, Sindh, North-West Frontier Province) had a similar constitution, with a governor appointed by the central government and a cabinet responsible to a single-chamber legislature.

The first six months of the new state were occupied in attending to the most urgent problems and hoping that some of the others would solve themselves if left alone. Gradually the government became aware of the resources available to it and the magnitude of the various claims upon them. By the spring of 1948 the first crisis was over, and it was clear that Pakistan was going to survive.

The struggle to achieve independence and the fight to maintain it had taken all the strength that Mr. Jinnah possessed. After a prolonged period of increasing weakness he died in September 1948. The nation had lost its Great Leader, the one man whose order was obeyed unquestioningly by all.

1948–1951

There was no dispute over the succession. Effective power passed to the Prime Minister, Liaqat Ali Khan, though his authority was never to equal that of Mr. Jinnah. The new Governor-General was the former chief minister of East Bengal, Khwaja Nazimuddin.

The government had to deal with a series of difficult issues—the framing of a constitution, Kashmir,[16] canal waters,[17] food production, industrialization, the balance of payments. It was unable to achieve any spectacular successes. A preliminary draft of the constitution was issued in 1950, but severe criticism was encountered from those who regretted the absence of distinctive Islamic provisions and those who

[16] See below, pp. 517–519.   [17] See below, p. 520.

wanted more autonomy for East Bengal. The draft was referred back to a committee of the Assembly.[18]

The progress made in other directions was real but not dramatic. Various economic development projects were begun, especially in the field of textile manufacture. A State Bank was established and monetary control extended over the economic system. There were no major changes in law or in administration. There was nothing that a man could point to at the end of a year and say, "This marks a distinct step forward."

There were some items to be counted as discredit. Political factions, especially in the provinces, began a process of intrigue that was to place in continued doubt the life of every government. A series of provincial ministers in Sindh was dismissed on grounds of corruption and political irregularities. Self-government had to be suspended in the Punjab in 1949 because of the impossibility of finding a stable and reliable ministry.[19] Official corruption, black-marketing, and general inefficiency were part of the price that had to be paid for the dislocation of government and economy caused by partition. The high hopes and firm faith that had sustained the people in the early months were being dissipated by petty frustrations and the absence of clear signs of substantial improvement. At this point, in October 1951, Liaqat Ali Khan was assassinated.

The murderer was an Afghan living as a political refugee in Pakistan, and his motive has never been clearly established. The consequences of his act were all too plain. In four years Pakistan had lost both of its preeminent leaders, and there was no one of equivalent stature to take their place.

1951–1954

Nazimuddin, whose piety and integrity have never been questioned, stepped down from the dignity of the governor-generalship and became Prime Minister. Ghulam Mohammed, the former Finance Minister, was elevated to the office of Governor-General. Most of the other members of the cabinet retained their offices, and a former civil servant, Chaudhri Mohamad Ali, was promoted to the Finance portfolio.

The problems facing the administration were not changed, and the

[18] A more detailed account of these developments may be found in Keith Callard, *Pakistan: A Political Study* (London: Allen and Unwin, 1957; New York: Macmillan, 1958), pp. 89–101.
[19] *Ibid.*, pp. 26–29.

government's ability to cope with them was lessened by the loss of its leader. Differences over the future constitution became aggravated. The advocates of an Islamic state demanded and received concessions. The East Bengalis also sought to advance the interests of their half of the country. The political situation in the provinces offered little chance of stable and vigorous administration.

In the early months of 1953 there were widespread riots in West Pakistan in support of demands which combined religious and political elements. And there was a food shortage that threatened large areas of the country with starvation. The Governor-General, whose position since Jinnah's death had been regarded as mainly formal, now intervened. He dismissed the Prime Minister and reconstituted the cabinet with Mohammed Ali, the former ambassador to the United States, at its head.

The Constituent Assembly, though dubious about the constitutional propriety of this action, did not openly challenge the new government. Technically it was still a government of the Muslim League, which filled almost every Muslim seat in the central and provincial legislatures. The League was split in many directions. There were those who wanted a constitution based on Islamic principles, and there were those who favored secularism in political life. Many of the Bengalis and some representatives from other provinces fought for provincial rights which they believed were being denied. There were supporters and opponents of the Governor-General and his nominee for Prime Minister. The political instability that plagued the provinces was now reproduced in Karachi.

The situation was made more complex by the result of the provincial election of 1954 in East Bengal. The eastern province, which contains more than half the total population of the country, voted overwhelmingly against the Muslim League and in favor of a coalition of parties that demanded greater provincial autonomy. This election did not affect the seats of the Bengal members of the Constituent Assembly, but it served to indicate that they had lost the confidence of their electorate.

A new provincial government, under the party label of the United Front, was installed. It found the province on the verge of major riots, and within a few weeks the central government suspended it from office. A strong governor, Major General Iskandar Mirza, was sent from Karachi to rule until it seemed possible to restore popular government without risking public tranquillity.

The Governor-General hoped to have a constitution approved without further delay. The Assembly was determined to limit the present and future powers of the Governor-General. The result was delay, intrigue, and maneuver. In September 1954 the Assembly passed bills aimed at reducing the power of Ghulam Mohammed. A month later he announced:

> The Governor-General having considered the political crisis with which the country is faced has, with deep regret, come to the conclusion that the constitutional machinery has broken down. He, therefore, has decided to declare a State of Emergency throughout Pakistan. The Constituent Assembly as at present constituted has lost the confidence of the people and can no longer function.[20]

1954–1958

A new cabinet was formed with the same Prime Minister and several other ministers, but also included were the commander in chief of the army (General Mohammed Ayub Khan, as Minister of Defense), a top civil servant with a military background (Major General Iskandar Mirza, as Minister of the Interior), a businessman, and representatives of groups that had opposed the Muslim League. Democracy seemed to be at a low ebb. Self-government was suspended in the eastern half of the country, and the national legislature had been dismissed. Further, the provincial ministers and legislators of West Pakistan were not outstanding for democratic practice.

The government proposed to frame a constitution by administrative order and to merge the western provinces into a single unit. However, the fundamental constitutional deadlock had already been referred to the courts.[21] A series of Federal Court decisions required a return to something resembling the pattern laid down by the Indian Independence Act. The government was forbidden to go ahead with making a constitution by administrative decree. A new Constituent Assembly was to be set up, elected by the provincial assemblies.

The court's ruling was accepted, and the second Constituent Assembly held its first meeting in July 1955. Shortly afterward the government was once more reconstructed. Chaudhri Mohamad Ali replaced Mohammed Ali as Prime Minister, and Ghulam Mohammed was succeeded as Governor-General by Iskandar Mirza. The com-

[20] *Gazette of Pakistan, Extraordinary*, Oct. 24, 1954.
[21] See Sir Ivor Jennings, *Constitutional Problems in Pakistan* (Cambridge, Eng.: Cambridge University Press, 1957).

mander in chief left the cabinet, which became once more a group of
political party leaders. The Muslim League was still the major component, but it had to share power with the United Front, since the
League could not claim the support of the new members from Bengal.

The initial party composition of the second Constituent Assembly
was as follows:

Muslim League	26
United Front	16
Awami League	13
Congress	4
Scheduled Castes Federation	3
United Progressive Party	2
Others	16
	80

In early 1956 many of the Muslim Leaguers and "others" joined the
Republican Party.

The new Constituent Assembly immediately began to work on three
major pieces of legislation. First, it had to clear away the legal and
constitutional tangle left by the dismissal of its predecessor and by
the interim of emergency rule. Second, it acted to amalgamate the
three provinces and the princely states of West Pakistan into a single
province. Finally, it adopted the new constitution. The draft, prepared by the government, was introduced in January 1956, debated
and passed in February, and proclaimed on March 23.

The adoption of the constitution was not to be a prelude to a period of political calm. The United Front, which filled most of the
seats in the East Pakistan [22] Assembly, had split into two major segments. It had been formed as an electoral alliance and began to dissolve as soon as victory was won. In West Pakistan the Muslim League
was about to disintegrate. One section adopted the name Republican
Party [23] and chose a leader, Dr. Khan Sahib, who had never been in
the League though he had joined the emergency cabinet in 1954. The
Republicans formed a provincial ministry and held a narrow majority in the West Pakistan Assembly. Although the League was in op-

[22] The constitution changed the name of East Bengal to East Pakistan, and the
other province was West Pakistan.

[23] A more detailed account of the political parties is given below in Chapter
XVII. See also Callard, *Pakistan*, ch. ii.

position to the Republicans at Lahore, both parties continued to support the central cabinet of Chaudhri Mohamad Ali. This unstable equilibrium lasted until September 1956, when the Muslim League moved into opposition at the center as well as in the provinces. Simultaneously one segment of the United Front—the Awami League —ousted the other from the government of East Pakistan. The national leader of the Awami League, H. S. Suhrawardy, who had been leader of the Opposition, was called on to form a government. This he was able to do, with the support of the Republicans who were at that time the largest party in the National Assembly. In October 1957 the Republicans broke away from the coalition. Mr. Suhrawardy resigned, and a new government was formed under the Muslim League leader, I. I. Chundrigar. This cabinet collapsed, in its turn, in December 1957, and Firoz Khan Noon (Republican) became Prime Minister. The Awami League supported the Noon ministry without joining it until in September 1958 they insisted on sharing the spoils of power. The resulting protracted and unedifying dispute among the parties over the allocation of ministerial portfolios was terminated only by President Iskandar Mirza's action in imposing martial law, abrogating the 1956 constitution, and abolishing political parties, on the night of October 7, 1958.

1958–1962

The "Revolution" brought an end to the parliamentary system in Pakistan. The Proclamation of October 7 dissolved the three legislatures and dismissed all the ministers and placed the country under the direction of General Mohammed Ayub Khan as Chief Martial Law Administrator. On October 27 Mirza resigned at the "request" of the generals, and Ayub became President. The office of Prime Minister was abolished and a presidential cabinet appointed, including three generals and eight (later ten) civilians, only one of whom had previous political experience. The governors of East and West Pakistan became responsible directly to the President for the administration of their provinces. Backing for the civil government was provided in each province by a general as martial law administrator, commanding a hierarchy of martial law authorities that was gradually withdrawn into the background as the new order stabilized itself. President, ministers, governors, and martial law administrators, with a few select high officials, met from time to time as the "Governors' Conference" to make the highest-level policy decisions.

The abrogation of the constitution having made a complete break with the past, the martial law regime was not limited as its predecessor of the 1954–1955 "emergency" had been. Proclaiming its purpose to "clean up the mess" and make possible effective democracy, the regime proceeded to attack the problems of smuggling, black-marketing, and corruption. Special commissions were assigned to investigate problem areas; of the reforms that resulted, the first and most dramatic was the West Pakistan land reform, accomplished under a martial law regulation of February 1959. The provincial administrations were studied and recast, with decentralization of powers to the divisional and district levels. On the first anniversary of Ayub's presidency he promulgated the Basic Democracies Order, providing for the establishment of elected union councils throughout the country and for appointed councils at the tehsil or thana,[24] district, and divisional levels, to be coordinated with the administration. In a presidential referendum on February 14, 1960, the 80,000 newly elected union councilors voted overwhelmingly to confirm Ayub in office for five years and to authorize him to prepare a new constitution. A Constitution Commission headed by Mohammed Shahabuddin, a former Chief Justice, was appointed to make a study and recommendations and submitted its report in May 1961. After further study by the cabinet, a presidential and quasi-federal constitution was promulgated on March 1, 1962, enshrining primarily Ayub's own constitutional ideas.

The dormant political life of the country immediately began to awaken. The first elections—in which again the union councilors were the voters—were held on April 28 for the National Assembly and on May 6, 1962, for the provincial assemblies. Martial law ended when the National Assembly met on June 8, and the conditional ban on political parties was lifted with the adoption of the Political Parties Act in July. The martial law ministers left office on June 8 and were replaced shortly by a cabinet of whom all but three "experts" (the Finance, Law, and Home ministers) were members of the National Assembly. The process of "group" formation in the National Assembly began immediately after the elections, and the new ministers were successful in rallying majority support for the government throughout

[24] A tehsil is an administrative jurisdiction below the district level in West Pakistan, primarily concerned with revenue collection. A thana in East Pakistan was originally a police jurisdiction, but is increasingly being utilized for other administrative purposes.

the first session in June and July. When the second session opened in late November 1962, the government majority consisted of the "conventionist" Muslim League plus some independents, and the principal opposition was the "Council" Muslim League led by Sardar Bahadur Khan, the President's brother. A similar situation prevailed in both provinces.

· XV ·

Economic and Social Structure

AT the time of the census of 1961, Pakistan had a population of about 94 million. Of these, over 50 million lived in East Pakistan. The vast majority was composed of poor and illiterate villagers. Those who could read and write in any language totaled 15.3 per cent of the total population—a decrease in the literacy rate since 1951 (partly explained by a change in the definition of literacy). Those who lived in cities and towns comprised about 22 per cent in West Pakistan, but only 5.5 per cent in East Pakistan.

There are immense contrasts between various sections of the country. One thousand miles of Indian territory separate East and West Pakistan. But this is not the only factor that keeps them apart. There are six main languages spoken in Pakistan. A small minority dispersed throughout the country possesses a knowledge of English, which is still the main vehicle of official and commercial transactions. In East Pakistan the language is Bengali, which uses a script derived from Sanskrit and serves to form a link with the Hindu Bengalis living in West Bengal on the Indian side of the border. The languages of West Pakistan are Urdu, Punjabi, Sindhi, and Pushtu. They have some elements in common, though they are far from being merely dialects of a central tongue. They are mostly written in the Urdu (or Persian) script and use a vocabulary that borrows heavily from Arabic and Persian. The cultural traditions of the two wings of Pakistan are, in consequence, substantially different. Persian is still the classical language for many West Pakistanis, and Persian verse is widely quoted. There are those who do not hesitate to say that Urdu is a more truly "Islamic" language than Bengali, which has been affected by its Hindu heritage. This, of course, is denied heatedly by Bengali Muslims.

The Economy

There are further grounds for difference beyond language. East Pakistan occupies the delta of the Ganges and Brahmaputra rivers, where these combine to form a massive flow of water. This water marks the main difference between the physical character of East and of West. The problem in the East is to drain it away to the sea. Each rainy season the delta is flooded, and the distributaries change their courses; for many months water is the only feasible means of transport in areas not served by the few railways. In the West, on the other hand, water has to be hoarded and shared out by an immense network of canals over the parched land or raised from wells by primitive means. The crops which give men their livelihood are also different. In the East rice is the staple food and jute the principal cash crop; in the West wheat and cotton are important.

Most of the cities and industry are in the West, and the average standard of living is lower in the East. Despite the West Pakistan land reform of 1959, 25 per cent of the land is still owned by slightly more than 1 per cent of the landholders, whereas in East Pakistan the State Acquisition process has eliminated the few large estates.[1]

Within West Pakistan there is a great variety of conditions. The North-West Frontier contains regions in which the life of the people must be much the same as when Alexander marched through. The basis of life is tribal, with the elders of each clan maintaining law and making the major decisions. Each man still carries a rifle on his shoulder and lives in a hut with thick mud walls, behind which his family and possessions are withdrawn at night. Thousands of Baluchis are nomads, pasturing their sheep and goats in the hills in summer and coming down to the plains in winter.

The women of Pakistan are mostly excluded from participation in the general life of the community. Where poverty requires it, the women work, either alongside the men in the fields or in groups in

[1] For further discussion of the land reforms, see the section "Economic Development" in Chapter XVIII.

the cities. But they keep themselves apart from strange men. And those families that can afford it, especially the middle classes, confine their women at home; but if they venture abroad, they do so under a veil that covers them from head to toe, and they are escorted by a male relative or servant. This custom of the seclusion of women does not exist without protest or attempts at reform. In 1961 the central government promulgated the Muslim Family Laws Ordinance, giving women legal safeguards in regard to marriage, divorce, and inheritance. Although applauded by emancipated women, the ordinance was attacked by conservative elements, and during the first session of the National Assembly in 1962 notice was given of a private member's bill to repeal it. The women immediately launched a political agitation to protect their rights, but such activity was of course limited to the governmental centers and large cities where foreign cultural and educational influences have been strongly felt.

Religion

The reason for the seclusion of women is the Islamic precept that a woman is to observe the strictest modesty. Islam is a factor that permeates every aspect of individual and social life in Pakistan. This is not surprising since the very reason for the creation of Pakistan was the feeling by Muslims that their faith and its associated tradition and culture placed them so far apart from their fellow Indians as to make them a separate nation. The central feature of the struggle for Pakistan was this sense of a separate identity as Muslims, as believers in Islam.

For a Muslim, his religion means obedience to the clear and definite commands of God as revealed by the Prophet Muhammad. These commands can be read directly in the Quran and understood almost equally well from the sayings and traditions of the Prophet. Such divine laws are not mere general principles, capable of being interpreted in widely differing senses. Many of them are precise and practical and regulate such matters as the manner of saying prayers, the proper laws of inheritance, the prohibition of alcohol and the flesh of swine, and the status of nonbelievers. The Muslim has tended to see the source of all law in his religion. If a matter is not explicitly provided for, it can be discerned by analogy from the nearest precedent or by deduction from an established principle.

This represents the traditionalist's view of the role of Islam. It was certainly not completely acceptable to Mr. Jinnah or to many other political leaders in Pakistan. In many instances the minds of these leaders operate on two levels. One is the realm of tradition and faith; the other, the area of their Western secular education. At one particular time and in one company they think in an Oriental language and organize their thoughts in Islamic terms; at another they think in English and use the vocabulary of John Stuart Mill or Woodrow Wilson. Such Pakistanis want all the advantages that can be learned from the experience of others, but, at the same time, they wish to feel the assurance that they are obedient to the word of Allah. Without Islam, Pakistan has no meaning. The nation's first Prime Minister said: "Pakistan was founded because the Muslims of this Sub-Continent wanted to build up their lives in accordance with the teaching and traditions of Islam, because they wanted to demonstrate to the world that Islam provides a panacea to the many diseases which have crept into the life of humanity today." [2]

The Islamic State

Throughout the long discussions prior to the adoption of the 1956 constitution there was a continuing demand that Pakistan should be an "Islamic State." In recognition of this, the country was designated the "Islamic Republic of Pakistan," and various constitutional clauses referred to Islam. While "no law shall be enacted which is repugnant to the injunctions of Islam," it was left to the legislatures to determine whether a proposal was or was not repugnant to those injunctions. To assist them, an Islamic Laws Commission was to report within five years on the question of modifying existing law and enacting Islamic requirements. The constitution was not in effect long enough for the meaning of these provisions to be clearly demonstrated.

Although the present constitution retains the requirement that the President be a Muslim, it has dropped the appellation "Islamic Republic." However, the preamble opens with the words: "In the name of Allah, the Beneficent, the Merciful. Whereas sovereignty over the entire Universe belongs to Almighty Allah alone, and the authority exercisable by the people is a sacred trust: . . ." As before, there are other allusions to Islam in the preamble and in the chapter on Principles of Policy, but these are unenforceable declarations of principle. The requirement that "no law should be repugnant to Islam" appears in the chapter on Principles of Law-Making, which sets out principles that are binding on the legislatures but are not enforceable at law.

[2] Constituent Assembly of Pakistan, *Debates*, V, 2, March 7, 1949.

If doubts arise concerning repugnancy—or any other of the Principles of Law-Making—the Assembly concerned or the President or governor may refer the question to the Advisory Council of Islamic Ideology, a presidentially appointed body of five to twelve persons with an "understanding and appreciation of Islam and of the economic, political, legal and administrative problems of Pakistan." Since its advice is not binding, the influence of the Advisory Council remains to be determined by political circumstances, including the prestige and authority of its members.

The Minorities

When Pakistan was formed, about one-quarter of its population consisted of non-Muslims. The upheaval of 1947 saw the transfer of millions of Muslims into Pakistan and the departure of millions of non-Muslims. The proportion of non-Muslims continues to decline, because of Hindu migration and greater Muslim fertility. The 1961 census indicated the non-Muslim population as 11.9 per cent of the total (see Table 8), compared with 14.1 per cent in 1951.

Table 8. Non-Muslim population (1961 census)

	East Pakistan	West Pakistan	Total
Caste Hindus	4,386,623	203,794	4,590,417
Scheduled castes	4,993,046	418,011	5,411,057
Christians	148,903	583,884	732,787
Buddhists	373,867	2,445	376,312
Parsis	193	5,219	5,412
Others	47,122	872	47,994
Totals	9,949,754	1,214,225	11,163,979
Percentage of minorities in total population	19.6%	2.8%	11.9%

Most of the Hindus in Muslim-majority areas either had a positive dislike for the prospect of Pakistan as a separate nation or were indifferent. There was no reason why they should feel the same emotional drive toward an Islamic state as their Muslim neighbors. On the contrary, the two-nation theory that lay behind the Pakistan movement seemed to imply that they would be reduced to the status of a permanent minority, excluded by their religion from full participation in citizenship of a Muslim state. The arguments for a separate Pakistan had always been twofold: first, that there was a bond which made all Muslims brothers; second, that Muslims were different from Hindus and did not wish to live under Hindu rule. The negative argument of fear of Hindu domination seemed at times to be stronger than the positive argument of the creation of a pure Muslim society.

The doctrine of Indian nationalism declared that men born in India were Indians first before the consideration of any claims of religious or local loyalties. The two-nation theory declared that a man was primarily a Muslim. Mr. Jinnah, however, always emphasized that this implied no threat to non-Muslims once the state of Pakistan was conceded. "Now I think we should keep that in front of us as our ideal and you will find in course of time Hindus would cease to be Hindus and Muslims would cease to be Muslims, not in the religious sense, because that is the personal faith of each individual, but in the political sense as citizens of the State." [3]

As can be seen from the figures in Table 8, the largest group of non-Muslims which remained in Pakistan consisted of the Hindus (caste and scheduled caste [4]) of East Pakistan. They raised objections to the proclamation of an Islamic state in 1956, and some Hindus have continued to leave the country for India. They have protested that the Hindu community is regarded with suspicion in Pakistan, and many feel that their sons will have opportunity for a better career if they transfer to the Indian side of the border where their coreligionists are in control. The position of those who wish to remain loyal Pakistanis is of course further compromised by such emigration, for example the expatriation of a Dacca High Court judge to Calcutta in 1958 and of the only Hindu member of the Civil Service of Pakistan in 1961.

The largest single grievance was the Muslim insistence on maintaining the system of separate electorates. This was introduced in 1909 to ensure adequate representation for the Muslim minority in the legislatures. It served to concentrate political divisions along communal lines and was always criticized by Indian nationalist leaders. It was continued in Pakistan because the Muslims had come to regard it as a proper safeguard of minority interests and because it prevented the Hindu electorate in East Bengal from being mingled with the

---

[3] Constituent Assembly of Pakistan, *Debates*, I, 20, Aug. 11, 1947.
[4] The scheduled castes are the low castes or outcastes.

Muslim voters. The system was carried farther in Pakistan, and a separate electorate was provided for the scheduled castes.[5] This split the Hindu community in two and reduced its political influence even more. The question of separate versus joint electorate was a major political issue, with the Muslim League on the side of segregation and the Awami League and the Hindus for joint electorates. The matter was left open by the 1956 constitution, but the Electorate Act of 1957 (as amended) provided for a joint electorate.[6] During the martial law regime the Basic Democracy elections were held on the basis of joint electorates, and the same principle has been recognized implicitly in the constitution of 1962.

One of the earliest committees established by the Constituent Assembly was that on fundamental rights and on minorities. Its report was substantially incorporated in the 1956 constitution, with guarantees of freedom of religion, religious education, equal opportunity for public employment, and the preservation of linguistic and cultural characteristics. Under the present constitution these guarantees, like the fundamental rights of the citizen generally, are set out in the Principles of Law-Making, binding on the legislatures but not justiciable without statutory implementation.

[5] Under the 1935 Government of India Act the scheduled castes were given reserved seats, but all Hindus voted for the various candidates.

[6] Keith Callard, *Pakistan: A Political Study* (London: Allen and Unwin, 1957; New York: Macmillan, 1958), pp. 240–254.

· XVI ·

The Structure of Government

THE first constitution of Pakistan was not adopted for almost nine years after independence. For twenty years those interested in public affairs had discussed the merits of the Government of India Act of 1935, even though its provisions were never fully implemented in their original form. The practical experience of the politicians, journalists, and students of government had been in relation to that constitutional act. The objections raised against it were seldom that it provided an unsuitable form of government but rather that effective power was confined to the wrong persons. Accordingly, although arguments in favor of a presidential or unitary system or both were presented, the constitution makers finally decided to proceed along lines that were already familiar, making some changes to meet the altered circumstances. Thus the 1956 constitution bore a strong resemblance to its parent, the 1935 Act, and hence to its brother the constitution of India.

The experience of 1956–1958 convinced Generals Mirza and Ayub, along with many others, that the parliamentary system that had been functioning in the provinces since 1937 and at the center since 1947 was not appropriate to Pakistani conditions. The drafters of the constitution of 1962 therefore attempted to evaluate the existing conditions of Pakistan and to work out a pattern of institutions that would be based on the realities of local experience rather than the ideals of British parliamentarism. The result owes something to the American example, to de Gaulle's France, and, very clearly, to the viceregal heritage of British India.

The Central Government

From 1947 until 1958 Pakistan functioned under a system of cabinet government, in the tradition of Britain and the older Commonwealth. Until 1956 Pakistanis owed formal allegiance to the Queen, although she herself had no role to play. Her representative was the Governor-General, and it was by virtue of his status as the agent of the Crown that Ghulam Mohammed was able to make the full use of his ill-defined powers in dismissing a Prime Minister and dissolving the Constituent Assembly. The Crown as a symbol was not appropriate for Pakistan, and it was not to be expected that the new nation would continue to regard a person of strange race and religion as its focus of allegiance. Pakistan therefore proclaimed itself to be a republic, with a President as head of state. The transition from Dominion to republic caused no disruption, and the last Governor-General became the first President, being elected by the Constituent Assembly. The break in continuity came in 1958, when President Mirza was forced to resign and General Ayub Khan assumed office as a "revolutionary" President.

Under the constitution of 1962 President Ayub Khan has been confirmed in office until August 1965, in accordance with the referendum of February 14, 1960. The conditions of office prescribed for future Presidents are rather complex. The President must be at least 35 years old and a Muslim. Normally he will have a term of five years, unless he dies, resigns, or is removed. He may be removed by impeachment on the charge that he has "wilfully violated this Constitution or has been guilty of gross misconduct" or medically on the grounds of physical or mental incapacity. In both cases the motion for removal must be brought by at least one-third of the total membership of the National Assembly and must be carried by a vote of three-fourths of the membership. In order to prevent frivolous or harassing attacks on the President, if the removal motion is supported by fewer than half the members then the original movers are automatically unseated. This penalty does not apply in case of a medical removal motion if the President has refused to submit to examination by a Medical Board defined in the constitution. If the President dissolves the National Assembly before the end of its term, his own term expires four months from the date of the dissolution. Thus the voters are called upon to resolve conflicts between the executive and the legislature.

Presidential (and all other) elections are conducted by an Election Commission composed of a permanent chief election commissioner aided by a High Court judge from each province, appointed *ad hoc* for each election. The right to vote in presidential and other elections is restricted constitutionally to the members of an electoral college, at least 40,000 in each province. The electors must be at least 25 years of age, and are in turn to be elected by adult suffrage. (The franchise is discussed further in the next section.) Presidential elections are to be held within four months before the end of a normal term and between two and four months after the date of a dissolution. A vacancy for any other reason is to be filled within three months. If the President has held office for more than eight continuous years, he is not eligible for reelection unless his candidature is approved by a secret ballot at a joint sitting of the two provincial assemblies (together with the National Assembly if it has not been dissolved). A further voice in choosing presidential candidates is given such a joint session in that by secret ballot it can decide which three of a numerous list of intending candidates (other than the incumbent) will be authorized to contest the election. There is no Vice-President; in the event of the absence of the President from the country or a vacancy in the office, the Speaker of the National Assembly acts as President (with certain limitations to his powers: e.g., he may not dissolve the National Assembly) until the incumbent returns from abroad or a new election is held.

The President is now head of the government as well as head of the state. Before 1958 the central authority was divided between the Prime Minister as head of government and the Governor-General/President as ostensibly a ceremonial figurehead in the British tradition. However, the relevant tradition in Pakistan was British Indian. The 1935 Act was framed with reference to the need for an independent executive, a Governor-General advised by ministers but with ultimate responsibilities of his own vis-à-vis the legislature. When the act was adapted for Pakistan in 1947, references to the discretionary powers of the Governor-General were eliminated, but the conventional notion of his exalted status remained. To this situation was added the unique identity of Qaid-i-Azam M. A. Jinnah, the unquestioned master of the Muslim League and of the leaders of Pakistan.

His ministers looked to him for guidance, and clearly he considered that he retained viceregal responsibilities under the 1935 Act. The three years of Nazimuddin's governor-generalship saw the initiative in the hands of the Prime Minister, suggesting that perhaps the normal pattern of cabinet government would be accepted. However, under Ghulam Mohammed the ascendancy of the Governor-General was restored. His successor, Iskandar Mirza, was also a man of authoritative temperament and a believer in seizing the initiative. Although he did not dominate his Prime Ministers, he refused to retreat into impotence and was continually accused of intriguing in party politics. Finally, rather than acquiesce in what he considered to be the dangerous game of the politicians, he used his position to overthrow the parliamentary order. When Mirza was ousted by Ayub, one of the new President's first actions was to abolish the office of Prime Minister, thus unifying central authority and responsibility within his own hands.

The President's council of ministers is in effect a return to a Governor-General's executive council. The President appoints ministers who serve at his pleasure, to assist him in the performance of his functions. They are not responsible to the National Assembly, and indeed according to the constitution as promulgated ministerial office is incompatible with membership of the Assembly. However, because in June 1962 members proved unwilling to give up their seats (and right to vote) in order to become ministers, the President used his powers under the transitional provisions (Article 224-3) to remove the incompatibility for a period of three years. Ministers in any case may attend and speak in the Assembly, as may the Attorney General. The constitution provides that for a period of twenty years the Defense Minister must be a retired officer of the rank of lieutenant general or its equivalent, unless the President himself has held such a rank. (In his first cabinet under the constitution President Ayub himself held the Defense portfolio.) Besides Defense there are ten other ministries: External Affairs, Finance, Commerce, Home and Kashmir Affairs, Industries and Natural Resources, Communications, Education and Information, Law and Parliamentary Affairs, Agriculture and Works, and Health, Labour, and Social Welfare. These ministries are divided into a total of seventeen divisions, and there are five divisions within the President's secretariat directly under his control (Cabinet, Establishment, Planning, Economic Affairs, and States and Frontier Regions). The President may appoint parliamentary secretaries from among the members of the National Assembly, one for each of the twenty-two divisions. It is to be expected that as before ministers and parliamentary secretaries will be appointed on a basis of provincial parity, and it seems likely that most ministers will be members of the Assembly.

The Central Legislature

The central legislature (no longer called a parliament) consists of the President and one house, the National Assembly. The constitution provides for 156 members elected in equal numbers from the two provinces, including three seats reserved for women from each province. The normal term of the Assembly is five years, but the first Assembly elected in 1962 is to serve for three years. Conduct of the elections, including the demarcation of constituencies, is the responsibility of the Election Commission. General elections are to be held within four months before the end of a normal term or within three months after a dissolution. Casual vacancies occurring within the last six months of an Assembly's term are not filled, but otherwise by-elections are conducted by the Election Commission. The reserved seats for women are filled by secret ballot of members of the provincial assemblies, grouped to form territorial zones (i.e., "constituencies"). A candidate for election must be a citizen of Pakistan, at least 25 years old, and not disqualified by the constitution or law. An individual may not be a candidate for more than one Assembly seat at one time: in other words, the old practice of multiple candidacies for "insurance" purposes is forbidden. If a member is elected to a provincial assembly, or is appointed as a governor or to any other disqualifying office, or is absent from the Assembly without leave for 30 (formerly 60) consecutive sitting days, his seat becomes vacant. In the 1962 legislative elections the electoral college was made up of the union councilors elected by adult suffrage in December 1959–January 1960. (See below, the section "Local Government.") However, many of the candidates spoke in favor of a widened franchise, and in July 1962 a Franchise Commission was appointed to consider possible changes. It seems likely, therefore, that the constitution will be amended and that the general elections in 1965 will see a return to adult suffrage.

The National Assembly is normally summoned, prorogued, and dissolved by the President. However, the Speaker may summon the Assembly at the request of at least one-third of the members, and only he can prorogue such a session. As an additional precaution, in case the office of President, Speaker, and Deputy Speakers are vacant the Chief Justice of the Supreme Court may summon the Assembly. The Assembly is required to meet at least once every six months. The President's power of dissolution is limited, as noted earlier, by the fact that dissolution requires him as well as the legislators to go before the voters. In addition, the Assembly cannot be dissolved within the last six months of its term of office or while a motion for removal of the President is being considered. In recognition of past Bengali dissatisfaction with the location of the national capital in West Pakistan, the constitution provides that Dacca shall be the principal seat of the National Assembly.

Formerly the general organization and procedure of the house followed the main lines of British practice, but the 1962 constitution has introduced changes. The Assembly elects a Speaker who remains in office (unless removed by a majority vote) until his successor is elected by the next Assembly after a general election. This eliminates former controversies over who shall preside at the first meeting of an Assembly and ensures that there will always be a Speaker to serve as acting President if need be. It has been established that the Speaker and the President should come from different provinces, and accordingly the first Speaker under the constitution is Tamizuddin Khan, who had been president of the first Constituent Assembly (1948–1954). To assist the Speaker there are two Deputy Speakers, senior and junior, one of whom according to seniority occupies the chair while the Speaker is absent or acts as Speaker if that office falls vacant. In case of vacancy in any of these offices a replacement must be chosen promptly. The rules of procedure are made by the Assembly itself, the members are guaranteed freedom of speech and vote, and the proceedings of the house may not be challenged in any court. The Speaker is required to "make such arrangements as are necessary" to instruct the members in their obligations as legislators, but there seems to be no way to force the members to attend such "classes." The Speaker is armed against unruly members with the power to refer a matter of "gross misconduct" to the Supreme Court; if the member is found guilty, he ceases to be a member of the Assembly.

Prior to independence the Indian central Assembly made use of standing committees to watch over the activities of government departments, and the practice was continued formally by the Constituent Assembly in its legislative capacity. However, these were more properly sleeping committees since they were habitually ignored by the ministers who felt their existence to be inconsistent with ministerial responsibility. Standing committees again assume importance as a link between the legislature and the administration with a return to an independent executive. There are now 19 committees, constituted on a basis of East-West parity; 16 are departmental, while the others deal with Unspecified Matters, Rules of Procedure and Privileges, and Public Accounts. The latter has ten members, the others six each. In addition, bills are normally referred to select committees for detailed consideration.

A bill, when presented to the house, may be debated on three occasions. First, there is a general discussion on the general principles of the measure. If approved and not referred to a select committee, the bill is discussed clause by clause, and detailed amendments may be moved. Finally, in amended form the measure is discussed once more and submitted for final approval.

When approved by the house a bill is presented to the President for his assent. Within thirty days he should either assent to the bill, declare that he withholds assent, or return the bill to the Assembly with a request for amendment. If he does none of these three, the bill becomes law automatically; there is no "pocket veto." The Assembly is competent to pass a rejected bill over the President's veto by a two-thirds majority, in which case he must either assent within ten days, dissolve the Assembly, or refer the bill to a referendum of the electoral college. If an absolute majority of the electors vote for the bill, it becomes law immediately. (Such a referendum may be used to resolve any question of conflict between the President and the Assembly.) Neither a general election nor a referendum would seem to be a desirable method of dealing with particular legislative issues, and undoubtedly the President will use the utmost of his influence to prevent the mobilization of a two-thirds majority against him. However, if he is unsuccessful, then the electors must have the last word.

Legislative control over the government has always centered upon the control of the purse. During the parliamentary era "budget time" was a period of great hazard for cabinets concerned with preserving their majorities. Since the cabinet need not now command a majority in order to remain in office, the constitution has severely limited the role of the Assembly in money matters. The annual budget statement must distinguish between expenditure charged on the Consolidated Fund (e.g., salaries of the President, ministers, judges, and so on), recurring expenditures (i.e., the normal expenditures of government), and new expenditure. The last category includes new items and increases of more than 10 per cent on the previous year's recurring expenditures. Whereas all of these categories may be discussed, only demands for grants (appropriations) for new expenditures must receive the assent of the Assembly. Further, the budget statement may include estimated expenditures in future years on particular long-term projects. Once the Assembly has approved such an estimate, the funds are committed and need not be approved again. Thus the government is assured of having in each fiscal year at least as much money as in the previous year and can plan for the future with confidence once a long-term project has been approved.

The procedure for the approval of the government's financial program provides the occasion for two general discussions of official policy as well as some probing into detail. There is a wide-ranging discussion immediately after the presentation of the budget. This is followed by individual demands for grants though parliamentary time never permits every item to be debated. Finally, when approval is being granted to tax measures another debate takes place on general or particular issues. The government need not fear either unwanted expenditures or alterations in the revenue, for neither demands for grants nor the "imposition, abolition, remission, alteration or regulation of any tax" may be moved without the recommendation of the President. Similar provisions existed in the previous constitution.

The public accounts of both the national and provincial governments are inspected by the Comptroller and Auditor-General, who is appointed by the President. Once appointed, he has the same security of tenure as a High Court judge. The national audit reports are submitted to the National Assembly and examined by the Public Accounts Committee. Examination at this stage is concerned more with financial regularity than with the wisdom of the policy that led to the expenditure.

A further method open to members of the National Assembly to criticize the actions of the government occurs at Question Time. As in Britain, a member may ask a particular minister for information on matters for which he is responsible. Notice must be given of such questions, but if the answer is not considered satisfactory, a "supplementary" question may be asked. The minister cannot, of course, be compelled to reply but naturally wishes to appear competent and well informed. Although the Assembly can no longer hope to overturn the government by a vote on a motion, the rules provide for adjournment motions and resolutions to express the feelings of members on the policies or action (or lack of it) of the government. Even an independent executive seeks to remain on good terms with the legislature, and therefore an unpopular minister might well find himself sacrificed in the interests of amity.

Emergency Provisions

Any government in Pakistan must bear in mind the fact that it is much closer to the threshold of disorder than is the case in longer-established democracies. The need to contemplate quick action in an emergency has therefore been recognized in the 1962 constitution as well as in its predecessors.

When the Assembly is not in session, the President has a general power to promulgate ordinances which have the same force as acts of the central legislature. An ordinance must be laid before the Assembly when it reconvenes and unless approved or disapproved sooner lapses six weeks from the day of the Assembly's meeting or six months after its promulgation, whichever is earlier.

There are further provisions to deal with a more serious emergency. "If the President is satisfied that a grave emergency exists a) in which Pakistan, or any part of Pakistan, is (or is in imminent danger of being) threatened by war or external aggression; or b) in which the security or economic life of Pakistan is threatened by internal disturbances beyond the power of a Provincial Government to control," he may issue a proclamation of emergency (Article 30). Such a proclamation must be laid before the Assembly, but for information only. During the emergency the President may promulgate ordinances even while the Assembly is in session, and the Assembly has no power to disapprove of them. Unless approved by the Assembly or repealed earlier by the President, emergency ordinances end with the emergency itself. Since there are no constitutionally guaranteed justiciable fundamental rights [1] and the central legislature retains overriding legislative powers in any case, Article 30 is a form of constitutional dictatorship under which all forms of political activity can be controlled by the central government and the liberty of the citizen can be restricted without means of redress. The courts would continue to function, and they and public opinion would pro-

---

[1] This question is discussed further in Chapter XVIII, in the section "A Free Society."

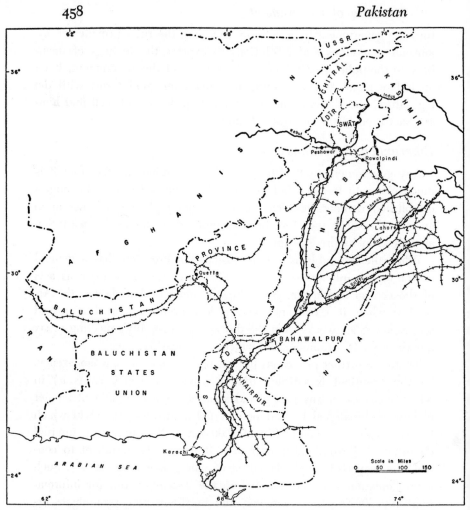

Map 8. West Pakistan. Note substantial difference of scale in Maps 8 and 9.

vide the only chance of exercising restraint upon a government that was prepared to abuse the emergency provisions.

The Provinces and Central-Provincial Relations

In 1947–1948 Pakistan contained eighteen "units" of government, each with some degree of local autonomy. There were the four governor's provinces (East Bengal, West Punjab, Sindh, and the North-West Frontier); each had a legislature and a full range of powers and responsibilities. Baluchistan was administered by a chief commissioner, and the four Baluchistan states were under the rule of local

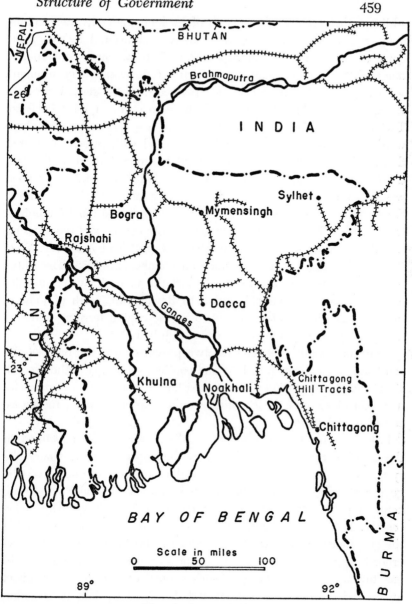

Map 9. East Pakistan.

princes, though they were soon to be merged into the Baluchistan States Union. There were four more small states under princely rule on the North-West Frontier. There were also the larger and more developed states of Bahawalpur and Khairpur. In 1948 the Karachi district was separated from Sindh to become the federal capital. In

addition, there remained a section of Kashmir under its own autonomous regime and extensive tribal areas administered by provincial
governments under federal supervision. The system of government
ranged from complete autocracy to full representative government.

East Pakistan has been a single province from the start. It was obvious, however, that changes would have to occur in West Pakistan.
The prospect of losing a separate identity was unpopular with those
who were in power in the smaller units and with those who feared
that local interests and traditions might be overwhelmed by the predominance of Punjab in any merger or federation. Little progress
was made in the first Constituent Assembly, and after its dissolution
the government proposed to amalgamate West Pakistan by administrative order. This move was blocked by the courts, and the measure
was therefore taken through the second Constituent Assembly. West
Pakistan became a single province on October 14, 1955. The status
of Karachi remained controversial until the martial law regime decided to move the national capital to Rawalpindi, north of Lahore,
in 1959. Karachi therefore ceased to be the capital territory and was
finally integrated into West Pakistan on July 1, 1961.

Parity or equality between the two provinces was the basis of the
constitutional settlement in 1956 and continues to underlie the present
structure. Disintegration of West Pakistan, as demanded by some elements in Sindh and the Frontier, would therefore reopen the entire
constitutional issue.

Provisions for the government of the provinces are contained in
the single constitution which covers the entire country. Under the
system of provincial autonomy prevailing from 1937 until 1958 the
governor under normal circumstances was a constitutional figurehead,
acting on the advice of ministers responsible to the provincial assembly. Martial law eliminated the legislature and ministers, making
the governor the sole executive. Under the 1962 constitution the governor is appointed by the President for an indefinite term and is subject to his direction. The governor's council of ministers is in effect
an executive council, appointed and dismissed by him in consultation with the President and not responsible to the provincial assembly.
Each provincial assembly has 155 members, including five reserved
seats for women, elected on the same basis as the National Assembly
and with analogous provisions in regard to Speaker and Deputy
Speakers, procedure, privileges, and so on.

Since the governor is responsible to the President whereas the provincial assembly is responsible to its electors, the possibilities for conflict between the two are obvious. If the assembly passes a bill over the governor's veto, he must either accept it or within ten days request the President to refer it to the National Assembly. If the National Assembly then approves the bill, it becomes law. However, if the National Assembly supports the governor in this or any other conflict referred to it, the governor with the concurrence of the President is empowered to dissolve the provincial assembly. If the electors then returned a new assembly hostile to the governor, the President presumably would have to yield and to find a governor and a policy more acceptable to the province.

A constant theme in the fifteen years since partition has been the demand for greater provincial autonomy. This has normally been countered by the central government's urging that limited resources and the risk of friction and instability make central control inevitable. It is hard to maintain that provincial self-government from 1947 to 1958 was an example of successful democracy and efficient administration. There was no one year during that period when at least one provincial government was not in danger of being overturned by intrigue within the ranks of its supporters.

To combat this political factionalism the central government made repeated use of its emergency powers. In the original form these had been designed to enable the Viceroy to suspend provincial autonomy in case local boycott or agitation by political parties made it impossible for the provisions of the constitution to be implemented. The centrally appointed governor then ruled as an agent of the central administration, exercising the powers of the legislature as well as of the cabinet. In Pakistan, before 1956, governor's rule was imposed on three of the four provinces for periods exceeding a year in each case. The primary reason in Punjab and Sindh was that no stable cabinet of politicians could be found. In East Bengal, in 1954, the newly elected United Front politicians were loudly demanding concessions that the center was not prepared to grant.

Because of provincial resentment—especially in East Pakistan— at central intervention, the 1956 constitution limited slightly the scope of the emergency power. Parliament was given the power to review a proclamation, which with approval could last a maximum of six months. During the life of the constitution governor's rule was invoked four times in East Pakistan and once in West Pakistan. The first two in East Pakistan during the summer of 1956 were to bridge a relatively minor constitutional hiatus, but the other two (in the spring and summer of 1958) were interventions by the central cabinet to preserve a provincial ministry whose support had evaporated. The suspension in West Pakistan in 1957 was for this same reason.

It is against this background of provincial instability and central intervention that the changes brought about by the present constitution are to be appreciated. Formerly authority within the provincial government was divided uneasily between responsible ministers and a governor who at any moment might be called upon to set them aside and rule alone. The result was suspicion and triangular intrigue involving the governor, provincial politicians, and central politicians and aimed at overthrowing or preserving the provincial ministry of the moment. Now, with the governor directly and continuously responsible to the President and the provincial cabinet independent of shifting majorities, both the former instability and the need for emergency powers of intervention have disappeared.

In short, formal provincial autonomy in the sense of a federal division of powers has now been eliminated, and the central-provincial relationship has returned roughly to the devolutionary pattern of the Government of India Act of 1919. The 1935 Act had introduced three separate lists of federal, provincial, and concurrent powers, and much controversy raged during the constitutional debates prior to 1956 over demands that the first be shortened and the second lengthened. In the end the 1956 constitution greatly extended the concurrent list, thus making the scope of provincial autonomy dependent on federal policy. The present constitution includes only a fairly short central list: defense, external affairs, external trade, national finance and economic planning, communications, nuclear energy, and gas and oil. All other matters are normally left to the provinces, except that the central legislature may make laws in the residuary field in the "national interest." The result is further to extend the areas of provincial jurisdiction, while permitting the center to take action wherever it seems necessary without the need to invoke "emergency" powers.

Actually provincial responsibilities have been greatly extended with effect from the fiscal year beginning July 1, 1962. The railway systems have been transferred to railway boards established by the provincial governments, separate East Pakistan and West Pakistan Industrial Development Corporations have succeeded the former central PIDC and have taken over the exploitation of mineral resources, and all major projects relating to health, education, food and agriculture, labor, social welfare, industries, and fuel and power have been transferred to the appropriate provincial agencies. Prior to the adoption of the constitution Water and Power Development Authorities and Agricultural Development Corporations had been established in the two provinces. All indications are that the central government intends to limit itself to planning and coordination functions for all matters other than those on the exclusive central list.

The granting of greater working autonomy to the provinces is reflected in financial arrangements under the constitution. Provincial tax resources remain much as before, the principal items being taxes on land and agricultural income, succession duties on agricultural land, and a variety of stamp duties and excises. Some provincial income is derived from rent and the profit on irrigation schemes and commercial activities. The remainder of provincial revenue comes from central grants and shared taxes. Shared taxes previously included income and sales taxes, jute export duties, and excises on tobacco, betel, and tea; to these the constitution adds corporation tax and cotton export duties. A Finance Commission including the central and provincial finance ministers is to make periodical recommendations concerning the distribution of shared taxes, the making of grants-in-aid by the center to the provinces, and the exercise of borrowing powers by all governments. An award of shared taxes made by a Finance Commission appointed in December 1961 considerably increased the provincial share over the 1952 settlement. Half the income and corporation taxes, 60 per cent of the excises on tea, tobacco, and betel, and 100 per cent of the jute and cotton export duties are allotted on the basis of population (i.e., a 50:44 ratio in favor of East Pakistan), and 60 per cent of the sales taxes are divided 70 per cent by population and 30 per cent by incidence.

The result of the award in 1962–1963 underlines the economic disparity between East and West Pakistan. With weightage in East Pakistan's favor, its share increased from Rs. 17.80 crores to Rs. 35.06 crores; its total budgeted revenue receipts were only Rs. 83.61 crores. West Pakistan's share increased from Rs. 26.66 crores to Rs. 34.76 crores, for a total revenue of Rs. 115.93 crores. On the capital side, the two provinces together received a total of Rs. 230 crores in development grants and loans from the central government. Still, West Pakistan's capital receipts and expenditures were almost twice those of East Pakistan.[2] In recognition of the seriousness of this economic gap, the constitution requires the Finance Commission to make a study before

[2] *Pakistan Times* (Lahore), June 13, 1962, pp. 6, 7. One crore equals 10 million rupees, roughly $2.1 million.

the end of each Five Year Plan period on the progress made and steps yet to be taken to remove regional disparities in per capita income. The commission's reports will be submitted to the National Assembly and to the provincial assemblies and will provide an opportunity for public and political pressures to be applied to the government. Given its overriding powers, the central government will not be able to avoid responsibility if all parts of the country are not enabled to share equitably in national progress.

Although the constitution makes no pretense at being federal, an amendment which would alter the limits of a province requires approval by a two-thirds majority of the provincial assembly before it can be introduced into the National Assembly. Amendments require approval by two-thirds of the National Assembly and must receive a three-fourths majority to pass over the President's veto. If this occurs, the President can either dissolve the Assembly or refer the matter to a referendum. In either case the ultimate decision lies with the elector.

Local Government

In some parts of the world local self-government has been credited with providing the foundation of democratic ideals and practices. The Indian subcontinent has always been a land of villages, and many local matters have always been decided by custom or group decision. In some parts of India and at certain periods the village panchayat or council of elders was a recognized institution of the local administration of justice. In the period preceding British rule the panchayat could not be regarded as a democratic system of local government. Appointed or hereditary local officeholders provided the link between the village and higher authority. The local sense of community has always been blurred by communal, caste, and other sectional loyalties.

During the period of British rule it was felt safest to begin experiments with representative government at the local level. Some kind of municipal body came into being quite early in the Presidency cities and most of the larger towns. Lord Ripon's Resolution of 1882 laid down the general principles of a system of local institutions in rural as well as urban areas. The details were left to each province to implement, but the main outline was similar in most cases. Municipal boards governed the towns and district and subdistrict boards were established for rural areas.

Unfortunately, especially after independence, local authorities in Pakistan found it difficult to concentrate on questions of sewers and streets and markets and public health. Instead of serving as local schools of responsible government, they became steppingstones to higher things and were exploited as tools in provincial and national party struggles. Elections were conducted in confusion and corruption, more so in West than in East Pakistan. By 1958 most of the district boards and many municipalities in West Pakistan were under suspension, and those that remained were superseded by the martial law authorities. The relatively more successful grass-roots union boards of East Pakistan were then used as prototypes for a new system of local government and administration evolved by President Ayub and embodied in the Basic Democracies Order of October 27, 1959.

The Basic Democracies system is a hierarchy of interlinked representative councils, inspired by the belief that to be effective democratic institutions must be on a scale comprehensible to the electorate called upon to work them. Direct election of councilors by adult suffrage therefore is limited to the primary units, the union councils with jurisdiction over some 10,000 people. The union councils elect their own chairmen, who are ex officio members of the council at the next level, the tehsil (in West Pakistan) or thana (in East Pakistan). The tehsil/thana council and the district and divisional councils (the two remaining tiers) also include among their members officials from the various government departments at the appropriate level. Although originally provision was made for the appointment of a limited proportion of additional nonofficials to the first two tiers to ensure the representation of minorities or special groups, the power was sparingly used. When the district and divisional councils were constituted in 1960, all the nonofficial members (at least half of whom had to be union chairmen) were appointed, but in June 1962 the Basic Democracies Order was amended to provide for indirect election. As the law now stands, the union chairmen in a district elect some of their number to the district council, and elected district councilors in each division elect some of their number to the divisional council. Since no more appointments of nonofficials are to be made at any level, in due course (all councils have a term of five years) the membership of the unions will be entirely elected and the membership of the other councils will be at least half indirectly elected and not more than half official.

The close links between the councils and the administration are indicative of the diverse responsibilities of the Basic Democracies. Union and district councils and town and municipal committees in urban areas have local government responsibilities, subject (as were previous local bodies) to fiscal controls and powers of direction and disallowance exercisable by the deputy commissioner, the commissioner, or, in a few instances, the provincial government. All councils are intended to help coordinate the activities of government departments, to supervise and guide any councils below them, and to sponsor and mobilize public support for development programs. Since tehsil/thana, district, and divisional councils are presided over by the executive officer responsible for the jurisdiction and include departmental officials as well as nonofficials some of whom sit on at least one other council, problems can be dealt with promptly by those most concerned. If lack of interest or noncooperation—either official or nonofficial—threatens to paralyze a council, a member who sits on a higher council can bring up the matter there for action. In order to minimize the obstructive effects of public apathy and official indifference, the government utilized the union elections of December 1959 and January 1960 and subsequent training programs for councilors and officials involved in the various tiers as part of a campaign to try to arouse a greater sense of civic responsibility and social service in the population generally.

In keeping with President Ayub's conviction that political parties were a major cause of the corruption and failure of the previous local government bodies, the Basic Democracy councils were originally intended to be nonpartisan. The first union elections were fought on the basis of personal reputation and influence, which meant in effect that tribal, caste, and clan affiliations were decisive. On the whole, the elected councilors were new to public life, largely middle and lower middle class, but they seem to have been unduly idealized as a new type of local leadership. Thus they were asked to participate in a "vote of confidence" in President Ayub on February 14, 1960, and under the constitution comprised the electoral college for the nonpartisan legislative elections of 1962. This electoral function is of course inconsistent with the belief that union councilors should be chosen only for their ability to serve local needs, and the revival of political parties inevitably involves them in national political considerations. The anticipated return to adult suffrage for national elections will end this direct involvement of councilors in provincial and national affairs, but it is most unlikely that parties will not make their presence felt in the various councils. Even under martial law factions and groups appeared in the municipal committees, and with the extension of the elected element to the district and divisional councils party identification would seem inevitable. In fact, party leadership may permit the strength developed in some councils to be communicated to others where vigorous local leadership has been lacking.

The Public Service

Contemporary Pakistan cannot be understood without giving due regard to the role of the bureaucracy. A special part of the present as of previous constitutions is devoted to this subject. It would be true to say that Pakistan could have survived since 1947 without politicians but that it would have collapsed without the civil service.

The Indian Civil Service, before 1947, was a remarkable organization. It was designed to keep the control of the essential parts of the machinery in the hands of those who would take orders from their duly constituted superiors and execute those orders without fear or favor. The ICS was the central service around which gravitated all other elements in the administration. Its membership never exceeded some 1,300 men. From 1870 some Indians had been included in its ranks, and by 1943 more than half were Indians. By a process of education, selection, training, and tradition these men had become assimilated to the pattern of the service as established by its British founders.

Not many of the ICS were Muslims, and a small number of these chose to serve in India rather than Pakistan. Approximately 100 Pakistani officials, with some British staff who agreed to remain, were thus the central core of the new administration. Recruitment has been proceeding year by year, but the total strength of the Civil Service of Pakistan (CSP) is still less than 400.

The CSP is fully conscious of the fact that it is an elite. Its recruiting announcement states: "The Civil Service of Pakistan is the successor in Pakistan of the Indian Civil Service, which was the most distinguished Civil Service in the world." [3] Its candidates are drawn from among the best university graduates. Those who are successful in meeting requirements go to the Civil Service Academy at Lahore for approximately two years' training, including a period of field training in East Pakistan. Formerly the second year was spent at Oxford

[3] Pakistan, Cabinet Secretariat, *Careers in the Pakistan Central Superior Services* (Karachi: Manager of Publications, 1954), p. 3.

or Cambridge, but in 1961 this was discontinued. The officer now can expect a tour of overseas training only after a few years in a district post.

CSP officers fill almost all senior administrative jobs at all levels of government, central, provincial, and in the districts. A limited number of senior posts in the provinces may be filled by promoted members of the provincial services, but most are reserved for the CSP provided that sufficient officers are available. Before independence the governorship of most provinces had been reserved for the ICS. In 1947 Pakistan appointed British ICS officers to three of the four provinces. Although the post of governor is not now reserved for CSP members, it is still possible for them to attain that position. A senior civil servant was governor of West Pakistan from August 1957 to April 1960.

In a district the CSP officer is the personification of the government. All government activities come under his command or supervision. Now known throughout the country as the deputy commissioner, he is in charge of the maintenance of law and order, revenue collection, and social services, presides over the district council, and is also a magistrate with substantial powers. There are 67 districts and tribal agencies in Pakistan, the largest of which contains over 7 million people. The deputy commissioner is responsible for all aspects of their well-being and acts as the agent of both central and provincial governments and as the supervisor of local authorities.

The districts are grouped into divisions, twelve in West Pakistan and four in East Pakistan, each under the control of a commissioner. The commissioner has general charge of the affairs of his division and presides over the divisional council. In West Pakistan, administrative reorganization during 1960–1962 has decentralized a number of departments—including public works, irrigation, education, health, and agriculture—to the divisional level or to groups of divisions. Their chiefs are subject to the policy control of a secretary in the provincial secretariat, who is a permanent official and usually a member of the CSP. Similar arrangements exist in the central government. Secretariat officials, provincial or central, are in most cases general administrators, although there is an increasing tendency to appoint "experts" to head technical departments. The role of the secretariat is to formulate policy alternatives for the minister in charge, while the executive departments, whether centralized or decentralized, implement the policy decided upon. A member of the CSP is liable to transfer to any assignment suitable to his rank in any department or any part of the country. However, because of the continuing shortage of officers from East Pakistan, most Bengalis serve in their home province. Tenure rules are designed to prevent overlong assignments to provincial or central headquarters and to ensure that the administrator is kept in contact with life in the districts.

This highly centralized structure of administrative services enables a few men in key positions to control the whole apparatus of government. The CSP, with the aid of the higher police officials who are also organized on a national basis, are able to govern the country by themselves—hence the ease with which the army and the permanent services took over the country in 1958. They had had the experience under British rule and again during the periods when self-government was suspended in the provinces. They form a small homogeneous group of high education, considerable administrative ability, and wide experience. In each capacity they tend to excel the elected politician, who is often tempted to resort to intrigue to lessen the dominant influence of the bureaucrat.

The martial law era was the apotheosis of bureaucratic authority. The army seized the reins of power from the hands of the politicians and challenged the bureaucracy to prove its worth. The public service was purged of those who had succumbed to the temptations of a corrupt political life, and in the process some fifteen members of the CSP itself were forced to retire. The administrative structure was reorganized, greater powers were delegated to district and divisional officials, and in the absence of the "third party"—the politicians—the wheels moved smoothly. However, President Ayub insisted that officialdom recognize that its purpose was to serve the people. The Basic Democracy councils were designed in part to bridge the gap between officials and people, and one of the most important tasks of the training program has been to convince officials at all levels that the people's views are important and that autocratic attitudes are no longer acceptable.

With the revival of political life under the constitution, the bureaucracy has come under fire again, for real as well as imagined faults. There are constitutional safeguards for the public services, to protect them from possible adverse interference by elected politicians. Under the constitution no disciplinary action may be taken against a public servant "by an authority subordinate to that by which he was appointed unless that subordinate authority has been expressly em-

powered to do so by an authority not so subordinate" (Article 177).
The words following "unless" have been added to the phrase appearing originally in the 1935 Act to restrict guarantees that are now considered excessive. In any disciplinary case the civil servant must be
given a chance to defend himself and is entitled to at least one appeal
against an adverse finding. The constitution also guarantees the status
of the central and provincial Public Service Commissions, which conduct recruitment and act as advisers on personnel policy and disciplinary cases. The members of the commissions are appointed by
the President or the governor concerned.

The Courts

The judiciary is part of the public services of Pakistan. In 1961
fifteen judges, including members of the Supreme Court, the High
Courts, and district courts, were members of the CSP. CSP officers are
generally allowed, after five years' service, to opt for judicial or executive appointments. If accepted for the judicial branch, the CSP
man—who will previously have tried cases as a magistrate—will serve
the rest of his career as a judge. Other judges are recruited from the
bar. Before being eligible for a High Court judgeship a person must
have practiced law for ten years, or have been a member of a civil
service for ten years and a district judge for three, or have held a
judicial office for ten years. Appointment to a High Court is made by
the President after consultation with the Chief Justice of the Supreme
Court, the governor of the province, and the Chief Justice of the High
Court concerned. To qualify for the Supreme Court, five years on a
High Court or fifteen years at the bar is required. The Chief Justice is
appointed by the President, and other members by the President after
consultation with the Chief Justice. All judges have security of tenure,
High Court judges retiring at 60 and Supreme Court judges retiring at
65. A judge of a High Court or of the Supreme Court can be removed
by the President only on the recommendation of the Supreme Judicial
Council, whose members are the three Chief Justices and the next two
senior judges of the Supreme Court.

The judiciary, especially in the higher branches, has been regarded
with pride and respect in Pakistan. Both Islamic and British traditions
lay stress on the rule of law. The system of jurisprudence owes more
to the common law than to the Sharia (the compilation of Islamic
law), despite the continuing demand for the codification and enforce-

ment of Islamic law. The legal system of British India consisted of the imposition of English procedures and prejudices on top of the complex mass of local rules and customs. The highest court of appeal until 1950 continued to be the Judicial Committee of the Privy Council. After that time Privy Council jurisdiction was exercised by the Federal Court, and the Supreme Court as the heir of the later continues to apply the broad principles of British legal interpretation. Under both the 1935 Act and the 1956 constitution the judiciary was charged with the interpretation of the constitution, and after 1956 with the enforcement of constitutionally defined fundamental rights. Under martial law the law as determined by the Supreme Court continued to be binding on all authorities, but the government had unlimited power to change the law if need be to undo the effect of a decision. The fundamental rights were no longer enforceable, but the Supreme Court and High Courts could and did issue writs such as habeas corpus and mandamus to protect rights under common or statutory law. During 1958–1962 the Chief Justice of the West Pakistan High Court became something of a popular hero for his fearless defense of personal rights and his public criticism of the regime's use of martial law regulations and military courts to bypass the normal procedures of the rule of law.

One of the most controversial aspects of the 1962 constitution as originally promulgated has been the curtailment of the powers of the courts vis-à-vis both the executive and the legislatures. The jurisdiction in the 1956 constitution to issue writs of habeas corpus, quo warranto, mandamus, and prohibition has been replaced by the power to issue orders that seem to have the same effect; however, since the traditional names are not used, the common law scope is avoided. Further, no order is issuable to a public servant in respect of his terms and conditions of service, except insofar as they are specified in the constitution, and no order of mandamus or prohibition is issuable that might injure the public interest. The intent and result of these provisions is to limit the former role of the courts in administrative matters and to prevent writ petitions from interrupting the essential activities of the government. The legislatures have been freed of judicial review, since no law can be challenged on the ground that the legislature that made it had no power to do so or on the ground that it disregards or violates any of the Principles of Law-Making in which fundamental rights are enumerated. In consequence, the role of the courts is now to interpret the law and to enforce rights under the law, but not to set limits to legislative action or to prevent the executive from implementing policies adopted by the legislature (as, for example, the land reform in East Pakistan was obstructed by litigation).

The Armed Forces

Until 1958 the military services in Pakistan remained scrupulously clear of involvement in politics. The heritage of the forces of British India was abstention from governmental affairs and support of the civil power in office. Pakistan received a share of the weapons and supplies of the former Indian forces, and a shattered military establishment. However, a large proportion of the fighting troops of the Indian army had been composed of Muslims from the Punjab and the Frontier. Muslims were less well represented in the technical branches and in the navy and air force, and Bengali Muslims practically unrepresented in the services. A number of British officers remained for years both in active commands and for training purposes while all the forces were being reconstructed and reorganized. Until the republic was proclaimed in 1956 the navy was the "senior service" as in Britain, but since then the army has held pride of place.

British influence is noticeable still in the character of the senior Pakistani commanders. They are nearly all men who received their training and early experience under British auspices. Some, like President Ayub Khan himself, are Sandhurst graduates. They are true professional soldiers in appearance and attitude of mind, and their principal concern with national politics has been the fear that political corruption might undermine the integrity of the forces. As a group they have favored any government that could make its will effective. In 1953 the army was called upon to use martial law to restore order in the Punjab,[4] and the experience was a vivid demonstration of the ability of the army to deal with the results of political ineptitude. In 1954 the army backed Ghulam Mohammed's new cabinet because the Governor-General seemed determined to deal firmly with the mess created by the politicians. However, at that time General Ayub refused to take complete power [5] and withdrew from the cabinet as soon as the new Assembly began to function. At the end of 1957 the

[4] Widespread rioting occurred in Lahore and elsewhere as the result of a campaign that combined religious and political features. The civil government lost control, and the army was called in. See Province of the Punjab, *Report of the Court of Inquiry . . . to Enquire into the Punjab Disturbances of 1953* (Lahore: Superintendent, Government Printing, 1954).

[5] See M. Ahmad, *My Chief* (Lahore: Longmans, Green, 1960), pp. 1–5.

economic situation in East Pakistan was so bad that the government turned to the army to stamp out smuggling. "Operation Closed Door" was briefly effective, until political influence brought it to an end. By October 1958, therefore, the army chiefs had become convinced that complete termination of the political regime was essential, in order to correct national ills before public despair spread to the ranks of the army. The imposition of martial law was therefore a matter of self-protection for the army, and as soon as the new regime was secure the military was returned to its proper defense functions.

Note: As this book went to press, the National Assembly was considering a government bill to amend the constitution in three principal respects: first, to describe Pakistan again as an "Islamic Republic" (cf. pp. 445–446); second, to transform the Principles of Law-Making into justiciable fundamental rights limiting the powers of the legislatures, and to extend the jurisdiction of the courts accordingly (cf. pp. 457, 471); third, to transfer the former "Principle of Law-Making" concerning the repugnancy of laws to Islam to the chapter on Principles of Policy, and to make appropriate changes in the functions of the Council of Islamic Ideology (cf. pp. 445–446). Controversy revolved around clauses safeguarding the martial law reforms by exempting from the effect of the fundamental rights all laws enacted between October 7, 1958, and the coming into force of the amendment.

On May 13, 1963, the President's effort to alter the constitution to permit ministers to retain their seats as members of an Assembly was declared unconstitutional by the Supreme Court, forcing a return to the original "separation of powers" conception of the constitution (cf. pp. 452, 498).

· XVII ·

The Political Process

IN the final stage before partition, Indian politics narrowed into a struggle between the Indian National Congress and the Muslim League, with the British government acting as referee and scapegoat. Other Indian parties and groups were forced aside or were compelled to merge with one of the main combatants. By 1946 the question "Should India be independent?" had been answered. The only issue remaining was whether there should be one or two successor governments.

The Muslim League was the party of Pakistan. Pakistan was the entire program of the Muslim League. Before 1947 an Indian living in the Punjab or East Bengal might be opposed to partition and the idea of a separate Muslim state. After 1947 such opposition amounted almost to treason. Those who believed that the Pakistan movement was mistaken had either to move to Indian soil or to hide their convictions as carefully as possible. Many of the leaders of anti-Pakistan parties went to India; such was the case of Kiran Sankar Roy, who had been chosen as the first leader of the Opposition in the Pakistan Constituent Assembly. Others—Abdul Ghaffar Khan, for example—were imprisoned or placed under official surveillance.

The months of rioting and bloodshed gave no time for the development of political opposition. The choice for the Hindu and the Sikh groups in West Pakistan was migration or death. When the turmoil subsided, the need for political representation of the non-Muslim was almost at an end in West Pakistan, and many of the leaders were missing from East Pakistan.

The Decline and Fall of the Muslim League

When Pakistan was created, Mr. Jinnah was the leader of the Muslim League. He became Governor-General and issued invitations to various individuals to join the cabinet. It was not a question of asking a party leader to form a cabinet of his own choosing. Liaqat Ali Khan had been Jinnah's principal lieutenant, and he and several other cabinet ministers were Muslim Leaguers of long standing. Others, such as Ghulam Mohammed, were included because of personal experience in administration rather than political leadership. The Muslim League was the progenitor of the state, and its function was to secure the stability of the new structure. There was little thought in 1947 of a struggle for political power within Pakistan.

The League had an overwhelming majority in the Constituent Assembly and all four provincial assemblies. The only organized party in opposition was the Pakistan National Congress, which was the successor in Pakistan to the Indian National Congress. Since it was composed almost entirely of Hindus from East Bengal, it could not hope to present itself as an alternative government in a predominantly Muslim country.

The Muslim League was the party of Pakistan—and of Jinnah. Political parties in India normally started at the top and later, if at all, achieved a broad popular base. This was especially true of the League. From its origin in 1906 until after the elections of 1937 it was composed mainly of the wealthy and the educated. It claimed to speak on behalf of the Muslim masses, but its composition was in no sense representative. When Mr. Jinnah returned from England in 1934, the League was little more than a name. He took charge of it, and within the party his authority was never seriously challenged. After the relatively poor showing in the 1937 election, Jinnah set to work to carry the League to the people. It was the case of a leader organizing a mass following, not that of a mass movement producing its own leaders.

The struggle for Pakistan required the submission of individual wills and ambitions to the overriding cause. There were many local leaders who faltered in this and either accepted office when Mr. Jinnah had decided to the contrary or cooperated with the Congress when Mr. Jinnah wished to oppose. They were expelled from the party and were supplanted by others more ready to obey the orders of their commander in chief.

In 1947 Pakistan was won, and within its boundaries the foes of the League were put to flight. The All-India Muslim League held its last meeting in December 1947 with Mr. Jinnah presiding. The Pakistan Muslim League then became its successor and proceeded to draw up a constitution. Under this constitution as amended up to 1956, the League consisted of the convention, the council, the Working Committee, and provincial, district, and city leagues. Membership in a primary league was open to a Muslim Pakistani, over 18 years of age, who was in agreement with the aims of the League and paid a triennial subscription of two annas ($.03).

The convention was an assembly of the members of the central and provincial League councils and was the ultimate authority within the party. No convention, however, was held up to 1958. Arrangements were made for a meeting in October 1954, but the political crisis of the dissolution of the Assembly forced a cancellation.

The League council was the principal controlling and policy-forming organ. It consisted of some 400 members—180 elected by each provincial council, League members of the National Assembly, party officeholders, and some nominated persons. The council was expected to meet at least twice a year, but in practice its sessions were less frequent. Meetings were summoned by the president, though any 75 members were entitled to demand a special session. The council elected the officers of the League and could amend the constitution. It had power to "affiliate, suspend, dissolve or disaffiliate a Provincial Muslim League." The council could delegate any of its functions to the Working Committee or to the president.

The office-bearers elected for three-year terms by the council were the president, the vice-president, the general secretary, the treasurer, and two joint secretaries. All these officers were members of the Working Committee, which also comprised not more than 22 members of the council nominated by the president. This committee had power to "control, direct and regulate all the activities of the various Provincial Leagues in consonance with the aims, objects, rules and declared policy of the Pakistan Muslim League." It could take disciplinary action against any individual member or constituent organization, subject to a right of appeal to the council.

An additional central organ of the League was the Parliamentary

Board elected by the council every three years. It consisted of 12 elected members (6 apiece from East and West Pakistan) and the League president as chairman. Its job was to select candidates for the central legislature and to supervise the provincial parliamentary boards when selecting provincial candidates. This process was known locally as allocating the party ticket and at times bore a marked resemblance to a competitive examination. The following announcement appeared in the press in 1951:

> The Central Parliamentary Board of the Pakistan Muslim League invites applications from persons wishing to seek election on the Muslim League ticket to the NWFP [North-West Frontier Province] Legislative Assembly in the forthcoming general elections.
>
> Applications should reach the Honorary Secretary of the NWFP Provincial Muslim League, Peshawar, by October 15 at the latest.
>
> Each application should be accompanied by a sum of Rs. 500 as application fee.
>
> In the case of applicants who fail to obtain the Muslim League ticket, three-fourths of the application fee will be returned, provided they fulfill the terms of the pledge [to be loyal to the successful candidate].[1]

In most democracies, politicians would agree—at least in theory—that party interests should never come before those of the state and its parliamentary institutions. Those countries that have recently attained independence have found it necessary to readjust their scale of loyalties. Before 1947 the state, for Indian Muslims, was British India, but the nation was the concept of Pakistan, as represented by the Muslim League. Support for the League was not a question of favoring the "ins" or the "outs" in the effort to install a new government for a term of office. The larger loyalty was to the League; the lesser, if any remained, was to the existing state. Some Pakistanis carried over this outlook into the age of independence. "I say to you," wrote Mr. Jinnah's sister, "support the Muslim League, because the League alone won Pakistan and can serve and consolidate Pakistan. . . . Don't oppose the League but come into it and remove its defects. If you destroy the League you destroy Pakistan."[2] The first Prime Minister, Liaqat Ali Khan, was making a similar point when he said: "So far as I am concerned, I had decided in the very beginning, and I reaffirm it today, that I have always considered myself as the Prime

[1] *Dawn* (Karachi), Oct. 3, 1951.
[2] *Pakistan Standard* (Karachi), Aug. 14, 1954.

Minister of the League. I never regarded myself as the Prime Minister chosen by the members of the Constituent Assembly." [3]

When Pakistan came into being, most of the senior leaders of the League became members of the various governments, and the role of the party receded into the background. Mr. Jinnah, while he lived, was the Great Leader in party matters as in all aspects of state policy. The party after its reorganization in 1948, however, chose Choudhry Khaliquzzaman as its organizer and, later, president. The party constitution of 1948 maintained the principle that the party should act as a watchdog over the central and provincial governments. Holders of party office were forbidden to hold cabinet posts, and members of the parliamentary boards were debarred from standing for election to the legislatures. The idea behind this arrangement was that the party could better represent the common people if its leaders were insulated against the temptations of power. Such a relationship was bound to lead to friction.

At the center Liaqat Ali Khan was strong enough to overcome any difficulties placed in his way, but there is no doubt that his position as a member but not the leader of his party's national organization was the cause of embarrassment. In the provinces the party machinery became the continuing source of opposition to the government. This led to prolonged instability in Sindh and the suspension of self-government in the Punjab in 1949.

The party constitution was amended in 1950, and the Prime Minister and the provincial chief ministers were chosen as party presidents. In the center, the change in the office of Prime Minister resulted in change of the party head. But the official appointment preceded the party election when Nazimuddin and then Mohammed Ali became Prime Minister—in this case there was a considerable interval when Nazimuddin, the dismissed minister, continued to be the titular head of the party which formed the government. The change when Chaudhri Mohamad Ali succeeded Mohammed Ali followed a different pattern. The Muslim League parliamentary party (members of the Assembly) elected Chaudhri Mohamad Ali, who then became Prime Minister. He was not a party politician by nature or experience, and he made no attempt to assume the presidency of the League. By this time the cabinet was a coalition, and he was able to balance its

---

[3] *Dawn*, Oct. 9, 1950. Still less, apparently, did Liaqat Ali regard himself as the Prime Minister chosen, according to the constitution, by the Governor-General.

sectional interests by maintaining a distance between himself and the League organization. In January 1956 the Prime Minister moved the nomination of Sardar Abdur Rab Nishtar as president, and at the same time the constitution was changed once more to separate the party leadership from the cabinet. Upon Nishtar's death in early 1958 he was succeeded by Khan Abdul Qaiyum Khan, former chief minister of the old Frontier Province.

The 1956 change in the party constitution resulted in a return to the earlier friction between the party leaders inside and outside the government. The Prime Minister was accused of disloyalty to his party. His reaction was sharp: "Let me make it clear that in any action that I have to take as Prime Minister I cannot be bound by a resolution of any political party. I have to do what I consider to be right under the constitution, and for that I am responsible to the Cabinet and to the Parliament." [4] Four months later Chaudhri Mohamad Ali resigned as Prime Minister and as a member of the League. He complained with some bitterness that the party had rendered his position untenable.[5] The League was not included in the following government, and the question of the relations between this party and the administration did not rise again until I. I. Chundrigar became Prime Minister in October 1957.

In the provincial Muslim Leagues the conflict between government and party was repeated, but the level of rivalry and intrigue was more intense. Between 1947 and 1955 there were seven ministries in Sindh and four in the Punjab, and each province suffered a prolonged suspension of self-government. Each of these ministries was, in name, a government of the Muslim League, and the party had at all times an immense majority in the legislatures. The size of the majority had much to do with the dissension within the party. When there is no fear that a strong opposition may overthrow the government, political loyalty gives way to individual maneuver. It would be true to say that no legislative session passed in these two provinces without some serious attempt to undermine the administration. Each government protected itself after its own fashion with carefully distributed favors for present or potential supporters and tangible signs of disapproval toward those who contemplated mutiny.

To judge by the wording of the League constitutions, the presi-

---

[4] *Pakistan Observer* (Dacca), May 15, 1956. This statement is in marked contrast with that of Liaqat Ali, six years previously.

[5] *Dawn*, Sept. 9, 1956.

dents, both central and provincial, should have had little trouble in dominating the party. Each appointed the majority of the members of his Working Committee, and the unwieldy councils were seldom in session. But this is to ignore the real nature of Pakistani political parties during the parliamentary era. (The situation does not seem greatly different in the period since the ending of martial law.) Political activity usually began with a few men of position and influence in a community. These might be landlords, businessmen, hereditary religious leaders, or simply young lawyers with a talent for oratory. The next step was to find a small nucleus of supporters and, if the would-be politician lacked money, a patron. Local politics became a struggle for predominance among groups of such men; provincial politics merely increased the scale of operations. Thus a few-score prominent men, each with a retinue of political liverymen, formed changing patterns of alliances to obtain and hold power. The ordinary member of the party—the two-anna man—was enrolled largely to give voting support to a particular local leader. It was often hard to join such a party since the officeholders made sure that prospective members were "sound" before allowing them to obtain enrollment forms.

There is nothing novel or improper in the idea that a party should be a tactical alliance for achieving power. What in the past distinguished the parties in Pakistan, especially the Muslim League, was the speed with which the alliances were made and dissolved. This was partly caused by the absence of a genuine opposition, though the tendency to dissolve into fragments persisted even after the emergence of large opposition groups. It was also due to the absence of any clear division of political forces by long tradition or by differences on major policies.

Before 1947 the policy of the Muslim League could be summed up in one word—Pakistan. The new state could be portrayed as all things to all men. And the struggle for Pakistan was a valid reason for postponing or eliminating all personal or sectional differences. Once the state was accomplished, the first tasks of the government were so clear and urgent that there could be little room for dispute except as to the appointments to office. All were agreed that Mr. Jinnah's leadership was beyond question, and some part of his political mantle fell on the shoulders of Liaqat Ali Khan.

The Muslim League was in power at all levels of government from 1947 to 1954. Nationally there was no call to face the prospect of a general election until 1958. Each of the four provinces, however, conducted one general election on the basis of an adult franchise, before the proclamation of the 1956 constitution. These elections were held in the Punjab and the North-West Frontier Province in 1951 and in Sindh in 1953. In each case members of the League won an overwhelming proportion of the seats, though a large number of independent candidates served to divide the popular vote. The League secured not less than 80 per cent of the seats in each province.

The façade of party unity was thus preserved, and the impression of public support was not seriously challenged. The real opposition was to be found within the ranks of the League, although in a few instances prominent individuals had taken their followers into opposition. Thus the main opposition party in the Punjab elections was led by the deposed chief minister, the Khan of Mamdot. In Sindh one deposed chief minister led an opposition group while another continued to lay claim to be the true head of the provincial Muslim League. The situation was confused, and the choice open to the voter was not very wide.

The electorate in Pakistan had no previous experience of an adult suffrage election. Unfortunately the examples of 1951–1953 could not be looked upon as a lesson in democratic procedures. An official inquiry reported: "It was widely and persistently complained that these elections were a farce, a mockery and a fraud upon the electorate." [6] H. S. Suhrawardy, then in opposition, used even stronger language: "The elections [in the Punjab] were a farce, intimidation and coercion, fraud and manipulation of ballot papers and ballot boxes were practised on an unprecedented scale." [7]

The Politics of East Pakistan

What has been said in the preceding paragraphs applies primarily to West Pakistan. Until 1954 East Bengal was politically quiescent. There were two chief ministers, Nazimuddin, who departed to take high office in Karachi, and his successor, Nurul Amin. There seemed to be no plots and counterplots, and the outward unity of the provincial Muslim League was unbroken. But the provincial government was strangely reluctant to contest by-elections or to dissolve the legislative assembly. The members of the legislature had been chosen be-

[6] Electoral Reforms Commission, Report, in *Gazette of Pakistan, Extraordinary,* April 24, 1956, p. 922. It should be noted that these elections were held before the establishment of the Election Commission.

[7] H. S. Suhrawardy, *Address to the Nation* (Lahore, n.d.), delivered at Dacca, May 8, 1953, pp. 6–7.

fore partition to sit in the assembly of undivided Bengal. Their term of office, however, was deemed to begin from the date of the first meeting after independence, in March 1948. Five years later the government hoped shortly to have a new constitution, and the life of the provincial house was extended until March 1954. The constitution was not adopted, and the election was finally held under the amended provisions of the Government of India Act.

Although the provincial government seemed secure, it had become clear that major differences had arisen between East Bengal and the central government. The basic grievance felt by the Bengalis has been a feeling that they were regarded as inferior by the rulers of West Pakistan.

Sir, I actually started yesterday and said that the attitude of the Muslim League coterie here was of contempt towards the East Bengal, towards its culture, its language, its literature and everything concerning East Bengal. . . . In fact, Sir, I tell you that far from considering East Bengal as an equal partner, the leaders of the Muslim League thought that we were a Subject race and they belonged to race of Conquerors.[8]

East Pakistan contains more than half the population of the whole country, but it is poorer and in 1947 was almost totally lacking in industry. Many Bengalis feel that a primary charge upon the national government should be the accelerated development of the east wing to the point where it possesses standards equivalent to the west. The central authorities, on the other hand, have often insisted that the utmost use of existing resources must be made and that the west is better suited for industrial development. This divergence of view has led to a series of requests by East Pakistan, many of which have not been met by the national government. The Bengalis have then proceeded to ask for greater decentralization to provide them with the authority and the resources to do for themselves what Karachi is unwilling to perform. To some extent this demand has been met in the 1962 constitution.

During the discussion of the 1956 constitution the members from Bengal pressed hard, with partial success, for increased authority for their province. They also fought vigorously for a distribution of seats in the national legislature that would not deprive them of the benefits of their numerical majority. A number of complex formulas were considered when it was expected that there would be four provinces and

---

[8] Constituent Assembly of Pakistan, *Debates*, I, 530, Sept. 7, 1955. The speaker was Ataur Rahman Khan, who was to become chief minister of East Pakistan.

two houses of the legislature. Finally, with two provinces and one house, the equal division of seats was accepted.

The issue which caused the greatest anger and resentment in East Bengal was that of the national language. Nearly 55 per cent of the total population speaks Bengali, whereas 28 per cent speak Punjabi and 7 per cent Urdu.[9] Bengali employs a script that is derived from Sanskrit, and Urdu and Punjabi use the Persian script. The principal language of the Indian Muslims before 1947 was Urdu, which can be understood over the greater part of the subcontinent. The West Pakistanis suspected Bengali because it forms a link with West Bengal (in India) and because much Bengali culture bears strong influences of Hinduism. Some of the advocates of Urdu as the main national language managed to convey the impression that the defense of Bengali was both un-Islamic and opposed to the interests of national unity.

It was made clear from the start that the national leaders intended to insist on Urdu as the state language. Mr. Jinnah made a speech in the capital of East Bengal which could leave no doubt concerning his own view. "But let me make it very clear to you that the State Language of Pakistan is going to be URDU and no other language. Anyone who tries to mislead you is really the enemy of Pakistan. Without one State Language, no nation can remain tied up solidly together and function."[10] When the first constitutional proposals were published, they contained the flat recommendation, "Urdu should be the national language of the State."

The subordination of Bengali was never acceptable to the people of East Pakistan. They suffered from many other disadvantages, and if this proposal were adopted, they would be separated further from influence and power by the barrier of language. The students of Dacca University protested violently against the imposition of Urdu, and in the resulting riot some of the demonstrators were killed. The issue had now become a sacred cause. After four years of growing bitterness the central leaders gave way and admitted equal status for Urdu and Bengali. The 1962 constitution recognizes this concession and provides further that English may be used for official purposes at least until 1972.

The national capital—formerly Karachi but now Rawalpindi—is more than a thousand miles from East Pakistan. The central government is therefore remote from the problems and feelings of Bengal. It

[9] Figures are according to the 1951 census. Language data from the 1961 census are not yet available.

[10] *Quaid-e-Azam Speaks* (Karachi: Pak Publicity, 1950), p. 133.

has recruited its civil servants and armed forces mainly from the west, although genuine attempts are being made to increase the proportion of Bengalis. Those Bengalis who go to the national capital as politicians or government employees tend to find either that they remain outsiders with no real influence or that they have been absorbed into the cultural pattern of West Pakistan and cease to act and feel as Bengalis.

Throughout this period of mounting Bengali irritation the position of the government of East Bengal was not easy. As a Muslim League administration it could not afford to quarrel openly with the national leadership. Yet its own sympathies were largely on the side of those who wanted increased autonomy and more consideration from West Pakistan and the central government.

In spite of known resentment against the center, informed observers still expected the Muslim League to win a majority in the new assembly, although it was conceded that a much stronger opposition was to be expected. The results of the election left no doubt as to the feelings of the electorate. Out of 309 seats the Muslim League secured 10, and the main coalition of opposing parties—the United Front—obtained more than 230. The monopoly of the Muslim League had been broken, and within three years that party was to find itself excluded from office in both provinces and at the center.

The Awami League

The largest single component of the United Front was the Awami (People's) League. This party had its origins in the period from 1949 to 1950 and was formed by grouping together a number of political leaders who had quarreled with the leaders of the Muslim League. In the North-West Frontier Province the Pir of Manki Sharif was forced out of the League and moved into opposition. In East Bengal, Maulana Bhashani, a former president of the Assam Muslim League, felt that a new party was needed to speak for the common people. In the Punjab the Khan of Mamdot was deposed as chief minister in 1949 owing to rivalry within the Muslim League. He organized his followers as the Jinnah Muslim League. Shortly afterward, he consolidated his group with the Awami League under the title Jinnah Awami Muslim League, and the new party gained 29 seats at the provincial elections.[11]

[11] In 1953 Mamdot and his adherents rejoined the Muslim League. In 1956 he transferred to the Republican Party.

The task of organizing these small opposition groups into a national party fell to H. S. Suhrawardy. He too had been a Muslim Leaguer and had been chief minister of undivided Bengal in the days immediately before partition, when he made an unsuccessful attempt to secure a united independent Bengal based on Hindu-Muslim cooperation. In 1947 he decided to remain in Calcutta working for communal peace between the Muslims and the Hindu majority in West Bengal. He had been elected to the first Constituent Assembly and even while living in India traveled to Karachi to participate in its sessions. In 1948, however, he was deprived of his seat on the ground of nonresidence in Pakistan. About a year later he moved to Pakistan and began to rebuild his political influence.

H. S. Suhrawardy is a professional politician with long experience as a legislator and cabinet officer during the period of British rule. He completed his education at Oxford and was trained for the bar. He is a fluent and persuasive speaker though not a great orator. Like many politicians he is noticeably more radical in his ideas and attitudes when in opposition. In office he has demonstrated a remarkable ability to maintain support and to outmaneuver his opponents.

The Awami League held a convention in Lahore in 1952. Its constitution was similar to that of the Muslim League, with a convention, council, and Working Committee, and Suhrawardy was convener. The manifesto of the party, adopted at that time, was filled with high-sounding phrases, but few of them had any concrete significance. The following proposal was advanced in the field of economic policy: "The State should be self-sufficient and even surplus in food and national requirements; it must be in a position to export finished products; the agriculturists must be assured a reasonable price for their produce, and the labourers a reasonable wage. The cost of living must be proportionate to the income."

During the period of its consolidation and growth the Awami League bore no responsibility for administration. Since it was also virtually excluded from the legislatures, it could hardly be called upon to bear the duties of a responsible opposition. It was able, therefore, to take advantage of almost all the feelings of discontent in any part of the country. In East Pakistan its supporters were mainly young men who had been no more than students during the struggle for Pakistan. Their general outlook was radical in economic and social matters, and they were ardent supporters of the demand for autonomy for East Bengal. The principal leader of this group was Ataur Rahman Khan.

A somewhat different style of politics, though with the same ends, was provided by Maulana Bhashani. The Maulana [12] was a born malcontent and a fanatic with millennial visions of what might be accomplished if only the rule of the saints could be established. He lived an austere personal life and attacked wealth and privilege. When the Awami League formed a government, he preferred to remain outside, acting as spokesman for the ordinary people. He had little knowledge of the problems of administration, finance, or international affairs. His appeal was less to the students of the colleges, who played such a prominent part in Bengali politics, than to the peasants in the villages.

Suhrawardy as national leader operated mainly from West Pakistan and established himself as a potential alternative Prime Minister. He stressed the need for a strong opposition.

Next, we believe that an opposition party is necessary for the proper functioning of democracy, this is the only influence that can keep the rulers in check and at work, and can create public opinion. The Muslim League, on the other hand, labels opposition as disruption, demands that there shall be no parties other than itself, and all other parties must be crushed out of existence. [13]

The first major chance to move toward power came with the East Bengal election of 1954. Late in the previous year the Awami League entered an alliance (the United Front) with the Krishak Sramik Party and some lesser groups. They agreed to sponsor a combined list of candidates against the Muslim League. Local committees chose the individual candidates, and it was often uncertain which section of the United Front claimed their primary allegiance. This prepared the way for prolonged confusion at a later stage over claims to predominance.

The United Front proclaimed a manifesto known as the Twenty-one Points. It contrived to promise something for everyone. It announced a firm adherence to Islam and urged that no laws should be passed contrary to the requirements of the faith. *Zamindari* (landlord system) was to be abolished without compensation, and the land was to be distributed to the peasants. The crucial item was point 19, the demand for provincial autonomy:

[12] Maulana is a religious title, the nearest Western equivalent of which might be doctor of theology.
[13] Suhrawardy, *Address to the Nation*, pp. 6–7.

Secure all subjects, including residuary powers, except Defence, Foreign Affairs and currency, for East Bengal, which shall be fully autonomous and sovereign as envisaged in the historic Lahore Resolution, and establish Naval Headquarters and ordinance factory in East Bengal so as to make it militarily self-sufficient.

When the elections were held, the United Front carried almost every seat it contested and emerged with a majority as great as that previously enjoyed by the Muslim League. A new ministry was appointed under the leader of the Krishak Sramik Party. The elections and their results had caused some commotion throughout the province. This erupted in two major riots in which hundreds of lives were lost. The central government had been alarmed by the program of the Front and by the character of some of its leaders. The riots provided the pretext for the proclamation of a state of emergency, and self-government was suspended before the new assembly had a chance to meet.

When the central cabinet was reorganized after the dissolution of the Constituent Assembly, Suhrawardy became Minister of Law. He was the only representative of the Awami League in a ministry still dominated by the Muslim League, and he found himself somewhat isolated. In the middle of 1955 he left the cabinet and became leader of the Opposition in the second Constituent Assembly. At the same time self-government was restored in East Bengal, but the Awami League was excluded from the new United Front ministry and formed the Opposition there also.

The next shift in the balance of political forces occurred a year later, after the 1956 constitution had come into operation. Chaudhri Mohamad Ali resigned as Prime Minister, and Suhrawardy formed a coalition government in cooperation with the Republican Party. The coalition split in October 1957, but after the brief interlude of the Chundrigar Muslim League ministry (October–December) a Republican-led coalition was formed with Awami support, which lasted until martial law was imposed.

In East Pakistan the United Front ministry, unable to rally a majority, was replaced in September 1956 by the Awami League, with some minority support. This ministry, under Ataur Rahman Khan, managed to cling to office with the assistance of the Awami-supported central government until October 1958 (including an interlude of governor's rule from June to August 1958).

The Krishak Sramik Party

The Krishak Sramik (Peasants and Workers) Party consisted of the personal following of the late A. K. Fazlul Huq. Fazlul Huq was a leading and highly controversial figure in the politics of Bengal for more than half a century. He participated in the founding of the Muslim League, and his subsequent career carried him in and out of that organization on several occasions. He was the mover of the Lahore Resolution in 1940. In 1937 he led his own Krishak Proja Party and secured a large number of seats in the Bengal Assembly. He became chief minister and held office for six years. After partition he accepted the office of advocate-general for East Bengal. In 1953 he broke with the Muslim League government and began to form a party to contest the forthcoming provincial election.

Fazlul Huq was a magnificent orator in Bengali, and though his technique did not appeal to the sophisticated, he had a mass following throughout his province. His main argument during the campaign was the demand for a greater measure of autonomy for East Bengal. He was the leading figure in the United Front, and there can be no doubt that his name and personal influence did much to swell the total vote against the Muslim League. After the March 1954 victory he became chief minister during the six weeks before governor's rule was proclaimed. His visit to Calcutta, while in office, was the occasion for a series of press reports indicating that he wanted complete independence for East Bengal and closer ties with West Bengal. The central government, after his dismissal, described him as a "self-confessed traitor to Pakistan." When the second Constituent Assembly was formed in 1955, however, the national government needed his assistance, and he entered the cabinet. At the same time his principal lieutenant became chief minister of East Bengal with a ministry composed mainly of the Krishak Sramik Party but with support from the non-Muslims and others. A few months later Fazlul Huq became governor of East Pakistan, a post that he continued to hold even after his party was replaced as the provincial government by the Awami League. He was dismissed by the central government in April 1958 after he had attempted to reinstall a KSP ministry in office by dismissing his Awami League cabinet.

During the summer of 1958 the KSP–Awami League struggle for ascendancy became extremely bitter. When neither side seemed able to maintain a majority, a two-month period of governor's rule was imposed. By the time the Awami League resumed office in late August, the Speaker and Deputy Speaker had become involved in the conflict. When the provincial assembly met at the end of September, the ministry succeeded in forcibly ousting the Speaker from office, infuriating the KSP opposition. A few days later the assembly met again with the Deputy Speaker in the chair. A riot broke out, the Deputy Speaker was fatally injured by something thrown by a member, and the house had to be cleared by the police. Parliamentary government was discredited, and martial law soon followed.

Non-Muslim Parties

In the various elections held before 1956 the non-Muslims voted in separate constituencies for candidates drawn from their own community. Although the Christians, Parsis, and Buddhists were represented at the center or in the provinces, the two major groups of non-Muslims were the Hindus and the scheduled-caste Hindus. The Pakistan National Congress was the principal representative of the upper-caste Hindus and had a substantial following among the scheduled (low) castes. The Congress was the official opposition in the first Constituent Assembly and in the assembly of East Bengal until 1954. Being confined to the Hindu community,[14] it could never hope to become a government with a majority. Its main role was therefore that of defender of minority rights and interests. It lay continually under the suspicion of disloyalty. Many of its members had opposed the creation of Pakistan and maintained friendly contacts with members of the Indian Congress across the border. Naturally the Congressmen could not be expected to have precisely the same feelings toward Pakistan as those of the Muslim nationalists.

The Congress Party fought on two main issues. First, it opposed the proclamation of an Islamic state and all features in the constitution that conferred a special status on one faith. Second, it argued vehemently against the continuation of the system of separate electorates, whereby the minorities were penned politically into little boxes and prevented from exercising effective influence on matters of wider concern. The Muslim League was pledged to the concept of two separate nations, the Muslim and the Hindu. It had fought for separate electorates to enhance its own position as a minority community. Both by tradition and by its line of reasoning the League wished to con-

[14] The Congress was open to members of all communities, but for obvious reasons very few Muslims in Pakistan wished to be connected with it.

tinue separate electorates to preserve the purity of Muslim politics and to ensure proportional representation of Hindus in the legislatures. The Awami League came round to the support of joint electorates, and in 1956–1957 the law was altered to provide simple territorial constituencies for the country as a whole.

The Scheduled Castes Federation also was the successor of an All-India organization. The scheduled castes had always had some doubts about their position under a predominantly caste Hindu administration. The Federation therefore pressed for special seats in the legislatures and for special quotas of jobs in the public services. The Muslim League had used members of the scheduled castes to substantiate their claim that the old Indian National Congress was primarily a body of upper-caste Hindus. Thus a scheduled-caste Hindu was named by the League to the interim government of 1946–1947 and was continued in cabinet office in Pakistan after partition. The community has often been divided in its political view, and members in the legislatures at times followed the lead of the Muslim League, the Awami League, the Krishak Sramik Party, and the Congress. The result has been that as a group the scheduled castes have had little political weight. The Federation, the largest political body representing the scheduled castes, obtained 27 seats (out of 309) in East Bengal and 3 (out of 80) in the second Constituent Assembly.

The Republican Party

The Muslim League won large majorities in all three provinces of West Pakistan, but these gave no stability since they were divided into a dozen major factions which struggled ceaselessly for power. One of the reasons for amalgamating the provinces in 1955 was the hope that, on a larger stage, the scope for petty conflicts would be lessened. The government of West Pakistan was appointed before the legislature came into being. M. A. Gurmani became governor, and Dr. Khan Sahib chief minister. Dr. Khan had been chief minister of the North-West Frontier Province immediately before partition. He was then a member of the Congress Party and had opposed the creation of Pakistan; the governor dismissed him a week after the new state came into existence. He was invited to join the emergency central cabinet of October 1954 as a sign that old quarrels had been forgotten and as an indication that in a moment of crisis all patriotic citizens should be prepared to serve the state.

The West Pakistan Assembly was chosen in January 1956 by election by the members of the old provincial assemblies. As was to be expected, a majority of its members belonged to the Muslim League. This made Dr. Khan Sahib's position somewhat equivocal. He had no party of his own and was unwilling to join the League. A large section of the League elected a party leader and demanded that he be summoned to form a government as the head of the largest party in the assembly. The chief minister responded by dismissing those members of his cabinet who were not prepared to be loyal to him. In April 1956 Dr. Khan Sahib announced the formation of the Republican Party. He was able to hold a narrow majority in the assembly, and most of the Muslim League members of the National Assembly joined the Republicans. In September the Muslim League members were dropped from the central cabinet, which was reconstituted under Suhrawardy with support from the Awami League, the Republicans, and some non-Muslims. The Republican majority in West Pakistan held through two short sessions of the provincial assembly, but the party was divided on the issue of separate or joint electorates. In March 1957, when the situation in the assembly was highly confused, self-government was suspended and the governor assumed power under Article 193. In July, Dr. Khan Sahib resigned as leader and was replaced by Sardar Abdur Rashid,[15] who was then called on to form a cabinet. He was succeeded in the spring of 1958 by M. A. Qizilbash, who retained office until martial law was instituted.

The Republican Party came into being solely because of the splits within the Muslim League. It was formed largely to prevent certain Muslim Leaguers, notably M. A. Khuhro and M. M. Daultana,[16] from taking power. Apart from personal loyalties and enmities and a desire to remain in office, there was little in common among the Republicans. In order to adopt a constitution and to work out a policy, the party held a convention in Lahore in September 1956. The constitution was basically similar to that of the Muslim League with a leader, national council, national convention, and provincial and local units. The only item of its program which was specific was related to the two-nation theory and its consequences:

To assert that there is more than one nation in Pakistan is to assert that some citizens of Pakistan are Pakistani nationals and some are not, that

[15] Rashid had been chief minister of the Frontier Province in 1953–1955 and had served in Dr. Khan's cabinet.

[16] M. A. Khuhro had been chief minister of Sindh, and Daultana chief minister of the Punjab. Both were in Dr. Khan's cabinet until April 1956.

Pakistan is the national homeland only of some of her citizens and not of all. To assert this is to free some of our nationals from the demands of allegiance to the State and loyalty to the country; it is to invite disloyalty and disruption.

Apart from this item, the other aims of the party were pious aspirations rather than proposals that could be implemented by an administration. Section headings included "the expedition of progress," "realisation of goodness," "disbursement of happiness," and "the consolidation of peace."

The National Awami Party

The parties described above have been based on personal and local factors rather than ideology. The Awami League, to a certain extent, developed a degree of responsiveness to the views of its ordinary members, but its policy was made mainly by a handful of leaders. In all cases it would be true to say that the leaders built the party rather than that the party produced its leaders. Fixed principles were normally subordinated to personal maneuvers to obtain power.

The National Awami Party (NAP) was, in this sense, also an association of leading figures, backed by their personal followings. But it also possessed a number of ill-assorted ideologies. This party was a union of malcontents, men who, by temperament, found themselves in opposition under any government. The party was formed in July 1957 as the result of an agreement between the leaders of eight minor groups.

In West Pakistan, for example, the Azad (Free) Pakistan Party had achieved a considerable measure of publicity largely owing to the character and position of its leader, the late Mian Iftikharuddin.[17] He was a minister in the Muslim League government of the Punjab immediately following partition, but resigned because that government was unwilling to adopt more radical solutions to social problems. His politics were of the extreme left, and he was often called a fellow traveler. In foreign affairs he was a principal critic of Pakistan's ties with the Commonwealth and the United States.

Other segments of the NAP were led by G. M. Syed and Abdul Ghaffar Khan. Syed was a major political figure in Sindh before partition and had been a member of both the Congress and the Muslim

[17] Iftikharuddin was a wealthy man and the proprietor of a leading newspaper, the *Pakistan Times,* until it was seized by the martial law authorities in 1959. He died in 1962.

League. He was a strong advocate of Sindhi interests and opposed the amalgamation of the provinces. Abdul Ghaffar Khan, the brother of Dr. Khan Sahib, used to be called the Frontier Gandhi. He was a member of the first Constituent Assembly, but for most of its duration he was in prison on security grounds. He wanted autonomy for the Pathan people of the frontier and also opposed the creation of West Pakistan.

Such minor parties in West Pakistan were mostly local organizations, but they were agreed in demanding the redivision of the province into linguistic units and radical social reforms. In 1956 they combined to form the Pakistan National Party. At first they supported Dr. Khan Sahib in the provincial assembly. Failing to obtain any reconsideration of the unification scheme, they withdrew their assistance. This led to the suspension of self-government in 1957.

In East Pakistan the National Awami Party had two main components. The Ganatantri Dal (People's Party) was formed in 1953. Its leadership was mainly Muslim, but it admitted others on equal terms and contested some non-Muslim seats. Its outlook was secular and socialist. There was also Maulana Bhashani, one of the founders of the Awami League. He was opposed to his party on issues of internal social reforms and on the question of Pakistan's alliances with the Western powers.

Bhashani attempted to bring the Awami League back to the path of virtue. Responsibility for the conduct of government in both Karachi and Dacca had induced a cautious outlook in the main leaders of the party. The Maulana was therefore outvoted in the Awami League council in his attempt to alter official policy. His response was to summon a convention to inaugurate the National Awami Party. The constituent resolution declared that the new party would "aim at freeing the country from imperialism, ameliorating the condition of the people and establish, through constitutional means, democracy in the country and autonomy in both the Wings of Pakistan." [18]

The NAP was the nearest facsimile to be found in Pakistan of a Communist-front organization. Both the Azad Pakistan Party and the Ganatantri Dal had been strongly influenced by Communists in the past, and they were followed into the NAP by the usual variety of leftists, idealists, and radical reformers. Whether accidentally or not, the statements and policy positions of the NAP echoed Communist slogans about "imperialism" and "peace" that had little relevance to

[18] *Dawn,* July 26, 1957.

the parochial interests of the Sindhi and Pathan romantics. The Communist Party as such had practically no success in Pakistan, and most of its efforts were concentrated on influencing labor, student, and political groups. The party was unsuccessful in provincial elections in West Pakistan, but by supporting the United Front in East Bengal in 1954 managed to elect four party members to the provincial assembly. In mid-1954 the Communist Party was banned by law, but one reputed Communist was elected to the second Constituent Assembly from East Pakistan. Thereafter, with its leaders arrested or under surveillance, the party was for all practical purposes crushed.

Because of its heterogeneous character, the NAP was a prime element of instability in both provinces and at the center. Its members found it impossible to follow a consistent policy, those in West Pakistan being willing to cooperate with the Muslim League, those in East Pakistan bitterly opposed. Its reversals contributed to the ministerial crisis that brought M. A. Qizilbash to power in Lahore in the spring of 1958 and to the bewildering changes in majorities in Dacca during the summer of the same year, culminating in the tragic scenes of late September.

Religious Parties

Although Pakistan is a predominantly Muslim state, political activity has not passed, to any substantial degree, into the hands of religious leaders. The Muslim League, which established Pakistan, was led by professional politicians, many of them lawyers by training. Men of rigid Islamic orthodoxy were to be found in most of the parties that have been described, but they controlled none of them.

This is not to say that religion plays no part in political life. Almost every Muslim, politician or layman, would agree that the clear injunctions of Islam ought to be followed in public as well as in private life. The attempt to give constitutional expression to Islamic ideals in 1956 and 1962 was much more than window dressing. Pakistan would indeed be without meaning if it failed to give Muslims a sense of being able to accomplish their own Islamic destiny.

Some politicians have attempted to ride into public favor by taking up a religious issue. Thus in West Pakistan the campaign against a particular Muslim religious sect was led by men who were both religious leaders and politicians. The result was explosive, involving widespread rioting and the imposition of martial law. On most issues public opinion has looked to the politician rather than to the man of religious learning. The cry of "Islam in danger" is, however, still powerful and might serve to produce a violent reaction if the interests of the faith seemed to be in danger.

Before martial law was imposed there were two parties which were religious in their leadership and policy. The more important was the Jamaat-i-Islami (Union of Believers). It was led by an able politico-religious theorist, Maulana Abul-ala Maududi. The Jamaat attempted to be more than a political party. It was a militant religious order owing obedience to its commander. It undertook social service activities as well as political teaching and agitation. Its members were subject to rigorous discipline and were expected to lead lives of austerity. Many individuals admired this spirit of devotion even if they did not agree with the political program of the group. During 1958 the influence of the Jamaat seemed to be growing, and it contested and did well in the Karachi municipal elections in April.

The second of the two religious parties was primarily based in East Pakistan, although in 1958 it absorbed a sympathetic group in West Pakistan led by former Prime Minister Chaudhri Mohamad Ali. The Nizam-i-Islam (Rule of Islam) Party was conservative and orthodox, and originated as the right wing of the anti-Muslim League alliance in East Pakistan in 1954. Although the radical and fundamentalist views of the Jamaat-i-Islami were quite different from the outlook of the Nizam-i-Islam, in 1958 there were indications of a possible alliance between the two in the anticipated general elections.

Martial Law

In his Proclamation of October 7, 1958, President Iskandar Mirza referred to the political process leading up to his intervention:

For the last two years I have been watching with the deepest anxiety the ruthless struggle for power, corruption, the shameful exploitation of our simple, honest, patriotic and industrious masses, the lack of decorum and the prostitution of Islam for political ends. . . . The disgraceful scene enacted recently in the East Pakistan Assembly is known to all. . . . The mentality of the political parties has sunk so low that I am unable any longer to believe that elections will improve the present chaotic internal situation and enable us to form a strong and stable Government capable of dealing with the innumerable and complex problems facing us today.[19]

All political parties were therefore abolished, their funds were later frozen, and ultimately their properties were forfeited to the govern-

[19] *Dawn,* Oct. 8, 1958, p. 1.

ment. Political activity was forbidden under martial law regulations, and some politicians were arrested. The heat and passion which had aroused a menacing popular ferment suddenly disappeared, amid a tangible sense of relief.

The collapse of the party system and the conventional political process left a void that could not remain unfilled. The army leaders were eager to remove their forces from involvement with the administration as soon as possible, to prevent the military from becoming a substitute channel of political pressures. At first the regime seemed to think that the bureaucracy itself could serve as the means of communication between the people and the government, but it was soon realized that this was unlikely and undesirable. In early 1959 President Ayub created a Bureau of National Reconstruction as a means of popularizing the "philosophy of the revolution," explaining government policies, and assessing public reactions, through local non-official National Reconstruction groups. Later the concept of the "Basic Democracies" as a means of combining local self-government with mass mobilization for national development was evolved. The Bureau of National Reconstruction organized the publicity drive with which the Basic Democracies were launched, and ultimately the two programs were merged. Until the end of martial law the various Basic Democracy councils provided the only legitimate channel for the expression of public grievances, supplemented from time to time by conventions of councilors.

The prohibition of organized political activity reflected President Ayub's oft-expressed belief that parties merely serve to divide the people, obscure issues, and prevent the exercise of the free judgment of the individual man. The union councils were so organized that illiterate voters could choose their councilors and councilors could determine issues on the basis of personal knowledge rather than party prejudice or doctrine. The close links between the voters and the unions, and between the various tiers of councils, were intended to encourage a sense of accountability and responsibility in all concerned. For provincial and national purposes, it was felt that adult franchise made the gap between the voter and the candidate too great, with the result that the voter was forced to choose blindly— or sell himself to a party—and no sense of mutual responsibility between voter and representative could exist. In order to make the electorate small enough that the elector could become personally acquainted with the candidates, it was decided to limit the franchise to a college composed of the elected union councilors. In President Ayub's words:

The broad masses of people elected the electoral college, who in turn elect National and Provincial institutions. The reason for this is simple. We are recognising an obvious truth that the ballot can only produce a true answer if those exercising it are asked questions in level with their horizon and knowledge. . . . the voters will be less liable to be exploited and misled in this system than in direct elections where they were driven as cattle to the polling booths.[20]

Thus it was hoped—rather naïvely—that political institutions could be devised to function without parties, with every voter and legislator acting as a free agent in the national interest.

Because martial law was not revoked until the National Assembly met, the elections of 1962 were held on a nonpartisan basis. The constitution requires that candidates have equal opportunity of addressing the electors and that the latter have the opportunity to question the candidates "face to face" (Article 173), in order to preclude undue advantage, party or otherwise. Meetings for this purpose were conducted by the Election Commission in every constituency and were presided over by retired judges with power to maintain decorum and prevent disruption and other time-honored preelection political practices. Article 173 also forbids parties to participate in elections unless so authorized by act of the central legislature. As the President commented:

I believe that if we can run our politics without the party system, we shall have cause to bless ourselves, though I recognize that like-minded people in the Assemblies will group themselves together. That is not serious, but what is dangerous is for these groups to have tentacles in the country. However, should this experiment prove unworkable, which I don't believe, then the party system could be revived only with the permission of the National Assembly.[21]

However, most candidates expressed themselves in favor of parties, and "groups" of "like-minded" members began to form immediately after the elections. In order to prevent parties from reviving as soon as martial law ended, in early May the President issued an ordinance banning them until the National Assembly could deal with the whole question.

[20] From the President's speech in presenting the constitution to the nation, March 1, 1962 (*Pakistan Times*, March 2, 1962, p. 7).
[21] *Loc. cit.*

Post–Martial Law Political Revival

At the time of his promulgation of the constitution President Ayub said that he believed in it wholeheartedly and that it could stand only as a whole—that it would collapse if any of its main elements were changed. One of its basic principles was the separation of the executive from the legislature and the incompatibility of ministerial office with membership in the Assembly. However, within days of its commencement (June 8), the President adapted the constitution by a dubious procedure [22] to permit members of the National Assembly and of the provincial assemblies to retain their seats if appointed as ministers. The assumption was that the ministers would be able to command blocs of votes and thus ensure the enactment of the President's (or the governor's) program. In the first session of the National Assembly, the late Mohammed Ali of Bogra mobilized a Democratic Group of some 35 East Pakistan members, and the government usually received the support of the Muslim Progressive Group of some 30 West Pakistan members and from some members of the approximately 30-strong Independent Group of former Muslim Leaguers led by Sardar Bahadur Khan (the President's brother). During the session it became clear that without parliamentary party organization and whips to mobilize speakers and votes it was difficult to carry on business smoothly and effectively. In addition, the demand for the removal of all restrictions on political activity, led by the People's Group of East Pakistan members under the leadership of Farid Ahmad of the Nizam-i-Islam Party, began to pose the danger that this issue might create a united front of all groups against the government. This apparently led the President and his ministers to decide to push their bill through the house to legalize political parties with some restrictions based on past experience. Thus the hope for a nonparty democracy died almost before it was born.

The Political Parties Act (passed on July 14, 1962) was intended to assure a return to normal political life within the framework of the new constitutional order by immobilizing and silencing the leaders of the parliamentary era and thus clearing the way for the growth

[22] He acted under Article 224–3, which permits adaptations to be made in the first three months "for the purpose of removing any difficulties" arising in bringing the constitution into effect. [While this book was in press, the Supreme Court, on May 13, 1963, held this "adaptation" to be in effect an amendment, and hence unconstitutional.]

of a new leadership. It was based on the assumption that political attitudes and behavior could be regulated by statute and that those affected adversely would respect the spirit as well as the letter of the regulation. During the six months after the adoption of the act it became evident that the intent of the legislation was being openly evaded and flouted, as political groupings led by disqualified politicians challenged not only the government but the new constitution itself. Finally, in early January 1963 the act was amended by presidential ordinance to make more explicit the restrictions imposed on certain politicians.

The personal disqualifications imposed by the Parties Act have been the most controversial aspect of it. Critics pointed out that if debarred from party membership and office, persons with political influence would pull strings from behind the scenes and thus would continue to wield power. The persons affected are those who (1) have been convicted of an offense involving moral turpitude and sentenced to more than one year in jail, with ineligibility to last for five years after release; (2) have been disqualified from holding public office for misconduct in ministerial office under the constitution; (3) have been dismissed from public service within the previous five years; or (4) have been disqualified by a tribunal or by retirement under the Elective Bodies Disqualification Order, 1959 (EBDO), until December 31, 1966. The last category is the most important since it affects the great majority of the former political leaders of the country.

EBDO was promulgated during the martial law period to permit the removal from public life of persons guilty of "misconduct"— very broadly defined but in general involving misuse of public money —in public office since August 14, 1947. Tribunals at the center and in each province, presided over by judges of the Supreme Court or High Court, conducted open hearings on charges made by the government against accused politicians, unless the individual concerned agreed to "retire" from public life rather than contest. Most of the leading politicians, including H. S. Suhrawardy, Firoz Khan Noon, Khan Abdul Qaiyum Khan, M. A. Qizilbash, Ataur Rahman Khan, and numerous other lesser ministers, were disqualified, although a few were fortunate enough to be exonerated. In addition, there were several categories of automatic disqualifications similar to those now provided in the Political Parties Act but without the time limits. All these persons were ineligible for the first Basic Democracy elections, and despite partial "amnesties" for some of the automatic categories most of them remained ineligible for the legislatures in 1962.

The attempt to exclude the "Ebdonians" from party activity as well as public office was naturally resisted by them and their supporters. By October 1962 a National Democratic Front had taken shape under the leadership of H. S. Suhrawardy and the so-called "Dacca Nine," a group of East Pakistan politicians who had denounced the new constitutional system shortly after it came into effect. Its leaders declared that the NDF was a "movement for the restoration of democracy" and not a party as defined in the Political Parties Act. Accordingly, the restrictions on the Ebdonians did not apply to their participation in the Front. In order to deal with this evasion of the intent of the act, the amendment of January 1963 clarified the definition of a political party to include "a group or combination of persons operating for the purpose of propagating any political opinion or indulging in any other political activity" and prohibited disqualified persons not only from becoming members or officeholders but also from "otherwise associating themselves" with any political party.[23] Further, the government was empowered to direct any disqualified person to refrain from any political activity—including press conferences or statements—for up to six months. In partial response to the contention that some of the EBDO disqualifications had been unfair, EBDO itself was amended to make explicit the President's power to remit a disqualification on application by the individual concerned.

Other restrictions contained in the Parties Act concern the objects for which parties can be formed. No party shall be "formed with the object of propagating any opinion, or acting in a manner, prejudicial to the Islamic ideology, integrity or security of Pakistan," nor shall any person "form, organise, set up or convene a foreign aided party or in any way be associated with any such party." [24] These clauses are aimed primarily at the thus-far ineffective Communist Party, but they could presumably be applied to the Congress Party because of its connections with India or to the groups that in the past made up the National Awami Party and recently have been supporting the National Democratic Front. If the government feels that a party falls within one of the forbidden categories, it is to refer the matter to the Supreme Court. If the Supreme Court, after hearing the persons con-

[23] Press release no. 1, Jan. 9, 1963, Embassy of Pakistan, Washington, D.C.
[24] Sec. 3. The text of the act is given in the *Pakistan Times*, July 15, 1962, p. 9.

cerned, upholds the government's contention, the party is to be dissolved, its properties and funds forfeited, and its officeholders disqualified for five years from election to the National Assembly or a provincial assembly. When the definition of a party was altered, the Law Minister hastened to assure the public that bar associations and social and educational forums would not be affected by these provisions.

A final provision of the Political Parties Act provides that anyone who gains election to an assembly as a member of a party must forfeit his seat if he withdraws from that party. This is intended to deal with the serious problem of former days posed by the instability of party memberships, with persons lured from one party to another by promises of various sorts. If an individual breaks with his party, he must now stand again at a by-election under his new political label, to enable his constituents to express their views through the ballot. This should go a long way indeed toward strengthening party discipline, because presumably a rebel member could be expelled from his party and thus lose his seat. However, it is questionable how appropriate this is in a system wherein the government is not supposed to be dependent on a legislative majority for its existence.

Having assented to the Political Parties Act, President Ayub gave some "advice" to prospective party organizers. In keeping with his consistent emphasis on national unity and discipline, he declared that he would like to see "the emergence of at least a couple of political organizations which are truly nationalistic in character, representing as wide a cross-section of people as possible from both the wings and carrying a programme based on unity, stability, development and all-round progress." [25] He urged parties to be so organized that people would join them freely "without the fear of internal intimidation and coercion which used to be experienced in the past."

Referring to announcements concerning the revival of various old parties, he made three suggestions: (1) that organizational deliberations be opened to all interested, not restricted to the old cliques; (2) that the structures should be built from the villages upward, with elections at all levels, to "ensure that the leadership grows with the consent of the people and inspires confidence"; and (3) that the parties should have "realistic and clear-cut" manifestoes, dealing with the many problems of the country. All these were eminently sensible suggestions, made with the hope that the political organizers would make

[25] *Pakistan Times,* July 18, 1962, pp. 1, 12.

Pakistani parties more relevant to the national good than in the past, so that "the new phase of political life in the country starts on a scientific and constructive basis."

The only political group that has made any pretense at following the President's advice is the "conventionist" Muslim League. This faction of the League, sponsored by central ministers (principally Z. A. Bhutto, now the Foreign Minister, and A. K. M. Fazlul Quader Choudhury, the Education Minister), held a convention in Karachi in early September 1962 to prepare for a campaign of recruitment and reorganization throughout the country. It endorsed the EBDO disqualifications and therefore was boycotted by Ebdonian Leaguers, who opposed a reorganization that would remove power from the control of their factions. Unfortunately the Convention-League has chosen as its chief organizer the 73-year-old Choudhry Khaliquzzaman, who was relatively unsuccessful in the same role in 1948 because of his lack of a following in Pakistan. Before long conventionist organizers became involved in local factional struggles, and the Convention-League began to lose supporters.

In order to preserve their dominance in the League, the Ebdonians backed a meeting of the League Council—which had been last elected in 1949—in Dacca in October. Because of the disqualifications imposed by the Parties Act they could not participate formally, but they ensured that "dependable" people were elected to party office. Thus the aged Khwaja Nazimuddin was persuaded to emerge from retirement to become president of the Council-League, and Sardar Bahadur Khan (President Ayub's brother) was elected general secretary. Both are considered loyal supporters of M. M. Daultana, the Ebdonian *éminence grise* from Lahore. The struggle between the two Muslim Leagues for the allegiance of the rank and file has been accompanied by efforts to bring about a reconciliation. The two factions are agreed in general on the acceptability of the presidential system and on the desirability of constitutional amendments in regard to fundamental rights and the franchise, but cannot reconcile their views on EBDO disqualifications. The Council-League therefore has continued to support the National Democratic Front in its contention that the government is undemocratic and to oppose the reorganization efforts of the Convention-League.

The National Democratic Front is an alliance of all those politicians who feel most at odds with the presidential system. Its major components are the various fragments of the old East Bengal United

Front of 1954 together with the Muslim League faction of their onetime sworn enemy Nurul Amin, plus most elements of the old National Awami Party in both provinces. Under Suhrawardy's leadership they demanded the removal of all political restrictions and a return to a parliamentary constitution. Submerging their normal hostilities and differences, the Ebdonian leaders of the NDF abjured the revival of their separate political parties until such time as the President should "restore democracy." Regardless of the merits of the NDF case against the presidential constitution, the Front's behavior has been sterile and a disservice to Pakistan. Its noncooperation policy has stultified the growth of normal political parties, thus increasing the likelihood of instability after the inevitable disintegration of the alliance. Such were the considerations that led the government to make the amendments of January 1963 in a further effort to deprive both the NDF and the Council-League of Ebdonian leadership.

The general demand for the "democratization" of the constitution has been supported by the two Islamic parties, the Jamaat-i-Islami and the Nizam-i-Islam Party. When the Parties Act came into effect, Maulana Maududi was the only leader able to summon his organization into being with the certainty that his word and influence were as authoritative as before. Maududi immediately endorsed the demand for the removal of political restrictions, although he refused to submerge his party into the NDF when it was formed. After some delay the Nizam-i-Islam Party, of which former Prime Minister Choudhri Mohamad Ali is the national leader and Farid Ahmad is the principal spokesman in the National Assembly, was revived as well. Both these parties are willing to accept the presidential constitution subject to amendments providing adult suffrage and fundamental rights, but in addition they have pressed for a return to the Islamic provisions of the 1956 constitution. Although there is little political or social sympathy between the NDF and the leaders of the Islamic parties, the latter have opposed the government's attempts to silence the Ebdonians by law.

Amid the ferment in which the first six months of the new political era closed, it was clear that no solution to Pakistan's long-term need for broad-based and responsible organs of political mobilization and expression has yet been found. The NDF and the Council-League represent the efforts of the old bosses and hierarchs to retain control of the political process, and the Convention-League has been unable thus far to show itself to be anything other than a new class of bosses.

At present the Jamaat-i-Islami is too elitist and the Nizam-i-Islam Party too conservative for broad appeal, but paradoxically they may present the best possibilities for future growth. President Ayub refuses to descend into the political arena to organize his own party in support of his beliefs, preferring to rely on the good sense of the masses and of the Basic Democrats.[26] His determination to eliminate the Ebdonian leadership as a political factor stems from his belief that only by depriving them of the mystique of party and public office can their authority and influence be broken to make way for new patterns of leadership. By forcing the parties to choose new officers the President hopes to foster the rise of new wielders of power who will refuse to give way to their erstwhile masters when the EBDO disqualifications expire.

Political life in Pakistan has reached the stage at which the people have begun to realize that they have power. The shock of martial law, the efforts of the President to speak directly to the masses, the Basic Democracy elections and the functioning of the various councils, the election of the legislatures, and the subsequent political controversies have all combined to extend political awareness and to bring into the effective political community new elements. Neither the governments nor the bureaucracies nor the parties can return completely to the old indifference to popular feelings. Neverthless, it is still too early to say that representative government is fully understood or accepted in Pakistan.

[26] While this book was going through the press, President Ayub joined the Convention-League on May 23, 1963, as an ordinary member.

· XVIII ·

Pakistan and Its Problems

IN the days before 1947 there were many who doubted whether Pakistan could ever be established as a working state. There is no existing parallel of a country which functions divided into two portions, almost equal in population but separated by a thousand miles of alien territory. True federalism is never an easy form of government to work since its very nature causes some degree of friction between the interests and attitudes of the component units. Federalism with only two components runs the risk of becoming a perpetual struggle for supremacy, yet a centralized administration in a divided country is difficult of achievement. The constitution of 1962, therefore, has provided for a quasi-federal arrangement, with the provinces enjoying broad powers under normal circumstances while the central government retains the last word on all issues.

"Federalism" can also be reflected in the notion that the central government should itself be composed and function as a representative body. Thus the cabinet should be evenly divided between East and West Pakistan. The civil service and the army should give equal attention to both wings of the country in their policies of recruitment and promotion. In the allocation of central expenditure the claims of each province should be considered equably. The standing complaint of East Pakistan as well as the cause of much hard feeling is that even after fifteen years of independence the province remains underprivileged and underrepresented.

National Unity

The first task of any government in Pakistan is that of holding the country together and maintaining the consent of the people at large to the continuance of the state if not of the government of the day. Of the pre–martial law parties, the Muslim League had the virtue that it was equally strong in both provinces at the outset; however, its policy alienated East Pakistan to the extent that the party was all but effaced there after 1954. The Awami League existed as a shadow in West Pakistan but drew its strength from the east, and the reverse was true of the Republicans. Coalitions were therefore uneasy alliances without real agreement on a clear policy. Martial law imposed unity by suppressing public debate of regional grievances and at the same time tried to deal with local differences as national problems. The presidential system gives a formal unity to the central government, but the President must still rely on balanced political support from both provinces. It remains to be seen whether the new political parties will be based on national distinctions of left and right or will return to the old pattern of parochial roots.

The principal problem in maintaining national unity is that of relations between East and West Pakistan. A second issue is the status of non-Muslims. Pakistan, by definition, is a state with a preponderance of Muslims, in which the principles of Islam shall guide social action. There is nothing in the constitution, however, that imposes significant discrimination upon non-Muslims. Nevertheless, there can be no doubt that the Hindu, in particular, does not feel himself to be a full citizen with standing equal to that of his Muslim compatriots. There has been a slow but steady drift of Hindus from East Pakistan to India, not entirely explainable by the historical attraction of the Calcutta metropolis for the peasantry of north and east Bengal. In the past the Christians have not felt the same sense of unease, but since the 1961 census revealed the extraordinary rate of growth of the Christian community there has been an increasing expression of anti-Christian sentiments among the Muslims. The government is genuinely concerned to protect the minorities, but the implicit attitude is that "we Pakistanis" must protect "them," not "those of us who are non-Muslims."

A Free Society

It is highly misleading to suppose that national independence and a free society are equivalent terms. Before 1947 Indians lived in a society that was free within limits defined by an alien power. Since independence those limits have changed—though not very much—but they are now set by a government that belongs to the country. There is a psychological difference, but to the man who finds himself in jail it is more apparent than real.

Any government must maintain order. In settled countries where the basic social purposes are a matter of general agreement, civil disorder is a minor concern. Pakistan is newly self-governing and emerged into separate existence during a period of turmoil and repression. The main laws and regulations limiting political activity which might endanger peace follow the pattern set under British rule.

Some of the limits on political activity are to be found in the ordinary criminal law. Thus section 144 of the Code of Criminal Procedure permits a magistrate to forbid a public meeting or to order a specified individual not to make a speech. Section 144 has been proclaimed with great frequency and is often in force for periods of several months. Other sections of the criminal law restrict what may be said or written in the course of political debate. A person who "brings or attempts to bring into hatred or contempt, or excites or attempts to excite, disaffection towards the Government established by law in the provinces" commits an offense punishable by a maximum sentence of transportation for life. (Before 1947 this meant exile to the penal colony of the Andaman Islands.) This clause has been used very rarely, but its presence alone can serve as a restraint.

The press in Pakistan is subject to control. Many newspapers, especially those printed in local languages, have been wildly irresponsible and malicious. In an illiterate society rumors can easily be started, and the truth is hard put to hold its own. The law therefore provides that publishers may be required to give deposits that are liable to forfeiture without a judicial trial. There is also provision for the suppression of a paper or for precensorship. In 1948 in Karachi the central government took action against seven newspapers, barring four and imposing censorship on three. During the martial law period the press was faced by the additional uncertainty of possible action under martial law regulations. In 1959 the central government seized the *Pakistan Times* of Lahore and its affiliated publications on the ground that they were subject to foreign (Soviet) influence and after auctioning the shares belonging to Mian Iftikharuddin and his son transferred the company in 1962 to its new owner.

The most serious limitations on civil liberties in Pakistan are the laws authorizing preventive detention. Such laws have a long history in the subcontinent. The Bengal State Prisoners Regulation of 1818 is still in force throughout Pakistan. More widely used have been the Security of Pakistan Act, 1952, and its provincial counterparts. Under the constitution the central legislature has exclusive jurisdiction to make laws concerning "preventive detention for reasons connected with defense, external affairs, or the security of Pakistan," with detentions for any other reason normally left to the provinces. The 1962 constitution also provides for the first time that no bill relating to preventive detention can be introduced or moved in a legislature without the prior sanction of the President or governor. This is in order to prevent private members' bills from being introduced and passed over the opposition of the government. Although the constitution imposes no absolute limits on the preventive detention power, the Principles of Law-Making recommend that detention should be made only in the interest of the security of Pakistan or of public safety and that a person should not be detained longer than three months without the authority of a board consisting of a Supreme or High Court judge and a senior government official. During the first session of the National Assembly in 1962 an act was adopted requiring detentions to be reviewed by the board within 45 days, permitting the *détenu* to appear in person and permitting detention without the approval of the board for a maximum of two months. These are the most extensive safeguards ever provided for *détenus* in Pakistan.[1]

When it was promulgated, the present constitution set out no judicially enforceable fundamental rights, thus reverting to the situation prevailing under the 1935 Act. Instead, the Principles of Law-Making declared that the law should respect the equality of citizens, freedom of expression, freedom of association, freedom of movement and the right to acquire property, the freedom to follow a vocation, and freedom of religion; it should provide safeguards in relation to arrest and detention, should not authorize retrospective punishment, should provide protections in regard to the compulsory acquisition of property,

---

[1] According to statements made in the various assemblies, in mid-1962 there were approximately 160 persons under preventive detention, most of them in East Pakistan.

and should not permit forced labor or slavery; it should secure equal right of access to public educational institutions and other public places, should not permit the practice of untouchability, and should not prevent any group from preserving its own language, script, or culture. Any bill was challengeable in the legislature on the ground that it departed from these principles or could be referred to the Advisory Council of Islamic Ideology on the same grounds, but once enacted the bill became law and was beyond challenge.

The task of reconciling the rights of the individual with the powers of the legislature in a constitutional formula having been avoided, the role of the courts in regard to personal liberties became one of defending the individual from the executive. Article 2 of the constitution declares that "to enjoy the protection of the law, and to be treated in accordance with law, and only accordance with law, is the inalienable right of every citizen . . . and of every other person for the time being within Pakistan." Further, no action injurious to a person shall be taken except in accordance with law, and no person shall be prevented from doing that which is not prohibited or compelled to do that which is not required by law. The assumption underlying this article was that the individual has inherent rights which can be infringed only by law, whether statute or otherwise. The responsibility for protecting personal rights was thus placed on the shoulders of the legislators rather than upon the judiciary. Popular respect for the judges was so great, however, and the commitment to the principle of constitutionally defined fundamental rights so deep, that the first amendment demanded by all political elements was for the reimposition of substantive limits on the powers of the legislatures. Accordingly, an amendment was to be enacted in the spring 1963 session of the National Assembly to make the rights included in the Principles of Law-Making enforceable in the courts, thereby returning to the position that had prevailed under the 1956 constitution.

Many free societies have laws upon their statute books which might severely limit the freedom of the citizen. Such laws are available for emergency use only, and it is clearly understood by the government as well as by public opinion that under ordinary circumstances they will not be employed. Pakistan has now lived through fifteen years of crisis, various emergencies, and more than three and a half years of martial law. Apart from this last period it would be wrong to suggest that political opposition has been prevented, and even then public criticism of the government's policies was not unknown. Certainly nothing like a reign of terror has ever existed. There has been on occasion a real danger of internal disturbance, and any government would have had to be armed to meet it. The exact steps taken may be open to criticism, but it is clear that after fifteen years Pakistan remains a country in which free political discussion and agitation are more the rule than the exception.

Economic Development

One of the chief aims of all nationalist movements struggling to achieve independence has been to accelerate the pace of economic development. The majority of the inhabitants of Pakistan live not far above the starvation line. They remember vividly the disastrous famine of 1943–1944 when the dead in Bengal were numbered by the hundred thousand. They hear of the prosperity and security of the workers in the economically advanced countries, and they insist that something must be done to raise local standards.

It was clear from the beginning that independence for Pakistan would harm the economy of the new state which consisted of two separated sections carved out of the economic unity of prepartition India. Pakistan was deprived of the commercial and industrial facilities formerly provided for those areas by the major economic centers of Bombay and Calcutta. Further, many of the businessmen and skilled workers of non-Muslim communities fled to India, and their place was only partially filled by refugees coming from the reverse direction. Those owners and operators of businesses who remained in Pakistan found an immense demand for their products and were able to make large profits. However, probably 90 per cent of the population were and are directly or indirectly dependent for their livelihood on the produce of the land. Accordingly, reform and improvement of the agricultural sector were recognized from the start as essential to any sort of national economic advance.

Unfortunately the attention of most of Pakistan's politicians was given to constitutional issues and the struggle for power. The landlords of West Pakistan were sufficiently strong and skillful to divert attention from land reform to other matters, and no major party before the imposition of martial law was able to adopt a systematic land reform program. Viewing the feudal land tenure pattern in West Pakistan as partly responsible for the failure of democratic institutions, President Ayub appointed a Land Reforms Commission in October 1958 and on the basis of its recommendations a martial law regulation was promulgated in early 1959. Under the reform no one can own more than 1,000 acres of unirrigated or 500 acres of irrigated land, and at the other extreme no subdivision below 12½ acres is permitted.[2] These limits have been entrenched in the constitution. Although the landlords remain powerful, their wings have been clipped and a precedent has been established that might lead to further reductions in the size of holdings later on.

In East Pakistan a complete revision of the pattern of land rights was begun under the State Acquisition and Tenancy Act, adopted by the Muslim League government in 1950. All rent-receiving interests between the cultivator and the state have been abolished, and a maximum holding of 125 acres has been set. For political reasons the United Front ministry attempted to acquire all holdings by one order in 1956, but the administrative machinery was totally unprepared to cope with the burden. During the martial law period the situation was straightened out, and the determination of rights was to be completed during 1962. In both provinces those who lost lands or rights are being compensated with long-term bonds on a sliding scale, and in West Pakistan the lands acquired by the Land Commission are being sold on easy terms to the cultivators. The consolidation of fragmented lands is also being pressed, and cooperative techniques are being encouraged. In 1961 Agricultural Development Corporations were established in each province to handle extension services and to supply such items as fertilizers and improved seeds.

No country is willing to remain a producer of primary products and rely upon others for its supplies of manufactured articles. Possession of large industries is a source of national pride even though the goods produced may be more expensive and of poorer quality than the imported article. Pakistan has undertaken a program of industrial development that is very large when measured against the available material resources. At the time of partition there were almost no industries in Pakistan. In fifteen years large numbers of jute, cotton, and woolen mills have come into operation, and the country is now an important exporter of cotton as well as jute textiles.

The program of industrialization has involved direct public investment, private initiative, and varying combinations of the two. For ten years the major government agency in this field was the Pakistan

[2] About 2.3 million acres were acquired by the Land Commission from 5,904 landowners and distributed to 150,000 cultivators (*Pakistan Times,* June 1, 1960, pp. 1, 7).

Industrial Development Corporation, which provided financial and technical backing for a large proportion of new industrial undertakings, particularly in East Pakistan. In 1962, as part of the decentralization of responsibilities to the provinces, the PIDC was bifurcated into the East and West Pakistan Industrial Development Corporations. Besides textiles, the two IDC's have enterprises in paper, sugar, chemicals, fertilizers, cement, shipbuilding, and engineering. The index of industrial production, which covers seventeen major industries, rose from 100 in 1954 to 213 in 1961.

Pakistan is not well endowed with natural resources. Iron ore has been discovered, but its quality and accessibility pose problems for economic use. However, steel mills are under construction in Karachi and Chittagong; imported materials are to be used at the start. There are coal deposits in West Pakistan, and large resources of peat in East Pakistan, but the latter is not yet exploited economically. Large reserves of natural gas have been discovered at Sui and elsewhere in West Pakistan, and in Sylhet in East Pakistan. In the West the gas is distributed to industrial centers by pipeline, while in the East the present output is entirely consumed in the manufacture of fertilizer. In 1947 Pakistan had only 5 per cent of the installed capacity for electricity in the subcontinent. By 1962 major hydroelectric installations at Warsak in West Pakistan and Kaptai in East Pakistan had come into production, supplemented by coal- and gas-burning stations.

The foreign trade of Pakistan has traditionally been made up of exports of raw materials and imports of machinery and manufactured goods, but the pattern is now shifting. Raw materials are increasingly consumed by domestic industries, and their products by home demand. Textiles and paper and other exported products must compete in the international market with older and more efficient producers. Total exports therefore fluctuate, while imports constantly increase with the demands of industrialization and the development program. Thus a current-account balance of payments surplus of $6 million in 1960 was followed by a deficit of $44 million in 1961. In 1949 when the pound sterling was devalued, the Pakistan rupee did not follow and maintained its higher value until 1955 in order to take advantage of continuing demand for Pakistan's exports of jute and cotton. Both imports and exports are subject to government control, but since 1958 there has been a steady liberalization in order to facilitate the industrialization process.

Pakistan had almost no class of capitalists and no developed invest-

ment market. Savings from the rural sector of the economy are traditionally hoarded or put back into the land. The industrial and commercial sector was small and composed largely of family enterprises.
Major industrial expansion has therefore needed state assistance or
foreign investment. Pakistan, like most newly independent countries,
has been reluctant to see vital industries controlled entirely by foreigners. Nevertheless, only in oil refining does the government "expect substantial participation of Pakistani capital in equity." There is,
however, strong encouragement to foreign firms to employ as many
Pakistanis as possible in senior positions. Apart from this, official
policy has welcomed foreign private investment. The main source of
private capital has been the United Kingdom, but increasing investments are now coming from the United States, West Germany, and
Japan.

With increasing industrialization the problems of urban labor have
increased. In 1962 there were reportedly 600 registered trade unions
with a total membership of some 500,000. Most of these are grouped
into the All-Pakistan Confederation of Labour, with a subordinate
federation in each province. However, the unions are weak and often
ineffective against hostile employers. Since 1958 the central government has sought to encourage the growth of unions in connection
with a general policy of industrial peace and improved working conditions. The Industrial Disputes Ordinance, 1959, provides for works
committees in industrial establishments and for industrial courts to
adjudicate labor-management disputes. Amendments to the Trade
Unions Act, 1926, require employers to recognize unions meeting
minimum conditions and permit unions to appeal to the industrial
court against the refusal of the registrar of trade unions to register
them. For years the leadership of unions has rested in the hands of
educated men who have no experience of the type of work performed
by the members and who often have exploited the members for political purposes unrelated to the workers' interests. In 1961 restrictions
were imposed by law providing certain disqualifications for trade
union office, including a bar on the election of more than 25 per cent
of the total number of officers from among outsiders.

There is general agreement that Pakistan must have a planned,
though not necessarily socialist, economy. Resources were too scarce
and the managerial class too small to consider uncontrolled investment, production, and distribution. In the early years the machinery
for economic planning was designed mainly to coordinate the activi-

ties of the State Bank and the various government agencies controlling imports, tariffs, and investment. In 1954, a Planning Board was established to review the progress of development, survey available resources, and prepare future plans. The First Five Year Plan (1955–1960) fell about $200 million short of its goals in the public sector, in part because of a lack of real planning consciousness in the government. In 1958 the Planning Board became the Planning Commission, with enhanced functions, and under its auspices the Second Five Year Plan (1960–1965) was launched. The revised plan envisions a total investment of some $4.8 billion, including about $2.3 billion in foreign assistance. This is expected from the international consortium including the United States, Great Britain, Canada, France, West Germany, and Japan. The plan aims at a 20 per cent increase in national income and emphasizes rapid development in East Pakistan. By 1962 the plan was on schedule, with some likelihood that a number of goals would be surpassed.

Social Policy

Pakistan is pledged by its constitution to the creation of a welfare state. The Principles of Policy are not enforceable in the courts, but they stand as a declaration of intent for the guidance of legislators and officials.

The well-being of the people, irrespective of caste, creed or race, should be secured—a) by raising the standard of living of the common man; b) by preventing the undue concentration of wealth and means of production and distribution in the hands of a few, to the detriment of the interest of the common man; and c) by ensuring an equitable adjustment of rights between employers and employees and between landlords and tenants.

Further, a system of social security and care for the sick and infirm is to be provided. In addition, "illiteracy should be eliminated, and free and compulsory primary education should be provided for all, as soon as is practicable."

These are noble ideals. Unfortunately they are so far from the existing state of affairs as to sound unreal to the ears of the "common man." In 1960, for example, Pakistan had one doctor for 9,600 persons as against one for 750 persons in the United States; one nurse for 44,500 persons as against one for 300 in Great Britain.[3] Underground drain-

[3] Pakistan, Planning Commission, *The Second Five Year Plan* (*1960–65*) (Karachi: Manager of Publications, 1960, p. 358.

age is available for sewage disposal to only a fraction of the urban population. Much has been done in recent years to clear refugee settlements in the major cities, the outstanding example being the Korangi colony built in Karachi in 1959–1960, but many remain virtually homeless. Community development work under the auspices of the former Village AID (Agricultural and Industrial Development) program and now through the union councils has improved village standards somewhat. However, the needs are so vast and the resources so limited that benefits to the general standard of living come slowly.

Foreign Policy

It is characteristic of all intense nationalist movements that the rest of the world appears merely as a background to the successive acts of the national drama. Thus the struggle for Pakistan was set amid the events of the Second World War and the early years of the cold war. It would be untrue to suggest that Pakistanis felt themselves unaffected by world politics, but their interest was focused primarily upon the achievement of national independence. Firoz Khan Noon, who was to become Prime Minister of Pakistan, said in 1946: "If the Hindus give us Pakistan and freedom, then the Hindus are our best friends. If the British give it to us then the British are our best friends. But if neither will give it to us, then Russia is our best friend." [4]

Once Pakistan had been established, the immediate concern of its foreign policy was to secure recognition of its sovereign statehood. Pakistan felt that the two new Dominions were equal successors to the international status of British India. The Indian government, on the other hand, considered that India was the principal heir and that Pakistan was a new state based on the decision of certain parts of the subcontinent to secede. The Secretariat of the United Nations seems to have taken the Indian view since the membership of India continued without reelection whereas Pakistan was admitted with no delay but only as the result of an application and election to membership.

The major problems of Pakistan's foreign policy arose from the partition of India. By all the factors of history, geography, and economics the interests of India and Pakistan were intermingled. The very boundaries of the two states were not defined until the day of

[4] Quoted in A. B. Rajput, *The Muslim League Yesterday and Today* (Lahore: Shaikh Muhammad Ashraf, 1948), p. 109.

partition had arrived. The definition of their respective territories was left to a Boundary Commission with members from each Dominion and Sir Cyril Radcliffe as chairman. Neither government was satisfied with the commission's award, which had to be decided by the vote of the chairman. An important area of the Punjab, in the district of Gurdaspur and with a Muslim majority, was allotted to India, and the Chittagong Hill Tracts, with a non-Muslim majority, went to Pakistan. There were many lesser causes of uncertainty and irritation.

The Boundary Commission had not decided the distribution of the princely states between the two Dominions. The British relationship with the Indian princes had been described as "paramountcy." This meant that the states retained internal self-government subject to the acceptance of guidance from British resident advisers. When independence came to British India, paramountcy lapsed, and it became the right of each prince (there were more than 600 of them) to decide for himself, with or without consulting his people, whether to join India or Pakistan or to try to achieve independent existence. The Viceroy urged the princes to make their choice between the two Dominions before independence day and to bear in mind the influence of geography, economics, and the composition of the population. The large majority had no alternative but to join India. Three states, however, were the cause of serious dispute between India and Pakistan. They were Junagadh, Hyderabad, and Jammu and Kashmir.[5]

Junagadh was a small state on the west coast of India about 200 miles south of the nearest territory of Pakistan. Its ruler was Muslim whereas the majority of the people were Hindus. The prince signed a formal accession to Pakistan but found himself opposed by a large section of his people. India massed troops on the border, and the ruler fled. His minister then invited India to enter the state to preserve order. A plebiscite was held later which decided in favor of union with India. The official view of the government of Pakistan is that the state legally forms part of its territory and that India's forcible occupation cannot be recognized.

Hyderabad constituted a much more significant example of a similar problem. It was the most important Indian state, and its ruler, the Nizam, was a man of immense wealth and great prestige. He was a Muslim, and his state had become a major center of Islamic culture. Osmania University had acted as an important stimulus to the growth

---

[5] Jammu and Kashmir had been one state for a century, but there were historical and cultural differences between the two regions.

of the Urdu language and literature. The majority of the state's population was Hindu, with the Muslims acting as a ruling class. Hyderabad had no coast line and was entirely surrounded by India. The Nizam's government tried to proceed toward complete independence and signed a "Standstill Agreement" with India in November 1947. The situation inside the state deteriorated rapidly, with Muslim and Hindu extremists resorting to violence and the Communist Party provoking a peasants' revolt. In September 1948 Indian troops marched into Hyderabad, and the issue was settled by force. Pakistan was not an immediate party to the dispute, but developments appeared to confirm Pakistani suspicions of India's aggressive intentions against areas under Muslim rule. Pakistani sympathies were, of course, on the side of the Muslim minority.

It is the quarrel over Kashmir that has proved the insuperable obstacle to friendly relations between the two countries. Kashmir was in a position shared by no other princely state, in that it could contemplate a real threefold choice—accession to India or to Pakistan or independence. Kashmir had frontiers with both new Dominions as well as with China, Tibet, and Afghanistan. Natural communications in 1947 were almost entirely with Pakistan. The Indian contact with the state was through the Gurdaspur district, which as a Muslim majority area Pakistan felt should never have been assigned to India. There was one poor road from India that was impassable in winter. The population of Jammu and Kashmir totaled more than 4 million of whom three-fourths were Muslim. There was a concentration of Hindus and Sikhs in Jammu, and a scattered population of Buddhists in the Ladakh region adjoining Tibet.

The Maharajah of Kashmir was a Hindu. He was on unfriendly terms with the Indian National Congress, which was opposed to autocracy, and with the Muslim League, which had no sympathy for Hindu princes. India and Pakistan have argued for ten years about the facts and the legal rights of the Kashmir dispute. The outline of events is clear. The Maharajah acceded to neither Dominion but entered into a Standstill Agreement with Pakistan. Rioting took place within the state and was soon converted into war by the invasion of Muslim tribesmen from the North-West Frontier of Pakistan. These tribesmen were armed and provided with transport to the border of the state, but it is not certain that the invasion was planned by the Pakistan government. The Maharajah, in danger of being driven out of the state, appealed to India for armed assistance. The Indians insisted that he first sign an instrument of accession to India, but at the same time they declared that the people of the state must be free to make the final decision once law and order had been restored. Indian troops were flown to the state's capital and routed the tribesmen who had lingered to indulge in looting and arson. Soon Indian forces were approaching the Pakistan frontier. The government in Karachi then ordered the army to intervene to prevent the whole of Kashmir from falling into Indian hands. The fighting continued through 1948 until a cease-fire was arranged in January of the following year.

In the meanwhile the issue had been taken to the United Nations. The Indian case was simple. Kashmir had acceded to India, and the presence of Pakistani troops was consequently an invasion of Indian soil. The Security Council should therefore condemn Pakistan as an aggressor, and India would then assume control of the state. After this had been done, a plebiscite could be held in peaceful conditions so that the will of the people might be ascertained.

Pakistan did not accept the validity of the accession of Kashmir to India. Prime Minister Mohamad Ali made this clear in a speech in the National Assembly. "If anything, here was an act of naked Indian aggression against a defenceless people, committed under cover of a fraudulent and invalid instrument of accession, surreptitiously obtained from a Hindu ruler who had lost the confidence and support of his people and whose writ had no longer any force within the state." [6] Pakistani indignation was made much greater because it seemed that India had been able to use force against Junagadh and Hyderabad to "rescue" Hindu people from Muslim princes but professed to be morally outraged when Pakistan wished to apply similar tactics in Kashmir.[7]

Essentially for both disputants the issue at stake is one of pride and prestige. Pakistan is utterly convinced that Kashmir must be a part of that country since it is a Muslim-majority area. Any other solution is unthinkable since it would deny the essence of Pakistan—the claim of the Muslims of India to be one separate nation with a right to a state of their own in areas where they constitute a majority. For India the converse is true. Indians claim that the reality of a secular democratic India will best be demonstrated if a Muslim-majority area be-

[6] National Assembly of Pakistan, *Parliamentary Debates*, I, 306, March 31, 1956.
[7] An account of the Kashmir dispute from the point of view of its effect on Indian foreign policy may be found in Chapter XIII, which also deals with the internal situation in that part of Kashmir held by India.

comes freely reconciled to its place within the Indian Union and that to surrender Kashmir would act as an irritant to extreme Hindu sentiment and might provoke increased communal tension with India. This is a continuation, after partition, of the old argument between Muslim separatism and a united India.

Serious discussion of the Kashmir question was resumed in late 1962, following pressures by the United States and Britain on India to attempt to come to terms with Pakistan in order to face the external threat from China. Freshly disillusioned over relations with China, Indian opinion was ready for a settlement—but in terms of an acceptance of the cease-fire line as a permanent border. To Pakistan, however, acceptance of the *status quo* is no settlement at all, but represents Indian intransigence and refusal to admit the Kashmiri right to self-determination. While India annexed the portion of the state occupied by Indian troops and in January 1957 indicated that the accession was irrevocable and a plebiscite outmoded, Azad Kashmir (on the Pakistan side of the cease-fire line) is not part of West Pakistan. Pakistan's commitment to a plebiscite was reflected in the fact that for years Azad Kashmir was ruled by a succession of provisional regimes in anticipation of the reunification of the state. Finally, in 1960, Basic Democracy elections were held, and in the fall of 1961 a president (K. H. Khurshid) and a twelve-man State Council were elected by the union councilors. If the ministerial discussions initiated in December 1962 fail to bring about a plebiscite at least in the Vale of Kashmir, demands will be made with increasing force that the government of Pakistan recognize the Khurshid regime as the legitimate government of an independent Kashmir state. This would further embitter Pakistan's relations with India, by making possible a Kashmiri appeal for Chinese intervention and increasing the likelihood of a violent attempt to oust the Indians.

The fighting in Kashmir in 1947–1948 produced a direct clash between the armies of India and Pakistan. On other occasions, the most recent in December 1961 during the Goa crisis, Indian forces have been massed near the Pakistan frontier and Pakistani counteraction has made war seem perilously close. In October and November 1962 the Western powers were greatly concerned lest Pakistan exploit India's involvement with China to attack in Kashmir. A small power directly confronting a larger neighbor always has reason for anxiety when relations between the two enter a period of friction. Pakistan is especially vulnerable in the event of war. Its territory is divided into two sections with a thousand miles of India in between. Communication between the two would be impossible by land or air, and the sea involves a prolonged voyage around India in the face of an Indian navy which is much larger than that of Pakistan. Pakistan's resources for the production of munitions are slight; the country has only two major ports, both of which would be vulnerable to blockade. The Pakistani air force is relatively small, although in recent years it has been supplied with the most modern aircraft from the United States, and most of its bases are within reach of Indian attack. The army of Pakistan is sizable and well trained, but with restricted supplies and air support its effect would be limited. War would be disastrous for both sides, even if some sort of victory could be won. Responsible leaders of the armed forces and the governments know this very well. Unfortunately the state of tension that has existed at times in the years since independence means that the possibility of war, however suicidal, cannot be ignored.

A further cause of bitterness between India and Pakistan was the lengthy dispute over the distribution of the waters of the Indus Basin. The Punjab contained one of the largest and most complex systems of irrigation to be found anywhere. Most of the irrigated land in 1947 lay in the West (Pakistani) Punjab. On the other hand, the upper reaches of five of the six main rivers lie in India or Indian Kashmir. The Indians wished to use some of this water for schemes of irrigation on their own side of the border, and they began to undertake projects that would reduce the flow of water to Pakistan. The World Bank was called upon to act as mediator, and finally in September 1960 an agreement was reached, allotting the three western rivers to Pakistan and the three eastern to India. An international consortium has agreed to finance the vast ten-year construction program necessary to build dams and canals in Pakistan so that the irrigation complex can be supplied from the western rivers. Although the solution of this problem has eased relations, similar frictions exist over the use of the Ganges waters in West Bengal and the possible consequences for projects in East Pakistan.

Other points of conflict between Pakistan and India have arisen from the attitude of each country toward its minorities. In 1961 serious anti-Muslim riots in central and northern India led to counter-demonstrations in Pakistan, and in 1962 trouble in West Bengal and Tripura, leading to an influx of refugees into East Pakistan, brought forth public demands that the Pakistan government take action. The steady emigration of Hindus from East Pakistan, already mentioned, was added to by the repercussions in border districts of the arrival of refugees from India. There have been lengthy arguments between the two governments on the subject of the disposition of property left behind by refugees, and no agreed scheme of compensation has been found. However, recently progress has been made on the return of bank deposits and other valuables. Between 1948 and 1951 there was a virtual stoppage of trade between the two countries since India refused to recognize the continued high value of the Pakistani rupee after its Indian counterpart had been devalued.

In all these issues Pakistanis have felt that India has never accepted their nation as an equal. The struggle for Pakistan before 1947 was in large measure the attempt to force the Indian National Congress to deal with the Muslim League as the representative of a separate but equal nation. The validity of this claim was never accepted by the Congress. Equality with (Hindu) India was therefore a dominant idea in the minds of Pakistanis even before their state came into being. This idea has continued to be the primary motive of Pakistan's foreign policy since 1947, and relations with all other countries are seen as they affect this basic objective.

Pakistan was created to be the homeland of the Muslims of the subcontinent. Accordingly the Pakistani nation can be expected to take an interest in the progress of Muslims everywhere. One of the constitutional Principles of Policy declares that "the bonds of unity amongst Muslim countries should be preserved and strengthened." Classical Islamic doctrine treats of Muslims as forming one people, and the institution of the caliphate preserved in theory the ideal of allegiance to a single ruler. In this sense the requirements of Islam cut across the concept of nationhood for Pakistan. Indeed, there were some religious leaders who opposed Pakistan because it tended to deify the nation and detract from the unity of all believers.

Many pious Muslims in Pakistan believe that their government should work steadily toward a pan-Islamic state or at least toward a Muslim bloc that would act as a unit when the interests of Muslims were in conflict with those of others. The government encouraged the activities of a number of unofficial organizations which aimed at closer understanding between Muslim peoples. It also originated a series of Muslim International Economic Conferences, the first and third sessions being held in Karachi in 1950 and 1954. In 1952 the prime ministers of twelve Muslim states were invited to Karachi, but the conference was abandoned because of the reluctance of some of the governments concerned. Heads of state or of government of Turkey, Iran, Iraq, Saudi Arabia, Jordan, Egypt, Syria, Indonesia, Afghanistan, Nigeria, and Malaya have exchanged visits with their Pakistani counterparts.

In the United Nations and elsewhere, Pakistan has given vigorous support to independence for Muslim peoples in Libya, the Sudan, Morocco, Tunisia, Algeria, and Malaya. There was also support for Iran during the oil dispute and for Egypt in the early stages of the Suez crisis. The Arab countries have been able to count on Pakistani influence in their conflict with Israel. "I would like to make it clear," said Prime Minister Suhrawardy in 1956, "that Pakistan has never recognized Israel, and my policy definitely is that we shall not recognize Israel under any circumstances." [8]

In these actions Pakistan has a genuine feeling of the duty of all Muslims to stand together. This is based on a simple code of friendship—that your friends are my friends and your enemies my enemies. Unfortunately the rest of the Muslim world has not been anxious to reciprocate, especially since the evidence of friendship demanded by Pakistan is support of its case against India. The Arab states, besides internal quarrels, have ambitions of their own which have little to do with the advancement of the realm of Islam. When Israel, Britain, and France attacked Egypt, the initial reaction in Pakistan was to offer support to the victim. Nasser, who hated the Baghdad Pact, was not impressed and refused to permit Pakistani forces in the United Nations Emergency Force or to receive a visit from Prime Minister Suhrawardy. Opinion in Pakistan felt betrayed. "It is nevertheless a matter of deep regret that in the veins of this turbulent egotist not the blood of Islam should seem to flow but the turbid waters of the Nile. Nasser will never be our friend; he will never think in terms of Islam except when it suits his own interest." [9]

It is unfortunate that Pakistan has not enjoyed good relations with neighboring Afghanistan. There had been a long record of friction between India and Afghanistan along the North-West Frontier. Afghan influence with the Pushtu-speaking tribes was considerable since they inhabit both sides of the border. After partition, the Afghans reopened old claims either for frontier adjustments or for an inde-

[8] *Pakistan News* (London), Nov. 24, 1956, quoting a statement of Nov. 14, 1956.
[9] *Dawn*, Dec. 1, 1956, editorial, "So This Is Nasser!"

pendent state of Pakhtunistan. Relations between the two countries reached a new low in 1961–1962, when Pakistan forced the Afghans to close their consulates and Afghanistan retaliated by breaking diplomatic relations and closing the border. Efforts of the Shah of Iran to mediate in the dispute in 1962 revived talk of some sort of confederation joining Iran and Pakistan with Afghanistan, but the Afghan rulers have shown no interest.

Relations with neighboring Iran and with Turkey have been strengthened through the erstwhile Baghdad Pact, now known as the Central Treaty Organization (CENTO). This alliance also provides a formal military link with Britain, supplementing informal Commonwealth arrangements. Pakistan's ties with Britain are of course historical in origin. The Muslim League tended to rely on the British for protection against the Congress prior to independence, and some measure of British sympathy was an essential condition for the creation of Pakistan. Immediately after independence, Pakistan hoped to rely on British and Commonwealth influence to guarantee fair treatment from India. Inevitably, Pakistanis became embittered when the British government, like those of other Commonwealth countries, declined to take sides in the differences between Pakistan and India and went out of their way to accommodate Nehru when India abandoned the Crown and became a republic.

This attitude has led to a feeling in Pakistan that membership in the Commonwealth is of no great advantage in the overriding issue of foreign affairs—relations with India. British policy in the Middle East has also drawn criticism, both from the left and from pious Muslims. Public denunciation of Commonwealth ties at the time of Suez was especially widespread. The proclamation of martial law seemed to herald closer relations with Great Britain, because of the personal inclinations of both General Mirza and General Ayub. The Duke of Edinburgh visited Pakistan in early 1959, and two years later Queen Elizabeth II and the duke made a full-scale royal tour of Pakistan (and India). These visits emphasized the traditional emotional and sentimental ties with Britain, but in subsequent months the treatment of Pakistani immigrants in Britain became the cause of renewed criticism of the Commonwealth.

The orientation to the West involved in Commonwealth membership was supplemented by an alliance with the United States in 1954. Pakistan was not seriously concerned by the threat of communism, internal or external, but desired friends as insurance against any possible threat from India. In default of more response from the Muslim world or the Commonwealth, Pakistan turned to the United States. The new Republican administration in Washington in 1953 was eager to find allies in Asia to stand against communism. In April 1953 the Governor-General dismissed Nazimuddin and replaced him with the then ambassador to the United States, who had become quite an admirer of things American. Subsequently Secretary of State Dulles visited Karachi, and the Governor-General, the Foreign Minister, and the commander in chief (General Ayub) went to Washington. The ultimate result was a Mutual Defence Agreement and, in due course, Pakistani participation in the SEATO and CENTO alliances.

Indian outrage at Pakistan's decision to join the Western alliance made this more acceptable internally than it might otherwise have been. The Awami League initially condemned the link with the United States, but when he came to power Suhrawardy found merit in it and became a staunch defender of the alliance and a major source of strength for the Baghdad Pact during the difficult Suez period. The alignment with the West has been aided inside Pakistan by a natural dislike of communism, combined with hostility produced by Russian support of both Indian and Afghan claims against Pakistan. However, there is a natural feeling in Pakistan that the alliance is valuable only if it strengthens the country against India.

President Ayub's government has made it clear that the alliance must be made effective or abandoned. The increasing tendency of Washington to cater to Indian needs, especially after the return of the Democrats to power, evoked strong criticism from Pakistan, so that President Ayub's planned state visit to the United States during 1961 was advanced by several months. The resulting high-level talks seemed productive, and President Ayub's personal impact increased general American awareness of Pakistan. The "indecent haste"—in the Pakistani view—with which the United States rushed arms to India in November 1962 led to bitter attacks in Pakistan on the alliance, with demands for a *rapprochement* with China and the USSR. The situation was somewhat improved by American and British pressures on India to reopen discussions on Kashmir. The disruptive possibilities of Kashmir in terms of the alliance were amply demonstrated during 1962 when Pakistan agreed with Communist China to demarcate the Sinkiang-Kashmir border. China has thus rejected India's claim to sovereignty over Kashmir and has won Pakistani gratitude. What this may ultimately mean for SEATO is unclear. What would happen to the alliance structure if the Russians changed their position on Kashmir can be better imagined than stated.

Constitutional Stability

National unity, a free society, economic development, a welfare state, national security—all these problems are intimately bound up with the need for constitutional stability. The present constitution was promulgated after a lengthy study and report by an independent commission and further study and consideration by the cabinet and the President himself. It was a sincere attempt to find an institutional framework appropriate to Pakistan, based on careful consideration of the experience of the past and the weaknesses and limitations of the existing society. It provides a unified and stable independent executive, a legislature that can be dissolved only if the President himself is willing to face the electors, referenda to resolve conflicts between the executive and the legislature by reference to the electors, and an independent judiciary. It also provides for autonomous provinces subject to over-all central review and coordination. But it is neither parliamentary nor truly federal, and as promulgated it did not provide for direct elections by adult suffrage, nor did it include justiciable fundamental rights as a limitation on both the legislature and the executive.

Clearly this constitution is not perfect. Its presuppositions in regard to political parties were naïve, but were abandoned almost immediately. Its provisions in regard to the franchise and fundamental rights fly in the face of the accepted democratic dogmas of the twentieth century, and accordingly will be altered in 1963. However, the over-all structure deserves a trial, to see whether it permits a more effective attack on national problems than was possible previously. Unfortunately, even after fifteen years the overriding concern of some Pakistani politicians is not the solution of national problems but the search for an ideal constitution. In pursuit of this Holy Grail they seem willing to go to any disruptive lengths, demanding still another Constituent Assembly and still another constitution. President Ayub's comments are à propos:

The spirit which made Pakistan is still there. It is only dormant. Let us activate it and get down to the task. There was so much to be done, so many national problems to be tackled and solved. Can we afford to dissipate our energies in petty hair-splitting over constitutional or political niceties? It is one thing to win freedom, quite another to sustain it. The latter is far more difficult a task. The country needs at this hour to turn to it with a singleness of purpose.[10]

It is to be hoped that the political leaders profit by the lessons of the past and press their views within the existing order. It will be a tragedy if the experience of Burma is paralleled in Pakistan.

SUGGESTED READING

For further reading on the Indian historical background, the student is referred to the bibliography at the end of the India section of this book.

INDIAN ISLAM AND THE PAKISTAN MOVEMENT

Aga Khan, H. H. the. *The Memoirs of Aga Khan: World Enough and Time.* London: Cassell and Co., 1954. The autobiography of one of the founders of the Muslim League.

Ahmad, Jamil-ud-Din, ed. *Some Recent Speeches and Writings of Mr. Jinnah.* Lahore: Shaikh Muhammad Ashraf. Vol. I, 5th ed., 1952; vol. II, 1947.

Albiruni, A. H. *Makers of Pakistan and Modern Muslim India.* Lahore: Shaikh Muhammad Ashraf, 1950. Short biographical sketches of Muslim leaders from Sir Sayyid Ahmad Khan to Liaqat Ali Khan.

Ambedkar, B. R. *Pakistan; or, The Partition of India.* 3d ed. Bombay: Thacker and Co., 1946. The demand for Pakistan as seen by the leader of India's untouchables.

Ameer Ali, Syed. *The Spirit of Islam.* London: Christophers, 1922. The classic modernist statement of Islam as a liberal and progressive faith.

Ashraf, Mohammad, comp. *Cabinet Mission and After.* Lahore: Muhammad Ashraf, 1946. Letters and documents covering negotiations leading up to the formation of the interim government by Congress in 1946, from the Pakistani viewpoint.

Baljon, J. M. S. *The Reforms and Religious Ideas of Sir Sayyid Ahmad Khan.* 2d ed. Lahore: Orientalia, 1958. A short but thorough study of the life and contributions of the father of the Aligarh movement and the Muslim revival.

Birdwood, Christopher Bromhead, Baron. *A Continent Experiments.* London: Skeffington, 1946. A British officer's sympathetic and understanding picture of the political situation in India at the close of the Second World War.

Bolitho, Hector, *Jinnah.* London: John Murray, 1954. A readable but not very profound biography of Pakistan's founder.

[10] From a speech at Montgomery, West Pakistan, July 14, 1962 (*Pakistan Times,* July 15, 1962, pp. 1, 12).

Campbell Johnson, Alan. *Mission with Mountbatten.* London: Robert Hale, 1951. A day-by-day record by Mountbatten's press attaché, who was critical of the part played by the Muslim League.

Coupland, Sir Reginald. *India: A Re-statement.* London: Oxford University Press, 1945. A summary of the following work, brought up to the end of the war.

——. *The Indian Problem.* New York: Oxford University Press, 1944. Published originally in England in three volumes: I, *The Indian Problem, 1833–1935* (1942); II, *Indian Politics, 1936–1942* (1943); III, *The Future of India* (1943). An indispensable survey of Indian political history, especially valuable for the period 1936–1943.

Dar, Bashir Ahmad. *Religious Thought of Sayyid Ahmad Khan.* Lahore: Institute of Islamic Culture, 1957. A Pakistani study of the life and work of Sir Sayyid Ahmad.

de Bary, William T., ed. *Sources of Indian Tradition.* New York: Columbia University Press, 1958. See sections by P. Hardy, "Islam in Medieval India," and Dr. I. H. Qureshi, "The Muslim Revival."

Dodwell, H. H., ed. *The Cambridge Shorter History of India, Part II: Muslim India.* Delhi: S. Chand & Co., 1958. A survey of the Muslim period in India, through the mid-eighteenth century.

Gibb, Sir Hamilton. *Mohammedanism: An Historical Survey* (A Mentor Book.) New York: New American Library, 1955. A brief study of the meaning of Islam by a leading authority.

Gopal, Ram. *Indian Muslims: A Political History (1858–1947).* London: Asia Publishing House, 1959. A Hindu account of the Muslim separatist movement, including much valuable information.

Griffiths, Sir Percival. *The British Impact on India.* London: Macdonald, 1952. A solid and scholarly assessment, written by a former senior official in British India.

Hunter, Sir William W. *The Indian Musalmans.* Reprinted from 3d ed., 1876. Calcutta: Comrade Publishers, 1945. A classic work, invaluable to the understanding of the growth of Muslim separatist sentiment.

Iqbal, Sir Muhammad. *The Reconstruction of Religious Thought in Islam.* Lahore: Shaikh Muhammad Ashraf, 1954. A reprint of lectures delivered in 1926 by one who is now considered the philosopher of the Pakistan movement.

Khaliquzzaman, Choudhry. *Pathway to Pakistan.* Lahore: Longsmans Pakistan Branch, 1961. The memoirs of the former leader of the Muslim League in the United Provinces, giving an inside view of the Pakistan movement.

Lumby, E. W. R. *The Transfer of Power in India.* London: Allen and Unwin, 1954.

Menon, V. P. *The Transfer of Power in India.* Princeton: Princeton University Press, 1957. A detailed record from 1939 to 1947 by a senior Indian civil servant who was close to the center of power.

Moon, Sir Penderel. *Divide and Quit.* London: Chatto and Windus, 1961. An account of the genesis of Pakistan and its consequences in the partition disturbances in Bahawalpur state in 1947.

——. *Strangers in India.* London: Faber and Faber, 1944. An excellent little book reviewing the problems of India through the eyes of a young civil servant and recently commended by President Ayub Khan for its insights.

Mosley, Leonard. *The Last Days of the British Raj.* London: Weidenfeld and Nicholson, 1961. A critique of the transfer of power in which Mountbatten loses some luster—a good antidote for Alan Campbell Johnson's adulation.

Rajput, A. B. *Muslim League, Yesterday and Today.* Lahore: Muhammad Ashraf, 1948. A rather poor account of the Muslim League from 1906, with emphasis on the Cabinet Mission period.

Ravoof, A. A. *Meet Mr. Jinnah,* 3d ed. Lahore: Shaikh Muhammad Ashraf, 1955. Jinnah's career up to 1946, as written by a disciple.

Saiyid, Matlubul Hasan. *Mohammad Ali Jinnah.* 2d ed. Lahore: Shaikh Muhammad Ashraf, 1953. A political biography of the Qaidi-Azam, much the best available.

Sarkar, Sir J. *Mughal Administration,* 3d ed. Calcutta, 1935. A brief survey by an acknowledged Indian authority.

Sen, Sachin. *The Birth of Pakistan.* Calcutta: General Printers and Publishers, 1955. The origins of Muslim separatism and the development of the Pakistan movement.

Sherwani, H. K. *Studies in Muslim Political Thought and Administration.* 3d. ed. Lahore: Shaikh Muhammad Ashraf, 1945. Includes a chapter on Sir Sayyid Ahmad Khan.

Smith, W. Cantwell. *Modern Islam in India.* London: Gollancz, 1946. An excellent analysis of Muslim social and political thought written when the author was in a Marxist phase.

Srivastava, A. L. *The Mughal Empire, 1526–1803.* 2d ed. Agra, 1957. Emphasizes administrative and social aspects of Mogul rule.

Symonds, Richard. *The Making of Pakistan.* London: Faber and Faber, 1950. A good introduction to modern Pakistan.

Titus, Murray. *Indian Islam.* London: Oxford University Press, 1930. A survey of intellectual and religious movements in Indian Islam.

Tuker, Sir Francis. *While Memory Serves.* London: Cassell, 1950. The Calcutta riots and communal troubles in eastern India as seen by the last British General Officer Commanding in Chief, Eastern Command.

POLITICS AND CONSTITUTION MAKING

Ahmad, Mohammed. *My Chief.* Lahore: Longmans Pakistan Branch, 1960. A short biography of President Ayub Khan by his former private secretary, recounting General Ayub's relations with Governor-General Ghulam Mohammed.

Ahmad, Munir. *Legislatures in Pakistan, 1947–58.* Lahore: Department of Political Science, University of the Panjab, 1960. An excellent study by a Pakistani student of the inner workings of the national and provincial legislatures.

Ahmad, Mushtaq. *Government and Politics in Pakistan.* Karachi: Pakistan Publishing House, 1959. A post-mortem on the parliamentary era, clarifying the political breakdown of 1958.

Binder, Leonard. *Religion and Politics in Pakistan.* Berkeley and Los Angeles: University of California Press, 1961. A detailed study of the religious factor in the working of the first Constituent Assembly, with some reference to the provisions of the 1956 constitution.

Calder, Grace. "Constitutional Debates in Pakistan," *Muslim World,* Jan., April, and July 1956, pp. 40–60, 144–156, 253–271. An easily accessible summary of the activities of the second Constituent Assembly.

Callard, Keith. *Pakistan: A Political Study.* New York: Macmillan, 1958. Although somewhat dated now, this is still the best over-all study of Pakistan politics available in the United States.

Choudhury, G. W. *Constitutional Development in Pakistan.* Lahore: Longmans Pakistan Branch, 1959. An analysis of the constitutional issues as dealt with by the Constituent Assemblies and embodied in the 1956 constitution.

Faruki, Kemal A. *Islamic Constitution.* Karachi: Khokhropar Gateway Publications, 1952. The outline of a constitution on an Islamic basis, representing a line of thought far removed from Western political ideas.

Feldman, Herbert. *A Constitution for Pakistan.* Karachi: Oxford University Press, 1956. An account of the political crises of 1953–1955.

Gledhill, Alan. *Pakistan: The Development of Its Laws and Constitution.* London: Stevens, 1957. As the title implies, a legal study.

Jennings, Sir Ivor. *Constitutional Problems in Pakistan.* Cambridge, Eng.: The University Press, 1957. The texts of the Federal Court's constitutional decisions of 1955, with an explanatory essay.

Jinnah, M. A. *Quaid-e-Azam Speaks.* Karachi: Pak Publicity, 1950. Mr. Jinnah's speeches, 1947–1948.

Maududi, Syed Abul Ala. *Islamic Law and Constitution.* Karachi: Jamaat-e-Islami Publications, 1955. This and the item below are pamphlets giving the fundamentalist ideology of the Jamaat-i-Islami.

530 *Pakistan*

Maududi, Syed Abul Ala. *Political Theory of Islam.* Lahore: Markazi Maktaba Jamaat-i-Islami, Pakistan, n.d.

Metz, William. *Pakistan: Government and Politics.* New Haven: Human Relations Area Files, Inc., 1956. A useful compilation of facts.

Pakistan, Cabinet Secretariat. *Report of the Constitution Commission, 1961.* Karachi: Manager of Publications, 1962.

Pakistan, Ministry of Law. *The Constitution of the Islamic Republic of Pakistan.* Karachi: Manager of Publications, 1956.

——. *The Constitution of the Republic of Pakistan.* Karachi: Manager of Publications, 1962.

Punjab, Province of the. *Report of the Court of Inquiry Constituted under Punjab Act II of 1954 to Enquire into the Punjab Disturbances of 1953.* Lahore: Superintendent, Government Printing, 1954. The Munir Report provides invaluable material on the problems of governing a country such as Pakistan.

Qureshi, I. H. *Pakistan: An Islamic Democracy.* Lahore: Institute of Islamic Culture, n.d. An essay by one of Pakistan's leading modernist scholars.

Sayeed, Khalid Bin. "The Jamaat-i-Islami Movement in Pakistan," *Pacific Affairs,* XXX (March 1957), 59–68.

——. "Martial Law Administration in Pakistan," *Far Eastern Survey,* XXVIII (May 1959), 72–79.

——. "Pakistan's Basic Democracies," *Middle East Journal,* XV (Summer 1961), 249–62.

——. *Pakistan: The Formative Phase.* Karachi: Pakistan Publishing House, 1960. A solid study of Pakistani politics under Liaqat Ali Khan, with reference to the background of the Pakistan movement and to the subsequent political breakdown.

Sharma, M. S. M. *Peeps into Pakistan.* Patna: Pustak Bhandar, 1954. An *émigré* Hindu writes with bitterness of politics in Karachi.

Smith, W. Cantwell. *Islam in Modern History.* Princeton: Princeton University Press, 1957. See especially ch. v. "Pakistan: Islamic State."

Zakaria, Nasim. *Parliamentary Government in Pakistan.* Lahore: New Publishers, 1958. A useful handbook, published just prior to the institution of martial law.

THE SOCIETY: ECONOMIC DEVELOPMENT AND FOREIGN POLICY

Ahmad, Mustaq. *The United Nations and Pakistan.* Karachi: Pakistan Institute of International Affairs, 1955. Written mainly for a Pakistani audience and showing their view of international affairs.

Ahmad, Nafis. *An Economic Geography of East Pakistan.* London: Oxford University Press, 1958. A valuable study of the economic and social setting of East Pakistan.

Akhtar, S. M. *Economics of Pakistan.* New and rev. (4th) ed. 2 vols. Lahore: Publishers United, 1956.

Andrus, J. Russell, and A. F. Mohammed. *The Economy of Pakistan.* London: Oxford University Press, 1958. Based mainly on the First Five Year Plan.

Arnold, F. B., ed. *Pakistan: Economic and Commercial Conditions, May 1954.* (Overseas Economic Survey.) London: H. M. S. O., 1955.

Beg, Aziz. *Captive Kashmir.* Lahore: Allied Business Corp., n.d. A Pakistani journalist's analysis of the Kashmir dispute and conditions on the Indian side of the cease-fire line.

Birdwood, Christopher Bromhead, Baron. *A Continent Decides.* London: Robert Hale, 1953. A review of the internal and external problems of Pakistan and India, with emphasis on Kashmir.

——. *Two Nations and Kashmir.* London: Robert Hale, 1956.

Brecher, Michael. *The Struggle for Kashmir.* Toronto: Ryerson Press, 1953. Based mainly on the proceedings of the United Nations.

Chaudhri, Mohammed Ahsen. *Pakistan and the Regional Pacts.* Karachi: East Publications, 1958. A competent brief review of Pakistan's affiliation with the Western alliances.

Crescent and Green: A Miscellany of Writings on Pakistan. London: Cassell and Co., 1955. Essays on history and culture, including one by Arnold Toynbee.

Davis, Kingsley. *The Population of India and Pakistan.* Princeton: Princeton University Press, 1951. A demographic study based on the 1941 census.

Hasan, K. Sarwar. *Pakistan and the Commonwealth.* Karachi: Pakistan Institute of International Affairs, 1950. Originally prepared for the Commonwealth Relations Conference at Bigwin Inn, Canada, in 1949.

——. *The Strategic Interests of Pakistan.* Karachi: Pakistan Institute of International Affairs, 1954. Originally prepared for the Pacific Relations Conference, Kyoto, 1954.

Ikram, S. M., and Percival Spear. *The Cultural Heritage of Pakistan.* Karachi: Oxford University Press, 1955. A collection of essays.

Islam, Ziaul. *The Revolution in Kashmir.* Karachi: Pakistan Publishers, 1948. A detailed account of events in Kashmir in 1947–1948.

Jafri, Haris, with Elizabeth K. Bauer and Nikki R. Keddie. *The Economy of Pakistan.* 2 vols. New Haven: Human Relations Area Files, Inc., 1956.

Karim, Nazmul. *Changing Society in India and Pakistan.* Dacca: Oxford University Press, 1956. A sociological study of Bengali society.

Khan, Liaqat Ali. *Pakistan: The Heart of Asia.* Cambridge, Mass.: Harvard University Press, 1950. The North American speeches of Pakistan's first Prime Minister.

Korbel, Joseph. *Danger in Kashmir*. Princeton: Princeton University Press, 1954. An account by a former member of the United Nations Commission, sympathetic to the Pakistan view.

Lakhanpal, P. L. *Essential Documents and Notes on Kashmir Dispute*. New Delhi: International Publications, 1958. A valuable collection of materials.

Liaqat Ali Khan. *See* Khan.

Maron, Stanley, ed. *Pakistan: Society and Culture*. New Haven: Human Relations Area Files, 1957. A collection of essays.

Mason, Edward S. *Promoting Economic Development: The United States and Southern Asia*. Claremont, Calif.: Claremont College, 1955. Written with reference to Pakistan.

Narasimham, S. C. V. *The Other Side*. Karachi: Sorodo Publications, 1955. Speeches by Hindu leaders in Pakistan.

Pakistan, National Planning Board. *The First Five Year Plan, 1955–1960*. Karachi: Manager of Publications, 1958.

Pakistan, Planning Commission. *The Second Five Year Plan (1960–1965)*. Karachi: Manager of Publications, 1960.

Peach, W. N., *et al*. *Basic Data of the Economy of Pakistan*. Karachi: Oxford University Press, 1959.

Qureshi, I. H. *The Pakistani Way of Life*. London: Heinemann, 1956. An introduction to the history and culture of Pakistan.

Stephens, Ian. *Horned Moon*. London: Chatto and Windus, 1953. Dealing with Kashmir and the North-West Frontier, this is a mixture of political reflections and travel diary by the former editor of a Calcutta paper who prefers Pakistan to modern India.

West Pakistan. *Report of the Land Reforms Commission*. Lahore: Superintendent, Government Printing, 1959.

PART FIVE : INDONESIA

By George McT. Kahin

· XIX ·

The Precolonial and

Colonial Background

GEOGRAPHY has had a strong influence upon the course of Indonesia's history and has always conditioned severely the course of its political development. It is the only major state based upon a widely flung archipelago; and whereas the four islands of Japan with their less than 150,000 square miles of area constitute in a practical sense one fairly integrated geographical unit, Indonesia's more than 736,000 square miles are spread out over several thousand islands covering an area which if set down in the Atlantic would stretch from New York to the Irish coast. Clearly Indonesia's problems of internal communication are much greater than those of any other major state. Indonesia's 1963 population of approximately 100 million—making it the world's fifth most populous country—is distributed over islands varying tremendously in size and density of population. Sumatra, whose area is slightly larger than Japan or California, supports a population of about 16 million. Bali with an area slightly less than half that of Connecticut almost equals it in population—just under 2 million. The 213,000 square miles of Indonesian Borneo are inhabited by just over 4 million people, but Java, with an area of only 48,500 square miles (slightly less than New York state), supports a population of about 65 million.

Constituting a bridge between Asia and Australia and lying athwart the principal channels of trade between the Indian and Pacific oceans, the Indonesian archipelago has for some two thousand years been a crossroads of both international commerce and outside ideas and culture. Whereas nearly two millennia of commercial contact with China appear to have had relatively limited cultural consequences for Indonesia, equally old trading contacts with India provided the channel for the introduction of Buddhist, Hindu, and later Muhammadan ideas.

Indonesia's fragmentation into a widely strewn archipelago tended to stimulate a degree of cultural, particularly linguistic, diversity among its islands' scattered groups of inhabitants. This was only partially offset by culturally integrating factors, such as the generally intensive commerce among the major islands and between them and the world outside—trade which served to spread the culture of the relatively powerful maritime political centers of Java and Sumatra, and later of Celebes and Borneo, along their coasts and often across the narrow seas to the smaller islands. Intra-Indonesian commerce diffused an Indonesian lingua franca (based chiefly upon the east coast Sumatran Malay from which the present national language stems) into the most distant of the port areas of the archipelago. And it was via these channels of commerce that Islam, an even more important element of cultural integration, was spread. By early in the twentieth century nearly 90 per cent of Indonesia's population was at least nominally Islamic, and today Indonesia is the world's largest Muslim nation. It should be noted, however, that, as in the case of Hinduism and Buddhism before it, the penetration of Islam into the indigenous cultural base has been very uneven. In some parts of Indonesia (especially in Sumatra, and most markedly in North Sumatra) it has almost eliminated any significant residuum of earlier religious belief. But in other areas (especially in Central Java and much of East Java), although becoming nominally dominant, Islam has in fact been obliged to work in harmony, or simply coexist, with equally powerful (and frequently culturally more influential) survivals of indigenous Javanese mysticism and Javanized Hinduism and Buddhism.

The Dutch established their first bridgehead in Java as early as 1619, but the expansion of their control was initially slow. Not until the middle of the eighteenth century were they firmly in control of all Java, and not until the eve of the First World War had they secured their position in areas of such intransigent resistance as Bali and northern Sumatra. Thus although it is true that Netherlands rule carved out Indonesia's present political boundaries and provided it with its longest period of sustained political integration, it is important to note that Dutch authority was not consolidated in many important areas of Indonesia until very recent times. Moreover, the impact of Dutch rule was markedly uneven. By the time of the First World War in nearly all of Java, in much of Sumatra, and in a few districts of Borneo and Celebes, Dutch administration impinged heavily, but with a few minor exceptions the remainder of the archipelago was largely untouched. Indeed, as late as 1950 at least half of Netherlands New Guinea had still never been brought under Dutch administration. The extent of political integration resulting from Dutch colonial rule should not, therefore, be overly emphasized.

Precolonial History and Government

Prior to the arrival of the Dutch, Indonesia was no mere geographical designation, and its present boundaries bear to some extent the stamp of its earlier history. Indeed, the domain ultimately administered by the Netherlands was roughly congruent with the areas dominated by the two great Indonesian empires of the ninth and fourteenth centuries, Shrivijaya and Majapahit. Shrivijaya, whose capital lay near the present site of Palembang in southern Sumatra, was a maritime state which for several centuries dominated Indonesian commerce and the international trade passing through the Indonesian archipelago. At the height of its power it appears to have exerted varying degrees of control over most of the politically important coasts of Indonesia, over the Malay peninsula, and possibly over some of the Philippines. Astride the currents of international commerce that eddied back and forth through the Straits of Malacca, Shrivijaya, and presumably the smaller kingdoms that preceded it, was at an early date in contact with religious ideas emanating from India—Buddhism in particular—and by the middle of the seventh century it had become a center of Buddhist learning of international renown. Buddhist ideas had also entered Java at an early date; however, toward the end of the thirteenth century, with the rise of the power of the state of Majapahit, Hinduism had clearly superseded it as the dominant religion. But Javanese Hinduism always incorporated important residues of Buddhism, indigenous mysticism, and animism. It was thus a religion whose Hindu elements had been severely conditioned by the Javanese cultural environment and adapted so as to harmonize with pre-Hindu religious ideas. At the zenith of its power, in the latter part of the fourteenth century, Majapahit's sea power and commerce dominated the Indonesian archipelago and the Malay peninsula. But if one can speak of Majapahit as an Indonesian empire, it must be pointed out that, as had been the case with Shrivijaya, it was at best a very loosely knit political entity wherein the power center's leverage on parts of Indonesia outside of Java and Bali was fitful and unsustained. By the middle of the fifteenth century its strength had begun to wane, and concurrently so did the position of Hinduism. Indeed, roughly coincident with Majapahit's decline was Islam's spread among the major port cities of the north Java coast, and with its final demise at the end of the sixteenth century Islam superseded Hinduism as the major religion of Java.

Islam penetrated Indonesia peacefully, not by the sword, but via commerce and missionaries. Although as early as 1292 Marco Polo had found a Muhammadan community near the northern tip of Sumatra, Islam's spread through Indonesia did not become rapid until the middle of the fifteenth century, its most spectacular period of expansion coming during the sixteenth and seventeenth centuries coincident with the impact of the power of the Christian Portuguese and Dutch. It is highly probable that this acceleration was related to the impingement of European Christian power, first Portuguese and later Dutch. The Portuguese aimed at eliminating the position of Indian Muslim merchants both in the Indian Ocean and farther east, and they were no less bent upon supplanting the substantial position in Indonesian commerce held by Javanese merchants and merchant princes —a policy later pursued by the Dutch with greater vigor and more success. Since Portuguese trade objectives were linked with a crusading missionary zeal in behalf of Christianity, it is understandable how the affinity of commercial interests between Muslim Indian traders and Indonesian harbor princes and merchants should help dispose these Indonesians to be receptive to Islam. When in 1511 the Portuguese finally captured the Malayan emporium of Malacca, key entrepôt of Indonesian trade, they found that the dominant political element in this great Islamic city was Javanese, its army largely Javanese, most of its shipbuilders and other craftsmen Javanese, and the major components of its extensive merchant class Javanese and Indian. Although strong enough to appropriate a considerable share of Indonesian trade, the Portuguese were not able to marshal sufficient power to subjugate the relatively small Javanese and Sumatran states that arose after the fall of Majapahit.

The Dutch arrived early in the seventeenth century in greater strength and, with their seizure of Malacca from the Portuguese in

1640, became the paramount European power in the Indies. Initially because of internal dissension among the Javanese states and skill in playing off one of them against the other, they were able with relatively small forces to maintain their tiny bridgehead in west Java at the port which they had occupied in 1619 and rechristened Batavia. Within the course of the century, however, they increased their strength and became the major power on Java, their expansion slowed only by the declining kingdom of Mataram. This state, founded in 1582 in what had been the heartland of the old empire of Majapahit, for a while controlled as much as two-thirds of Java and small parts of southern Sumatra and Borneo, but never approached Majapahit or Shrivijaya in power. In the middle of the seventeenth century it was obliged to come to terms with the Dutch. With a steadily diminishing power and a shrinking area, it maintained a tenuous semi-independence until 1755, when the Dutch divided its residual area into two small states, Surakarta and Jogjakarta. Following a spirited but unsuccessful Jogjakarta-based rising from 1825 to 1830, the Dutch severely reduced the size of even these remnants of old Mataram, leaving them as they existed until the end of Netherlands rule—two tiny enclaves in south central Java, each granted a partial autonomy, with its *sunan* or Sultan maintaining his palace and court entourage, but reigning rather than ruling.

Little is known concerning the political organization of precolonial Indonesia. Very early two rather different kinds of states began to emerge. The most numerous, and usually the smaller, were the harbor principalities which dotted much of the coast of Sumatra and Java. A few of these were also to be found along some of the coasts of Borneo and parts of Celebes, where they constituted enclaves flanked by vast territories inhabited by tribal political groups. These states were based primarily upon inter-Indonesian and overseas trade, and only secondarily upon control over adjacent hinterlands with rice-producing peasants. Their rulers were either themselves directly involved in this commerce or else received considerable indirect benefit from it. The second type were the inland, predominantly agricultural, semibureaucratic states of central and eastern Java. Several of them, Majapahit in particular, developed substantial interests in inter-Indonesian and overseas commerce and in the process absorbed many of the harbor principalities; but their initial, and usually their major, basis of power rested on inland rice-growing areas, generally river plains where irrigation played an important part and where high concentrations of agrarian population were possible. All these precolonial states appear to have been characterized by a considerable degree of decentralization. Only their heartland areas seem to have been politically and administratively integrated, their lesser, but often important, outlying districts usually enjoying considerable independence. Moreover, within the confines of both Mataram and its semivassal states, as well as within the contemporary independent west Java sultanate of Bantem, numerous villages lying some distance from the capitals appear to have usually enjoyed substantial autonomy, a quality verging on virtual independence among those most distant. Even before the consolidation of Dutch rule there appears to have been among the villagers of Java a tradition of jealously guarded autonomy and of striving to keep the power of the capital at a distance. Although in the villages, particularly among those in the outlying districts, there may have been elements of democratic government, the capital and central areas of these states were organized along authoritarian lines with power concentrated in the hands of an autocratic ruler and his court entourage.

These precolonial states, especially those on Java, appear to have shared a roughly similar political ethos, what Heine-Geldern has termed "the cosmological basis of state and kingship," [1] belief in the parallelism between the natural universe and the world of men. The political community was regarded as being constantly and critically influenced by natural forces, both terrestrial and extraterrestrial, the principal purpose of the state being to harmonize itself and the human activity which it encompassed with these forces. Man, and thereby political activity, was to conform and to work in harmony with this cosmological environment. The ruler was believed to be the incarnation of a god and to have magical or mystical properties enabling him to contact the natural forces and their divine representations. Thus he was in a pivotal position to mediate between these forces and his subjects and to secure harmony between them. Being *au courant* with the posture of these forces, he could tell when their shifting patterns of order reflected a harmony propitious for important decisions.

This idea of individual and state activity harmonizing with the cosmos, so vital to the political order of pre-European and particularly pre-Islamic Indonesia, is not dead today. Although certainly much less influential now than in the past, it is of greater significance in the individual and political lives of present-day Javanese than most West-

[1] Robert Heine-Geldern, *Conceptions of State and Kingship in Southeast Asia* (Southeast Asia Program, Cornell University, Data Paper no. 18; Ithaca, N.Y., 1956).

erners are aware. The important contemporary residue of this sort of thinking is the still widely revered idea of harmony—harmony with the forces of nature, harmony within the political community—and conversely the conviction that inharmonious conduct is a disruptive force which society should rightly frown upon. It is this outlook which undergirds the still prominent belief in Java and many other parts of Indonesia that basically important political decisions should be an expression of full harmony and should not be based upon a 51 per cent, or even a 90 per cent, majority. And there are not a few Western-educated Indonesians in important government posts today inclined to avoid or defer certain important decisions unless they feel through mystical insight, or are informed by a wise man better endowed with this quality, that the configuration of the cosmic forces is appropriate.

Netherlands Control through Indirect Rule

The authoritarian political organization which characterized the central area of Mataram during its period of vigor was taken over by the Dutch as they absorbed its districts and in its essentials was extended by them throughout almost all of Java. Thus a political system, which in the pre-Dutch period had in actual practice been highly authoritarian largely in areas near to the capital and lesser administrative centers, was so strengthened with Dutch power that the outlying districts as well were forced into the same political mold. Commanding limited resources and being expected to show a high annual profit on its small capital, the Dutch East India Company was not in a position to pay the high costs that a system of direct administration would have entailed. The inexpensive system of indirect rule that it pursued was sufficient to secure the sort of political control necessary for the attainment of its economic objectives. In essence this provided for the utilization of the indigenous power structure, or more precisely its amenable elements. The Dutch maintained the aristocratic character of the societies of Java, taking over for themselves the apex of the pyramid of power and retaining at the second and third echelons of authority that considerable portion of the indigenous aristocracy willing to work with and under them.

Because the company's economic objectives demanded that new and additional burdens be placed on the peasants, it enlarged and strengthened the power of the cooperating elements of the aristocracies of Java vis-à-vis the peasantry. Since these aristocrats could if threatened call upon Dutch military force to back them up, they were able to disregard the interests and sentiments of the peasantry in a way which previously had rarely been possible outside the heartland areas of the old states. Vis-à-vis Dutch authority the position of the indigenous aristocracy of Java became weaker, but in its relationship to the Javanese peasantry it became strengthened. This increased power could be exercised all the more effectively because concurrently the peasantry in the outlying areas was progressively losing its traditional bargaining power—namely, the ability to abandon the area of a harsh king or local aristocrat and move on to the district of one whose rule was less onerous or to virgin areas distant from the center of any aristocrat's power. For the *pax Nederlandica,* however oppressive, eventually put an end to the frequent warfare and raids that had previously been so common among the Javanese states, thus promoting conditions favoring the rapid growth of Java's population and the consequent decrease of virgin arable lands.

The central role of the aristocratic Javanese agents of the Dutch was to ensure that the indigenous population of their areas delivered them a large proportion of their crops, a fixed proportion of which they passed on to the company. In return they were granted important benefits, being permitted to impose exactions of *corvée* labor as well as crop deliveries over and above what the company demanded. Indeed, they were generally free to add as much more as could be squeezed out of the villages in the areas under their control.

Well before the demise of the Dutch East India Company in 1798 the Chinese had come to occupy a key position in its system of economic exploitation in Java, one equal in importance to that of the indigenous aristocracy. Each of these elements was indispensable both to the successful functioning of the company and to the roughly similar system pursued by the government of the Netherlands soon after the end of company rule. Neither of these systems, nor for that matter the social legacy of Dutch rule as a whole, can be understood without some mention of the tremendous expansion of the economic role of the Chinese in Indonesia under the aegis of Netherlands rule. Although prior to the establishment of Dutch power Chinese merchants had been active throughout the Indies, the Indonesian princes severely limited and controlled the area of their settlement, and their principal function was limited to that of intermediaries in the exchange of goods between the Indies and China. But with the spread of the Dutch East India Company's power in Java, the scope and intensity of Chinese activity expanded greatly. The company consciously promoted this, initially regarding the Chinese as its special protégés, protecting and favoring them because of the conviction that its exploitation of the Indies could be most efficiently achieved through them.[2] Although at first the company's territorial administrative agents were nearly all recruited from the indigenous aristocracy, increasingly it came to lease areas of Java to Chinese entrepreneurs, a practice often taken over by its Javanese aristocratic agents who themselves frequently subleased their authority to Chinese. In addition, the company farmed out various monopolies to them—exclusive rights to collect road tolls, levy bazaar fees, collect customs, and sell salt. Because of this and their hold on the rice trade stemming from their control of the economies of leased villages, the Chinese came to dominate the internal commerce of Java. In the process Java's indigenous merchant class was largely eliminated, never again recovering its strength. This fact has had an important influence upon the character of present-day Indonesian society, on its ideological orientation, and on the economic policies its leaders have pursued.

Rampant and widespread corruption in its administration in Indonesia combined with a reckless financial policy under which stockholders were paid dividends averaging 18 per cent per year led to the collapse of the Dutch East India Company in 1798. The area it controlled was then placed under the direct authority of the Netherlands government. There was no real break with the company's policies, however; its key economic and political institutions were retained. During the brief interlude of British rule (1811–1816) attendant upon the Napoleonic Wars, efforts were made by Stamford Raffles to reduce the powers of the Javanese aristocracy; but very little of his program was realized, and much of what was accomplished was abandoned following the return of Netherlands authority.

After the withdrawal of the British in 1816 the policy of the Netherlands government until 1830 was indecisive and wavered between opening the Indies to individual enterprise and reverting to a system of government monopoly very much along lines the company had followed. Finally, primarily as a result of financial considerations stemming from the large-scale rebellion in central Java of 1825–1830 and the

[2] These Chinese were in Indonesia on sufferance of the Indonesian rulers, with the government of China at this time giving them no support; on the other hand, the Javanese merchants were generally closely tied in with indigenous power. Thus it was understandable why the Dutch preferred working through the alien Chinese who were the more tractable because they could not look for support to any Javanese prince.

costs of the unsuccessful war with Belgium, the Netherlands government adopted a system providing for government monopoly. The new
system, known variously as the Cultivation System and the Net Profit
Policy, lasted as a whole until 1877, after which it was progressively
restricted until it was completely abolished in 1919. From the standpoint of the Netherlands its success can be measured by the fact that
as of 1877 it had paid off the East India Company's and subsequent
government debts of 178 million guilders and in addition brought to
the Netherlands home treasury a net profit of 664.5 million guilders.[3]
In theory the Cultivation System called for one-fifth of the peasant's
rice fields being planted with a commercial export crop designated by
the government, with the peasant exempted from paying a land tax;
in practice not only was he forced to continue payment of this tax,
but rarely was he able to limit to one-fifth of his total the area of his
land planted with the government crop. "One-third, one-half, and even
the whole of these irrigated fields were used for growing designated
crops for the Government, and instead of 66 days per year, which
originally was the normal period, the interest of certain Government
cultures necessitated those liable to service working 240 days and even
more." [4]

Under the Cultivation System the fundamental elements of the partially eroded system of political relationships developed by the company were reestablished. Indeed, it could hardly have succeeded without the support of the Javanese aristocratic hierarchy. The supervisory
staff of European civil servants was increased, but local authority was
no longer leased to Chinese, and throughout practically all of Java
this aristocracy was the only real point of contact between Dutch power
and the indigenous population. To secure the aristocracy's effective
support the government actually enhanced the position of its upper
ranks, the regents, to a point beyond that which they had enjoyed
under the company. Their office was made hereditary; they were frequently given a modest grant of land; their powers were strengthened
as against lesser officials including the village headman; and, of key

---

[3] Indonesian nationalist leaders were later to remark that of this sum 236 million
guilders was applied to the reduction of the Netherlands public debt, 115 million
for the reduction of Dutch taxes, 153 million for the construction of the Dutch
state railways, and 146 million for the improvement of fortifications in the Netherlands (J. S. Furnivall, *Netherlands India* [New York: Macmillan, 1944], p. 210).

[4] G. H. van der Kolff, "European Influences on Native Agriculture," in B.
Schrieke, *The Effects of Western Influence on Native Civilizations in the Malay
Archipelago* (Batavia, 1932), pp. 108, 111.

importance, they were given a direct financial interest in the system's operation—a percentage of the crops collected from the peasantry. As a prominent Dutch jurist in the Indies was later to write concerning this system:

Over against his subordinate civil servants and the population the regent was elevated to become a feudal prince, who in turn, however, had to carry out the will of the resident [the top territorial Dutch administrative official]. From the population servile submission was demanded and even the village leadership, by nature identical with the interest of the people, was made a tool in the hands of the regents and their subordinate district heads.[5]

The Cultivation System, its basic elements roughly the same as under the Dutch East India Company, thus tended to solidify the pattern of Java's social structure which had begun to emerge under company rule. The authoritarian content of Javanese society was increased, in particular the relationship between the village and the political structure above it. Throughout Java the village headman came to be dependent for his position on the Dutch and the Dutch-backed aristocratic hierarchy above him to an extent approximating what had existed earlier between headman and Sultan in the limited heartland of Mataram. The collectivist aspect of peasant society, probably already reinforced during the period of company rule, became much stronger during the forty years of the Cultivation System. As Furnivall has pointed out, "So great were the demands on landholders, that landholding was no longer a privilege but a burden which occupants tried to share with others."[6]

In 1877 with the beginning of what was termed the Liberal Policy, the Cultivation System gradually gave way, in many areas very slowly indeed, to a laissez-faire system which for the first time allowed private capital considerable freedom. In Sumatra, Borneo, and Celebes Dutch authority penetrated into areas where its writ had previously been absent or only nominal, generally instituting a system of indirect administration through the local aristocracies and opening the way for large-scale private investment by Western (largely Dutch) capital in plantation agriculture and mining. Whereas this was important in Sumatra and to a lesser extent in Borneo and Celebes, it had relatively little impact on Java. Not only was the Cultivation System maintained in parts of Java until very late, in some areas until 1919, but elsewhere

---

[5] P. H. Fromberg, "De Inlandsche Beweging," *Verspreide Geschriften* (Leiden: Leidsche Uitgeversmaatschappij, 1926), p. 558.

[6] *Netherlands India*, p. 141.

on the island the pattern of the economy changed slowly. In those areas of Java not affected by Western plantation agriculture the ending of forced cultivation, individual liability for taxation, and an increasing pressure of the population on the available arable land gradually broke down the collective landownership that the company and the Cultivation System had fostered. The increased supplanting of collective by individual landownership did not, however, entail a commensurate disintegration of the collectivist (communal) pattern of social relationships. Although the chief objective characteristic of agrarian collectivism—common ownership and/or disposition of land—has for the most part disappeared,[7] much of the collectivist psychology induced by this previously long period of collectivist organization remains.

Among the most important measures introduced by the government following the switch to a laissez-faire policy were its land laws of the 1870s. While allowing the European entrepreneur to rent, for a limited period, land cultivated by an Indonesian, they forbade its purchase by any non-Indonesian. This enlightened policy had long-term consequences beneficial to Indonesian society. It was spared the large-scale alienation of peasant landholdings to Western, Chinese, or Indian creditors such as occurred in many other parts of Southeast Asia. Consequently the pattern of agrarian society during the last few decades of Dutch rule in Java, and indeed throughout most of Indonesia, was relatively balanced and free of the socioeconomic extremes which characterized most other Asian agrarian communities. In Java, the rapidly mounting population was, however, already beginning to undermine this balance. And because of the diminishing reserves of noncultivated arable land and the growing disparity between the agricultural base of the village and the population dependent upon it, the number of landless peasants increased significantly during the 1930s. This in combination with the decrease in communal lands was beginning to induce a greater degree of economic differentiation at the village level than had previously obtained. Nevertheless, the long period of collectivist agrarian organization had left most Javanese villages with a set of values which has helped preserve social equality in the face of diminishing economic equality.

The colonial society which we have been describing was, then, one

---

[7] As late as 1882, 53 per cent of landholdings in Java were collectively owned (either as general village lands or for the support of village officials), 35 per cent of landholdings being in this category as late as 1907, with 17 per cent (the last year for which statistics are available) in 1932.

wherein the indigenous elite's surviving elements had come to terms
with the colonial power, serving as its key agents in an inexpensive but
effective system of indirect rule and as a political buffer between Dutch
authority and a peasantry which still looked to this elite for guidance.
On Java this was matched by a roughly similar buffer in economic relationships, one originally provided by the Javanese aristocracy and
Chinese jointly, at the end of the nineteenth century by the Chinese
alone. Although commencing about 1910, coincident with a set of
more enlightened policies designed to improve village conditions, the
number of Dutch officials having some direct contact with the peasantry
became for the first time significant, until the end of Netherlands rule
a probable majority of Indonesians still viewed the political order as
one where power which affected them issued primarily from the hands
of their own traditional aristocratic ruling class. And for the most part
these traditional leaders continued to serve more as the agents of the
Dutch colonial regime than as representatives of their people's interests.

Emergence of a New Indonesian Elite and the Rise of Nationalism

Beginning in the second decade of the twentieth century a new,
Western-educated elite finally began to emerge. But its numbers remained so few and the Dutch so circumscribed its role that throughout the course of Netherlands rule it was unable to effect a sufficiently
widespread and sustained relationship with either the peasantry or
urban and plantation labor to educate them to the realities of their
political environment. For a brief period this new elite, led by a small
group of influential Islamic leaders strongly influenced by recently
generated Modernist Islamic currents emanating from Cairo and elsewhere in the Near East, was able to establish enough contact with the
peasantry of Java to create the first and only peasant-based nationalist
organization during the entire period of colonial rule. This movement,
Sarekat Islam (United Islam), grew so fast, by 1919 enrolling the support of more than 2 million members, that the Dutch became thoroughly
alarmed and saw to it that henceforward contact between Indonesian
nationalist leaders and the peasantry was made extremely difficult.
Thereafter, the repression of the colonial authorities so limited the
political activities of these leaders that never again during the period
of Netherlands rule were they able to develop the contacts with the
peasantry that had been basic to the burgeoning of Sarekat Islam.
One consequence of this was that most of the men who emerged at the

end of the Second World War as leaders of an independent Indonesia had little understanding of the basic character and outstanding problems of their country's peasantry.

Soon after the spectacular rise of Sarekat Islam an intense competition ensued for control over its membership between its original Islamic leadership and that of the newly founded Indonesian Communist Party, during the course of which Sarekat Islam lost most of its mass backing. And when at the end of 1926 the Communists attempted a revolt, they so lacked supporters and their effort was so weak and uncoordinated that the Netherlands East Indies government suppressed them with ease and dispatch. Thereafter, until the Japanese occupation, the Communists, few and divided among themselves, operated underground and quite ineffectively, and the Sarekat Islam was unable to recapture its previous commanding position. During this period the dominant role in the nationalist movement was played by secular, non-Communist Indonesians, among whom Soekarno was the outstanding leader. The repressive apparatus now at the disposal of the Dutch was so powerful, however, that he and other prominent nationalists, such as Mohammad Hatta and Soetan Sjahrir, were unable to build up the organizations necessary to provide the movement with sufficient power to challenge the Dutch. After a few years of moderately successful organizational work in the late 1920s and early 1930s these three leaders along with a number of others were summarily arrested and not released from their places of detention until the Japanese invasion.

Neither in its prewar phase nor in its postwar revolutionary period was the Indonesian nationalist movement headed by either a landed aristocracy or a substantial middle class. The modern Indonesian political elite—the men who led their country's nationalist movement and struggle for independence and who are the political leaders of Indonesia today—has been the product of an only recently available Western education and to a lesser extent of the impact of Modernist Islamic thought. Although in Indonesia education has traditionally been highly esteemed, the Islamic educational facilities existing there in the first decades of the twentieth century, and those available to the considerable number of Indonesians who went to Mecca for study, were not well suited to equip Indonesians to meet their country's modern needs. For this, as an increasing number of them were aware, modern Western education was necessary. Not until very late, however, was such education, particularly secondary education, made available to Indonesians, the Dutch trailing the British in India in this respect by approximately half a century. Moreover, for some time even the limited facilities open to Indonesians were reserved for the sons of aristocrats, and even for them opportunities were exceedingly limited. Those who held the dominant positions in the formation of Dutch colonial policy had no interest in preparing Indonesians for independence and little interest in training them for responsible positions in government or business. The meager amount of educational facilities opened to Indonesians was enough to spark the nationalist movement, but far too little to prepare Indonesians for the efficient administration of their own country.

Opportunities for Indonesians to acquire a secondary education were so few that during the period 1910–1914 in all of Indonesia an average of only 4 Indonesians graduated from high school per year. The yearly average had increased to 11 for the period 1920–1921, to 157 during the years 1929–1930, and by 1940 had reached only 240 (out of an Indonesian population of around 70 million). This stands in sharp contrast to the situation obtaining in British India. Although the quality of its high schools and colleges was probably on the average lower than that of those in Indonesia, opportunities for Indians to attend were vastly greater than for Indonesians in colonial Indonesia. With its population approximately only four times as large as that of Indonesia, British India by 1917 was providing a high school education to 216,160 students, as against 7,474 receiving such education in Indonesia twenty-three years later, in 1940. Moreover, while the preponderant majority of those receiving this education in India were Indians, only 1,786 of the 7,474 were Indonesians—most of the facilities in Indonesia being reserved for Europeans. For Indonesians the situation with regard to college-level education was even worse. The first technical college in Indonesia was opened only in 1919, the first law school in 1924, and the first medical college in 1926. In British India as early as 1891 there were 15,589 students enrolled in college, and by 1920 more than 50,000 were enrolled as against just 2 Indonesians attending college that year in Indonesia. As late as 1940 there were only 630 Indonesians attending colleges in Indonesia with only 37 being graduated in that year. (A much smaller number were enrolled in colleges abroad.) In the same year there were 12,179 students attending public colleges in the Philippines, a country with a quarter the population of Indonesia.

This situation was not in any sense indicative of a lack of desire among Indonesians for Western education. Rather it reflected a dearth of opportunities resulting from limited facilities and a heavy discrimination against Indonesians. Even before the great depression of 1929–1930, the Netherlands Indies government had shown a reluctance to expand opportunities in Western education for Indonesians, the nature of the Dutch colonial regime not being attuned to this. Thus an extensive survey made by a government commission just prior to the depression determined that 25 per cent of all Indonesians who had graduated from Western schools were unable to find jobs in which their education could be utilized and concluded that Western education for Indonesians was on too large a scale and that the "tempo of expansion exceeds the scope of social development." There were two major reasons why this commission was obliged to come to these conclusions. First, again in contrast to India, the Indonesian commercial class capable of taking advantage of Western education was pathetically diminutive, and additionally European business firms were generally averse to hiring Indonesians.[8] Second, and again in contrast to the situation in British India, the Dutch administration in the Indies was reluctant to take Indonesians into the upper levels of its bureaucracy.

Indonesia at the conclusion of Dutch colonial rule was a country with practically no indigenous middle class. If one can speak of an Indonesian middle class on Java, its commercial element had been almost eliminated. The tiny remnant still surviving at the end of the Cultivation System may have received some minor benefit from the introduction of a laissez-faire economy, but there appears to have been little or no increase in its numbers. The conditions of the company and the Cultivation System had so blunted the sensitivity of the native population on Java to the urges of capitalist economics that in Java there was little response among them to any opportunities for entrepreneurial activities which the new system may have opened up.[9] Into the resulting vacuum crowded the aggressive, already-established resi-

---

[8] Even during the year just previous to the depression of 1929–1930 Western business firms in Indonesia employed only 126 Indonesians in positions paying $100 per month or more (computed from figures appearing in *Hollandsch-Inlandsch Onderwijs-Commissie*, vol. VIa, *De Werkgelegenheid in Nederlandsch-Indië voor Nederlandsch Sprekenden* [Opportunities for Employment in the Netherlands Indies for Speakers of Dutch; Weltevreden, 1931], pp. 28–29).

[9] In Sumatra, Borneo, and Celebes—by contrast—opportunities in copra and small-holder's rubber production and trade probably somewhat strengthened the position of Indonesian entrepreneurs. Any increase in the number and/or wealth of Indonesian entrepreneurs outside of Java would appear, however, to have been more than offset by a decline in their numbers on Java, with a resultant over-all decrease for Indonesia as a whole.

dent Chinese merchant class supplemented by thousands of immigrants from southeast China. Armed with industriousness and commercial ability acquired in the fiercely competitive society of their own country, they eagerly exploited opportunities which the Indonesian population was rarely equipped to dispute with them and which did not tempt most Netherlanders. Nearly all of that part of the middle class in Indonesia which was not European was Chinese. There existed only a handful of Indonesian entrepreneurs, a most meager handful in Java, and what hard data are available suggest that the numbers of even this tiny residual element were declining rather than growing during the last years of Dutch rule.

In 1941, of those Indonesians who had received a Western primary education or above and who had found employment in which this education was utilized, probably about two-thirds worked as civil servants in the Netherlands East Indies government. Insofar as there did exist an Indonesian middle class at the close of Dutch rule, it was preponderantly a bureaucratic middle class. This majority element, as well as the sizable minority of Western-educated Indonesians unable to secure jobs which made any effective use of their education, had no direct stake in capitalism, regarding it as something largely outside of their own sphere of life, the province of alien Europeans and Chinese. They were not opposed to government's having a major role in economic affairs and tended to be warmly receptive to the socialist ideas to which Western education had given them access. These Indonesians, and in particular those who assumed positions of leadership in the nationalist movement and the revolution, usually tended to regard capitalism as an aspect of colonialism, many actually equating the two. By and large they looked on capitalism as the way of the European overlord and his Chinese associates, a system whose benefits bypassed Indonesians.

It is thus understandable why Marxism, in particular Marxist ideas concerning the relationship between capitalism and colonialism, has had such a wide appeal for Indonesians. Although an undoubted majority of the modern Indonesian political elite have been affected by these ideas, most of them have been highly eclectic in their approach to Western political thought and often mix their Marxism with the ideas of non-Marxist political theories. Whereas most of them have been attracted to and influenced by Lenin's analysis of colonialism, often profoundly, the large majority have been drawn to revisionist strands of Marxism leading in the direction of democratic socialism rather than communism. There has, however, always been a significant minority who have espoused communism. Another by no means insignificant minority, though eschewing communism, has undertaken (sometimes more unconsciously than consciously) to wed Marxian economic con-

Chart 5. Economic differentiation in the nonagrarian sector of colonial Indonesian society in 1940, indicating percentage of each population group in the several income categories: Income in guilders (the guilder equaling approximately one-half U.S. dollar) * as shown by income tax assessments †

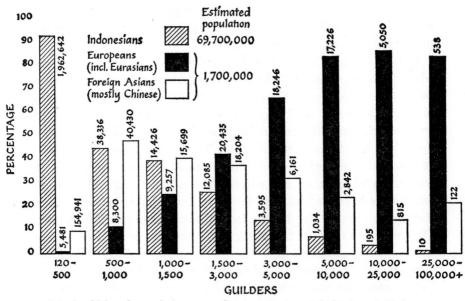

* It should be observed that many living costs, particularly that of food, were considerably less in Indonesia than in the United States at that time.

† This chart is based upon statistics appearing in the Netherlands East Indies official government statistical yearbook, *Indisch Verslag,* 1941, vol. II, Table 110, p. 181, and Table 110A, pp. 184–185.

cepts with largely indigenously rooted ideas of paternalistic authoritarianism. Finally, it should be noted that most of the strongly Islamic political leaders, especially those most receptive to Modernist Islamic ideas, are socialistically oriented, some of the most influential calling themselves "religious socialists." They have argued that Muhammad preached socialist economic doctrines twelve centuries before Marx, but their socialism, though probably fully harmonious with any enlightened interpretation of Muhammad's teachings, also bears the print of the social democratic strand of Marxism.

The fact that so large a proportion of the Indonesian middle class found jobs with the civil service should not induce the conclusion that the Netherlands provided the Indonesians with any significant preparation for self-government. The facts were quite different. Although during the last decade of their rule the Dutch were giving their own colonial officials a training which was probably superior to that provided by any other colonial power, in Indonesia they built up no equivalent of the Indian Civil Service. Whereas the British during the last decades of their rule in India turned over a very substantial amount of the country's administration to highly trained Indians, this was decidedly not the case with the Dutch in Indonesia. A breakdown of the component elements of the Netherlands Indies Civil Service at the end of Dutch rule makes this abundantly clear. As late as October 1940, out of the 3,039 higher-ranking civil service positions only 221 were held by Indonesians. The other Indonesian civil servants held posts largely devoid of any real decision-making function wherein the chief requirement was to carry out decisions arrived at by the generally paternalistic-minded Dutch officials who stood above them. Even in the upper-middle ranks Indonesians filled no more than 40 per cent of the positions. "Function must be equivalent to education" was the official Dutch rationale for this system; and so long as they were denied this education, Indonesians could thereby be barred from the positions where they might have had the training in governmental administration which their counterparts in India and the Philippines enjoyed and which contributed so much to the political viability of those countries following their independence.

Not only was the record a somber one with regard to preparation of Indonesians in governmental administration. In addition, again in contrast to the record of the British in India and Burma and of the United States in the Philippines, Indonesians were allowed no real experience with the institutions of national self-government, parliamentary or other. The most that the Netherlands was willing to countenance was a largely advisory People's Council on which elected Indonesians as late as 1940 held only 19 out of 60 seats and which had no significant function other than providing a sounding board heeded or disregarded at will by Dutch colonial officials.

Thus during the colonial period Indonesians were denied access to constructive political roles. Those who were forthright in pressing demands for independence were arrested, jailed, and deported to remote islands. Those who tried to cooperate with the colonial authorities in the expectation that this would lead to significant grants of administrative responsibility to Indonesians within an increasingly autonomous, though Dutch-controlled, Indonesia were bitterly disappointed. Being thus denied any really constructive role or responsible position in colonial society, educated Indonesians assumed the only posture consistent with their nationalist convictions—one of opposition, an opposition without responsibility. For the independent Indonesia that emerged after the Second World War, this was to have unfortunate consequences not confined to lack of administrative training and experience in self-government. Because of this condition, many Indonesians could not entirely rid themselves of their negative attitude toward government in general. Their long participation in a politics of opposition had endowed them with an opposition orientation which, though useful during the period of revolution and the long struggle against the Dutch, militated against a constructive role in government once Indonesia had attained its independence. This residuum in conjunction with another derived from the same set of colonial circumstances, namely, a reluctance to assume responsibility for decisions, particularly when confronting new problems demanding new answers, constituted in their combination a colonial legacy hardly suited to the political and administrative exigencies confronting the Indonesian elite upon the attainment of independence.

· XX ·

The Revolution and the

Revolutionary Government

THE Indonesian elite's dissatisfaction with Dutch rule was such that many welcomed the Japanese invasion of early 1942, believing that under Japan their situation could not be worse and might well be better. The harshness of Japanese rule soon disabused them of any such expectations. The sufferings of Indonesians at the hands of the Japanese reinforced their nationalism and did not dispose them to welcome the return of the Dutch. The weak, halfhearted defense put up by the Dutch army dealt a heavy blow to Netherlands prestige, and Indonesians tended to hold the Dutch responsible for their sufferings inasmuch as the Netherlands was regarded as having neither effectively protected Indonesia nor permitted Indonesians to bear arms to protect themselves. This and the persistent anti-Dutch propaganda of the Japanese spread anti-Dutch sentiment more widely among the mass of the population than ever before.

The Japanese Occupation

Nationalism grew apace during the three and a half years of Japanese occupation, but in the various parts of the archipelago its growth as an organized movement was rather uneven, there being three sepa-

555

rate Japanese military occupation zones in Indonesia.[1] Each was administratively distinct, with little intercourse between them. One Japanese army occupied Java and, although responsible to the Japanese Southeast Asia command headquarters in Saigon, enjoyed considerable autonomy. Under it the Indonesian nationalist movement was given the greatest latitude for development. Sumatra was administered by a separate Japanese army, likewise directly responsible to Saigon but inclined to give nationalists less scope. Celebes, Borneo, the Moluccas, and the Lesser Sundas were under a division of the Japanese navy, with headquarters at Macassar, which followed a severely repressive policy that in general allowed Indonesian nationalists no more latitude than had the Dutch.

On Java long-exiled influential nationalist leaders were allowed substantial freedom of movement; some were permitted a contact with the Indonesian masses which, although limited and controlled, was much greater than had been countenanced by the Dutch. The Japanese were willing to grant them such opportunities in order to secure their help in harnessing Indonesia more effectively to Japan's wartime economic requirements—in particular assistance in mobilizing forced labor and in organizing peasant deliveries of rice. Those nationalist leaders willing to lend themselves to this work, Soekarno in particular, were given opportunities for touring the countryside, making speeches to the peasantry, and utilizing the radio network. In the process they were able to engage in a considerable amount of nationalist propaganda.

The Japanese occupation greatly furthered the spread of an all-Indonesian language. This language, based primarily upon Sumatran Malay (and closely related to the old commercial lingua franca of the Indonesian port cities), had earlier been promoted by Indonesian nationalists with only modest success. After the outlawing of Dutch and an abortive attempt to get the Indonesians to use Japanese in schools and in administration, the occupation command authorized the use of Indonesian for these key functions. As a consequence a national lan-

---

[1] For accounts in English of the Japanese occupation see Benedict R. O'G. Anderson, *Some Aspects of Indonesian Politics under the Japanese Occupation: 1944–1945* (Cornell Modern Indonesia Project, Interim Reports Series; Ithaca, N.Y., 1961); M. A. Aziz, *Japan's Colonialism and Indonesia* (The Hague: Nijhoff, 1955); H. J. Benda, *The Crescent and the Rising Sun* (New York: Institute of Pacific Relations; The Hague: van Hoeve, 1958); Williard H. Elsbree, *Japan's Role in Southeast Asian Nationalist Movements, 1940–45* (Cambridge, Mass.: Harvard University Press, Institute of Pacific Relations, 1953).

guage, a basic vehicle of any nationalistic movement, took real root in Indonesia.

One of the most important results of the occupation was the virtual social revolution which expediency obliged the Japanese to put through, a measure which gave a sharp fillip to the growth of nationalist sentiment. Arriving with almost no military government personnel and believing it necessary to intern practically all Netherlanders, they were obliged to turn to Indonesians to help them staff many administrative and technical positions previously held by the Dutch. Until the last months of the war the Japanese filled the top posts themselves, but Indonesians who had formerly occupied the lower ranks of the services frequently were suddenly pushed up into positions two or three levels above what they had held in the Dutch colonial administration. Generally they were able to fill these positions with a degree of competence which quite surprised them. It became apparent to many that the skills of the Dutch colonial official, whom for so long they had been taught to regard as their superior, were well within the compass of their own abilities. This realization engendered a powerful self-confidence which increased their belief in their ability to govern themselves. Moreover, those who had personally benefited from this revolutionary upward social mobility naturally had a vested interest in maintaining these changes. To them, this meant resistance to any return of Dutch rule; for they felt that its reestablishment would mean loss of their new posts.

Toward the end of the war expectation of an Allied attack on Java persuaded the Japanese that to have any hope of the Indonesians' support they would have to promise them independence and yield them some upper-level administrative posts. Beginning in early October 1944, just after an announcement by the Japanese Prime Minister that Indonesia would be given independence "in the very near future," occupation authorities on Java began to relax controls over the activities of nationalist leaders, giving them greater opportunities for contact with the people. By early 1945 the Japanese began to take some short and halting steps in the direction of limited Indonesian self-government. A significant number of top-level administrative positions were gradually opened to Indonesians. (Again it was only on Java, and to a much lesser extent on Sumatra, that the Japanese made these concessions to Indonesian nationalism; in the areas administered by the navy the lid was clamped tight until almost the very end.) Although these positions remained usually under close Japanese supervision and always under ultimate Japanese control, they were important in generating a feeling of self-confidence among the Indonesian elite, a belief in their ability to handle the key positions previously held by Dutch officials.

Expectation of an Allied attack also brought the Japanese to establish an auxiliary army, a lightly armed militia known as the Peta. It was this Japanese-trained, but Indonesian officered, militia which was to provide the principal military force behind the revolution, both in its early stages, when ironically it turned on the Japanese troops and fought them, and later when it fought British and subsequently Dutch forces. In addition, the Japanese gave a very limited military training— but no arms—and the function of security guards to a considerable number of village and urban youth; when the Peta later as a revolutionary army expanded its ranks, it was able to draw on this source.

In March 1945 the Japanese appointed a committee of some 60 Indonesians, most of them prominent, representing the principal social and ethnic groups of Java and Madura, and 7 Japanese to work out plans for the political and economic organization of an independent Indonesia. At meetings in May and July its members reached agreement on a set of broad national political principles. The Indonesians appear to have dominated these discussions, the Japanese members, for whatever reasons, taking relatively modest parts. The major role was played by Soekarno; much of the discussion was between him and certain Islamic leaders who wished the principles to have a more strongly Islamic cast than he believed was consistent with that religion's relatively undogmatic character in most of Indonesia and with the fact that the country had important non-Islamic minorities. Soekarno prevailed, and the set of five principles, *Pantjasila,* finally adopted —through a compromise between differing views held by the committee members—was a synthesis wherein his own thinking was dominant. In fact the *Pantjasila* was Soekarno's own statement made in an off-the-cuff speech (and recorded stenographically) toward the end of the meeting wherein he presented his own ideological synthesis in an effort to bridge his position and that of the more doctrinaire Islamic leaders while changing his own views as little as possible in the process.

The *Pantjasila,* although vague and not fully acceptable to some nominally Islamic Western-educated Indonesians as well as some prominent Islamic leaders, was to become the nearest approach to an official Indonesian national philosophy. The Five Principles in the order then presented by Soekarno were nationalism, internationalism (or humanitarianism), representative government, social justice, and belief in God in a context of religious freedom. His nationalism had a geopolitical element and defined the Indonesian nation as covering "the entire archipelago of Indonesia from the northern tip of Sumatra to Papua." It was not, however, to be chauvinistic, but was to harmonize with other nationalisms to form an international community, "one family of all nations," wherein each member would maintain his national identity. Representative government would incorporate the Islamic principle of consultation, and the envisaged house of representatives would provide Muslims with ample opportunity for working toward an Islamic political order while at the same time giving adherents of other religions an equal chance to advance their own ideas. But representative government would mean little if not undergirded by social justice. In America and the countries of Western Europe, Soekarno argued, "the capitalists are in control," and in them political democracy is unaccompanied by economic democracy. "Political democracy," he stated, citing the French revisionist socialist Jean Jaures, does not ensure "economic democracy." If social justice was to be secured for the Indonesian people, both kinds of democracy would be necessary; "if we are seeking democracy, the need is not for the democracy of the West, but for . . . politico-economic democracy."

Late in July 1945 the Japanese command on Sumatra provided for the establishment of a roughly similar committee to make preparations for independence, but in the areas under its control the Japanese navy made no such concession. Not until August 7, 1945, when Japan's Southeast Asia headquarters ordered the establishment of an all-Indonesian Independence Preparatory Committee, was it possible for Indonesian nationalists from the navy-administered areas to come to Java to consult with Javanese and Sumatran leaders. This committee, with Soekarno as chairman and Mohammad Hatta as vice-chairman, was composed of 11 members from Java, 4 from Sumatra, 2 from Celebes, and 1 each representing the Lesser Sundas, the Moluccas, and the Indonesian Chinese community. Its announced function was to make preparations for transfer of governmental authority to it by the Japanese.

The Revolutionary Struggle

Japan's surrender resulted in the sudden removal of the repressive apparatus that had for so long held the Indonesian nationalist movement in check. It found the Indonesian members of the Peta anti-Japanese as well as anti-Dutch and equipped with the arms necessary to contest any reimposition of outside control. When the Japanese commander in Java made clear that rather than promote Indonesian independence he would obey the Allied orders to maintain the *status quo* pending the take-over by Allied troops, Soekarno and Hatta, urged on by the anti-Japanese underground organizations and student groups, on August 17, 1945, proclaimed Indonesia's independence.

Some Japanese officers, stupefied by their country's sudden surrender, acquiesced to the Indonesians' seizure of stocks of arms in their custody; but others ordered their troops to resist the Peta and students. The scope and tempo of this fighting quickly increased, with the Peta, reinforced by newly armed student organizations, engaging in heavy fighting against Japanese forces for control of key cities. The first phase of the Indonesian revolution had begun. Sumatra followed Java's example, and in parts of that island, too, fighting broke out between Indonesians and Japanese. This was not the pattern, however, in Borneo, Celebes, the Lesser Sundas, or the Moluccas. There the Japanese had not allowed Indonesian nationalists to organize or to form militias, and consequently they had little trouble in maintaining control until Allied troops, generally Australian, took over. The Australians, not confronted by any strong and active Indonesian nationalist organization with which they felt obliged to come to terms, did not hesitate to reinstall Dutch civil administrators promptly.

In Java and Sumatra the situation was very different. When the British, the Allied troops assigned there, first landed in Java some six weeks after the declaration of independence, they were amazed to find the newly born Indonesian Republic a going organization, possessing an effective militia and a functioning, if somewhat rudimentary, administration. Moreover, they soon discovered that the Republican regimes on Java and Sumatra were solidly linked to and backed by the Indonesian masses. Although the Indonesians were glad to have the British accept the surrender of Japanese troops and send them home, they naturally could not agree with that part of the Allied mandate which called for the British to turn over authority to the Dutch before pulling out. Heavy fighting resulted. The British ultimately had to send Japanese troops into battle to shore up an Indian division which except for its Ghurka component had proved unreliable, several hundred Indians deserting to the Indonesian side.

It rapidly became clear to the British that unless they were willing to bring to Indonesia a greatly increased strength of soldiers and equipment they would have to alter their policies and find some measure of common ground with the leaders of the Indonesian revolution. Continuation of a military policy found no backing at home, and the British soon began to deal with the Republic of Indonesia as a *de facto* government. In addition they urged the Dutch, whose troops they had meanwhile begun to shoehorn into some of the port areas they held, to negotiate with the Republic so that a peaceful compromise might be effected. Following the disarming and removal of the Japanese, Britain put great pressure on the Netherlands to come to such an agreement, making it clear that all British troops would leave Indonesia by November 1946.

Late in November, Netherlands and Republican authorities finally signed an ambiguously worded document, the Linggadjati Agreement, which it was hoped would avert the outbreak of war and meet the basic demands of both parties. This provided for the protection of Dutch economic interests in Indonesia and for Dutch recognition of the Republic's *de facto* authority over Java and Sumatra. Ultimately the Republic was to be merged in an Indonesian federation containing at least two other units—Borneo and "the Great East" (Celebes, the Lesser Sundas, the Moluccas, and Western New Guinea). This federal state would then cooperate with the Netherlands in establishing a vaguely defined Netherlands-Indonesian Union to emerge at the beginning of January 1949.[2] During the ensuing eight months of relative peace the Dutch consolidated their control over the islands outside of Java and Sumatra and reinforced their troop strength in the Javanese and Sumatran port cities turned over to them by the retiring British. Dutch efforts to reassert political control over Indonesia followed two courses: first, an attempt to destroy the Republic and its armed forces by military means and, second, a politics of divide-and-rule calculated to isolate the Republic from other areas of Indonesia and create a political system—a so-called federal order—wherein pro-Republican elements would be smothered, or at least decisively outvoted, by representatives from a congeries of some fifteen Dutch-sponsored and Dutch-controlled component states.[3] But successful prosecution of their tactics of indirect rule, however refined and skillful, was ultimately dependent

[2] For a full account of the Linggadjati negotiations and an analysis of the agreement see Charles Wolf, Jr., *The Indonesian Story* (New York: John Day, 1948).
[3] For an account of the strategy and tactics employed by the Dutch see G. McT. Kahin, *Nationalism and Revolution in Indonesia* (Ithaca, N.Y.: Cornell University Press, 1952), pp. 351–390.

upon the other prong of their strategy, a decisive and crushing military victory over the forces of the Republic—an objective they were to find unobtainable.

In July 1947 the Dutch charged the Republic with violating the Linggadjati Agreement, refused to abide by its arbitration clause, and launched an all-out attack. After their forces had overrun the Republic's richest districts in Java and Sumatra, they were induced by the United Nations to halt further advance and to sign in January 1947 another military truce and political agreement with the Republic, the Renville Agreement. In essence this gave the Dutch temporary control of the areas they had penetrated in return for their pledge to hold a UN-sponsored plebiscite in them to determine whether or not their populations wished to be governed by the Republic. It was very clear that in any such plebiscite an overwhelming majority would declare for the Republic, and the Dutch never held one. Instead, and likewise in contravention of the Renville Agreement, in these disputed areas they energetically set about to sponsor and build up amenable puppet or semipuppet states such as they had already begun establishing in Borneo and Celebes.

Into the truncated territory left the Republic on Java, a deficit food area, fled approximately a million refugees from those parts Dutch forces had entered. A tight Dutch blockade, extending even to medical supplies and quite in violation of the Renville Agreement, made living conditions extremely harsh. Because of this and because Indonesian leaders saw the United States and the European democracies unwilling to take effective measures to bring the Netherlands to live up to its commitments under the agreement (while they for the time being regarded Soviet Russia as supporting the Republic), the pro-Communist minority inside the Republic grew in numbers and influence. The Stalinist Communists were emboldened and, apparently responding to the new international line, laid plans for taking over the government and ousting Soekarno and the cabinet headed by Hatta. Their preparations were only partially completed when their effort was prematurely triggered by second-echelon Communist leaders operating from the central Java city of Madiun. After bitter fighting lasting from mid-September through mid-November 1948, the Republic's army (the large majority of its units remaining loyal) suppressed the rebellion.[4]

Just six weeks later, in defiance of the UN-sponsored Renville Agree-

---

[4] An account of the Madiun rebellion and its background can be found in Kahin, *Nationalism and Revolution*, pp. 256–303.

ment, the Netherlands launched an all-out military campaign against the Republic's weakened forces. But Indonesian resistance was determined and sustained, and by the late spring of 1949 it was clear that the Dutch could not marshal sufficient military strength in Indonesia to enforce a political decision through military power. It was likewise clear that any prolongation of their costly military effort would result in an even more widespread destruction of the Netherlands' 2-billion-dollar investment in Indonesia and be a continuing heavy drain on its manpower and wealth at home. As Dutch holdings were increasingly exposed to the Republic's scorched-earth policy, more and more Dutch businessmen joined liberal elements in the Netherlands long committed to the idea of Indonesian independence. This in conjunction with powerful adverse world opinion, including substantial pressure from the United States, finally brought the Netherlands government to come to terms with the realities of Indonesian nationalism. At the Round Table Conference held at The Hague during the late summer of 1949 a settlement was reached which ended the hostilities and provided for Indonesia's full independence. In essence the Dutch yielded their claim to sovereignty over all Indonesia except Western New Guinea (with the proviso that its status be decided during the coming year on the basis of negotiations between Indonesia and the Netherlands) in return for the preservation of their economic stake in Indonesia and a shipping agreement and a debt settlement distinctly favorable to the Netherlands, Indonesia being saddled with nearly $1,130,000,000 of the colonial regime's obligations, much of which had been incurred since 1945 in financing the effort to suppress the Republic.[5]

Effect of the Revolution on Indonesian Government

The circumstances attending Indonesia's long and difficult struggle for independence decisively shaped the nature of its government. The political institutions forged during the heat of nearly five years of revolution were developed under unique conditions, quite different from those obtaining after independence. By its very nature the revolutionary struggle exerted powerful centripetal pressures which greatly eased the tasks of government. The necessity for Indonesians to stand

[5] For the most scholarly and comprehensive account of the Dutch-Indonesian negotiations and their culmination in the Round Table Conference, see Alastair M. Taylor, *Indonesian Independence and the United Nations* (Ithaca, N.Y.: Cornell University Press, 1960).

shoulder to shoulder against a common enemy induced a consciousness of common political purpose and a political integration, at the
same time enhancing the individual's willingness to sacrifice for the
common good. The Republic was able to wage a war against tremendous odds for more than four years on a printing-press currency
backed by nothing more than the symbols of nationalism and independence. Thus during the long period of struggle there was no great
pressure to provide formulas of political organization calculated to
satisfy regional sentiments.

The character of the revolutionary Republic's political institutions,
institutions which were to have a profound influence upon postrevolutionary Indonesian government, was also strongly affected by the
struggle for power within the ranks of revolutionists.[6] And to some
extent it was influenced by a belief (which reinforced the position of
certain leaders) that Indonesia's bargaining position against the Dutch
in the forum of world opinion would be stronger if it had a government
which was rid of any important residue of the Japanese occupation
and any suggestion of fascist orientation.

At its first meeting on August 18, 1945, the Independence Preparatory
Committee elected Soekarno and Hatta respectively President and
Vice-President of the newly proclaimed Republic of Indonesia and appointed a commission of seven, including these two leaders, to make
a final draft of a national constitution, a document already largely
written during the last month prior to the Japanese capitulation. Within
a week this work was completed and the constitution promulgated.
Though considered definitely provisional, it was not replaced until the
end of 1949.

The 1945 constitution described a political order somewhat like
the American. The center of power was to be lodged with a President
assisted by an appointed cabinet directly responsible to him. In addition to holding executive powers the President would share legislative
power with an elected Congress. The major departure from the American system was the provision for a sort of periodical constitutional
convention to be known as the Consultative Assembly. This large
elected body was to meet every five years and would be charged with
electing the President and Vice-President (who would be responsible
to it), initially formulating the definitive constitution—in later meetings
amending it if necessary—and determining the broad lines of general

---

[6] An account of the internal politics of the revolution in this early, formative
period can be found in Kahin, *Nationalism and Revolution*, pp. 147–212.

governmental policy. There was also provision for a High Advisory Council, whose composition was to be defined by law and which was to advise and provide information requested by the President and have the right to submit proposals to the government.

Although the 1945 constitution envisaged three major repositories of power—an elected Consultative Assembly, the presidency, and an elected Chamber of Representatives—the circumstances of the revolution never allowed sufficient opportunity to hold the national elections which were the necessary antecedents for creation of the Consultative Assembly and the Chamber of Representatives. Only the transitional provisions of the 1945 constitution were in an operational sense of importance. These stipulated that until the formation of the two elected bodies all state powers would be exercised by the President assisted by a central national committee which would have a purely advisory function. Thus on August 29 Soekarno dissolved the Independence Preparatory Committee and in its place established the Komite Nasional Indonesia Pusat (Central Indonesian National Committee), or KNIP as it came to be known. Assisted in his selections by Hatta, he appointed 135 members to the new body, including those of the dissolved Independence Preparatory Committee. Those selected were considered to be outstanding Indonesian nationalists and the most important leaders of the principal ethnic, religious, social, and economic groups in Indonesia; few could be classified as amenable political stooges. A cabinet directly responsible to the President was appointed, for the most part made up of those Indonesians who had served as department heads under the Japanese during the last months of their rule. Thus the government established at the outset of the Indonesian revolution was one in which power was largely concentrated in the presidency.

This system lasted for only two and a half months, until November 15, 1945. Widespread opposition to its concentration of power soon emerged, a large part of the criticism being equally concerned with the survivals of Japanese rule evidenced by the cabinet's membership. Much of the pushing power behind the revolution came from the armed youth organizations, whose members were deeply affected by the ideas of the most prominent of the leaders who had refused to work with the Japanese, in particular by Soetan Sjahrir and Amir Sjarifuddin. These youth groups along with a large minority of the KNIP accused several key members of Soekarno's cabinet of being close to the Japanese in their thinking and of possessing what they termed "fascist mentalities." They were disturbed that these men were in control of key sectors of government and in positions to exert substantial influence on the course of policy. And, although the majority were reconciled to Soekarno's assumption of the principal post of leadership in the revolution, they opposed his exercising the overwhelming and unrestrained power called for in the transitional regulations of the constitution.

In response to this powerful sentiment, on October 7, 1945, 50 members of the KNIP presented a petition to Soekarno urging that legislative authority be shared by the President with the thus far advisory KNIP. Cognizant of the strong backing of this element and fearful of the challenge from a third group headed by the nationalist-Communist leader Tan Malaka, Soekarno gave in to this demand (undoubtedly with Hatta urging him to do so). Thereby he strengthened his ties with the Sjahrir and Sjarifuddin groups and those who shared their dislike of some of the high officials left in office by the Japanese. On October 16, 1945, a presidential decree, signed by Vice-President Hatta, provided that pending the establishment of the Consultative Assembly and Chamber of Representatives called for in the constitution the KNIP would be vested with their legislative authority, thereby sharing legislative power with the President. All legislation now had to be approved by the KNIP as well as by the President, with the KNIP having the same right as he to introduce legislation. The decree also stipulated, as had been requested in the petition, that the KNIP delegate its powers to a small permanently sitting representative body known as the Working Committee (Badan Pekerdja) which was to be composed of members of the infrequently convoked parent body (the KNIP) and responsible to it. Although the KNIP was required to convene a minimum of only once a year, the Working Committee was to meet at least every ten days. The KNIP elected the two men who had been the principal leaders of the anticollaborationists—Sjahrir and Sjarifuddin—respectively as chairman and vice-chairman of the newly established Working Committee. They accepted their posts on condition that they be empowered to select its other 13 members, a demand which the KNIP granted. Thereupon the Working Committee became a key factor in the Republic's government, exercising to the full its colegislative powers and under Sjahrir overshadowing both President and cabinet.

At the end of October 1945, Sjahrir published a small booklet, *Our Struggle* (*Perdjuangan Kita*), which had great impact upon the thinking of politically active Indonesians, especially those who remained dissatisfied with the still substantial power in the hands of the cabinet and regarded its members as too close to the Japanese in their thinking. Sjahrir strongly castigated what he described as the fascist and opportunistic mentality of many members of the government, both in the cabinet and in the upper level of the bureaucracy. He warned that these men might lead the government in the direction of fascist totalitarianism and jingoist nationalism and called for their prompt removal from office.[7] There was a heavy rallying behind him; those who had earlier called for the President's sharing power with the KNIP now demanded that the cabinet be responsible to the KNIP rather than to the President. The positions of those in the cabinet and in the bureaucracy who owed their posts to the Japanese were seriously weakened, and although Soekarno had not been included in the attack, there is no doubt that it temporarily decreased his political stature. Sjahrir's position was further strengthened because of the feeling among a number of influential Indonesians that a government required to deal with the victorious Allies ought to show as little residual Japanese influence as possible.

Thus on November 11 the Working Committee called for the introduction of cabinet responsibility to parliament, that is, to the KNIP. Soekarno and Hatta promptly accepted this proposal, dismissing the old cabinet and opening the way for establishment on November 14, 1945, of a new cabinet headed by Sjahrir, one no longer under the authority of the President and responsible only to the representative body of the government. With the Working Committee (now under a new chairman and vice-chairman) still serving as deputy of the KNIP during the long periods between its meetings, the cabinet in effect became responsible to the Working Committee. Although not specifically spelled out at this time, it was expected that should a difference arise between cabinet and Working Committee the matter would be referred for resolution to the KNIP. In practice all disagreements which arose were resolved between them without an appeal by either one to the KNIP. The Working Committee never challenged the cabinet's assumption of the major executive role, but reserved the right to scrutinize closely its discharge of that power through a frequently employed right of

[7] Sjahrir was himself later of the opinion that his attacks upon these men had been unduly strong and resulted in an embitterment and alienation which carried over into the postrevolutionary period, making it unnecessarily difficult for him and his party to work harmoniously with them (conversations with the writer, 1954–1955).

interpolation. In the legislative field the Working Committee came close to being the cabinet's peer. One reason for the positive and efficient role played by the Working Committee was its small size. Until March 1947 its membership did not exceed 24, and thereafter it was increased to only 45. This made possible discussion along traditional Indonesian lines, that is, discussion resulting in a conclusion based upon the broad consensus of the group as a whole rather than one based upon majority vote. Whereas the KNIP, had it been disposed to be an active legislative body, was much too large for discussion and decision making along traditional Indonesian lines, the Working Committee was of optimal size and usually followed this process in arriving at its most important decisions. Another reason for the Working Committee's efficiency was its members' freedom from close connection with political parties and their usual tendency to view issues apart from party considerations, showing themselves in most cases to be above party in their conduct.

During its month's operation under Sjahrir's chairmanship (October 16, 1945—November 12, 1945) prior to the establishment of cabinet responsibility to parliament, the Working Committee had called for the creation of a diversity of political parties. It took this important measure largely to obviate the possible growth of a totalitarian political order—one of the reasons which had prompted it to demand that the KNIP be transformed into a body with legislative authority and which later brought it to demand that the cabinet be responsible to the KNIP rather than the President. The Working Committee was particularly concerned lest a monolithic party organization be established wherein those who had worked with the Japanese would exercise control because of their still dominant position throughout most of the bureaucracy.[8] It was to preclude this and ensure that these elements would be politically undercut that the Working Committee on October 30, 1945, called for the formation of several political parties reflecting various trends of opinion. This position was promptly endorsed by the cabinet and the President in a government regulation of November 3 which noted that "if democratic principles are to be observed it is not permissible that only one party should be allowed to function." Parties proliferated, but they did not develop real roots in the popula-

[8] An abortive move to establish such a party had been made on August 22, 1945, when the Independence Preparatory Committee had decided on the formation of a single national party. Ten days later this decision was withdrawn and the proposal shelved, but there was considerable expectation that it might be reactivated.

tion; for national elections, although repeatedly scheduled, were not held during the revolutionary period. The impact of the parties on the political scene was not immediate. But whereas in the formation of his first cabinet (November 14, 1945—March 12, 1946) Sjahrir was able to disregard them completely, in forming his third and last cabinet (October 2, 1946—July 3, 1947) he was obliged to meet them halfway in their demand for cabinet representation.

Although it is true that during the four-year revolutionary period the principal legislative and executive roles were played by the Working Committee and the cabinet, one should not minimize the importance of the presidency. Soekarno and Hatta appear to have participated in all major governmental decisions, and as far as can be ascertained, none was ever taken to which they were strongly opposed. Promulgation of any law or decree was regarded as requiring the signature of either the President or the Vice-President, and it was Soekarno's position that signing was no mere formality but an indication of presidential approval which he had the right to withhold when he was in disagreement. Thus to the writer he stated: "Theoretically I can veto any law of parliament. However, I have never done so, because my system was to keep in very close contact with Assaat [chairman of both the Working Committee and the KNIP] and to influence the Working Committee. Agreements were worked out ahead of time, and thus collisions between presidency and Working Committee were avoided." The fact that both President and Vice-President generally acted in close concert during this period helped ensure that their views would usually diverge little from those held by the cabinet and the Working Committee. For in the process of finding common ground between themselves the two leaders were likely to be that much closer to the views of these other two organs of government.

Soekarno, in addressing an important session of the KNIP in February 1947, stated that in his opinion, pending elections which would determine the composition of the representative bodies of the state, it was the task of the President himself to nominate and appoint KNIP members "because of the fact that the President himself is regarded as the representative of the whole people." Even then his views concerning the proper qualities of a representative body foreshadowed the controversial position which he was to take in 1957: he held that the KNIP should incorporate members of occupational groups, the regions, the principal non-Indonesian minorities, the armed organizations, as well as of the political parties. In the KNIP as he and Hatta enlarged it in 1947 the parties actually held only 222 out of 514 seats, and the appointments reflected Soekarno's view that a party's representation should be determined not merely by the number of its members, but also by its degree of organization and integration. Thus while acknowledging that the major Islamic party, the Masjumi, enrolled several times as many members as either the Socialist, Labor, or Communist parties, he held that nevertheless because of greater integration and superior organization these last three were entitled to 35 seats each in the KNIP as against 60 for the Masjumi.[9] This same philosophy was reflected in the composition of the Republic's High Advisory Council, one of the few organs of government provided for in the 1945 constitution which functioned as described. Its membership of 10 to 19 members, selected by Soekarno in consultation with Hatta, related only incidentally to party and embraced distinguished regional leaders as well as individuals representing important religious and ethnic groups.

In times of acute crisis when for one reason or another the cabinet could not function effectively, plenary emergency powers were exercised by the President. It was, however, never clear to what extent the decision to vest the President with them was a prerogative of the President or lay within the competence of cabinet and/or Working Committee.[10]

The relative efficiency and quality of Indonesia's government during the revolutionary period may be explained in part at least by three important factors. One was the previously noted solidarity induced by the common struggle against the Dutch. A second was the generally smooth working relationship between the government's representative body and the cabinet, a situation which was not to obtain during most of the postrevolutionary period. In practice the cabinet had to deal only with the Working Committee of the representative body (KNIP) and for all practical purposes was responsible only to it. With the Work-

[9] Conversation of the writer with President Soekarno, Jogjakarta, December 12, 1948. Soekarno stated that in determining party strength he consulted with Hatta after having received reports from local officials giving estimates of party strength within their areas.

[10] See A. K. Pringgodigdo, *The Office of President in Indonesia as Defined in the Three Constitutions in Theory and Practice* (Cornell Modern Indonesia Project, Translation Series; Ithaca, N.Y., 1957), pp 15–16. Soekarno's own position was clear. To the present writer he stated: "I have the right to declare a state of emergency, during which I can govern by decree, and to do so I do not need consent of parliament, though of course I would always talk it over with the ministers beforehand" (Muntok, Bangka, May 4, 1949).

ing Committee composed of a small group of competent men, it was reasonably easy for them to reach agreement in a short time. Thus the cabinet could generally count upon the Working Committee's knowing its own mind and reaching a decision fairly quickly, qualities which were much more difficult to develop in the large, heterogeneous, and loosely organized KNIP and which were to prove equally difficult to achieve in the postrevolutionary parliament. Moreover, the size and quality of the Working Committee's membership meant that discussion, informal as well as formal, between it and cabinet members could yield mutual understanding, common ground, and finally agreement relatively quickly. Such rapport would not have been possible had the cabinet been obliged to deal directly with the KNIP, and it was not to prove possible between cabinet and parliament in the postrevolutionary period when the intermediary Working Committee had been abolished.

A third reason for the relative effectiveness of government in the revolutionary period lay in the generally harmonious relationship between President and Vice-President. The policies emanating from the presidency were moderated by the fact that such cooperation implied a degree of compromise between the views of these two men. In addition, when during the last two years of the revolutionary period the hardening of party lines made it increasingly difficult in times of crisis to form cabinets based upon a parliamentary majority, this harmony ensured that emergency, transitional "presidential cabinets" could be formed with Vice-President Hatta acting as Prime Minister. The composition of such cabinets did not become a question of bargaining between the various political parties, the key post being held by a man of great prestige who stood above party, and it was generally believed that a cabinet so established could not be forced to resign by a vote of nonconfidence in the KNIP. During periods of crisis two such cabinets were formed. The first was established following the Renville Agreement on January 29, 1948, in order to ensure that the Republic undertake the unpopular task of implementing it and endured until August 4, 1949. It was not based upon a party coalition commanding a majority in parliament, although the major parties were represented in it, and Hatta conducted his government in a way which in fact ensured consistent majority support. The second, essentially a reshuffle of the first, lasted from August 4, 1949, to December 20, 1949, and was created under Hatta's leadership to set the stage for the final negotiations with the Dutch at The Hague. It should be reiterated that the possibility of establishing such presidential cabinets was dependent upon a reasonably harmonious relationship between Hatta and Soekarno, a harmony which was to decrease rapidly after 1950 and give place to a complete rupture by 1956.

Government in Sumatra and in the Dutch-controlled Areas

During the first two years of the Republic's existence, that is, until the first Dutch military campaign of July 1947, its authority extended to all of Java and Sumatra except for a few enclaves embracing those major ports held first by the British and later by the Dutch. In the remainder of Indonesia, it will be recalled, the Dutch were enabled to take over with very little trouble. Although most politically conscious Indonesians in Borneo, Celebes, the Lesser Sundas, and the Moluccas were strongly pro-Republican, the Dutch were able to put down their few efforts at armed resistance with relative ease. The central government of the Republic, with its capital during most of this period at Jogjakarta in central Java, certainly spoke for that large majority of Indonesians on Java and Sumatra (well over four-fifths of Indonesia's population), but its relationship with Java was much closer than with Sumatra. The Netherlands navy and air force so effectively controlled communications between the two islands that only rarely were the Republic's officials able to run their blockade. Following the military campaigns of the summer of 1947, wherein approximately one-half of Java and about a quarter of Sumatra (including almost every important port) were overrun by Dutch troops, the problem of communication became even more difficult. Thus, although during the revolutionary period the top administrative posts in Sumatra were held by officials appointed or endorsed by the central government of the Republic and though many of its major policies were followed insofar as possible by the Sumatran Republican administrations, of necessity these administrations were highly autonomous. Financially they were completely independent of the central government, printing their own currencies, usually tying them to the Straits dollar. The Republic's armed forces in Sumatra were obliged to finance themselves, often quite independently of the local civil administrations, and to rely primarily upon the local Indonesian population for food and supplies. Thus during the course of the revolution the several regions of Sumatra by and large governed themselves through their own highly autonomous Republican administrations, operating only under broad directives from the central government and doing so only to the extent that they regarded this as feasible. They fended for themselves militarily against the Dutch, financed themselves, and undertook directly the local measures which they deemed necessary for their economic and social well-being.

Meanwhile in the substantial areas controlled by the Netherlands outside of Java and Sumatra, and after mid-1947 in those parts of these two islands which its army had overrun, the Dutch endeavored to establish a new political order of their own. By early 1949 they had created in these areas fifteen so-called "states" which were represented to the outside world as being run by local Indonesians and possessing a high degree of self-government. Although elaborate governmental façades were set up, in every case the outwardly Indonesian regime was controlled tightly and effectively by the Dutch colonial administration. In those states created in former Republican territory following the military campaign of mid-1947, Republican guerrilla units sometimes controlled as much of the area as the Dutch; but in those set up outside of Java and Sumatra, Netherlands military and police control was effective, and pro-Republican elements were either jailed or induced to keep quiet because of the overwhelming force which they confronted. In some of these areas the Dutch were able to win the support of a small minority which foresaw that under the Republic its aristocratic status and semifeudal privileges would be lost. And in almost every case there were a few political opportunists from other walks of life willing to collaborate in a positive sense in order to benefit from the financial remuneration, the automobiles, and the other things that the Dutch made available to them. Other Indonesians grudgingly cooperated in order to secure a living for their families, but remained pro-Republican at heart. The overwhelming majority of the Indonesian populations of these Netherlands-sponsored states were, however, opposed to the regimes with which they were saddled and looked wistfully to those areas of Java and Sumatra still able to hold out against the Dutch, regarding them as champions of their own cause.

It should be noted, then, that throughout the long period of the revolution only on Sumatra and Java, and after the middle of 1947 only in parts of these islands, were the Indonesian people administratively linked to the Republic. And only on Java itself (only half of Java after mid-1947) were they effectively incorporated into its government. Thus the major part of the Indonesian archipelago went through the more than four years of the revolution either as highly autonomous units with ties more psychological than substantive connecting them with the Republic's central government (as on Sumatra) or as units completely separated from it and under Netherlands control. The desire for independence and common opposition to the Dutch rallied all these areas and ensured a psychological unity throughout the revolution, one demanding a united and fully independent Indonesia. But this psychological bond was a mixture of positive and negative elements. True, it was to an important extent based upon an increasing sense of national identity and the belief that independence would open the way to a better life. At the same time, however, it was activated by the powerful negative dynamic of opposition to colonial rule—a component of Indonesian nationalism which was to lose much of its strength as a force for national cohesion once independence had been won.

· XXI ·

Postrevolutionary Indonesia: The Period of Parliamentary Democracy (1950-1957)

FOUR years of revolution with a common objective and the attendant spread of a national language brought to Indonesians a great increase in political consciousness and national awareness. Particularly marked among urban elements, this was often discernible at the village level as well, the turmoil of Japanese occupation and revolution having done much to break down the introverted parochialism previously characteristic of most Indonesian villages. The rapid spread of a national educational system, down to and including the village, significant even during the revolution but tremendous in scale (if not always in quality) thereafter, considerably reinforced this tendency.

Heightened Expectations

Another important psychological residue of the revolution was the heightened expectations which the achievement of independence induced. They characterized in particular the outlook of educated and semieducated elements, especially those who had played the most active roles in the revolution, but were also to be found in varying degrees among a large part of urban and plantation labor and in some areas

575

among the peasantry. Economic benefits as well as social and political status formerly seen as having been preserves of the Dutch were now regarded as the legitimate right of Indonesians. This feeling was understandably strongest among those who had won new self-confidence during the revolution and Japanese occupation by demonstrating ability to handle a wide range of positions previously regarded as outside the scope of their competence. But the idea was widespread that careers should be open to talent and that positions should be based upon ability and upon achievement demonstrated during the revolution. Education was seen as the postrevolutionary generation's principal channel of advancement, an avenue of social mobility extending down to the village. Although within a few years party connection increasingly became a criterion for career advancement, initially it did not supersede education in importance.

This emphasis upon education as a basis for advancement, though undoubtedly salutary in general, frequently penalized the middle generation—the young men and women in their twenties and early thirties who had provided so much of the vanguard of the revolution, often shouldering aside their more timorous colonial-conditioned elders and at decisive moments assuming the leadership and taking the decisive actions without which the revolution would have failed. Having in so many cases dropped out of school or college during the Japanese occupation and/or shelved their schooling to throw all their energies into the four-year revolutionary struggle, they were in educational terms a "lost generation." Beginning in 1950 some were able to return to their studies, but most had been out for so long, often having a wife and children to support, that this was quite impossible. Thus they were in an awkward position, for although their revolutionary record and practical experience gave them a claim to the positions or responsibility they had assumed or aspired to, on educational grounds they were in a weak position to compete. And now many of the older-generation revolutionary nationalists who had been happy to give them their head during the revolution felt that the time had come to reassert a position of superiority based on education as well as age, and since a reasonable degree of security was now attached to the upper governmental and political positions, the older nationalists wished to ensure that these should rest largely in their own hands.

Although many of the younger ex-revolutionaries did not actually lose their government or party posts, often they were smothered by new positions opened up above and beside them and filled by their elders. Those so bypassed became understandably bitter and discouraged, their expectations frustrated. Thereby their country was deprived of much of the imaginative thinking and willingness to take resolute action which had made this group's service so valuable during the revolution. In failing to provide its young revolutionary vanguard with opportunities for social service commensurate with the positions it filled during the revolution, the leaders of postrevolutionary Indonesia dissipated one of their country's most valuable assets, contributing to its problems as well as weakening its political viability.

Economic Conditions

Postrevolutionary expectations operated in an unpromising economic milieu. For after the revolution Indonesia was immensely poorer in developed economic resources than during the prewar colonial period; the wartime bombing raids, long and bitter fighting in the revolution, and frequent recourse to scorched-earth policies, both preceding the Japanese occupation and during the revolution, had resulted in the devastation of wide areas. The extent of damage or total destruction to transportation and communication facilities, oil installations, plantation equipment, sugar centrals, and the few industrial enterprises which the prewar economy had supported was tremendous; their restoration would require great effort, large financial outlay, and a substantial period of time. With respect to the government's financial substance, it should be recalled that as a consequence of the Round Table Agreement Indonesia had been saddled with a heavy indebtedness to the Netherlands, one which from the outset was a significant drain upon its economy. Moreover, because of the destruction of some of the few prewar industrial and processing enterprises, Indonesia's postwar economy was even more lopsided, even more preponderantly dependent upon the export of a few generally unprocessed raw materials (rubber, tin, oil, and copra) than before the war. And, as then, the prices of most of these exports on the world market fluctuated widely, making it difficult for the government to undertake long-term economic planning. With the government dependent primarily upon export and import taxes for its revenue, this problem was to become especially crucial.

Although the revolution and the Japanese occupation had seriously eroded the economic base of the country, its population had increased considerably, at least 15 per cent over the prewar figure, with most of this increase in already-overcrowded Java. During the revolution the

Javanese peasantry did temporarily improve its position by repudiating
its indebtedness to Chinese moneylenders, but the ratio between peasants and the available supply of arable land had become more unbalanced. Concentration of landownership and absentee landlordism
remained slight, but the average peasant's plot on Java had become
smaller and his level of living had probably dropped, with the substantial degree of economic equality which persisted being maintained
"through a division of the economic pie into smaller and smaller
pieces," a sort of "shared poverty." [1]

Most of Indonesia's economy above the village level remained
capitalistic in character and still preponderantly in the hands of non-
Indonesians, primarily Netherlanders and Chinese. Although the
amount of Western capital invested in postwar Indonesia remained
large (Dutch investments despite destruction suffered during the revolution still standing in the neighborhood of a billion dollars), its political leverage was now infinitely less than had been the case during
the colonial period. Western economic enterprise now had to deal with
a government whose leaders were nearly all strongly socialist, many
of them unsympathetic to any increase in the role of foreign capital
and most of them dedicated to the idea of its eventual displacement
by socialization or transfer to the hands of Indonesian capitalists. In
addition, business, both Western and Chinese, was now confronted by
large, militant trade unions, something the colonial government had
never countenanced. Formation of these labor unions had been encouraged by the revolutionary government, and the postrevolutionary
government remained sympathetically inclined toward them, framing
legislation advantageous to their growth and to their bargaining position vis-à-vis capital. Membership in these unions soon reached between 1.5 and 2 million, and it was precisely in the plantations, oil
fields, and industrial enterprises where Western capital was most active
that they enrolled most of their members. Increasingly the trade unions
took on a political orientation, the majority of them becoming adjuncts
of political parties, in particular the Indonesian Communist Party.

Just as during the colonial period, Indonesia's 2.5 to 3 million Chinese continued to dominate the lower and middle levels of the capitalist
sector of the economy. As a consequence of the revolution they had to
a large extent lost their previously strong position as dispensers of

---

[1] Clifford Geertz, "Religious Belief and Economic Behaviour in a Javanese Town:
Some Preliminary Considerations," *Economic and Cultural Change,* IV, no. 2
(Jan. 1956), 141.

agrarian credit, most of them leaving the countryside for the cities and thereby swelling the proportion of Chinese domiciled there; but they were quick to move into those sectors of economic enterprise from which European capital was withdrawing. As government policy sought to promote the economic interests of Indonesians, primarily through granting highly preferential treatment in distributing import licenses, some traditional Indonesian trading elements, largely in Sumatra and Borneo, were able to take direct advantage of these opportunities. In many areas, however, particularly in Java, these measures indirectly benefited Chinese more than they helped Indonesians. Most Indonesians lacked the requisite entrepreneurial experience and subleased their privileges to Chinese so endowed with this quality as to make substantial profit even though required to give the Indonesian license holder a sizable cut. An undoubted affinity of economic interests developed between such Indonesian "fronts" and their Chinese associates, but this was to result in no discernible social integration. The Chinese community continued to stand apart from the Indonesian, the distance between them having if anything been increased during the course of the revolution when most Chinese took what they termed a "neutral" position, one hardly likely to elicit sympathy from the hard-pressed Indonesians. Even that majority of the Chinese population willing to accept Indonesian citizenship was not regarded as Indonesian by most ethnic Indonesians and found itself discriminated against by governmental economic policy.[2] Thus the role of Indonesians in the capitalist sector of their country's economy remained almost as small after the revolution as before, the slight increase of their importance between 1950 and 1957 stemming primarily from preferential governmental policies.

The Bureaucracy

A great and striking difference between postrevolutionary and colonial Indonesian society was in the bureaucracy. Whereas before the revolution Western-educated Indonesians had been given only very slight access to its middle and upper ranks, these had now become their exclusive preserve. In the bureaucracy heightened expectations could to a degree at least be rewarded; for, as traditionally, it was still regarded by Indonesians as a profession of great prestige. The economic rewards were, however, disappointing, salaries (in terms of purchas-

[2] See Donald E. Willmott, *The National Status of the Chinese in Indonesia 1900–1958* (Cornell Modern Indonesia Project, Monograph Series; Ithaca, N.Y., 1961).

ing power) being much smaller than during the colonial period. This resulted not only from the poverty of the postrevolutionary government and an increasingly serious monetary inflation, but from inflation of the bureaucracy itself. By the early 1950s the national civil service had become four times as great as before the war, over 600,000 as against approximately 150,000.

The necessity of incorporating the Dutch-sponsored Federalist civil service into that built up during the revolution in the Republic induced from the outset a loss in morale among both elements. Those from the Republic felt that revolutionary service and sacrifice should be rewarded; they were often disillusioned in finding themselves placed under someone who had greater experience or educational qualifications but who had served in one of the Dutch-controlled states and whom, as a consequence, they frequently regarded as opportunistic and lacking in patriotism. On the other hand, former Federalists working under a civil servant whose only training had been acquired under the revolutionary Republic frequently felt aggrieved because the Republican lacked their experience or education.

Unfortunately it proved virtually impossible to stiffen the administrative backbone of the new state by utilizing experienced Dutch and Eurasian civil service personnel. From the standpoint of cold logic the government's dismissal of so many of the undoubtedly competent Dutch and Eurasian administrative officers and technicians who had served the colonial government may seem unreasonable. But the nature of Indonesian nationalism ran counter to such logic. Distrust of the Dutch was increased as a result of an attempted coup against the new Indonesian government (the Westerling Affair) by demobilized officers and men of the Dutch colonial army less than two months after the Netherlands had formally relinquished sovereignty. As a consequence many actually loyal and capable Dutch civil servants were regarded with suspicion and kept from positions in which they could have been very useful. Moreover, Indonesia is perhaps unique among the newly emancipated Asian nations in that its Eurasian population, which had competently filled many of the upper-middle administrative positions in the colonial bureaucracy, with few exceptions declared unequivocally for the colonial power, during the revolution aligning themselves solidly with the Dutch against the Republic. Thus, although many Eurasians remained in Indonesia after the Netherlands' withdrawal, they were rarely welcome in the higher administrative and technical positions, even though often better trained than Indonesians.

The Indonesian bureaucracy was not a harmonious and unified group.

The postrevolutionary loss of morale was soon increased as the competition of political parties resulted in its growing politicization, appointments frequently being made more in terms of political patronage than merit. As they maneuvered for control of parliament, and especially as they prepared for the national elections, the parties often utilized their power to influence appointments to the bureaucracy as a means of filling strategic positions in the territorial administrations as well as in certain key ministries with men who could be relied upon to advance party interests. Consequently, although the bureaucracy was a force of some consequence in the Indonesian political scene, its impact was not as great as might have been expected on the basis of the high proportion of the Western-educated Indonesian elite it incorporated. Where the influence of its members was felt, this was frequently in terms of party advantage rather than calculated to promote views or interests of the bureaucracy as a whole.

This, then, was the bureaucracy called upon to be the instrument of a government covering the world's geographically least integrated major state, a bureaucracy charged not merely with routine administration, but also with carrying out a wide range of social services far surpassing those previously undertaken by the highly trained officials of the colonial government. It was a bureaucracy notable primarily for its size, too large for the government to pay its members adequately, lacking in efficient organization, and bereft of the high morale and *élan* that had previously existed among that part of its membership which had served the revolutionary government. Most crucial of all, there were few possibilities for improving its quality, the overwhelming majority of its members being woefully lacking in experience and only a very small proportion equipped with even a secondary education. Thus postrevolutionary Indonesia emerged without the governmental capital so vital to the political viability of a new state—a well-trained civil service such as India fell heir to or at least the well-trained nucleus for one such as Pakistan inherited. Nor had the Netherlands' colonial legacy provided any substantial pool of educated men which might have been drawn upon to compensate for this lack. Indonesia began its postrevolutionary existence with what was undoubtedly the weakest civil service by far of any contemporary major state.

The Army

With respect to its armed forces, too, Indonesia did not enjoy as substantial a colonial inheritance as India or Pakistan. Instead of an integrated monolithic army with members having a common background of training and led by highly trained professional officers with substantial careers behind them, Indonesia's postrevolutionary army was highly heterogeneous and only a handful of its officers had prewar experience. It incorporated two broad components—the semiguerrilla revolutionary army and sizable elements of the disbanded Dutch colonial army (KNIL). Not only were they poorly suited to work harmoniously with one another, but even within the larger of them, the revolutionary army, there were ideologically diverse elements, frequently with different backgrounds of training.

According to the Round Table Agreement, troops of the Royal Netherlands Army, numbering about 80,000, were to be withdrawn from Indonesia as rapidly as possible, and the Netherlands Colonial Army (KNIL)—a predominantly Christian Indonesian and Eurasian force of some 65,000 men—was to be dissolved by July 26, 1950. Actually the demobilization of the KNIL took considerably longer and was not completed until June 1951. This was a delicate process, inasmuch as only a very small number of these troops elected to settle in the Netherlands, most of them wishing to stay in Indonesia. Indonesian leaders were understandably reluctant to incorporate these former adversaries into the new Indonesian army. But it was believed even more dangerous to return all of them to civilian life, thereby setting free of military discipline a formidable group of professional fighting men whose loyalty to the new government was at best dubious and many of whom would be further antagonized if denied the opportunity to continue in their chosen career. Consequently it was regarded as necessary to absorb approximately half of this ex-colonial force into the new army. Very soon the government experienced serious trouble from some of those demobilized elements not incorporated into the new army; it was from this group that Captain "Turk" Westerling recruited the soldiers for his abortive *coup d'état*. Westerling, a recently retired Dutch officer, already notorious because of his responsibility for atrocities during 1946 in southern Celebes, on January 23, 1950, led a force of recently demobilized Netherlands colonial troops into battle against a small Indonesian army unit quartered in Bandung, drove them out, and briefly occupied the city. Three days later his men infiltrated Jakarta for the purpose of launching a coup against the government, but were discovered and ejected by former Republican forces before they could act. Shortly thereafter Westerling fled to Singapore in a Dutch military plane.

An equally grave question centered about the future of some 100,000

Republican guerrilla soldiers in Java, Sumatra, Celebes, and Borneo who had not been part of the regular forces of the revolutionary army. Clearly, unless they were incorporated into the new army, provision had to be made for absorbing them into civilian life—a task which was hard enough as a psychological problem, but was particularly difficult because of the economic and administrative weakness of the government.

Even within the major component of the new Indonesian army, the regular detachments of the revolutionary forces, there were many serious factors impeding unity. Only the revolution itself, common battle against the colonial enemy, had kept its diverse elements together during 1945–1949. But with this integrating factor removed, their differences tended to be accentuated. Except for a tiny handful who had received training as noncommissioned officers, and even more rarely as commissioned officers, during the last years of the colonial regime, its officers were divided into two major groups—those who had been trained by the Japanese and subsequently fought for the Republic in the revolution and those who had not had any previous military training but received all their experience during the course of the revolution itself. A large proportion of this second group were men of some education, mostly former teachers or high school students. A significant proportion of the Japanese-trained and indoctrinated group tended to feel that the army should quite properly have a voice in politics, often taking a sympathetic view of authoritarian political organization and holding democratic government in low regard.[3] A majority of those officers trained exclusively during the revolution were initially inclined, however, in part because of their educational background, to view politics as something that an army officer should eschew; but, with the ineffectiveness of civilian government increasingly evident to them, many came within a few years to change their minds.

A further important division within the officer corps—one already discernible during the last two years of the revolution—became extremely important during the postrevolutionary period, its growth being stimulated by the dispatch of a sizable minority of the younger and

---

[3] Within the group of Japanese-trained officers there was a small but influential element, particularly heavily indoctrinated by the Japanese, who were strongly attracted to the political and social code of the Japanese officer caste, especially to the ideas of Toyama, leader of the Black Dragon Society, and to the sort of thinking evidenced among the Japanese army's Young Officers group. These were advocates of a highly authoritarian political order wherein the army would be regarded as "the soul of the nation" and entitled to play a central role.

generally better-educated officers abroad for advanced training, especially to the United States. Such experience often increased the generally existing propensity among the better-educated officers to urge a
reorganization and rationalization of the army in order to make it
smaller, more efficient, and technically better trained—more like the
professional armies of the West. Their point of view understandably
generated strong opposition among that large component of officers
trained under the Japanese—a group which possessed less education
and fewer technical qualifications and which consequently feared,
with some justification, that under such a program they would be regarded as the most expendable element. For their part they argued
that what was needed was a large army, trained and organized as during the revolution, with emphasis upon guerrilla tactics and revolutionary spirit.

Equally important were the divisions which emerged in the army on
the basis of regional identification. The course of the Indonesian revolution, with its long period of grueling guerrilla warfare, enforced a
pattern of military operations which made for a divided and regionally
rooted military establishment, one effective in fighting the Dutch but
not well suited to maintaining a unified military organization once
independence had been achieved. There was a natural tendency for
army personnel to be recruited in the regions where they fought, and
to conduct successful guerrilla warfare the revolutionary army had
to develop close and sympathetic rapport with the local populations.
There resulted an identification of local army units with the inhabitants of the regions in which they operated and a tendency for soldiers
and officers to regard themselves as representatives of the local population, a conviction which did not die with the attainment of independence. Thus in the postrevolutionary period a large part of the
troops stationed in the various regions (particularly in Sumatra) were
those which had fought there during the revolution and developed
roots among the population. These roots were strong and in many cases
were maintained afterward. During the revolution, moreover, many
officers had become accustomed to playing roles which were in part
political as well as military. It was not merely a matter of regarding
themselves as the vanguard of the revolution, often seeing themselves
in this respect as peers of the political leaders in Jogjakarta. In addition, the nature of the military struggle against the Dutch frequently
required commanders to exercise a wide range of political and administrative functions in the areas where they operated. So accustomed

did many of them become to playing these extramilitary roles that following the revolution they were often reluctant to relinquish them.

It should be therefore apparent why from the outset postrevolutionary Indonesia was beset by security problems of great magnitude, problems that were to tax seriously its limited financial and administrative resources. For a country as vast and geographically unintegrated as Indonesia the problem was made more acute because of the lack of adequate air and naval forces and the absence of trained personnel to man larger forces. During the first year of its existence the new government was, after great difficulties, able to cope with and largely eliminate the problem posed by adventurers and recalcitrants among demobilized (though sometimes still intact) units of the Dutch colonial army. But the problem of rehabilitating some 100,000 ex-guerrillas, training them and finding them places in civilian life, was to prove more difficult, and the close of 1957 found it still only partially solved. In the mountains of western Java and the interior of southern Celebes militantly Islamic ex-guerrillas dedicated, ostensibly at least, to the proposition of establishing a theocratic Islamic state (Darul Islam) maintained substantial armed forces and sustained until 1962 (when most of them surrendered) a violent and destructive hit-and-run guerrilla warfare against the government.[4]

The Political Elite

Government and politics in postrevolutionary Indonesia have been dominated by a handful of people, probably no more than a couple of thousand. During the period 1950–1957 most of this tiny political elite was drawn from the upper ranks of the bureaucracy, the cabinet, the leadership of the political parties (both in and outside parliament), the army, journalism, and the universities. Although incorporating a number of influential people whose education had been leavened by a considerable Modernist or orthodox Islamic ingredient and in a few instances by heavy doses of Japanese indoctrination (especially in the case of some army officers), the outstanding characteristic of nearly all members of this elite was Western education, secondary school or above. This similarity in educational background and a common colonial and revolutionary conditioning tended to promote considerable

[4] For a more comprehensive discussion of the army's evolution and political role, see Guy J. Pauker, "The Role of the Military in Indonesia," in J. J. Johnson, ed., *The Military in Underdeveloped Areas* (Princeton: Princeton University Press, 1962).

homogeneity in their approach to socioeconomic problems, nearly all of them espousing some variant of socialism. A very minor portion were attracted to communism, and a few, including a small but active number of army officers, inclined toward other types of totalitarianism. The preponderant majority, however, were in varying degrees proponents of democratic ideas. Nevertheless, during this period increasing disunity developed, even among those who had been united during the revolution. There were differences over whether and to what extent the state should be organized along Islamic lines and whether or not the Communists should be permitted a part in the government; and there were differences over Soekarno's proper role in government and the extent of his authority in the army, the urgency of the West Irian (New Guinea) issue and the right way of solving it, the kind of decentralization best suited to Indonesia's interests, the proper way to reorganize the army, the manner in which national elections should be carried out, and the necessity for and proper nature of a drive against corruption. But purely personal differences were frequently of greater importance. Given the tremendous possibilities in postrevolutionary society for rapid upward advance, the very minuteness of this elite may well have been detrimental to its inner harmony. With the floodgates of social mobility opened, it was perhaps natural that the sudden availability of many new and heretofore unobtainable positions should generate a competitive scramble, one rendered particularly sharp because the competitors knew one another (and one another's limitations and virtues) so well. The situation might not have been characterized by such bitterness had the competition been more impersonal—as could presumably have been the case if the elite had been larger, less intermarried, and less knowledgeable of one another's character. The numerous political parties, moreover, based as much (or more) on personalities as on issues and platforms, tended to aggravate the situation, the multiparty system working frequently against solidarity and providing channels for promoting intra-elite conflict.

During the 1950–1957 period (as subsequently) Indonesia's political elite generally exercised its leadership without the necessity of any great amount of consultation with the mass of the population. (The major exceptions were the national elections of 1955–1956 and the provincial elections of 1957.) The village level of society presented a more democratic character than before the revolution, and the village leaders—most of them now elected—were often obliged to come to terms with a more politically conscious village populace and new and sometimes aggressive unofficial local leaders. Nevertheless, by and large the villagers—leaders and led—still looked (as they do today) to governmental levels above them for initiative in a number of traditional as well as new spheres of activity. They remain used to and still expect the exercise of authority from above, and in general the relationship between the national or regional capital and the village has remained strongly authoritarian in character, with little or no feeling on the part of its inhabitants that the government in Jakarta or the regional capital is "their" government or is in any way their agent.

There were occasionally, however, some relatively important decisions taken by the elite where an area of consensus broader than its own membership was required and where the area was expanded to incorporate what might be termed the literate subelite. This sector of the population roughly corresponded with the more politically conscious elements among Indonesia's two to three million newspaper readers, generally individuals possessing an education which had stopped at or gone no more than a couple of years beyond the primary level. During this period the Indonesian press was for the most part vigorous, forthright, and often politically sophisticated; consequently where it was necessary that a decision on a political issue be based in a relatively broad consensus, the press was usually effective in arousing the political concern of the literate subelite. Moreover, several of the political parties were sometimes able to mobilize significant sectors of public opinion on such occasions through rallies and verbal agitation as well as through their newspapers.

On those very rare occasions when governmental decisions required an even broader base, this subelite—working primarily, though not exclusively, within the political parties and the labor and peasant organizations or through such components of the bureaucracy as the Ministries of Information, Interior, or Religion—served as the link between the elite and the masses. The literate subelite could as yet only to a limited extent be characterized as mediator between the two, since the relationship was still largely one-sided, that is, from the top down. But its mediating role was increasing.

Some Traditional Factors Affecting Decision Making

Despite the revolution, the hierarchical cast of government inherited from the colonial and precolonial periods remained strong during the 1950–1957 period and remains so today. Persistence of traditional attitudes toward authority has discouraged the growth of self-reliance among subordinate officials, the majority of whom have felt uneasy about exercising initiative and have continued to look upward in the hierarchy for instruction concerning many matters which they should be capable of resolving themselves. With few exceptions, the expectation has persisted that initiative should emanate from the top, and it has usually been deemed improper for a subordinate to introduce something new. Many even of those qualified individuals in the highest levels of government have continued to show the imprint of a colonial experience wherein they were conditioned to eschew important decisions and leave them to paternalistic Dutch officials, a conditioning which frequently results in deferring or avoiding decisions of pressing importance. Where there is no way of evading a decision, the attempt is all too frequently made to escape full responsibility by sharing it with others, particularly with those relatively few colleagues who are not averse to shouldering responsibility. The resultant number of meetings concerned with relatively trivial problems has been, and remains, staggering. These cut deeply into the time and energy of the few key men in the government, whose preoccupation with minor matters hinders the formation of governmental policy and delays administrative decisions.

The problem was exacerbated during the 1950–1957 period because of the limited number of Indonesians who received administrative training or higher education under the Dutch, with most of those who did being absorbed into the very top levels of the bureaucracy and into the ministries. In other words nearly all of the few experts were lodged at the very top of the governmental decision-making pyramid. Because of both traditional factors and the limited supply of *expertise* the system forced a host of routine as well as important decisions— political, administrative, and technical—to the top levels of the hierarchy. Thus many more decisions were passed to the top than was true in probably any other major nontotalitarian country.

A traditionally rooted element in the decision-making process which has continued to have importance is the emphasis upon social solidarity and harmony—a cultural value particularly strong among the Javanese which begets the widely shared conviction that openly stated conflict is to be avoided as disruptive. It is this precolonial legacy which underlies and helps explain the distinctively Indonesian approach to group decision, the coming to agreement through extensive discussion (*musjawarat*) aimed at yielding a synthesis of views, an often implicit consensus known as *mufakat*. Such generally sensed agreement is reached not through majority vote, but in a way somewhat reminiscent of the Quaker "sense of the meeting." This is a consensus which is felt rather than physically measured. It eschews voting, for voting produces an opposition minority as well as the majority. Hence a number of influential Indonesian political leaders have remained averse to decision-making procedures that involve voting. They are convinced that these stimulate disharmony and make differences explicit, crystallizing points of view to an extent where they are too hard to be mellowed or melted down into a common synthesis through further discussion.

Mufakat procedure appears usually to have worked well at the village level, where the sphere of decision making is well charted and largely concerned with matters of traditional concern, most of them easily relatable to past precedent. But while *mufakat* is possible on a small scale (we have noted that this was one reason for the success of the Working Committee in the revolutionary government), it is not easily adapted to decision making by large bodies of individuals with considerably different backgrounds such as made up Indonesian parliaments both before and after the elections of 1955. Parliamentary decisions were reached on the basis of a simple majority vote and came to be regarded by many Indonesians as contributing to and reinforcing national differences of opinion.

Despite undoubted virtues, the *mufakat* system does slow the process of decision making. In both parliamentary and postparliamentary cabinets the usual practice has been for most decisions of major importance to be made on this basis rather than by simple voting. This has also been the general pattern in a number of the top-level bureaucratic councils. With such a paucity of people qualified to take decisions in behalf of the government, the few key men must attend an unending number of deliberative sessions to arrive at decisions generally made by a single responsible individual in most governmental systems; in addition, those sessions which involve major decisions are often very long, sometimes a whole series of meetings over a considerable span of time being required to arrive at the consensus necessary before action can be taken. For in order to maintain harmony it is frequently necessary to discuss and debate a question for a long time if a common denominator sufficiently precise for laying the basis of a new policy is to be discovered. Sometimes the inability to attain *mufakat* results in the shelving of a major issue, since it is regarded as more important

to maintain harmony—even though the problem remains—than to
arrive at a decision based upon a simple majority and a consequent
open disruption of solidarity.

Formation of a Federal Government

The Round Table Conference agreement signed at The Hague in
November 1949 stipulated: "The Netherlands unconditionally and
irrevocably transfers complete sovereignty over Indonesia to the Republic of the United States of Indonesia and thereby recognizes said
Republic of the United States of Indonesia as an independent and
sovereign state." The latter accepted this sovereignty "on the basis of
the provisions of its Constitution which as a draft has been brought to
the knowledge of the kingdom of the Netherlands." The transfer of
sovereignty was therefore explicitly unconditional, and there is no justification for interpreting acceptance as binding Indonesia to the constitution operative at the time or as limiting its right to amend or
basically change that constitution at will. But part of the price of the
Netherlands' relinquishment of its claim to sovereignty had been the
stipulation that transfer of authority be made not to the Republic alone,
but to a federal Indonesia wherein the Republic would be merely one
of sixteen component units. Although the federal system of government
bequeathed by the Hague Agreement remained intact for only a scant
six weeks and thereafter progressively disintegrated until replaced by
a unitarian form of government in mid-August 1950, less than eight
months after its inception, this legacy was to have long-term consequences significant in shaping the character of the subsequent government and the problems confronting it, some of which still persist.

Much of the groundwork for the Hague Conference had been laid
in Java during the middle of 1949 in the course of preliminary negotiations, the Inter-Indonesian Conferences, held between delegations
from the Republic and from the "Federalists"—the representatives of
the fifteen Dutch-created states. Foremost among the accomplishments
of these conferences were the outline draft of a constitution for the envisaged federal order and the agreement that its constituent states
should have no military forces of their own. This last provision, reaffirmed later at the Hague Conference where it was also stipulated that
the Dutch colonial army was to be dissolved, meant that the supporting
bayonets upon which these Dutch-created states rested would soon be
withdrawn, leaving nothing but the federal constitution itself to protect
them from the popular demand that they be liquidated.

After some reworking by the Republican and Federalist delegations to the Hague Conference the draft constitution agreed upon earlier at the Inter-Indonesian Conferences emerged as the constitution of the projected federal Republic of the United States of Indonesia (RUSI), being signed by both delegations on October 29, 1949. This federal state to which the Republic's representatives were obliged to agree was a weirdly unbalanced and distorted organism. Its very composition testified to the artificial nature of the federal system which the Dutch had been sponsoring and made clear that in constructing it they had been more concerned with promoting a strategy of divide and rule, calculated to eventuate in a political order which they could indirectly control, than in establishing a federal system honestly dedicated to Indonesia's very real need for a political decentralization consistent with basic geographic, economic, and cultural factors. The constitution provided for a federation composed of sixteen states. Whereas the largest component, the Republic of Indonesia (the residual area left to the revolutionary Republic following the Renville Agreement, comprising approximately half of Java and three-quarters of Sumatra), had a population of more than 31 million, the coequal state of Riau, comprising the tiny Riau archipelago just off Singapore, had a population of only about 100,000. The small islands Bangka and Billiton each constituted a state, and the meager population of Indonesian Borneo was divided into no less than five. Each of these sixteen states, regardless of its population, was represented by two senators. The Senate was granted colegislative authority with the House of Representatives on matters "referring particularly to one, several or all participant territories or parts thereof, or concerning the relations between the Republic of the United States of Indonesia" and these constituent states. Only a two-thirds majority of the members of the House at a session where at least two-thirds of its total membership was present could override the Senate in such matters. Further protection was provided the Dutch-created federal components by a provision that 100 of the 150 members of the House should come from the 15 Dutch-created states (apportioned according to their respective populations), whereas the Republic of Indonesia, the federation's major component, would have only 50 representatives (approximately 10 less than it was entitled to on a basis of population). Since each of the states was free to decide on the matter of selecting its representatives to both houses of the parliament, whether by election or appointment, it appeared that the elements installed in power by the Dutch would be able to maintain their positions by seeing to it that those representing their states were "reliable."

The position of the Dutch-sponsored states in the new political

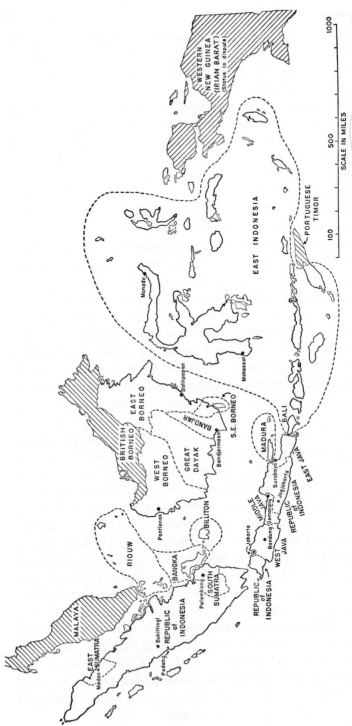

Map 10. Federal Indonesia. Boundaries shown are of the Republic of the United States of Indonesia on December 27, 1949. (Pasundan is designated here as West Java.) With the exception of Middle Java, whose boundaries date from early March 1949, all approximate the boundaries of fourteen or more months previously. The major exception is West Borneo, whose southwest corner had for a brief period been detached to form the short-lived autonomous area of Kota Waringen. (From *Nationalism and Revolution in Indonesia*, by George McTurnan Kahin, copyright 1952, Cornell University Press.)

order was not, however, as strong as these provisions might suggest. Quite apart from the fact that the overwhelming majority of their populations were in opposition to the regimes with which the Dutch had saddled them, the constitution incorporated provisions which in the long run were to make possible their legal dissolution. Although the "Government" (cabinet plus the President) was obliged to share legislative power with the House of Representatives on all matters and with the Senate as well on those matters in the compass of its authority, it was expressly stipulated that the cabinet would not be responsible to either of the existing representative bodies. It was held that since most of their members had not been elected (and those few who were had been chosen under conditions which fell far short of any democratic norm) cabinet responsibility was not appropriate. Elections were scheduled to be held within a year, after which (so the constitution implied but did not expressly stipulate) cabinet responsibility to the two representative bodies would commence. In addition, Article 139, one that was to assume great importance in the liquidation of the Dutch-sponsored constituent states, stated that "the Government on its own authority and responsibility has the right to enact emergency laws for the regulation of such matters of federal governing power as demand immediate provisions on account of urgent circumstances," these regulations requiring, however, the subsequent endorsement of the House. Moreover, the prospects for the survival of this federal system were weakened because of the unsympathetic attitudes of the federal government's President and Prime Minister—Soekarno and Hatta.[5]

[5] The Inter-Indonesian Conferences had established a National Preparatory Committee, composed of Federalist delegates from the Dutch-sponsored states and delegates from the Republic, and had charged it with, among other things, selection of the President of the projected United States of Indonesia and of the *formateurs* of its first cabinet. Although this committee contained 60 Federalists as against only 20 Republican members, the prestige of Soekarno was so great and the relative stature of the leading Federalists so puny by comparison that even the most intransigent of the Federalists realized that it would be a travesty to elect anyone other than this man who had become the principal popular symbol of the revolution. On December 16, 1949, a sixteen-man *ad hoc* committee, which was selected by the larger National Preparatory Committee and in which each member state had one vote, unanimously elected Soekarno President of the United States of Indonesia. (The federal constitution, it may be noted, did not provide for a Vice-President.)

An agreement reached at the Inter-Indonesian Conferences, and later incorporated into the federal constitution, provided that the President "in agreement with the delegates" of the component states select a group of three men charged with the formation of a cabinet (actually four were appointed—two Republicans

The Unitarian Movement and Creation of a Unitary Government

Immediately upon its assumption of office the Hatta cabinet was confronted by growing local demands, given encouragement by Soekarno and a number of other high government leaders, that the federal legacy of the Netherlands be scrapped in favor of a unitarian political order. Indeed, the dominant and overshadowing political development during the eight-month Hatta cabinet (December 1949—July 1950) was the unitarian movement, a widely based and increasingly powerful popular demand for replacing the federal order, regarded as a tainted vestige of colonial control, by a unitary system of government which would restore the revolutionary Republic to a position of dominance. Thus a major part of the time and energies of Hatta and his cabinet were absorbed in the effort to keep this transition orderly and confined to constitutional channels.

The active phase of the movement was precipitated by the attempted coup of demobilized Netherlands colonial soldiers led by Captain Westerling. Not only did this do serious harm to Indonesian-Dutch relations, sowing deep distrust and suspicion among Indonesians with regard to Netherlanders still in Indonesia. In addition, the incident caused grievous damage to the position of the Federalists, since it was discovered that Sultan Hamid, one of their chief leaders and a member of the cabinet, had played a major part in planning the affair. Evidence that some officials of the Dutch-sponsored Pasundan (West Java) government had ties with Westerling further discredited the Federalists. Popular indignation was so strong and widespread that Federalist representatives in parliament had no recourse but to support the cabinet's emergency law of February 8 calling for Pasundan's relinquishing its powers to a state commissioner appointed by the cabinet. This set in train a whole series of similar moves, wherein under strong local pressure the governments of most of the federal states undertook to end

---

and two Federalists). Just as Soekarno had dwarfed every Federalist who might have had the temerity to present himself as a candidate for the presidency, so did Hatta overshadow every possible Federalist candidate for the post of Prime Minister. In the cabinet which was formed on December 20, 1949, the Republican element held a dominant position, eleven posts as against five for the Federalists, Hatta serving concurrently as Prime Minister and Minister of Foreign Affairs and the Federalists holding only one key portfolio, Internal Affairs, which went to Anak Agung.

their existence, symbolizing the change by amalgamating themselves with the old Republic. The process was held up in East Indonesia where troops of the recently demobilized Netherlands Indies Army temporarily resisted the landing of former Republican troops. By early May, however, following a conference between Hatta and the heads of the states of East Indonesia and East Sumatra, these last two of the fifteen Dutch-created states agreed to give up their identities and join the old Republic in the establishment of a new unitary Republic of Indonesia.

On May 19, 1950, leaders of the federal government (acting in behalf of the governments of the states of East Indonesia and East Sumatra) reached an agreement with those of the Republic of Indonesia on the basic character of the new unitary state.[6] During the next two months representatives of the federal government's House of Representatives and of the Republican KNIP met together to work out a draft unitary constitution based upon this agreement. By July 20, 1950, they had completed their work and presented their draft to the federal House and Senate and to the Working Committee of the KNIP for approval, with the understanding that these bodies could not amend it, but only approve or disapprove. After some three weeks of discussion they reached general agreement and by large majorities approved the draft, which on August 15 was signed by President Soekarno and Soepomo, Minister of Justice in the federal (RUSI) government, and promulgated as the "Provisional Constitution of the Republic of Indonesia." It is this unitary constitution which, despite its provisional and expected short-term history, remained fully operative until early 1957 and which was not completely superseded until mid-1959.

---

[6] Its provisional constitution was to be framed "through revision of the RUSI [federal] Provisional Constitution in such a manner that it . . . contain the essentials of the Constitution of the Republic of Indonesia . . . and additionally appropriate sections of the Provisional Constitution of the RUSI." It was to be drawn up by an "Assembly for Changing the Constitution" made up of the House of Representatives of the outgoing federal government and the Working Committee of the Republic's KNIP, and it was understood that as soon as possible elections would be held for a constituent assembly which would frame a final constitution. Until superseded by new legislation, existing acts and regulations were to remain in force, "with the understanding that, wherever possible, the laws of the member-state, the Republic of Indonesia . . . be adhered to." It was agreed that the Senate would be abolished, that the cabinet would be made responsible to a unicameral parliament, that Soekarno would be President and (implicitly at least) that Mohammad Hatta would be Vice-President. The new state's provisional unicameral legislature was to be created out of the combined memberships of the federal House of Representatives and the Working Committee of the Republic's KNIP with a provision that other members could be added.

Although pro-Republican sentiment and the demand for the liquidation of the remnants of the old Dutch-created federal system had triumphed, an important residue survived. In order to ensure the smooth transition from a federal to a unitary government Republican leaders believed it necessary to placate the largely Dutch-selected representatives from the Dutch-sponsored states who held seats in the outgoing RUSI Senate and House. Thus, in conformance with the Charter of Agreement of May 19, the unitary constitution made a major concession to this group by providing that the new state's unicameral legislature incorporate the memberships of the federal government's Senate and House of Representatives together with those from the Republic's High Advisory Council and KNIP Working Committee.[7] As a consequence, more than 40 per cent of the membership of the parliament which was to govern Indonesia from mid-1950 until the spring of 1956 was made up of individuals who had worked with the Dutch in the states established by them and who for the most part owed their current parliamentary positions to this earlier collaboration. Some were men of political probity and ability, but there were many whose careers had been marked by political opportunism and frequently by widely known involvement in governmental corruption. Not only did this make the unitary state's largely nonelected parliament less representative than had been the Republic's nonelected parliament, it also introduced at the outset an unhealthy political atmosphere, weakening both the moral authority and the ability of the representative body that was charged with governing Indonesia during the critical six-year period prior to the national elections; and there is no doubt that the long delay in holding these elections stemmed, to an important extent, from the fact that many of these men realized that elections would spell the end of their parliamentary careers.

[7] In the new House of Representatives 130 members could be classified as Republicans and 106 as Federalists (it should be recalled, however, that some Federalists had actually been strongly pro-Republican in outlook). Of those classified as Republicans, 46 had been members of the KNIP's Working Committee (as of 1950), 13 had been members of the Republic's High Advisory Council, 50 had constituted that one-third of the federal government's House of Representatives drawn from the Republic's KNIP, another 19 had been appointed by the Republic, while it was a constituent unit of the federal government, to represent the former territory of Pasundan after that state's amalgamation with the Republic in February 1950 following the Westerling affair, and 2 had been drawn from the Senate. Of those classified as Federalists, 27 came from the Senate and 79 from the federal government's House of Representatives.

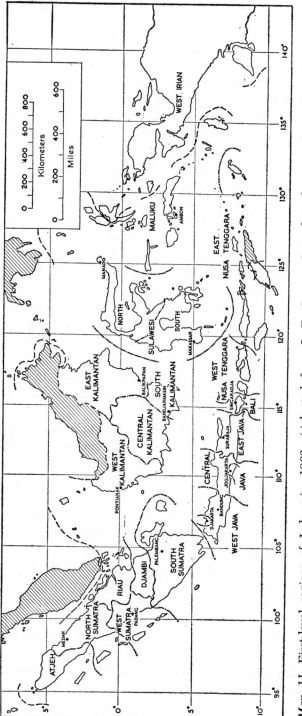

Map 11. First-level regions of Indonesia, 1963. (Adapted from J. D. Legge, *Central Authority and Regional Autonomy in Indonesia,* frontispiece; reproduced by permission, Cornell University Press.)

Soekarno

A central factor in the government and politics of postrevolutionary Indonesia has been the country's President, Soekarno. He has been a major political force in his own right, one might even say the strongest organized political force in Indonesia. He has consistently maintained that in filling the office of President he is not obliged to diminish his role as his country's revolutionary nationalist leader. Although the extent to which he has continued to play this politically charged extra-constitutional role has often not been agreeable to a considerable proportion of the political elite, it undoubtedly has been to millions of the Indonesian rank and file, particularly in Java. For over thirty years he has been regarded by Indonesians as their chief nationalist leader. He has been a charismatic personality without peer in Indonesia, and, indeed, in few other countries in the world. His powers of oratory and his personal charm and dynamism have provided him with the means for enlisting mass backing that no Indonesian leader has been able to rival. Had he constituted himself a political party and run for office in the elections of 1955, he would probably have emerged with more votes than any other party. And undoubtedly the fact that he did indirectly back the Indonesian Nationalist Party (PNI) in those elections was a major reason for its emerging as the party with the largest number of votes.

Although he has shown great talent as a nationalist and revolutionary leader and has continued to display an unrivaled shrewdness in politics, Soekarno has not demonstrated comparable aptitude in providing Indonesia with the leadership it has needed to meet some of the most important of its postrevolutionary problems. From the outset he realized that the problem of national unity would be a formidable one, estimating in 1949 that its achievement would require another ten years;[8] but his approach to this problem has not always been marked by sympathetic understanding of the sentiments of the areas outside Java, and he has not demonstrated leadership in working out a formula to provide for the governmental decentralization best calculated to promote such unity. Soekarno has brought together Islamic, Javanese mystical, and Western political thought—including a considerable component of the revisionist Marxism of the 1920s—in a synthesis which has had widespread appeal as a nationalist ideology. But some of those who have been his close supporters have observed that in general he

[8] Discussions with the writer, Muntok, Bangka, May 2–4, 1949.

has given little attention to relating this synthesis in any concrete and effective sense to economic realities and that the revisionist Marxism upon which he has drawn has manifested itself in a rather rigid cast with insufficient adaption to changing conditions.

During the period 1950–1957, one of Soekarno's major political pre-occupations was with what he conceived to be the very real threat of an Islamic political order. The fact that the Masjumi was never able to settle upon a definition of an Islamic state did not diminish the concern of Soekarno and other secular nationalists. For although the top Masjumi leaders could not agree among themselves on the attributes an Islamic state should have, the fact that these men—most of whom were actually quite moderate in their outlook—were on record as being in principle committed to this end left open the possibility that some of the more aggressive dogmatists in the party might force through a radical definition that would commit the Masjumi as a whole. While it is perfectly true that the ideas of such Masjumi leaders as Mohammad Natsir, Dr. Sukiman, and Mohammad Roem were not in themselves likely to cause great alarm to the non-Islamic communities in Indonesia, there was no firm assurance that these moderates would be able to withstand pressures from the more extreme elements in the party. Insofar as Soekarno's opposition to the Masjumi was based upon concern over the prospect of an Islamic state, he had strong and consistent support from a wide range of political opinion, including leaders of the Catholic and Christian parties as well as those of the PNI and the Indonesian Communist Party (PKI). Soekarno and these men were concerned not only over the dangers that might arise should governmental power pass into the hands of narrow, intolerant religious zealots. They were also worried over the threat which would be posed to Indonesian unity, fearing that any attempt to introduce an Islamic state would provoke secession by areas with Christian majorities—such as Ambon, Flores, Timor, Northern Celebes, and the Tapanuli district of North Sumatra.

Undoubtedly this widespread fear of an Islamic state stemmed in no small measure from the fanatical conduct and militant advocacy of the leaders of Darul Islam, the insurgent group whose armed forces had held control since 1948 of shifting areas of the mountain districts of central West Java.[9] In practice in governing areas under their

[9] On breaking with the Republic of Indonesia in 1948, the leaders of Darul Islam held that in implementing that part of the Renville Agreement calling for withdrawal of the Republic's troops in areas of West Java penetrated by Dutch

control the leadership of Darul Islam soon abandoned any real adherence to the tenets of Islam, relying largely on brutal terrorism to dragoon local support. In theory, however, the movement remained dedicated to the proposition of an Islamic state whose control was to be extended over all Indonesia. The capacity of its forces in waging guerrilla warfare was of a very high order, and not until 1962 was the Indonesian army able to administer a really decisive defeat and capture Kartosuwirjo, Darul Islam's top leader. Throughout the 1950s Darul Islam constituted an ominous cloud on Jakarta's political horizon. Although some Masjumi leaders, such as Mohammad Natsir, did make genuine efforts to induce Darul Islam to lay down its arms, they were completely unsuccessful, and the suspicion remained strong with Soekarno and the non-Islamic parties that some of the less moderate leaders of the Masjumi were pleased that Darul Islam forces were able to resist government troops and thus maintain a political and military presence. The fact that Masjumi leaders were reluctant to condemn the organization unequivocally, generally maintaining that government policies and the heavyhandedness of government troops were responsible for its continuing militancy, served to nourish the suspicion that some Masjumi leaders did in fact have friendly relations with Darul Islam. To appreciate Soekarno's attitude toward the Masjumi, it must also be noted that his personal relationships with most of the party's leaders (the major exceptions being Dr. Sukiman and, until they withdrew from the Masjumi in 1952, the leaders of the Nahdatul Ulama) were distinctly lacking in cordiality, these men being much less amenable to his influence than were most top leaders of the PNI and several of the smaller parties. Moreover, since the Masjumi was the only major party with relatively strong support in the outer islands, the mounting anti-Javanism of these areas added another discordant overtone in its relations with Soekarno.

Certainly the principal touchstone of Soekarno's political strategy throughout most of the 1950s was his unflagging effort to weaken the Masjumi's power. And in this he had strong support from the non-Islamic parties, leaders of the Christian Party as well as the PNI viewing the Masjumi as a greater threat than the Communists. Only after

---

forces, the government of the Republic was betraying the revolution. The strongly Islamic irregular forces which had served as an auxiliary of the Republic's army refused to evacuate this area; they continued to fight the Dutch, and it was this group that formed the nucleus of Darul Islam's army. Later, a number of other armed groups, some of them long engaged in banditry and having little interest in the tenets of Islam, joined these forces.

the unexpected displays of Communist Party strength in the election of 1955 and particularly in the provincial elections of 1957 did leaders of the secular nationalist parties develop reservations about the political realism of this anti-Masjumi preoccupation and begin to question the wisdom of Soekarno's order of priorities. But even after this impressive growth in Communist strength, Soekarno remained less concerned with their political potential than with that of the Masjumi. This was a view which he maintained until the Masjumi's power was scotched in the course of the 1958 rebellion, whereupon the political potential of the army became his chief worry. Although Soekarno remained consistently opposed to the Communists' developing too much strength and ultimately supported measures calculated to weaken their bases of power, he was convinced of his ability to cope with them and keep them sufficiently in check. His assurance was increased by his belief that he would be able to domesticate them sufficiently so that their primary loyalty would be to Indonesia rather than to the requirements of Moscow or Peking—a view shared by few other Indonesian political leaders. But in any case, Soekarno appeared confident that if the Communists should become intractable he would have no difficulty in marshaling the power necessary to crush them.

The Presidency

It has earlier been noted that a major weakness of Indonesia's government was the nonelected, conglomerate parliament which functioned from 1950 until 1956—a body which because of the nature of its membership lacked moral authority from the outset. A second important weakness stemmed from the 1950 constitution's vagueness in defining the position and role of the President. The powers it clearly granted the President were themselves hardly impressive. He had the explicit right of designating those who were to form a new cabinet (the *formateurs*), selecting one or several individuals to fulfill this function. In accordance with the recommendation of the formateur or formateurs, he appointed the Prime Minister, who might or might not be one of the formateurs.[10] In addition to various ceremonial functions, the only other clear-cut constitutional power of the President was his right to appoint the unitary state's first Vice-President, though even this was "upon the recommendations submitted by the House of Represent-

---

[10] A. K. Pringgodigdo, *The Office of President in Indonesia as Defined in the Three Constitutions in Theory and Practice* (Cornell Modern Indonesia Project, Translation Series; Ithaca, N.Y., 1957), p. 23.

atives." Under the 1950 constitution it was, then, only with regard to these two matters that the President was given the prerogative to act without reference to the cabinet.

There were, however, several attributes of the constitution which greatly facilitated Soekarno's assumption of a major governmental role. First was the provision that "the President and the Vice-President are inviolable," a term borrowed from the phraseology relating to the monarch in the Dutch constitution. This meant that there was no method of impeaching or removing in any way the President (or Vice-President) from office or of calling him to account for his actions. Moreover, it was stipulated that the President (and the Vice-President) could not be replaced prior to an elected constituent assembly's drafting of a new constitution which would designate the provisions for election to these offices,[11] and it was clear that it would be a considerable period before an elected constituent assembly would draft a new constitution. (The Constituent Assembly elected in 1956 deliberated unsuccessfully until mid-1959, when it was dissolved.) In addition, the President was granted the right to dissolve the House of Representatives, being required to order the election of a new House within thirty days. Although it was argued that such an action would need cabinet support, this was not made explicit in the constitution, and the President might well have been able to assert such a prerogative successfully. He never attempted to do so, but the possibility that he could gave him at least indirect influence with parliament over and above that of his own personality as the great revolutionary leader and ceremonial head of state.

Sitting in his constitutionally unassailable position and responsible constitutionally to no one, Soekarno was free to interpret a number of ambiguous provisions in the constitution in ways which allowed him to play a role far in excess of what was usually regarded as its spirit and intent, but not necessarily in excess of its letter. Much of this ambiguity centered about the term "the Government," a term which was defined in the 1949 constitution as comprising President plus one or more cabinet ministers, but which was not defined at all in the 1950 constitution. Article 83 of the 1950 constitution, seemingly one of explicit clarity, stipulated that "the Ministers shall be responsible for the entire policy of the government; jointly for the entire policy, and each Minister individually for his share in the government." The intent of the article itself would therefore seem to have given to a cabinet and

[11] See Pringgodigdo, *The Office of President in Indonesia,* p. 30, and Article 141 and the official Elucidation to the provisional constitution.

the parliament to which it was responsible sole authority for all legislation and other governmental regulations, sharing this authority with the President only with respect to the relatively few cases where the constitution explicitly conferred authority on him, namely, dissolution of parliament, award of decorations, granting of pardons, conclusion and ratification of treaties and other agreements with foreign powers, appointment of diplomatic representatives, declaration of war (to be concurred in by parliament), and declaration of a state of emergency. According to this interpretation, except in these functions the President did not share with the cabinet in the exercise of power, but acted within the government only as agent of the cabinet, promulgating and countersigning its legislation—fulfilling this function automatically and in full conformance with its wishes.

In view, however, of the historic definition of the term "Government" in Indonesia and the constitution's explicitly absolving the President of governmental responsibility, there was also basis for arguing that although the cabinet was indeed "responsible" for all legislation it shared *authority* for it with the President, he and the cabinet together constituting "the Government." Quite apart from whichever interpretation was right, there was certainly nothing in the constitution to restrain a President should he wish to assert his own judgment and refuse to endorse his name to and promulgate a particular piece of legislation put forward by the cabinet. And, as has been noted, during the revolution Soekarno was convinced that he did have this right of veto, even though then too he never employed it openly. Thus, although until 1957 Soekarno did not publicly challenge the cabinet's right to play the paramount role in initiating legislation, on a number of important occasions between 1950 and 1957 he quietly, but effectively, delayed or vetoed legislation of which he did not approve. Whatever the wisdom of his stand on these occasions, such actions tended to undermine the principle of cabinet responsibility to parliament. When confronted by such presidential interference, a cabinet had no alternative but to acquiesce or resign—except in those situations where it was in close enough rapport with dominant elements in the army to secure their support in offsetting the power exerted by the President.

Another unhappy ambiguity in the constitution was that concerning the President's relationship to the armed forces. Article 85 of the constitution can be read only as indicating that authority over the armed forces was to be shared by President and cabinet, stating as it did that "all decrees of the President, including those concerning his authority over the armed forces of the Republic of Indonesia, shall be counter-signed by the Minister(s) concerned." On the other hand, Article 127, with equal explicitness, stated that "the President is in supreme command of the armed forces." Although these statements could be interpreted as being fully compatible and providing for presidential subordination to the cabinet in such matters, it is also possible to argue (and frequently was argued) that authority over the armed forces was shared by President and cabinet and even that in this sharing the initiative for appointment of officers lay with the President.

In addition, Soekarno on a number of important occasions exerted substantial political influence by appealing over the heads of cabinet and parliament to the people in public addresses which sometimes deviated considerably from policies of the cabinet in question, on occasion making statements in clear defiance of the Prime Minister's request not to. Important also was his close connection with one of the largest political parties, the Indonesian Nationalist Party. Standing in particularly close relationship to its older-generation leaders, he sometimes induced them to reverse a position already taken in parliament or in cabinet meeting.

Soekarno's great political stature, his continuing insistence upon playing the part of revolutionary nationalist leader over and above that of President, and the constitution's vagueness in defining his position meant that he was often able to pull decisive levers of power without having to assume constitutional responsibility for the consequences. Thus even before 1957 and his controversial call for a drastic change in the political order—a "guided democracy"—Soekarno was already playing a major role in postrevolutionary Indonesian government and politics. This role was not consistent with and far exceeded what is generally considered the proper function of a President in a constitutional parliamentary system. It might well have been much better, as Mohammad Hatta and Mohammad Natsir along with some of those still close to Soekarno argued, to have endowed Indonesia in 1950 with a presidential system explicitly providing much greater scope to the office but at the same time clearly locating responsibility.

Hatta and the Vice-Presidency

The 1950 constitution stipulated that the first appointment of a Vice-President in the new unitary state would be made by the President in accordance with recommendations of parliament. Mohammad Hatta, as the national leader second in stature only to Soekarno and the man who had filled this office during the revolution, was inevitably the unanimous choice. Coming from central Sumatra and regarded by most Sumatrans as their chief representative in government, Hatta was a fitting complement to the Javanese Soekarno. Since he is looked upon as a much more devout Muslim than Soekarno, his presence in the vice-presidential office tended to reconcile those Islamic leaders made uneasy by some of Soekarno's ideas. As heads of government, Soekarno and Hatta constituted a well-balanced team, supplementing one another in qualities of personality and leadership and functioning together in something like a co-presidency. While Soekarno has been weak in economics and in his capacity to work out practical economic policies for the country, this field was Hatta's particular strength.[12] Thus Hatta brought to the vice-presidency a prestige and ability which lent the office a stature considerably beyond that suggested by the 1950 constitution.

The constitution stated merely that "in the exercise of his duties the President is assisted by the Vice-President" and that in the event of the President's death or disability the Vice-President would assume his functions. It did not permit the Vice-President to be Prime Minister. Therefore formation of a presidential cabinet such as existed over considerable periods during the revolution was not possible. Hatta did take over the reins of the presidency rather briefly during the summer of 1955 when Soekarno, coincident with an adverse political situation centering around a refusal of top army officers to agree with his selection of a chief of staff, departed on a pilgrimage to Mecca. In general, however, Hatta's role was primarily a symbolic one, symbolic particularly of national unity. This was in contrast to the active role he played in government during the revolution and the first year thereafter.

An increasing divergency of views gradually emerged between Hatta and Soekarno as to the basis for solving salient national problems and with regard to Soekarno's attitude toward the Communists and the Masjumi. Their estrangement, noticeable as early as 1952, became increasingly serious. It led to the deterioration of an important symbol of national unity and to Soekarno's becoming less and less receptive to Hatta's advice. By 1956, in the face of the evident inability of the Indonesian parliament and cabinet to meet the tremendous problems confronting the country, the possibility of Hatta's resigning the vice-

[12] Hatta was the principal organizer and promoter of the cooperative movement in Indonesia. See his *The Co-operative Movement in Indonesia* (Ithaca, N.Y.: Cornell University Press, 1956).

presidency in order to receive an appointment by Soekarno as Prime
Minister of a new and effective government was ruled out. The distance between the two men had become far too great, and this sort
of teamwork was no longer possible. The completeness of Hatta's break
with Soekarno was symbolized by his resignation in December 1956
from the office of Vice-President. Hatta dissociated himself from the
government, and subsequently no new Vice-President was appointed.

Cabinet and Parliament

We have seen the extent to which the cabinet's functioning was circumscribed by the vaguely defined, but important, role of the President. This meant that harmony between the two was generally dependent upon the personal relations between the Prime Minister and
the President. When they were cordial, as during the cabinets of
Ali Sastroamidjojo and Dr. Sukiman Wirjosandjojo, cooperation was
generally smooth and made the cabinet's work considerably easier.
When they were not cordial, as during those of Natsir, Wilopo, and
Burhanuddin Harahap, the cabinet's task was made extremely difficult
and its governmental effectiveness decreased.

We have noted that the right to dissolve parliament lay explicitly
with the President and that only implicitly did the cabinet share in
this function. This imposed a serious limitation upon the effectiveness
of cabinet government in Indonesia, inasmuch as without presidential
backing a cabinet had no way to call parliament to account. In
every case where a cabinet felt inclined to press for dissolution, it
was on poor terms with the President. Moreover, dissolution would have
had to be followed by elections, and not until April 4, 1953, was an
election law passed. Even after this it was widely argued that parliament could not properly be dissolved in view of the constitution's pre-
scription that elections be held within thirty days of a dissolution, a
requirement widely regarded as impossible to fulfill because technical
and administrative preparations for elections were seen as requiring
ten to fourteen months. Indonesia's cabinets were thus denied effective
power to dissolve parliament, an attribute important to the viability
of parliamentary government in most Western democracies. This
militated seriously against responsible conduct among many members
of its parliament, allowing them to pursue their own personal courses,
no matter how opportunistic, without being held accountable. The
deficiency was compounded because usually the party, too, had little
means of disciplining a member who sat in parliament. It was often

obliged to be extremely circumspect and gentle in dealing with errant M.P.'s, since if pushed too hard they might leave the party (as a number did), joining another or maintaining themselves as independents —sometimes available to the highest bidder. Party discipline was strengthened just before the 1955 elections, because a party's national headquarters had the right to determine whether or not an M.P. would be entered on its election list and whether he would stand near the top or bottom of the list. (Those at the top had first claim on the votes the party won.) Following the elections the situation gradually became similar to what it had been before, the only important sanction remaining in the hands of the party's leadership being patronage. Except for the Indonesian Communist Party and the much smaller Indonesian Socialist Party, Indonesian political parties were unable to exert party discipline over any considerable period of time.

The number of political parties represented in parliament worked against efficient government. In the parliament that existed from August 1950 until early 1956, no party ever held more than 52 out of 236 seats, and even following the elections of 1955 none had more than 57 seats in the new 273-member parliament. Indonesia's multiparty system thus always required a coalition government. This introduced the same general difficulties as in France. The multiplicity of parties in combination with the fluctuating character of their relationships, a situation made all the more fluid and unpredictable in Indonesia as a result of the repeatedly shifting balances of power within the parties, seriously undermined stability. The problem was made more serious and complicated because of the frequent divergence in attitude between those representing the party in the cabinet and the leaders at party headquarters as well as between both of these and the representatives in parliament. The general lack of party discipline made all these relationships unpredictable.[13]

---

[13] Moreover, since a party was frequently not represented in the cabinet by its strongest leaders, cabinet members were generally obliged to refer back to party headquarters before making any important decisions. When this was not done, party representatives in the cabinet often found themselves repudiated and denied backing by the party's top leadership. Since the party leadership itself was often divided, the requirement that cabinet members representing the party consult with the divided party leadership often meant that they had to wait a long time before discovering its position, thus delaying cabinet decisions on important matters longer than usual. And if the cabinet member felt he could not wait for instructions from his party's high command and took a position on his own responsibility in cabinet meetings, he might well find his position repudiated by his party afterward.

The effectiveness of parliamentary government was further undermined, after as well as before the elections, because of the frequently
irresponsible role of the parties not represented in the cabinet. Rarely
was their opposition constructive. Their frequent opportunism and lack
of responsibility undoubtedly derived in part from the previously mentioned residue of the colonial period, the posture of negativist obstructionism. And among the sizable ex-Federalist minority, most of whom
attached themselves to one of the major Republican political parties,
there were many whose conditioning during their period of collaboration with the Dutch undoubtedly helped to dispose them to opportunism and irresponsibility. There were strong hopes that national
elections would result in greatly reducing irresponsibility among parliament members, but these expectations were not fulfilled. To some
extent this was a consequence of the nature of the elections. The system involved overly large multimember constituencies where the candidates were selected and ranked on the party election list by party
headquarters in Jakarta, often with too little regard for local opinion.
Dependent upon their party's national headquarters rather than on
anything approximating a local primary, candidates usually tended to
feel that their chief responsibility was to Jakarta headquarters and not
to their local constituents. Following the elections the relationship
of most party representatives in parliament with their constituencies
became even more tenuous than before. This undoubtedly contributed
to the irresponsibility so many displayed in parliament.

Thus parliament severely limited the cabinet's ability to act with
dispatch and carry out a really efficient legislative role. Time and again
it held up or sidetracked the cabinet's legislative proposals or distorted
them with amendments, sometimes refusing to pass even legislation
advocated by cabinet representatives of parties holding a majority in
parliament. Parliament also slowed up the legislative process through
its insistence upon time-consuming interpolations and the convening
of meetings at which ministers were requested to attend and explain
cabinet policies. All this resulted in a tremendous backlog of government bills. In really pressing circumstances the cabinet was able to
circumvent parliamentary obstructionism by promulgating emergency
legislation. Emergency measures were valid unless rejected by the
House of Representatives at its next session, but such legislation was
rarely annulled, so long as the cabinet which promulgated it was still
in power when the House of Representatives reconvened. The cabinet's
scope of action was usually not circumscribed by budgetary commit-

ments, no cabinet except Wilopo's and Burhanuddin's presenting parliament with its annual budget until the year which it was designed to cover was well along.

Political Parties

Indonesia's political parties have been built from the top down, the leader organizing the mass following rather than a mass movement thrusting up its own leader. The elections of 1955 showed that, except for the Communist Party and the very small Indonesian Socialist Party, the organization of political parties in Indonesia bore little resemblance to that of those operating in the Western democracies. With these exceptions they have consisted of loosely articulated aggregates of political backing clustered about locally influential individuals—to a major extent district officials, village headmen, and religous leaders. The primary function of the generally nationally prominent party elite has been to supply the political attraction, to find the funds and patronage necessary to bring these local leaders into the party fold, and to provide a skeletal nation-wide organization attuned primarily to the waging of the election struggle.[14] In the words of an able Indonesian political analyst:

The numerical strength of the political parties as shown by the election results, or more precisely the political power of the particular elite groups leading those parties, is therefore, not so much, and not only a reflection of the measure of acceptance of either ideology or leadership, but also a reflection of such groups' ability to manipulate the traditional power relationships within the village.[15]

Not long after the national parliamentary elections of late 1955 and the Constituent Assembly elections held in the months immediately

[14] No major party financed its operations—particularly its election campaign—solely from membership dues. The Communists developed their own unique system of raising money, but among the other important parties a major source of funds was contributions from those receiving the patronage which the party was able to dispense because of its position in government. Probably an equally important source was a formula whereby those granted lucrative import licenses frequently were expected to make a substantial contribution to the party's election chest. With Indonesian society largely devoid of a middle class or a wealthy upper class upon which a party might draw for financial support, participation in the government was of particularly great importance in financing party activity. Those in the opposition were at a much greater disadvantage in this respect than they are in most other countries.

[15] Soedjatmoko, "The Role of Political Parties in Indonesia," in Philip W. Thayer, ed., *Nationalism and Progress in Free Asia* (Baltimore: Johns Hopkins Press, 1956), p. 131.

afterward there was a rapid loosening, and sometimes a dissolving, of the bonds holding together the various nuclei of local leadership in the major parties, only the Communists maintaining an integrated political organization. Moreover, even during elections the parties did not incorporate all the major power factors in Indonesian society, the most important lying outside the party organization (or only partially effective through it) being the army, certain regional elites, and an increasing proportion of secondary and college students.[16]

Prior to mid-1952 the Islamic Masjumi (Madjelis Sjuro Muslimin Indonesia—Council of Indonesian Muslim Associations) was easily the largest political party in Indonesia. Thereafter, following the withdrawal of one of its major constituent organizations, the Nahdatul Ulama, it was in at least second place. Although the Nahdatul Ulama's departure reduced the Masjumi's representation in the 236-member preelection parliament from 52 to 44, it still held two more seats than any other party. In the elections of 1955 it won the second largest number of votes, 7,903,886 (21 per cent) and thereby 57 out of 273 parliamentary seats. It polled nearly 50 per cent of its vote outside Java (mostly in Sumatra and South Celebes), a little over 25 per cent in West Java and Jakarta, and only 25 per cent in East and Central Java combined. Its voting strength was much more evenly distributed throughout Indonesia than that of any other party, since it won the largest number of votes in 10 out of the 15 electoral districts.[17] Enrolling

[16] In addition to the four major parties—the PNI, the Masjumi, the Nahdatul Ulama, and the Communist—there have been several minor parties. Primarily because no major party has ever commanded a majority, the latter have played a role in Indonesian government disproportionate to their size. The largest, the Partai Sarekat Islam Indonesia (PSII), held 4 seats in the preelection parliament and 8 thereafter, thanks to an election poll of 1,091,160 (just under 3 per cent). Second largest in the 1955 elections was the Christian party, which garnered just over 1 million votes (2.6 per cent) and increased its number of seats in parliament from 5 to 8. It has been a predominantly regional party, with strength primarily among the Lutheran Bataks of North Sumatra and Protestants in the Minahassa area of northern Celebes and in the South Moluccas. Next in size, the Catholic Party polled 770,740 votes (2 per cent) and held 6 seats in the elected parliament as against 8 in the preelection parliament, its major strength being in the eastern Lesser Sundas, especially Flores. With slightly fewer votes in the 1955 elections (753,191), the Indonesian Socialist Party won 5 seats, against 14 before elections. Despite its size this party has had a significant influence on the course of Indonesian politics because it numbers several able and influential intellectuals, including former Prime Minister Soetan Sjahrir, among its members. After the elections 27 political parties, organized into 17 parliamentary alignments, were represented in parliament.

[17] See Herbert Feith, *The Indonesian Elections of 1955* (Cornell Modern Indonesia Project, Interim Reports Series; Ithaca, N.Y., 1957).

most of the nation's most prominent Muslim leaders, the Masjumi was able through its influence over district and village religious leaders to tap a wide reservoir of peasant support at election time. Although originally incorporating a probable majority both of the slender business element of the Indonesian middle class and of those Indonesian landowners owning in excess of the amount necessary to support their families (few could be called landlords in the usual Asian sense) and a relatively small proportion of the middle class's bureaucratic sector, the party's platform was nevertheless predominantly socialist.[18] Its leaders realized, however, that it would be a long time before Indonesians could run many sectors of the economy efficiently and that foreign capital would be badly needed for a considerable time to come. In general the Masjumi was more hospitable to foreign capital and consistently took a more hardheaded attitude toward nationalization than any other major party. In the words of the party's chairman, Mohammad Natsir: "Nationalization should not outrun the government's ability to accumulate sufficient capital and to train sufficient administrators and technicians; the government's initial efforts in the economic sphere should therefore be to invest in new enterprises rather than take over old ones." [19]

The fact that the Masjumi, despite its composition, was consistently a proponent of socialist goals attested to the influence within the party of the Religious Socialist group. Led by Natsir and enrolling the support of such prominent men as Sjafruddin Prawiranegara, Mohammad Roem, and Burhanuddin Harahap, the Religious Socialists—all of them proponents of Modernist Islamic ideas and convinced of the necessity for Islamic leaders to know Western culture well—had come by the close of the revolution to be the most influential element in the direction of the party. They did not, however, dominate the party's thinking concerning the relationship of Islam to the constitutional basis of government (specifically concerning the nature of an Islamic state) to the same extent that they did its approach to socioeconomic ques-

---

[18] Islam and socialism have been regarded as fully compatible, and socialism mixed with a system of cooperatives has been regarded as the economic order best suited to Indonesian society. When, however, small-scale capitalist enterprise is controlled in conformity with the interests of Indonesian society, it is considered as socially healthy because it develops individual initiative and responsibility. Only when it is economically efficient to do so should such enterprises be integrated into cooperatives. The government's participation in the economy should be limited to sectors having a "social character," e.g., transportation, power, communication, mining, and heavy industries.

[19] Statement to the writer during talks in Jakarta, March 1955.

tions. Nor did they fully control party organization. The Masjumi was never a well-integrated party. Although it enrolled a large number of individuals, it was also heavily dependent upon its constituent "special members," a loose federation of semiautonomous Islamic social and educational organizations such as the Modernist Muhammadijah and until mid-1952 the more conservative Nahdatul Ulama.[20]

In mid-1952 the Masjumi was dealt a serious blow with the withdrawal of one of its two major component groups, the Nahdatul Ulama (Council of Ulemas)—a defection which removed its major basis of support in eastern and central Java. In leaving the party fold the Nahdatul Ulama (NU) carried off only 8 of the Masjumi's 52 parliamentary representatives, but in the 1955 elections it won 6,955,141 votes (18.4 per cent) and 45 out of 273 seats, polling 86.6 per cent of its vote in Java with nearly three-quarters of its total in East and Central Java. There were important political reasons for the NU's defection, but religion played a significant part. Its leadership is drawn primarily from predominantly rural areas of East Java, little influenced by Modernist political thinking. The NU was in fact founded as a nonpolitical organization in 1926 partly in protest against these ideas. Its leaders are wed to a conservative variant of Islam and at the same time are much more tolerant of and willing to compromise with pre-Islamic Hinduistic and Javanese mystical ideas, still strong in much of Java, than are adherents of Modernist doctrine. While Islamic Modernism encourages the study of Western learning, the usually locally rooted religious teachers prominent in the NU have been probably less exposed to Western education than any other set of important political leaders in Indonesia.

Even after the NU's departure the Masjumi lacked cohesion. Personal as well as ideological differences militated against harmony and efficiency of effort among its leaders. Dr. Sukiman Wirjosandjojo, with a following primarily in Central Java and the only top party leader on close terms with Soekarno,[21] although ideologically much closer to the Modernist Islamic element than to the leaders of the Nahdatul Ulama, had enjoyed a leading position in party circles during the revo-

[20] Until 1948 it also included as one of these member organizations the residuum of a prewar nationalist party, the PSII. In July 1947, as a result of a political deal between Amir Sjarifuddin, who needed Islamic political support in the cabinet he was then trying to form (the Masjumi having refused to participate), several older-generation PSII leaders to whom he had promised cabinet posts defected from the Masjumi, bringing a rump PSII with them.

[21] Natsir and the other Religious Socialists have been much closer to Hatta.

lution in large part because of his ability to moderate between and straddle these groups. His strength in party circles became less after the revolution, in particular after the collapse of his cabinet in early 1952. Thereafter, especially following the NU's withdrawal, he was more and more eclipsed by Natsir, but he continued to command sufficient influence within the party to make him a significant factor in its internal politics.

The increasing influence of Isa Anshary, chairman of the Masjumi's West Java branch, which was noticeable as early as 1952, introduced the most incompatible element into the party's leadership. Dogmatic in his approach to Islam, he was aggressively intolerant of what he considered to be the backsliding and religiously compromising conduct of many other members of the Islamic community, in particular of members of the Nahdatul Ulama. He regarded as heretical their willingness to blend Islam with a considerable dose of Javanese mysticism and surviving elements of Hinduism. Although he was never able to challenge the dominant position of the Religious Socialists in the party, his strength in West Java was so substantial and his oratorical abilities so considerable that he could not be fully controlled. Indeed, his bitter public denunciations of "un-Islamic" Indonesians and "un-Islamic" activities earned him the sobriquet of "our Joe McCarthy" from his uncomfortable colleagues in the party's leadership. Whereas Natsir's approach to the place of Islam in politics was, at least until 1957, moderate and consistent with Indonesian realities—and if ever fully understood would probably not have alarmed Indonesian Christians, Soekarno, or the members of the Indonesian Nationalist Party [22]—this was not true of Isa Anshary. His demands concerning an Islamic state incorporated ideas which were much more dogmatic and extreme and which understandably caused non-Islamic leaders real concern. Ironically, the more the other major parties and Soekarno isolated the Masjumi politically —keeping it out of the government and pushing it to the opposition end of a political polarization—the more the position of Isa Anshary and his followers in the party was strengthened. After the elections, however, it was clear that his extremism had hurt the Masjumi's electoral appeal, especially in Java, and subsequently his influence declined. Despite this, the antagonism of Soekarno and parts of the Indonesian Nationalist Party toward Natsir and his group in the Masjumi continued and the struggle between them for political ascendancy was no less bitter.

[22] This evaluation is based upon extensive talks with Mohammad Natsir in Jakarta, March–April 1955 and August 1956.

Prior to the elections of 1955 when it held 42 parliamentary seats, the Indonesian Nationalist Party (Partai Nasionalis Indonesia, generally referred to as the PNI) was clearly at least the second largest party in the country. It emerged from the elections with the largest vote— 8,434,653 (22.3 per cent)—and 57 seats. The major base of its power has been the bureaucracy. The PNI has been easily the most popular party among the upper and middle strata of the bureaucrats, probably incorporating a majority of them. Broadly speaking, the PNI has been the party of the bureaucratic middle class and of the *pamong pradja* —the traditional Indonesian territorial civil service, the element with the strongest ties with the old Javanese aristocracy. It has found its widest following in Java, winning 86 per cent of its total vote there in the 1955 elections and more than 65 per cent of its total in East and Central Java.[23] With nearly all of its top leaders coming from Java, it has understandably been referred to as a "Javacentric" party. Through its strong position in government, both in Jakarta and through the regional civil service, the PNI was able, particularly in Java, to muster substantial local support in elections through the powerful group of civil servants affiliated with it.[24]

The PNI has never possessed a really consistent and comprehensive ideology, particularly with regard to socioeconomic affairs. Its members have been for the most part only nominal Muslims, many of them being both contemptuous and fearful of Islamic orthodoxy. The party's official credo, *Marhaenism* ("Proletarianism"—with as much rural as urban emphasis), is borrowed from President Soekarno, with whom the party has usually had a particularly close relationship. It has also been the most consistent of all parties in supporting his *Pantjasila*. The PNI in fact bears the name of Soekarno's prewar nationalist party, and although there is no organic connection between them many of its older-generation leaders were Soekarno's close associates in the prewar nationalist movement. All Indonesian political parties are strongly nationalistic, but the PNI's nationalism has shown a particularly strong emotional charge. Indeed, one of the party's prominent leaders has

---

[23] Feith, *Indonesian Elections.*

[24] Of the various ministries through which it has exerted influence, it has probably been able to achieve most through the Ministry of Information and its multitude of local branches. In this ministry PNI influence has been dominant throughout most of the postrevolutionary period. Until the fall of the Wilopo cabinet, the Masjumi could partially match this influence through its control of the Ministry of Religious Affairs; thereafter this ministry, along with its regional branches, came increasingly under the control of the Nahdatul Ulama.

characterized its leadership as incorporating two major groups: the "irrational, emotional nationalists" and "the rational nationalist group." [25] There has also been a third component—one incorporating many of the older civil servants, not particularly dynamic, and usually most influenced by the prewar nationalist leaders in the party. Initially it threw its support to the "irrational" group, but following the 1955 elections its members became alarmed at the Communists' impressive showing in Central and East Java; it was subsequently less willing to follow such leadership and showed more independence. The "rational nationalist group" had by 1957 come to attract support from the largest proportion of educated, younger-generation party members, but with the possible exception of the first months of the Wilopo cabinet it was never quite able to match the strength in party circles of the other two groups.[26]

The Indonesian Communist Party (PKI) has differed from the other major parties in that it has been both well organized and able to maintain substantial party discipline. By the middle of 1957 it appeared to have become the biggest political party in Indonesia, probably slightly larger in its following than the PNI, the Masjumi, or the NU and certainly larger in its active membership. Its attainment of major party status came relatively late, the period of rapid growth not beginning until late 1952. With only 17 seats in the preelection parliament, the PKI increased its stature strikingly in the 1955 elections, winning 6,176,914 votes and 39 seats. Of its total vote in this national election 88.6 per cent came from Java, 75 per cent from East and Central Java alone. Whereas the organizations of the other three major parties were weakened after the 1955 elections, the Communists increased both the strength of their organization and the size of their following, winning first place in the East Java and Central Java provincial elections of mid-1957 (27.5 per cent of the total vote).

During, and particularly in the first two years after, the revolution

[25] In conversations with the writer in 1955 and 1958–1959.

[26] The nature of the PNI's nationalism was such that the party was considerably less hospitable to foreign capital than was the Masjumi. Many influential members were not, however, averse to building up Indonesian capitalists, especially if they were party members, through discriminatory government action, especially through the granting of import licenses and of privileged access to credit from government banks. This disposition was certainly not absent among other parties wed to a socialist program, but after the fall of the Wilopo cabinet the PNI became the major practitioner of this art. Although this did not square with the party's socialism, it did with its nationalism, inasmuch as this process was regarded as an aspect of the Indonesianization of the economy.

the Communists were poorly organized. They had been crippled by
the Madiun rebellion—a taint which still, though diminishingly, em-
barrasses them—and not until 1952 did they have much success in
rebuilding their strength.[27]

Early in 1951 D. N. Aidit—27 years old and recently back from a
year in Communist China and North Vietnam [28]—with a group of
other young men unsullied by any leading role in the Madiun rebellion, wrested control of the party from an older group, of which the
intellectual leader was Tan Ling Djie, an Indonesian of Chinese de-
scent. In the first half of 1952 Aidit and his two very able lieutenants—
M. H. Lukman and Njoto—apparently felt securely enough in control
to announce a radical change in party policies—a switch from a small
elite party to one with a mass organization and the inauguration of a
National Front program calling for a largely constitutional role and
cooperation with other "anti-imperialist parties." This entailed a policy
of consistent enmity toward the Masjumi (which the Communists saw
as their most dangerous rival) and support of the PNI and later the

[27] In August 1951 they received another setback, although much milder and
temporary. Reacting to an increasing level of terrorist activities which were
aimed at disrupting the production of East Java estates and tying up port areas
and which the Communists had been carrying out for more than a year, Prime
Minister Sukiman, backed by Soekarno, ordered the arrest and temporary jailing
of a large number of PKI leaders. Following their release an underground element
of the party concentrated the previously scattered armed groups in an area in
Central Java comprising the northern slopes of the Merapi volcano and Mt.
Merbabu and the hills peripheral to it. Here they reinforced an older base dating
from the Madiun rebellion and gave intensive military and political training to
youths brought in from East and Central Java for short periods on a rotating basis.
From this base, known as the "Merapi-Merbabu Complex" (MMC), they tied
down between 3,000 and 4,000 government troops during 1952–1953. At the
end of 1953, soon after the fall of the Wilopo cabinet (a PNI-Masjumi coalition)
and the formation of the PNI-dominated cabinet under Ali Sastroamidjojo—incorporating the NU but with the Masjumi, the Socialist, and the Christian parties in
opposition—the MMC troops suddenly ceased aggressive activities. It was reported
that this had been ordered by Communist Party leaders as a result of an understanding which they had been able to reach with the new Ali government, one
which they apparently considered made it worth while to cooperate with his
government and concentrate on preparing for the coming elections. In 1954–1955
the pro-Socialist Party Governor of Middle Java, Budiono, initiated a vigorous
military campaign which resulted in defeat of the MMC troops and elimination of
their base.

[28] In an interview with the writer, Aidit stated that he was in south China
as a journalist during the Chinese Communist take-over, but that they paid little
attention to him. He said that after this he went to northern Vietnam, where
he stayed a longer time and met a number of Vietminh leaders, but not Ho Chi
Minh (Jakarta, January 1961).

NU in an effort to drive a further wedge between them and the Masjumi—a strategy which was pursued with considerable success. After 1952 the Communist leaders seem to have realized more and more that their party's fortunes would largely be determined by their ability to clothe it in the symbols of Indonesian nationalism. They therefore not only ceased criticizing Soekarno but became vociferous exponents of his *Pantjasila,* backed up with vigor his every move to win Western New Guinea (West Irian), and did their best to increase his and PNI leaders' concern over the dangers of an Islamic state.

In late 1953 soon after the formation of Ali's cabinet the Communists radically altered their conduct in parliament. They now made a major effort to get along with the government in power. Communist deputies in parliament consistently supported Ali's coalition cabinet, whose majority was so slender and so dependent on several of the fickler minor parties that it welcomed the Communists' support. One possible *quid pro quo,* either tacit or explicit, was the acquiescence of Ali and his cabinet to largely unrestricted Communist Party organizational drives and election preparations.

The Communists were able to develop increasing influence via a number of Communist-front and Communist-influenced organizations. Through the principal labor federation, the SOBSI (Sentral Organisasi Buruh Seluruh Indonesia), they controlled or at least strongly influenced about 1.5 million trade unionists, well over half of those in Indonesia. In addition, through the Barisan Tani Indonesia (Indonesian Peasant Front), an organization which they tightly controlled, they developed considerable peasant backing, particularly in plantation areas. In some of the poorer districts of East and Central Java, where in the 1955 national elections the Nahdatul Ulama and Masjumi were competing for peasant support, the Communists frequently offered an agreeable alternative to peasants who were only nominally Muslim. In some parts of Java the Communist Party was much more successful than the PNI, and it was particularly in these districts that, thanks to its continuing organization, it captured many of the votes in the provincial elections of 1957 which had gone to the PNI in 1955.

The Communist Party's spectacular growth during 1954–1957 is explainable in large part by the ability of its top- and middle-rank leaders and by their dedication to the party cause, but there were other important reasons for its success. One was the continuing belief of President Soekarno and some of the most influential leaders of the PNI that the Communists posed less of a threat, at least in an im-

mediate sense, to Indonesia and their own political fortunes than the
Masjumi. They felt that the Masjumi had a real chance of emerging
victorious from the elections and that the Communists did not. This
made it easier for the Communists to promote a political polarization
which served to isolate the Masjumi.

Another important reason for the Communists' success has been
financial: their party has undoubtedly become the wealthiest in Indonesia. Their financial resources have derived only partially from
membership fees. Although they have not, like the other major parties,
been able to secure financial resources through participation in government, they have compensated by their ability to tap the Chinese
business community in Indonesia for substantial funds. In securing
these funds they have had important cooperation from the Chinese
Communist government's embassy and consulates in Indonesia and
from the Bank of China. While many Chinese businessmen undoubtedly
have been far from eager to make these contributions, they have done
so because of the difficulties which they might otherwise encounter.[29]

Political Developments (1950–1957)

From September 1950 until April 1957 [30] Indonesia had six parliament-based cabinets. The first of these, lasting from September 6,
1950, to April 27, 1951, and led by the Masjumi's Mohammad Natsir,
was formed following an unsuccessful attempt to establish a Masjumi-
PNI coalition cabinet, attempts to do so having broken down over
disagreement on the apportionment of cabinet seats. Natsir's cabinet
was based upon a coalition of the Masjumi and several of the smaller
parties, including the Socialist and Christian parties but excluding
the PNI and the then small Communist Party. Lack of PNI support
was a major weakness, and PNI opposition in conjunction with increasing friction between Natsir and Soekarno finally forced the cabinet

[29] Responsible Indonesian officials believe that usually Indonesian-domiciled
Chinese businessmen contribute because of persuasion or pressure from the Chinese
embassy or pressure from the Communist-controlled labor unions and the threat
of retaliatory action (boycott, labor trouble, or denial of credit) in case of non-
compliance. Moreover, in remitting funds to relatives in China Indonesian-domiciled Chinese have been obliged to utilize the channels provided by the Chinese
Embassy and its adjunct, the Bank of China. Indonesian officials are convinced that
much of the Indonesian currency so secured has been made available to the
Indonesian Communist Party.

[30] For the most scholarly and comprehensive account and analysis of developments during this period see Herbert Feith, *The Decline of Constitutional Democracy in Indonesia* (Ithaca, N.Y.: Cornell University Press, 1962).

to resign. A major reason for Soekarno's opposition was his impatience with what he considered Natsir's lack of vigorous action in dealing with the West Irian problem. Further friction arose over their differing views as to the President's proper role in the government.

With the fall of the Natsir cabinet Soekarno selected two formateurs, one from the Masjumi and one from the PNI. Dr. Sukiman, the Masjumi formateur, being relatively close to Soekarno and the PNI, was able to form a coalition cabinet, based upon the Masjumi, the PNI, and several of the smaller parties, which lasted from April 27, 1951, to April 3, 1952. Sukiman's cabinet was the only one that fell over a foreign policy issue. The crisis was precipitated by an agreement negotiated with the United States for economic assistance. The American ambassador exceeded his instructions from Washington and, quite unnecessarily, prevailed upon the Indonesian Foreign Minister to subscribe to a statement widely interpreted by Indonesians as signifying their country's abandonment of an independent foreign policy and committing it to alignment with the United States. (Foreign Minister Achmad Subardjo had been led to believe by Ambassador Merle Cochran—quite at variance with Washington's intent—that refusal to subscribe to this statement would result in cessation of American economic assistance to Indonesia.) In this case both major political parties strongly condemned the agreement, and this in conjunction with a vociferous popular protest brought the cabinet down.

Formateurs appointed by the President from each of the two major parties unsuccessfully attempted to put together a new cabinet. Following their failure, Soekarno appointed Wilopo, a leader of the more "rational" element in the PNI. He was successful in drawing support from the younger leaders within his party as well as from the Masjumi, Socialist, Christian, and Catholic parties. In the caliber of its members the Wilopo cabinet (April 3, 1952, to August 1, 1953) was probably the strongest of all cabinets in postrevolutionary Indonesia. Within a few months, however, its position was weakened by increasing friction with President Soekarno over control of the armed forces and by dissension among the army's officers—dissension that was rendered acute by cabinet attempts to rationalize and modernize the army. This process was envisaged by a number of officers and by Soekarno as leading to the ultimate dismissal of a substantial proportion of the less-well-educated men who had been trained initially during the Japanese period, the group which, on the whole, stood closest to Soekarno. Indications that efforts at rationalization were being frustrated by parliament members led by older-generation PNI leaders close to Soekarno provoked an attempted coup (the October 17 Affair) by anti-Soekarno officers aimed at forcing him to dismiss parliament. This move was actually directed against Soekarno and officers close to him more than it was against parliament itself. There was a sufficient rallying to Soekarno of officers opposing rationalization to enable him to stand up to the proponents of parliamentary dissolution and refuse. With division in the army and continued pressure from Soekarno and the strongly pro-Soekarno wing of the PNI, the cabinet finally fell over the refusal of parliament, including most of the PNI members, to support it in its attempt to remove peasant squatters from government-owned tobacco lands in North Sumatra.

The fall of the Wilopo cabinet was symptomatic of the widening split which was developing between the Masjumi and the PNI. Attempts to form a new cabinet based upon a PNI-Masjumi coalition were unsuccessful, and only after two months was a cabinet finally formed by a leader of one of the minor parties, Wongsonegoro of the PIR (Persatuan Indonesia Raja). This cabinet centered on the PNI—with one of its leaders, Ali Sastroamidjojo, as Prime Minister—and included the Nahdatul Ulama and several of the small parties. The Masjumi, Socialist, and Christian parties were now in the opposition. Despite mounting criticism of the government's ineffectiveness in promoting economic reconstruction and development, of increased governmental corruption—relating in particular to activities of the cabinet's Minister of Economic Affairs, Iskaq Tjokrohadisurjo—and a serious revolt of the strongly Muslim Atjehnese of northern Sumatra which broke out almost immediately after it took office, Ali's government managed to remain in power from August 1, 1953, until August 12, 1955. Soekarno's influence in government increased greatly during this period, and one reason for the longevity of Ali's cabinet was the consistent support which he gave it. Other reasons were its ability to hold its members and supporting M.P.'s in line due to a more lavish dispensation of patronage than had ever before occurred and the previously mentioned change in Communist tactics giving the Ali cabinet sustained support. In addition Ali's initiative in holding the Asian-African Conference earned his cabinet helpful domestic prestige.

During the course of the Ali cabinet an increasing polarization emerged in Indonesian politics. This resulted primarily from the maneuvering for elections and produced an increasing tendency for the President, the PNI, the Nahdatul Ulama, and the Communist Party to work together for defeat of the Masjumi. In this situation the Nahdatul Ulama held a pivotal position, being courted by both the President and the PNI on the one hand and by the Masjumi on the other. Throughout this period President Soekarno, backed by the cabinet, made a sustained effort to strengthen his position in the army. It was in fact the attempt of the pro-Soekarno Minister of Defense, Iwa Kusumasumantri, to install a chief of staff desired by Soekarno but not acceptable to the majority of top-ranking army officers that precipitated the cabinet's fall.

The last cabinet to be formed prior to the 1955 elections was one whose formateur was designated by Vice-President Hatta, because President Soekarno had left the country on a pilgrimage to Mecca after meeting defeat over the army issue. This cabinet led by Burhanuddin Harahap of the Masjumi's Religious Socialist group lasted from August 13, 1955, until March 24, 1956. It was based upon a coalition of the Masjumi, the Nahdatul Ulama, the Socialists, and some of the smaller parties. However, the NU's support was generally either apathetic or unreliable. With the PNI in opposition and President Soekarno upon his return clearly hostile, the cabinet had a difficult time from the outset. It picked up some popular support because of a vigorous anti-corruption drive, but it lost prestige over its unsuccessful attempt to control the air force, whose commander in chief—clearly backed by Soekarno—refused to countenance the installation of a deputy chief sponsored by the cabinet. When the outcome of the elections became known in December and it was clear that the PNI had received more votes than the Masjumi, the cabinet's position became even weaker. Because of this and a continuing lack of support from Soekarno, its effectiveness during its last months as a caretaker government pending the formation of a new cabinet based upon the results of the elections was less than that of any previous cabinet.

Following the elections the Masjumi and the "rational" and older groups in the PNI, all alarmed over the unexpectedly large vote won by the Communists, worked to reestablish sufficient cooperation to permit their joining together in a cabinet which would exclude the Communists. At the end of March 1956 such a cabinet was formed, under the prime ministership of the PNI's Ali Sastroamidjojo. In addition to the PNI and Masjumi, the cabinet incorporated the NU and representatives of several of the smaller parties.[31] Thereby it could look to

[31] Soekarno had appointed Ali as formateur rather than Wilopo, whose name had been offered by the PNI along with that of Ali. Soekarno criticized Ali's cabinet

a wide base of support in parliament, but from the outset it never commanded strong backing from Soekarno. Moreover, party differences that had become more rigid during the course of the election campaigns were ineffectively bridged in the cabinet, and one could hardly say that it functioned as a harmonious team. Patronage continued to be dispensed on a large scale, a process which nourished governmental corruption. An attempt by Natsir to induce Prime Minister Ali to undertake a vigorous anticorruption cleanup, regardless of who in the Masjumi or the PNI suffered, was turned down. The Prime Minister was widely criticized for being more concerned with foreign affairs and the welfare of his party than in addressing himself to the country's pressing domestic problems. Continuing indications of corruption in high places, mounting inflation, and the government's ineffectiveness in dealing with Indonesia's major economic and administrative problems brought keen disappointment to the many Indonesians who had expected that elections would provide some sort of political panacea and bring effective government. As a consequence, disillusionment with parliamentary democracy became increasingly widespread. Understandably the Communist Party benefited from this situation. As the only major party not represented in the government, it could avoid responsibility for the discouraging situation while growing in strength through its effective organization. Although criticizing the government, it generally remained careful not to antagonize the PNI, directing its major barbs against the Masjumi.

The second half of 1956 was marked by growing regional dissatisfaction and a coincident decrease in the cabinet's control over military leaders, who were now playing an increasingly important political role. The regions outside Java were becoming intensely dissatisfied with the government's failure to take effective action to further their economic development and to meet even their most immediate economic problems or—alternatively—to provide sufficient administrative and fiscal decentralization to allow them to undertake this themselves. The conviction that Jakarta was utilizing for the benefit of Java a disproportionate amount of the country's foreign exchange, approximately three-fourths of which was earned by areas outside Java, heightened this dissatisfaction. The government's failure to allocate to army com-

---

list for incorporating no Communist Party supporters and urged that they be included, arguing that since the Communist Party had emerged as fourth largest in the elections national unity would best be served by including them. The PNI refused to go along with this suggestion.

manders sufficient funds to pay their men and provide them with adequate food and housing led regional commanders in Celebes and North Sumatra as early as mid-1956 to enter into illegal barter trade in copra and rubber. Thereby they took over directly foreign exchange which would otherwise have been channeled through Jakarta. One of the first open indications of the army's increasing political role (and of widening divisions within it) was the narrowly averted attempt in August 1956 by Colonel Kawilarang, commander in West Java, to arrest Foreign Minister Abdulgani on charges of corruption just as he was about to depart for the London conference on Suez. In the middle of November, Colonel Zulkifli Lubis, former deputy chief of staff, launched an abortive coup against the government designed to oust Chief of Staff Nasution as well as Prime Minister Ali and to clean up corruption. His plot was discovered before he could move certain army units from Bandung to Jakarta, and it failed.

Differences among political parties and between Soekarno and Hatta continued to grow. Because the Masjumi had emerged from the elections as definitely the major party outside Java—particularly in Sumatra—and because its representatives in the Ali cabinet held a clearly subordinate position in which they were able to accomplish very little toward promoting measures calculated to assuage the mounting regional restiveness, the party's central leadership found itself under great pressure from regional leaders as well as from Isa Anshary to pull out of the cabinet and go into opposition. Natsir, however, argued that to do so would further weaken national unity and benefit only the Communists, and he managed to keep the Masjumi in the government until January 9, 1957, when the Sumatran coups, Soekarno's continuing call for a new governmental system, and the withdrawal of one of the smaller parties made the cabinet's position completely untenable.

Soekarno, never enthusiastic about Ali's second cabinet, increased his criticism of it and eventually of the whole system of parliamentary government. Late in October 1956 he remarked that political parties might best be "buried" in order that national unity be advanced. On November 10 in his opening address to the Constituent Assembly [32] he stated that "the freedom to set up political parties does not consti-

---

[32] In the elections for the Constituent Assembly, held in December 1955 just after the elections for parliament had been concluded, the PNI received 9,070,218 votes and 119 seats (out of 514 elected seats for the whole assembly), the Masjumi 7,789,619 votes and 112 seats, the Nahdatul Ulama 6,989,333 votes and 91 seats, and the Communist Party 6,232,512 votes and 80 seats (Feith, *Indonesian Elections*, p. 65).

tute the only means to keep the democratic system going" and that Indonesian democracy should be unique and not a copy of imported systems. The weaker groups in Indonesian society should be protected from the stronger, he argued, this necessitating that Indonesia's system of democracy should "see to it that one group should not be exploited by another; this means that for the time being, our democracy must be a guided democracy." Soekarno's call for a guided democracy and his attacks upon the system of parliamentary democracy widened the breach with Hatta, a separation which was formalized with Hatta's resignation as Vice-President on December 1, 1956. Hatta's departure from the government was seen by the outer regions, particularly Sumatra, as depriving them of their principal representative in the government, and their discontent with Jakarta increased. During late December three successive bloodless coups by army commanders in North, Central, and South Sumatra resulted in their administrations' being taken over by army-led councils which announced that they no longer recognized the Ali cabinet. Jakarta was able to manage a countercoup in North Sumatra that ended in a progovernment commander's regaining control of Medan and some other parts of that province. The regional councils of Central Sumatra and South Sumatra led respectively by Lieutenant Colonel Achmad Hussein and Lieutenant Colonel Barlian remained in power.

Following mounting indications of regional dissatisfaction with the Jakarta government and the cabinet's continuing inability to control regional military and civilian leaders in their arrogation of more local powers, Soekarno on February 21, 1957, made a major address in which he set forth his recommendations for a drastic change in Indonesia's political system. The whole structure of government, he stated, "must be rebuilt, renewed right to the very foundation, and a new, completely new edifice constructed." Noting that every cabinet had had to cope with recurrent crises arising because of a lack of authority and because of sustained opposition from various groups in parliament, Soekarno concluded:

I have finally come to the conclusion that the cause lies in our practicing a system not suited to our specific requirements, in our indiscriminate adoption of every feature of the system that is known as western democracy. . . . The more I look back on our experiences of the last eleven years the more I am convinced that the system of democracy that we have taken over is, in fact, incompatible with the Indonesian outlook. . . . The principles of western democracy, the parliamentary democracy of the western countries, incorporate the concept of an active opposition, and it is precisely the adoption of this concept that has given rise to the difficulties we have experienced over the last eleven years. By accepting this concept we have come to think in a manner that is alien to the Indonesian way of life.

As a remedy Soekarno suggested that a new kind of cabinet be created in which the ministers would be drawn from all major parties represented in parliament, making clear that this should include the Communist Party. In addition, he proposed that there be created a National Council which would be "representative of every section of the Indonesian people without exception . . . [with a] membership drawn from all groups in the community—occupational, social, religious, cultural—along with the chiefs of the armed forces and of the police, the Attorney General," and "those ministers of the cabinet holding key portfolios." Soekarno himself would be chairman. Its function, he said, "will be to advise the cabinet, to submit recommendations to the cabinet at the request of the cabinet or without a request of the cabinet." Just as the cabinet would be a "concentrated reflection of the composition of parliament," the National Council would be a "concentrated reflection of the Indonesian nation." Cabinet and council would be closely linked, and by reason of their composition "a firmly established bridge would be created between the parliament and the dynamic forces of society."

Hatta's public criticism of Soekarno's proposal was prompt and trenchant. Incorporation of the Communists into the cabinet, he said, would not promote political solidarity but would introduce a disruptive element inasmuch as the Communists were dedicated to quite different objectives from the other parties. "If co-operation with the Communists were to be imposed on the other parties, the existing antagonisms would only be heightened and the prospect of national unity would become even more remote." Moreover, being "a segment of an international movement dedicated to world revolution . . . and a dictatorship of the proletariat," the Communists, if represented in the cabinet, would make it impossible for Indonesia to follow an independent foreign policy since they would subordinate Indonesia's interests to those of Soviet Russia. To include the Communists in the cabinet would be as futile as "to try to mix water and oil"; their proper place was in the opposition:

These faults and the malpractice of allocating appointments on the basis of party affiliation will not be corrected by the installation of a composite cabinet and the elimination of opposition in the chamber of representatives. The situation can only be remedied by an efficient government comprised of honest and capable ministers under the leadership of the President.

Establishment of a National Council, Hatta added, would be unconstitutional and would in effect be a duplication of parliament; the attainment of a stable government with unquestioned authority could best come by formation of a presidential cabinet headed by Soekarno himself, with the President assuming clear responsibility. Whenever useful the President could hold regular meetings with cabinet members, party leaders, and nonparty experts to discuss urgent political issues. Consequently there would be no need for a National Council.

Soekarno's proposals were accepted by the PNI and the Communist Party and also, in somewhat altered and watered-down form, by the reluctant Nahdatul Ulama; but they were never accepted by the Masjumi, whose leaders viewed his proposals much as did Hatta. The proposals provoked more dissatisfaction in the major islands outside Java, precipitating during the first week of March 1957 coups by the military commanders in Celebes and Indonesian Borneo, who established army-led councils similar to that set up in Central Sumatra. The rump Ali cabinet on March 14 signed an emergency decree declaring a state of martial law ("War and Siege") for all Indonesia and then promptly resigned. This had the immediate effect of strengthening the positions of Soekarno and the army, making both of them even less dependent than before upon the support of the political parties. While this regulation merely confirmed the existing arrogation of civil powers by commanders in the areas outside Java, it initiated the transfer of a wide range of these powers to army commanders in Java, and it enhanced the authority of the army chief of staff, Major General A. H. Nasution.

The Failure of Indonesia's Parliamentary Democracy

With the collapse of Ali Sastroamidjojo's cabinet, Indonesia moved away from a system of parliamentary democracy toward a new and different kind of government. By analyzing the weaknesses of the old system and determining some of the main reasons for its failure, it should be easier to understand why by 1957 so many politically conscious Indonesians had become proponents of, or at least receptive to, a basic change in their system of government. This should also provide some insight into the factors which condition and delimit the possibilities for the new system's success.

It should be noted, however, that the political order which operated in Indonesia from 1950 to 1957 was neither a reasonable copy of one of the more suitable Western democratic systems nor an adequate synthesis of Western and traditional elements. No real attempt to adapt the Western system to Indonesian conditions was made. For the most part the Indonesian constitution of 1950 was an unimaginative, rigid, and doctrinaire adaptation of the constitution of the Netherlands. The inappropriateness of this constitution to Indonesian conditions was considerably increased by operating it, as in the Netherlands, through a multiparty system, based upon multimember constituencies and proportional representation. However well the 1950 constitution and the party system coupled to it reflected Dutch cultural values, the Netherlands' social structure, economic development, and political history, they did not conform to Indonesian realities.

It is possible that even with considerable adaptation to meet Indonesian conditions the basic elements of Western constitutional democracy could not have been made to work effectively in the Indonesia of the 1950s. But whatever chances such an adaptation might have had, no fair test of constitutional democracy, whether of the parliamentary or presidential variety, has yet been made in Indonesia.

However important the deficiencies in the Indonesian constitution, they were not in themselves the really fundamental factors in explaining the ineffective functioning of parliamentary government in the 1950–1957 period. More basic, at least in combination, were surviving elements of traditional culture, the conditioning of the Indonesian elite under Dutch and Japanese rule, Indonesia's social structure, the lack of a consensus on several important matters, and especially the balance of power prevailing in the period when the system was tried.

Despite the influence of egalitarian democratic concepts among many of the small Western-educated elite, even among them, and certainly among Indonesians generally, the traditional belief was still strong that government should properly be of an authoritarian, albeit paternalistic, cast. Society and its governmental projection were still seen as overwhelmingly overshadowing the individual; and in the powerfully surviving and widespread traditional view the individual could not easily be identified as a discrete entity, endowed with rights of his own, with which society was obliged to come to terms. Thus the idea of individual rights vis-à-vis government was weak except among some of those with a Western education—and many from this group appear to have had distinct reservations as to its suitability in an

Indonesian context. Government was generally seen not as the servant of the people, but rather, similar to traditional times, as their steward. Responsibility was still conceived to be primarily upward, those at the apex of governmental power regarding themselves (and being popularly regarded) as responsible to a moral, cosmological totality —but not to the people, to the electorate. The propensity to accept authoritarian government as normal had, understandably, been maintained by the nature of Dutch colonial rule and the Japanese occupation. As was noted earlier, under colonial rule Indonesians were given no opportunity to become acquainted with the workings of the parliamentary system. The fact that they were denied access to any really constructive political roles or responsible administrative positions in colonial society left not a few future members of the Indonesian parliament with outlooks warped by oppositionism and a negative view of government in general. Such attitudes were, of course, hardly conducive to responsible political conduct and were not consistent with the outlook required in a responsible parliamentary opposition.

Nor were they consistent with the still strongly surviving cultural values of solidarity and harmony. And certainly these values could not easily be reconciled with the institutionalization of an active opposition in government, or with the bitter internecine warfare conducted so regularly among the congeries of political parties which operated in parliament. Solidarity and harmony were values which were also clearly incompatible with decision by majority vote. For such a system was seen by Indonesians as abetting and guaranteeing political division and as serving to point up and register publicly differences of opinion, whereas according to the precepts of Indonesian, especially Javanese, culture these differences should be bridged, or if not bridged at least muted. And of course these values could not find congenial a system of elections which served to advertise and describe in sharp relief the issues which divided society, thus exacerbating them and rendering them the more dangerous.[33] Had the elections been based upon single-member constituencies, different political mechanics might well have been set in motion, and conceivably the electoral process might then, as in Great Britain, have served to bridge differences rather than to increase them. However, Indonesians never became acquainted with this potentiality of parliamentary government.

[33] Described by Herbert Feith as "an organized sharpening of social tensions." See his *Indonesian Elections*.

Another factor working against the success of parliamentary government in Indonesia was the lack of consensus on a number of important matters. This deficiency would, of course, have worked against the success of any kind of government, but the particular nature of Indonesia's system of parliamentary government tended to reinforce and make these divisions the more prominent. Undoubtedly the most dangerous was the persistent issue of a secular versus an Islamic state. The Indonesian political community became increasingly split over this matter; the issue dominated all others in the deliberations of the Constituent Assembly which had been elected in 1955 and finally, in 1959, brought the assembly to the bitter stalemate culminating in its dismissal. Of lesser, but nevertheless considerable, importance was the lack of agreement on such matters as regional autonomy versus centralism (i.e., should really significant authority and responsibility be delegated to regional administrations or not); whether the army should be represented in government councils or be a politically neutral instrument of government; whether elections were a source of legitimate governmental authority; and whether government should have a representative as well as a directive role, few Indonesians other than some of the Western-educated minority viewing representation as a normal attribute of government.

From the very outset there was a division of opinion as to the desirability of a parliamentary system of government. Although the system initially enjoyed some prestige among Western-educated Indonesians, partly because it was associated with several of the most powerful and technically advanced countries of the world, it was a way of government to which few of the political elite appear to have had any really strong ideological commitment. In any case, support for parliamentary government and the multiparty system associated with it had been probably less a reflection of the elite's persuasion of their suitability to Indonesian conditions than a result of political expediency. The system's initial acceptance during the early period of the revolution, it will be recalled, had been partly prompted by a desire to present an acceptable face to the major Western powers, whose alienation might have prejudiced chances for the revolution's success. And it had been to an even greater degree a consequence of a domestic power struggle wherein a multiparty parliamentary-based cabinet system provided for certain elements of the political elite a means of ensuring that a competing and initially ascendant group controlled by those who had worked closest with the Japanese would not dominate the government.[34]

The lack of consensus in these matters had not been immediately apparent. For during the revolutionary period differences over these issues were muted and obscured because of an overwhelming preoccupation with the struggle for independence and the tremendously strong integrating force of nationalism. But with the withdrawal of Dutch power, some of the cement of nationalism tended to wash out from many of the major cracks in the foundation of national consensus, revealing them so clearly that they could no longer be ignored.

Of great importance in understanding why parliamentary government in Indonesia failed, and in particular why the governments based upon it lacked sufficient authority to ensure the system's viability, is the fact that political power was much too widely dispersed. The political elite was disunited, and the government did not rest upon a sufficiently substantial consolidation of the power elements in Indonesian society; important political forces remained outside of government and unrepresented or much underrepresented in parliament. Indeed, one might say, then, that the collapse of parliamentary government in Indonesia was incidental to and predetermined by a prior problem—that of an insufficient power base on which to build the system. And since the nature of Indonesia's particular parliamentary system was not well suited to expanding that initial power base, its prospects for survival were slim at the outset.

This fragmentation of power can perhaps be better understood if it is recalled that government in independent Indonesia did not derive from any unified, anticolonial nationalist movement. Conditions in Indonesia and the weight of Dutch and Japanese repression worked against such a development as occurred in India and a number of other colonial areas. Indonesia, then, lacked the sort of single powerful nationalist organization which if carried forward into the period following independence could have contributed to political unity.

Moreover, in Indonesia there was no orderly transition to independence. Independence issued from an extremely disruptive revolution which, because of the extent of Japanese power, could not be planned in advance and which was actually a largely spontaneous explosion with very little initial coordination or focus of power. It was not the planned product of any one dominant and cohesive group; rather it involved concurrent pushes by several different groups, with central

[34] See pp. 565–568.

power having to be built up during the course of the revolutionary process and in confrontation with competing domestic power groupings. Furthermore, the revolution was set in train without any single dominant political philosophy apart from attachment to often vaguely perceived variants of socialism and, of course, the strong sense of nationalism and opposition to the reimposition of Dutch control.

The basic problem in postrevolutionary Indonesia was that of *creating* governmental power as such; effective governmental power was the essential and all-too-lacking prerequisite. In a sense one could say that a vicious circle developed: lacking sufficient power at the outset, the government found that what initial authority it did possess was progressively undermined because of its continuing inability to exert enough power to govern effectively. In other words, deficiency of power led to deficiency of performance, which in turn led to a decrease of the government's moral authority with the public, and a further weakening of its power.

Certainly the power base of Indonesian parliamentary government as it operated from 1950 to 1957 was a narrow one, with several major centers of power largely outside government and unrepresented in cabinet or parliament. Under the 1950 constitution neither of the two major national figures—Soekarno and Hatta—was given a role at all commensurate with his political stature. Soekarno, restive and frustrated by such an artificial situation, did find ways of interpreting the constitution which countenanced his somewhat more considerable role in government, and at times he managed to exert significant political influence which was contrary to the spirit if not the letter of the constitution. His political activities being at least as much outside as within the framework of parliamentary government, on the whole they served to weaken the system's authority. Had this principal personification of Indonesian nationalism been granted at the outset constitutional power and responsibility commensurate with his national stature, Indonesia's government might well have been more effective than it was.

Another major power factor, the Indonesian army, also stood apart and distinct from the political parties which in their shifting combinations formed the power base of parliamentary government. And this was an army increasingly dominated by a group of officers who felt strongly that their vital roles in the struggle for independence and their exercise of civilian authority during the revolutionary period entitled them to an important place in government as well as to the material benefits and social prestige enjoyed by the civilian elite. Although con-

stitutionally denied a political role even more decisively than Soekarno, the army's leadership increasingly from 1955 directly or indirectly applied important extraconstitutional pressures upon the government.

On several important occasions, then, the government's effectiveness
was critically impaired by generally unpublicized interference by
Soekarno and by both covert and open interference by the armed forces.
Whether or not such interference was prompted by wise and sensible
objectives (and sometimes this was no doubt the case), its effect was
not merely to reduce the functional effectiveness of parliament, but
also—and in the long run this was more important—to lower its prestige
and authority with the public.

It should also be noted that some of the most influential of the
regional elites from outside Java were either unrepresented or much
underrepresented in the political parties and in parliament. Frequently
their locally domiciled civilian leaders had close ties with the territorial
army commanders, for, especially in Sumatra, Borneo, and Celebes
(just as in Java), these officers tended to be local men, sensitive to local
problems and needs. It was natural that these two elements of the
regional elites should be drawn together, both in their promotion of
local interests and in their growing antagonism to a central government which was all too often insensitive to their views.

Thus, of the several repositories of political power, parliament was
based in only one—the political parties. It is, therefore, important to
appreciate the nature of this all-too-narrow base. To begin with, Indonesia was and remains badly lacking in indigenous social elements
economically independent of government and endowed with sufficient
financial resources to support the sort of political parties requisite to
the effective operation of parliamentary democracy. The nonbureau-
cratic component of the Indonesian middle class (the Chinese minority apart) was far too small and weak to finance party activity; nor was
there a landed gentry substantial enough to do so. In Western-type
democracies it is, of course, taken for granted that a political party
can secure access to sufficient nongovernmental financial means to ensure its viability, at least until it is once again in power and has access
to governmental patronage. In Indonesia, however, for every major
political party except the Communist, the government constituted the
major, and essential, source of financial support. Only by actual participation in government could the major non-Communist parties secure
the funds necessary for large-scale political activity. Such participa-

tion meant not only access to patronage and the ability to build party backing through providing supporters with posts in the bureaucracy. In addition, it made possible dispensation of various privileges, such as the highly profitable import licenses, whose recipients were expected to express their appreciation in financial terms. Equally important, there were various devices whereby 5 or 10 per cent of loans from foreign countries could be siphoned into the coffers of the parties which formed the government. These devices were by no means of exclusive benefit to the party organizations, for frequently considerable amounts went into the pockets of individual cabinet members and prominent party officials.

In short, then, during the period 1950–1957 party activity was increasingly financed by governmental corruption, and inevitably, as this corruption grew and became known to the public, the image of the parties became badly tarnished. When even the elected government of Ali Sastroamidjojo showed no signs of abandoning such practices, and corruption in fact became greater, popular disgust with and repudiation of the party system became considerably more widespread. Despite the dedication and honesty of the Chairman of Parliament, Sartono, and of a considerable number of that body's membership, all too many M.P.'s were regarded by the public as corrupt as well as factious and irresponsible. In any case, the corruption so pronounced in the party system tended to rub off on parliament, and in the public eye that institution as a whole, as well as the parties, was widely regarded as corrupt.

As was noted earlier, the plethora of parties meant that government was necessarily made up of coalitions of several of them—all too generally shifting and often fickle coalitions, whose effectiveness would in any case have been diminished by the shortness of their lives. The instability of cabinets was further aggravated, it will be recalled, not only because of their inability to dissolve parliament, but also because the center of gravity of party power generally lay outside of parliament —with party leaders who were frequently unresponsive to the representatives of their own party that sat in either parliament or cabinet. Toward their party's membership the attitude of most of these leaders was highly autocratic: "We know what's good for you; we will lead you." Usually the party bosses were a law unto themselves, running party headquarters in Jakarta without responsibility to the constituencies which in theory the parties were supposed to represent. And insofar as members of parliament felt responsibility to anyone, it was usually to their party bosses rather than to any geographic constituency.

An additional reason for the discrediting of elected authority in general, and of parliamentary democracy as it operated in Indonesia, was the situation at the intermediate levels of government (provinces and *kabupatens*) where, in the eyes of the population, were mirrored in microcosm all the weaknesses of the Jakarta political stage. For, with the introduction at the beginning of January 1957 of the decentralization legislation so vigorously championed by the political parties, local authority in Java and several other areas was progressively transferred from the old professional centrally directed administrative civil service (pamong pradja) to elected regional heads and elected regional councils. All too often the political parties did not run well-qualified locally rooted men of prominence for these positions, and as a consequence a great many second- and third-rate individuals were put in office. Their frequent lack of stature and qualifications and their almost immediately apparent ineffectiveness and political partisanship quickly outraged local public opinion. And, quite apart from overly great emphasis on party and personal interests as against those of the local population, too many of the individuals put up for election by the parties were "town-bred members of the intelligentsia who locally commanded neither social prestige nor popular confidence and were ignorant of local problems and needs." [35] Among politically conscious Indonesians this experience at the local level considerably reinforced the increasingly widespread sentiments generated by the dismal record of parliamentary government at the national level—namely, that election was no proper basis for authority and that the influence of political parties in government was disrupting and corrupting.

Finally, even that all-too-limited decision-making authority which the government did possess was not matched by a power of decision implementation, for it did not command a bureaucratic instrument capable of effectively exercising that authority. The government's continuing inability to carry out satisfactorily many of those decisions which it was able to take contributed to the diminution of its authority and served to damage further the reputation of parliamentary democracy.

In any attempt to provide a balanced discussion of the reasons for the failure of Indonesia's system of parliamentary democracy, it should,

[35] Selo Soemardjan, *Some Social and Cultural Implications of Indonesia's Unplanned and Planned Development,* paper presented at the tenth Pacific Science Congress, Honolulu, August 21–September 6, 1961.

however, be reiterated that the particular variant which Indonesians experienced was hardly an appropriate example of the system in general and that the circumstances obtaining in Indonesia during the period in which it operated scarcely permitted a fair test. This distortion of the system and unfairness of the test were compounded by the often inferior caliber of the men who sat in the cabinets with which the system has been identified. Especially was this so during its major test, the cabinet led by Ali Sastroamidjojo from early 1956 until March of 1957—the one and only cabinet to be based upon a parliament which had been elected. It would be unfair not to note that some of its members could scarcely have brought credit to any cabinet, parliamentary or otherwise. But this Ali cabinet in particular tended to color the general Indonesian view of parliamentary democracy. Thus, the general term "parliamentary democracy" came to be something of a scapegoat not only for the undoubted weaknesses of the *particular* parliamentary system which Indonesia experienced, but also for the deficiencies of certain individuals who sat in its cabinets.

· XXII ·

The Introduction of Guided

Democracy (1957-1962)

BY EARLY 1957 it seemed evident that most politically conscious Indonesians had come to regard parliamentary democracy as a system which had failed and which was unsuitable for Indonesia. Indeed, the ease with which Soekarno and army leaders during the next few years were able to eliminate its institutions and move on toward their announced goal of Guided Democracy reflected this profound disillusionment with the old political order and the strong popular desire to see it replaced by a more effective system. Not only Soekarno's supporters, but also many of his opponents, were in agreement that to be effective any new system would for at least a considerable time need to be fairly authoritarian. There was, then, a widespread receptivity to drastic political change, and in many cases to almost any sweepingly different political system, whether or not it was called Guided Democracy. "Guidance" was in these circumstances a welcome word, for to Indonesians it seemed all too clear that government and political life in general stood badly in need of this quality.

What, then, were the objectives of Soekarno and the army?

Soekarno's Views

Soekarno's criticism of parliamentary democracy and the multiparty system and his persuasion that they were unsuited to Indonesia were of long standing. These sentiments had been strengthened as a consequence of the manifest ineffectiveness of the Indonesian system of parliamentary government; and they were undoubtedly further reinforced when the 1955 elections rendered the PNI and the NU (the two major parties previously most amenable to his influence) less dependent upon him, and therefore less disposed to respond to his wishes. But his views cannot be understood simply in terms of his own political ambitions and his conviction that his proper role in Indonesian history is a political one far outstripping that provided under a parliamentary system.

It is Soekarno's contention that his basic political and economic ideas are today the same as they were even before the Indonesian revolution; what have changed, he says, are not his views, but conditions in Indonesia.[1] And, indeed, there is much in the record which supports this assertion. His emphasis on political unity, with all elements united into one harmonious whole, was clearly foreshadowed in the strategy which he advocated for the Indonesian nationalist movement more than thirty years ago. Even at that time Soekarno was anything but a political pluralist. Social divisions and competing interests were quite as uncongenial to him as they were incongruous with traditional Javanese values of solidarity and harmony. In his view, the component elements of the state should complement one another, not in an equilibrium of divergent forces, but in a consciously sought-for harmony. Unity of power and of leadership is regarded as essential. The leader is no mere broker for the ideas and demands of various interest groups. His function is positive and paternally authoritarian, but his effectiveness is dependent upon his rapport with and sensitivity to the views and wishes of the people. Through consultation with them he secures advice and guidance as a basis for deciding what is best for them and for taking the initiative in attaining this.

Soekarno has seen in the *musjawarat-mufakat* decision-making process of the Indonesian village [2] a method which he believes to be consistent with his views and which can be adapted for use at the national level of government. The generally idealized model of this process calls for a period of free discussion during which consensus is gradually achieved; the village headman senses the crystallization of opinion and announces the consensus, this being regarded as binding upon the villagers. Soekarno emphasizes that even at the village level

[1] Interview with the writer, February 14, 1959.
[2] See pp. 588–589.

this system will not work unless coupled with strong leadership; in other words, there must be an able, widely respected headman with the prestige and personality to lead opinion himself and—most important —to state a final judgment as to what synthesis the consultations have yielded.[3] Thus, although the system does provide for consultation and exchange of opinion, it is in fact, even under favorable circumstances, unworkable without a considerable authoritarian element—personified in the headman or whoever else is charged with discovering and announcing the consensus. For apart from the initiative he will have to take in launching and guiding the discussion, under most circumstances the consensus spokesman will have to be somewhat arbitrary and autocratic if he is to describe a synthesis of sufficient substance and precision of outline to provide a really useful basis of action.

Soekarno's reservations about parliamentary democracy had long been held and sometimes publicly voiced. At the outset of the revolution he was among those who took the initiative in creating a single monolithic national party, and he was opposed to the introduction of a multiparty system a few months later. In the 1945 Indonesian constitution, in whose drafting he played an influential part, the kind of government envisaged was not a parliamentary cabinet system, but rather one based in a powerful presidency, with the cabinet appointed by and responsible to the President. If during the early years of the revolution Soekarno's power had been greater and subject to fewer political challenges, this presidential government would not have given way in November of 1945 to a parliamentary system. In his major speech of December 17, 1949, he was clearly appealing for a different system from the parliamentary democratic one soon to be written into the 1950 constitution. "There is a difference," he said, "between our democracy and the democracy of other places. . . . Democracy of the East, or more precisely Indonesian democracy, is a democracy accompanied by leadership."

To all this must be added the fact that by 1957 Soekarno had come to feel a deep concern over the manifest inability of Indonesia's government to achieve any significant degree of economic development or to move any real distance toward the egalitarian socioeconomic goals of the revolution. Indeed, the political phase of the revolution seemed to have waned without ushering in any important change in the coun-

---

[3] "At no matter what level," stated Soekarno, "the system can only work where there is leadership; there must be a leader capable of stating what the decision is" (interview with the writer, March 19, 1959).

try's economic life except that the political parties which controlled government had managed to build up a favored, artificially protected group of Indonesian importers—a "new bourgeoisie," small it is true but hardly consistent with the socialist slogans to which these parties still paid lip service. In contrast with this, Soekarno had just viewed during his trip to Communist China, in the middle of 1956, the striking advances in economic development achieved through Mao Tse-tung's success in organizing and harnessing the energies of the Chinese people. Although still persuaded that communism was not appropriate for Indonesia, Soekarno was highly impressed by the methods of social organization and discipline developed by the Chinese Communists. He was disposed to explore the possibility of borrowing and adapting some of these techniques for Indonesian use, with the idea that he, at the head of a quite different monolithic political organization, might approximate in Indonesia what the Communist Party had accomplished in China. It should be emphasized that Soekarno did not contemplate that the Indonesian Communist Party should fill the central role.

Thus, what Soekarno had by 1958 come to advocate was the abolition of all existing political parties and their replacement by a single national leadership party. This new monolithic party he envisaged as a well-integrated governmental organization subordinate to and controlled by him and charged with mobilizing the energies of the population to serve government and build up the country. This National Front, as he came to call it, would be an organization with a radical left, but non-Communist, orientation which in harnessing popular energies to the service of government would function something like the Communist Party in China. In mobilizing the population, the National Front would work through component elements which Soekarno termed "the functional groups"—organizations of the youth, peasantry, labor, veterans, army, and so on. Soekarno had not worked out the details, but he was confident that with all political power thus channeled into a single organization progress could be made toward the revolution's economic goals. He saw himself as leading the National Front and being identified with it, the people regarding it as Soekarno's organization. He thought of it as the mass organization par excellence, one which would overshadow and ultimately subsume the political parties.

With political parties abolished, parliament would be superseded by new deliberative bodies designed to provide a better channel for the people's revolutionary demands. These bodies would be composed of individuals representing functional groups (the largest being the peasantry, labor, and the armed forces) and religious and ideological currents. In appointing their representatives Soekarno expected to recruit a new leadership closer to the people and more fully reflecting their revolutionary urge than had the representatives of the "ossified and sterile parties." In these deliberative bodies there was to be no place for a permanent institutionalized opposition, and there was to be no vote by majority. Instead, following a sufficient period of closed discussion, decisions would be taken on a *musjawarat-mufakat* basis, with no votes and no divisions, through a unanimous agreement by acclamation.

As an interim measure prior to an ultimate elimination of all political parties and their members' absorption into the projected National Front, there would be a cabinet composed of all major political parties, including the Communist Party.

Soekarno realized that under the system of Guided Democracy which he envisaged, he would be obliged to shoulder a great deal more responsibility than had earlier been the case.[4] But at the same time, wherever possible, he was anxious to spread this responsibility, sharing it as much as he could with all important political groups, while at the same time retaining for himself the key decision-making power. Thus the National Council (and its successor in 1959, the High Advisory Council) had two functions: to advise Soekarno, by elaborating his ideas, testing some of them in its discussions, and occasionally by introducing new ones; and to share responsibility with him for his decisions. When one appreciates this responsibility-sharing function of the body, one can better understand Soekarno's insistence that it include significant representation from both the Communist Party and the army.

The Army's Views

In understanding the army's increasingly critical attitude toward parliamentary government and its subsequent championing of Guided Democracy, it is important to bear in mind the rather special historical conditioning of its officers. It will be recalled that Indonesia did not emerge from Dutch control with anything comparable to the Sand-

---

[4] "Under the new system," he stated, "I will have to carry a great deal more weight upon my shoulders—for I will not only lead the government, but the National Council and the National Front; to lead the National Front will require much work and energy from me" (interview with the writer, March 19, 1959).

hurst-trained officer cadre inherited by India—professionals whose training endowed them with an unquestioning conviction that the armed forces were properly an obedient instrument of civilian political authority. The outlook of most Indonesian officers was forged in the crucible of the revolution. Many emerged from the long struggle with the Netherlands convinced that since the army had been the principal element in winning its country's independence, its leaders had a clear right to a major political role. Among those officers who had received their initial training from the Japanese this conviction was often particularly strong, for their Japanese instructors had emphasized that military officers had not merely the right but indeed the mission to give leadership in government. Moreover, during the course of the four and a half years of revolutionary struggle army officers had become quite used to playing a major part in government. This circumstance has been obscured because, beginning in 1950, following the withdrawal of Dutch power, the army pulled back from most of the political and administrative functions which it had exercised and did indeed become much more a mere instrument of civilian authority. But the officers who had for so long played these extramilitary roles could not easily forget their experiences; and the propriety of resuming these roles seemed all the greater when during the mid-1950s the effectiveness and moral probity of the civilian government declined so considerably.

Army criticism of the political parties and their government was aggravated by the efforts of several cabinets, including the election-based government of Ali Sastroamidjojo, to extend the influence of particular political parties among the officer cadre—making for politicization and factionalism which were destroying army unity. To understand the fervor with which many top officers, including General Nasution, advocated the abolition of political parties, it is necessary to understand how strongly they were antagonized by such party activity. This feeling was such that many of them concluded that government by the political parties (and the parliamentary government associated with them) was by its nature incompatible with maintenance of the army's unity. But it was toward the Communist Party (PKI) that army officers were most hostile. This anti-PKI posture was not only a consequence of their antagonism toward the parties in general and their belief that because the PKI had become the strongest party it was most likely to be in a position to influence government policy if parliamentary democracy were continued. Army officers were also convinced that the PKI was the party most strongly opposed to their keeping their recently acquired economic positions and perquisites and the least disposed to countenance their maintaining any significant role in government policies. And, of great importance, they could not agree with Soekarno that the PKI could be "domesticated"; for they saw it as linked with Soviet Russia and Communist China and consequently as a threat to Indonesian security and independence. There were also a good many officers who were opposed to the PKI on religious grounds, not believing its protestations of religious toleration. Although, almost without exception, senior army officers were agreed as to the desirability of ultimately eliminating the PKI, they differed as to the appropriate timing and the steps to be taken. While some were on the *qui vive* for a sufficient excuse to crack down on it with all available force, there were others who were reluctant to provoke a four-square confrontation lest this also lead to a confrontation with Soekarno. And some were concerned lest such a move provoke insurrectionary activity which, though they were confident they could suppress it, might cause serious economic damage and social disruption. Thus, in looking forward to a new political order to replace parliamentary democracy, a clearly defined and unwavering objective of the army was the abolition of political parties. Although some officers had reservations concerning the wisdom of such a blanket policy, their colleagues pointed out that it would be awkward to abolish only the Communist Party and not the others as well.

The army's leaders were also united in desiring that parliamentary democracy yield place to more authoritarian and purposeful government, with Soekarno (and for many of them Hatta as well) assuming a major role and major responsibility. But in any such scheme they insisted that there be clear provision for the army's having an important voice in the formulation of government policy. General Nasution held that to ensure its appropriate voice, the army should, even in normal times, be represented in the cabinet as well as in all advisory and policy-making bodies of government.[5]

Although by early 1957 Soekarno's ideas about the new political order which he wished to see introduced had already begun to take shape, his power was not sufficient for him to impose them. He was obliged to compromise considerably and to move ahead slowly and

[5] Interview with the writer, January 15, 1959. General Nasution went on to say that in periods of crisis (such as he said existed at the time of this interview) the army's representation should be enlarged.

cautiously. Nor were the chief of staff of the army, General Nasution, and his colleagues at headquarters strong enough to insist on any full implementation of their much less clear plans for changes in the political system. For not only was there a lack of any full agreement between Soekarno and the army on the political changes to be introduced; even with respect to those aspects upon which they could agree they were opposed by the leaders of the political parties and by the increasingly powerful and highly autonomous military-led regimes in Sumatra and Celebes. These outer-island military leaders desired the diminution of both Soekarno's and General Nasution's powers and proposed quite different solutions to remedy Indonesia's political and economic ills; and they were strong enough to oblige these two leaders to hold back in promoting their new plans. Thus it was not until the power of the intransigent regional leaders had been broken that Soekarno and the army had any substantial scope for carrying them out. Indeed, until mid-1959 the movement toward Guided Democracy was gradual and the steps taken were short, halting, and sometimes indecisive.

1957–1958: A Period of Crisis

Despite widespread demands, particularly from areas outside Java, that he appoint Hatta as formateur of the new cabinet, Soekarno on March 15, 1957, gave this mandate to Suwirjo, chairman of the PNI, instructing him to form a coalition cabinet of all major parties and to establish a National Council. Unable to bring the major parties— including his own—to accept inclusion of the Communists in the cabinet, Suwirjo returned his mandate a week later. Soekarno then gave him a second mandate, this time instructing him to form a cabinet of experts, whose selection would not necessarily correspond to party strength. Again Suwirjo failed. Thereupon, instead of turning to the Masjumi, the other first-ranking party, Soekarno undertook the unprecedented action of appointing himself, "Citizen Soekarno," as formateur for the purpose of establishing an "emergency extra-parliamentary cabinet of experts." Within a week he had succeeded in lining up a group headed by Djuanda Kartawidjaja, an able and respected nonparty man with considerable experience in earlier cabinets as Minister of Communications and of Economic Planning. His cabinet incorporated members of the PNI, the NU, and a few of the small parties, as well as several nonparty people. It contained no member of the Communist Party, but two nonparty ministers (Agriculture and Mobilization of National Strength for Reconstruction) were regarded as being sympathetic to it. Although not represented in this cabinet, the Communist Party gave it strong support in parliament. The Masjumi refused to enter the government, labeling it unconstitutional.

Both Soekarno and Djuanda stated that the new cabinet would be responsible to parliament, but in fact its responsiveness to the President was considerably greater. From then on, the strength of parliament and the scope of its authority progressively declined and contracted in the face of the increasing governmental roles played by the President and the army. Soekarno, with his appointment of the Djuanda cabinet, and the army, under the country-wide declaration of martial law, took their first significant steps in the direction of Guided Democracy. Almost immediately Soekarno went ahead with his plan for a National Council, he and Djuanda signing an emergency decree on May 6, 1957, establishing this body of forty-three members.[6]

The remaining months of 1957 were marked by continuing dissension among the political parties and mounting disagreement and tension between General Nasution's headquarters and the regional commanders in Sumatra and Celebes, who were asserting an increasing degree of independence in administrative and economic matters. The commanders in these outer islands insisted that army unity depended upon a reconciliation between Hatta and Soekarno, Hatta's installation as Prime Minister, and the removal of General Nasution (along with some of his aides) as chief of staff. The success of the Communists in the Java provincial elections of mid-1957 (wherein they won 27.5 per cent of the vote and emerged as by far the largest party) did alarm the other three major parties sufficiently to bring them to talk of the necessity of cooperation against the Communists, but in fact no common front was forged and differences between the non-Communist parties remained as great as before. And between Soekarno and the Masjumi the breach became broader, and mutual suspicion greater, than ever before. Although the central government did make an effort to meet regional demands—granting considerably larger monetary subventions to the areas outside Java and drafting legislation providing

[6] It was provided that all appointments and removals of council members would be the prerogative of the President, that the President would be its chairman, and that "members of the council shall be appointed from functional groups within the society, persons who can bring regional problems to the fore, the holders of military and civilian posts as necessary and ministers as necessary." In the official explanation attached to the decree it was stated, "In our further constitutional development it is clear that other efforts are necessary to accommodate the growth of active forces in our society which are not channeled effectively by existing institutions."

for much greater administrative autonomy—it was unable to halt the drift toward an even greater degree of regional independence. Indeed, Jakarta was now faced by the dissident areas' increasing arrogation of control of foreign-exchange-earning exports, a circumstance which aggravated the government's already serious economic situation. Political tensions in Jakarta increased. Colonel Lubis, leader of the abortive coup of November 1956, was believed to be preparing a second attempt, to be directed against both Nasution and Soekarno; and he undoubtedly had a part in the hand-grenade attack against Indonesian Communist Party headquarters in July of 1957.

In an effort to deal with these increasingly grave problems, to reconcile Soekarno and Hatta, and to bridge the divisions within the army and in the political community, Prime Minister Djuanda in September 1957 organized two successive national conferences of prominent regional, military, and civilian leaders. Through them Soekarno and Hatta were brought together for talks and promised to try to work together for solution of the nation's problems. The two men, however, remained divided on several key issues and were unable to agree on the scope of Hatta's role in any new cabinet that might replace Djuanda's or on whether the Communists would be included in such a cabinet. Soekarno remained unwilling to meet Hatta's minimum terms as to the degree of real authority the latter would exercise in any such cabinet. The conference did result in the establishment of a committee of seven of the country's top leaders, who were charged with the task of restoring unity within the army. Its members were Soekarno, Hatta, Djuanda, Dr. Johannes Leimena, the Sultan of Jogjakarta, Dr. Aziz Saleh, and General Nasution.

In the midst of this committee's deliberations, an attempt—which came very close to succeeding—was made to assassinate President Soekarno, reportedly by agents of Colonel Lubis. Soekarno escaped unscathed, but this experience understandably left a deep imprint on his political thinking. The fact that Lubis was closely associated with the dissident colonels from Sumatra and Celebes made the task of restoring army unity all the more difficult. Moreover, the principal agent in the assassination attempt, although apparently operating without any connection with the Masjumi party's leaders and without their knowledge, had previously been closely associated with at least one of them. In view of the bitter relations already existing between Soekarno and the top Masjumi leaders, it is not surprising that he was convinced that they, as well as Colonel Lubis, were behind the plot to assassinate

him. Soon after this incident, the committee of seven charged with restoring unity in the army ceased its efforts, and prospects for an over-
all military and political settlement looked dimmer than ever.

Just one day before the assassination attempt a vote in the United
Nations General Assembly had fallen short of the two-thirds majority
necessary to endorse Indonesia's petition that the Netherlands be called
upon to negotiate over the status of West Irian. Soekarno had warned
of the serious reaction which such a refusal would provoke in Indonesia, and during the first weeks of December there was wide-scale
seizure of Dutch properties and a campaign calling upon the some
46,000 Netherlanders still resident in Indonesia to leave. Soekarno was
the major promoter of this move, but labor unions—prominent among
which were elements of the Communist-dominated SOBSI—took the
major role in the seizures. The take-overs indicated a lack of planning
and central coordination and resulted in considerable economic disruption until the Djuanda government ordered the army to move in
and take over establishments from the squads sent in by the labor
unions. The army was able to keep most of these enterprises going,
but the departure of a sizable proportion of the Netherlanders who had
been key personnel in their operation led to their markedly decreased
efficiency. The attempt to take over Dutch interisland shipping backfired, with the Dutch ultimately withdrawing their ships from Indonesia and leaving the country badly short of transport needed for
interisland commerce.

The precipitate nature of these actions and the lack of preparation
brought strong criticism from Hatta and even more vigorous criticism
from several of the Masjumi leaders. The stand of the Masjumi was
quickly exploited by their opponents, who accused its leaders of being
pro-Dutch and of lacking proper patriotism, a refrain taken up by
a newspaper controlled by Soekarno. Among those most vigorously
attacked was Sjafruddin Prawiranegara, governor of the Bank of Indonesia. He resigned his position in the bank and with a number of
other Masjumi leaders, including Natsir, suffered many threats from
politically motivated youth groups, some of whose members marched
repeatedly around their houses, intimidating their families. Protection
from the police and army was not forthcoming, officers making it clear
that without authorization from Soekarno they could not interfere. A
cousin of Natsir was arrested in the latter's house and accused of
involvement in the July hand-grenade attack on Communist Party headquarters. Another former Masjumi Prime Minister, Burhanuddin Hara-

hap, heard that he was to be charged with involvement in the assassination attempt against Soekarno and was due for arrest. In the face of this situation Natsir, Sjafruddin, and Burhanuddin Harahap removed to Padang, capital of the already virtually autonomous central Sumatran regime headed by Lieutenant Colonel Achmad Hussein. Here they found preparations for a major confrontation with Jakarta well advanced. Several of the top military commanders of Sumatra and the Celebes, together with Colonel Lubis and an ex-Socialist Party Minister of Finance, Professor Sumitro Djojohadikusumo, had already agreed on some sort of challenge to the government calculated to effect changes—on the exact nature of which there was no complete agreement. Natsir held back, initially refusing any full commitment to the enterprise, and joined only after the die had been cast and he had no option but to go along. But Sjafruddin entered eagerly into the discussions, pushing Colonel Lubis aside as the principal planner.

The attitude which the dissident regionalists took toward Jakarta appears to have been strengthened by the expectation of considerable outside support. It is difficult to ascertain to what extent they indulged in wishful thinking, but in any event foreign agents did make commitments to them and one shipload of supplies reached Padang before the rebellion was launched. Soon afterward considerable quantities of modern American military equipment were flown to the rebels, mostly from Formosa. Acting somewhat more precipitously than might otherwise have been the case, in order to take advantage of Soekarno's temporary absence abroad, the regionalist leaders, with Colonel Hussein as their spokesman, on February 10, 1958, issued an ultimatum to the central government. They demanded that the Djuanda cabinet resign within five days, that Hatta and/or the Sultan of Jogjakarta form a nonparty cabinet of experts with a mandate to govern until the next national elections, and that Soekarno resume a purely constitutional position.[7] The Djuanda cabinet refused to comply with the ultimatum, and on February 15 at Padang the dissident leaders proclaimed the Revolutionary Government of the Republic of Indonesia, with Sjafruddin as Prime Minister. The revolutionaries, expecting wide support from other parts of Indonesia, believed that Jakarta would accede to their demands, if not initially at least soon thereafter. However, the only open support came from Central Sumatra, the district of Tapanuli and part of Atjeh in North Sumatra, and North Celebes. Varying de-

---

[7] Not in this original ultimatum, but one of the rebels' demands, was that all members of the PKI be denied participation in government.

grees of sympathy—and this tended to wane rather rapidly in most areas—was the only support forthcoming from other parts of Indonesia; and this included South Sumatra, a rich and important province already highly autonomous of Jakarta, whose military leader, Colonel Barlian, had been privy to the rebels' plans and upon whom they had counted for support. American military supplies to the rebels continued to arrive in considerable quantities, but despite several encouraging statements by Secretary of State Dulles the United States did not recognize their regime or even grant it belligerent status.

After considerable uncertainty upon the part of the Jakarta government as to how it should respond to the situation and an initial period of wavering upon the part of Soekarno when he seemed to favor Hatta's counsel for a negotiated settlement, a reply in military terms was finally decided upon. Had the rebels not openly broken with the Jakarta government, had they not fractured Indonesian national unity by setting up a competing government, had they not openly attacked so major a symbol of Indonesian nationalism as President Soekarno, it would probably have proved impossible to secure the acquiescence of army commanders and influential civilians in Java in the marshaling of Javanese troops for the attacks which were finally mounted on rebel-held territory in Sumatra and Celebes. On March 7, 1958, crack government paratroopers landed near the oil fields of eastern Sumatra, and the rebel soldiers fled. This easy success steeled the government's resolve to effect a solution by force, and thereafter its troops advanced rapidly. By early May they had captured both Padang and the inland rebel stronghold of Bukittinggi, with the rebels offering virtually no resistance and with remarkably few shots being fired in anger. Some rebel troops went over to the government; most of them withdrew discreetly from the towns; and their resistance was soon reduced to guerrilla level. In North Celebes the fighting was considerably stiffer and more prolonged, but by the end of July even there no major town remained in rebel hands. Although resistance in the form of guerilla activity was to continue for another two and a half years, by June 1958 the back of the rebellion had clearly been broken.[8]

As a consequence, one of the major power factors—the dissident regional leaders—had been removed from the national scene, and the

[8] For an excellent account of the rebellion, particularly its internal politics, the conditions surrounding its conclusion, and its effect on national politics, see Herbert Feith and Daniel S. Lev, "The End of the Indonesian Rebellion," *Pacific Affairs*, vol. XXXVI, no. 1 (Spring 1963).

pattern of power relationships which remained was a simpler one. But the rebellion and its suppression accomplished more than this; it resulted also in a considerable strengthening of Soekarno and of Nasution and the central army leadership. The army emerged more united than it had been for many years, and because of this it had greater political strength and influence than before the rebellion. For Soekarno, not only were many of his regionalist critics weakened and discredited; but along with them the Masjumi—the political party most strongly opposed to him—had been implicated in the rebellion, and as a consequence its power in national politics was drastically reduced. (The same was true for the Socialist Party which, though opposing the rebellion, had to some extent been implicated, primarily because of Professor Sumitro's involvement.) It should be noted, too, that the Communist Party, although watched closely by the army, had been able to utilize the first year of the rebellion to build up its strength and to penetrate some new areas, such as part of Central Sumatra, where its members were sometimes given authority in civilian affairs because they were deemed reliable in terms of their opposition to the rebels.

Power Relationships (1958–1962)

With the back of the rebellion broken, the road to Guided Democracy lay more open to Soekarno and the army than before, and to the extent that they could agree together on a program there were few political obstacles to impede them. But cooperation was not always easy. Although both remained agreed in principle on certain major aspects of the political order which they envisaged—such as abolition of the political parties and establishment of a National Front—they could not come to a satisfactory arrangement as to which would control the decisive levers of power. Even though he was as fully dedicated as the army to the elimination of all political parties, Soekarno deemed it wisest to hold back in the execution of such a policy pending assurance that he would be able to assert exclusive control over the monolithic National Front which he envisaged as replacing the parties. As late as February 1963 he had not attained that objective: nor, even then, did it seem likely that he would.

Being unable himself to exercise dominant influence and control over the now much more unified and politically powerful Indonesian army, Soekarno could not afford to see the political parties liquidated. For he feared isolating himself and being obliged to stand alone in confronting the army on the chessboard of power. By maintaining the political parties, he could assure himself of a broader base for political maneuver and of organized support on at least some of the issues wherein he differed from the army. Thus Soekarno became reconciled to shelving his plans for eliminating the parties; though willing to have them weakened, he undertook to halt the process and to rescue the most amenable of them, permitting them a limited, but controlled, existence. The problem which he has had to face has been how to keep the parties weak enough to control yet strong enough to serve as an effective ally against the army.

In view of his need to maintain parties as a political counterpoise to the army, Soekarno felt it especially necessary to resist army plans for outlawing and eliminating the Indonesian Communist Party, since by late 1958 it was the only political party commanding substantial organized mass backing.

There now remained only three power factors of any real consequence—Soekarno, the army, and the Indonesian Communist Party. The nature of their relationship decisively circumscribed the course of political events during the period 1958–1962 and exercised a decided influence on the way in which Guided Democracy developed. At the risk of some oversimplification, this set of relationships can be depicted in terms of a rather lopsided triangle, with a long, gently sloping right-hand side, representing the army, and a much shorter, steeper left-hand side, representing the Communist Party—these two sides leaning in to an apex, representing Soekarno. With great tactical skill Soekarno balances off one authoritarian organization against the other, to the end that his own position is supported. He has no substantial organization of his own; his power derives largely from his skill in playing off these two forces against each other—in a way permitting him to utilize both of them—combined with his remarkable ability to communicate and maintain rapport with the mass of the population, which could be said to form the base line of the triangle described above. Thus Soekarno is engaged in a constant effort to balance the army and the Communist Party against one another, in order to ensure that neither becomes so strong as to challenge his ascendancy or too weak to serve as a counterpoise to the other. The major amendment that complicates this representation stems from the fact that the army's potential of power is so formidable that Soekarno, being unable to dominate the army himself, has felt obliged to make a sustained effort to keep it from becoming more solidly united. Thus he has consistently tried to ensure that the loyalty of at least some territorial commanders will be greater to him than to the chief of staff and that no chief of staff grows to a stature very much beyond that of a *primus inter pares*. For if the army were to become truly monolithic under a commander popular enough and strong enough to secure absolute obedience from all senior officers (regardless of Soekarno's representations), Soekarno's power relative to the army's would decline. It would also then be unlikely that the PKI (with or without the support of the other parties) could constitute a sufficiently powerful counterpoise to make workable the triangular political formula so important to the maintenance of Soekarno's ascendancy and his latitude for political initiative. As the situation has existed during this period, a viable political *modus vivendi* has been maintained because within this triangular relationship there has been a reciprocity of need. This has been a sort of double marriage of convenience wherein Soekarno is the bigamist: he has needed the army's support, and the top army officers have required his backing; he has needed the Communist Party's support, and it has remained dependent upon him for protection against the army.

The Communist Party (PKI) is useful to Soekarno in other ways as well. It has been the one group, other than the army, with an effective organization capable in many areas of reaching down to and activating the mass of the population, and therefore Soekarno has regarded it as important to Indonesia's economic stability and development. In view of the Communists' strong position among much of the peasantry (particularly on Java) and with organized labor (urban and industrial as well as plantation), he has felt it more advantageous to harness the PKI in with the government's efforts than to run the risk of its sabotaging them.

Moreover, by protecting the PKI from those army commanders bent upon destroying it and by maintaining cordial relationships with its leaders, he is generally believed to have helped ensure Communist bloc diplomatic support (deemed especially important in the struggle to secure control over West Irian) and large credits from the Soviet Union for the purchase of military supplies and for a wide range of economic assistance. Thus, although content to see the strength of the PKI contained and occasionally cut back, Soekarno has remained opposed to those army leaders advocating its forceable elimination.

There is another important reason, but probably the least understood, for Soekarno's unwillingness to countenance attempts to eliminate the PKI or to remove its members from governmental representative bodies. This is his conviction that it is politically dangerous to disassociate in the public's eye the Communists from government. Particularly following his own assumption of paramount governmental responsibility in 1957, he has felt it unwise to exclude Communists from government and thereby from *responsibility* for government inadequacies and failures. Soekarno has remained extremely sensitive to the danger posed by a Communist Party which, by standing outside of government and free from any association with its failures, could become the principal vehicle for popular discontent with and opposition to the government. Thus, despite the persistent opposition of most senior army officers, Soekarno has continually pressed for bringing the Communists more fully under the strong light of governmental responsibility, hoping in particular to bring them into the cabinet. He has no intention of handing over to them positions of key authority which could be utilized for any significant enhancement of their power, but he does wish them to hold posts of nominal importance which will clearly identify them with government. Although unable to overcome army opposition to Communists' holding cabinet portfolios,[9] Soekarno has managed to put them into positions of enough prominence in the several appointed national representative bodies as to identify them sufficiently with his government to make it appreciably more difficult for them to capitalize upon its mistakes and failures.

The Communist Party's Dilemma

From the Communists' point of view, of course, some representation in government is helpful because this makes it awkward for the army to outlaw them. But it is a moot question (and muted differences among top Communist leaders testify to this) whether in the long run through this arrangement the PKI is not losing more than it is gaining—in particular whether short-term calculations of expediency designed to husband its strength are compatible with building the public image necessary to ensure it sufficient support if at a later date conditions should be more propitious for an actual bid for power.

In order, then, to secure Soekarno's protection, the PKI has been obliged to make it worth his while. This has meant a full public support of his ideology and policies. Necessarily this has blunted the PKI's sword of criticism, obliging the party usually to restrict its attacks to the actions by the army or civil officials inconsistent with or ineffective

[9] In the cabinet formed in March 1962 two members of the PKI were formally designated members but held no portfolios and have not been invited to attend its regular meetings.

in implementing Soekarno's policies. But with the army ever watchful against unauthorized mass demonstrations and zealous in cracking down on journalism which it regards as provocative, the scope open to the PKI even for this has been limited. Where it has undertaken to exploit governmental failures and champion popular grievances arising from administrative shortcomings and harsh economic conditions, the PKI has generally been obliged to do so as a calculated risk, weighing the advantages of such action against the expectation that in most cases this will be followed by army reprisals which will by no means always be contrary to Soekarno's interests. Despite the many and widespread grievances of the population which are available for exploitation, the Communists have been permitted very little scope for making political capital out of them. The fact that in some areas they have succeeded in sufficiently representing the interests of peasants and plantation labor to develop a reasonably favorable public image has undoubtedly been due to hard work, able leadership, and courage. However, the abilities of local cadres have been uneven, and in some districts army commanders have become more astute in denying them such opportunities.

The collapse of the parliamentary system had caught the PKI ideologically as well as physically unprepared. With the overwhelming majority of army officers ranged against it and desiring its elimination, the PKI had—short of armed action which it was not in any position to undertake successfully—no recourse but to accept Soekarno's terms, giving him an even fuller measure of support than before.

Pursuit of these tactics has not made for easy ideological explanation, especially in terms of class analysis. Rationalization of the party's support for Soekarno's government has been, as in the second half of the parliamentary period, primarily in terms of the national struggle against imperialism. This has been given priority over the class struggle, even as this is defined in the new class analysis—an analysis which has been adapted to the situation to single out the "bureaucratic capitalists" and "fascists" (both terms, in PKI parlance, referring to the army) as the proletariat's principal enemy. The class analysis which has emerged is clearly one of tactical expediency. It regards Indonesia as being divided between two major social forces—pro-Manipol (i.e., supporters of Soekarno's Political Manifesto, his principal formulation of Guided Democracy) [10] and anti-Manipol. The former includes workers, peasants, petty urban bourgeoisie, national bourgeoisie, and the intelli-

[10] See below, p. 661.

gentsia. Anti-Manipol forces include imperialists, landlords, compradors (e.g., Indonesians associated with foreign business interests), and bureaucratic capitalists. By "bureaucratic capitalists" the PKI means the many inactive or retired army officers who manage the former Dutch properties as well as those on the active list spread out through governmental administrative offices.

In Aidit's report to the Extraordinary Congress of the PKI of April 7–25, 1962, repeated assurances of the party's full support for President Soekarno and his policies were balanced by forthright criticism of the army, particularly its economic role. The bankruptcy of liberal democracy, stated Aidit, had taken place under unfavorable circumstances in which the people's power was not sufficiently strong for them to assume full control. In the period of Guided Democracy which had followed, corruption and bureaucratic abuse had continued; Soekarno's formulations of Guided Democracy had been ruthlessly and cynically abused by "fascist" and "bureaucratic capitalist elements," who sought to tighten their control over the population; and "guidance" was stressed to the near elimination of "democracy." Despite the fact, he said, that the President had insisted that Manipol should guide the "rifle," in many areas the rifle appeared to be controlling Manipol. The state enterprises taken over from the Dutch had not been truly nationalized but had come under the control of "bureaucratic capitalists and thieves," who should be completely purged from these enterprises.

In this most recent statement, as earlier, Aidit went out of his way to stress that the party eschewed responsibility for the government's shortcomings. The reactionaries, he said, were stating that one advantage of the recent cabinet reshuffle (wherein the PKI had been given nominal representation without holding any portfolios) was that the party would be obliged to assume responsibility for the deteriorating economic situation. The PKI, he said, would always refuse to accept the blame for policies over whose execution it could exercise no control. He went on to warn that economic conditions would not noticeably improve under the new cabinet, for in it the PKI had very little influence.

The expediency of the PKI's tactical program was not, however, being easily accepted by an influential minority of the party's leadership. Aidit testified to this when he stated before the party's April 1962 congress that, although internally the party suffered from "contradictions" as a result of "differences concerning a correct policy," these were being overcome. Given the domestic political context within

which the party was obliged to operate, it seemed likely that contradictions between short-range tactical expediency and long-term strategy
and ideological tenets would continue. Domestic considerations would
probably remain paramount in shaping the PKI's policies. But the increasing sharpness of the ideological dispute between Moscow and
Peking might well serve to increase strife within the PKI by hardening
differences between the party factions; the more militant minority
might perhaps find a useful congruence between some of their views
and those of Peking. It seemed likely that during 1963 Aidit's undoubted
qualities of leadership and intraparty statesmanship would be subject
to one of their greatest tests.

Rivalry between Partners in Power: Soekarno and the Army

Although much of the maneuvering in the competition for power
between Soekarno and the army was hidden from public view, most
of the actual confrontations could not be. In July of 1959 General
Nasution, having just become Minister of Defense in Soekarno's new
cabinet while maintaining his position as chief of staff of the army, was
able to frustrate Soekarno's effort to place the air force directly under
presidential authority. A month later Soekarno managed to obstruct
persistent efforts by army leaders to prevent the PKI from holding its
sixth National Congress. The army did force postponement of the
congress several times, but Soekarno was ultimately able to insist that
the party be granted permission, then underlining his defiance of the
army by addressing the Congress himself.

The next important conflict came in September 1959, several months
after Soekarno had appointed a new Attorney General, charging him
particularly with eradicating corruption wherever he found it in government. Almost immediately this man, undoubtedly with Soekarno's
knowledge, began investigations among several top-ranking army
officers in General Nasution's headquarters, finding ample evidence
of corruption centering in illegal barter activities. There was considerable speculation that these investigations constituted an effort by
Soekarno to weaken elements in the army unaligned with him and
generally to decrease the army's influence in government. General
Nasution (himself completely untarnished by corruption) stood firmly
by his officers and ordered the arrest of the Attorney General. Given
the fact that a good many other officers had been involved in corrupt
practices, General Nasution found little difficulty in securing sufficient

backing to resist Soekarno on this issue. Although able to secure the
release of the Attorney General, Soekarno was not in a position to
insist upon his reinstatement in office.

A third major confrontation occurred toward the end of the year,
and extended well into 1960, as a consequence of a government regulation of November 10, 1959, prohibiting aliens from engaging in retail
trade in rural areas. This was aimed against the Indonesian Chinese,
who had long dominated such activity. The army command in West
Java on its own initiative issued an ordinance, applicable only to that
region, which obliged Chinese from rural areas to move to towns, regardless of their occupation, and which was sometimes invoked even
against those who had opted for Indonesian citizenship. Following
provocative interference by consular agents from Communist China,
which only served further to antagonize local army officers and make
them even more fervent in applying this ordinance, Soekarno intervened. Despite Peking's angry response, he insisted that the campaign
against the Chinese be pressed forward. But he sought a quick and
honorable settlement with China (albeit largely on Indonesian terms)
rather than the more severe anti-Chinese campaign advocated by the
army's West Java command, some of whose officers seemed to relish
twisting the dragon's tail. Soekarno was ultimately able to moderate
the army's zeal in responding to the emotionally charged anti-Chinese
feeling, which was particularly prominent in West Java, and negotiated
a very favorable settlement with Peking. One of the consequences of
Soekarno's action was to ease the situation for the PKI, which had
been the only party to criticize these discriminatory measures against
the Chinese. Thereby the PKI had laid itself open to the accusation
that it was acting as part of an international Communist movement and
in deference to Peking rather than in accordance with Indonesian
national interests.[11]

On July 8, 1960, the Politbureau of the PKI released a statement
juxtaposing high praise for Soekarno with severe criticism of the cabinet
and the army. This charged the cabinet with ineffectiveness in carrying out Soekarno's policies and accused the army of profiteering through
the management of the properties seized from the Dutch and of dividing its attention between the rebels and the PKI, dissipating energies

---

[11] For a fuller account see below, p. 686; see also G. William Skinner, "The
Chinese Minority," in Ruth T. McVey, ed., *Indonesia* (New Haven: HRAF; due
to be published in 1963), and David P. Mozingo, "New Developments in China's
Relations with Indonesia," *Current Scene*, I, no. 24 (Feb. 5, 1962), 1–7.

in trying to control the latter which should have gone into its effort to suppress the rebellion. This public criticism elicited a sharp and immediate response from the army. Publication of the statement was forbidden; one Politbureau member was arrested; and Aidit was interrogated. Soon thereafter, the army commanders of South Borneo, South Celebes, and South Sumatra banned all PKI activity in these areas. In his efforts to protect the PKI, Soekarno was obliged to suspend all party activity in Indonesia for a three-month period, at the end of which time he had only partially salvaged its position. Although the situation in Java was eased for the Communists, the three military commanders who had moved against the party in the outer islands maintained repressive measures against the PKI, giving it little or no scope for activity in these areas.

Persistent efforts by Soekarno to bring the Communists into the cabinet reached a climax at the beginning of 1961, but the army was again successful in restraining him. The most Soekarno was able to secure, in the reorganization of his cabinet in March 1962, was inclusion of two of the Communist Party's leaders (Aidit and Lukman) in largely honorary positions as ministers without portfolio. On balance, however, the cabinet's membership now reflected somewhat greater army influence and a more decidedly anti-Communist orientation than obtained before the reorganization.

In the last major confrontation, in June 1962, Soekarno appeared to have strengthened his position by his success in "elevating" General Nasution to a new post of Chief of Staff of the Combined Armed Services and promoting General Jani to Chief of Staff of the Army. Although, like Nasution, strongly anti-PKI, Jani was regarded as being in some respects more easily influenced by Soekarno. General Nasution retained his post as Minister of Defense, but it was generally believed that President Soekarno had thereby strengthened his position against General Nasution and against the army as a whole. Shortly thereafter the strongly anti-Communist territorial commanders of South Sumatra, South Borneo, and South Celebes—the three who had gone farthest in restricting PKI activity—were transferred.

Army cohesion and prestige had increased with the final successes against the rebel forces and the negotiations (undertaken on the initiative of General Nasution rather than Soekarno) which culminated in the surrender of all important remaining rebel groups in Celebes and Sumatra during the course of 1961 (and of the West Java Darul Islam in mid-1962). But in the eyes of the Indonesian public Soekarno won

greater kudos than the army as a consequence of victory in the campaign to eliminate Dutch control over West Irian, finally consummated
in August 1962.

Of more importance, Soekarno's position has been strengthened by
virtue of a rising and increasingly widespread popular reaction against
the incursion of army power into areas of administration and economic
management previously reserved to civilians. Continuing evidence of
corruption among many army officers and noncoms engaged in such
work and their frequent heavyhandedness in dealing with civilians
have created a resentment and concern among leaders of all political
parties that has brought them to regard Soekarno as a champion of
civilian supremacy and the only political force capable of preventing
the further spread of army power. Thus not only the leaders of the
Communist Party, but also those of the other legal parties as well,
look to Soekarno as an ally against the army, even if Soekarno's terms
for this alliance are highly unpalatable.

Soekarno's efforts to reduce the army's role in civil affairs became
more direct in December 1962 with his announcement that in May
1963 (with the transfer of West Irian's administration from the United
Nations to Indonesia) martial law would be lifted. Although General
Nasution, General Jani, and several other senior officers publicly endorsed this objective, it was by no means certain—even if martial law
was officially declared ended—that the army would in fact relinquish
a really substantial part of its civil authority.

It would be difficult to predict the outcome of this Soekarno-army
rivalry—one between two watchful partners in power. The uneasy
equilibrium still existing between them at the beginning of 1963 might
endure for a considerable time, with a continuation of the marriage of
convenience between the two obliging each to keep on accommodating
its policies to the requirements of the other.

The Shaping of Guided Democracy (1958–1962)

Undoubtedly Soekarno would rather not have been dependent upon
the Communists for the support which they found it expedient to give
him; he would have preferred to work through what was to have been
the keystone institution in his Guided Democracy—a National Front,
the monolithic political organization wherein all the political parties,
including the PKI, would merge their identities. But the army was,
understandably, quite as keen as he to control such an organization.
With each being unwilling to yield control to the other, the inner

articulation and lines of command within the two successive variants of a National Front that were constructed [12] were such as to render the organization ineffective as a political instrument, for, of course, a monolithic political structure can scarcely be workable where it rests in two separate power bases. Although efforts during this period to establish an effective National Front were all abortive, there was a sufficient area of agreement between Soekarno and the army to permit a number of significant changes in the system of government.

The decisions taken resulted in the political order's assuming a progressively more authoritarian cast. Freedom of speech and freedom of assembly were drastically restricted. Newspapers critical of the government were closed down, and by 1960 the once free and vigorous Indonesian press was fully bridled—becoming a conformist instrument of governmental policy. Recourse to legal protection, never highly developed, was made increasingly difficult, and the judicial system became increasingly an adjunct of governmental policy. Utilizing its martial law powers, the army progressively undercut the strength of labor unions, both non-Communist and Communist, declaring strikes illegal in more and more industries and plantations.

The army's role in government increased dramatically. Indeed, the close meshing of military and civil power has become one of the salient features of Guided Democracy. Since the middle of 1959, the armed forces (but primarily the army) have held on the average approximately one-third of all cabinet positions. Army officers have come to occupy a number of key offices in important government bureaus, and they have been assigned a good many diplomatic posts previously reserved for civilians. Particularly after mid-1959 the armed forces have had a substantial number of seats in all important governmental representative bodies—in the new appointed parliament, in the High Advisory Council, in the interim Consultative Assembly, as well as in the two successive National Fronts.

In conformity with provisions of the State of War and Siege (martial law) army participation was extended substantially throughout most areas of civil administration and in the management of government-owned sectors of the economy. In the management of the Dutch enterprises seized in December of 1957, the army's role was clearly domi-

[12] The first of these, the National Front for the Liberation of West Irian, was initiated in early 1958 by the army; the second, known simply as the National Front, was initiated by Soekarno approximately three years later. A more comprehensive account of the development of Guided Democracy is given in Herbert Feith, "The Dynamics of Guided Democracy," in McVey, ed., *Indonesia*.

nant. In other sectors of the economy army administrative supervision, although differing in degree from one territorial command to another, reached even to the village level, where officers and noncommissioned officers were frequently authorized to exercise control over rice milling and to purchase rice for the government at prices it had set. In the more traditional areas of civilian administration, both in Jakarta and in provincial and district capitals, places were found for an increasing number of army officers, their positions often being parallel with, but in authority usually superior to, existing civilian officials. In effect, a sort of dual administration was emerging in a number of sectors of government administration, with the extent of army participation varying from one military district to another. In some regions, within as well as outside of Java, the authority of army territorial commanders (although a great deal less than in the 1957–1958 period) was sufficiently autonomous of Jakarta and sensitive to local requirements and opinion as to develop some of the attributes of a federal system.

The army's greatly expanded role in civil administration and economic management made available to General Nasution and his staff resources of patronage which could be utilized to strengthen the army's unity and to rationalize the organization of its components. The availability of so many new positions meant that surplus officers could be absorbed and loyal conduct rewarded. This was of course not the only basis for such extramilitary appointments; but where these considerations were uppermost, they were obviously often not consistent with securing the officers best qualified to fill administrative and managerial positions. Thus the efficiency of civil administration and the management of the government's economic enterprises often suffered. Moreover, some officers could not resist the wide opportunities for graft which these positions opened up, often learning about such opportunities from their civilian associates, but sometimes displaying considerable initiative of their own. In any case, with these positions there generally went important material perquisites—housing, repair allowances, an automobile, and so on. Thus, in terms of both function and wealth, officers were given access to social positions which previously were largely a preserve of the political elite. Because of its new role the army was in a sense becoming something of a political party, its officers united not only by nationalism and anticommunism but also by a substantial vested interest—a common stake in defending their lucrative and prestigeful bureaucratic positions.

In the shaping of the ideology of Guided Democracy the army has played virtually no role, the initiative here being almost entirely Soekarno's. His principal public formulation was his speech of August 17, 1959, entitled "The Rediscovery of Our Revolution." Later referred to as the Political Manifesto (Manipol), this statement was elaborated and refined during September by Soekarno in conjunction with the High Advisory Council and its chairman, Roeslan Abdulgani, and was then designated as the official basis of state policy under Guided Democracy. In addition to justifying the return to the 1945 constitution, Manipol called for a return to the spirit of the revolutionary period of 1945–1949. Emphasizing that the revolution's economic and social goals had not yet been achieved—that a "just and prosperous society" had yet to be attained—Soekarno insisted that the Indonesian revolution be resumed so that the "deviations" from its original principles and goals could be overcome. (Indeed, a subsequent official inference from Manipol was that the revolution was the supreme law of the land, superior even to the 1945 constitution.) Manipol incorporated five fundamental principles: the 1945 Constitution, Indonesian Socialism, Guided Democracy, Guided Economy, and Indonesian Identity (personality). Collectively these were known as USDEK (a word formed by combining the first letters of each of the five principles as expressed in Indonesian), and the official term for the state ideology became known as Manipol-USDEK. Although these principles were not defined with any great precision, they were consistent with Soekarno's basic political and economic ideas (as described above) and were meaningful to many Indonesians, providing them with some degree of psychological security—a feeling that the government had a sense of direction and a set of goals. Increasingly, however, these principles came to have a negative function, with government campaigns for their indoctrination being aimed at enforcing ideological conformity and measuring and ensuring political loyalty.

The freedom and scope of the political parties were rapidly curtailed. The first major blow, and one aimed primarily at the PKI, came in the announcement of Prime Minister Djuanda (speaking as much for Soekarno as for the army) in late September of 1958 that the parliamentary elections scheduled for September 1959 would be deferred until sometime in the following year. The non-Communist parties, fearful of the waxing strength of the PKI and the likelihood that it would emerge with by far the largest vote in any fair election, were privately pleased with this reprieve. However, they were in a poor position to make use of it, for since they no longer controlled the cabinet, they lacked access to the funds and patronage previously available to them. The PNI and the NU especially were further weakened by the government's draconian monetary purge of mid-1959 when, in a futile effort to counter inflation, it reduced by 90 per cent the face value of all 500- and 1,000-rupiah notes and confiscated 90 per cent of all bank accounts above 25,000 rupiahs.[13] As a result, many of the private firms which these parties had sponsored in the past and which had continued to provide them with a source of income were ruined or greatly weakened.

The first major confrontation with the parties came over the issue of a new election law. Having discovered that it was to his interests to maintain the parties rather than to liquidate them, Soekarno was now trying to give substance to his formula of keeping the parties weak enough to control yet strong enough to serve as an effective ally against the army. By this time the leaders of all the parties were quite as concerned as he over the army's increasing power and equally desirous of stemming its further encroachments into the residual areas of civilian administration. The formula which Soekarno put forward was one supported by the army but one that went too far in undermining the parties' position in parliament to win even their most grudging agreement. He stipulated that the new election law provide that 50 per cent of the representation in parliament be from members of functional groups elected from lists drawn up by the government (in effect, Soekarno in consultation with the army). The parties insisted that functional-group representation in parliament not exceed 33⅓ per cent and demanded some say in the selection of functional-group candidates.

The impasse which resulted lasted until February 20, 1959, when the government came forward with a dramatically new proposal, one subscribed to by Soekarno but stemming from the initiative of the army, particularly General Nasution. This called for a return to the 1945 constitution, which would then open the road to Guided Democracy. (The 1945 constitution, it will be recalled, provided that the principal locus of governmental power would be the presidency.[14]) The government announced its intention of coupling with the 1945 constitution—in itself a revolutionary symbol to which it was awkward for any political party to object—a new election law which would

---

[13] The rupiah was then exchanged at 35 to the U.S. dollar at the official rate and several times more at the black-market rate.

[14] See pp. 564–565.

provide that half the members of parliament be elected under the banner of a National Front headed by Soekarno. The Front's election list would be made up of members of the various functional groups, representatives of the armed forces being appointed by the heads of their services rather than elected. Qualifications of the parties for participating in the elections would be worked out in accordance with an as yet not fully defined party simplification law.[15]

Meantime, the Constituent Assembly, elected in December 1955, was still sitting, deadlocked primarily on the issue of the place of Islam in the state, with neither the Islamic bloc nor the secular parties being able to muster anything like the necessary two-thirds majority required for adoption of constitutional principles. In the judgment of Wilopo, Chairman of the Constituent Assembly, if this one major problem of the place of Islam in the state could have been solved, other questions could have been worked out relatively easily.[16] But the minimum acceptable to the Muslim bloc (headed by the Masjumi and NU) was that the President be a Muslim and that the Islamic population of Indonesia (but not the non-Islamic population) be required to follow Islamic law (*Sjariah*).

In late February 1959 the cabinet, speaking for President Soekarno, indicated that it would request that the Constituent Assembly resolve its impasse by voting for the 1945 constitution in its entirety and without amendment. The only gesture to be made in the direction of the Islamic bloc would be incorporation of a statement in the preamble to the constitution (which is, of course, a nonoperative part) that adherents of Islam would have the obligation of following Islamic law. Initially, 53 per cent of the Constituent Assembly (including the PNI and the PKI) declared themselves in favor of returning to the 1945 constitution, but there was a rather widespread expectation upon the part of the secular parties that the NU could be induced to join

[15] In a conversation with the writer, President Soekarno indicated that he also expected the political parties to incorporate members of functional groups in their own election lists, with every other person on each party's list indicated as representing one of them. He stated that he hoped to be able to exert significant influence on the parties' choices of their functional representatives, and he anticipated that, with the parties' functional-group representatives added to the exclusively functional-group representation of the National Front, well over half the members of parliament would speak for the functional groups. He stated that it was his intention to caucus with the functional-group representatives in parliament—both those elected on the list of his National Front and those elected under the party lists—with the intention of organizing them and working with them as the parliamentary majority (Jakarta, March 19, 1959).

[16] Interview with the writer, March 11, 1959.

them and thereby provide the necessary two-thirds majority. Blunder-
ing tactics on the part of the PNI and considerable skill by Masjumi
leaders in the Constituent Assembly frustrated this expectation, and
with the NU lined up firmly with the Masjumi in opposition, hopes
ended for the Constituent Assembly's endorsement of a return to the
1945 constitution.

In the face of this impasse and with Soekarno then away on a two
months' trip abroad, Chief of Staff Nasution banned all political activities temporarily. On July 5, 1959, shortly after his return, Soekarno,
with full backing from the army but with little constitutional authority, dissolved the Constituent Assembly and declared by decree that
the 1945 constitution had replaced that of 1950. Again with solid backing from the army, Soekarno moved ahead vigorously, relying where
necessary upon a provision in the 1945 constitution which empowered
the President to enact government regulations in place of laws in
cases of emergency—a power which he was to use generously thereafter. In the new cabinet which Soekarno then appointed, the army's
representation was considerably stronger and all ministers were enjoined from holding membership in any political party. A further blow
was struck at the parties a few weeks later when upper-level civil servants throughout the government were ordered to sever all party ties
or else resign their positions.

Two advisory councils were now established under the President:
a High Advisory Council (its chairman, Roeslan Abdulgani, had been
vice-chairman under Soekarno in the earlier National Council, now
being replaced) and a National Planning Council, with a non-Communist, radical socialist confidant of Soekarno, Mohammad Yamin, as
chairman. Masjumi and PSI representatives were excluded from both
of these councils. The army's proscription of party activities was lifted,
but scope for such activities was limited, army permission being required for party meetings.

Especially damaging to party strength and prospects—and particularly hard on the PKI—was a decree by Soekarno in September 1959.
This aimed at ending the substantial regional administrative autonomy,
introduced two and a half years before and already well established
in most of Java and several other areas, and restoring centralized direction of local government. Fully backed by the army, Soekarno's
new ordinance provided that governors of first-level regions (equivalent to the old provinces) were to be appointed by the President,
while heads of second-level regions were to be appointed by the Min-

ister of the Interior, subject to the President's approval.[17] With these officials no longer elected and with a regulation following soon thereafter forbidding members of the regional legislatures' executive boards from having any party affiliation, the position of the political parties was drastically undercut.

Five months later Soekarno delivered his last major blow against what remained of the parliamentary system. On March 5, 1960, following parliament's refusal to accept his government's budget, he dissolved it and announced that its composition was to be altered so that its membership would be more in conformity with the spirit of the constitution of 1945.

So stunned and angered by this were most members of parliament that a significant minority of even PNI and NU party leaders joined a protest movement, the Democratic League, initiated primarily by members from the Masjumi and from the PSI and several other small parties. During April and May, with Soekarno on a trip abroad, branches of the Democratic League were established in most areas of Indonesia, usually with either the conscious tolerance or moral support of army commanders. Probably a majority of these commanders gave the League an opportunity to grow more because of its anti-PKI posture than because of its opposition to Soekarno's move against parliament. The League was unable to attract sufficient backing from either the PNI or NU to pose any real problem for Soekarno, and if its leaders had been led to expect significant support from the army, they were soon disappointed.

Shortly after his return, Soekarno proceeded with his plans for the establishment of a new and fully appointed parliament composed of both party and functional representatives. To this new parliament, formally installed in June 1960, he appointed 132 members of functional groups (of whom 36 represented the armed forces) and 130 nominees of the political parties—assigning 44 seats to the PNI, 36 to the NU, 30 to the PKI, and 20 in all to minor parties; no representation was given to either the Masjumi or the PSI. Although in Soekarno's apportionment of party seats the PKI was clearly underrepresented, it compensated by being able to influence a relatively larger proportion of the representatives from the functional groups. The role of the new parliament was minor indeed—little more than that of a truncated

[17] For the fullest discussion of these developments see especially pp. 209–229 of J. D. Legge, *Central Authority and Regional Autonomy in Indonesia: A Study in Local Administration, 1950–1960* (Ithaca, N.Y.: Cornell University Press, 1961).

and partly artificial sounding board. It was clearly overshadowed by the High Advisory Council, which remained the principal advisory organ of the President. Like that body and the National Planning Council, the new parliament was enjoined from arriving at decisions through voting, all of its decisions having to be unanimous in accordance with the *musjawarat-mufakat* system. And as with these other bodies, in cases where such accord could not be reached the problem at issue was simply to be referred to Soekarno for his disposition.

Soekarno's final move to bring the political parties under his control came in July of 1960 with his introduction of regulations to implement presidential ordinances of December 31, 1959, on "The Conditions for and Simplification of Parties." If these rules did not ensure the complete tractability of the parties, they did provide ample means for threatening or eliminating any which were unwilling to give Soekarno the cooperation he desired. And they provided a basis for outlawing the Masjumi and the PSI and for holding a constant threat over the head of the PKI. To be legally recognized, all parties were required to be of a certain minimum size and to demonstrate their loyalty to Soekarno's government by declaring themselves in full ideological alignment with Soekarno and giving explicit pledges of unqualified support to his major ideological pronunciamentos.[18]

On April 14, 1961, Soekarno announced that eight parties were recognized: The PNI, Partindo (a small party which had split off the PNI's left wing), IPKI (a small party with army connections), the NU, the Catholic Party, that section of the PSII (a small Islamic party) led by those of its leaders closest to Soekarno, the PKI, and the Murba (a small nationalist-Communist party). Three months later the Parkindo (Protestant) and Perti (a small Islamic party) were added to the approved list. Not only were the Masjumi and PSI proscribed, but any possibility that those of their leaders who had not been involved

[18] The ordinance provided that the President, "after consultation with the Supreme Court" (which in effect meant at his own discretion), was authorized "to dissolve any political party presently involved in rebellion," i.e., if its leaders were participating in or clearly supporting a rebellion or if a party failed to announce officially its formal disapproval of such a rebellion. (Although the Masjumi had failed to publish any such formal disapproval of the rapidly waning rebellions in Sumatra and Celebes, the PSI had made such a formal disclaimer; nevertheless, in August 1960 both parties were declared illegal and ordered to dissolve). In addition, political parties had to demonstrate that they enrolled a minimum membership of 150,000 members with branches in at least 25 per cent of Indonesia's 21 provinces (first-level regions) and in at least 25 per cent of the country's approximately 300 *kabupatens* (second-level regions), this requirement to be met no later than February 28, 1961.

in the rebellion might continue to play a political role was removed when, in January 1962, most of them with any stature were summarily arrested; as of February 1963 they had still not been brought to trial or released. Among them were Soetan Sjahrir and Subadio Sastrosatomo of the PSI and Prawoto Mangkusasmita and Mohammad Roem of the Masjumi.

In the first months of 1960 Soekarno proceeded to establish the one remaining political institution stipulated in the 1945 constitution—the People's Consultative Assembly. Under that constitution this body was to be the highest organ of the state, electing the President, who was to remain responsible to it, and setting the broad lines of state policy; for these purposes it was to meet once every five years. Although the constitution provided that this body was to be elected, Soekarno, in accordance with the transitional provisions of the constitution (originally designed to meet the chaotic conditions attending the outbreak of the revolution), undertook to appoint 216 of its 499 members as representatives of functional groups. The balance of the membership, in accordance with the constitution, was made up by parliament—the membership of which Soekarno had only recently appointed. Thus the only political body to which Soekarno acknowledged legal responsibility was one whose members he himself had appointed.

The People's Consultative Assembly, under its Chairman, Chairul Saleh—a non-Communist radical leftist, appointed by Soekarno—has met just once, in November 1960. At this meeting it promptly endorsed the political structure and political ideology which Soekarno had developed. It then approved the National Planning Council's recently prepared Eight Year Plan—a massive, vague, unintegrated, and quite utopian projection of economic development, important primarily for its political symbolism. (It was regarded, at least for a time, as an earnest of the government's concern with economic problems and has been useful in establishing the impression of national purpose and direction; but it is not in itself a feasible working plan.)

In the establishment of a National Front the army had originally seized the initiative from Soekarno. Actually its National Front for the Liberation of West Irian appeared to be at least as concerned with containing and rolling back Communist Party influence at the local level, while generally expanding that of the army, as with mobilizing support for the struggle to win the still Dutch-controlled half of Irian (New Guinea). In association with this Front, local army commanders established cooperation organizations between the army and various functional groups—labor, peasantry, veterans, youth, and so on. By obliging leaders of these groups to cooperate with it at the local level, the army was provided with a means of policing Communist activity and countering Communist penetration into these sectors of society while at the same time expanding its own influence and control.

Dissatisfied with a National Front controlled by the army, Soekarno at the beginning of 1961 undertook to establish a new National Front, with a secretariat which he himself had appointed. But his efforts to build this into an effective political organization under his exclusive control have been unsuccessful. Army influence within it has been considerable; and the representatives of the legal political parties have been insufficiently cooperative and differed too much among themselves to make possible that minimum of organizational integration and consolidation of purpose which would have been necessary for the National Front to become the powerful political instrument which Soekarno originally envisaged.

Soekarno thus continued to be without a major political organization of his own. In order to maintain a reasonable degree of political ascendancy he was obliged to balance the legal parties (among which the Communist Party alone had any real strength) against the army and to sustain a sufficient influence among senior officers to keep army leadership divided and incapable of presenting a hostile united front against him. No further institutional changes of any real significance have been introduced, and Guided Democracy remains an incomplete and internally inconsistent system, its further development being aborted by a continuing dispersion of power.

It is difficult to measure the effectiveness thus far of Guided Democracy with respect to the normal activities of government, and economic development in particular. For the system's emergence coincided with a major rebellion, followed by a prolonged crisis over West Irian, events which have absorbed most of the government's administrative and financial resources. An outstanding question, and one which assuredly concerns Soekarno, is whether the new system can marshal and apply the nation's energies to economic growth. The question is also raised as to whether this system can be operated successfully without some focus more dramatic than the long-term and relatively prosaic course of economic development. That Soekarno is not fully confident of his ability to cope with this situation—and particularly to grapple with Indonesia's formidable economic problems—would seem to account in part for the persistence of repressive measures against his critics and for his continuing emphasis upon psychological means of control and legitimation. Much energy continues to be devoted to political exhortation and indoctrination, which place great emphasis upon ideological conformity and focus attention on nationalist symbols and pageantry. There is a continuous effort to keep alive a sense of national crisis. It is reiterated that the revolution—at least in a social, economic, and cultural sense—is still continuing. And it is alleged that antipatriotic domestic elements persist in opposing it. Although the struggle for West Irian has been won, Indonesia is described as still confronting external forces—colonialism, neocolonialism, and imperialism—dangerous to its security and/or incompatible with its revolutionary principles. Indonesian opposition to a Malaysian federation and support for the Brunei rebels are undoubtedly well suited to sustaining this atmosphere of crisis.

· XXIII ·

Some Major Problems

MUCH of the previous discussion has dealt directly or indirectly with Indonesia's central political problem, the continuing dispersion of power. The still-unresolved power struggle continues to absorb a vast amount of time and energy which are needed for the more constructive purposes of government. Soekarno may live a good many more years, and while he lives he is likely to remain the strongest single political factor. Although he may be able to increase his political power relative to that of the army (as he did during 1962), it appears unlikely that he will ever be able to dominate it fully. Soekarno's death would not resolve the power struggle, although, by removing the major buffer between the army and the PKI, it might precipitate a more decisive phase. An army-PKI rivalry would then probably dominate the political scene. But the power struggle might well be complicated by the resurgence of Islam as a political force, a process which is likely to be accelerated with Soekarno's death.

The Army

With or without Soekarno, the army is almost certain to remain a major political factor. The changes which its extramilitary role in Indonesian society have imposed on its character should strongly affect the extent of its continuing political influence. Clearly the public's attitude toward the army will influence the outcome of its rivalry with both

Soekarno and the PKI. If army cohesion can be maintained without the cement provided by corruption and special perquisites and amenities for officers and noncoms and if army personnel become less heavy-handed in dealing with the public, then the army may be able to establish a reasonably favorable public image. It would undoubtedly be assisted in this task if the armed forces acquiesce to a significant reduction in their share of the national budget; this would involve a decrease in the size of the army and a sharp reduction in the enormously expensive programs for the purchase of foreign (mostly Russian) ships and planes by the navy and the air force.[1] A better relationship with the public might also ensue if the army's recently announced civic action program of public works and economic development leads to the effective utilization of its resources of manpower and technical and engineering skills.

Efforts by civilian leaders to keep the army divided in order to make it more amenable to civilian control have worked against the attempts of such men as General Nasution to eradicate corruption in the army. For with divisions obtaining or threatening, the army's chief of staff has been reluctant to press for the removal of officers guilty of corrupt practices lest this lose him the support of other officers, likewise involved, whose backing he needs in order to maintain unity. Although the patronage made available by the army's access to new extramilitary administrative and managerial positions may have had

[1] At the end of 1962 the army was reported to number about 350,000 men, the navy around 40,000, and the air force over 30,000. The Indonesian navy was reported to have one 19,000-ton cruiser of the Soviet postwar Sverdlov class, with a second large Soviet-built cruiser to be delivered in 1963 (both being designed as missile launchers); four Soviet-built Riga-class frigates (believed to be equipped with ship-to-ship guided missiles); at least seven modern destroyers (including five of the Soviet Skoryi class); about twenty submarines (at least twelve of them being long-range Soviet W class); two submarine depot ships; twelve patrol craft; and twenty or more motor torpedo boats. The air force (also largely Soviet-equipped) was reported to have ten TU-16 pure-jet bombers (with a range of nearly 5,000 miles); twenty to thirty IL-28 turbojet bombers; ten to twelve long-range, 1,200-mile-an-hour MIG-21 twin-jet fighters; and approximately a hundred Soviet MIG-15, 17, and 19 fighters; a battery of Soviet-built ground-to-air guided missiles; American C-130 transports; a number of Soviet troop carriers; and a large number of older, smaller aircraft, largely of American make. The Russians were also reported to have turned over a squadron of anti-submarine helicopters, with a second squadron promised for 1963. Most of the army's equipment is still of American make. It is generally believed that much of the Soviet air and naval armaments which have been sold to Indonesia (especially those which are most modern) have not been available to the government of Communist China.

a short-term effect of contributing to greater unity, it has at the same time led to a widespread increase in graft and corruption among army officers and noncommissioned officers. Such practices create discord and tension between the officers involved in corruption and the group which refuses to have anything to do with it; and this constitutes a long-term factor working against army unity. The withdrawal of the army from many of its extramilitary administrative and managerial positions would, of course, remove many opportunities for graft; but this would immediately generate another factor working against unity —the discontent of a great many newly superfluous officers. Unless they could be given positions in civilian life approximately as attractive as the military positions they were being asked to relinquish—a highly unlikely possibility—then resentment would undoubtedly be acute and create a situation dangerous not only for army unity, but perhaps politically as well.

The more responsible and politically sophisticated army leaders are certainly aware of this danger. They also recognize that the present level of corruption in the army poses a serious threat to morale and discipline and is likely to alienate further that still considerable group of officers who have not become involved in graft. Morale and discipline are also threatened by the resentment of those officers who participate in corrupt practices but become disgruntled at what they regard as an unequal division of the spoils. If one or more of these sources of discontent should become stronger, a situation might develop wherein the loss of morale and/or discipline would lead to a reluctance on the part of some officers, noncoms, or soldiers to carry out orders to use force against organized mob activity protesting legitimate civilian grievances. This could, of course, have important political consequences.

When the government was endeavoring to marshal sufficient military strength to mount a campaign capable of wresting West Irian from the Netherlands by force, it was possible to justify the expenditure of over 75 per cent of the national budget on the armed forces. Since the acquisition of West Irian, however, it has been difficult for the service chiefs to justify so large an amount.[2] In the face of strong public

---

[2] It has been suggested that in view of the pressure for demobilization some army leaders may find it advantageous to press for a military build-up in Indonesian Borneo, with the argument that major forces need to be readied in case developments across the border require Indonesia's intervention. However, it is unlikely that a campaign in support of anti-Malaysia rebels in Brunei and/or other British Borneo territories, even if accompanied by an all-out effort designed to rally

feeling, supported by Soekarno, that the size of the recently expanded army should be reduced, but with the fear that such a program would increase internal army strains and promote disunity, General Nasution and General Jani have endeavored to resist such pressure by pledging the army's manpower and engineering skill to projects useful to the country's economic development. They announced a program at the end of 1962 whereby army units—down to platoons at the village level—would be assigned to building roads, bridges, irrigation ditches, and so on and to opening up new lands in the outer islands to agriculture. If undertaken on a sufficient scale and if efficiently managed, such a program might make an important contribution to Indonesia's economic welfare; however, even under optimal conditions, it would be unlikely to promote significant economic development unless supplemented by substantial imports of capital goods, raw materials, and spare parts. Such imports require large outlays of foreign exchange, the present and future availability of which is limited considerably by the heavy expenditure of Soviet credits on very costly naval and air armament recently undertaken in connection with the military build-up over the West Irian issue.

The servicing of this huge Soviet arms debt of some $600 million to $750 million will absorb a sizable share of Indonesia's foreign exchange earnings. Moreover, since this Soviet equipment must be maintained under tropical conditions and with far too few trained Indonesians to care for it, deterioration is bound to be abnormally extensive. Thus, except in the unlikely case that the Soviet Union agrees to supply on a gift basis the necessary spare parts and other expensive attrition replacements, merely to keep this equipment in operative condition will annually absorb a significant amount of what remains of Indonesia's foreign exchange after costs of debt servicing have been met.

The incompatibility of maintaining the armed forces at their present level of manpower and equipment with the availability of sufficient financial resources to improve the country's declining economic situation is becoming increasingly apparent to politically conscious Indonesians. Whether the situation is simply permitted to continue or whether efforts are made to resolve this incompatibility, the political consequences are sure to be significant.

---

popular backing, would be generally regarded as providing justification commensurate with the West Irian struggle for absorbing a preponderant share of governmental expenditure.

Regionalism and Decentralization

Regionalism is still an important force in Indonesia—scotched, but not eliminated, by the suppression of the 1958–1961 rebellion and having today considerable potential strength. The course of the rebellion and its overwhelming defeat demonstrated the strength of Indonesian nationalism to be greater, or at least more enduring, than most outside observers had assumed. But many of the conditions which led to the rebellion remain. The provinces' discontent with Jakarta's paternalism is still profound. Local dissatisfaction with the central government and the belief that decentralization of administrative authority and fiscal power would permit the regions to promote their own welfare more effectively remain strong. Nor are these feelings confined to that portion of the Indonesian population which lives outside of Java; these views are found in Java as well, and particularly in West Java. It remains evident that the attempt to control the details of local administration from Jakarta is out of tune with Indonesia's geography and persisting regional economic and cultural differences.

Under Guided Democracy individuals from the various regions are included in the High Advisory Council and other representative bodies in Jakarta. They do not fulfill a genuinely representative function, however, and many of them would certainly not be the first choices of their regional compatriots; and in any case their influence on government is generally slight. To a significant extent, however, this lack of formal civil administrative decentralization and regional representation has been compensated for by the army's territorial commanders. Most of the regional military commanders, often men from the local ethnic group, have been responsive to local needs and sentiments. They have frequently moderated the application of Jakarta's policies, modifying them so that they accord better with local conditions. In addition, on their own initiative they have often carried through measures of local benefit which have been quite independent of Jakarta and have occasionally even deviated from its policies. But helpful as the territorial military commanders often are in championing local needs, they do not furnish an adequate substitute for a regular, institutionalized system providing reasonable autonomy for all the regions and for their effective representation in Jakarta.

Moreover, a greater degree of administrative and fiscal decentralization might well stimulate Indonesia's economic development. Wider direct local participation in the planning and execution of projects would be likely to excite additional local interest and to bring more active public participation. If this were accompanied by greater fiscal decentralization, permitting a larger proportion of locally levied and collected taxes to be made available for local economic development, more revenue could probably be collected than at present.

Economic Problems

During the last decade Indonesia's economic growth has lagged considerably behind its population increase, and average per capita income has declined. The volume and value of exports are less now than they were ten years ago; with the exception of oil, production of all of Indonesia's major exports is below the prewar level. The production of rubber, traditionally Indonesia's major export, fell by 10 per cent between 1950 and 1960 and has continued to decline since. Rubber trees are becoming overage, and increasingly sterile as producers, at a rate far exceeding new planting. Rice production has risen by only approximately 10 per cent during the last two decades, while the population has increased by more than 30 per cent. Indonesia is now one of the world's major importers of rice. During the last few years most industry has been operating at only 50 to 60 per cent of capacity, mainly because of a lack of spare parts and raw materials.

A government budget which has been in deficit every year except for 1951 (with its Korean War export boom) has stimulated inflation without providing for a significant degree of government investment in economic development. Although private Indonesian citizens play such a minor entrepreneurial role and although private foreign capital has been discouraged from investing in Indonesia (American oil companies being the only significant exceptions), the average ratio of government investment to total government expenditure has been extremely low, far lower than in China, India, Japan, or Pakistan. The already serious inflation accelerated rapidly during the course of the 1958–1961 rebellion and the final phase of the West Irian campaign. This inflation has stimulated speculation and the hoarding of essential raw materials and spare parts—thereby greatly hampering industrial output—and continues to make realistic economic planning almost impossible.

Between 1951 and 1961 the consumer price index increased approximately 700 per cent, and it rose by at least 150 per cent more between mid-1961 and mid-1962. Only substantial governmental subsidization of rice purchases, housing, and so on has made it possible for most civil servants to get along. Even so, the great majority of these people have been under intolerable pressure and have made ends meet only by taking extra jobs (which compete for their time and energy to the detriment of their work for the government) and/or partaking of the illegal income which is now widely available through the corrupt practices permeating so much of the governmental administration.

The 1958–1961 rebellion and the campaign for West Irian undoubtedly added significantly to the strains on Indonesia's economy, but they are not the basic reasons for the country's major economic problems. The single most important cause has been mismanagement. Indonesia's political leaders have been successful in dismantling most of the inherited capitalist-colonialist sector of their economy, but largely unsuccessful in building up the socialist system that was to take its place. They have shown little understanding of what is required to make a socialist economy function effectively. Soekarno and most of his advisers (the exceptions have been appallingly few) have confined themselves primarily to projecting desirable, albeit sometimes rather Utopian, goals and drawing up the broadest and most elementary of blueprints; but they have not been disposed to work out the detailed infrastructure of administrative and fiscal measures necessary for the realization of these plans. And they have been impatient with and largely unreceptive to the advice of those better-trained Indonesians who argue the necessity of providing for these prerequisites and who point to the many mundane problems which must be solved before any real progress in the development of a socialist economy can be achieved.

Another aspect of the problem has been put very well by a recent observer:

The notion that government should play a leading role in directing the economy is taken as self-evident. Yet the level of competence and discipline required to manage a "guided economy" along the lines contemplated would tax the capacity of the most experienced and stable governments. The government has shown neither the will nor the disposition to impose the discipline required for economic development under socialism. While the Yugoslavian approach, for example, is widely admired, one finds no disposition to move in that direction by providing the savings which made possible Yugoslavia's impressive increase of output. . . . Most of the economic problems are the familiar and predictable results of government attempts to direct the economy without understanding that every system has its own inner discipline.[3]

Indonesia has been able to defer a rational hardheaded approach to the problem of economic development because of two remarkable factors—one of them artificial and both rapidly disappearing. First, Indonesia's agrarian situation has been relatively healthy, there being little of the distortion in agrarian relationships, especially landlordism, such as has existed in India and Pakistan; and, second, Indonesia has received a large amount of foreign economic assistance.

Although shielded from many ill effects of inflation, much of Indonesia's peasant population has in recent years suffered a distinct deterioration in economic status. Certainly this has been true for most of the Javanese peasantry, of whom only about 40 per cent are now believed to be landowners. Java is now the most densely populated major area of the world, with more than 66 million people crowded into its 48,500 square miles. This predominantly rural population increases by approximately 1.5 million per year, the government doing nothing to promote birth control.[4] With Java's supply of unused arable land exhausted, the resulting pressure on the land weakens the position of tenants and promotes a rapid increase in the already large number of landless peasant laborers. This is not a situation which land reform alone can appreciably mitigate. The major difficulty is not absentee landlordism, which, though apparently increasing, is still far less common and involves much smaller plots than in India and Pakistan, but the fact that on Java there is simply not enough land to go around. And it is, of course, on Java that most of Indonesia's peasantry live.[5] Unfortunately programs of rural economic development—whether in the form of industrialization, emphasizing small-scale scattered enter-

[3] Don D. Humphrey, "Indonesia's National Plan for Economic Development," *Asian Survey*, II, no. 10 (Dec. 1962), 12–21. Professor Humphrey was head of an American government team which visited Indonesia in mid-1961; it should be noted that in their report he and the members of his team indicated full sympathy with Indonesia's desire to build a socialist economy.

[4] For Soekarno's attitude toward birth control see Louis Fischer, *The Story of Indonesia* (New York: Harper, 1959).

[5] Agrarian reform laws introduced in 1961, even where implemented (and the government lacks the bureaucratic and fiscal means for proper implementation), can be ameliorative only, and even then of benefit to merely a minority of the most depressed elements of the Javanese peasantry. The bulk of the swelling ranks of Java's landless peasants have not been helped at all and cannot be helped in view of the limits of arable land existing on Java.

prises, or adequately capitalized and administered programs for re-settlement of Javanese peasants in appropriate areas of Sumatra and Borneo—are still so limited as to benefit no more than a small propor-tion of the rural population and lag appallingly far behind its rate of increase. And with Java's urban-based industries expanding at a rate insufficient even to keep pace with the growth of urban unem-ployment, there can be few opportunities for landless peasants in the cities. On the basis of the government's present grossly inadequate program of economic development, the level of living of most of Java's peasantry is bound to decline further.

No matter how enduring the social cohesion and communalistic outlook of the Javanese village (and in many places these qualities appear to be diminishing), there are limits to the village's ability to serve as a social security agency for its depressed elements. Rural poverty can be shared only so far, and in much of Java the limit would seem to be in sight, if not actually exceeded. It is, of course, not poverty itself, but how people feel about poverty that nurtures radicalism. The Javanese peasant has not been politically insulated. Having been aroused by revolution, the elections of 1955–1957, and the emphasis on social justice in the slogans of Soekarno's Manipol-USDEK, and having witnessed during his own lifetime a deterioration in his eco-nomic condition, he is likely to become increasingly politically con-scious. To crystallize the views of a sizable portion of this peasantry might not take a great deal more agitation than the PKI—hampered though it has been by the army—has thus far managed to carry out. Unless the government soon makes a much greater effort to meet the problem of Java's rapidly increasing peasant population, the prospect of political dissidence in rural Java is likely to become strong, and in a few more years only dedicated and courageous leadership might be needed for the materialization of such dissidence on a really sub-stantial scale. In this situation the PKI would be the political element best prepared and most likely to benefit.

Another minatory political factor deriving from Indonesia's lack of economic growth is the widening disparity in the rates of growth of the country's economy and its rapidly expanding educational system. Because of this gap, there is an increasing number of secondary school and college graduates who are unable to find jobs reasonably com-mensurate with their education. With the government able to absorb a smaller proportion each year of these young people into its already badly bloated bureaucracy or into the armed forces, it would seem inevitable that a growing number of them will become discontented and politically restive. Similarly it seems likely that political ferment will grow among those still in school because of their discouragement at the bleak prospects for future employment. With such "objective social factors" shaping up in both urban and rural areas, it is understandable why many Indonesian Communist leaders believe that time is on their side.

Most of what little economic development Indonesia has undertaken during the past decade has been made possible by foreign aid. Increasingly in recent years this source has also covered a considerable portion of operational costs of government having nothing to do with economic development. Outstanding foreign indebtedness at the end of 1962 was believed to total approximately $1.6 billion. Of this, approximately $883 million was owed the Soviet bloc—about three-quarters of which was for the purchase of arms. (Of a Soviet arms credit totaling between $800 million and $1 billion Indonesia was believed already to have used up about 75 per cent; but it had thus far drawn upon only about one-quarter of Soviet bloc economic credits totaling about $600 million—of which approximately $368 million had been advanced by the USSR.) Approximately $182 million was owed the United States. The remainder of Indonesia's outstanding debt as of the end of 1962 was apportioned approximately as follows: International Monetary Fund $83 million, Yugoslavia $83 million, Japan $80 million, West Germany $70 million, France $63 million, United Kingdom $37 million, Italy $16 million, India $8 million, UAR $3 million, and short-term commercial debts about $40 million. These figures do not include grants-in-aid from the United States totaling approximately $300 million (primarily surplus agricultural commodities) and around $400 million in war reparations from Japan.[6]

Foreign aid has temporarily relieved Indonesia from the necessity of working out the means for raising capital domestically. Ultimately these must be developed, but the possibility of Indonesia's successfully marshaling its own energies and resources for an effort in that direction is seriously undermined by the weight of the indebtedness already incurred. Although the terms of repayment for most of these debts are moderate, the burden of servicing them is very heavy.

[6] For estimates of foreign economic assistance during the period 1950–1961 see Alexander Shakow, "Foreign Economic Assistance in Indonesia: 1950–1961" (Ph.D. dissertation, London School of Economics, 1962). Of the total indebtedness to the Soviet bloc at the end of 1962 probably no more than $40 million was owed Communist China.

Annual service charges absorbed an estimated 25 to 30 per cent of Indonesia's foreign exchange earnings in 1962 and in 1963 were due to increase to about $238 million, severely reducing the amount available for necessary imports. Several of Indonesia's creditors may agree to extend the period for repayment, but this will only postpone the reckoning. And that reckoning will ultimately be all the more severe unless the government undertakes a sustained program of economic stabilization involving drastic reductions in governmental expenditures (on the armed forces especially) and other realistic measures to combat inflation.

Foreign Relations

Geography shields Indonesia from some of the realities of international power politics which the other major Asian states must more directly confront (and vis-à-vis Communist China the presence of the U.S. 7th Fleet provides a useful if publicly unacknowledged insulation). Probably more than any other Asian state, Indonesia's posture in foreign relations is conditioned by its colonial experience, in particular the arduous fight for independence. As with other ex-colonial countries, long subjection to colonial rule has engendered an extreme aversion to anything that can be interpreted as subservience to any foreign power. But among Indonesians this concern is heightened as a result of their revolutionary experience, in particular their interpretation of the roles of the United States and Soviet Russia during that period. Indeed, one cannot fully understand the insistence of every Indonesian government to date upon an independent foreign policy without reference to this. Indonesian leaders tend to view the records of both the United States and Soviet Russia during 1945–1949 as having been actuated much more by calculations of self-interest than by the principle of self-determination for Indonesia.[7] They believe that during the first three and a half years of their struggle for independence both the United States and Soviet Russia, whatever their public statements may have been, either left the Republic of Indonesia to fend for itself against heavy odds or gave indirect help or encouragement to its enemies, the Dutch or the Communists.[8]

[7] For an excellent account of Soviet Russia's attitude toward and relations with Indonesia during the revolution see Ruth T. McVey, *The Soviet View of the Indonesian Revolution* (Cornell Modern Indonesia Project, Interim Reports Series; Ithaca, N.Y., 1957).

[8] The United States is generally regarded as having enabled the Netherlands to mount its military offensives in Indonesia by giving major financial assistance to

Indonesia's "neutrality" is not one of isolation from world affairs, but rather a refusal to commit itself to either of the two great power blocs. The country's leaders have been jealous guardians of an independence of action brooking no advance commitments—what they have termed "an independent and active foreign policy." Insistence upon this policy has also been symptomatic of their protest against the failure of the major powers to consult sufficiently with them (and other Asian leaders) in matters concerning Asia. This feeling was important in bringing Indonesian leaders to sponsor the Asian-African Conference at Bandung in 1955. Since then, but especially after March 1957 with Soekarno's increasing domination of the formulation of foreign policy, Indonesia has aspired to an important role in international affairs. Soekarno has regarded his country as having a special mission both as a major leader of the world's nonaligned countries and as a champion of all peoples still under colonial rule.

Of all foreign policy issues, that of West Irian (Western New Guinea) has been by far the most important to Indonesians, and it is one which has had particularly strong domestic political overtones. There is some basis for the belief that this dispute was sometimes used to promote a psychological atmosphere conducive to national consciousness and unity and that on occasion it served to divert attention from a government's shortcomings in domestic matters. Regardless of this, the issue had a deep intrinsic reality for most politically conscious Indonesians. They believed West Irian to be an integral part of their nation, their government's claim to it just and legitimate, and its continuing occupation by the Dutch intolerable.

The Irian issue has also constituted one of the principal touchstones, with Soekarno especially, for measuring the friendship of foreign countries. Indonesian leaders have been grateful for Soviet Russia's and Communist China's sedulous support of their claim to West Irian, a fact which helps to explain why since 1956 Indonesia's neutralism has often tended to incline in favor of these two Communist countries. (And as a consequence of their support it was much easier for the PKI to convert the West Irian issue into important

---

the Dutch home economy which made it possible for the Netherlands government to utilize a large part of the country's domestic economic substance for support of its costly military effort in Indonesia. Many Indonesians regard Soviet Russia as having encouraged, if not instigated, the attempted *coup d'état* of the Communists at Madiun in 1948, a revolt which, though effectively suppressed, certainly weakened the Republic's military strength on the eve of the second Dutch offensive.

domestic political capital.) The position of neutrality so long maintained by the United States in the dispute was interpreted by Indonesians as favoring the Netherlands—a neutral position being regarded as acquiescence to the *status quo*. Even before the Indonesian
Communist Party threw its propaganda campaign into high gear,
moderate Indonesian leaders, including those of the Catholic Party and
the Masjumi, were in agreement with Mohammad Hatta that the
neutral position of the United States in fact constituted support of the
Netherlands. Later there was wide agreement with Hatta's view that
it was because of the United States stand and its influence in the United
Nations that Indonesia's request to the General Assembly in 1957 for
the opening of discussions on West Irian with the Netherlands fell short
of the two-thirds vote which was required for it to pass.[9] The conviction
among Indonesians that the United States sided with the Netherlands
was reinforced shortly thereafter when Secretary of State Dulles
abruptly recalled and transferred the American ambassador, John
Allison; for they understood that Allison had just recommended that
the United States support the Indonesian claim to West Irian.

With the increasing evidence that the Dutch intended to hold New
Guinea and give no further consideration to negotiations, anti-Nether-
lands sentiment in Indonesia grew deeper and more widespread. This
resulted in 1956 in Indonesia's unilateral abrogation of the Round
Table Conference Agreement of 1949 and the government's repudiation
of that major part of its indebtedness to the Netherlands assumed under
that agreement which Indonesians calculate to have been incurred
through Dutch military operations against them. And in December of
1957, with the Netherlands' continuing refusal to negotiate, Dutch
properties in Indonesia were seized, and strong and effective pressure
was exerted upon the Dutch community of some 46,000 still resident
there to evacuate to the Netherlands.

For a time the government's preoccupation with the rebellions in
Sumatra and Celebes overshadowed the West Irian dispute. But by
August 1960, following its abrogation of diplomatic relations with the
Netherlands, the Indonesian government was prepared to initiate a
more militant phase in its struggle for the control of the economically
and culturally backward residue of the Dutch East Indies. Meantime,
the United States having refused to sell them the large quantities of
arms they had requested, the Indonesians had turned to Soviet Russia.
The Russians agreed to sell Indonesia a large amount of modern equip-

[9] See Mohammad Hatta, "Indonesia between the Power Blocs," *Foreign Affairs*,
XXXVI, no. 3 (April 1958), 486.

ment and to advance the credit for its purchase. In the largest of these arms agreements, announced early in 1961, the $450 million Soviet credit was described as being granted for the purpose of liberating West Irian. The Indonesian armed forces were expanded, and in November 1961 Soekarno publicly threatened military action if the Dutch did not yield control. With small Indonesian guerrilla units having already been landed along the West Irian coast (and also dropped farther inland), it was clear that he was serious. Public opinion in the Netherlands had swung away from a policy likely to lead to war, but some formula was needed which would avoid humiliation for the Dutch.

The Kennedy Administration, having already evidenced a much more knowledgeable understanding of the West Irian problem than its predecessor—including the effect the dispute was having on Indonesia's domestic politics and foreign policy—moved closer to the Indonesian position and undertook to persuade (the Dutch would say "pressure") the Netherlands to make concessions. With the help of U Thant, the UN's Acting Secretary General, Washington was finally successful in sponsoring negotiations, which in August 1962 discovered the necessary face-saving formula. This provided for United Nations control over West Irian until December 31, 1962, and joint UN-Indonesian administration from then until May 1, 1963; following this the Indonesian government was to have exclusive control of the territory, but with the obligation to provide the inhabitants an opportunity before the end of 1969 to indicate through an "act of self-determination" whether they wish to remain with or sever their ties with Indonesia. As the Indonesian government has up to six years to administer and educate the inhabitants before they make their choice and as the UN has charged Indonesia with the primary role in making the arrangements for that choice to be registered, West Irian is likely to remain with Indonesia.[10]

The American role in the resolution of the West Irian issue did much to improve relations between Jakarta and Washington, but Indonesian distrust of the United States was by no means completely overcome. The fact that mistrust persists can be attributed primarily to United States actions during the first months of the 1958–1961 Sumatra-Celebes rebellion. Indeed, Indonesia's current attitude toward a number of countries is still influenced by the positions they took in 1958—whether or not they gave moral and material support to the rebels. Indonesia's

[10] For a good analysis of the agreement see Alastair M. Taylor, "Nederlands Nieuw-Guinea Becomes Irian Barat," *International Journal*, XVII, no. 4 (Autumn 1962), 429–435.

leaders regard the United States as having been the rebels' principal source of outside support. Soekarno became convinced, and remains so today, that Secretary of State Dulles and the CIA were out to overthrow him. Some of Dulles' public statements were widely regarded, outside as well as in Indonesia, as calculated encouragement of the rebels. Western correspondents confirmed (albeit more often privately than publicly) Indonesian allegations that American agents were training the rebels to use modern American military equipment shipped to them by sea and air, mostly from Formosa. Several Americans described by Secretary Dulles as "soldiers of fortune," but regarded by the Indonesians as CIA agents, flew planes for the rebels on bombing missions resulting in considerable material destruction and the loss of life among Indonesian civilians as well as military personnel. One such American pilot is regarded by Indonesians as responsible for sinking one of their navy's principal ships, most of her officers and crew going down with her. The consequent bitterness among Indonesian naval officers may have had some bearing upon their later willingness to turn to Soviet Russia for the purchase of naval vessels.

The Philippine government earned Indonesian distrust by making no apparent move to restrain rebel pilots from using facilities at the U.S. air base at Clarke Field. Distrust of the British resulted from the belief that rebel pilots were for a time permitted to use a Singapore airfield and that several British firms had advanced credit to the rebels.

The conviction among Indonesian leaders, Soekarno especially, that the Malayan Prime Minister, Tunku Abdul Rahman, favored the rebel cause and that the rebels on Sumatra were able to arrange for supplies in Malaya has strongly affected the Indonesian government's attitude toward that country. This belief and the resentment it has engendered reinforce Indonesia's current opposition to Abdul Rahman's plans for a Malaysian federation.[11]

An already critical attitude toward Chiang Kai-shek's Formosan re-

---

[11] His plan provided that the three territories of British Borneo (Sarawak, Brunei, and North Borneo) and Singapore were to be federated with Malaya. It was primarily in protest against this plan that A. M. Azahari, head of Brunei's only substantial political party (which had in August 1962 won an overwhelming victory giving it all of the elected seats in the Brunei legislature), led an unsuccessful rebellion in December 1962. Soekarno declared Indonesia's support of the rebels; and, like Azahari, the Indonesian government has held that the British Borneo territories should first be given full independence, after which they can decide whether or not they will join with Malaya. As of April 1963, Malayan and British plans (endorsed on February 7, 1963, by the Sultan of Brunei) still called for the direct federation of these Borneo territories by August 1963, without an intervening stage of full independence.

gime became much stronger because of its support (in the shape of arms and military instructors) for the rebels in Celebes. Syngman Rhee hardly endeared his country to Indonesia by his informal but public offer to send South Korean volunteers to support the rebels. (This was followed by Peking's offer of assistance to the Jakarta government, neither offer being accepted.)

However prepared Secretary Dulles may have been to recognize an anti-Soekarno regime in Indonesia, successive rebel defeats soon indicated that there would be very little to recognize. The tone of his statements changed; they could no longer be construed as implying moral support of the rebels, and they stressed that the rebellion was an internal affair to be settled by the Indonesians. In August 1958 the air-borne arrival in Jakarta of a token American shipment of arms signaled a major shift in American policy, one based upon a view more consistent with Indonesian political realities. It proved impossible, however, for the Indonesian government to induce the United States to sell it more than a minor fraction of the arms which Indonesia's service chiefs believed they needed—and far less than was required to equip their forces to mount an effective invasion of Dutch-held West Irian. Thus Indonesia turned to Soviet Russia, securing from the Soviet bloc by the end of 1962 $800 million to $1 billion in credits for purchase of the Soviet-built ships and planes which now predominate in the Indonesian navy and air force. (The army, however, is still equipped primarily with American arms.)

Indonesia remains committed to a nonaligned foreign policy. But its present need for outside economic assistance (as noted above) has become so serious that its international orientation is likely to become more influenced than previously by the extent to which the United States and Soviet Russia come to its support.

Indonesian leaders have a healthy respect for Communist China's power. However, they do not worry about the possible direct impingement of its power as do those who head the governments of some of China's more immediate Asian neighbors. This is partly a consequence of the distance between China and Indonesia (and the existence of a water barrier dominated by American and British Commonwealth naval and air power), but it also stems from the strength of Indonesian nationalism. Relations between the two countries have been affected significantly by the existence of Indonesia's large Chinese minority of approximately two and a half million—a substantial portion of whom feel their primary loyalty to be to China—and by the long-ingrained, widespread antagonism of many Indonesians toward them.

Jakarta exchanged diplomatic recognition with the Peking regime in 1950 and subsequently has consistently backed its claim to represent China in the United Nations. Relations between the two countries were, however, quite cool until, beginning in 1953, Communist China made a persistent effort to win Indonesian friendship. In 1955 Peking made a major concession by agreeing to conclude with Indonesia the first dual-nationality agreement China had ever negotiated. This was to end the traditional Chinese claim that all persons of Chinese blood living in Indonesia be regarded as of Chinese nationality—whether or not they considered themselves Indonesians. The agreement provided that all persons of Chinese ancestry who lived in Indonesia could hold only one nationality—Indonesian or Chinese.[12]

However, before the details could be worked out and the treaty ratified, a major crisis intervened which for a time badly strained relations between the two countries. This was the previously mentioned Indonesian regulation [13] which prohibited aliens from engaging in retail trade in rural areas and which required in some areas that they move to towns. Since aliens in this trade were almost exclusively Chinese and since this constituted one of the major occupations of Indonesia's Chinese community, the Chinese government naturally regarded the measure as discriminatory and anti-Chinese. After formally protesting to no avail, Peking ordered its embassy and consular personnel in Jakarta to visit the rural areas and urge local Chinese to disregard the regulation. This action encouraged some Chinese to resist the measure, but it angered Indonesian officials, particularly army officers, who responded by using force where necessary to implement the regulation. The Indonesian government protested strongly to Peking, restricted the movements of the Chinese embassy and consular staff, and demanded that several of them return to China. Peking's countermove was to invite all Chinese resident in Indonesia who no longer desired to remain there to come back to China on ships provided by China. Peking was apparently unprepared for and shocked at the extent of the response. In the twelve-month period beginning in December 1960 almost 100,000 were repatriated. The magnitude of the response eventually brought the Chinese Embassy to discourage

[12] For the fullest account of the political status of the Indonesian Chinese during the twentieth century and the course of negotiations between Indonesia and China on nationality through 1958 see Donald E. Willmott, *The National Status of the Chinese in Indonesia, 1900–1958* (Cornell Modern Indonesia Project, Monograph Series; Ithaca, N.Y., 1961).

[13] See p. 656.

those who were not students or who did not have special skills.[14] Shortly thereafter nearly all remaining Chinese who had planned to leave appear to have changed their minds when they learned that most of those who had been repatriated were obliged to settle in state farms on Hainan Island and there were informed that "they must develop the spirit of labor and accept the idea that they are settled on the farm permanently." [15]

Peking had hardly been successful. It had failed to prevent enforcement of the Indonesian regulation aimed at the local Chinese and for most of them had only made matters worse. It had antagonized Indonesian government leaders and "damaged China's prestige in wide circles of Indonesian opinion," had embarrassed the Indonesian Communist Party,[16] and in its repatriation program had incurred considerable expense.

Both Jakarta and Peking apparently felt that it was to their interests to effect a *rapprochement,* and this did develop during the latter half of 1960 and early 1961. The most important step was the signing of an implementing agreement on December 24, 1960, finally making the Dual Nationality Treaty operative. Thereby Chinese resident in Indonesia were given a two-year period to indicate whether they elected Indonesian or Chinese nationality; the Indonesian government insisted that those who did not choose Indonesian and simultaneously reject Chinese nationality before an Indonesian court were to be regarded as Chinese.[17] The provisions of this agreement, like the resolution of the dispute over rural retailing, are symptomatic of the fact that under present conditions maintenance of cordial relations between Peking and Jakarta will probably have to be primarily on Indonesian terms.

[14] David P. Mozingo, "New Developments in China's Relations with Indonesia," *Current Scene,* I, no. 24 (Feb. 5, 1962), 2–3; G. William Skinner, "The Chinese Minority," in Ruth T. McVey, ed., *Indonesia* (New Haven: HRAF; due to be published in 1963). (Mozingo and Skinner spent one to two years in Indonesia studying Sino-Indonesian relations and problems of the local Chinese.) For a good general account of recent Sino-Indonesian relations see also Lea E. Williams, "Sino-Indonesian Diplomacy: A Study of Revolutionary International Politics," *China Quarterly,* July–Sept. 1962, pp. 184–199.

[15] Skinner, *loc. cit.,* citing *Jen-min jih-pao,* Feb. 15, 1961, as translated in *China News Analysis,* no. 362 (March 3, 1961), p. 7; Mozingo, *loc. cit.,* p. 3.

[16] Mozingo, *loc. cit.,* pp. 2–3.

[17] Children are not bound by their parents' decision and have the right to choose Indonesian nationality within two years of their eighteenth birthday. Skinner, *loc. cit.,* has estimated that when the final count is made the number of Chinese holding Indonesian citizenship will be between 600,000 and 800,000.

SUGGESTED READING

Historical Background

Allen, G. C., and Audrey G. Donnithorne. *Western Enterprise in Indonesia and Malaya.* London and New York: Macmillan, 1957. Useful for its account of the colonial period, but not a well-balanced treatment.

Bastin, John. *The Native Policies of Sir Stamford Raffles.* Oxford: Clarendon Press, 1957. A scholarly and useful study.

Benda, Harry J. "The Communist Rebellions of 1926–1927 in Indonesia," *Pacific Historical Review,* May 1955, pp. 139–152.

——. *The Crescent and the Rising Sun: Indonesian Islam under the Japanese Occupation.* The Hague and Bandung: van Hoeve, 1958. Contains a good account of Dutch Islamic policy.

——, and Ruth T. McVey, eds. *The Communist Uprisings of 1926–1927 in Indonesia: Key Documents.* (Cornell Modern Indonesia Project, Translation Series.) Ithaca, N.Y., 1960. This includes a substantial and valuable introductory essay.

Boeke, J. H. *The Evolution of the Netherlands Economy.* New York: Institute of Pacific Relations, 1946.

——. *The Structure of Netherlands Indian Economy.* New York: Institute of Pacific Relations, 1942. Tendentious, but useful.

Bousquet, G. H. *A French View of the Netherlands Indies.* Trans. by Philip E. Lilienthal. London and New York: Oxford University Press, 1940. An imaginative and provocative critique of Dutch colonial policy, particularly of Dutch Islamic policy and attitudes toward Indonesian nationalism, by a distinguished French Islamic specialist and colonial civil servant.

Broek, Jan O. M. *Economic Development in the Netherlands Indies.* New York: Institute of Pacific Relations, 1942.

Burger, D. H. *Structural Changes in Javanese Society: The Village Sphere and The Supra-Village Sphere.* Trans. by Leslie Palmier. (Cornell Modern Indonesia Project, Translation Series.) Ithaca, N.Y., 1956 and 1957. Useful analysis of Indonesian society by an established Dutch scholar.

Cator, W. L. *The Economic Position of the Chinese in the Netherlands Indies.* Chicago: University of Chicago Press, 1936. A scholarly and valuable study.

Cole, Fay-Cooper. *The Peoples of Malaysia.* New York: Van Nostrand, 1945.

Coolie Budget Commission. *Living Conditions of Plantation Workers and Peasants on Java in 1939–1940.* Trans. by Robert Van Niel. (Cornell Modern Indonesia Project, Translation Series.) Ithaca, N.Y., 1956. An important, but hitherto classified and unpublished, report of the Netherlands Indies government.

Day, Clive. *The Policy and Administration of the Dutch in Java.* New York:

Macmillan, 1904. A useful, though somewhat uncritical, historical study.

Emerson, Rupert. *Malaysia: A Study in Indirect Rule.* New York: Macmillan, 1937. An imaginative, but sound and scholarly analysis of colonial rule in Indonesia and Malaya—a classic, but unfortunately out of print.

Furnivall, J. S. *Colonial Policy and Practice: A Comparative Study of Burma and Netherlands India.* New York: New York University Press, 1956. The treatment of Indonesia is less full than in the author's *Netherlands India*, but is nevertheless very useful; contains a full exposition of his theory of plural economy.

——. *Netherlands India: A Study of Plural Economy.* New York: Macmillan; Cambridge, Eng.: Cambridge University Press, 1944. The best treatment of colonial rule in Indonesia; an excellent general history.

Geertz, Clifford. *The Development of the Javanese Economy: A Sociocultural Approach.* Cambridge: Massachusetts Institute of Technology, Center for International Studies, 1956. An imaginative and valuable analysis.

Haar, B. ter. *Adat Law in Indonesia.* Ed. and with an introduction by E. Adamson Hoebel and A. Arthur Schiller. New York: Institute of Pacific Relations, 1948. A good description of the customary law of the principal indigenous communities.

Hall, D. G. E. *A History of South East Asia.* 2d ed. London: Macmillan; New York: St. Martin's Press, 1963. The most comprehensive and scholarly general history of the area. Its coverage of Indonesia is excellent.

Harrison, B. *A Short History of South East Asia.* London: Macmillan; New York: St. Martin's Press, 1954. A much shorter survey than that by Hall, but nonetheless very useful.

Heine-Geldern, Robert. *Conceptions of State and Kingship in Southeast Asia.* (Southeast Asia Program, Cornell University, Data Paper no. 18.) Ithaca, N.Y., 1956. Useful to an understanding of the traditional (precolonial) political ethos.

Higgins, Benjamin. "The 'Dualistic Theory' of Underdeveloped Areas," *Economic Development and Cultural Change,* IV (Jan. 1956), 99–115. A substantial answer to Dr. Boeke's controversial theory, with particular relevance to Indonesia.

Kat Angelino, A. D. A. de. *Colonial Policy,* vol. II. Trans. from the Dutch by G. J. Renier. The Hague: M. Nijhoff, 1931. Comprehensive and solid description of the colonial government and of Dutch colonial policy.

Kennedy, Raymond. *The Ageless Indies.* New York: John Day, 1942. A well-written, though rather skimpy, survey.

Klerck, Edward S. de. *History of the Netherlands East Indies.* 2 vols. Rotterdam: W. L. and J. Brusse, 1938. A comprehensive and detailed coverage, rather turgid.

Pelzer, Karl J. *Pioneer Settlement in the Asiatic Tropics.* New York: American Geographical Society, 1945. Contains an excellent description of prewar agrarian conditions in Java and of Dutch-sponsored efforts to transplant Javanese peasants in the outer islands.

Purcell, Victor. *The Chinese in Southeast Asia*. London: Oxford University Press, 1951. Contains a useful history of the Chinese minority in Indonesia prior to the revolution.

Raffles, Sir Thomas Stamford. *History of Java*. London: Black, Parbury, and Allen, 1817.

Schrieke, B. *The Effect of Western Influence on Native Civilizations of the Malay Archipelago*. Batavia: G. Kolf and Co., 1929. Contains several excellent essays. See particularly those by G. H. Van der Kolff and J. W. Meyer Ranneft.

——. *Indonesian Sociological Studies*, part I. The Hague and Bandung: van Hoeve, 1955. *Ruler and Realm in Early Java*, part II. The Hague and Bandung: van Hoeve, 1957. Recently translated selections from the works of an outstanding Dutch scholar. These are important studies of aspects of precolonial and colonial society.

Snouck-Hurgronje, C. *The Atjehnese*. Leyden: late E. J. Brill; London: Luzac and Co., 1906.

Vandenbosch, Amry. *The Dutch East Indies: Its Government, Problems, and Politics*. Berkeley and Los Angeles: University of California Press, 1944. The fullest account in English of government organization in the prewar period.

Van Leur, J. C. *Indonesian Trade and Society*. The Hague and Bandung: van Hoeve, 1955. Translation of the principal work of one of the most imaginative and provocative of Dutch scholars, who marshals convincing data to challenge the previously dominant European-centered view of Indonesian history.

Van Niel, Robert. *The Emergence of the Modern Indonesian Elite*. Chicago: Quadrangle; The Hague: van Hoeve, 1960. A study of the origins of Indonesian nationalism and Dutch policy toward it during the period 1900–1927.

Vlekke, Bernard H. M. *Nusantara: A History of the East Indian Archipelago*. 2d, rev. ed. Cambridge, Mass.: Harvard University Press, 1958. A useful history, especially with regard to the precolonial period.

Williams, Lea E. *Overseas Chinese Nationalism: The Genesis of the Pan-Chinese Movement in Indonesia, 1900–1916*. Glencoe, Ill.: Free Press, 1960. A comprehensive study based upon research into previously unsurveyed colonial records.

The Revolution and the Revolutionary Government

Alisjahbana, Takdir. "The Indonesian Language—By-Product of Nationalism," *Pacific Affairs*, XXII (Dec. 1949), 388–392.

Anderson, Benedict R. O'G. *Some Aspects of Indonesian Politics under the Japanese Occupation: 1944–1945.* (Cornell Modern Indonesia Project, Interim Reports Series.) Ithaca, N.Y., 1961. Important data and insights unavailable elsewhere.

Aziz, M. A. *Japan's Colonialism and Indonesia.* The Hague: M. Nijhoff, 1955.

Benda, Harry J. "The Beginnings of the Japanese Occupation of Java," *Far Eastern Quarterly,* XV (Aug. 1956), 541–560.

——. *The Crescent and the Rising Sun: Indonesian Islam under the Japanese Occupation.* The Hague and Bandung: van Hoeve, 1958. By far the most scholarly and valuable study of the Japanese occupation.

Coast, John. *Recruit to Revolution.* London: Christopers, 1952. An exciting, somewhat flamboyant account incorporating considerable significant data by a Britisher who worked closely with the Foreign Ministry of the Republican government in London, Bangkok, and Jogjakarta during the period 1945–1948.

Gandasubrata, S. M. *An Account of the Japanese Occupation of Banjumas Residency, Java, March 1942 to August 1945.* Trans. by Leslie Palmier. (Southeast Asia Program, Cornell University, Data Paper no. 10.) Ithaca, N.Y., 1953. Firsthand observations by the Resident of Banjumas.

Kahin, George McT. *Nationalism and Revolution in Indonesia.* Ithaca, N.Y.: Cornell University Press, 1952.

Schiller, A. Arthur. *The Formation of Federal Indonesia.* The Hague and Bandung: van Hoeve, 1955. A scholarly, highly legalistic account concerned with the formal documents describing the Dutch-sponsored federal order of 1946–1949, but eschewing consideration of its political context or objectives.

Selosoemardjan. *See* Soemardjan, Selo.

Sjahrir, S. *Out of Exile.* Trans. by Charles Wolf, Jr. New York: John Day, 1949. The very readable personal journal of a leading Indonesian intellectual who was later to become Prime Minister of the Republic. All but the first chapter, dealing with the 1945 period, were written while he was in exile during the 1930s.

Soekarno. *The Birth of the Pantja Sila.* Jakarta: Ministry of Information, 1952. The original formulation by the future President of the Republic of his Five Principles of State.

Soemardjan, Selo. "Bureaucratic Organization in a Time of Revolution," *Administrative Science Quarterly,* II (Sept. 1957), 182–199. A keen piece of sociopolitical analysis by an Indonesian who was in a key position to observe.

Taylor, Alastair M. *Indonesian Independence and the United Nations.* Ithaca, N.Y.: Cornell University Press, 1960. An excellent study, giving a full and balanced coverage of the diplomatic aspects of the dispute and valuable insights into domestic conditions which helped to shape it.

van Mook, H. J. *The Stakes of Democracy in South East Asia.* New York: Norton, 1950. The personal views of the last Dutch Governor-General.

Wehl, David. *The Birth of Indonesia.* London: George Allen and Unwin, 1948. An interesting and useful account of the 1945–1947 period by a writer who was apparently an officer in the British occupation forces. Although this is not a balanced account, it contains considerable important information and a useful appendix of documents relating to the Dutch-Indonesian negotiations.

Wolf, Charles, Jr. *The Indonesian Story.* New York: John Day, 1948. An account of the 1945–1949 period containing by far the most reliable coverage of the Indonesian-Dutch negotiations culminating in the Linggadjati Agreement.

The Postrevolutionary Setting

Bank Indonesia. The yearly reports of this central bank contain the fullest body of economic data available.

Biro Pusat Statistik (Central Bureau of Statistics). *Statistical Pocket Book of Indonesia, 1960.* Jakarta: Biro Pusat Statistik, 1961. Useful compilations of statistics bearing on a wide range of governmental activity.

Geertz, Clifford. *The Religion of Java.* Glencoe, Ill.: Free Press, 1960. A major contribution which incorporates insights useful to an understanding of Indonesian political activity, especially at the local level, based upon extensive field research.

——. "Religious Belief and Economic Behaviour in a Central Javanese Town: Some Preliminary Considerations," *Economic Development and Cultural Change,* IV (Jan. 1956), 134–158.

——. *The Social Context of Economic Change: An Indonesian Case Study.* Cambridge: Massachusetts Institute of Technology, Center for International Studies, 1956. Mimeograph. A study of the sugar industry in Java and of its social context and impact.

Geertz, Hildred. *The Javanese Family.* Glencoe, Ill.: Free Press, 1961. Family relationships and values among social groups in an East Java town: a scholarly study based upon substantial research in the field.

Grader, Charles J. *Rural Organization and Village Revival in Indonesia.* (Southeast Asia Program, Cornell University, Data Paper no. 5.) Ithaca, N.Y., 1952.

Human Relations Area File. *Indonesia.* Subcontractor's Monograph. 3 vols. New Haven, 1957. Of uneven quality, but useful for reference on a variety of subjects.

Jay, Robert R. "Local Government in Rural Central Java," *Far Eastern Quarterly,* XV (Feb. 1956), 215–227. A very useful study.

Kennedy, Raymond. *Field Notes on Indonesia: South Celebes, 1949–1950.*

Ed. by Harold C. Conklin. New Haven: Human Relations Area Files, 1953. Useful, though not completely digested, data on rural life.

Koentjaraningrat. *Some Social-Anthropological Observations on Gotong Rojong Practices in Two Villages of Central Java.* Trans. by Claire Holt. (Cornell Modern Indonesia Project, Monograph Series.) Ithaca, N.Y., 1961. A solid and illuminating study.

McVey, Ruth T., ed. *Indonesia.* New Haven: HRAF. This general survey, due to be published in 1963, incorporates chapters by highly qualified specialists and should prove extremely useful. It will include chapters on agriculture (Karl J. Pelzer), the Chinese (G. William Skinner), cultures and communities (Hildred Geertz), the economy (Douglas S. Paauw), history (Robert Van Niel), labor (Everett D. Hawkins), and politics (Herbert Feith).

Palmier, Leslie H. *Social Status and Power in Java.* London: Athlone Press, 1960. A study of social status and relationships in a Javanese town, based on field research in 1951–1952 and 1953–1954.

Selosoemardjan. *Social Changes in Jogjakarta.* Ithaca, N.Y.: Cornell University Press, 1962. An unusually valuable study of social, economic, and political change in an area of key political importance by an able sociologist who has had a rich and varied experience at several levels of the Jogjakarta administration and served as private secretary to the Sultan of Jogjakarta.

Skinner, G. William, ed. *Local, Ethnic, and National Loyalties in Village Indonesia: A Symposium.* (Southeast Asia Studies, Yale University, Cultural Report Series.) New Haven, 1959. Includes material on villages in East Central Java (Clifford Geertz), West Java (Andrea Wilcox Palmer), Bali (Hildred Geertz), Tapanuli (Edward M. Bruner), and Sumbawa (Peter R. Goethals) and an introductory essay, "The Nature of Loyalties in Rural Indonesia," by the editor.

Supomo. "The Future of Adat Law in the Reconstruction of Indonesia," in Philip Thayer, ed., *South East Asia in the Coming World.* Baltimore: Johns Hopkins Press, 1953. Pages 217–236.

van der Kroef, J. M. "Economic Development in Indonesia: Some Social and Cultural Impediments," *Economic Development and Cultural Change,* IV (Jan. 1956), 116–133.

——. "Indonesia: Centrifugal Economies," in James W. Wiggins and Helmut Schoeck, eds., *Foreign Aid Re-examined: A Critical Appraisal.* Washington, D.C.: Public Affairs Press, 1958. Pages 197–220. An interesting and useful account.

——. *Indonesia in the Modern World.* 2 vols. Bandung: Masa Baru, 1954, 1956. A collection of essays of rather uneven quality, incorporating some useful (though not always completely reliable) data and stimulating (though not always soundly based) ideas.

van der Veur, Paul. "The Eurasians of Indonesia: Castaways of Colonialism," *Pacific Affairs*, XXVII (June 1954), 124–137. A solid treatment based upon substantial research.

Wertheim, W. F. "Changes in Indonesia's Social Stratification," *Pacific Affairs*, XXVIII (March 1955), 41–52. A discussion of individualist and collectivist tendencies in contemporary society.

——. *Indonesian Society in Transition*. 2d ed. The Hague and Bandung: van Hoeve, 1959. An analysis of past and present Indonesian society by a leading Dutch sociologist which is most useful for its account of prewar society.

Willmott, Donald E. *The Chinese of Semarang*. Ithaca, N.Y.: Cornell University Press, 1960. An objective study by a sociologist. It is based on field research and has significance transcending the Chinese community in Semarang.

Willner, Ann R. "Social Change in Javanese Town-Village Life," *Economic Development and Cultural Change*, VI (April 1958), 229–242.

Woodman, Dorothy. *The Republic of Indonesia*. New York: Philosophical Library, 1955. A good introduction, but uneven in quality. The best chapters deal with the British occupation and the role of the United Nations in the Indonesian-Netherlands dispute.

Postrevolutionary Government and Politics

Bone, Robert C. "The Future of Indonesian Political Parties," *Far Eastern Survey*, XXIII (Feb. 1954), 17–24.

Brackman, Arnold C. *Indonesian Communism: A History*. New York and London: Praeger, 1963. Because of the writer's considerable experience in and knowledge of Indonesia, this should be an important and useful study.

Budiardjo, Miriam S. "The Provisional Parliament of Indonesia," *Far Eastern Survey*, XXV (Feb. 1956), 17–23. A good discussion of an important aspect of governmental weakness in the postrevolutionary period.

Feith, Herbert. *The Decline of Constitutional Democracy in Indonesia*. Ithaca, N.Y.: Cornell University Press, 1962. A scholarly, comprehensive, and detailed study of postrevolutionary Indonesian government and politics through 1957 based upon extensive field research. This is a work of unusual depth and quality.

——. "Indonesia," in George McT. Kahin, ed., *Governments and Politics of Southeast Asia*. 2d ed. Ithaca, N.Y.: Cornell University Press (in progress). An excellent general introduction.

——. *The Indonesian Elections of 1955*. (Cornell Modern Indonesia Project, Interim Reports Series.) Ithaca, N.Y., 1957. The most comprehensive and reliable account.

——. *The Wilopo Cabinet, 1952–1953: Turning Point in Post-Revolutionary Indonesia*. (Cornell Modern Indonesia Project, Monograph Series.) Ithaca,

N.Y., 1958. A full description of a key period in postrevolutionary politics, incorporating keen and illuminating political analysis.

——, and Daniel S. Lev. "The End of the Indonesian Rebellion," *Pacific Affairs*, vol. XXXV, no. 3 (Spring 1963). An excellent account by two very knowledgeable writers.

Fischer, Louis. *The Story of Indonesia*. New York: Harper, 1959. A well-written report of his visit in 1958, during which he had a number of interesting conversations with Soekarno.

Goethals, Peter R. *Aspects of Local Government in a Sumbawan Village (Eastern Indonesia)*. (Cornell Modern Indonesia Project, Monograph Series.) Ithaca, N.Y., 1961. Based upon two years of field research by an able anthropologist, this study provides unusually deep insight into important aspects of the political process at the village level.

Hanna, Willard A. *Bung Karno's Indonesia*. New York: American Universities Field Staff, 1960. A series of reports by a lucid writer who has become bitterly disillusioned. The study incorporates a number of keen and valuable insights, but it lacks balance and perspective.

Hatta, Mohammad. *Past and Future*. (Cornell Modern Indonesia Project, Translation Series.) Ithaca, N.Y., 1960. A brief but important address by the Vice-President on the eve of his resignation in December 1956, describing aspects of his political philosophy and his criticism of the course of political developments at that time.

Hindley, Donald. "President Sukarno and the Communists: The Politics of Domestication," *American Political Science Review*, vol. LVI, no. 4 (Dec. 1962). A useful account, much of it based on field research, which helps to balance the often distorted analyses of the relationship under discussion.

Legge, J. D. *Central Authority and Regional Autonomy in Indonesia: A Study in Local Administration, 1950–1960*. Ithaca, N.Y.: Cornell University Press, 1961. An excellent description and analysis of the changes in regional administration during a decade when the system's pattern turned full circle.

Lev, Daniel S. "The Supreme Court and Adat Inheritance Law in Indonesia," *American Journal of Comparative Law*, II, no. 2 (Spring 1962), 205–224. A perceptive analysis of the often important legislative function of the Supreme Court. This provides, incidentally, the fullest description in English of the contemporary Indonesian judicial system.

Mackie, J. A. C. "Indonesian Politics under Guided Democracy," *Australian Outlook*, XV, no. 3 (Dec. 1961), 260–279. Especially useful for the period 1959–1961.

McVey, Ruth T., ed. *Indonesia*. New Haven: HRAF (due to be published in 1963). Especially the chapter on politics by Herbert Feith.

——. "Indonesian Communism under Guided Democracy," in A. Doak Barnett, ed., *Communist Strategies in Asia*. To be pub., Praeger, 1963.

Mossman, James. *Rebels in Paradise*. London: Jonathan Cape, 1961. An interesting account of the first and critical months of the 1958 rebellion on Sumatra by a perceptive British journalist.

Mozingo, David P. "The Sino-Indonesian Dual Nationality Treaty," *Asian Survey*, vol. I, no. 10 (Dec. 1961). A valuable account of recent relations.

Natsir, Mohammad. *Some Observations concerning the Role of Islam in National and International Affairs.* (Southeast Asia Program, Cornell University, Data Paper no. 16.) Ithaca, N.Y., 1954. Important insights into the thinking of the chairman of the Masjumi Party.

Pauker, Guy J. "The Role of Political Organizations in Indonesia," *Far Eastern Survey*, XXVII (Sept. 1958), 129–142. A stimulating analysis.

——. "The Role of the Military in Indonesia," in J. J. Johnson, ed., *The Military in the Underdeveloped Areas.* Princeton: Princeton University Press, 1962. A description and analysis of the army's political role, 1945–1961.

Pringgodigdo, A. K. *The Office of President in Indonesia as Defined in the Three Constitutions in Theory and Practice.* Trans. by Alexander Brotherton. (Cornell Modern Indonesia Project, Translation Series.) Ithaca, N.Y., 1957. The author was a distinguished scholar who served as director of the cabinet of the President.

Selosoemardjan. *Social Changes in Jogjakarta.* (See same reference above, in the section "Postrevolutionary Setting.")

——. *Some Social and Cultural Implications of Indonesia's Unplanned and Planned Development.* Paper presented at tenth Pacific Science Congress, Honolulu, Hawaii, August–September 1961. A sociologically oriented account incorporating a number of illuminating observations.

Soedjatmoko. "The Role of Political Parties in Indonesia," in P. W. Thayer, ed., *Nationalism and Progress in Free Asia.* Baltimore: Johns Hopkins Press, 1956. Pages 128–140. A keen analysis of the role of political parties in the 1955 elections.

Soekarno. *Marhaen and Proletarian.* (Cornell Modern Indonesia Project, Translation Series.) Ithaca, N.Y., 1960. A lecture given in mid-1957 which Soekarno regards as one of the most important expositions of his political philosophy.

——. *Towards Freedom and the Dignity of Man.* Jakarta: Department of Foreign Affairs, 1961. Five of the President's major speeches, including "The Birth of Pantja Sila" (1945) and his Political Manifesto of August 17, 1959.

Sutter, John O. *Indonesianisasi: Politics in a Changing Economy, 1940–1955.* (Southeast Asia Program, Cornell University, Data Paper no. 36.) Ithaca, N.Y., 1959. A useful study, encyclopedic in coverage, pertinent to an understanding of both economic and political developments during this fifteen-year period. Its four volumes discuss respectively the last years of Dutch rule, the Japanese occupation, the revolutionary period, and the years 1950–1955.

Tedjasukmana, Iskandar. *The Political Character of the Indonesian Trade Union Movement.* (Cornell Modern Indonesia Project, Monograph Series.) Ithaca, N.Y., 1959. A very useful study by a former Minister of Labor.

van der Kroef, J. M. "The Dilemmas of Indonesian Communism," *Pacific Affairs*, XXXV, no. 2 (Summer 1962), 141–159. A generally balanced and useful treatment.

van Marle, A. "The First Indonesian Parliamentary Elections," *Indonesië* (The Hague and Bandung), IX (June 1956), 257–264.

Widjojo Nitisastro and J. E. Ismael. *The Government, Economy and Taxes of a Central Javanese Village.* (Cornell Modern Indonesia Project, Translation Series.) Ithaca, N.Y., 1959.

Widjojo Nitisastro and Wilopo. *The Socio-economic Basis of the Indonesian State.* (Cornell Modern Indonesia Project, Translation Series.) Ithaca, N.Y., 1959.

Major Problems

Ekonomi dan Keuangan Indonesia (Economics and Finance in Indonesia). Published monthly or bimonthly beginning in 1953 by Pembangunan, Jakarta. This is a scholarly journal edited by a group of Indonesia's leading economists, with contributions by foreign economists concerned with Indonesia as well as by Indonesians. Usually each issue has at least one article in English. In general a high standard has been maintained, many of the contributions being unique in coverage and extremely useful.

Fryer, D. W. "Economic Aspects of Indonesian Disunity," *Pacific Affairs*, XXX (Sept. 1957), 195–208.

Glassburner, Bruce. "Economic Policy-Making in Indonesia, 1950–1957," *Economic Development and Cultural Change*, X, no. 2 (Jan. 1962), 113–133. A very useful article incorporating a good historical running account and a stimulating analysis by an economist who knows Indonesia well.

Hatta, Mohammad. *The Co-operative Movement in Indonesia.* Ithaca, N.Y.: Cornell University Press, 1957. The only full account of the development of cooperatives. Also gives considerable insight into the economic and political views of the former Vice-President.

Hawkins, Everett H. D. "Prospects for Economic Development in Indonesia," *World Politics*, VIII (Oct. 1955), 91–111. Outdated, but still useful.

Higgins, Benjamin. *Indonesia's Economic Stabilization and Development.* New York: Institute of Pacific Relations, 1957. An account of economic problems and of plans for economic development as projected in 1956. It incorporates significant observations by Guy Pauker on political aspects of these problems.

——, ed. *Entrepreneurship and Labor Skills in Indonesian Economic Development.* (Southeast Asia Studies, Yale University, Monograph Series no. 1.) New Haven, 1961. Includes an interesting introduction by Professor Higgins.

Humphrey, Don. D. "Indonesia's National Plan for Economic Development," *Asian Survey*, II, no. 10 (Dec. 1962), 12–21. An account of economic conditions with some very good analysis.

——, et al. *Report to the President: Perspectives and Proposals for United States Economic Aid*. Washington, D.C.: Economic Survey Team to Indonesia, 1962; New Haven: Yale University Southeast Asia Studies, 1963. An extensive and informative survey of conditions in 1962 and prospects for economic growth.

Hutasoit, M. *Compulsory Education in Indonesia*. UNESCO, 1954. An account of Indonesia's rapid and substantial expansion of its educational system by the secretary-general of its Ministry of Education.

Legge, J. D. *Central Authority and Regional Autonomy in Indonesia: A Study in Local Administration, 1950–1960*. (See same reference above, in the section "Postrevolutionary government.")

Mackie, J. A. C. "Indonesia's Government Estates and Their Masters," *Pacific Affairs*, XXXIV, no. 4 (Winter 1961–1962), 337–360. A good account of the nationalization of Dutch firms and some of the political consequences.

McVey, Ruth T., ed. *Indonesia*. (See same reference above, in the section "Postrevolutionary Setting.")

Maryanov, Gerald S. *Decentralization in Indonesia as a Political Problem*. (Cornell Modern Indonesia Project, Interim Reports Series.) Ithaca, N.Y., 1958. Especially useful with respect to the relationship of political attitudes to regional differences.

——. *Decentralization in Indonesia: Legislative Aspects*. (Cornell Modern Indonesia Project, Interim Reports Series.) Ithaca, N.Y., 1957. A useful and full account of the earlier legislation.

Massachusetts Institute of Technology, Center for International Studies, Indonesia Project. *Stanvac in Indonesia*. New York: National Planning Association, 1957. A critical evaluation of the operations of the major U.S. business enterprise in Indonesia.

Paauw, Douglas S. *Financing Economic Development: The Indonesian Case*. Glencoe, Ill.: Free Press, 1960. The most substantial study of modern Indonesian economic problems.

Palmier, Leslie. "Occupational Distribution of Parents of Pupils in Certain Indonesian Educational Institutions," *Indonesië* (The Hague and Bandung), X (Aug. and Oct. 1957), 320–348, 349–376.

Pelzer, Karl J. "The Agrarian Conflict in East Sumatra," *Pacific Affairs*, XXX (June 1957), 151–159. An important article based on thorough and extensive research.

Soedjatmoko. *An Approach to Indonesian History: Towards an Open Future*. (Cornell Modern Indonesia Project, Translation Series.) Ithaca, N.Y.,

1960. A brief, but very good discussion of the problems raised by national-ist bias and distortion in the writing of Indonesian history.

——. *Economic Development as a' Cultural Problem.* (Cornell Modern In-donesia Project, Translation Series.) Ithaca, N.Y., 1958. A brief but useful analysis.

FOREIGN RELATIONS

Bone, Robert C. *The Dynamics of the Western New Guinea (Irian Barat) Problem.* (Cornell Modern Indonesia Project, Interim Reports Series.) Ithaca, N.Y., 1958. Based upon several years of intensive research in In-donesia and the Netherlands.

Collins, J. Foster. "The United States and Indonesia," *International Concilia-tion,* March 1950.

Djajadiningrat, Idrus Nasir. *The Beginnings of the Indonesian-Dutch Nego-tiations and the Hoge Veluwe Talks.* (Cornell Modern Indonesia Project, Monograph Series.) Ithaca, N.Y., 1958. A deep and searching analysis of the early period of negotiations—one that was of great importance in establishing attitudes which dominated the later and better-known periods of negotiation.

Emerson, Rupert. "Reflections on the Indonesian Case," *World Politics,* I (Oct. 1948), 59–81.

Finkelstein, Lawrence S. "Indonesia's Record in the United Nations," *Inter-national Conciliation,* no. 475 (Nov. 1951), pp. 513–546. A good survey of 1950 and the first half of 1951.

Hatta, Mohammad. "Indonesia between the Power Blocs," *Foreign Affairs,* XXXVI (April 1958), 480–490.

——. "Indonesia's Foreign Policy," *Foreign Affairs,* XXXI (April 1953), 441–452.

Henderson, William. *Pacific Settlement of Disputes: The Indonesian Ques-tion, 1946–1949.* New York: Woodrow Wilson Foundation, 1954.

Kahin, George McT. *The Asian-African Conference, Bandung, Indonesia, April 1955.* Ithaca, N.Y.: Cornell University Press, 1956.

McVey, Ruth T. *The Calcutta Conference and the Southeast Asian Uprisings.* (Cornell Modern Indonesia Project, Interim Reports Series.) Ithaca, N.Y., 1958. A useful supplement to previously much oversimplified accounts.

——. *The Soviet View of the Indonesian Revolution.* (Cornell Modern In-donesia Project, Interim Reports Series.) Ithaca, N.Y., 1957. A scholarly and pioneering study of high quality.

Mozingo, David P. "New Developments in China's Relations with Indo-nesia," *Current Scene,* vol. I, no. 24 (Feb. 5, 1962). An excellent account by a knowledgeable scholar.

——. "The Sino-Indonesian Dual Nationality Treaty," *Asian Survey,* vol. I, no. 10 (Dec. 1961).

Palmier, Leslie H. *Indonesia and the Dutch*. London: Oxford University Press, 1962. An interesting account, but one which suffers from an undue preoccupation with divisions of interest between Javanese and non-Javanese Indonesians and from an endeavor to interpret Indonesian domestic politics and external policy too much in terms of this factor.

Pauker, Guy J. "The Soviet Challenge to Indonesia," *Foreign Affairs*, XL, no. 4 (July 1962), 612–626. A pessimistic analysis and prognosis.

Smith, T. E. "The Brunei Revolt: Background and Consequences," *World Today*, XIX, no. 3 (April 1963), 135–138.

Taylor, Alastair M. *Indonesian Independence and the United Nations*. (See same reference above, in the section "The Revolution.")

van der Veur, Paul. "West Irian: A New Era," *Asian Survey*, II, no. 8 (Oct. 1962), 1–8. An informative report based on field research in West Irian shortly before the Dutch withdrew.

Williams, Lea E. "Sino-Indonesian Diplomacy: A Study of Revolutionary International Politics," *China Quarterly*, July–Sept. 1962, pp. 184–199.

Willmott, Donald E. *The National Status of the Chinese in Indonesia, 1900–1958*. (Cornell Modern Indonesia Project, Monograph Series.) Ithaca, N.Y., 1961. A substantial, balanced, and very useful study.

INDEX

Index

(C = China; I = India; Is = Indonesia; J = Japan; P = Pakistan)

Abdullah, Sheikh, 309-310
Afghanistan, 522-523
Agha Khan, the, 424
Agrarian problems, *see* Economic problems *and* Peasantry
Agrarian Reform Act of 1950 (C), 54
Agricultural Association (J), 209
Agricultural Co-operative Association (J), 209
Ahmad, Farid, 498, 503
Aidit, D. N., 616, 654-655, 657
Akali Dal Party (I), 347
Akbar, 273
Aksai Chin Plateau, 69, 72, 74, 104, 125
Ali, Chaudhri Mohamad, 435, 437, 439, 478-479, 487, 495, 503, 518
Ali, Maulana Muhammad, 426-427
Ali, Mohammed (of Bogra), 436, 478, 498
Ali Sastroamidjojo, 606, 620-623; cabinets of, 616-617, 620-623, 626, 633, 635, 641
Aligarh, 423
All-China Congress of Soviets: First, 37; Second, 38
All-Japan Trade Union Congress, 207
All-Pakistan Confederation of Labour, 513
Allied Occupation of Japan: purge, 229-230; reform policies, 172
Allison, John, 682
Ambedkar, Dr. B. R., 311, 316, 347-348
American occupation, *see* Allied Occupation of Japan
Amin, Nurul, 481, 503
Amir Ali, Syed, 427
Amoy, 130
Anak Agung, a Federalist, 594n; *see also* Federal government

Ancestor worship, 12
Andhra: communism in, 356; creation of, 366
Annam, *see* Vietnam
Annihilation campaigns (C), 37-38
Anshary, Isa, 613, 623
Antirightist struggle (C), 64
ANZUS Treaty, 130
Armed forces (C): Chinese Red Army, 35-37, 43, 45, 54; First Front Army, 38; Second Front Army, 39; Fourth Front Army, 39; Eighth Route Army, 41; New Fourth Army, 46
Armed forces (I), 308-309; *see also* British Indian army *and* Indian National Army
Armed forces (Is), 561, 572, 581-585, 595, 599-600, 610, 619, 621-626 *passim*, 645-646, 653-654; control over, 586, 603-604, 619, 621-622, 629, 645-646, 672; economic program, 671, 673; extramilitary role, 583-585, 631-632, 636, 640-644, 649, 653, 657-658, 670-672; modern build-up, 671n; *see also* Peta *and* Power struggle
Armed forces (J): Cherry Blossom Society, 168; Control faction, 170; discontent, 167-170; factions in, 170; Imperial Way faction, 170; National Defense Force, 251; National Police Reserve Force, 251; National Safety Force, 251; role in government, 164, 170, 177; *see also* Militarism *and* Rearmament
Armed forces (P), 472-473, 484, 496, 505, 520
Aryans, 269-270
Ashida, Hitoshi, 231

Asian-African Conference, 59, 127, 620, 681
Asian Solidarity Committee, 123
Asoka, 271
Assam, 69, 72
Association of Political Friends (J), 212
Atjehnese, revolt of, 620
Atom-free zone, 114
Atomic weapons, protests against testing (J), 257
Attlee, Clement, 296, 297
Aurangzeb, 273, 274
Australia, 130, 560; China's relations with, 70, 106, 122
Autumn Harvest Rising, 35, 36
Awami League (P), 438, 439, 448, 484-493 *passim,* 506, 524
Azad, Abul Kalam, 427, 430
Azad Pakistan Party, 492-493
Azahari, A. M., 684; *see also* Malaysia, Federation of
Aziz Saleh, 645

"Backyard steel" campaign, 66
Badan Pekerdja, *see* Komite Nasional Indonesia Pusat
Baghdad Pact, *see* CENTO
Bahawalpur, 430, 459
Bakshi Ghulam Mohammed, 310
Baluchistan, 430, 458; States Union, 459
Ban, 233
Bandung Conference, *see* Asian-African Conference
Barisan Tani Indonesia, 558; *see also* Peasantry
Barlian, Lt. Col., 624, 648
Basic Democracies (P), 440, 465, 466, 469, 496, 500, 504; district councils, 440, 465-467; divisional councils, 440, 465-467; tehsil/thana councils, 440, 465-466; union councils, 440, 465, 496, 515
Bengal, partition of: *1905-1912,* 424-425; *1947,* 430, 485, 516
Bengal, East, *see* East Pakistan
Bengali language, 442-443, 483
Bentinck, Lord William, 276
Beria, Lavrenti, 60
Berlin, 120
Bhashani, Maulana Abdul Hamid Khan, 484, 486, 493
Bhave, Vinoba, 355, 374, 379-380; *see also* Bhoodan Yagna movement
Bhoodan Yagna movement, 351, 355, 379-381
Black Dragon Society, 583n
Bolshevik Revolution, 34, 52, 84
Bose, Subhas Chandra, 291-293

Boxer Rebellion, 19, 20
Brainwashing, 96
British, in India: *to 1857,* 274-277; *1857–1945,* 277-294; transfer of power (1945–1947), 294-300
British Borneo, 127
British East India Company, 276, 278
British Indian army, 280
British occupation (Is), 543
Buddhism, 8, 108, 446, 489, 536, 537
Budiono, 617n
Bureau of National Reconstruction (P), 496
Bureaucracy and civil service: in China, 13; in India, 279, 334, 553; in Indonesia, 549-554, 560, 576, 577-585 *passim,* 587-589, 611, 614, 634, 640-641, 676 (see also *Pamong pradja*); in Japan, 166, 195-198, 232, 242-244; in Pakistan, 440, 467, 468-471, 484, 496, 505; Civil Service of Pakistan (CSP), 467, 468, 469; Indian Civil Service (ICS), 279, 467, 468, 553
Burhanuddin Harahap, 606, 609, 611, 621, 646-647
Burma, 69, 70, 127; Burma Road, 43; China's relations with, 6, 104-107 *passim,* 116, 122, 124
Business community: in India, 377; in Indonesia, 578-579, 611, 618, 639; in Japan, 204-205

Cabinet Mission, 1946 (I), 430
Cabinets (I), *see* Council of Ministers
Cabinets (Is): *revolutionary,* 565-574; and KNIP, 570-571; and parliament, 567, 570; problems of, 573-574; *post-revolutionary,* 592-594, 618-626; and parliament, 601-603, 606-609, 620-625, 633, 639-640, 665-666; and the president, 602-604, 606; formateurs, 593n, 601, 619, 621n, 643; problems of, 626-632; six parliament-based cabinets, 618-626; *see also* Federal government *and* Presidency
Cabinets (J), 192-195
Cabinets (P), 435, 437, 439, 452, 473, 487, 491, 505; provincial, 460
Cairo Conference, 134, 138
Calcutta: riots in (1947), 304; Youth Conference, 117
Canton, 15, 20, 26-27, 29, 42, 50; Canton Commune, 35
Capitalism (J), 160, 167, 177-179
Capitalism, Indonesian view of, 550, 551, 611n, 615n, 653-654
Caste system, 270; *see also* Untouchables, in India

Castro, Fidel, 73, 121, 128
Catholic Party (Is), 599, 610n, 619
CC Clique, 30, 43
Celebes Rebellion, *see* Sumatra-Celebes Rebellion
CENTO, 522, 523, 524
Central Asia, 4, 7; China's relations with, 4, 8, 9
Centre-state relations, 320, 329
Ceylon, 74, 122, 134; China's relations with, 106, 122, 124, 129
Chahar, 94
Chairul Saleh, 667
Chamber of Commerce and Industry (J), 204-205
Chamber of Representatives (Is), 565
Chamdo, 94, 101
Chang Kuo-t'ao, 39, 40, 44
Chang Tso-lin, 23
Changchun, 47
Changchun Railway, 55
Changsha, 36, 37
Charter Act of 1833 (I), 276
Chelmsford, Lord, 285
Ch'en Ch'eng, 134, 135
Ch'en Kuo-fu, 30, 33
Ch'en Li-fu, 30-33
Ch'en Shao-yü, *see* Wang Ming
Ch'en Tu-hsiu, 24, 34, 35
Chen Yi, 134
Ch'en Yün, 77
Cheng Feng, *see* Rectification
Chengtu, 50
Chiang Ching-kuo, 135, 136
Chiang Kai-shek, 27-42 *passim,* 72, 130-131, 135-138
Ch'ien-lung Emperor, 10, 15
Ch'in dynasty, 5, 7, 8, 12
Ch'in Pang-hsien, *see* Po Ku
Ch'in Shih Huang Ti, 5
China: censorate, 13; Central, 35, 37; East, 41, 60; Emperor, 7, 12-13; empire, 4-15, 101-102; North, 4, 8, 9, 21, 34, 42, 46; Northeast, 5, 23, 25, 28, 43; prehistory, 4; renaissance, 24; revolution, 21, 23; South, 5-9 *passim,* 21, 27, 35, 54; Southwest, 5, 28, 43, 46; Western impact upon, 3, 10, 15-25 *passim*
China, Communist, *see* China, foreign relations; Chinese People's Republic; *and* Communist China, governmental bodies
China, Communist Party of, 9; agricultural policy, 61, 65-66, 98-99; alliance with Kuomintang, 27-28, 29, 33; cadres, 54, 79, 95-96, 107; Central Committee. 46, 61, 74, 76-77, 81, 83,
86, 98; Congresses: First (1921), 34; Second (1922), 34; Sixth (1928), 35, 46; Seventh (1945), 46, 76; Eighth (First Session, 1956), 65, 76-77, 79, 83, (Second Session, 1958), 65, 76-77; Ninth, 81; constitution: of 1945, 74, 76; of 1956, 76, 78; Control Commission, 77; economic policy, 3, 59-60, 63-67 *passim,* 98-107, 131; factional differences, 80-81; fiscal policy, 54; foreign policy objectives, 115-116; foundation of, 24, 34; General Office, 77; history of (to 1949), 34-41; local organizations, 78; membership, 78; military committee, 77, 111; National Party Congress, 74; Organization Department, 77; Politburo, 60, 76-77, 93, 111-112; Propaganda Department, 77; regional bureaus, 60, 70, 77-78; Rural Work Department, 77; Secretariat, 76, 77; Social Affairs Department, 77; succession to Mao, 80-81; United Front with National Government, 40-43; United Front Work Department, 77, 82
China, foreign relations with: Africa, 118, 122, 127-128; Albania, 71, 106, 118, 122-123; Algeria, 106-107, 116, 128; Arab states, 122; Brazil, 129; British Commonwealth, 122; Cambodia, 73, 106, 122, 124-125, 129; Canada, 70, 106, 122; Chile, 129; Congo, 128; Egypt, 106; France, 15, 17, 58; Guinea, 106, 125, 128; Laos, 122, 126; Nepal, 70, 72, 106, 116, 122, 124; Netherlands, 15, 122; Pakistan, 73, 122, 125-126; Philippines, 125, 138; Somalia, 128; South Africa, 122; Switzerland, 122; Yemen, 106; Zanzibar, 128; *see also* Australia, Burma, Central Asia, Ceylon, Cuba, Germany, Great Britain, India, Indonesia, Japan, Korea, Malaya, Mongolia (Outer), New Zealand, Southeast Asia, Soviet Union, Thailand, United States, Vietnam, *and* Yugoslavia
China, National Government of (1928-1949), 29, 38, 41, 43, 104; functioning of, 32-33; State Council, 31; united front with Communist Party, 40-43
China, Republic of (1949-), 56, 68, 71-72, 85, 113, 117, 122, 129, 130-138
Chinese, migration of, 5-7, 133; *see also* Overseas Chinese
Chinese dynasties: dynastic cycle, 7; role of gentry in, 7, 8, 10, 11, 13
Chinese People's Republic: Central Peo-

Chinese People's Republic (*cont.*)
ple's Government Council, 86, 88, 90; Chairman of, 88, 90; constitution of 1954, 61, 82, 86-88; history of, 52-74; local government, 91-93; mass organizations in, 83-85; Ministry of Defense, 88, 90, 111-112; Ministry of Public Security, 96; minor parties in, 51, 78, 82-83; National Defense Council, 88, 111; Organic Law, 85-86; People's Armed Police, 96; People's Congresses, 85-86; People's Revolutionary Military Council, 88; regionalism in, 60-61, 91; State Council, 90, 91, 93-94; Supreme People's Court, 91; Supreme People's Procurator's Office, 91; totalitarianism of, 101-102; views regarding possible future world war, 112-113; *see also* Communist China, governmental bodies

Chinese People's Volunteers, 57, 67

Ch'ing dynasty, 10, 13, 18, 20; fall of, 21, 47

Chinggis Khan, 9

Choshu, 162, 228

Chou dynasty, 5

Chou En-lai, 35-44 *passim,* 55, 57, 59-63, 69, 71, 77, 80-81, 87, 90, 98, 111-112, 125

Christian Party (Is), 599, 600, 610n, 613, 617, 618-619

Christianity: in China, 15-16, 17, 25, 108; in Indonesia, 547; in Pakistan, 446, 489, 506

Ch'ü Ch'iu-pai, 35

Chu Teh, 36, 38, 39, 77

Chundrigar, Ismail I., 439, 479, 487

Chungking, 42, 43, 50

Civil liberties: in India, 328; in Japan, 183-184; in Pakistan, 448, 457, 471, 473, 508-509

Civil service: *see* Bureaucracy and civil service

Clive, Robert, 275

Coalition government (C), 45-48

Cochran, Merle, 619

Comintern (C), 34-39; alliance with Kuomintang, 26-28, 35; Seventh Congress, 40

Common law (P), 470-471

Common Market, 120

Common Program (C), 82, 85, 87

Commonwealth, the: and India, 322; and Pakistan, 492, 515, 523

Communalism (I), 302-304; communal parties, 344-348

Communism: in India, 353-355; in In-donesia, 562, 586, 617n, 680, 681n; Soekarno's views on, 599-601, 639; in Japan, 210-211, 217; *see also* specific Communist parties

Communist China, governmental bodies: Chinese People's Political Consultative Conference, 52, 82, 85, 87; Major Administrative Committees, 60-61, 91; National People's Congress, 66, 81-82, 86-94 *passim;* State Planning Committee, 59-60, 90; Supreme State Conference, 61, 63, 88, 90, 98; *see also* Chinese People's Republic

Communist International, *see* Comintern

Communist Party, in Pakistan, 493-494, 500

Communist Party, Indonesian, 548, 562, 570, 578, 601, 607, 609-610, 615-626, 639, 643-646, 647n, 649, 651, 654-657, 661, 663-667, 670, 678, 680n, 681n, 687; fund raising, 618; growth of, 617-618; Murba, 666; Soekarno's views concerning, 592-599, 605, 625, 642, 651-652, 657; *see also* Communism *and* Power struggle

Communist Party, Japanese, 210, 214; Cominform criticism of, 210, 217

Communist Party of China, *see* China, Communist Party of

Communist Party of India, 353-359; and Chinese Communists, 357, 358; divisions within, 358

Communist Party of the Soviet Union, 76, 78; Twentieth Congress, 62; Twenty-second Congress, 71; *see also* Moscow

Communist Youth League, 76, 79

Community Development Program (I), 332

Confucianism, 8-13 *passim,* 29-30, 109

Congo, 128

Congress, Pakistan National, 438, 475, 489, 490, 500

Congress Party (I), *see* Indian National Congress

Constantine, Emperor, 15

Constituent Assembly (I), 295-296, 311, 322; consideration of constitution of India, 312

Constituent Assembly (Is), 602, 609, 623n, 663, 664; dismissal of, 629

Constituent Assembly (P), 434-437, 448, 460, 472, 475, 478, 485, 487, 488, 489; dissolution, 437, 450, 460; function of, 434; membership in, 434, 438, 490, 493, 494

Constitution (I), 302, 310; drafting of,

Constitution (I) (*cont.*)
312; nature of, 313-316, 321; operation of, 321-334

Constitution (Is): *of 1945,* 564-565, 570-571, 590-595, 638, (return to) 660-667; *of 1949* (Federal), 590-593, (Article 139) 592; *of 1950* (Unitary), 594-597, 601-605, 627, 638, 663; *see also* Hatta *and* Soekarno

Constitution (J): *of 1889,* 164-165, 181-182; *of 1947,* 182-186, 218, 251

Constitution (P): *of 1956,* 438-439, 448, 449, 461-462, 471, 482, 487; *of 1962,* 440, 448-454 *passim,* 460, 462, 471, 482-483, 497, 503, 505, 508; amendment of, 464, 473, 509; Islamic principles in, 445-446, 473, 503; principles of law making, 445-446, 448, 471, 473; principles of policy, 445, 473, 514, 521

Constitutional Association (J), 212

Consultative Assembly (Is), 564-565, 659, 667

Contradictions, Doctrine of, 63-64

Co-operative Movement in Indonesia, 605n

Corruption, 586, 596, 606-608, 621-623, 633, 654-660, 672, 676

Council of Ministers (I), 317, 318, 325

Cripps, Sir Stafford, 292, 294

Crown prince (J), 187

Cuba, 121; China's relations with, 106, 122, 128; Cuban missile crisis, 73, 128; *see also* Castro

Cultivation System, 544-547

Curzon, Lord, 283

Dairen, 56

Dalai Lama, 69

Dange, S. A., 356-358, 375

Darshan, 374

Darul Islam, 585, 599-600; *see also* Islamic State (Is)

Daultana, Mian Mumtaz Muhammad Khan, 491, 502

Decentralization (Is): in precolonial period, 540; in modern period, 586, 591, 598, 622, 634, 644-645, 674-675

Decision making, 144, 207, 208, 323, 325, 568, 587-590, 634, 640; *see also* Harmony and *Musjawarat-mufakat*

Defense problems (J), 250-254

Delhi Sultanate, 272

Democracy (Is), 540, 586; Democratic League, 665; Indonesian views on, 559, 624-625, 627-628; *see also* Guided Democracy *and* Parliamentary democracy

Democracy (J), 258-259

Democratic centralism (C), 26, 29, 74, 76, 86

Democratic Party (J), 215-216

Democratic Republic of Vietnam, *see* Vietnam

Democratic Socialist Party (C), 135

Democratic-Socialist Party (J), 207, 217

Depression, the, 33

Dictatorship of the proletariat, 82, 84

Diem, Ngo Dinh, 59n

Dienbienphu, 58

Diet, *see* Imperial Diet *and* National Diet

Disarmament, 114-115, 120-121

District officer (I), 279, 331

Djuanda Kartawidjaja, 643-648, 661

Dual-nationality agreement (Is), 686-687; *see also* Overseas Chinese, in Indonesia

Dulles, John F., 648, 682, 684-685

Dupleix, Gov.-Gen., 275

Dutch East India Company, 541-543

Dyarchy and Government of India Act: *1919,* 286; *1935,* 289

East Pakistan (East Bengal), 431, 434, 442, 443, 447, 458, 460, 461, 465, 467-469, 474, 475, 481-490, 505; autonomy for, 435, 436, 486-88; economic development in, 463, 473, 482, 512, 520; elections in, 436, 481, 484, 486, 488; politics in, 438, 439, 481-490, 493-495, 500, 506; provincial assembly, 438, 481, 482, 489, 490, 495

Eastern Railway (C), 25

Economic development (C), 11; agriculture, 5, 24, 103-104, 131, 132, 137; *see also* Agrarian Reform Act *and* China, Communist Party of

Economic development (Is), 537-539, 546-547, 550-551, 577-579, 637-639, 651, 668, 673, 675-677, 679-680

Economic development (J), 104, 249

Economic development (P), 510-514

Economic problems (Is), 547, 550-551, 562-563, 579-583, 622, 643-645, 654, 660, 662, 667-668, 672, 675-680; Chinese economic role in Java, 542-543; debt settlement with Netherlands, 563; foreign indebtedness, 679

Economic problems (J), 245-250

Education: in India, 549: in Indonesia, 547-550, 553, 575-576, 581, 584; in Philippines, 549

Eisenhower, Dwight D., 69, 118, 130, 137, 253-254

Elder Statesman (J), 164, 177
Election Commission (P), 451, 453, 497
Elections (I): electoral procedures, 364, 367, 368; in British India, 290, 295; in Republic of India, 320, 362-364, (1951-1952) 302, 364, (1957) 302, 364-368, (1962) 302, 369-370; preparations for, 362, 363; states' elections, 367
Elections (Is), 565, 569, 586-587, 593, 596, 602, 608-615, 617, 620-623, 628, 634, 647, 661-663, 667
Elections (J), 213, 215; campaign expenditures for, 232, 237; coercion in voting, 239; "election brokers," 237; electoral behavior, 233-240; electoral districts, 237, 239
Elections (P), 451, 453, 480-481, 501; electoral colleges, 451, 453, 466, 497; for Basic Democracies, 1959-1960, 448, 500; legislative indirect elections, 1962, 440, 497; presidential, 451; provincial, 480-481, 484, 490, 494 (*see also* specific provinces); referenda, 440, 455, 464, 466; separate electorates, 447, 448, 489-491
Elective Bodies Disqualification Order, 1959 (P), 499-500, 502-504
Emergency powers (P), 457, 461-462, 509-510; governor's rule, 435, 461-462, 487, 488, 491, 493; state of emergency, 437-438, 440
Emperor (J), 154-155, 164, 175, 182, 186-189, 218; as symbol, 186-188; Imperial House Law, 182; Imperial Household Ministry, 177, 188; political role of, 188-189
Empress Dowager, the, 19-20
English language, 442, 483
Eurasians, in Indonesia, 581–582
Europe, Eastern, 55-56, 63-64, 82, 96, 117, 123
Extraterritoriality, 16, 33

Family, the (J), 173-175
Farm Organizations (J), 208-209
Farmers (J), 208-209
Federal Court (P), *see* Judicial process (P)
Federal government (Is), 590-596; Federalists, 561, 573, 580, 590-591, 593-594, 608; *see also* Constitution (Is)
Federalism: in India, 314, 320, 329; in Pakistan, 463-464, 505
Federalists (Is), *see* Federal government

Federation of Economic Organizations (J), 204-205
Federation of Housewives (J), 209
Feng Yü-hsiang, 23, 29
Feudalism: in China, 5; in Japan, 155-157, 162
Filial piety, and political loyalty (J), 174-175, 186
Finance Commission (P), 463, 464
Finland, 124
"Five Anti" campaign, *see* Wu Fan campaign
Five Principles of Peaceful Coexistence, 55, 61
Five Year Plan (I): First, 302, 384-385; Second, 302, 385-386; Third, 302, 386-387
Five Year Plan (P), 514
Foochow, 130
Foreign relations, *see* separate country headings
Foreign trade: Japan, 159, 249-250; Pakistan, 512
Formosa, *see* Taiwan
Formosa Resolution, 130
Fukien, 17, 29, 38, 134
Functional groups (Is), 639-640, 663-665, 667-668; *see also* National Front
Fundamental rights (I), 328
Fundamental rights (P), 448, 457, 471, 473, 508-509
Furnivall, J. S., 544n, 545

Ganatantri Dal (P), 493
Gandhi, Mohandas K., 286, 374, 379; assassination of, 345; at second Round Table Conference, 288; in Calcutta (1947), 304; noncooperation campaign, 287, 291; on Khilafat movement, 287; on partition, 297; on role of Congress Party after independence, 338; salt march (1930), 288
General Council of Japan Labor Organizations, 206
General Council of Trade Unions of Japan, 206-207, 222
Geneva Conference, on Indochina, 58-59
Genghis Khan, *see* Chinggis Khan
Geography, influence of (Is), 536, 581, 585, 674, 680, 685
Germany, 117; China's relations with, 17, 22, 29
Goa, 275, 519
Gokhale, G. K., 283
Government of India Act: *1919*, 285-286; *1935*, 289, 313, 428, 433, 448n, 449-452, 462, 470-471, 482, 508

Governor-General (P), 433, 436, 437, 450-452, 472, 478n, 524; *see also* Presidency, in Pakistan

Governors (P), *see* Provincial government (P)

Great Britain, foreign relations, 58, 73
with China, 15-17, 33, 43, 122
with India: before independence, 274, 300; since independence, 400; *see also* British, in India
with Pakistan, 523

Great Leap Forward (C), 65-66, 68, 80, 103, 107, 109, 112, 118, 119; termination of, 70, 100, 102, 132

Great Wall, 4, 5

Green Island, 135

Guerrilla warfare (C), 36-37, 43-44, 55, 58

Guided Democracy (Is), 604, 624-625, 636-669, 674, 676

Guided economy (Is), *see* Economic development (Is)

Gupta empire, 271

Gurmani, Mushtaq Ahmad, 490

Hague Conference, *see* Round Table Conference

Hainan, 45, 134

Hamid, Sultan, 594

Han dynasty, 7, 8

Hankow, 21, 27-28, 42

Harmony, Indonesian emphasis upon, 540-541, 559, 628, 637; *see also* Decision making

Harsha, 271

Hastings, Warren, 276

Hatoyama Ichiro, 216-217, 228, 231

Hatta, Mohammad, 548, 556-572 *passim*, 612n, 621-626, 631, 643-645, 648; and the vice-presidency, 604-606; cabinet of, 594-596; on Soekarno's proposed cabinet, 625-626, 682n; resignation of, 606, 624

Hawaii, 20

Hay, John, 18

Heilungkiang, 94

High Advisory Council (Is), 564-565, 570, 596, 659, 664, 666, 674; *see also* National Council

Hindu Code Bill, 328

Hindu Mahasabha (I), 345, 346

Hinduism: in India, 269, 270; in Indonesia, 536-538, 612-613; in Pakistan, 431-433, 446-448, 474-475, 489-490, 506

Hirano Rikizo, 234

Hitler, Adolf, 31

Ho Chi Minh, 58, 59n

Ho Lung, 39

Holy See, 16, 108

Hong Kong, 20, 105

House of Councilors (J), 191

House of Peers (J), 189

House of Representatives (Is): federal, 591, 593; unitary, 595, 596, 601, 602, 608

House of Representatives (J), 164, 191-193

Hsiang (rural district), 92

Hsien (county), 13, 32, 91

Hsuchow, 50

Hu Shih, 24

Huhehot, 95

Hunan, 35-36, 39, 42

Hundred Days Reform, 19

Hundred Flowers Campaign, 63, 98

Hungary, 1956 crisis in, 62-63, 119

Hunza, 105

Huq, A. K. Fazlul, 488

Hurley, Patrick J., 45

Hussein, Lt. Col. Achmad, 624, 646

Hyderabad, 516-517, 518

Iftikharuddin, Mian, 492, 508

Ikeda, Hayato, 231

Imperial Agricultural Association (J), 208

Imperial Diet (J), 164, 182, 189-190

Imperial Rule Assistance Association (J), 171-172, 214

Independence Preparatory Committee (Is), 559, 564, 568n; replaced by KNIP, 565; *see also* Komite Nasional Indonesia Pusat

India, foreign relations, 106
concern for persons of Indian origin, 399
factors conditioning, 388-390
foreign policy of Indian National Congress, 391-392
nonalignment policy, 388, 389, 392-393, 402
with Arab states, 399
with China, 56, 58, 118, 122, 124-126, 388-389, 393, 398-399; Sino-Indian border dispute, 69, 71-74, 116, 118-119, 125
with Great Britain, 400
with Indonesia, 536
with Pakistan, 394-397; canal waters question, 394-395; dispute over Kashmir, 395-397
with South America, 399
with Soviet Union, 106, 397-398
with United States, 400, 401

Indian Civil Service, *see* Bureaucracy and civil service

Indian Independence Act (1947), 437

Indian Independence Bill, 298

Indian National Army, 291-293

Indian National Congress, 280, 287, 337-343, 424-433 *passim*, 474-475, 490, 492, 517; All-India Congress Committee, 341; Avadi resolution (1955), 340, 383; Congress Party in Parliament, 326; crisis of 1950-1951, 339; founding of, 282; ministries, formed by 1937, 290, by 1946, 295; moderates and extremists in, 283-284; noncooperation during Second World War, 291, 292; organization of, 341-342; organizational problems of, 338-339, 342; position in Indian states, 330, 331; resolutions on foreign policy, 391; Working Committee, 323, 341-342

Indian states: Centre-state relations, 320, 329; directive principles of Indian states policy, 316; government of, 319; Part "A" states, 316, 319; Part "B" states, 316, 319; Part "C" states, 316, 319, 320; reorganization of, 320, 365; States Reorganization Commission, 302, 366

Indochina, *see* Vietnam

Indonesia, foreign relations, 679-680, 681-687; with China, 69, 70, 73, 106, 118, 122, 124, 127, 129, 536, 617-618, 639, 656, 680-681, 685-687 (*see also* Overseas Chinese); with Formosa, 647, 684-685; with Great Britain, 560-561, 684; with Korea, 647, 685; with Malaya, 672n, 684; with Soviet Union, 106, 651, 673, 679, 681-685; with United States, 563, 619, 647-648, 679, 680n, 682-685; *see also* Japan

Indonesian language, 536, 556, 557

"Informal government" (J), 176, 179-180, 227

Intellectuals, *see* Political elite and intellectuals

Inter-Indonesian Conferences (1949), 590; National Preparatory Committee, 593n

Inukai Tsuyoshi, 169, 212

Iqbal, Sir Muhammad, 428

Iraq, 118, 128

Irian Barat, *see* West Irian

Iskaq Tjokrohadisurjo, 620

Islam (C), 8, 108

Islam (I), 272, 274

Islam (Is), 536-538, 558-559, 585, 598, 605, 613, 617, 670; *see also* Islamic State *and* Modernist Islamic thought

Islam (P), 444-445, 446, 470-471, 494-495, 500, 521; Advisory Council of Islamic ideology, 446, 473, 509; Islamic Laws Commission, 445; modernist thought in, 445; traditionalism in, 444, 494; *see also* Islamic State (P)

Islamic State (Is), 585, 599, 611, 613, 617, 620, 663; *see also* Darul Islam, Masjumi, *and* Partai Sarekat Islam

Islamic State (P), 433, 434, 436, 445, 446, 447, 489, 494; *see also* Jama'at-i-Islami-Pakistan *and* Nizam-i-Islam Party

Isolation policy (J), 159-160

Ito Hirobumi, 163, 212

Iwa Kusumasumantri, 621

Jama'at-i-Islami-Pakistan, 495, 503, 504

Jammu, *see* Kashmir

Jan Sangh Party (I), 345

Jani, Gen., 657, 673

Jao Shu-shih, 60, 77, 80, 91

Japan, foreign relations: influence of occupation upon Indonesia, 565-568, 575-577, 583-585, 619, 627-628, 630, 641; occupation of Indonesia, 555-569, 628, 630; with China, 4, 8, 17, 19-20, 22, 24, 28, 32-34, 40-46, 55, 57, 61, 105, 126-127, 134, 137, 138, 167-168, 170-171, 218, 250, 255-256; with Korea, 256-257; *see also* other country headings *and* Sino-Japanese War

Japan Farmers' Union, 208

Japan Federation of Employers' Associations, 204-205

Japan Management Association, 204-205

Javanese aristocracy, Dutch use of, 541-547, 614; regents, 544-545

Jehol, 33, 95

Jenghiz Khan, *see* Chinggis Khan

Jesus, Society of, 15-17

Jiban, 236-237

Jinnah, Mohammed Ali, 293, 295, 420, 428-434 *passim*, 444, 447, 475-478, 480, 483; as Governor-General, 433, 451, 475; death of, 434; on Hindu-Muslim relations, 296n

Jinnah Awami Muslim League (P), 484

Jiyuto (J), 162, 211, 214

Juchen, 8, 9

Judicial process (J), 198-200; attitudes toward law, 200-201; Supreme Court, 198-200

Judicial process (P), 470-472, 473, 509; Code of Criminal Procedure, 507; High Courts, 451, 470, 471, 499, 508; Supreme Court (formerly Federal Court), 437, 454, 470, 471, 473, 498n, 499, 500-501, 508; Supreme Judicial Council, 470; writ jurisdiction, 471
Judiciary, *see* Judicial process
Juichin, 36, 37, 38
Junagadh, 516, 518

Kaban, 237-238
Kadar, Janos, 71
Kaishinto (J), 162, 212
K'ang Yu-wei, 19, 20
K'ang-hsi Emperor, 10, 16
Kansu, 39, 101
Kao Kang, 60, 62n, 80, 91, 94
Karachi, 431, 483, 495; federal district, 459; merger with West Pakistan, 460
Kartosuwirjo, 600
Kashgar, 104
Kashmir, 69, 73, 101, 104-105, 434; Azad Kashmir, 460, 519; Indo-Pakistan dispute over, 308, 309, 395-397, 517-519, 524; Maharajah of, 309; position in Indian Union, 310
Kassem, Abdul Karim el, 128
Kato, Takaakira, 212
Kautilya, 270
Kawilarang, Col., 623
Kazakhs, 101
Kennedy, John F., 131, 683
Kerala, 69, 121, 324; Communist government in, 353, 357
Khairpur, 430, 459
Khaliquzzaman, Choudhry, 478, 502
Khan, Abdul Ghaffar, 474, 492-493
Khan, Ataur Rahman, 482n, 485, 487, 499
Khan, Khan Abdul Qaiyum, 479, 499
Khan, Liaqat Ali, 295, 434-435, 475, 477-478, 480
Khan, Field Marshal Mohammed Ayub, 437-438, 440, 449-450, 452, 466, 469, 472, 496-498, 501, 504, 510, 523, 524-525
Khan, Sardar Bahadur, 441, 498, 502
Khan, Sir Sayyid Ahmad, 282, 423, 427
Khan, Tamizuddin, 454
Khan Sahib, Dr., 438, 490-492
Khilafat movement, 287, 425, 427
Khitan, 9
Khrushchev, Nikita Sergeievich, 61, 67-73, 113-114, 118-119, 120; attack on Stalin, 61-62
Khubilai Khan, 9

Khuhro, Mohammed Ayub, 491
Kiangsi, 36-38, 40
Kirin, 94
Kishi, Nobusuke, 231, 253-254
Kita, Ikki, 169
KNIP, *see* Komite Nasional Indonesia Pusat
Kokutai, 186
Komite Nasional Indonesia Pusat (Central Indonesian National Committee), 565-571; Working Committee (Badan Pekerdja), 566-571 *passim*, 589, 595n, 596; *see also* Sjahrir, Soetan
Korea, 130; China's relations with, 4, 10, 15, 22, 56-57, 67, 106, 116, 123, 125
Korean War, 59, 116, 130, 137, 675; armistice negotiations, 58; Chinese role in, 54, 56-57, 102, 116, 117
Kripalani, Acharya, 339, 351
Krishak Sramik Party (P), 486, 487, 488-489, 490
Krishna Menon, V. K., 72, 73; electoral victory in Bombay (1962), 370
Kuang-hsü Emperor, 19, 20
Kung, H. H., 33
Kuomintang, 22, 23, 26, 135, 136-138; alliance with Comintern, 26-28, 35; Central Advisory Committee, 136; Central Committee, 136; Central Executive Committee, 31, 32, 136; Central Reform Committee, 136; Central Supervisory Committee, 136; decline of, 43, 48-50, 98; foundation of, 21; in power, 28-33; Political Council, 31; struggle with Communists, 28, 29, 34, 35-40, 42, 43-50, 55; Youth Corps, 135
Kuomintang, Left, 28-30, 37
Kwangming Daily, 83
Kwangsi, 42
Kwangsi Ch'uang Autonomous Region, 91
Kwangsi Clique, 29
Kweichow, 39
Kweisui, 95

Labor: in China (forced labor), 96-97; in Japan, 205-208; in Pakistan, 513
Labor-boss system (J), 227
Labor-Farmer Party (J), 213
Labor organizations: in Indonesia, 556, 578, 646, 653, 659 (*see also* SOBSI); in Japan, 205-208
Ladakh, 69, 72
Lahore Resolution, 291, 432, 487, 488
Lanchow, 101

Land laws of 1870s (Is), *see* Land ownership

Land reform (J), 179

Land reform (P): East Pakistan, 443, 472, 486, 511; West Pakistan, 440, 443, 510-511

Land tenure (J), *see* Landlords

Landlords (J), 179, 208

Landownership: in Indonesia, 545-546, 578, 611; in Japan, 159, 226

Languages (I), 321

Latin America, 71, 118, 122, 128-129

Leadership (I), 325, 330

Lebanon, 67, 118, 128

Legalism (C), 5, 12

Legislatures (C), *see* China, Communist Party of; China, National Government of (1928-1949); Communist China, governmental bodies; National Assembly (C); National People's Convention; *and* People's Political Council

Legislatures (Is), *see* House of Representatives (Is), Komite Nasional Indonesia Pusat, National Council, Parliamentary democracy, *and* Senate

Legislatures (J), *see* House of Councilors, House of Peers, House of Representatives (J), Imperial Diet, *and* National Diet

Legislatures (P), *see* Constituent Assembly (P), National Assembly (P), *and* Provincial government (provincial assemblies)

Lei Chen, 136

Leimena, Johannes, 645

Lenin, Vladimir Ilyich, 25, 26, 44, 45, 70, 119n

Lhasa, 69, 101, 104

Li Li-san, 35, 36, 37, 46

Li Teh, 38

Li Tsung-jen, 29

Liang Ch'i-ch'ao, 19, 20

Liaoning, 94

Liberal Democratic Party (J), 217-220, 232

Liberal Party (J), 214-217, 229-230

Lin Piao, 50, 68, 77, 91

Lin Po-ch'ü, 77n

Linggadjati Agreement, 561-562

Linguistic states question (I), 329, 340-341, 367; Dar Commission, 366

Liu Lan-t'ao, 91

Liu Po-ch'eng, 91

Liu Shao-ch'i, 60, 65, 66, 76, 77, 80, 81, 88, 90, 111, 117, 132

Local government (I), 331; municipal government, 332

Local government (Is): Sumatra, 572-574; village, 586-587, 637-638, 660; *see also* Regionalism

Local government (J), 159, 201; Local Autonomy Agency, 202; Local Autonomy Law, 202

Local government (P), 464, 465; municipal, 464, 465, 466, 467, 495; *see also* Basic Democracies *and* Provincial government

Lohia, Ram Manohar, 352

Long March, 38-39

Lubis, Col. Zulkifli, 623, 645, 647; abortive coup, 623

Lucknow Pact, 287

Lukman, M. H., 616, 657

Lumumba, Patrice, 128

Ma Yin-ch'u, 107

MacArthur, Douglas, 134, 251

Macaulay, Lord, 276-277

McMahon Line, 69, 72-74

Madiun rebellion, 562, 616, 681n

Madjelis Sjuro Muslimin Indonesia (Council of Indonesian Muslim Associations), *see* Masjumi

Mahendra, King, 124

Mahrattas, 273, 274-275

Majapahit, 537-539

Malaya, 76, 127; China's relations with, 122, 124, 125

Malaysia, Federation of, 127; Indonesian view of, 669, 672n, 684

Mamdot, Khan of, 481, 484

Manchu dynasty, *see* Ch'ing dynasty

Manchu Reform Movement, 20

Manchukuo, 170; *see also* Manchuria

Manchuria, 7, 17, 23, 25, 33, 40, 45-48, 55-56, 60, 62, 94, 104; Japan's invasion of, 168-169

Manchus, 10, 23, 25

Mandarin, 110

Mandate of Heaven, 12

Manipol-USDEK, 653-654, 661, 678; *see also* Economic development (Is)

Mao Tse-tung, 35-40, 60-64, 66, 70, 71, 76, 77, 80-81, 85, 90, 98, 99, 111-112, 119, 132, 138, 639; and Stalin, 44, 45, 46, 55; *On Coalition Government*, 46; *On the People's Democratic Dictatorship*, 50-51, 85; revolutionary strategy of, 36, 44-45, 50, 110, 117

Maoerhkai Conference, 39

Marhaenism, 614

Marriage Law of 1950 (C), 108

Marshall, George C., 47-48

Martial law (Is), 626, 644, 658, 659-660

Martial law (P), 472, 506; imposition in 1958, 439, 440 460, 469, 471, 473, 489, 491, 495-497, 507; revocation in 1962, 440, 497

Marxism: in Indonesia, 551-552, 598-599; in Japan, 213, 222-223

Marxism-Leninism, 34, 36, 62, 74, 107

Masjumi (Is), 570, 599-601, 605, 610-626 *passim*, 644-646, 649, 663-667, 682; economic platform, 611

Mass campaigns, 80-83

Mass line, 84

Mataram, kingdom of, 538-540, 545; Jogjakarta and Surakarta, 539

Matsus, 130

Maududi, Maulana Abul Ala, 495, 503

Mauryan empire, 271

May Fourth Movement, 24

May Thirtieth Movement, 24-25

Mehta, Asoka, 352, 353

Meiji, 160; Emperor, 160, 164; oligarchy, 162-165, 228; restoration, 160-161

Menon, V. K. Krishna, *see* Krishna Menon, V. K.

Menon, V. P., 289-290, 292, 298; on aftermath of partition, 305; on integration of princely states, 306; on refugees in Delhi, 304; Secretary of States Ministry, 299

Merapi-Merbabu Complex (MMC), 616n

Merchants, in China, 11

Middle class: in Indonesia, 548, 550-554, 578-579, 611, 614, 632; in Japan, 176-177

Middle East, 4, 118, 127, 128

Middle Kingdom (C), 4

Mikoyan, Anastas, 62n

Militarism (J), 166-170; reaction against, 167, 172, 177, 252

Military Affairs Commission (C), 32

Military Clique (C), *see* Whampoa Clique

Ming dynasty, 9-10

Minor parties: in China, 82-83; in Indonesia, 610n; in Japan, 214, 216

Minorities, 446, 518-519; in China, 5, 86-87, 91-94, 100-101, 116; Muslims in India, 485, 517, 520-521; non-Muslims in Pakistan, 446, 447, 448, 474-475

Mirza, Major Gen. Iskandar, 436, 437, 439, 449, 450, 452, 495, 523

Mitsubishi, 212

Modernist Islamic thought, 547-548, 552, 611-612; Muhammadijah, 612; see also *Pantjasila*

Modernization (J), 161, 163

Mogul empire, in India, 272-274, 278

Mohammed, Ghulam, 435, 437, 450, 452, 472, 475

Mongol empire, 9

Mongolia, Inner, 7, 10, 34, 47, 91, 92, 94-95, 100

Mongolia, Outer, 23, 43, 61, 100, 104, 122; China's relations with, 106, 122-123

Mongolian People's Republic, *see* Mongolia, Outer

Montagu, Samuel, 285

Mookerjee, Dr. S. P., 345

Morley, Lord, 285

Morley-Minto reforms, 284-285, 424

Moscow, 35, 36, 61, 121; 1960 Communist conference at, 70-71, 118

Mountbatten, Lord, 296-297, 309, 430

Mughal empire, 420

Mukden, 10

Murba, *see* Communist Party, Indonesian

Musjawarat-mufakat, 588-590, 637, 638, 640, 666

Muslim League (I), 290, 291, 292; and Constituent Assembly, 295, 296; and interim government (1946), 295, 296; electoral victories, 295; policy during Second World War, 293

Muslim League (P): "Convention" League, 441, 502, 503, 504n; "Council" League, 441, 502, 503; preindependence, 424-433 *passim*, 474, 475, 523; *1947-1958*, 436-438, 448, 475-481, 484, 485-494 *passim*, 506, 511, 517

Muslims: in British India, 419, 422, 424, 426, 427, 428, 477; in India, 485, 517, 520-521; in Pakistan, 444, 447; Muslim bloc, 521, 522, 523; Muslim Family Laws Ordinance of 1961, 444; Muslim International Economic Conferences, 521-522

Mutual responsibility (J), 159

Mysticism, Javanese, 536-537, 612-613

Nagaland, 72, 302

Nagy, Imre, 62

Nahdatul Ulama, 600, 609-617 *passim*, 620-621, 623n, 637, 643, 662-663, 665-666; foundation of, 612; withdrawal from Masjumi, 612

Nanchang Rising, 35

Nanking, 21, 28, 42, 50

Nanking, Treaty of, 16

Narayan, Jayaprakash, 374; and
Bhoodan movement, 351; talks with
Nehru (1953), 340, 351
Nasser, Gamal Abdel, 128
Nasution, Gen. A. H., 623, 626, 641-
645, 649, 655, 657, 660, 662, 671,
673
National Assembly (C), 32, 46, 48, 135
National Assembly (P), 440, 444, 450,
451, 452, 453, 454-457, 461, 464,
473, 491, 497, 498, 503; committees
of, 454, 455, 456; procedure, 454,
455, 456; Speaker and Deputy Speakers of, 451, 453, 454
National Awami Party (P), 492-494,
500, 503
National Council (Is), 625-626, 639n,
640, 643-644; Hatta's views on, 626;
role of President, 644; *see also* High
Advisory Council
National Democratic Front (P), 500,
502-503
National Diet (J), 190-192, 232, 240-
242; standing committees in, 191-192,
241
National Front (Is), 639-640, 649, 658-
659, 663; first, 659, 667, 668; second,
658-659, 668; PKI program, 616
National People's Convention (C), 31
National Planning Council (Is), 664,
666; Eight Year Plan, 667
National Preparatory Committee (Is),
see Inter-Indonesian Conferences
National Public Service Law (J), 197
Nationalism (C), 24-25
Nationalism (I), 280; Muslim nationalism, 282
Nationalism (Is), 547-548, 551, 555-
561 *passim*, 563-565, 574-577, 580,
598-599, 604, 609n, 612n, 614-615,
617, 625, 630-631, 637, 648, 660,
669, 674, 681, 685; of the PNI, 615n;
see also Nationalist Party, Indonesian;
Partai Sarekat Islam; *and* Regionalism
Nationalism (J), 169, *see also* Militarism
Nationalist Party, Indonesian, 599-600,
607, 609, 610n, 613-619, 620-622,
623n, 662-666; Soekarno's backing of,
598, 604; *see also* October 17 Affair
Native states (I), *see* Princely states
Natsir, Mohammad, 600, 604, 606, 611,
613, 618-619, 622-623, 646-647
Natural resources (J), 154
Nazimuddin, Khwaja, 434, 435, 452,
478, 481, 502, 524
Nehru, Jawaharlal, 69, 73, 121, 288,
297, 311, 325, 338, 339, 349, 374;

as foreign policy spokesman, 391;
heads interim government (1946),
295; influence of public opinion on,
372; on India's foreign policy, 392-
393; on India's independence, 300;
talks with J. P. Narayan (1953), 340
Neo-Confucianism, 8
Net Profit Policy (Is), *see* Cultivation
System
Netherlands, and Indonesia, 536-557,
560-564, 570-574, 577-578, 581, 585,
588, 595, 627-628, 630, 641; colonial
army (KNIL), 582, 585, 590; debt
settlement, 577; Liberal Policy, 545;
Netherlands-Indonesian Union, 561;
Pasundan government, 594; People's
Council, 553; *see also* Federal gov-
ernment, West Irian, *and* Westerling
Affair
Neutralism: in Indonesia, 633; in Japan,
251
New Democracy (C), 59
New Democratic Youth League, 76, 79
New Guinea, Western, *see* West Irian
New Life Movement, 33
New Zealand, 130; China's relations
with, 122
Nieh Jung-chen, 90n
Nine Power Pact, 25
Ningsia Hui Autonomous Region, 91
Nishtar, Sardar Abdur Rab, 479
Nizam-i-Islam Party (P), 495, 498, 503,
504
Nizam of Hyderabad, 308
Njoto, 616; *see also* Communist Party,
Indonesian
Noon, Firoz Khan, 439, 499, 515
North East Frontier Agency (C), 69,
72, 74, 125
Northern Expedition, 27-28
North-West Frontier Province (P), 422,
430, 434, 443, 458, 459, 472, 484,
490, 491; elections in, 477, 481; tribal
areas in, 443, 460, 517
NU, *see* Nahdatul Ulama
Nuclear weapons (C), 65, 112, 114,
131, 132
Nurhaci, 10

October 17 Affair, 621
October Revolution (C), *see* Bolshevik
Revolution
October Revolution (P), 439
Oda, Nobunaga, 155
Offshore islands (C), 113, 115, 131
Okada, Keisuke, 169
Okinawa, 257-258
Open Door Policy, 18, 25

Opium, 15, 16, 17, 20; Opium War, 16, 18

Organization Clique (C), *see* CC Clique

Our Struggle, see Sjahrir, Soetan

Overseas Chinese, 6, 69, 76, 85-87, 106, 116, 125, 127, 138
  in Indonesia, 541-544, 546-547, 550-551, 578-579, 618, 656, 685; dual-nationality agreement, 686-687; re-patriation program, 686-687; trade restriction, 656, 686

Pai Chung-hsi, 29

Pai-hua, 24

Pakhtunistan, *see* Afghanistan

Pakistan, foreign relations, 515-525; with China, 519, 521; with Commonwealth, 492, 515, 523-524; with India, 515-521, 524; canal waters dispute, 520; Kashmir dispute, 517-519, 524; with United States, 492, 523-524; *see also* Muslims *and* other country headings

Pakistan Industrial Development Corporations, 462, 511-512

Pakistan Resolution, *see* Lahore Resolution

Pamong pradja, 614, 634

Panchayat, 272, 316, 332, 464

Panchayati Raj, 331, 332

Panchsheel (*Panch Shila*), 393

Pantjasila, 558, 614, 616; *see also* Modernist Islamic thought

Pao-chia, 33

Paotow, 101

Parkinson's Law, 90n

Parliament (I), 319, 325, 326; committees of, 326, 327; role of, 327; role of Congress Party in, 326; role of opposition parties in, 326

Parliamentary democracy (Is), 575-638, 640-641, 653, 665; unique aspects of, 627, 635; *see also* Cabinets, post-revolutionary

Parliamentary government (Is), *see* Parliamentary democracy

Partai Sarekat Islam Indonesia, 547-548, 610n, 612n, 666

Partition of India, 297-300, 303, 430-431, 515

Pasundan government, *see* Netherlands, and Indonesia

Patel, Vallabhbhai, 311, 325; and integration of princely states, 299, 305-307, 339

Pathet Lao, 126

Patronage (Is), 581, 607, 609, 618, 620, 622, 625, 633, 659, 660, 662, 671

Peace Preservation Law (J), 213

Peaceful coexistence (C), 59, 80

Peasantry (C), 8, 11

Peasantry (I), 376

Peasantry (Is), 541-548, 556, 578, 587, 617, 620, 677-678; *see also*, Barisan Tani Indonesia, Economic problems (Is), Landownership, *and* Public opinion

Peasantry (J), 158, 160; *see also* Farmers

Peiping, *see* Peking

Peking, 19, 21, 22, 24, 28, 33, 42, 50, 52, 60, 61, 63, 68, 70, 71, 86, 87, 91, 117, 119n, 128, 131

Peking University, 107

P'eng Te-huai, 68, 91, 112

People's communes, 65-66, 70, 79

People's Congress, 92, 94

People's Consultative Assembly, *see* Consultative Assembly

People's Council (C), 92, 94

People's Council (Is), *see* Netherlands, and Indonesia

People's Daily, 83

People's Democracy (C), 82

People's Democratic Dictatorship, 82, 87

People's Liberation Army, 50, 56-57, 68, 72, 86, 96, 101, 111-112, 113; Field Armies, 91; Field Armies abolished, 61, 91; General Staff, 88, 111, 112; Public Security Forces, 96; Second Field Army, 55

People's Political Council, 42-43

Persatuan Indonesia Raja (PIR), 620; *see also* Wongsonegoro cabinet

Persian language, 421, 442-443, 483

Peta, 558, 560

Philippines, contact with Indonesia, 537, 684

PIR, *see* Persatuan Indonesia Raja

PKI, *see* Communist Party, Indonesian

Planning Commission (I), 383-384

Planning Commission (P), 514

PNI, *see* Nationalist Party, Indonesian

Po Ku, 37, 46

Poland, 64; 1956 crisis in, 62-63, 123

Political Consultative Conference, 48

Political elite and intellectuals (Is), 547, 548, 551, 585-587, 598, 607, 609-610, 627, 629-630, 632, 660; negative attitude toward government, 554

Political elite and intellectuals (P), 480, 493-494

Political parties (I), 335-360, 361; atti-

Political parties (I) (*cont.*)
tudes toward, 335; *see also* specific parties

Political parties (Is), 564, 568-570, 576, 585, 587, 589, 608-618, 627, 636-637, 663-665; discipline of, 606-607; fund raising, 609, 617-618 632-633; multiparty system, 568, 581, 586, 607, 628-629, 633, 636, 638; role in government, 610-615, 631-635; Soekarno's control of, 666; *see also* Minor parties, National Front, Power struggle, *and* specific parties

Political parties (J), 165-166; army attitude toward, 214; campaigning tactics, 239-240; minor, 214, 216; postwar, 214-224; prewar, 211-214; recruitment of members, 220; social basis of, 221-224; *see also* specific parties

Political parties (P), 438-440, 466, 495-498; Political Parties Act (1962), 498-504; *see also* specific parties

Political Science Clique, 30

Political Tutelage, 26, 28, 31, 32; in practice, 28-33

Population (C), 3, 86, 107, 131

Population (Is), 535, 539, 546, 577, 591, 675, 677-678

Population (J), 153-154

Population (P), 442, 446; non-Muslim, 446, 447

Port Arthur, 55, 61

Potsdam Conference, 47

Power struggle (Is), 627-634 *passim*, 636, 644; PKI and, 652-653; with army, 641-643, 651-655; with Soekarno, 651-654; Soekarno with army and political parties, 621, 629, 636-639, 643-652 *passim*, 655-658, 661-671

Prasad, Dr. Rajendra, 311, 312, 323

Prawoto Mangkusasmita, 667

Premier, *see* Prime Minister

Presidency: in India, 317, 318, 323-324; in Indonesia, 564-572, 601-604, 644n, 664-666; in Pakistan, 439, 445, 446, 450, 451, 452-457, 461-462, 506, 508

Presidential cabinets, 571-572, 605, 626

Press, the: in China, 33, 95; in India, 373-374; in Indonesia, 587, 646, 653, 659; in Japan, 213; in Pakistan, 492n, 507-508

Pressure groups: in India, 375-381; in Indonesia, *see* Power struggle; in Japan, 211

Preventive detention (P), 508

Preventive Detention Act (I), 328

Prime Minister: in India, 318; in Indonesia, 571, 593, 601, 604-606, 621, 644; in Japan, 194-195; in Pakistan, 434-439, 450-452, 477-479, 487

Prime Minister's Secretariat (J), 194

Princely states (I), 280; integration of, 299, 301, 305-307

Privy Council (J), 164, 177, 182, 188

Progressive Party (J): Kaishinto, 212; Shimpoto, 214, 229-230

Provincial assemblies (P), *see* Provincial government

Provincial government (P), 439, 462, 465, 479; chief ministers, 478, 487, 488, 490, 491; governors, 439, 460, 461-462, 468, 488, 490, 508; Provincial assemblies, 434, 460, 461, 464, 473, 475, 481, 489, 495, 498

PSI, *see* Socialist Party, Indonesian

PSII, *see* Partai Sarekat Islam Indonesia

Public administration (I), 333, 334

Public finance (P), 455-456, 463

Public opinion: in China, 95, 102, 125-136; in India, 371-374; in Indonesia, 553, 575-576, 587-588, 632, 634, 652, 670-674 *passim;* in Japan, 254

Punjab, 422, 472, 474; in Pakistan, 434, 435, 458, 460, 461, 472, 478, 479, 481, 484, 492, 520; partition of, 303, 430-431, 516; Sikhs in, 367

Qaid-i-Azam, *see* Jinnah, Mohammed Ali

Qizilbash, Muzaffar Ali, 491, 494, 499

Quemoy, 68,114, 118, 130

Quran, 444

Radcliffe, Sir Cyril, 298, 516

Radhakrishnan, Dr. Sarvepalli, 324

Raffles, Sir Stamford, 543

Rajagopalachari, C. R., 343

Ram Rajya Parishad, 346

Rashid, Sardar Abdur, 491

Rashtriya Swayamsevak Sangh, 346

Rearmament (J), 218, 251-254

Rectification (C), 44-45, 64, 78-79

Refugees: in India, 301, 304, 305; in Pakistan, 510, 521

Regents, *see* Javanese aristocracy

Regionalism (Is), 572-574, 584-585, 622-623, 629, 631-632, 643-644, 649, 656-657, 660, 664-665, 674-675; regional commanders, 583-585, 624, 626, 645-646, 674; *see also* Decentralization *and* Sumatra-Celebes rebellion

Religious Socialists (Is), 552, 611, 612-613, 614-618, 621

Renville Agreement, 562, 571, 599
Republic of China (1912-1928), 21-25
Republic of Indonesia, 591, 595, 596; establishment of new unitary Republic, 595; proclamation of, 565; unicameral parliament, 595, 596
Republic of the United States of Indonesia (RUSI), 590-596; map of, 592
Republican Party (I), 347, 348
Republican Party (P), 438-439, 487, 490-492, 506
Returned Students (C), 36-38
Revisionism (C), 67, 70, 118, 119
Rhee Line, 256
Ripon, Lord, 279, 331
Rites Controversy, 16
Roem, Mohammad, 599, 611, 667
Roeslan Abdulgani, 623, 661, 664
Round Table Conference or Hague Conference, 563, 577, 582, 590, 682
Round Table Conferences (1930-1932), 288, 432
Roy, Dr. B. C., 330
Roy, M. N., 354
Roy, Raja Ram Mohan, 280
Russia, *see* Soviet Union
Russo-Japanese War (1904-1905), 17, 20, 166

Samurai, 155, 158, 160-162
San Fan campaign, 54
San Francisco Peace Treaty, 252; regarding Okinawa, 257
San Min Chu I, *see* Three Principles of the People
Sartono, Chairman of Indonesian Parliament, 633
Sarvodaya society, 379
Satsuma, 162, 228
Satyagraha, 287
Scheduled castes, in Pakistan, 489
Scheduled Castes Federation: in India, 347-348; in Pakistan, 438, 490
"Scramble for Concessions," 19, 20
SEATO, *see* Southeast Asia Treaty Organization
Seiyukai, *see* Association of Political Friends
Senate (Is): federal, 591, 593; unitary, 595-596
Senkyoya, 239
Seoul, 57
"Sepoy Mutiny" (1857), 275, 277-278, 280, 421, 423
Shahabuddin, Mohammed, 440
Shanghai, 25, 27, 30, 33, 36, 42, 50, 91
Shansi, 29
Shantung, 17, 22, 24, 28, 46, 47, 50

Sharia, compilation of Islamic law, 470
Shensi, 5, 39-41, 46
Shensi-Kansu-Ningsia Border Region, 41, 46
Shidehara, Kijuro, 231
Shigemitsu, Mamoru, 231
Shih (municipality), 91
Shimpoto (J), 214, 229-230
Shoda, Michiko, 187
Shogun, 156
Showa Emperor, 166
Shrivijaya, 537-539
Sian, 40
Sikang, 94
Sikhs, 431, 433, 474
Sikkim, 105
Simla Conference (1945), 293-294
Simon Commission, 288, 432
Sindh: elections in, 481; province of, 420, 430, 431, 434, 435, 458, 460, 461, 478, 479, 492, 494
Singapore, 127
Sinkiang, 10, 23, 25, 39, 43, 56, 61, 91, 100, 101, 104
Sino-Japanese War: *1894-1895,* 19, 20, 22, 166; *1937-1945,* 41-46, 50, 170
Sino-Soviet Friendship Association, 84
Sino-Soviet relations, *see* Soviet Union, foreign relations with China
Sjafruddin Prawiranegara, 611, 646-647; *see also* Republic of Indonesia
Sjahrir, Soetan, 548, 566-569, 610n, 667; head of cabinet, 567-569; *Our Struggle (Perdjuangan Kita),* 566-567
Sjarifuddin, Amir, 565, 566, 612n
SOBSI (Sentral Organisasi Buruh Seluruh Indonesia), 617, 646
Social Democratic Party (J), *see* Socialist Party (J)
Social structure: in China, 11-12; in Indonesia, 546, 548, 550, 576, 577, 586, 627, 632; Communist version of, 653-654
Socialism: in China (transition to), 59; in India, 348-349; in Indonesia, 551-552, 578, 586, 611, 631, 676; in Japan, 164, 213-214
Socialist Party (I), 350; Congress Socialist Party, 349, 350; Praja Socialist Party, 351-353; Socialist Party of India, 352
Socialist Party (J), 126, 214-219, 231, 233, 238
Socialist Party, Indonesian, 570, 609, 610n, 619, 621, 649, 664-665; *see also* Religious Socialists
Soekarno, 548, 556-572 *passim,* 586, 593-601, 605-606, 612-619, 631-632,

Soekarno (*cont.*)
642-644, 652; and Guided Democracy, 636-640; and seizure of Dutch properties, 646; and six parliamentary based cabinets, 618-626; attempted assassination of, 645; cooperation with Hatta, 571-572, 605-606, 640, 644-645, 670-671; on proposal for National Council, 625-626, 643-644, 664-665
Soepomo, Minister of Justice, 595
Soldiers, in China, 11
Soong, T. V., 30, 33
Soong Ching-ling, 88n
Southeast Asia, 6; China's relations with, 9, 57-58; relations with Japan, 257
Southeast Asia Treaty Organization, 125, 130, 524
Soviet Union, 4, 58, 63, 84-85, 92, 93, 96, 100, 102, 104, 106, 110, 116, 117, 124, 126
debate at Bucharest, 70
foreign relations with: China, 15, 17, 23, 25, 43, 44, 46-47, 55-56, 57, 60-61, 62n, 64, 65, 67, 68, 69-73, 80, 100, 105, 106, 110, 111-115, 117-122, 125, 127, 132, 133-134, 671n; India, 397-398; Indonesia, 651, 673, 677, 681, 685; Japan, 255; Pakistan, 524
intercontinental ballistic missile, 65, 113
Sputnik I, 65, 113, 117, 128
Soviet Union, Communist Party of, *see* Communist Party of the Soviet Union
Sparta, 5
Spheres of influence, 17
Stalin, Iosif Vissarionovich, 27, 28, 35, 36, 39, 40, 44-47, 50, 55-60, 62, 63, 78, 82, 92, 98, 102, 112, 119
Starlinger, Wilhelm, 3-4 (cited)
State of war and siege (Is): *see* Martial law (Is)
States Reorganization Bill (1956), 366
Student organizations: in India, 376; in Japan, 209
Subadio Sastrosatomo, 667
Subardjo, Achmad, 619
Suez Canal, 423, 522, 523, 524
Suez crisis, 127
Suhrawardy, H. S., 439, 481, 485-487, 491, 499, 500, 503, 522, 524
Sui dynasty, 8
Suiyuan, 95, 101
Sukiman Wirjosandjojo, 599, 600, 606, 612, 617n, 619
Sultan of Jogjakarta, 645, 647
Sumatra, government in revolutionary period, 560-563, 572-574, 647

Sumatra-Celebes rebellion, 562, 647-649, 657, 666n, 674, 675, 682-683
Sumitro Djojohadikusumo, 647, 649
Sun Fo, 30
Sun Li-jen, 136
Sun Yat-sen, 20, 21, 25, 27-30; ideas of, 25-26, 29, 31-32
Sun Yat-sen, Mme, 88n
Sung Chiao-jen, 21-22
Sung dynasty, 8-9
Supreme Court (I), 315, 319, 327
Suwirjo, 643
Swatantra Party, 343-344
Syed, G. M., 492
Sylhet, 430
Syrian crisis, 118, 128
Szechuan, 39, 42, 101

Taiping Rebellion, 18
Taisho Emperor, 164-165
Taiwan, 10, 50, 54, 72, 85, 113, 115, 130-138 *passim*; crises in, 68, 71-72, 114-118, 130-131, 138; Taiwan Strait, 56, 131, 138
Tan Ling Djie, 616
Tan Malaka, 566
Tanaka, Giichi, 212
Tandon, Purshattamdas, 339
T'ang dynasty, 8, 9
Taoism, 108
Tara Singh, Master, 347
Taxation (J), 155, 160, 163
Taxation (P), *see* Public finance
Tehsil councils, *see* Basic Democracies
Teiseito (J), 162, 212
Telengana affair, 355
Teng Hsiao-p'ing, 76, 77
Thailand, 76, 124, 127; China's relations with, 6, 124, 125
Thana councils, *see* Basic Democracies
Third International, *see* Comintern
"Three Anti" campaign, *see* San Fan campaign
Three Principles of the People (C), 25-26
Tibet, 5, 6, 8, 10, 23, 25, 39, 50, 69, 70-72, 94, 101; "liberation" of, 23, 54, 55
T'ien Shan, 7, 8
Tientsin, 33, 50
Tilak, B. G., 283-284, 285
Tirana, 118
Tito, Josip Broz, 67, 118, 123
Tokugawa shogunate, 157-160
Tokyo, 138
Tokyo Imperial University, 166, 196, 242
Trade unions (I), 375
"Treaties, unequal," 16

Treaty ports, 17
Treaty tariff, 16
Truman, Harry S., 47, 130, 137
Tsunyi Conference, 39
Tung Pi-wu, 88n
T'ung-chih Restoration, 18
Tunku Abdul Rahman, 684
Twenty-one Demands, 22
Twenty-one Points (P), 486-487
Twenty-eight Bolsheviks, *see* Returned Students
Two Chinas, 122, 129, 131
Tz'u-hsi, *see* Empress Dowager

Union councils, *see* Basic Democracies
Unitarian movement (Is), 590, 594-597; unicameral legislation, 595-596
United Arab Republic, 106, 128
United Front (P), 436, 438, 439, 461, 484, 486, 487, 488, 494, 502-503, 511; *see also* Awami League *and* Krishak Sramik Party
United Kingdom, *see* Great Britain
United Nations, 56, 105, 128, 129; and Indonesia, 562, 646, 682-683; and Pakistan, 515, 518, 522; role in Kashmir dispute, 396
United States, 56, 67, 73, 102, 106, 110, 118, 120, 124, 126, 127; China policy of, 17-18, 43, 45-48, 54-55, 68, 72, 105, 112, 115, 116-117, 129-131, 137-138; China's relations with, 33, 43, 55, 57, 105, 113-115, 125, 129-131, 132, 135; relations with India, 400, 401; with Indonesia, 562-563, 583-584, 619, 647-648, 680-684; with Japan, 199, 252-254, 257, U.S. aid, 248, U.S. bases, 252; with Pakistan, 492, 523
United States of Indonesia, *see* Republic of the United States of Indonesia
United States Security Treaty with Japan (1960), 253
United States Seventh Fleet, 55, 130, 137
Untouchables, in India, 270, 315, 320, 347, 348
Urdu language, 421-422, 442-443, 483, 517

Versailles Conference, 24
Vice-presidency: in India, 318; in Indonesia, 564, 569, 571, 601, 604-606, 624
Vietnam, 124, 127; China's relations with, 4, 6, 10, 56, 58-59, 62, 112, 116-117, 123, 124-125, 126; Vietminh, 58
Village aid (P), 515

Vitalism, 30
Vladivostok, 25

Wang Ching-wei, 29, 30, 41-42
Wang Ming, 37, 46
Warlords, 22, 28, 49-50
Washington Conference, 25
Water and Power Development Authorities (P), 463
West Irian, 499, 501, 527, 541, 558, 559, 580-581, 658, 667-675 *passim*, 681-683; act of self-determination, 683
West Pakistan, 436, 438, 440, 442-443, 459, 460-463, 465, 468, 474, 475, 482, 510, 512; politics in, 437, 438, 486, 490-492, 493, 494, 506; provincial assembly, 438, 490, 491
Westerling Affair, 580, 582, 594
Whampoa Clique, 30
Whampoa Military Academy, 26
White-collar class in Japan, 223
Wilopo, 606, 609, 614n, 615, 617n, 619-620, 621n, 663
Women's organizations (I), 376
Women's organizations (J), 209
Wongsonegoro cabinet, 620
World Court, 74
World Federation of Trade Unions, 70, 117, 123
World Peace Council, 123
World War I, 17, 22, 167, 285
World War II, 44, 104, 109, 120, 172, 291
Wu, K. C., 134, 136
Wu Fan campaign, 54
Wuchang, 21

Yalta Conference, 47
Yamin, Mohammad, 664
Yangtze River, 4, 5, 17, 27, 42, 46, 50, 104
Yellow River, 4, 5, 50, 104
Yen Hsi-shan, 29
Yenan, 46, 78
Yoshida, Shigeru, 215-216, 231
Yoshihito, *see* Taisho Emperor
Young Pioneers (C), 79
Youth Party (C), 135
Yuan, the five, 26, 31, 32, 135
Yuan dynasty, 9, 13
Yuan Shih-kai, 20, 21-22
Yugoslavia, 63; China's relations with, 122

Zaibatsu, 166, 177, 212
Zengakuren (J), 210-211, 253
Zenro, 207